D0407140

THE FACTS ON FILE DICTIONARY OF

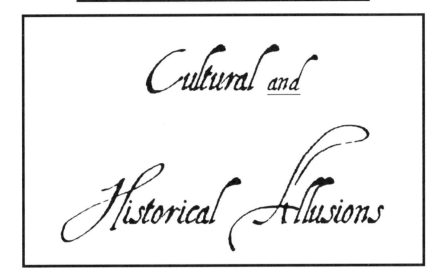

Cultural and

Historical Allusions

THE FACTS ON FILE DICTIONARY OF

Cultural and

Historical Allusions

SYLVIA COLE

ABRAHAM H. LASS

Facts On File, Inc.

Facts On File Dictionary of Cultural and Historical Allusions

Facts On File, Inc.
132 West 31st Street
New York, NY 10001

Library of Congress Cataloging-in-Publication Data
Cole, Sylvia.
    The Facts on File dictionary of cultural and historical allusions /
Sylvia Cole, Abraham H. Lass.
        p. cm.
        Rev. and expanded ed. of: The Facts on File dictionary of 20th-century allusions.
        ISBN 0-8160-4057-5 (acid-free paper)
        I. Lass, Abraham Harold, 1907– II. Cole, Sylvia. Facts on File dictionary of
    20th-century allusions. III. Title.
        031.02—dc21   00-021995

Facts On File books are available at special discounts when purchased in bulk quantities for businesses, associations, institutions or sales promotions. Please call our Special Sales Department in New York at (212) 967-8800 or (800) 322-8755.

You can find Facts On File on the World Wide Web at http://www.factsonfile.com

Text design by Sandra Watamabe
Cover design by Cathy Rincon

Printed in the United States of America

MP Hermitage 10 9 8 7 6 5 4 3

This book is printed on acid-free paper.

Contents

Introduction

Some years ago, an anecdote in the *New York Times* described a pickup basketball game in a local park. One player, to the embarrassment of his teammates, made wild passes at the basket whenever the ball came to him:

> His fifth shot, awkwardly launched, hit the backboard and went in! A cynical cheer rose up and from its midst a voice boomed, "It's a Scud!" Everyone understood. I felt I was witnessing the birth of a new word in our living language.

(Richard Povill, "Metropolitan Diary," *New York Times,* January 30, 1991)

In fact, the writer of this anecdote was witnessing not so much the birth of a new word as the birth of a new allusion. After all, "Scud" had been for several decades a military code word for a Soviet-made missile. What had not been known about the Scud before its use in the Gulf War was its erratic performance: it turned out to be not a precision instrument but instead a hit-or-miss projectile that did not always find its target. In the anecdote, the ball had acted like a Scud; therefore, metaphorically, it *was* a Scud. In this context, "Scud" is an allusion summing up in one word the similar attributes of both the missile and the basketball shot.

Our language is chock full of allusions, which enable us to describe in a word what otherwise might take a paragraph or even several pages to explain. Consult a dictionary and you will find allusion defined as a casual reference, something alluded to. In that case, anything or anybody could be an allusion: the asparagus we had for lunch; Aunt Sophie's pet parakeet; a childhood memory of cleaning board erasers in the schoolyard—anything. As this book uses the term, an allusion is not a mere reference but a reference that has been transformed into a metaphor; a reference that stands for a certain set of attributes or circumstances. Thus, a brilliant student or, sarcastically, a very stupid one may be hailed as "an Einstein." A person of selfless devotion to the sick and the poor may be referred to as "another Mother Teresa." Comical linguistic blunders are malapropisms, from Mrs. Malaprop, a character who mangled the English language in Richard Sheridan's 18th-century play *The Rivals*. More currently, such blunders are often referred to as "Goldwynisms," after Sam Goldwyn, the Hollywood producer, or "Berraisms," after Yogi Berra, the baseball player. A highly touted product that turns out to be a dismal failure is "an Edsel," from the name of the Ford car that bombed. The word for a slick substance applied to cooking utensils to render them non-stick becomes an allusion in the appellation "the Teflon president," to describe Ronald Reagan.

Some allusions call up a more complex set of attributes and circumstances. In the sentence, "In our negotiations with Milosevic we must guard against another Munich," "Munich" is not merely a city in Germany; it is an allusion standing for appeasement. It refers to the 1938 Munich Pact, in which the prime minister of Britain, Neville Chamberlain, in the vain hope of achieving "peace in our time," allowed Adolf Hitler to annex the Sudetenland area of Czechoslovakia. How much more meaningful in this context is the allusion, with all its historical overtones of frightful consequences, than the word "appeasement"!

Similarly, we may come upon a scornful allusion to somebody as "a Walter Mitty." If we are familiar with James Thurber's short story "The Secret Life of Walter Mitty," we conjure up a vision of a poor henpecked schnook who compensates for his insignificance by daydreaming endlessly of glamorous adventures in which he plays the conquering hero. If we do not know the origin of the allusion, however, its full meaning and import are lost on us.

One more example: We are all familiar with the blatant deception with which classrooms, summer camps, old-age homes, even certain concentration camps have been prettied up on the eve of inspections. Such false facades are known as "Potemkin villages," an allusion to the cardboard façade with which the 18th-century Russian prince Grigory Potemkin covered the miserable dwellings of an entire village through which Empress Catherine II (Catherine the Great) would have to pass on her scheduled visit. The question arises: Why use the allusion rather than the bald and more accessible description of façade? Because the allusion, in a word, enriches and vitalizes the description with a reference to its colorful source.

The Facts On File Dictionary of Cultural and Historical Allusions explains allusions of the past millennium, roughly from 1000 to A.D. 2000. To compile the book, we revised and expanded *The Facts On File Dictionary of 20th-Century Allusions,* originally published in 1991, and combined it with more than 600 entirely new entries that cover allusions from the Middle Ages to the 20th century. (Allusions from the classical and biblical eras have already been collected in *The Facts On File Dictionary of Classical, Biblical and Literary Allusions.*) It has been a prodigious task but a rewarding one, yielding insights into the changes that have occurred in our civilization and in the language that mirrors it.

Culture before the middle of the 19th century was disseminated and handed down mostly through the written word by and for an educated, literate elite, an aristocracy of wealth or genius. Most of the allusions from that time refer to authors and the characters they created in poetry, novels and plays; to artists and their subjects; to intellectuals and their ideas; and to the leading figures and events in politics and war. To mention a few: "Rabelaisian" (ribald), "Lilliputian" (diminutive or petty), a Becky Sharp (opportunistic), "Hogarthian" (satirical), "Napoleonic" (grandiosely ambitious).

In our own time, language borrows more and more from mass culture: movies (Rambo), radio ("Who's on first?"), television (Ozzie and Harriet), cartoons (Charlie Brown), politics ("read my lips"), sports (full-court press) and commercial products (Marlboro Man), among other sources. In the alphabetical order in which these allusions are arranged, high and low culture mingle without prejudice: Michelangelo is followed by Mickey Mouse.

This book provides the source and original meaning of each allusion, as well as its meaning and use in our language today. Examples and cross-references are supplied where necessary. Of course, some allusions are so far-ranging in scope that they do not lend themselves to short, easy definitions, so the appropriate meaning to fit a particular use must be extrapolated from various possibilities. The word "Faulknerian," for example, calls up a complex pattern of Southern social castes, racial violence, religiosity, obsession with the antebellum past, morbid sexuality, alienation, hallucinatory and rhapsodic language, as well as rambunctious humor. In a similar way, the precise meaning of such allusions as "Chaucerian," "Shakespearean," "Dickensian" and "Kafkaesque" depends on the context; our definitions try to summarize the complex visions and strategies such allusions represent.

We hope this dictionary provides a useful and reader-friendly reference for becoming acquainted with those allusions of the distant and more recent past that have survived and become part of the contemporary culture.

a

Abbott and Costello   Bud Abbott (the tall, debonair one) and Lou Costello (the short, explosive one) were the top money-making comedy team in movies of the 1940s, then became the most watched, most syndicated TV performers (1951–53). The critics hated them and the show itself. The audience loved them and the show itself.

Essentially, Abbott (1895–1974) and Costello (1906–59) were reusing material that they had been using on stage and in film since the 1930s. The Abbott and Costello show consisted largely (the critics maintained *exclusively*) of lowbrow slapstick; outrageous puns; knockabout, physical, "pratfall" comedy routines; contrived, improbable situations; frenzied, unrelated sights and gags. Nonetheless, out of this mad, hilarious melange came such classic routines as "Who's on First?"

ABCs   The first three letters of the alphabet. Children learn to read by studying their ABCs. By extension, apprentices must first learn the ABCs of their trade; that is, the most elementary or basic requirements. Or, a concept may be "as easy as ABC."

Abelard and Héloise   Unlike such fictional lovers as Romeo and Juliet and Tristan and Isolde, Abelard and Héloise were historical figures who have been enshrined in the pantheon of great lovers.

Peter Abelard (1079–1142) was one of the most brilliant teacher-philosopher-theologians of his day. As the head of his own school, he made Paris the intellectual center of the Western world. He was a forerunner of scholasticism, predating Thomas Aquinas. He believed that reason could be used to prove articles of faith. His best known work was entitled *Sic et Non.*

When Abelard was 38, he became tutor to Héloise (1101–64), the 17-year-old niece of Canon Fulbert of Nôtre-Dame. Abelard and the beautiful, intellectually gifted Héloise fell in love. They had a son together and, to assuage Fulbert's fury, they were married in a secret ceremony. Fulbert's ill treatment of Héloise prompted Abelard to place her in the convent of Argenteuil for safety. Fulbert hired thugs to castrate Abelard. Abelard fled to the monastery of St-Denis. Héloise wrote him passionate letters that have been preserved and published.

Abelard was buried at Paraclete, a monastery he had founded. In 1164 Héloise was buried beside him. In 1817 their remains were removed to the Père-Lachaise cemetery in Paris.

Abelard and Héloise are still known today as legendary lovers whom no vicissitudes of fortune, no tragedy could separate.

abracadabra   Magic charm first used by Gnostics in the second century to ward off evil spirits. Like an acrostic, it was said to be made up of the first letters of the Hebrew words *Ab* (Father), *Ben* (Son) and *Ruach Acadascha* (Holy Spirit). Engraved on parchment, it used to be worn around the neck as a good luck amulet.

"Abracadabra" is a word now generally used by magicians as a kind of dramatic introductory salvo before the production of a rabbit from a hat and other tricks. It is also used as a magic incantation for any kind of inexplicable or illogical evocation, or hocus-pocus, or sleight-of-hand.

according to Hoyle   Edward Hoyle (1672–1769) was a British authority on card games, especially whist. His compilation of the rules governing these card games achieved worldwide acceptance.

Hoyle's name has entered the language in the phrase "according to Hoyle." By extension, it has come to mean behaving honorably, fairly, following the rules faithfully.

Use: "Gentlemen, we're undertaking a very important project. The company's survival may very well depend on how well we do our job. Everyone will be watching us. I want everything done according to Hoyle, no sharp practices, no corner-cutting."

Adams, Ansel (1902–1984)   Photographer famous for his wide-angle American West landscapes of towering, snowcapped mountains and great trees. His pictures, which have been reproduced in more than 35 books, helped to establish photography as a legitimate art form with its own way of seeing.

Addams, Charles (1912–1988)   American cartoonist who for 50 years contributed his outrageously macabre humor to the *New Yorker*. He created an Addams family, an Addams house and Addams situations that are all ghoulish. In one well-known cartoon he shows a slinky, witch-like family on the roof of their haunted-looking Victorian house. It is Christmas and they are about to pour upon the carolers below a cauldron-full of boiling oil. In another cartoon Addams depicts a weird-looking man waiting outside a delivery room. The nurse is saying, "Congratulations! It's a baby!" His spooky, archetypical work antedated and paved the way for "black humor."

A Charles Addams is any weird person, house or situation that suggests a macabre sense of humor, a topsy-turvy sense of values.

Adler, Polly (1900–1962) As practitioner and entrepreneur in prostitution, the "oldest profession," Polly Adler was widely known as "the last of the great madams" and her establishment as "New York's most famous bordello."

In her autobiography, *A House Is Not a Home,* Polly Adler boasts of "a clientele culled not only from *Who's Who* and *The Social Register*—but from *Burke's Peerage* and *The Almanac de Gotha.*" Her "guests" also included politicians, gangsters (Dutch Schultz, Frank Costello, Lucky Luciano), writers, etc. She and her "girls" worked out of fashionable, lavishly decorated apartments equipped with bars and dining rooms.

After a highly colorful career, Polly Adler retired from her "business" in 1944 to write her autobiography and to pursue other, non-"business" activities.

Adlerian In accordance with psychoanalytical theories and treatment formulated by Alfred Adler (1870–1937). Adler started out as a disciple of Freud but broke away from the Master because he rejected Freud's emphasis on sex. To Adler the individual's drive for power, his desire for superiority, often to compensate for feelings of inadequacy, was at the heart of neurosis.

Adler coined the phrases "inferiority complex" and "superiority complex."

Afghanistan In December 1979, Soviet troops invaded the small central Asian country of Afghanistan in order to prop up their unpopular communist puppet regime in Kabul. For 10 years they were unable to prevail against the Afghan Mujahedeen, Islamic guerrilla warriors who controlled the mountain passes with arms supplied mostly by the United States, West Germany and Japan. In spite of almost universal condemnation by the United Nations, the loss of thousands of lives and the drain on its resources, the Soviet Union did not pull out its forces until 1989. The fire that Leonid Brezhnev started was finally put out by Mikhail Gorbachev.

Afghanistan was to the Soviet Union what Vietnam was to the United States, a humiliating defeat of a great power by a tiny country.

Agincourt Site in northern France of a battle fought on St. Crispin's Day, October 25, 1415, in which King Henry V of England routed the numerically superior French forces. The masses of lightly clad English yeomen, using their longbows, unseated the armor-encased French knights, who fell from their horses into the mud and could not rise again. The armor of chivalry became obsolete that day.

Afterward, a tidal wave of pride and patriotism flooded England. This euphoric sense of destiny is magnificently expressed in act IV of Shakespeare's *Henry V* when, on the eve of the Battle of Agincourt, Henry addresses his soldiers:

> *And Crispin Crispian shall ne'er go by,*
> *From this day to the ending of the world,*
> *But we in it shall be rememberèd—*
> *We few, we happy few, we band of brothers. . . .*

A reference to Agincourt implies a triumph against vastly superior forces, a triumph of homely means against sophisticated weaponry.

Ahab   Captain of the *Pequod,* the whaling vessel in Herman Melville's novel *Moby Dick* (1851). Ahab's monomaniacal pursuit of the fierce white whale, MOBY DICK, who tore off one of his legs in a previous encounter, ends in tragedy.

An Ahab has come to mean anyone in single-minded, obsessive pursuit of a goal.

Aladdin, or the Wonderful Lamp   A tale from *Mille et une Nuits* (c. 1710) by Antoine Galland, published in English as *The Arabian Nights* (1721). Aladdin, a poor boy in China, is locked in a cave by a magician. There the boy finds a lamp, which, when rubbed, calls up a jinn (genie) who is ready to fulfill every one of Aladdin's requests. The boy acquires instant transportation home, great riches and treasures, a beautiful palace and eventually a princess's hand in marriage.

What has survived of this tale in modern parlance is the notion that, like Aladdin, one can rub a metaphorical lamp and immediately a genie will materialize to do one's bidding and grant one's wish.

Alas! Poor Yorick   An expression used by HAMLET in the grave-digger's scene (act V, scene 1) of Shakespeare's tragedy. Hamlet has returned to Denmark, having foiled Claudius's scheme to have him killed in England. He comes upon a man singing and jesting as he digs a grave and unearths a skull. The skull, he tells Hamlet, is that of Yorick, the court jester when Hamlet was a lad.

Hamlet is moved to reflect upon the vanity of life:

> Alas! poor Yorick. I knew him, Horatio; a fellow of infinite jest, of most excellent fancy; he hath borne me on his back a thousand times; and now, how abhorred in my imagination it is!

The phrase "Alas! poor Yorick" is often used somewhat ruefully and humorously to mean: Where are past glories or vainglories now?

albatross   A white sea bird with narrow wings and a 10- to 12-inch wingspan. An excellent glider, the albatross was thought by superstitious sailors to bring good luck. In "The Rime of the Ancient Mariner," a poem by Samuel Taylor Coleridge, the mariner, out of a dark impulse, shoots the albatross with his crossbow and brings down disaster upon the ship and its crew.

> *Ah! Well-a-day! What evil looks*
> *Had I from old and young.*
> *Instead of the cross, the Albatross*
> *About my neck was hung.*

Only when the mariner spontaneously blesses the "happy living things" in the deep does the albatross fall off and sink "like lead into the sea."

An albatross around one's neck is a cross to bear, a burden, a curse.

See also ANCIENT MARINER.

Alcatraz   In 1868, the United States War Department established a prison for deserters on Alcatraz, an island in San Francisco harbor. In 1934 Alcatraz was taken over by the Department of Justice as a "super-prison for super criminals" who couldn't be contained in the regular federal prisons.

The warden, James A. Johnston, ruled "The Rock" (as Alcatraz was known) with an iron hand. Under his stern, unsentimental administration, Alcatraz became known as America's Devil's Island, characterized by maximum security, minimum privileges, a rule of silence, prisoners locked up 14 hours a day, no trustee system, bad behavior punished by beatings and special handcuffs, straitjackets and solitary confinement ("the hole").

Some inmates tried to escape. None succeeded. Some tried suicide. Others became insane. The infamous Al Capone, master criminal, was sent here. He was paroled in 1939, suffering from advanced syphilis. Widespread criticism of Alcatraz's methods led to its closing in 1963.

Alcatraz has become a symbol for escape-proof, harsh, cruel prisons.

Alden, John   See "WHY DON'T YOU SPEAK FOR YOURSELF, JOHN?"

Aleichem, Sholem   See SHOLEM ALEICHEM.

Alger, Horatio, Jr. (1832–1899)   American writer of 119 boys' books, in which the heroes begin as poor newsboys or bootblacks and rise to great wealth and influence. He encapsulated in each book the American dream of rags to riches.

Ali Baba   See OPEN SESAME.

Alibi Ike   Main character and title of a 1924 short story by RING LARDNER (1885–1933). Later, a comic strip.

An Alibi Ike is a person who always has a ready excuse.

Alice in Wonderland   Shortened and more frequently used title for *Alice's Adventures in Wonderland* (1865) by Lewis Carroll (pseudonym for Charles Lutwidge Dodgson, 1832–98). Carroll wrote the story for ten-year-old Alice Liddell, one of three young daughters of his friend H. G. Liddell. The original illustrator, who created the definitive images of Alice and the other characters in the book, was Sir John Tenniel.

Alice, a little girl with long, blonde hair, pursues the White Rabbit down a rabbit hole. She falls a long, long way and lands in Wonderland. She experiences many puzzling changes and meets a succession of strange characters: the Cheshire Cat, the Mad Hatter, the March Hare, the Caterpillar, the Queen of Hearts and others. She cannot understand their topsy-turvy logic, their parodies of well-known poems and songs, their outrageous puns and other wordplay.

An Alice-in-Wonderland is somebody in a world of inspired nonsense, a world in which the rules of logic have been suspended.

All-American   Originally, an honor conferred on the outstanding football players at each team position. In 1889, the first All-American team was chosen by the famous football player, coach and authority, Walter Camp, for the magazine *Weeks' Sports*. Today, All-American athletes are chosen in many other sports.

The term "all-American" now stands for general, all-around excellence.

"all animals are equal, but some animals are more equal than others"
From George Orwell's satirical fable *Animal Farm* (1945). The animals on Mr. Jones's farm stage a revolution against their human masters and drive them out. The pigs, under their leader Napoleon, take over. Corrupted by power, they in turn become tyrannical and rationalize their hegemony with the above slogan.

Used cynically or satirically to demolish the hypocrisy of claims to absolute equality in the face of a privileged elite.

Allen, Woody (1935–   )   United States film director, writer, actor, comedian, born Allen Stewart Konigsberg. Allen uses autobiographical material, especially his own soul-searching for meaning in the universe. A Woody Allen movie is usually funny, philosophical, cerebral, satirical, with a New York City, middle-class Jewish milieu. His films include *Sleeper* (1973), *Bananas* (1971), *Annie Hall* (1977),

Manhattan (1979), *Hannah and Her Sisters* (1986), *Radio Days* (1987) and *Bullets over Broadway* (1994).

All in the Family   See BUNKER, ARCHIE.

"all quiet on the western front"   Phrase used in military communiqués and newspapers during World War I to indicate no dramatic action, only the usual attrition in the trenches. Erich Maria Remarque used the phrase with irony and bitterness in his 1929 novel *All Quiet on the Western Front,* about the German infantry in World War I, because men were still suffering and dying when it was "all quiet on the western front."

The phrase has been used in nonmilitary situations, but always with irony, as when tensions in a school over certain incidents are hushed up and someone mordantly observes, "all's quiet on the western front."

Almanac de Gotha   The European social register first published in Germany in 1763, a *Who's Who* of royalty and titled individuals or families.

Use: If the Kennedy family represents the nearest approximation to royalty in the United States, then the list of guests assembled at the Kennedy compound last weekend read like an American *Almanac de Gotha.*

Alphonse and Gaston   A super-polite pair of Frenchmen created by the gifted cartoonist Fred Opper for Hearst's Sunday papers in the early 1900s. Flamboyantly dressed as 19th-century French dandies, they observed a code of highly artificial good manners:

"You first, my dear Alphonse."
"No-no-you first, my dear Gaston."

They were universally understood as symbols of excessive politeness.

Alps   Majestic chain of mountains in south-central Europe, its valleys and peaks covering parts of Switzerland, Austria, Germany, France, Italy, and the former Yugoslavia. They soar from a base of 3,000–4,000 feet to 15,772 feet at Mont Blanc, eternally snow-covered, as are the Matterhorn and the Jungfrau.

Although the Himalayas are even higher, it is the Alps that have become the symbol of unreachable height—as in Alexander Pope's famous lines in "An Essay on Criticism" that compare the rigors of learning to climbing the Alps.

American Dream   A vision of America as a land of opportunity, a land in which every individual may achieve his or her innate potential regardless of sex, color, religion, class or circumstances of birth. The dream drew millions of immigrants to the United States and propelled them across a continent. The dream is often corrupted to mean a mere drive for materialistic values. The tragic toll taken by the pursuit of the American Dream has been portrayed in such utterly different novels as *Giants in the Earth* (1924) by Ole Rölvaag, *An American Tragedy* (1925) by Theodore Dreiser and *The Great Gatsby* (1925) by F. Scott Fitzgerald.

American Gothic   Painting by American regionalist Grant Wood (1892–1942). The 1930 canvas is filled with a closeup of an American farm couple posed stiffly against their house. The couple looms almost as large as the house, which has a Gothic, arched attic window. They are immaculately and precisely dressed in farm clothing, the man in a jacket and overalls and carrying a pitchfork; the woman in a coverall apron over a Peter Pan–collared dress. Their expression is determined, dour, even fierce. The artist's treatment of them seems double-edged—half epic, half ironic.

The popular use of the term "American Gothic" certainly is meant to indicate satirically stiff, upright, precise and correct.

American Legion   National organization of military service veterans chartered by Congress in 1919, with posts throughout the country and a strong lobby in Washington, D.C. Associated with veterans advocacy, super-patriotism, flag-waving and parades, and fervid opposition to communism.

An American Tragedy   Novel published in 1925 by Theodore Dreiser (1876–1945), based on the Chester Gillette–Grace Brown murder case of 1906. The protagonist, Clyde Griffiths, is ashamed of his poverty-stricken, street evangelist parents. He yearns for the wealth, the easy living, the mobility of the world he first encounters as a bellhop in a hotel. At his uncle's home in upper New York State, he comes in contact with high society. His ambitions flare, especially when he senses the possibility of marrying the very wealthy Sondra Finchley. Unfortunately, he has already impregnated a poor factory girl, Roberta, who refuses an abortion. Faced with this dilemma, Clyde daydreams of murdering Roberta. Matters are taken out of his hands after Roberta drowns when their rowboat capsizes. Clyde is arrested, tried and sentenced to death. Dreiser, through the defense attorney, indicts society for the crime, for filling youthful heads with false, tawdry, glittering illusions. Dreiser exposes the shoddy American dream of success based on materialistic values.

America's Sweetheart   Nickname given to Mary Pickford (born Gladys Smith, 1893–1979), for 23 years the most popular screen star in the world.

Pickford invariably played Little Mary, the pure, innocent but self-reliant girl with the long blonde curls and the sweet smile, just on the verge of womanhood. She appeared in many films, including *Poor Little Rich Girl, Daddy Long Legs,* and *The Little American.* The marriage of America's Sweetheart to Douglas Fairbanks, the all-American male, represented in real life a kind of epiphany of movie dreamland.

Now used tongue-in-cheek for a too-sweet, too-pure, too-popular girl.

Amos 'N' Andy   A "blackface" radio comedy created by Freeman Gosden (Amos) and Charles Correll (Andy), it appeared in 1929 on NBC, sponsored by Pepsodent. It was an immediate, overwhelming success, one of the first truly original creations of early radio. A vast audience was charmed by its wit and warmth.

In 1950, *Amos 'N' Andy* moved into television—only to discover that a new era had come into being, demanding an end to "blackface" comedy. All black characters henceforth were to be played by black actors.

With superb actors, directors and writers, *Amos 'N' Andy* continued to charm its new audience. But the growing civil rights movement found the depiction of blacks in *Amos 'N' Andy* offensive and damaging to the image of blacks in America. Continued pressure led to the withdrawal of *Amos 'N' Andy* from syndication in 1966.

ancien régime   Literally, the old order. A term used by the leaders of the French Revolution to describe the government and the governing class under the Bourbons (1589–1793): cruel, aggressive, addicted to lavish living, unconcerned about the welfare of the rest of society.

Applied pejoratively to earlier times, governments, and societies.

Use: "I was an adolescent under the ancién régime—before, that is, organized play, psychological understanding, and the birth-control pill came into existence." (Aristides [Joseph Epstein], in *American Scholar*)

ancient mariner   The central figure in Samuel Taylor Coleridge's "The Rime of the Ancient Mariner" (1798), a ballad about sin and atonement.

The ancient mariner has committed the sin of killing a harmless ALBATROSS. In the course of the terrible suffering that he and his shipmates have endured as a consequence, he has learned compassion.

> *He prayeth best, who loveth best*
> *All things both great and small;*
> *For the dear God who madeth us,*
> *He made and loveth all.*

After his ordeal and survival, the ancient mariner is seized from time to time with the obsessive need to tell his tale.

In modern usage an "ancient mariner" is one who holds you with his "skinny hand" and "glittering eye" and won't let go until he has finished his interminable story.

angry young man   Expression applied to certain British playwrights and novelists of the 1950s and to the characters they created. Their heroes were usually lower-middle-class, anti-establishment rebels. Outstanding examples are: John Osborne in *Look Back in Anger* (1956, play); Kingsley Amis in *Lucky Jim* (1954, novel); and Alan Sillitoe in *The Loneliness of the Long Distance Runner* (1959, novella).

Anna Karenina   Tragic heroine of the great Russian novel of the same name (1873–76) by Leo Tolstoy (1828–1910). Beautiful, charming, generous, intelligent, Anna is married to Karenin, a humorless man and a rather rigid, conventional but important bureaucrat. She has a young son, Seryozha, whom she adores.

Anna is drawn reluctantly but inexorably into a passionate affair with the dashing army officer Count Vronsky. Deeply in love with Vronsky and pregnant with his child, she leaves her husband and is forced by Karenin to give up Seryozha. Vronsky sacrifices his brilliant career and his friends in the army to devote himself exclusively to Anna. Society, in its hypocrisy, turns against Anna, not because she is having an adulterous affair, but because she has violated society's cardinal rule in such matters: Be discreet!

Anna and Vronsky become totally dependent on each other's love. Anna becomes febrile, demanding, obsessive, possessive and jealous. Finally, fearing that Vronsky is about to leave her for another woman, Anna throws herself under the wheels of a train. Vronsky is left desolate.

Tolstoy intended *Anna Karenina* to be an object lesson in the deterioration of a woman who transgresses the moral law, but Anna remains a towering tragic figure who inspires us with pity and terror.

Annie Oakley   In baseball, a free ticket to a game. So named by American League president Ban Johnson because complimentary tickets to a baseball game have holes punched in them and they look like the playing cards that the legendary sharpshooter Annie Oakley shot full of holes in Buffalo Bill's Wild West shows in the 1880s.

By extension, an "Annie Oakley" has come to mean any free ticket, such as a pass to a theater.

Antietam, Battle of   The bloodiest battle of the Civil War, it took place on September 17, 1862, at Sharpsburg, Maryland. General Robert E. Lee had prepared to attack the Union forces, but a copy of his plan fell into Union hands, allowing Union general George B. McClellan to anticipate Lee's strategy. When the smoke of battle cleared, over 10,000 casualties lay on the battlefield.

"Antietam" stands for a fight to the finish, a no-holds-barred bloody conflict, especially between opponents within a single entity; e.g., Pat Buchanan versus George Bush vying in the primaries to be the Republican Party's nominee for president.

Antonioni, Michelangelo (1912–)   Italian film director. Antonioni created strangely haunting landscapes against which indolent women drift in an atmosphere of melancholy ambiguity tainted with corruption. Antonioni achieved international recognition with his trilogy: *L'Avventura* (1960), *La Notte* (1961) and *L'Eclisse* (1962). His 1967 film *Blow-Up* explored Antonioni's obsession with illusion and appearance. His photographer hero, spying on a couple making love in a London park, fails to see an extraordinary thing, which shows up only in the blow-up of his pictures— the corpse of a murdered woman among the trees. Seeing, like beauty, is in the eyes of the beholder. Antonioni's cinematography has suggestive power. Out of a sequence of everyday images he projects mystery, solitude, alienation and despair.

Antony, Marc   A character, based on a historical figure (82–30 B.C.), defined in two of Shakespeare's plays, *Julius Caesar* (c. 1599) and *Antony and Cleopatra* (c. 1607). In the former, Marc Antony delivers the savagely ironic funeral oration over Caesar's body ("Friends, Romans, countrymen, lend me your ears; I come to bury Caesar, not to praise him"), an oration that turns the mob against the conspirators led by Cassius and joined by Brutus. The assassins flee Rome. Antony, with Lepidus and Octavius, defeats them at Philippi. Both Cassius and Brutus commit suicide.

In *Antony and Cleopatra,* Marc Antony neglects his responsibilities as a member of the triumvirate ruling Rome. He has abandoned his wife in Rome because he has fallen under the sensual spell of Cleopatra. He returns to Rome when his wife dies. He appeases Octavius by marrying his sister Octavia, but when Antony is once more irresistibly drawn to Egypt and Cleopatra, Octavius initiates war against the adulterous pair. In the end, disgraced and defeated in battle, Antony falls upon his sword. Cleopatra too commits suicide.

Marc Antony is depicted as a passionate man, an able general and administrator who could have ruled an empire but who gave up all for love and deemed the sacrifice a world well lost.

apartheid   From the Afrikaans word for "apartness" or separation. Until March 1992, in the Republic of South Africa apartheid was the comprehensive and rigid institutionalization of racism. Its intention was to separate the races, not only black from white, but also nonwhite groups from one another. The white minority ruled dictatorially over the nonwhite majority. Blacks had no representation in government and no civil rights. They were forced into separate townships; they worked for pittance wages in menial or in dangerous jobs (as in the mines); they were forbidden all social intercourse with whites and had to use separate facilities. They were brutalized by the police on any suspicion of rebellion or disobedience. Their condition has been powerfully dramatized by such South African novelists as Peter Abraham (*Mine Boy*), Alan Paton (*Cry, the Beloved Country*) and Nadine Gordimer (*My Son's Story*).

The principal architect of South Africa's strict apartheid laws was Prime Minister Hendrik Verwoerd, who was assassinated on the floor of Parliament in 1966 by a white man who claimed that Verwoerd was favoring the blacks at the expense of the whites. Verwoerd's policies continued under Johannes Vorster and Pieter Botha.

Rising black rebellion against apartheid under the leadership of the African National Congress (ANC) led to increased oppression and large-scale imprisonment or exile of dissidents. In the 1980s 12 Western countries imposed economic sanctions on South Africa because of its policy of apartheid. The United Nations followed suit. Not until F. W. de Klerk became president were repressive restrictions against blacks loosened. Most political prisoners, including ANC leader NELSON MANDELA, imprisoned for 27 years, were released. In a plebiscite in 1992 the white people of South Africa voted to continue de Klerk's policies of lifting apartheid. On May 10, 1994, Mandela was elected the first black president of South Africa.

Apart from its specific reference to racial segregation, in America the word "apartheid" is used today to denote any kind of segregation, as of men and women in orthodox synagogues, or haves and have-nots in separate neighborhoods.

Appalachia   A region in the Appalachian Mountains of the United States associated with poverty, backwardness and ignorance—home of the hillbillies. Its people were depicted with sensitivity in the 1930s photographs of Walker Evans and in the poetic prose of James Agee in *Let Us Now Praise Famous Men* (1939).

apple pie   Traditionally regarded as the quintessential American dish. Now a homely metaphor for American values.

Use: He's a true American. What he's advocating in the Senate is as American as apple pie.

Appleseed, Johnny (John Chapman) (1774–1847)   For 50 years, Johnny Appleseed led a nomadic existence preaching and teaching settlers how to establish and care for their orchards. It is said that four states (Pennsylvania, Ohio, Indiana, Illinois) owe their orchards to him.

His mission brought with it extraordinary acts of kindness and generosity to people and animals. A man of great courage and endurance, he is said to have set out alone, during the War of 1812, to warn the backwoods settlements about the fall of Detroit and imminent Indian attacks.

In 1923, Vachel Lindsay (1879–1931) wrote a poem celebrating Johnny Appleseed as an American folk hero.

A Johnny Appleseed is a person who helps people to help themselves by teaching them to use the tools of self-sustenance. He is one who may scatter the seeds of ideas in people's minds.

Appointment in Samarra   Title of a 1934 novel by the American writer John O'Hara. Although the novel is about the tragic life of Julian English, the head of a Cadillac agency in Gibbsville, Pennsylvania, the exotic title comes from a legend felicitously narrated by Somerset Maugham. This legend is used as a kind of epigraph and parable for the book. It is called "Death Speaks" and tells of a servant who was jostled by Death in a Baghdad market. Terrified, he jumped on his master's horse and galloped away to Samarra, where Death would not find him. The master asked Death why he had threatened his servant. Death replied, "That was not a threatening gesture . . . it was only a start of surprise. I was astonished to see him in Baghdad, for I had an appointment with him tonight in Samarra."

Thus, an "appointment in Samarra" is an inescapable rendezvous with death.

Après moi le déluge   Reproved for her extravagant expenditures, MADAME DE POMPADOUR (1721–64), the witty, beautiful, influential mistress of Louis XV of France, is said to have replied with characteristic arrogance, *"Après moi le déluge"* (After me, the flood). In common parlance, the phrase has come to mean "I don't care what happens after I'm dead," or, "After I'm gone, this whole structure will collapse."

Use: "In their last lame-duck session, the Democrats decided to call the Republicans' bluff by recommending a repeal of their own tax increase, an '*après moi le déluge*' gambit that would almost certainly bankrupt the states' coffers and force the Republicans to raise taxes on their own." (*New York Times,* January 13, 1992)

"April is the cruelest month"   Opening words of T. S. Eliot's poem *The Waste Land* (1922):

April is the cruelest month, breeding
Lilacs out of the dead land, mixing

13

Memory and desire, stirring
Dull roots with spring rain.

Often used superciliously with mock sensitivity to the stirrings of spring, or as a joking reference to the April 15 income tax deadline.

Aquinas, St. Thomas (c. 1225–1274)

One of the great names among medieval Scholastics, the most brilliant philosopher-theologian of the 13th century, a renowned teacher at Paris and in Italy, Saint Thomas Aquinas in the *Summa Theologica* and other works argued that reason and faith are reconcilable, two separate but harmonious paths to knowledge. Reason arrives at knowledge through the senses and logic; faith arrives at knowledge through divine revelation. Both come from God, the ultimate source of truth. Saint Thomas applied Aristotelian logic to problems of religious doctrine. In 1879 Pope Leo XIII proclaimed Thomism to be the "official" philosophy of the Roman Catholic Church.

In modern usage, to think of somebody as a Thomas Aquinas is to imply that he is brilliant and subtle in argumentation, that he can reconcile the irreconcilable.

Arabian Nights

See SCHEHERAZADE.

Arbeit macht frei

German for "work makes you free," the motto inscribed over the entrance gates to the Nazi concentration camp at Auschwitz (Oswiecim, Poland); cynical, in view of the forced labor, starvation and almost certain death that awaited the inmates.

Used sarcastically today when imposing an unwelcome chore or task. See also AUSCHWITZ.

Arbuckle, "Fatty"

Roscoe Arbuckle, a former plumber's helper, became one of Mack Sennett's original KEYSTONE KOPS, a grotesque, slapstick silent film comedian. His name describes a grossly fat person.

Archie

First appearing in 1941, *Archie* quickly became one of the most widely-read comics. It dealt with the teenagers of the day as seen through adult eyes: Archie Andrews, the quintessential high school student; Jughead, whose passion for hamburgers exceeded his passion for girls; Reggie, Archie's black-haired rival; and Betty and Veronica, Archie's girlfriends and rivals for his attentions. At its peak, *Archie* was selling over 1,000,000 copies a month.

Archie, like *Batman*, *Superman* and a small handful of others, has transcended comic books and become pure Americana.

Areopagitica   An impassioned tract written in 1644 by the English poet and pamphleteer John Milton (1608–74), arguing for freedom of the press. It urged the repeal of a law that required the licensing of all books before publication and that in effect established the principle of prior censorship by an office of the government.

What the MAGNA CARTA is to the Constitution of the United States, the *Areopogitica* is to the First Amendment guarantee of freedom of speech and the press.

Use: The American Civil Liberties Union (ACLU), in innumerable briefs before the Supreme Court, has in essence voiced an ongoing, ever-vigilant Areopagitica against infringement of First Amendment freedoms.

Ariel   A delicate, airy spirit in Shakespeare's *The Tempest,* Ariel was imprisoned in a tree by the witch Sycorax. PROSPERO releases Ariel and promises eventual freedom if Ariel will faithfully carry out Prospero's wishes. This comes to pass at the end of the play. Ariel sings some of the most beautiful songs ever written by Shakespeare:

> *Full fathom five thy father lies*
> *Of his bones are coral made. . . .*

and

> *Where the bee sucks, there suck I*
> *In a cowslip's bell I lie.*

An "Ariel" is someone light, fleet, delicate, lovely; someone seemingly without human grossness.

See also CALIBAN.

"Arkansas Traveler, The"   A well-known piece of American folklore in the form of a skit with dialogue and music. The Arkansas Traveler, on horseback, is lost, tired, and looking for lodging. He comes upon a squatter who is fiddling outside a log cabin. The fiddler pretends to misunderstand all of the traveler's questions. A battle of wits ensues in which the traveler is placed in the role of straight man:

> Traveler: Where does this road go to?
> Squatter: It ain't gone anywhere since I been here . . .
> Traveler: Is it far to the next town?
> Squatter: It seems farther than it is but you'll find it ain't.

Traveler: Which way to the post office?
Squatter: I don't know.
Traveler: You don't know much, do you?
Squatter: No, but I ain't lost.

Traveler: Why don't you put a new roof on your house?
Squatter: Because it's rainin'.
Traveler: Why don't you do it when it's not raining?
Squatter: It don't leak then.

(From Alan Lomax, *American Ballads & Folk Songs*,
and Carl Sandburg, *The People, Yes.*)

In the course of the skit, which could go on with improvisations for more than half an hour, the traveler notices that the squatter keeps playing the first half of the tune "The Arkansas Traveler" over and over again. Evidently the squatter doesn't know the rest of it. When the traveler offers to teach him the second half, he wins the squatter's enthusiastic trust and hospitality. At this moment, the traveler turns the tables and engages in a contest of wits in which the squatter becomes the straight man.

The origin of this folktale is in dispute. The best scholarship points to Colonel Sandford C. Faulkner of Little Rock who, while touring the state in the election campaign of 1840, got lost in the mountains. Upon his return he told the story of his encounter with the squatter. It proved to be so amusing that he was called on to repeat it again and again.

An Arkansas Traveler ostensibly is a country bumpkin who surprises us with his native wit. Common usage has confused the country bumpkin, or squatter, with the Arkansas Traveler.

armchair quarterback   See MONDAY MORNING QUARTERBACK.

Armstrong, Louis Henry "Satchmo" (1900–1971)   Jazz trumpeter. His friends called him "Satchelmouth" because his mouth was unusually large. Later, they abbreviated his name to "Satchmo." To millions the world over, he was a living legend.

Henry Pleasants is quite sure that "almost everything we have heard in the past 40 years in jazz . . . short of folk and rock . . . derives from Armstrong."

Equally certain is Leonard Feather that "Americans, unknowingly, live part of every day in the house that Satch built."

Satchmo had no imitators. He was, in fact, not imitable. His distinctive, gravelly voice was immediately recognizable. He made music for its own sake because, as he once said, "I'm just glad."

Arno, Peter (1904–1968)   American cartoonist for the *New Yorker* magazine. Born Curtis Arnoux Peters, of a prominent family in Rye, New York, Arno was educated at Hotchkiss Preparatory School and at Yale University. Oddly enough, he chose to delineate in his cartoons low-life characters such as might have crashed one of Jay Gatsby's bizarre parties: half-naked flappers, exotic dancers, speakeasy types, boors and drunks.

Use: Jack Kroll, in a review of *Jerome Robbins' Broadway* in *Newsweek* (March 6, 1989), wrote: "The 'Charleston' from *Billion Dollar Baby* (1945) whips the entire jazz-age 20's into a whirligig of flouncing flappers, boozing socialites, collegiates in pink raccoon coats, mobsters and bootleggers; it's like a giant Peter Arno cartoon brought to life!"

Arnold, Benedict (1740–1801)   Considered one of the most despicable characters in American history, a traitor to his country, Arnold began as a courageous military commander who raised his own militia in the Revolutionary War and fought alongside Ethan Allen to capture Fort Ticonderoga from the British. Eventually he was made commander of West Point. Embittered by what he considered his shabby treatment by the Continental Congress, Arnold planned to surrender West Point to the British. When his contact with the British, Major John André, was caught and hanged by the Americans, Arnold fled to the British side and fought against his countrymen. After the war, Arnold lived in exile in Canada and in England.

Benedict Arnold is the classic traitor. To be called "a Benedict Arnold" is to be given a special niche among the infamous.

Arrow Collar Man   In 1924, the Arrow collar ad that made the Arrow Collar Man the most popular of contemporary male icons. Perfectly clad in Arrow shirts, square-jawed, pink-cheeked, clean shaven, elegantly groomed, young and handsome by any standard, he fluttered female pulses throughout the land.

Arrowsmith, Martin   The protagonist of Sinclair Lewis's novel *Arrowsmith* (1924). A young doctor and medical researcher, he must fight various temptations to abandon his ideals in exchange for wealth and fame. In his struggle to maintain his integrity he is influenced by his mentor and idol, Dr. Max Gottlieb, a German-Jewish refugee dedicated to science. In the end Arrowsmith, together with his friend Terry Wickett, retires to a quiet place in Vermont to devote himself to pure research. The novel is a kind of *Pilgrim's Progress* for the medical profession and has been the prototype for others in the genre, e.g., *The Citadel* by A. J. Cronin.

arsenal of democracy   President Franklin Delano Roosevelt's description of the United States as it undertook to supply the Allies with the weaponry and materiel needed to fight the AXIS countries of Germany and Italy, before the United States (and Japan) entered World War II. This was initially called a "lend-lease" program. By the end of the war, the United States had supplied $48.5 billion worth of military equipment to 42 countries.

Use: The United States has remained an arsenal of democracy, supplying most of the technologically advanced air power in places such as Bosnia and Kosovo to fight "ethnic cleansing."

Artful Dodger   The nickname of Jack Dawkins, an expert pupil of FAGIN in the art of pickpocketing and other nefarious tricks in Charles Dickens's *Oliver Twist* (1837–39). It is the Artful Dodger who is sent by the suspicious Fagin to trail Nancy when she steals out on Oliver's behalf to a meeting with Mr. Brownlow. Fagin reports Nancy's "disloyalty" to Sikes, who murders her in retaliation.

As the name implies, an "artful dodger" is a shifty, petty criminal, expert in evasion.

Arthur, King   The legendary king of the Britons who, according to one account, decisively defeated the Saxons at Mount Badon in A.D. 516. He supposedly died in the Battle of Camlan in 537. (See Nennius, *History of the Britons.*)

Arthur became the center of an ever-growing group of legends, myths, romances and fairy tales generally gathered under the rubric King Arthur and the Knights of the Round Table. The mysteries surrounding his birth, education and ascension to the throne; his indestructible sword, EXCALIBUR; his guiding magician, MERLIN; his blindness to the adulterous affair between his wife, Guinevere, and his bravest and most trusted knight, Lancelot; his betrayal by his own son, Mordred; his death and removal to AVALON, have intrigued writers and poets all over the world throughout the ages. The tragic element of Arthur's story, the fall from innocence, has added profundity to his legend.

King Arthur represented the highest ideals of medieval chivalry. He was a model to all his knights in such virtues as loyalty, bravery, integrity, the fair dispensing of justice, gallantry to women, charity to the poor and defenseless.

The adjective "Arthurian" often is used to describe a person who seems to embody these qualities. Similarly, the name of King Arthur's legendary capital, CAMELOT, has come to stand for an ideal city or society.

Ash Can School   Twentieth-century art movement. Ugly subjects can make beautiful paintings, if the technique is lively and emphatic. So taught Robert Henri (1865–1929), an American artist who was the spokesman and the leader of a group of painters who came to be known as the Ash Can School. They included William Glackens (1870–1938), George Luks (1867–1933), John Sloan (1871–1951), Everett Shinn (1876–1953), George Bellows (1882–1925) and Henri himself. They flourished just prior to World War I. Akin to the naturalists in literature (Zola, Dreiser), they based their art on the observation of the seamy side of American urban life: Bowery bums, prizefighters, bored office workers, prostitutes, subway commuters, tenement dwellers, scrubwomen, breadlines, overflowing garbage cans and dirty slums. Their style derived from their original experience as illustrators. In England their counterparts led by John Bratby were called the Kitchen Sink School.

Thus we refer to certain obsessions with ugly, realistic subjects in books, printing or real life as belonging to the Ash Can School.

Ashley, Lady Brett   Heroine of *The Sun Also Rises* (1926), a novel by Ernest Hemingway. She is a beautiful, abandoned Englishwoman in love with Jake Barnes, the hero; but because he has been rendered sexually impotent by war wounds, she engages promiscuously in a series of love affairs with Jake's friends in Paris. In Pamplona, where the group has gone for the bull-running, she seduces Pedro Romero, a star torero. In the end, she gives Romero up for his own good, thus achieving in renunciation the feminine counterpart of the Hemingway hero code.

"ask not what your country can do for you; ask what you can do for your country"   These memorable words were spoken by President John F. Kennedy at his inauguration on January 20, 1961. They were an inspiring call to Americans to rededicate themselves to the ideals upon which the nation had been founded.

They are often used today by politicians, but also by those who simply substitute another word for "country." For example, Ask not what your mother can do for you; ask what you can do for your mother.

assembly line   Moving belt used by Henry Ford in the manufacture of the Model T automobile. It made mass production quick, easy and cheap, each worker contributing a single maneuver as the object on the moving line went by him. It also made for boredom on the part of the worker.

Today the assembly line idea seems to be used not only in industry but in human affairs as well. The trend in health services, for example, is toward assembly-line medicine, as the patient is passed from one "specialist" to another.

Astaire, Fred (1899–1987)   Born Fred Austerlitz in Omaha, Nebraska, he became what many people believe to be America's greatest dancer. Slim, graceful and stylish, Astaire was sophisticated perfection in white tie and tails. Together with his best partner, Ginger Rogers, with whom he appeared in several movie musicals between 1933 and 1939, he made routines of dazzling bravura seem effortless. His films include: *Top Hat, Shall We Dance, The Gay Divorcee, Flying Down to Rio, Roberta,* and *The Story of Vernon and Irene Castle.*

The name Fred Astaire is synonymous with elegant male sophistication and debonair grace on the dance floor and off.

Astor, John Jacob (1763–1848)   One of 12 children born to a poor German butcher, Astor became an enormously successful American fur trader and New York City real estate investor.

Asked if he'd have done anything differently with his life, he replied with characteristic bluntness that he regretted he had not bought all of Manhattan Island.

When he died, he was the richest man in America. For his ruthless operations, historians have placed him among the contemporary ROBBER BARONS.

To be called an "Astor" is to be counted at the very peak of the financial élite. However, the term is also used ironically, as when someone habitually short of cash is described as "a regular John Jacob Astor."

Atlas, Charles (1894–1972)   In his early years, Atlas was a poor physical specimen: anemic, lacking in strength, listless, underweight. Depressed by his physical condition, he set about building himself up with his own regimen, which he called "dynamic tension." In time, he won the title of "The World's Most Perfectly Developed Man." He opened his own gym where he worked up his original physical development system, which he offered by mail order. His potent advertising campaign drew tens of thousands of responses yearly from individuals who wanted to do something quick and dramatic about their physical plight. They all saw themselves as the "80 lb. weakling" that Atlas depicted himself as having been—before he developed into the magnificent persona that dominated every ad. They fervently believed that he would rescue them from a life of weakness and inferiority.

atom bomb   Awesome explosive weapon deriving its power from splitting the atom (atomic fission); used radioactive uranium for its production. First tested and exploded on July 16, 1945, at Alamogordo, New Mexico. The first bomb was dropped in wartime on August 6, 1945, on Hiroshima, Japan, with greater power than 20,000 tons of TNT. The second and final atom bomb ever to be used against a civilian population was dropped on August 9, 1945, on Nagasaki, Japan. So ruinous was the effect of these bombs that Japan surrendered on August 14, 1945. The United States had a monopoly on the manufacture of the atom bomb until the U.S.S.R. exploded one in 1949. Eventually Great Britain, France, Communist

China, India and Pakistan tested bombs of their own. The ultimate weapon; the ultimate threat; destructive power.

"attention must be paid"   Phrase spoken by Linda, the wife of WILLY LOMAN in the play *Death of a Salesman* (1949) by Arthur Miller. She has discovered evidence that Willy is planning suicide. Willy is an embittered man, a failure as a provider and especially as a father. She says to Biff, the estranged son who has failed to live up to Willy's expectations: "I don't say he's a great man. Willy Loman never made a lot of money. His name was never in the paper. He's not the finest character that ever lived. But he's a human being, and a terrible thing is happening to him. So attention must be paid. He's not to be allowed to fall into his grave like an old dog. Attention, attention must be finally paid to such a person . . ."

Attica   A maximum security prison in New York state. On September 9, 1971, the prisoners mounted what was said to be the most violent prison riot in American history. It involved about 1,000 inmates, who seized part of the compound and held 30 guards and civilian workers as hostages.

Negotiations continued for almost a week between inmates and an "observers' committee" consisting of representatives of government, newspapers, etc. Russell G. Oswald, state commissioner of correction, accepted most of the prisoners' demands. He rejected their demand for no reprisals and total amnesty for the rioters. The inmates answered Oswald by displaying a number of hostages with knives at their throats. The assault on the prison followed. State troopers, prison guards and 1,500 sheriffs' deputies finally smashed the revolt. Twenty-eight prisoners and nine guards were killed. Attica left a stain on the administration of New York state's penal system.

Attica has become synonymous with extreme brutality and misguided zeal in the handling of prisons and prisoners.

Attila   King of the Huns from A.D. 433 to 453. Although he appears to have been a reasonably just ruler of his own people, he inspired terror abroad. Having squeezed as much tribute as the traffic would bear from the cowed Eastern Roman emperors, he turned westward from present-day Hungary. In the year 451 he invaded Gaul with 500,000 troops. These Mongol hordes were defeated by a coalition of Germanic tribes. Attila then marched into Italy and became part of the barbarian invasions that toppled the Roman Empire. Attila, his army struck by pestilence and shortage of supplies, returned to Hungary, where he died in 453.

Attila's name has become associated with barbaric savagery, as has the term "Hun." Killing, pillaging, ransacking, carrying off booty have become the trademarks of Attila and his Huns. He became known as the Scourge of God.

Augustine, St. (354–430)   Born Aurelius Augustinus of a Christian mother and a pagan father in Roman North Africa, he was educated in Carthage and became a teacher of rhetoric in Rome and later in Milan. The essence of Augustine's story is contained in *The Confessions* (400), the chronicle of his dramatic conversion to Christianity after an early life of hedonism. He had fathered an illegitimate child and he had been "lazy, lustful and mischievous". His soul hungered "restless to find its rest in God." During Easter week in 387 he was baptized.

Although Augustine became a founder of Christian theology, especially as set forth in his 22-volume work *The City of God* (413–426), it is as a sincere and devout convert who found faith after "great doubt and mental disquietude" that he is still read.

Auschwitz   Nazi death camp in southwest Poland. Between 1942 and 1944 about two million Jews were exterminated at Auschwitz (Oswiecim, in Polish), gassed in gas chambers and their bodies burned in adjacent crematoria. Terrorized by brutal SS guards and dogs, convoys of newly-arrived Jews were lined up for "selection:" those who were to die immediately and those who were to live for a while. Everything of conceivable value was confiscated and used by the Nazis: clothing, possessions, gold fillings, hair, even the ashes. The camp was liberated by Soviet troops on January 27, 1945.

Auschwitz is synonymous with ultimate, premeditated horror, with man's inhumanity in its most brutal and deadly form, carried out with mechanistic efficiency. See also DACHAU.

automatic pilot   A mechanical device on an airplane that, when switched on, takes over the guiding or steering of the plane from the human pilot. Metaphorically, the phrase is used for activities other than guiding a plane or a boat or a balloon, with the implication that someone is being lazy or inattentive, as in the following quotation from a review by Michiko Kakutani in the *New York Times* (April 8, 1999): "Such scenes . . . remind us what this talented writer can do when he isn't coasting along on automatic pilot."

Avalon   The isle to which King ARTHUR is taken when he is mortally wounded and from which it is said he will return to lead his people once again.

Avalon in Celtic mythology is the island of Blessed Souls and an earthly paradise. A 1989 movie about a Jewish family that has immigrated to America, the *goldeneh medina* (golden land), in search of liberty and prosperity was called, symbolically, *Avalon*.

Axis   Term coined by Italy's Benito Mussolini in 1936 after signing an agreement with Hitler. He said that Berlin and Rome would form "an axis around which all European states can assemble." Actually, the Axis in World War II comprised only Germany, Italy and Japan, with a little help from Bulgaria, Hungary and Rumania. An "axis" is an alliance of two or more states for coordinating foreign and military affairs. Today, it's any alliance, as in Senator Lloyd Bentsen's statement upon learning he had been chosen to run as vice presidential candidate on the Democratic ticket in 1988: "The Massachusetts and the Texas axis was good for the country and good for the Democratic Party in 1960 and it's going to be a real winner in November of '88."

ayatollah   Among Shiite Muslims, a religious leader who has achieved great understanding of Islamic laws. The word became well known in the Western world after Ayatollah Khomeini succeeded in ousting the shah of Iran and in imposing his fundamentalist government on his country. Now it stands for any highly repressive, punitive, rigidly fundamentalist person; a theocratic despot.

Babbitt, George F.   Main character in Sinclair Lewis's satirical novel *Babbitt* (1922). His name has added a word to the English language. A Babbitt is a "typical" American midwesterner. He is a standardized man, a product of 20th-century mass production, with a standardized family, a standardized house and car and other appurtenances of the materialistic life. He is a conformist, a joiner, a booster, a philistine, a man of conventional morality and conservative politics who "thinks" in clichés and platitudes. If ever he questions the worth of his own mode of life, his attempt to stray results in cheap, tawdry, futile affairs, such as that of George Babbitt and Janis Judique, and he is glad to return to the haven of middle America.

"Babes in the Wood"   The title of a popular English broadside ballad also known as "The Children in the Wood, or the Norfolk Gentleman's Last Will and Testament" (1595). The story tells of two very young children who are placed by their dying parents in the care of an uncle. This evil man hires two assassins to murder the orphans so that he can come into their large inheritance. One of the hired killers, however, is so taken with the children that he kills his obdurate partner and then abandons the tots to fend for themselves in the woods. After some days of wandering, the children die in each other's arms. A robin covers the bodies with leaves. The wicked uncle and the man who abandoned the children are severely punished. In some later versions, the tragic ending is exchanged for a happy one: The children are found asleep in the woods and are rescued.

In modern usage, babes in the wood are people so naive and innocent that they are easily misled.

Baby M   Infant girl born in 1986 to surrogate mother Mary Beth Whitehead and the natural father William Stern. After the baby's birth, Mrs. Whitehead reneged on her contract to give up the baby to Mr. and Mrs. Stern for a payment of $10,000. She rejected the money and fought to retain the child. After a long, complicated battle fought in the courts, the media and every household, Judge Harvey R.

Sorkow in March 1987 awarded the baby to Mr. and Mrs. Stern and presided over the adoption of the child by Mrs. Elizabeth Stern. Baby M became Melissa Elizabeth Stern.

On February 3, 1988, however, the New Jersey Supreme Court ruled that surrogate motherhood contracts involving an exchange of money violated the law against the sale of children. It ruled, too, that Baby M would be reared by the Sterns but that Mrs. Whitehead retained full parental rights, including visitation. The adoption of Baby M by Mrs. Stern was voided.

Baby M has become a catchword for legal and ethical problems arising out of surrogate parenting.

back street   From the novel of the same name (1931) by Fannie Hurst (1889–1968) about a married man and his mistress who carry on a longstanding secret affair in one of the "back streets" of town.

"Back street" refers to the nonrespectable part of town where illicit affairs and illegal transactions are hidden from public view.

bad seed   This term refers to *The Bad Seed* (1955), a play by the American play-wright Maxwell Anderson, based on a novel by William March, about a seemingly innately wicked child. Destroying the illusion of the natural innocence of child-hood, it raises the question of the genetic source of evil; in other words, can a bad seed be implanted within the human embryo? The term "bad seed" is resorted to as an explanation of otherwise inexplicable criminal behavior in children. A case in point is the real-life story of Mary Bell, a girl of 11 living in Newcastle-upon-Tyne, England, who in 1968 murdered two little boys. She showed no remorse and was sentenced to 12 years in detention. In the United States there has been a rash in recent years of murders by children, such as the April 1999 shootings at a high school in Littleton, Colorado, in which two students killed about 20 of their class-mates and teachers before killing themselves. The cause: nurture or nature? Upbringing or genetic bad seed?

Baedeker   Named after its publisher, Karl Baedeker (1801–59), the granddaddy of travel guidebooks appeared in 1829. This first volume was followed by a series of detailed, exhaustive guides to most European countries, parts of North America and the Orient. These guides covered everything from history to cuisine, and even provided early ratings of accommodations.

The early Baedekers were published in German, and later appeared in French and English translations.

In their day, the Baedeker guidebooks dominated the travel field. Today, the new Baedekers include Michelin, Frommer's, Fodor's and others.

The term "Baedeker" now describes almost any kind of extensive guide, as a Baedeker of the best restaurants, a Baedeker of historical monuments, or a Baedeker of important museums.

"Baedeker" also is sometimes used derisively, as in "she can't even walk down her own street without a Baedeker."

Baghdad   From ancient times the hub of desert commerce and travel, the city was founded in A.D. 762 on the west bank of the Tigris (in modern Iraq) by the caliph Mansur. Under the caliph Harun-ar-Rashid it became a center for scholars, artists and merchants and enjoyed great wealth. Baghdad is the setting for many of the stories in the ARABIAN NIGHTS. It is a city associated with exotic bazaars, crowded streets, international intrigue. New York City, for example, has been called "Baghdad on the Hudson."

Balanchine, George (1904–1983)   Choreographer. Born Georgi Militonovich Balanchinadze in St. Petersburg, Russia. In the 1920s, after training at the Petrograd Imperial Ballet Company, Balanchine became the chief choreographer for Diaghilev's Ballets Russes. He formed a friendship with Igor Stravinsky, whose music inspired him to his best innovative ballets for the rest of his life. In 1934, he came to New York at the invitation of Lincoln Kirstein. There he founded the School of American Ballet and in 1948, the New York City Ballet, with its permanent headquarters since 1964 at the State Theater in Lincoln Center. Balanchine grafted the tradition of Russian classical ballet onto American soil, but he went on to create a new, spare style with plotless ballets and long-legged ballerinas.

balkanize   From the Balkan Peninsula, made up of Albania, Bulgaria, Greece, Romania, the former Yugoslavia and the European part of Turkey. These small, contentious states (and their predecessor states) engaged in the First and Second Balkan Wars in 1912 and 1913. In 1914, the assassination of Archduke Francis Ferdinand of Austria-Hungary by a Serbian nationalist in Austrian-held Sarajevo was the immediate cause of World War I.

After World War II and after the death of Tito, the Balkan Peninsula was further fragmented by the breakup of Yugoslavia into six constituent republics: Serbia, Croatia, Macedonia, Slovenia, Montenegro and Bosnia. Within some of these republics ancient ethnic hatreds flared up, stoked by nationalist dreams of a "greater Serbia." Thus began the horrors of ETHNIC CLEANSING, especially in Bosnia (1991–95) and in Kosovo (1995–99), and the further fragmentation of the Balkans.

To balkanize now means to divide and conquer; to divide groups or areas into small, contending and ineffectual factions—that is, to prevent minorities from exercising political power by "balkanizing" them, one against the other.

Use: "At the same time the field [sociology] became balkanized as schools began offering degrees in competing disciplines like black studies, Jewish studies and women's studies." (Joseph Berger, "Sociology's Long Decade in the Wilderness," *New York Times,* May 28, 1989)

Ball, Lucille See *I LOVE LUCY.*

ball game Originally applied to sports, as in baseball or football. Now extended to mean a set of circumstances or conditions involving two or more contenders or opponents, as in the phrase "a whole new ball game."

Balzacian See *COMÉDIE HUMAINE.*

banality of evil See EICHMANN, ADOLPH.

Band-Aid Trademark for a small strip of adhesive bandage with gauze in the center; used to cover or protect minor cuts, wounds, abrasions. Invented by Earle Dickson and commercially launched by Johnson & Johnson in 1921. Has come to mean a temporary solution that does not meet long-range, basic needs; limited or makeshift help; a temporary, stop-gap remedy, as in "Our Band-Aid approach to economic development must be changed . . ."

Banquo's ghost Banquo is a foil to the main character in Shakespeare's tragedy *MACBETH* (1606). At the beginning of the play, Macbeth and Banquo are victorious generals and noble thanes (lords) in Scotland. Both are accosted and tempted by the three witches. Banquo remains loyal to King Duncan; Macbeth murders Duncan and becomes king of Scotland.

When Macbeth learns from the witches that Banquo's descendants shall be kings of Scotland, he arranges to have Banquo and his son, Fleance, killed. Later, at a banquet to which he has invited all of his thanes, Macbeth pretends to be annoyed at Banquo's absence. At this point, Banquo's ghost appears in Banquo's seat. Only Macbeth sees it. Macbeth is completely unnerved by the appearance of the ghost. He shouts "Never shake thy gory locks at me" and reacts in a way incomprehensible to his guests, although some of them have begun to suspect Macbeth as the murderer of their king. The banquet breaks up in disorder.

The expression "Banquo's ghost" has come to symbolize an unwanted reminder of misdeeds, an embodiment of a guilty conscience.

Bara, Theda Born Theodosia Goodman (1890–1955). Dark-haired beauty of the silent movie era, she played the evil vamp (short for vampire) who lures men, ruins them and tosses them aside. "Kiss me, you fool," a line from her 1914 film *A Fool There Was,* is still quoted satirically.

Barbie Doll   Trade name of a very popular, blue-eyed, blonde, teenaged doll with a stylish wardrobe. Named after Barbie Handler, daughter of the owners of the Mattel Toy Company, it first went on the market in 1958. Today it is a term applied to a bland, saccharine, superficial person.

barefoot boy   A term from a poem (1855) by the American poet John Greenleaf Whittier (1807–92) that celebrates the bucolic joy of a country childhood; the simplicity, naïveté and openness of youth; the general sweetness and kindness that envelops young people growing close to "nature."

The opening lines set the idyllic mood of the poem: "Blessings on thee, little man / Barefoot boy with cheeks of tan."

The barefoot boy has come to refer to any fresh-faced young man, and implies a certain innocence.

"Barkis is willin'"   In Charles Dickens's novel *David Copperfield* (1850), an expression of assent used by Barkis, a man of few words, a carrier who courts and wins Peggotty, David's devoted and jolly nurse, by having David convey the message "Barkis is willin.'"

In today's parlance, "Barkis is willin'" is a humorous way of accepting a task or a relationship.

Barnes, Jake   Central character in Ernest Hemingway's novel *The Sun Also Rises* (1926). An American journalist, sexually impotent because of war wounds, he is in love with the beautiful and promiscuous Lady Brett Ashley. Deeply frustrated, he moves in a circle of aimlessly drifting expatriates in Paris. With them he is drawn to wherever he can find excitement, as to Pamplona for the bull-running festival.

Jake Barnes is a prototype for those who try to overcome psychological wounds in pointless drinking, drifting, cynicism. He is representative of the "lost generation."

Barney Google   The creation of cartoonist Billy DeBeck, Barney Google appeared in a daily comic strip sequence called *Take Barney Google, For Instance* (June 17, 1919). The American public took Barney to itself immediately. It couldn't resist Barney, his wife Lizzie (three times his size), his horse Spark Plug (a carefully draped blanket covered his knock-knees) and their dizzyingly varied adventures. He won and lost fortunes, wooed heiresses, got involved in murders, hijackings, secret trips to Cuba and Europe. For more than 80 years, the feisty, top-hatted, diminutive Barney has enjoyed America's unbounded affection.

Barnum, Phineas Taylor (P. T.) (1810–1891)   Born in a poor, rural community (Bethel, Connecticut), Barnum was driven by a powerful desire to make good. Convinced that "there was no limit to the public's gullibility," Barnum in the 1840s started touring the United States with a series of fabulous "attractions": the midget Tom Thumb, the Rubber Man, the Thin Man, the Elephant Man, and others. Later, Barnum opened the successful private Museum of Curiosities, located on Broadway in New York City. The museum housed such "freaks of nature" as the Bearded Lady, the Fat Lady, the Wild Man of Borneo and Jumbo, the African Elephant, billed as the "world's only surviving mastodon."

In 1870, in partnership with James H. Bailey, Barnum launched "The Greatest Show On Earth," the most spectacular circus in the world.

In his time, Barnum was one of the most celebrated living Americans—the great pioneer in the creation of mass amusement, a master showman, probably the most adroit manipulator of the public attention. Convinced that Americans (and Europeans, too) wanted to be "humbugged," Barnum ran his life and his enterprises according to this motto: "There's a sucker born every minute."

A Barnum is an original, clever, resourceful, unprincipled exploiter of the mass mind and emotions, a quintessential showman.

baroque   An ornate, exuberant, dramatic style of architecture that originated in Rome during the final phase of the RENAISSANCE and spread throughout Europe during the 17th and the first half of the 18th centuries. It started as a revolt against the classicism of Palladio, but, carried to excess, the style became known as ROCOCO. In France, the baroque was the style of Louis XIV. Two of the great names associated with baroque architecture are Gianlorenzo Bernini (1598–1680) in Italy and Johann Fischer von Erlach (1656–1723) in Austria.

The term "baroque" has also been applied to sculpture, painting, music and literature. It has come to mean convoluted, complex and decorative.

Barrymore   Stage name of an American theatrical dynasty, the "royal family of the American stage." Their real name, never legally changed, was Blythe.

Maurice Barrymore married Georgianna Drew, the daughter of John and Louisa Drew (both well-known actors). Maurice and Georgianna had three children: Lionel Barrymore (1878–1954); Ethel Barrymore (1879–1959); and John Barrymore (1882–1942). These three were outstanding in classical as well as modern roles, in tragedy as well as comedy, on the stage as well as on the screen. Lionel is remembered for his annual Christmas interpretation on radio of Ebenezer

Scrooge in Dickens's "A Christmas Carol." John Barrymore, after his brilliant performance as Hamlet in 1922, was considered the greatest Shakespearean actor of his day. The Barrymores were all very handsome people, but John acquired the nickname of "the Great Profile" because of his aquiline nose. The dynasty is continuing with Drew Barrymore, who began her acting career at the age of six in *E.T.: The Extraterrestrial,* a Steven Spielberg film. The name Barrymore is the standard against which all other acting performances are measured.

Barton, Clara (1821–1912)   During the Civil War, so inadequate was the care of the wounded soldiers that disease killed more troops than did bullets. The War Department's bureaucracy seemed unable to get the food and medical supplies to where they were needed. Clara Barton was prominent among those who stepped in to bring some order into the War Department's inadequate efforts. Her devotion and superior organizational ability made a significant contribution to the welfare of the soldiers.

Later, when the Franco-Prussian War (1870–71) broke out, she got a firsthand look at how the well-organized International Red Cross operated in the war theater. When she returned from Europe, Clara Barton embarked upon an arduous campaign to get Congress to establish a Red Cross organization in the United States. In 1872, she became the first president of the American Red Cross. Under her leadership, Red Cross chapters sprang up all over the United States. She resigned in 1904, but remained actively involved in Red Cross work until her death at age 91.

For her devotion to humanitarian causes, Clara Barton has come to stand as a symbol of selfless sacrifice in the nursing profession.

basket case   This term probably originated during World War I to refer to young soldiers who had lost all their limbs, becoming quadriplegic and thus totally incapable of getting around on their own or doing anything for themselves. Dalton Trumbo's harrowing novel *Johnny Got His Gun* (1939) tells the story of one such "basket case." Today, a basket case refers dismissively to any person or even nation considered so inept as to be utterly helpless and hopeless.

Bastille   Originally a royal chateau built for King Charles V of France in 1370, the Bastille had become, by the 18th century, an infamous prison, housing among its inmates such prominent political prisoners as Voltaire.

On July 14, 1789, as the French Revolution began, a mob of angry Parisians stormed this "symbol of absolutism." In France, July 14 is a national holiday commemorating the fall of the Bastille.

An attack on any bastion of terror and oppression, a blow struck for freedom, is often referred to as "storming the Bastille."

Bataan   Battle in the Philippines lost in 1942 by the American and Filipino forces under General Douglas MacArthur. After having been ordered to escape by President Franklin D. Roosevelt and upon arriving in Australia, MacArthur announced the now famously prophetic words, "I shall return."

Bataan is notorious for the "Death March" and for other brutalities to which the Japanese victors subjected their prisoners of war.

Use: "The unbroken sound of our footsteps was beginning to feel ominous like the Bataan death march." (Ella Leffland, *Rumors of Peace*)

Batman   In May 1939, Batman made his debut in *Detective Comics.* By day, Batman is Bruce Wayne who has inherited a great fortune. Orphaned when his parents were killed in a street holdup, he devotes his life to fighting crime or, occasionally, to "one-man vigilante justice."

By night, Wayne becomes Batman, "self-trained strong man, gymnast, acrobat"—the scourge of criminals whom he pursues with relentless zeal. As Batman, he wears a bat-like cape and cowl.

Batman has no superpowers. He catches criminals by employing his superior intelligence. Despite some of his unsavory, questionable behavior, Batman has maintained his hold on his vast audience for a half-century. His crime-plagued readers still find security and solace in his swift if occasionally crude and unconstitutional treatment of criminals.

bat a thousand   In baseball, to achieve a perfect record, to get a hit every time at bat—an obvious impossibility. This expression has come instead to mean compiling an outstanding, extraordinary record.

In popular use, to bat a thousand is to be highly successful.

batting average   In baseball, a number expressing a player's batting performance or ability. It is arrived at by dividing the number of hits by the number of times at bat—and carrying the result to three decimal places.

Batting average now applies to any measure of achievement.

Use: Among the salesmen in the Eastern division, Garfield has the best batting average.

Battle of the Bulge   In December 1944, a dent about 60 miles deep was created by the German counterattack against the Allied line in Belgium-Luxembourg. When America's General Anthony McAuliffe received an ultimatum from the

Germans to surrender, he answered with the now-famous, laconic "Nuts!" In January 1945 the Allies advanced and straightened the bulge. Now the term is applied humorously to heroic efforts at dieting to reduce bulges—of the flesh.

Baudelaire, Charles (1821–1867)   French poet, author of *Fleurs du Mal* (1857), a book of poems. See also HYPOCRITE LECTEUR.

Use: "[The] . . . Paris [of Balzac] is not just a city, but a spiritual condition: brilliant, corrupt, built on broken hopes and ruined lives, the city of Baudelaire's poetry." (Brooks Wright)

Bauhaus   Influential school of design founded in 1919 in Weimar, Germany, by the architect Walter Gropius (1883–1969). Its original faculty included Wassily Kandinsky, Paul Klee, Lyonel Feininger, Marcel Breuer, Herbert Boyer and, after 1923, Laszlo Moholy-Nagy. In 1926 it moved to Dessau. In 1928, Mies Van Der Rohe, the German architect, became its head. In 1933, because of Nazi hostility, it was dissolved. Its staff was dispersed and its influence spread throughout the world.

The Bauhaus philosophy was encapsulated in the tenet: "Form follows function." All design, whether of a building, a household object like a chair or a lamp, an industrial machine or an entire city, should be based strictly on the function and needs of that entity and upon a close scrutiny of the nature of the materials used. The Bauhaus stressed the importance of the craftsman-designer in the manufacture of mass-produced objects. Its style was clean, unadorned, severe, refined.

The Bauhaus had a beneficial influence in calling attention to the need for beauty in everyday objects, and to the use of modern materials and techniques in their manufacture. The Museum of Modern Art in New York City has a special department for award-winning industrial design based on Bauhaus principles.

Bauhaus refers to anything—glass buildings or pots and pans or chairs—that shows refinement of line and shape coming from economy of means and an understanding of the materials of construction.

Bay of Pigs   Site of the April 25, 1961, invasion of Cuba by anti-Castro Cuban exiles living in the United States. This counterrevolutionary attempt, encouraged by President John F. Kennedy, was easily repulsed by the Cuban military, in large part because the United States failed to provide air cover as promised.

Now used as an example of an ill-conceived, badly managed, disastrous military adventure, a fiasco, a military betrayal.

beast of Buchenwald   Ilse Koch, wife of the commandant of the Buchenwald concentration camp (near Weimar, Germany), infamous for having lampshades made out of the skin of her victims. She committed suicide in September 1967, while serving a life sentence for atrocities that even SS officers deemed excessive.

Beat Generation   From "beat," meaning worn-out, pooped, exhausted, plus "beatitude," meaning bliss. Members of the Beat Generation hoped to achieve out of the lowest depths of despair that spiritual illumination that leads to the peace that passeth understanding. The Beats represented a Bohemian revolution against the mores and values of a "corrupt, materialistic, military-minded" society. They adopted unconventional modes of dress and behavior. They sought release from moral restriction in hallucinogenic drugs, alcohol, sexual experimentation and poverty.

The term was first applied in the 1950s to the poets who gathered at the City Lights Book Store in San Francisco: Allen Ginsberg, Gregory Corso, Lawrence Ferlinghetti and, later, Gary Snyder; and to the prose writers Jack Kerouac and William Burroughs. See also BEST MINDS OF MY GENERATION.

Beatles   British rock-and-roll quartet: John Lennon (1940–80); [James] Paul McCartney (1942–); George Harrison (1943–); Ringo Starr [Richard Starkey] (1940–).

In 1961, this popular singing group burst out of their hometown of Liverpool, England, to conquer the world and alter the style and substance of a segment of popular music. Discovered by manager Brian Epstein, they made musical history.

In the 1960s the Beatles' albums sold more than 250 million copies—a musical milestone. Lennon and McCartney wrote most of the songs. Lennon added complexity and a heightened social consciousness to the lyrics. McCartney wrote the immensely appealing melodies. The Beatles' distinctive hairdo made long hair a token of disaffection.

beatnik   Member of the BEAT GENERATION.

Beatrice   Probably Beatrice Portinari (1266–90) of Florence, Italy, whom the poet DANTE first met when he was nine years old and again when he was 18. She died in 1290 when Dante was only 25. She had married Simone de' Bardi, and Dante in 1293 married Gemma Donati, who remained in Florence when Dante was exiled for life in 1302.

The love of Dante for Beatrice was an ideal, spiritual love. She was his muse and inspired much of his writing. "La Vita Nuova" (1292) tells in prose and poetry the story of that love. In *The Divine Comedy*, Dante's masterpiece, Beatrice guides Dante through Paradise. She is the symbol of divine revelation, and leads Dante to the beatitude of salvation.

A Beatrice, therefore, is an ideal beloved, an inspiration to spiritual wholeness and creative endeavor—a muse.

Beatrice and Benedick   Witty young sparring partners in the game of love in Shakespeare's comedy *Much Ado About Nothing* (1600). They seemingly run from each other, waiting breathlessly to be caught. Involuntarily drawn together, they resort to badinage to disguise their true feelings from each other and from themselves. Although Hero and Claudio are technically the main characters in this play, Beatrice and Benedick steal the show with the spirited exchanges in their "merry war."

On television and radio shows, husband-wife or other male-female pairs will often assume a Beatrice-and-Benedick relationship for the entertainment of the audience, who enjoy witty infighting.

beat to the punch   In boxing, the boxer who lands a punch before or faster than his opponent is said to beat him to the punch. In general, to act faster, to get an advantage over a competitor.

Use: "Carrel seemed to be the best man for the job. But he never got it. Bradley beat him to the punch."

Beau Brummel   (George Bryan Brummel) (1778–1840) Born in London of wealthy parents, educated at Eton and Oxford, he became prominent in London society. An original, elegant trendsetter in London men's fashions, he cut an unusual figure for his sartorial style, earning him the title Prince of the Dandies.

A Beau Brummel is the quintessentially best-dressed man.

Beauty and the Beast   Appearing first as *La Belle et la Bête* (1756), by Mme Leprince de Beaumont, this French fairy tale was translated into English in 1757. In 1946, Jean Cocteau adapted it into a great film classic.

In order to save her father's life, Beauty, the youngest of his three daughters, agrees to live in an isolated place inhabited only by a frightful Beast. Although she refuses to marry the Beast, she gradually finds herself looking forward to his daily visits. After three months, the Beast allows her to go home to her father, provided she returns within a week. Detained by her selfish sisters, she finally returns to the castle to find the Beast dying of heartbreak. She realizes that she has fallen in love with the ugly but gentle Beast. She tells him that she can no longer live without him. Immediately, he turns into a handsome young prince; the spell that had imprisoned him within the Beast's body is broken. They marry and live happily forever after.

The phrase "Beauty and the Beast" is generally applied—sometimes seriously, sometimes jokingly—to a seemingly ill-matched couple: a beautiful woman and an ugly man.

Becky Sharp   The vivacious and opportunistic heroine of *Vanity Fair* (1847), a novel by the English writer William Makepeace Thackeray (1811–63).

The character of Becky (Rebecca) Sharp shows up in high relief against that of Amelia Smedley. The two meet as students in an exclusive finishing school, Amelia as the gentle, well-bred daughter of a wealthy merchant and Becky as an ambitious charity girl, an orphan who teaches French for her board. *Vanity Fair* recounts the seesaw fortunes of these two friends.

Amelia is kind, unselfish and generous to Becky. On the other hand, Becky will stop at nothing to achieve wealth and status. She goes after Amelia's brother Jos, only to have him snatched away from her and sent back to the army in India. Becky then takes a job as a governess in Sir Pitt Crawley's household and secretly marries his second son, Rawdon Crawley. She is appalled at her own blunder when Sir Pitt, a far wealthier man, subsequently proposes to her. Later, Becky takes up with the lecherous, unscrupulous but immensely wealthy Lord Steyne. Rawdon discovers their liaison and leaves Becky for good. Excluded from society, down and out, Becky picks up one man after another in various spas.

Eventually, Becky once more attracts Jos Smedley, now returned from India, and becomes his mistress. She makes him take out a sizable insurance policy, with herself as the beneficiary. Jos subsequently dies under mysterious circumstances. Becky Sharp finally has achieved her goal: She has become a rich woman.

Becky Sharp is aptly named. "Becky" sounds hard, impervious. "Sharp" suggests cunning, unscrupulousness, ruthlessness. Nevertheless, the reader is grudgingly forced to admire this social climber's indomitable drive to succeed in a hypocritical society where wealth, not virtue, makes the livin' easy.

A Becky Sharp is an unscrupulous, indomitable social climber.

Bedlam   Short for *Bethlehem*. Originally a priory built in 1247, the Bethlehem Royal Hospital was converted to an insane asylum in the late 14th century. It remains the oldest mental hospital in England. In the 17th century, it was moved from Bishopsgate to Moorfields, where for a small fee anybody could gain admission to stare or even jeer at the patients.

"Bedlam" today means not an official asylum but any place that *seems* to be a madhouse, a place where confusion reigns. There are classrooms, for example, where the kids are out of control, that are sheer bedlam.

behind the eight-ball   In the game of pocket billiards the players must pocket all the other numbered balls before pocketing the eight-ball—a black ball with a small white circle in the center. To be positioned behind the eight-ball makes it impossible for the player to strike any other ball without striking the eight-ball first. Therefore he is in danger of losing the match, if by chance he pockets the eight-ball before all the other balls have been put into the pockets.

"Behind the eight-ball" has come to mean being in a difficult, awkward, unpleasant, untenable position.

Beirut   Capital city of LEBANON. During the Lebanese Civil War of the 1970s and 1980s, the city suffered great damage and its inhabitants lived in fear as rival factions fought for control.

Use: "The project was 'once a good place to live.' Now, however, it's a small-scale Beirut, where rival drug-selling gangs use guns and razors in a vicious struggle to monopolize sales." (*New York Times* editorial, June 16, 1989)

bell the cat, to   In common parlance, "to bell the cat" is to accept a hazardous mission to help others. Once upon a time, a family of mice lived peacefully in an old house. One day, the mistress of the house adopted a young, vigorous cat. The cat's natural appetite for mice soon reduced the mouse population and spread terror among the survivors. In desperation, the mice held a meeting to decide how to deal with the feline menace.

One bright young mouse suggested tying a bell around the cat's neck. The tinkling of the bell would warn the mice of the cat's approach. Appreciative applause from the assembled mice lasted briefly. "A great idea," said one of the veteran mice, "but who will bell the cat?"

"Belle Dame sans Merci"   See "LA BELLE DAME SANS MERCI."

Belle Époque   See LA BELLE ÉPOQUE.

bench   In baseball, the bench is where the players sit when they are not playing in a game. To bench a player means to keep him out of the game for poor performance, injury or other reasons. Use of the word has been extended to areas beyond sports, as in business.

bench warmer   In sports, a player who seldom plays. Generally a substitute, he sits on the bench and "warms" it. By extension, anyone who does not play an active role in any enterprise.

Bennet, Mrs.   The mother of five marriageable daughters in Jane Austen's novel *Pride and Prejudice* (1813), Mrs. Bennet subscribes wholeheartedly to the opening declaration of the novel: "It is a truth universally acknowledged, that a single man in possession of a good fortune, must be in want of a wife."

Mrs. Bennet is a silly, ignorant, garrulous, fluttering woman whom her caustic husband barely tolerates. Her vulgarity so offends the aristocratic Mr. Darcy that for a long time his pride prevents him from accepting that he has fallen in love with her sprightly daughter Elizabeth. Nor can he believe at first that Elizabeth's older sister, Jane, is truly in love with his friend Bingley, since he ascribes to Jane the materialistic motives of the mother in seeking a wealthy suitor. Mrs. Bennet is so singleminded in marrying off her girls that she is overjoyed when a third daughter, Lydia, elopes with Wickham, an officer and a scoundrel.

Benny, Jack (1894–1974)   Born Benjamin Kubelsky, he was one of the finest comedians of radio and television, "a comedian's comedian," a master of timing and inflection, and the "pregnant pause"—best illustrated in one of his famous routines:

He is held up on a dark street. A nervous robber threatens him: "Your money or your life, mister."

Benny makes no move to comply. He is silent—for a long, long fraction of a minute.

The by-now anxious robber prods him: "Hurry up, mister. Your money—or your life."

Benny's slightly impatient reply: "I'm thinking! I'm thinking!"

Benny projected a unique comic persona: pathologically stingy (he kept his money in a vault); the butt of insults and humiliations from lesser characters; his below-par violin playing; his pose of elegant inadequacy; his special relationship with Eddie Rochester, his sardonic, gravel-voiced valet.

Benton, Thomas Hart (1889–1975)   American regionalist painter from Missouri who used only American themes, most of them rural. Benton depicted in muralist style the landscape and farm workers of the Midwest. His figures are sculptural and are endowed with energy and vitality. He rejected foreign influences, modernist aesthetics and urban culture as decadent. He aimed to create an authentic American epic style based on themes from American life and history. *Cradling Wheat* (1938) is typical of his style. Benton is associated with the epic treatment of American rural life.

Bergen, Edgar (1903–1978) **and Charlie McCarthy**   Edgar Bergen, a deft, sophisticated ventriloquist, and Charlie McCarthy, his fresh, master-of-back-talk dummy, were among radio's most listened to, pre-television pair.

Bergen's understated, witty thrusts and Charlie's irreverent retorts and equally irreverent comments about institutions and people delighted audiences everywhere. Bergen later added Mortimer Snerd, a dull simpleton, often capable of unexpectedly fey repartee.

When Bergen decided that his performing days were over, he donated Charlie to the Smithsonian Institution.

Use: "I like it. It's as good a way out as any, maybe the best. You got this kid up there, you gotta do something with him, so why not make him out a dummy? He fits—a regular Charlie McCarthy." (*The Last Hurrah* by Edward O'Connor)

Bergman, Ingmar (1918–)   Swedish film director who gathered about him a company of exceedingly gifted actors (Liv Ullmann, Bibi Andersson, Max von Sydow), cameramen (Sven Nykvist and Gunnar Fischer) and technicians, whom he used with stunning effect in all his pictures. His masterpieces are dark, brooding meditations upon large themes: the silence of God; the nature of appearance and reality; the terrible isolation of man; the ambiguity of evil; the absence of faith and love; the duality of the artist in society; the intensely erotic psychosexuality of women in confined environments. Although he has tried his hand at comedy, it is as a tragic visionary that he has set his stamp upon the cinema. His films include *The Seventh Seal* (1956), *Wild Strawberries* (1957), *Persona* (1966), *Cries and Whispers* (1972), *Scenes from a Marriage* (1974), *Autumn Sonata* (1978) and *Fanny and Alexander* (1983).

Bergman, Ingrid (1915–1982)   Swedish-born film actress whose films include *Intermezzo* (1939), *Casablanca* (1943), *For Whom the Bell Tolls* (1943), *Spellbound* (1945), *Notorious* (1946) and *Autumn Sonata* (1978), among others. Her image of radiant natural beauty and wholesomeness was tarnished when she had an extramarital affair with Italian movie director Roberto Rossellini and gave birth to his child. The world was scandalized at the time and Bergman was ostracized. Sexual mores changed, however; eventually Bergman's transgression was forgiven and she continued her interrupted career.

Berkeley, Busby (1895–1976)   American film director and choreographer who created dazzling effects of "patterned drill" in the Hollywood musicals of the 1930s. In such movies as *42nd Street, Gold Diggers of 1933* and *Footlight Parade,* he thrilled audiences with seemingly perfect kaleidoscopic patterns made with huge companies of beautiful chorus girls.

Berle, Milton (1908–)   A pioneer of the television variety show, the American entertainer Milton Berle made his raucous debut on June 9, 1948, as host of the

Texaco Star Theater. A graduate of the vaudeville and burlesque circuits, Berle brought with him the gags and routines he had mastered: rowdy, off-color, sure-fire and played for belly laughs.

The new television audiences found Berle's clowning and irreverent humor irresistible. Before long, he became the first television superstar, affectionately dubbed "Uncle Miltie" and "Mr. Television." In a sense, Berle was the one who really popularized the new medium.

Berle's antics are synonymous with noisy, lowbrow, occasionally tasteless comedy. He is uniquely American.

Berlin Wall   A concrete wall replacing a barbed-wire fence first strung up on August 13, 1961, by armed East German soldiers to stop the exodus of East German refugees to the West. A confrontation between U.S. and Soviet tanks on either side of the wall threatened for a time the uneasy peace of the COLD WAR. The wall finally came down in November 1989.

The Berlin Wall was a symbol of the ideological divide between East and West. See also IRON CURTAIN.

Bernhardt, Sarah (1844–1923)   Great French actress who came to be known as "the Divine Sarah" and mockingly, among lesser mortals, as "Sarah Heartburn." Her acting technique, unlike the more natural bent of her most famous rival, Eleanora Duse, was operatic, exaggerated, mannered. She was famous for her long death scenes and her equally long-drawn-out murder scenes, as in *Phèdre* by Racine and in *la Dame aux camélias* by Dumas, in which latter play she made her American debut. She even played such men's parts as Hamlet and L'Aiglon.

Born Henriette Rosine Bernhard in Paris, the illegitimate child of a Dutch Jewish mother and an Amsterdam merchant father, she was baptized as a Roman Catholic and educated in a convent school. She studied at the Paris Conservatoire and in 1862 made her debut at the Comedie-Française in *Iphigénie en Aulide* by Racine. Beautiful, graceful, with a magnificent speaking voice, she became a star among stars and eventually an actress-manager in her own theater. In 1914 one of her legs was amputated, but she continued her career. Her talent for showmanship and her much advertised love affairs entranced the public of two continents.

Today if a child has a tantrum or if a woman seems to be self-dramatizing, somebody might say, "Look at Sarah Bernhardt." Her name has come to stand for overacting.

Berraisms (also Yogi-isms)   Linguistic mutilations attributed to the great Yankee catcher Yogi Berra (1925–). As with GOLDWYNISMS, questions have been raised about the authenticity of some of these Berraisms:

- Sometimes you can observe a lot by watching.
- It ain't over till it's over.
- No wonder nobody comes here—it's too crowded.
- A nickel ain't worth a dime anymore.
- Even Napoleon had his Watergate.
- I want to thank all the people who made this night necessary.
- Why don't you pair them up in threes?
- Ninety percent of this game is half mental.
- Half the lies they tell me ain't true.

"The best lack all conviction, while the worst are full of passionate intensity"   These lines close the first stanza of "The Second Coming," a poem by William Butler Yeats (1865–1939), the Irish poet and playwright. The stanza conveys the disorder, the chaos threatening to swamp the world in a tide of anarchy. In the lines above, Yeats refers to well-meaning people who are no longer sure of their values, and to the ideologues and fanatics who are all too sure of theirs, being ready to kill for them.

These lines are often quoted and applied to the newest demagogues, authoritarians and despots, as well as to those like Hitler, Stalin, Mussolini, et al., who have disappeared but have left their horrible mark on the world.

"best minds of my generation"   From the opening line of Allen Ginsberg's poem *Howl* (1956), which denounces the mechanistic dehumanization of a society whose God is Moloch, a god that demands human sacrifice. Ginsberg sees the most sensitive young men of his generation "destroyed by madness, starving hysterical naked / dragging themselves through the negro streets at dawn looking for an angry fix, / angelheaded hipsters . . ." Ginsberg is their spokesman in this incantatory Jeremiad, the opening salvo of the BEAT GENERATION.

beyond the pale   "Pale" comes from the Latin word *palum,* a stake, broadened to mean a fence, a territory with exact limits; first applied to an area of eastern Ireland ruled by the Angevin king Henry II (1154–89). By the 15th century, the area encompassed four counties: Louth, Meath, Dublin, Kildare. Anything "beyond the pale" was considered, in a sense, beyond the bounds of civilization.

Later, "beyond the pale" encompassed such related meanings as beyond the boundaries of civilized speech or behavior.

In 1772, Russia established its own Pale of Settlement—designating the only areas in Ukraine, Lithuania, Poland, White Russia, Bessarabia and Crimea where Jews were allowed to live. In essence, the Jews were placed in a geographical straitjacket. Jews found outside the Pale of Settlement were arrested and punished—

unless they had special travel or residential permits. During the 19th century, Jews in the Pale of Settlement were subjected to cruel repression, forced conversions to Christianity, involuntary baptism, extortion and, finally, POGROMS and massacres.

Bhopal   A city of about 200,000 inhabitants in India where, on December 3, 1984, a deadly leak of methyl isocyanate gas from an insecticide plant owned by Union Carbide killed more than 2,000 people. Thousands more were hospitalized with symptoms of choking, vomiting, dizziness, sore throat and burning eyes. Many were blinded. Those who could, fled to escape the noxious fumes. Union Carbide was sued for $15 billion and eventually a settlement was reached. In an age in which environmental concerns have reached the forefront of international attention, Bhopal stands for man-made industrial catastrophe on a huge scale. It is equaled, perhaps, only by the meltdown at Chernobyl in the Soviet Union.

Bible, the   Generally refers to the Christian Bible, containing the Old Testament (sacred writings of Judaism) and the New Testament (sacred writings on Jesus Christ). The Bible is considered to have been divinely inspired and therefore author-itative. Although the term "Bible" used to be reserved for religious scripture, as in "The Koran is the Bible of the Muslims," it has come to be used in modern times for every book that purports to treat any subject, however trivial, in a full, exhaus-tive and fundamental way, as in the following titles: *The Chocolate Bible* (1997) by Christian Tenbver; *The Bartender's Bible* (1991) by Gary Regan; *Earl Mandell's Vitamin Bible* (1991).

Bible Belt   Areas in the South and Midwest of the United States where religious fundamentalism is a powerful political force. Publishers of textbooks, for example, must consider how their treatment of evolution will go over in the Bible Belt. Librarians are often pressured to remove from their shelves certain books that are offensive to the mentality of some Bible Belt readers, and politicians are often judged by their position on single-issue causes fanatically held by Bible Belt voters.

big bang   Generally accepted theory of the origin of the universe in a single big explosion of a highly compacted bit of matter. That happened about 15 billion years ago, and the universe has ever since been expanding outward from the center of the initial explosion. Used colloquially for any big explosion.

Big Bertha   Huge siege cannon used by the Germans in World War I. Said to be named after Bertha Krupp, a member of the German ammunitions family.

Large, amply endowed women used to be referred to as Big Berthas—unchar-itably.

Big Brother   In George Orwell's *1984* (1949), the despotic "leader" of Oceania, whose ubiquitous portrait stares out of countless posters that bear the caption "Big Brother is watching you." He represents the pervasive presence of totalitarian rule, the invasion of privacy.

Big Lie   Technique used by the Nazi propaganda machine under Goebbels. If the lie was big enough, outrageous enough, how could people fail to give it credence even though it contradicted all the evidence? After all, who could invent so big a lie? One of the biggest lies that the Nazis succeeded in getting accepted was the story that the deportation of Jews to Eastern European concentration camps and extermination centers was just a "resettlement" program. Another was to depict as "subhumans" the Jews whom they had systematically dehumanized through brutality, intimidation, starvation, imprisonment and murder.

In the spring of 1989 the Chinese government tried to use the Big Lie after they fired indiscriminately at crowds of unarmed students and workers demonstrating for democracy in Tiananmen Square, Beijing. The presence of TV cameras and satellite broadcasting made the Big Lie more difficult to get away with.

big stick   From the maxim coined by President Theodore Roosevelt in 1901 to describe his interventionist policies in Latin America: "Speak softly and carry a big stick, and you will go far." A "big stick" is the threat of force to achieve one's way.

billingsgate   Foul language associated with workers in the fish market located at Billings Gate, an ancient gate into the city of London on the north bank of the Thames. The Billings Gate goes back to the 13th century, the fishmarket to the 17th century.

Today, "billingsgate" is a synonym for any coarse, abusive, vituperative language.

Billy the Kid (1859–1881)   Born William A. Bonneville, one of the old West's most infamous desperadoes, he is said to have killed 21 men by the time he reached the age of 21—something of an exaggeration.

In his spectacular career of murder and cattle rustling, Billy cut a wide swath through the American Southwest. Following his shooting of Sheriff Brady in 1880, he was captured by Sheriff Pat F. Garrett and sentenced to hang. While under guard, he escaped, killing two deputies. At large for seven weeks, he was finally discovered and fatally shot by Sheriff Garrett at Fort Sumner, New Mexico, on July 15, 1881.

Billy the Kid is probably the most written-about Western outlaw. He was the stuff of which myths are made, yet the reality of his exploits needs no embroidery or amplification. Today, any desperado may be referred to as "a Billy the Kid."

Birth of a Nation, The Landmark silent film directed by David Wark Griffith in 1915, based on Thomas Dixon's novel *The Clansman* (1905). Its three-hour-long dramatization of the events leading up to and through the Civil War and the Reconstruction that followed established the film medium as an art form. It is notable for its realistic and spectacular battle scenes. However, it has become an extremely controversial film because of the anti-Negro bias in the Reconstruction scenes, when the hero, an aristocratic Confederate veteran, joins the newly formed Ku Klux Klan.

Use: "I've tried to produce a synthesis between the traditional view of Reconstruction—the old *Birth of a Nation* image—and the revisionist view, the continued hold of racism and federalism." (Eric Foner, quoted by Herbert Mitgang in the *New York Times* Book Review, May 22, 1988)

Bismarck, Otto Von (1815–1898) The "Iron Chancellor" who ruled Prussia according to this precept: "The great questions of the day will be settled not by resolutions and majority votes . . . but by BLOOD AND IRON." A MACHIAVELLIAN statesman, he succeeded in unifying Germany by means of "the iron fist in the velvet glove."

Bitburg To commemorate the 40th anniversary of the end of World War II, President Ronald Reagan planned to lay a wreath on the graves of German soldiers in Bitburg, Germany, where Nazi SS troops were also interred. This created a furor in the United States. To make matters worse, Reagan said that the Bitburg dead were just as much victims of Nazism as the ones who died in concentration camps. Elie Wiesel took the president to task in an eloquent and impassioned talk in which he "spoke truth to power." But Reagan, for political reasons, had to keep his commitment to the German chancellor to visit the site.

bite the bullet In the days before anesthesia, many surgeons gave their patients a soft, lead bullet to bite on—to divert their minds from the excruciating pains of surgery and to inhibit their screaming.

Today, to "bite the bullet" means to do something painful but necessary, or to make a tough decision.

black belt A rating of "expert" in various arts of self-defense (such as judo and karate).

In informal use, someone who is expert in any field.

Use: "In a highly competitive field, Jerry Barat has been judged a black belt by his peers."

blackboard jungle   From a 1955 movie, based on a novel of the same name by Evan Hunter, telling of a teacher's harrowing experiences with a gang of kids in a New York City school. The term has become a metaphor for the terror, chaos and mayhem in many inner-city schools.

Black Death   An epidemic of the bubonic plague that wiped out more than one-third of the population of Europe between 1347 and 1350. It has been called the greatest calamity ever visited on the Western world. A contemporary chronicler wrote that people believed it was the end of the world.

The plague started when sailors from the Crimea entered the port of Messina. It spread, through fleas that live on diseased rats, from Sicily, northward to Italy, France and the rest of Europe. The rat-infested, filthy towns of the Middle Ages were hit hardest. All normal life ceased. Death and the fear of death reigned supreme. Those few who dared to administer last rites became the next victims. The dead were thrown into mass burial pits. Livestock died by the thousands in the fields.

The bubonic plague reappears periodically. It broke out, for example, in the Great Plague of London in 1665. This calamity was described from firsthand observation in the *Diary of Samuel Pepys* (1633–1703) and, in a fictional account, in *Journal of the Plague Year* (1722) by Daniel Defoe. In 1947 Albert Camus wrote a compelling novel about bubonic plague in the Algerian port of Oran. It is called *The Plague* (*la Peste*). Over the years the term "Black Death" has come to have application to any uncontrollable epidemic.

black hole   A black hole in astronomy is not strictly speaking a hole at all, but a mass of such great density that nothing can escape its gravitational pull, not even light rays, which it absorbs (hence, *black* hole). The theory is that black holes originated in the explosions of very dense stars at a time when the universe was very young.

The term is used figuratively in everyday language to connote a deep hole from which one cannot extricate oneself, such as a "financial black hole."

black hole of Calcutta, the   On June 20, 1756, Suraj-ud-daula, Nawab of Bengal, captured Calcutta and imprisoned 146 members of the British East India Company in a stifling dungeon measuring 18 feet by 14 feet 10 inches, known as the Black Hole. All but 22 men suffocated overnight.

The expression "black hole of Calcutta" has come to mean any badly ventilated, dark place. It is also a punishment cell in military barracks, a "solitary confinement" prison cell for recalcitrant, unmanageable prisoners.

Black Monday   Monday, October 19, 1987, when the Dow Jones average on Wall Street fell about 500 points and set off fears of a 1929-type crash and depression.

The term refers generally to a collapse or wildly fluctuating prices on Wall Street.

blackout   The practice of extinguishing all lights or covering windows at night during the London Blitz of World War II. Now used for a blackout of news, or a power blackout as a result of heavy use of electricity.

Blackpool, Stephen   A character in Charles Dickens's novel condemning utilitarianism, *Hard Times* (1854), Blackpool is a hardworking, honest weaver in the Coketown factory of Josiah Bounderby. No matter how hard he tries, he cannot rise above the poverty inflicted on him by a heartless, greedy industrial system. In a labor dispute at the factory, he is caught between a ruthless boss and a ruthless union leader. Siding with neither, he is ostracized by the workers and fired by his boss. While seeking work elsewhere, he finds out that in his absence he has been falsely accused of a robbery actually committed by Tom Gradgrind, the rich spoiled son of the main character. On his way back to vindicate himself, Blackpool falls into a ditch and dies.

Stephen Blackpool is a victim, a man of simple, earnest integrity, crushed in the deadly conflict between capital and labor in a for-profits-only system that exploits and degrades the workers.

Blarney Stone   Those who kiss the Blarney Stone are said to be magically and instantly endowed with the gift of gab. They can smooth-talk you, lie to you, flatter you outrageously, and still enchant you.

The Blarney Stone is actually a triangular stone near the top of the wall of Blarney Castle in the village of Blarney, just north of Cork in Ireland. On it one reads: "Cormac McCarthy fortis me fieri, fecit A.D. 1446." According to one legend, a descendant of McCarthy, the original builder, in 1602, refused to surrender the castle to the English Crown. He stalled Queen Elizabeth's emissary with fine-sounding promises. Blarney became a word for smooth talk.

Blavatsky, Madame Helena Petrovna (1831–1891)   Born in Russia, Madame Blavatsky cofounded the Theosophical Society in the United States in 1875 and became "a priestess of the occult." She had traveled widely in India and in the mountains of Tibet, where she had met masters of the sacred essence, in harmony with the Universal Oversoul. She said they shared their secret wisdom with her.

Theosophy is a philosophical system that rejects scientific rationalism and espouses the spiritual nature of the universe. Its adherents seek to establish contact with the Divine through contemplation, revelation and spiritualist seances.

In 1887 William Butler Yeats heard Madame Blavatsky lecture on theosophy in London. He immediately fell under her spell and joined her society. Theosophy supplied Yeats with the cosmology for his mystic visions of the universe.

A "Madame Blavatsky" is a practitioner of the occult.

blimp   Originally a "B-limp" type of airship, meaning of a British, World War I, non-rigid design. These were used mostly for coastal patrol. Now a "blimp" metaphorically is a fat person with the shape of a dirigible.

blitzkrieg (or blitz)   German for "lightning war." Unlike the slow, holding technique of trench warfare in World War I, the German technique in World War II was the blitzkrieg. This involved the element of sudden surprise attack, softening the target with air strikes, and the use of swift motorized units to surround and cut off resistance. Thus were Poland, Denmark, Norway, Belgium, the Netherlands, France, Yugoslavia and Greece each conquered within a few days or weeks. The shortened form "blitz" described the bombing strikes on civilian populations, as in the London blitz. Frequently used today in the phrase "media blitz," to denote an intensive advertising promotion or political campaign.

blockbuster   Four-ton bombs dropped by the RAF in 1942; called blockbusters because they could destroy an entire city block. By the end of the war the Allies were dropping bombs of up to 11 tons on enemy cities. Now a blockbuster is anything gigantic, effective, impressive or having wide popular or financial success; e.g., a movie or a sales campaign can be a blockbuster.

Blondie   One of the most famous comic strip characters. Blondie, a "harebrained flapper," is pursued by DAGWOOD Bumstead, the playboy son of a tycoon. In 1933, Dagwood is married to Blondie and promptly disinherited by his father.

Blondie, now head of the household, becomes a devoted, affectionate, levelheaded wife, getting Dagwood out of his many misadventures. The family is in a state of constant agitation. Yet they are happy and optimistic.

Blondie has been translated into many languages. Once its readers numbered in the hundreds of millions.

blood and iron (Blut und Eisen)   With characteristic bluntness, Otto von BIS-MARCK (1815–98) set down his political and military philosophy for the Prussian

Reichstag in 1862: "The great questions of the day will be settled not by resolutions and majority votes—but by *blood and iron.*"

Moved by Bismarck's vaulting nationalism and diplomatic skill, Prussia succeeded in consolidating the German states into the German Empire with Prussia as its central, dominant force. Bismarck became its first chancellor (1871), naturally dubbed the "Iron Chancellor."

Bismarck's policies, expanded and carried forward by his successors, inevitably propelled Germany and Europe into two horrendous wars: World War I and World War II.

"Blood and iron" has come to stand for fervid nationalism and ruthless militarism.

"blood, toil, tears and sweat"   "I have nothing to offer but blood, toil, tears and sweat," declared Winston Churchill on May 10, 1940, in his first address to the House of Commons as prime minister of Britain. Churchill was referring to the task of fighting Hitler in World War II. This phrase has been shortened generally to "blood, sweat and tears" and is used to suggest nothing but sacrifice in a prospective task or relationship.

Bloom, Leopold   If *Ulysses,* the 1922 novel by James Joyce, hangs upon the framework of Homer's *Odyssey,* then Leopold Bloom represents the wandering Odysseus; Molly Bloom, the not-so-patient Penelope; and Stephen Dedalus, Telemachus searching for his father. Stephen ultimately finds a father in Leopold Bloom, a middle-aged Jew who is portrayed as an everyman wandering through all the venues of Dublin, from business offices to bars to brothels to funeral parlors to his own bedroom, on a single day: June 16, 1904. He is the ultimate antihero.

Use: "[Richard] Ellman was drawn to genius, yet was himself an ordinary man—the Leopold Bloom of biography." (*New York Times* Book Review, January 13, 1991)

Bloom, Molly   The epitome of female sensuality, she is married to Leopold Bloom, the main character in *Ulysses* (1922) by James Joyce. Her lengthy, unpunctuated, erotic stream of consciousness as she lies in bed at the end of the day—the day on which the entire action of the novel takes place, June 16, 1904—waiting to receive her husband from whom she has been estranged, closes the novel and is undoubtedly the most famous interior monologue in literature. Her last word is "yes," an affirmation of love and life and experience. Molly, in the Homeric scheme of the novel, represents Penelope, but a lusty one. Molly was modeled on Joyce's wife, Nora Barnacle.

Bloomsday   June 16, 1904, the day on which all the events of James Joyce's *Ulysses* (1922) take place. Joyce is said to have picked this date for his novel to commemorate the anniversary of his first walk with Nora Barnacle who was to become his wife. Every June 16 people who have a passion for *Ulysses* celebrate "Bloomsday" by following the route taken by Leopold BLOOM through Dublin (if they are in Ireland) or by a nonstop, oral reading of the entire novel.

Bluebeard   "Once upon a time," begins this tale by Charles Perrault (1697), there was a very rich man with a blue beard so ugly that women felt repelled by him. Nevertheless, he had married six times, although nobody knew what had happened to his wives. Soon after he married a seventh time, he had to leave on a business trip. He handed all the keys to his bride but warned her *not* to unlock the door to the room at the end of the corridor. Curiosity overwhelmed her. She entered the room to a grisly sight: Hanging on the walls were the bodies of his former wives with their throats slit.

Upon his return, Bluebeard knew immediately that his wife had disobeyed him. "You wanted to enter the little room!" gloated Bluebeard. "Well, Madam, enter it you shall—you shall go and take your place among the ladies you have seen there." In the nick of time she was saved by her two brothers, who came galloping into the castle and ran the villain through with their swords.

In Perrault's morality tale, women are warned to curb their curiosity, as if the fault were theirs. In modern times the more heinous vice would seem to be Bluebeard's murderous sadism. The macabre elements of the tale have often been parodied and spoofed. Some writers have understood the tale of Bluebeard to be a satire on King Henry VIII.

Today, a Bluebeard is a cruel, boorish man—especially one with a series of wives.

blue bird of happiness   The object of a search by the woodcutter's children Tyltyl and Mytyl in Maurice Maeterlinck's drama *The Blue Bird* (1909). Used symbolically today for elusive happiness.

bluestocking   This word has a long history. It originated in Venice in the 1400s when a group of Venetian ladies and gentlemen formed a society whose members were distinguished by the blue stockings they wore. By 1590 the blue stocking fad had reached Paris. By 1750, it had arrived in England. Here, under the aegis of Lady Elizabeth Montagu, the blue stocking became an emblem of sorts for the literary, scholarly women who met at her home.

Today, a "bluestocking" is a woman, an intellectual snob or pedant, especially one who tends to neglect the feminine graces.

boat people   Refugees from South Vietnam who tried to escape the communist takeover at the end of the Vietnam War by piling into flimsy vessels of every description and heading for neighboring territories. Many drowned; many were turned into a seemingly endless odyssey through pirate-infested coastal waters. It is estimated that 1.5 million Vietnamese and other Indo-Chinese have fled from their homelands since 1975. The phrase "boat people" has come to stand for any refugees desperate to find safe harbor from oppression.

Boccaccio, Giovanni (1313–1375)   Florentine author known chiefly for *The Decameron* (1348–53). In that book, 10 young patricians (seven girls and three young men) flee from the plague in Florence to a villa in the hills of Fiesole. They spend their time in telling stories: Each tells one story during a cycle of 10 days. The result is 100 stories encompassing almost every literary genre: romance, fairy tale, folk story, fable, anecdote. Many of these tales have been adapted again and again, as for example the story of the submissive wife, "The Patient Griselda." But what *The Decameron,* and Boccaccio, have become associated with over time are the bawdy tales.

Thus, although Boccaccio was a learned man who wrote about Dante and explicated *The Divine Comedy* in public lectures; although he was a humanist responsible for the recovery of many of the classics; although he was a biographer, a poet, a friend of Petrarch and Dante; and had a profound influence on the use of the Italian vernacular, what Boccaccio has come to stand for in the popular imagination is licentiousness, even pornography.

Bogart, Humphrey (1900–1957)   American actor, the star of such film classics as *The Petrified Forest* (1934), *The Maltese Falcon* (1941), *Casablanca* (1942), *The Treasure of Sierra Madre* (1948) and *The African Queen* (1951).

Nicknamed "Bogey," he played a lean and tough guy with narrowed eyes made narrower from the smoke of a cigarette clenched between his teeth. He hid idealistic values beneath a seemingly impenetrable veneer of cynicism.

bohemian   Originally, a gypsy or vagabond thought to have migrated to Western Europe from the ancient realm of Bohemia. During the 15th century, these "Bohemians" were prohibited from entering Paris. They were forced to remain outside the gates of the city in St. Dénis. Ironically, the modern use of the term is often associated with inhabitants of the Left Bank in Paris. In the opera *La Bohéme* (1896), for example, Puccini tells the story of four young impoverished students who share a garret on the Left Bank.

Another place that has been associated with bohemians is Greenwich Village in New York City, especially in the 1910s and '20s when such writers, artists and radicals as Edna St. Vincent Millay, e.e. cummings, Eugene O'Neill, Edward Hopper, Max Eastman, Delmore Schwartz and Emma Goldman lived there.

A bohemian has come to stand not only for intellectuals and artists and political radicals but also for any person who lives an unconventional, free-style life in dress, manners and morals. A bohemian would rather starve in an attic than take a 9-to-5 job. He or she feels infinitely superior to the bohemian's opposite, the bourgeois.

Bolívar, Simón (1783–1830) To South Americans he is known as the Liberator, the greatest Latin American hero, the father of a continent. He won the war of independence against Spain after many reverses and with the use of guerrilla fighters. He was elected president of Greater Colombia (comprising what is now Colombia, Venezuela, Ecuador and Panama). He organized the government of Peru and created Bolivia, named after him. In the end be became a dictator, dramatically surviving an assassination attempt, only to die of tuberculosis, poor and despised. Posthumously, his reputation has been rehabilitated. A passionate, headstrong visionary in life, be became a revered icon after death.

A Bolivar is a great patriot, a champion in a fight for national independence.

Bolshevik Member or adherent of one of the two main branches of Russian socialism. Vladimir Ilyich Lenin gained a brief majority for this radical branch in 1903; established as a separate party in 1912. In 1917, after 11 years of exile, Lenin returned to Petrograd (now Saint Petersburg) after the abdication of Czar Nicholas II. On November 7, 1917, the Bolshevik Party, organized into workers' councils, overthrew the moderate provisional government of Alexander Kerensky and seized power. The first thing the new Marxist government did was to start peace negotiations with Germany. The Russians had already lost 3.7 million people in World War I. The Bolsheviks (under Lenin and Trotsky) were on their way to establishing a "dictatorship of the proletariat."

"Bolshevik," in general parlance, denotes a fiery radical with Marxist ideology.

Bond, James Agent 007, British super-spy played originally by Sean Connery, and later by David Niven, George Lazenby, Roger Moore, Timothy Dalton and Pierce Brosnan in films based on the novels of Ian Fleming, including *Dr. No* (1962), *Goldfinger* (1964), *From Russia With Love* (1963), *You Only Live Twice* (1967). Always involved in foreign intrigue, Bond is good-looking, suave, irresistible to women, pleasure-loving, equipped with the latest gadgetry for destruction, expert in the martial arts. He always plays his part with tongue-in-cheek bravado.

bonfire of the vanities See SAVONAROLA.

Bonnie and Clyde   American film (1967) with Faye Dunaway and Warren Beatty, based on two real-life outlaws, both in their 20s, Texans Bonnie Parker and Clyde Barrow. Their four-year spree of violence, bank holdups and 12 murders throughout the Southwest in the early 1930s ended in their being ambushed and riddled with bullets by a posse of Texas Rangers. The film romanticized them and turned them into folk heroes.

booby trap   In World War II, a hidden explosive designed to go off on contact, or when detonated by some remote control device; designed to harass or kill enemy forces.

   Now "booby trap" has come to mean a seemingly harmless ploy or arrangement that conceals trouble for an opponent in business or, perhaps, for an adversary in an argument, an unforeseen pitfall.

boondocks   An uninhabited backwoods or marsh. Now any remote area far from the activities of big-city life. For example, in trying to save their children from the dangers and temptations of Manhattan, the Lewises moved to Queens, which, as far as they could see, might just as well have been out in the boondocks.

Boone, Daniel (1734–1820)   Well-known American frontiersman, born in Reading, Pennsylvania, to Quaker parents. Enamored of the virgin wilderness around him and the promise of a free, independent life, Boone became a hunter at the age of 12. He was captured and adopted by the Shawnee Indians. After he returned to his people, he devoted the rest of his life to the exploration and settlement of Kentucky. Despite attacks and harassment by the Indians, Boone continued to hack out the Wilderness Road, building Boonesboro, one of several forts. From 1774 to 1778, as a captain in the United States Militia, Boone defended the Kentucky settlements he had so ardently worked to establish. Boone spent the latter years of his life in Missouri doing what he loved most, exploring new land and hunting.

   James Fenimore Cooper modeled Natty Bumppo of the *Leatherstocking Tales* on Daniel Boone. Boone has become the archetypal American frontiersman.

Borden, Lizzie (1860–1927)   Lizzie Andrew Borden lived with her mother and stepfather in Fall River, Massachusetts. On the night of August 4, 1892, someone entered Mrs. Borden's bedroom and murdered her with 19 ax blows to the skull. Mr. Borden arrived home later that night and lay down to take a nap in the downstairs sitting room. He was dispatched with 10 strokes of an ax.

   Lizzie Borden was charged with the two murders. After a sensational trial that attracted nationwide attention, she was acquitted.

Though the crime was never solved, interest in it persisted. Edmund Lester Pearson, in his book *The Trial of Lizzie Borden* (1937), thought Lizzie was guilty. Edward Rudin's *Lizzie Borden: The Untold Story* (1961) declared Lizzie innocent.

Lizzie Borden achieved a kind of minor immortality in contemporary, anonymous doggerel:

> *Lizzie Borden took an ax, and gave her mother forty whacks.*
> *When she saw what she had done, she gave her father forty-one.*

Accused female murderers of parents are frequently called Lizzie Bordens.

Borgia   An Italian Renaissance family who earned a reputation for villainy and vice that included murder, fratricide, incest, lust for power and cynical opportunism.

The founder of this tribe was Alonso Borgia (1385–1458), who became Pope Calixtus III in 1455. His nephew Rodrigo Borgia (1431–1503) became Pope Alexander II in 1492. This pope promoted the fortunes of his progeny, Cesare and Lucrezia, more than he did the interests of the church.

Cesare Borgia (1476–1507) became the model for Machiavelli's *The Prince*. At the age of 17 he was already a cardinal; but, more interested in political than in spiritual power, he resigned from his office after the death of his older brother, in which he was said to have had a hand. Thereafter, he made an alliance with Louis XII of France, married Charlotte d'Sebret, sister of the king of Navarre, and seized towns and states throughout Italy. At one point he lured his chief enemies to a castle and had them all strangled. He himself seemed to have nine lives. He was poisoned with the same poison that did his father in, but Cesare survived. Arrested by Pope Julius II, he escaped to Naples, thence to Spain and finally to the court of Navarre. He died fighting for the king.

Lucrezia Borgia (1480–1519), whom some historians have tried to reclaim from infamy, was married three times. Her first marriage to Giovanni Sforza was annulled. Her second husband, Alfonso II of Naples, was murdered by her brother Cesare in 1500. She had more luck with her third husband, Alfonso d'Este, the duke of Ferrara. In Ferrara, Lucrezia gathered around her artists and poets (Ariosto, among them) and reigned over a brilliant court. In spite of historical revisionism, Lucrezia is still associated in the popular imagination with poison rings, incestuous affairs with her father and brother, and general mayhem.

A Borgia is ruthless, unscrupulous and treacherous in the pursuit of power.

borking   Term derived from Robert Heron Bork (1927–   ), American jurist whose nomination to the Supreme Court of the United States in 1987 by President Ronald Reagan was defeated by a Senate vote of 58 to 42 after a lengthy, no-holds-barred assault by liberals against his amply documented conservative views and decisions on civil rights, abortion, privacy and other issues. He resigned in 1988 from his judgeship on the Federal Court of Appeals for the District of Columbia to become a resident scholar at the American Enterprise Institute.

"Borking" has come to mean "the trashing of a conservative candidate by ideological warriors of the left." See SATURDAY NIGHT MASSACRE.

borscht belt   A string of hotels, boarding houses and rooming houses in the Catskill Mountains of New York catering mostly to Jewish vacationers. It was named by *Variety* editor Abel Green after the cold beet soup popular with Jewish gourmets. The borscht belt hotels were famous not only for their superabundant food but also as the testing ground for such well-known stand-up comics as Milton Berle, Buddy Hackett, Danny Kaye, Mel Brooks, Jackie Mason, Lenny Bruce and many, many others.

Bosch, Hieronymus (c. 1453–1516)   Dutch painter whose best known work is his triptych *The Garden of Earthly Delights* (1500). Although chronologically Bosch belongs to the Renaissance, he seems medieval in content and spirit. The three sections of *The Garden of Earthly Delights* depict, from left to right, (1) the creation of man and woman in Eden; (2) the cavorting of people in carnal pleasure and sin on this earth; and (3) their consignment to torture in the burning fires of hell. His is a pessimistic view: man's life proceeds from innocence to damnation.

Bosch's canvas is crowded with strange, fantastic images: glass bubbles, colossal fruits, demons, animals real and imaginary, exotic birds and fish, clusters of nude people copulating, men riding all kinds of animals around a pool of prostitutes, a vast surreal phantasmagoria of lust and procreation inhabited by peculiarly asexual figures. However, the symbolism of these configurations has not been satisfactorily ascertained.

Boston Strangler   Between June 1962 and January 1964, 13 women were murdered in Boston, all elderly, all living alone, all sexually assaulted, all strangled. When caught, Albert H. de Salvo (1933–73), the Boston Strangler, confessed, furnishing details of the murders that only he could have known. Sentenced to life imprisonment, he later was stabbed to death by one or more of his fellow inmates.

Use: The rash of murders of women led the police to believe that a new Boston Strangler was on the loose.

Boswell, James (1740–1795)   Scottish lawyer, writer, friend of many of the literary men of his time, James Boswell met the great Samuel Johnson (1709–84) in 1763. Developing a deep admiration for him, Boswell managed to overcome

Johnson's initial dislike and indifference and eventually became a warm friend and confidant. Early in their relationship, Boswell decided to make Johnson his "great subject." He spent considerable time with Johnson in open-ended conversations and long trips together. Boswell virtually became Johnson's "shadow." During these many meetings Boswell took notes on Johnson's brilliant conversation. These notes and recollections would eventually become his *Life of Samuel Johnson* (1791).

The *Life* is among the greatest of biographies. With dramatic fidelity, Boswell rendered Johnson fully alive, vital, crusty, warm, humane, encompassing: a towering, unforgettable man. Macaulay called Boswell the "Shakespeare of biographers."

A Boswell is a faithful, selfless biographer and companion.

Botticelli, Sandro (1444–1510)   Born Alessandro di Mariano Filipepi in Florence, Botticelli became one of the great painters of the Italian Renaissance and a favorite of the MEDICI circle. His most representative paintings are *La Primavera* (c. 1478) and *The Birth of Venus* (c. 1485), two of a series on pagan subjects with Neoplatonic themes.

The Birth of Venus shows the nude but modestly posed goddess of love standing at ease on a scallop shell that is being wafted over the sea by two winged zephyrs, looking like angels, at her left. To the right of Venus is a female figure, the personification of spring, who is about to drape a flower-patterned cloak over her. Venus has all the earmarks of what has come to be known as a Botticelli girl: the elongated, ethereal figure; the idealized head with flowing blonde tresses; the benign expression of innocence in the face. She is sometimes jokingly referred to as "Venus on the half-shell."

Bottom   One of the "mechanicals" (tradesmen) in Shakespeare's comedy *A Midsummer Night's Dream* (c. 1595). Undeterred by his own ignorance or vulgarity, Bottom thrusts himself forward as leader of the rehearsal of *Pyramis and Thisbe,* a play that he and his loutish friends plan to present at the nuptials of King Theseus and Hippolyta. They have chosen as their rehearsal ground a grassy grove not far from the bower of Titania, Queen of the Fairies. To this enchanted wood have also run the two pairs of lovers: Hermia and Lysander, Helena and Demetrius.

The shenanigans, intended and accidental, of Bottom and his group supply the farcical elements of the play. Bottom somehow finds himself transformed with an ass's head upon his shoulders. Titania, with love juice sprinkled on her eyelids by Puck, awakens to fall incongruously in love with the creature next to her, Bottom. All the lovers go round and round until everything is disentangled at the end of the play.

Bottom is a clownish character: aggressive, know-it-all, busy-bodyish, ungainly, undaunted and yet ultimately endearing. He is the one with an ass's head, both literally and figuratively.

bottom line   Originally, the line at the bottom of a financial statement that indicates either a net profit or a net loss. The use of the term has been extended to cover the end result of any dealings, practices, theories, or emotions or to identify the crux, the essential point involved in them. It has been further extended to suggest practicality, a concern with profit.

Bourbon   A French royal dynasty (1589–1792) descended from a powerful family living in Bourbon, France, from the 10th century. In 1272 Robert of Clermont, the sixth son of Louis IX, married Beatrice of Bourbon. In 1589 Henry IV became the first Bourbon king of France. His son was Louis XIII; his grandson, Louis XIV. Bourbon rule in France ended with the French Revolution.

The Bourbons were autocratic and stubborn. Talleyrand said of them that they forgot nothing and learned nothing. Today the term "bourbon" indicates a political or economic reactionary.

bourgeois   The term *bourgeois* refers to a middle-class society with middle-class values and a shopkeeper's mentality. In the Middle Ages the bourgeois were neither the aristocrats nor the peasants; they were, literally, the people of the burg, the town. Concerned mainly with property and acquisition, they could not be romanticized, as the other two classes could be, nor could they successfully aspire to climb into the upper class. They were condemned, even when wealthy, to be labeled the nouveaux riches. This is exquisitely demonstrated in Molière's play *Le Bourgeois Gentilhomme* (1670), in which M. Jourdain tries to rise to the position of a gentleman but remains a bourgeois and a boor.

"Bourgeois" still has a pejorative connotation. To be labeled a bourgeois is to be accused of worshipping respectability at all costs; to have no aspirations other than a desire for conformity, conventionality, security, money and comfort.

Bovary, Emma   The protagonist of *Madame Bovary* (1857), a novel by Gustave Flaubert (1821–80). Emma Rouault, the daughter of a prosperous farmer, receives a convent education. She longs for the finer things in life, things she has learned about in romantic novels: beautiful clothes, a fine home, a brilliant husband, a glamorous life in Paris. But she marries a devoted, sentimental and inept doctor, Charles Bovary, and lives in the dull provincial town of Yonville l'Abbaye. She is bored, restless, sick with disappointment, disillusion and idleness. Her romantic yearnings lead her into febrile adulterous affairs, first with Rodolphe and then with Léon, both of whom tire of her wild, insatiable demands upon them. Meanwhile, she has gone heavily into debt for all kinds of luxuries supplied to her by an unconscionable merchant, Lheureux. Unable to get help to repay her debts, and in disgrace over public auction of her goods, Emma takes arsenic and dies a painful, ugly death, while her husband, who has truly loved her all along, stands by helplessly.

In the French language, *Bovarisme* has become a word that stands for romantic illusions and unfulfilled expectations. Emma Bovary is a pathetic character, delineated with supreme realistic artistry by Flaubert.

Bow, Clara   See "IT" GIRL.

bowdlerize   This term refers to Dr. Thomas Bowdler (1754–1829), a British physician. When he retired, he applied his considerable energy to "cleaning up" Shakespeare's plays, Gibbon's *Decline and Fall of the Roman Empire* and other literary works. Setting himself up as critic and judge of what his contemporaries should be allowed to read, he applied his censorious editorial scalpel to "Whatever is unfit to be read by a gentleman in a company of ladies. . . ." He excised those words that could not "with propriety be read aloud in a family."

In 1818, Bowdler published his *Family Shakespeare* in 10 volumes. He had manhandled famous speeches and some major characters, and had dropped altogether some "bawdy" characters. Bowdler's *Family Shakespeare* became a best-seller.

To "bowdlerize" is to engage in self-righteous, often trivial, prudish censorship; to eliminate anything the self-appointed critic feels could possibly offend.

Bowery   Street in Manhattan, once associated with flophouses, derelicts, drunks and vagrants; often the last stop on the way down. For example, George Hurstwood, a tragic character in SISTER CARRIE (1900), a novel by Theodore Dreiser, ends his life on the Bowery. He has fallen from prosperity and a stable family life to joblessness, penury, drunkenness and despair.

The Bowery was New York City's SKID ROW.

boy next door   The 1930s stereotype of the nice, wholesome, ideal boyfriend or sweetheart. This quintessentially sweet, kind, wholly loving and lovable character is enshrined in Hugh Martin and Ralph Blane's song, "The Boy Next Door," sung by Judy Garland in the movie *Meet Me in St. Louis* (1944). The term "girl next door" has similar connotations.

Boy Scout   Member of the Boy Scouts of America, founded in 1910 by William Boyce, a wealthy Chicago publisher, and modeled on the British Boy Scouts, started in 1908 by Colonel Robert Baden-Powell with the motto "Be Prepared." A quasi-military organization with "troops" and uniforms, it proposed to build skills and develop character, self-sufficiency, courage, courtesy, citizenship, in every boy who joined. A boy could advance from level to level, all the way to the top—Eagle Scout. Every president of the United States automatically becomes an honorary Scout.

The term "boy scout" has come to be used half-derisively to describe a goody-goody type.

bra burner   Some activists for women's rights have regarded the bra (brassiere, in its original form) as a "demeaning symbol" of the way women dressed (or felt compelled to dress) to appeal to men. Spurred on by men who burned their draft cards at anti–Vietnam War demonstrations in the 1970s, some of the more zealous advocates burned their bras in public—a symbol of their liberation. "Bra-burner" is a pejorative term for any militant proponent of women's rights.

Brady, Mathew (1823–1896)   American pioneer in the art of photography. Brady's photographs of contemporary figures and events established him as the outstanding chronicler of his time.

In 1840, Brady opened his studio at the intersection of Broadway and Fulton Street in New York City, where he attracted prominent sitters. As his business grew, Brady moved to Washington, D.C., where his pictures of influential figures brought him fame and fortune.

Brady achieved his greatest success during the Civil War. He organized a group of Civil War photographers to follow the armies and to record what they saw. The result was one of the greatest photographic collections of a historical event, an incomparable record of the war years and a massive contribution to the National Archives.

Brady exerted a profound influence over the burgeoning "documentary" photography of the 1930s. Today he stands as a key figure in the development of photography as art and documentation.

Brady Gang (Wild Bunch)   The most widely hunted gang of the 1930s. They terrorized the Midwest and, in the process of robbing banks and engaging in other criminal activities, killed two clerks and three police officers. They were imprisoned—but escaped. On October 12, 1937, they entered a Maine sporting goods store to place an order for two revolvers. The clerk recognized them and told the gang members that the guns would be ready in a few days. Meanwhile, he alerted the FBI. When the gang returned to pick up their purchase, they were ambushed by a team of FBI men. Al Brady and Clarence Shaffer died in the shoot-out. Dalhover was tried and executed. See also BUTCH CASSIDY AND THE SUNDANCE KID.

Brahmin   A worshiper of Brahma, and the highest caste in the Hindu priestly order. The original American designation of Brahmin was applied to the social, literary, political aristocracy of Boston by Oliver Wendell Holmes (1841–1935). Today the intellectual and political linkage to Boston has vanished. "Brahmin" applies, sometimes pejoratively, to an influential group in politics, education, law and other fields. The name carries connotations of élitism and snobbishness.

brain drain This term originally referred to the recruitment in the early 1960s of highly trained professional talent from England to the United States with the promise of high salaries. One U.S. ad for help in a London newspaper read: "Brain Drain—or the Chance of a Lifetime." Later the term was applied to students from third-world countries who came to the United States to learn and stayed to earn.

The term now means any raid on talent, especially scientific, from one country to another, from one university to another, or from one industrial laboratory to another.

brain trust Originally, intellectuals and university professors who were invited to Washington, D.C., to help fashion the New Deal programs of President Franklin Delano Roosevelt. They formed a kind of unofficial cabinet of advisers to the president. Among them were Harry Hopkins, Raymond Moley, Adolph A. Berle, Jr., and Rexford Tugwell. President John F. Kennedy also surrounded himself with a "brain trust."

A body of eggheads or intellectuals whose combined knowledge and expertise are used to run a governmental, educational or business enterprise, the term sometimes is applied to brilliant students as well.

Brancusi, Constantin (1876–1957) Romanian sculptor who lived in Paris from 1904 and studied with Modigliani. His *Bird in Space* (1926) is quintessential Brancusi: a polished bronze abstract shape that suggests in the simplest possible form the soaring, upward-curving motion of a bird in flight.

Brando, Marlon (1924–) American stage and screen star. Brando's image was definitively set in his very first stage role, Stanley Kowalski, in Tennessee Williams's play *A Streetcar Named Desire* (1947; screen version, 1951). He played the part of an uncouth, inarticulate, macho Polish-American worker, married to the sister of a faded, rather poetic Southern belle named Blanche du Bois. Extremely physical, brutal, indifferent to the amenities of civilized behavior, alternately mumbling and shouting obscenities, he proved to be both repellent and attractive to the sensitive Blanche. Brando also starred in *The Men* (1950), *The Wild One* (1953), *On the Waterfront* (1954), *The Godfather* (1972), *Julius Caesar* (1953), *Last Tango in Paris* (1972), *Viva Zapata* (1951) and *Apocalypse Now* (1979), among others. Brando speaks with his body, suggesting pent-up passion or violence.

Braque, Georges (1882–1963) French painter who together with Pablo Picasso created one of the great innovative movements in 20th-century art—

cubism. His early cubist paintings tend to be monochromatic and indistinguishable from those of Picasso. He painted mostly still lifes, e.g., *Black Fish* (1924), *Cafe Table* (1911), reducing objects to layered geometrical forms as they would seem if seen simultaneously from many points of view. Later, he introduced the techniques of collage, pasting pieces of newsprint and chips of wood to his canvases. In the 1950s, he did a series of paintings of birds with utter simplification of form. See also CUBISM.

"brave new world"   An exclamation uttered by Miranda in act 5, scene 1 of William Shakespeare's final play, *The Tempest* (c. 1611–12). Miranda has lived with her father, PROSPERO, on an enchanted isle inhabited only by spirits like ARIEL and subhumans like CALIBAN. Before Prospero engineers the shipwreck of those in Milan who usurped his dukedom, Miranda has never seen other people. When she is introduced to these men, Miranda exclaims:

> *O, wonder!*
> *How many goodly creatures are there here!*
> *How beauteous mankind is!*
> *O brave new world*
> *That has such people in't!*

Brave New World was the ironic title of Aldous Huxley's sinister novel (1932) about a utopia in reverse, a society whose members are, by genetic engineering and cultural conditioning, created to perform their separate functions in society.

The expression "brave new world" is often used, however, to express surprise in a discovery or a new insight, as Miranda did.

bread and circuses   From the Latin, *panem et circenses.* Juvenal (60–140), the Roman satirist, cynically remarked, "The people eagerly want two things—bread and circuses." The Roman government supplied these in lavish quantities: public spectacles or entertainments designed to distract the people from the failures of government but providing no solutions to its problems. Hence any cynical, governmental diversion or distraction from the people's central concerns is characterized as a "bread-and-circuses" approach.

Brechtian   Suggestive of the theories and plays of the German dramatist Bertolt Brecht (1898–1956). Brecht is associated with "epic theater." He rejected suspension of disbelief as a working theory of drama and also rejected the Aristotelian aim of catharsis. His aims were didactic and his methods smacked of agitprop (agitation and propaganda). He saw the theater as spectacle and often used the music of composer Kurt Weill, as in *The Threepenny Opera* (1928) and in *The Rise and Fall of the City of*

Mahaganny (1929). Brecht wished to create distance between the audience and the players and often used a narrator to address and instruct the viewers as to what they should be seeing. His plays proceeded in a succession of swiftly changing, brief scenes rather than in the traditional three-act format. Their mood was heavy, as though outlined in black, like the paintings of the German expressionists. Their viewpoint was Marxist; their tone cynically and mordantly critical of modern society.

Other Brecht plays are *Mother Courage and Her Children* (1939), *The Good Woman of Setzuan* (1938), *The Caucasian Chalk Circle* (1944) and *The Life of Galileo* (1937).

Bridge of San Luis Rey, The   Pulitzer Prize–winning novel (1927) by Thornton Wilder (1897–1975) about five travelers who are killed on Friday noon, July 20, 1714, when a bridge over a canyon in Peru collapses. A witness to the disaster, Brother Juniper, a Franciscan friar, decides to investigate the events that brought the five together at that moment to share a common fate. Was it simply an accident or was it divine providence?

The bridge of San Luis Rey has become a symbol of shared disaster by persons otherwise discrete, as in a plane crash.

Bridge of Sighs   An enclosed 16th-century Venetian bridge that led from the Doge's palace to the former Pozzi Prison. Trials were held in the ducal palace. Condemned prisoners then passed through the bridge as they were led to the prison.

A "bridge of sighs" is a journey toward retribution.

brinkmanship   The fine art of almost going to war, an art defined and practiced by John Foster Dulles, secretary of state under President Dwight D. Eisenhower from 1953 to 1959. Dulles was the chief architect of America's cold-war policy toward the Soviet bloc in Eastern Europe. He threatened to use nuclear power to stem U.S.S.R. aggression.

Used generally for stepping to the brink of hostilities, for using a variety of strategies short of all-out fight. A kind of flirtation without consummation in affairs other than belligerence, as in love or business or diplomacy. See also COLD WAR; IRON CURTAIN.

Broadway   A street that runs north-south on the West Side of Manhattan in New York City and gives its name to the theater district alongside of it. Broadway is a mecca for all ambitious theater people: actors and actresses, playwrights, directors, producers, designers and technicians. Nicknamed the Great White Way, it is illuminated by marquees that have blazoned forth the names of all the glamorous theatrical greats of the 20th century. To play on Broadway is to reach the zenith of professional theatrical recognition.

Brobdingnagian   An inhabitant of the land of Brobdingnag in Book Two of *Gulliver's Travels* (1726), a satire by Jonathan Swift (1667–1745). Just as in Book I Gulliver finds the Lilliputians and everything around them to be diminutive, so in Book II he finds the Brobdingnagians and everything in their world to be gigantic. Brobdingnagians are 60 feet tall and their houses, furniture, roads, conveyances are magnified to scale. Even cats, dogs, mosquitoes, hailstones are frighteningly huge to the "normal" Gulliver, who is displayed as a marvelous, talking, thinking, tiny freak at Brobdingnagian fairs.

Brobdingnagian in modern usage still means huge, gigantic, colossal, such as Brobdingnagian portions at a restaurant.

Bronx cheer   A sputtering noise made by extending the tongue between the lips and forcibly expelling air. Sometimes called the "razberry" (raspberry).

The Bronx cheer is generally confined to sports contests—especially baseball. Avid, highly partisan, excitable fans employ the Bronx cheer to express feelings of contempt or derision for individual teams or players—and especially for umpires' decisions.

The Bronx cheer is also known as "the Bird," an expression of disapproval or contempt, often accompanied by hissing and booing.

Brook Farm   An idealistic community founded by George Ripley in 1841 as the Brook Farms Institute of Agriculture and Education, an experiment in living by transcendental and communist philosophical and social concepts. Following a creed of "plain living and high thinking," each member shared in the manual labor necessary to make the group self-sufficient.

Located on about 200 acres of attractive farmland in Roxbury, Massachusetts, Brook Farm attracted the attention of such notables as Nathaniel Hawthorne and Charles Dana. Hawthorne actually used Brook Farm as a model in his *The Blithedale Romance* (1852).

In its brief existence (1841–46), Brook Farm drew mixed reviews. William Henry Channing called it "a great college of social students." Ralph Waldo Emerson took a somewhat dimmer view of it, characterizing the project as exchanging one prison for another.

In 1846, the community's uncompleted and uninsured main facility burned down and the following year the members of Brook Farm disbanded.

A "Brook Farm" is a well-meaning but unworkable communal society.

Brooklyn Bridge   Suspension bridge over the East River connecting Manhattan and Brooklyn in New York City, built from 1867 to 1874, the work of J. A. Roebling. With its magnificent, vaulting Gothic arches, it has inspired many artists.

The term "Brooklyn Bridge" has become associated with gullibility: e.g., "he is so convincing that he could sell you the Brooklyn Bridge"; or, "he is so naive, he'd agree to buy the Brooklyn Bridge"; or, "he's so dishonest, he'd sell you the Brooklyn Bridge."

Brothers Karamazov, The (1880)   The three brothers in this great Russian novel by Fyodor Dostoevsky (1821–81) are the passionate Dmitry, the rational Ivan, and the guileless Alyosha; another character, Smerdyakov, is said to be their illegitimate brother. All four have been sired by the coarse, sensual, buffoonish, provincial landowner, Fyodor Karamazov, with three different women. The women have died of abuse; the children have been grossly neglected and tormented by the father. In the course of the novel the father is murdered. Which of the brothers has murdered him?

Circumstantial evidence points to Dmitry. He has quarreled violently with his father over his inheritance. Besides, he and his father are rivals for the fickle affectations of the wayward Grushenka. Passionate and irascible, given to gambling yet impulsively generous, proud but sometimes self-abasing, Dmitry has a turbulent nature full of contradictions. Dmitry is arrested, tried, found guilty and sentenced to prison in Siberia. Although he insists that he did not kill his father, and although he is offered a means of escape, he accepts his sentence because in his heart he was guilty of desiring his father's death.

Who, then? The killer is Smerdyakov, a lackey full of resentment at his debased position in the Karamazov household; insolent, ambitious and greedy, he has perverted Ivan's ideas to think that anything is permissible. Smerdyakov told Ivan that he could facilitate the murder of the father by Dmitry. Dmitry would be sent away and he, Smerdyakov, and Ivan would share the inheritance. Smerdyakov takes Ivan's silent horror at the proposal as acquiescence. In Smerdyakov we find cynicism translated into evil. Ivan, realizing his unintentional part in the murder and his guilt in Dmitry's punishment, goes insane.

In Dostoevsky's world view, insanity and evil are the ultimate results of rationalism and nihilism. Simple belief in God leads to goodness and salvation.

The Brothers Karamazov represent three ways of modern man: the emotional, the rationalistic, the spiritual; or, body, mind and soul.

Brown, Charlie   Central character in *Peanuts,* the most successful comic strip of all time. Created, written and drawn exclusively by Charles M. Schultz (1922–2000), the strip first appeared on October 2, 1950, and ran as a daily feature 18,250 times, during a period of almost 50 years, up to the day of the cartoonist's death. It has been translated into more than 20 languages worldwide, adapted for books, TV and movie animation, and used to promote commercial products from toys and lunchboxes to sweatshirts and greeting cards. It has brought in revenues of more than $50 million a year.

Charlie Brown is a hapless, round-headed little boy who, no matter how patiently he perseveres, never succeeds. He always strikes out at bat (except once after 43 years of no-hits); his baseball team never wins; he never gets a chance to kick the football; his kite always becomes entangled in the branches of a tree (once he held on to the kite strings for eight full days); his love is never requited. He is the very essence of meek failure. Asked why Charlie Brown always had to lose, Schultz replied, "You can't create humor out of happiness."

Charlie Brown is surrounded by a permanent cast of Li'l Folks (the original title of the strip), including Snoopy, a beagle with fantasies of achieving what is beyond a mere dog to achieve; Linus, intellectually precocious but unable to function without a security blanket; Lucy, a sharp-tongued fuss-budget; Schroeder, a Beethoven enthusiast on a toy piano; Sally, Charlie Brown's romantic little sister; and Peppermint Patty, a consistent D-minus student.

Charlie Brown and his circle embody the angst and neuroses of modern civilization.

Brown, John (1800–1859) A lifelong opponent of slavery, Brown was a zealot, abolitionist and insurrectionist determined to rid the United States of this immoral scourge, even if he had to use force against the government. In 1859, Brown rented a farm near Harper's Ferry, Virginia. Here, on October 16, he and 21 followers attacked and occupied the federal arsenal. In the federal counterattack, 10 of Brown's followers were killed; the rest were captured. Brown was convicted of treason and hanged on December 21, 1859.

During the trial, Brown appeared as his own defense attorney; according to contemporary accounts, he was "a powerfully inspired and selfless martyr"—as well as an out-of-control fanatic.

Brown was celebrated in a Union marching song, "John Brown's Body Lies A-Moldering In The Grave," during the Civil War, and later in Stephen Vincent Benet's great epic poem *John Brown's Body* (1928).

John Brown remains a symbol of fanatical zeal destroying itself in its passion to right a grievous wrong.

Brown v. Board of Education See SEPARATE BUT EQUAL.

Bruegel, Pieter (c. 1525–1569) Flemish painter, famous for his landscapes and scenes of peasant life. He was probably influenced by the crowded canvases of HIERONYMUS BOSCH and by the calendar paintings of the seasons in such 15th-century illuminated manuscripts as *Les Très Riches Heures du Duc de Berry.*

Bruegel paints large colorful panoramas of country folk engaged in everyday work and play and homely ceremonies: e.g., *The Harvesters* (c. 1565), *Peasant Dance* (c. 1568), *Peasant Wedding* (c. 1568). These are closely observed scenes of humble but robust people who are coarse, funny and appealing.

Brunhild (or Brunhilde)   A VALKYRIE, a heroine in the Scandinavian cycle of legends, *The Volsunga Saga,* which was the source of Richard Wagner's epic opera cycle *Der Ring des Nibelungen.*

In the original story, Brunhild is awakened from a long sleep by Sigurd (or Siegfried), the hero who has killed the dragon Fafnir and has taken from him a treasure hoard of gold as well as a magic ring with a curse upon it. Brunhild and Sigurd fall in love and become betrothed. Sigurd, however, leaves Brunhild to continue his adventures. Brunhild creates a magic circle of fire around herself to guard against other suitors. Meanwhile, a magic potion has made Sigurd forget Brunhild. He falls in love with Gudrun, a daughter of the Rhine king. Gudrun's brother Gunnar has designs upon Brunhild and convinces Sigurd to help him. Sigurd deceives Brunhild. In the shape of Gunnar, he breaches the circle of fire and extracts from Brunhild a promise of marriage. Sigurd and Gudrun, Gunnar and Brunhild have a double wedding.

When Brunhild learns of the deception, she has Sigurd killed and she herself commits suicide.

A Brunhild is generally a large, blonde, Nordic-looking woman who suggests Amazonian strength and heroic potential. In Wagnerian operas she is often portrayed by a physically imposing dramatic soprano.

bubble   Metaphorically, the word "bubble" refers pejoratively to any scheme, especially for a financial enterprise, that turns out to have been grossly inflated, insubstantial or fraudulent. Eventually the bubble bursts and thousands of deceived investors are ruined.

A notorious example was the South Sea Bubble. The South Sea Company of England, founded in 1711, proposed to assume the entire British national debt of nine million pounds in exchange for an annual payment of six percent on its stock and a monopoly of British trade with the South Sea Islands and South America. Speculation drove the price of its stock from £128 to £1,000 per share. In 1720 the bubble burst: the value of the stock plummeted, banks failed and investors were stripped bare.

Some financial analysts warned that the inflated value of Internet stocks in the late 1990s was a bubble waiting to burst.

Buchenwald   Nazi concentration camp near Weimar, established in July 1937, where 50,000 people died from forced labor, starvation, beatings and the gas chambers. Many intellectuals from all over vanquished Europe were murdered here. Some were used as guinea pigs for infernal "medical" experiments. American forces that liberated the camp on April 12, 1945, found 20,000 living skeletons, and corpses stacked like firewood awaiting incineration. See also BEAST OF BUCHENWALD.

Buckley, William F(rank), Jr. (1925–) Erudite, witty, articulate, ubiquitous spokesman for conservatism in America, Buckley was born in New York City and launched his career in 1951 with the publication of *God and Man at Yale,* in which he castigated his alma mater for turning the sons of its wealthy supporters into "atheistic socialists." In the same vein, he once said: "I would rather be goverened by the first 2,000 people in the telephone directory than by the Harvard University faculty."

In 1955 he founded and became the editor of the foremost conservative journal in the United States, *The National Review.* At its inception he said that he wanted to repeal much of the liberal social legislation of the preceding two decades. His magazine would "stand athwart history, yelling 'Stop'." He is the author of the column "On The Right." He has written many books, including *McCarthy and His Enemies* (1954), *Up From Liberalism* (1959), books on sailboat racing and, most recently, novels of mystery and intrigue. His instant recognition by the public, however, came from his hosting of the long-running Public Television debate show *Firing Line.* Not one to suffer fools gladly, on the air he took every opportunity to demolish his opponents with formidable knowledge of the facts, daunting skill as a polemicist, polysyllabic abstruse words and withering wit, together with an icy charm and frequently raised eyebrows.

Buck Rogers The first American science fiction comic strip, it appeared on January 7, 1929. Awakening from a five-century sleep, former U.S. Army Air Force lieutenant Buck Rogers finds his beloved America in the hands of Mongol invaders. Aided by attractive young Wilma Deering, he liberates his country and prepares to take on a host of new enemies: "tiger men of Mars," "pirates from outer space," his arch-foe, "Killer Kane." With the help of a scientific prodigy, Dr. Huer, Buck will eventually conquer all enemies and prevail over all the dangers that lie ahead.

Buck Rogers is the conqueror that all of us in our helpless state would like to be—strong and victorious against our known and unknown enemies. The young, especially, unable to cope with a world they never made and could not master, found that they could deal with a hostile and threatening universe—as Buck Rogers.

"buck stops here, the" President Harry Truman, in his feisty way, was fond of using this slogan. It was his way of saying that ultimate responsibility lay with him,

as when he fired General Douglas MacArthur from his post as supreme commander of U.N. forces in Korea in 1951; or when he ordered the atomic bombing of
Hiroshima in 1945. "The buck stops here" implies putting an end to the practice of
"passing the buck," or shifting the responsibility to somebody else.

Buffalo Bill   He was born William Frederick Cody (1846–1917). A highly
accomplished horseman and marksman, Cody was also a man of many careers:
rider of the pony express, a scout for the U.S. Army, a soldier in the Union Army
and a master showman. He got his nickname Buffalo Bill for his zeal in hunting buffalo for a company building the Kansas Pacific Railroad. During the period of his
employment (1876–78), he is said to have killed 4,861 buffalo. Legend has it that,
in the wars against the Indians, Cody also killed and scalped Yellow Hand, the chief
of the Cheyenne Indians.

Cody's colorful personality and extraordinary exploits made him a national
hero. Through his sensational Wild West Show, with its cast of cowboys, Indians,
sharpshooters, roughriders, and dramatizations of CUSTER'S LAST STAND and stagecoach robberies, he brought the romance of the Wild West to all of America. In
1887, he took his show to Europe. For 30 years Cody played himself as the true
hero of the Wild West.

Cody was a "natural" for the "dime novelists" (see DIME NOVEL) of his day. To
these somewhat inflated fictional accounts of his life and exploits, Cody added his
own more tempered *The Life of Wm. F. Cody* (1878) and *Story of the Wild West and
Campfire Chats* (1879).

Buffalo Bill stands as the almost mythical symbol of the Wild West: reckless,
daring, resourceful and successful.

Bumppo, Natty   See *LAST OF THE MOHICANS.*

Bunker, Archie   Central character in *All in the Family,* a revolutionary TV sitcom
that made its debut on January 12, 1971. As far away from the pieties of OZZIE AND
HARRIET as one could imagine, *All in the Family* confronted formerly taboo issues
with openness and raucous squabbles. Race, ethnicity, feminism, homosexuality,
and other unmentionable topics were finally out of the closet. In this four-member
family, Archie Bunker, a blue-collar worker played by Carroll O'Connor, took the
part of an incorrigible racist and bigot; his daughter, played by Sally Struthers, was
a feminist; his son-in-law, played by Rob Reiner, was a leftist liberal; and his wife,
Edith, played by Jean Stapleton, became the shrill-voiced befuddled peacemaker.
Because Archie, a loudmouth, expressed outrageously benighted opinions, be
became the butt of the audience's laughter rather than anger. He voiced what many
a Neanderthaler thought but dared not express in an age of political correctness.

Bunker Hill   Site, in Massachusetts, of one of the earliest battles of the American Revolution (June 17, 1775). During the siege of Boston by units of the Continental Militia, American forces under William Prescott took up a defensive position on a hill. They succeeded in repelling the first two attacks by the British under William Howe, but they ran out of ammunition and were finally dislodged by a third assault upon the hill. In spite of their ultimate defeat, their fierce resistance and courage, as well as their infliction of heavy damage on the British, served to bolster colonial morale.

Use: Frank Rich of the *New York Times* has called the STONEWALL riots "the Bunker Hill of the modern gay civil rights movement."

Bunthorne   Hero of the satirical Gilbert and Sullivan operetta *Patience* (1881), Bunthorne is a spoof of the long-haired, sighing, attitudinous, super-aesthetical poet. Modeled on Oscar Wilde, he wears the clothes of a dandy and walks around with a long-stemmed lily in his hand. His affectations win him the rapturous, if fickle attentions of "Twenty Love-Sick Maidens."

A "Bunthorne" is an aesthete.

Bunyan, Paul   Legendary hero of tall tales told by the lumberjacks of the American Northwest, he was of gargantuan size and superhuman strength. Carl Sandburg writes in *The People, Yes:* "The Pacific Ocean froze over in the winter of the Blue Snow and Paul Bunyan had long teams of oxen hauling regular white snow over from China." Paul Bunyan is said to have cut out the Grand Canyon just by dragging his pick behind him. He owned a prize blue ox named Babe, "measuring between the eyes forty-two ox-handles and a plug of Star tobacco exactly," according to Sandburg. Bunyan built a hotel so tall, he had the "last seven stories put on hinges so's they could be swung back for to let the moon go by."

These stories were first collected and illustrated by W. B. Langhead in "Paul Bunyan and His Blue Ox" (1914), an advertising pamphlet published by the Red River Lumber Company.

Any allusion to Paul Bunyan implies great size and great strength.

Burns and Allen   A husband-and-wife team on radio, in the movies and finally on television, George Burns (Nathan Birnbaum, 1896–1996) and Gracie Allen (1906–64) continued to delight their audiences until 1958 when Gracie retired. Subsequently, George tried to make it on his own, since he wouldn't hear of looking for a substitute for Gracie. Finally, he took to doing a one-man show, cast as a geriatric roué. He lived to the age of 100.

The Burns and Allen formula looked deceptively simple. George was in show business, the center of problems created by "nutty friends, wacky neighbors, and a zany wife—Gracie." George, an ever-present cigar as his prop, played acerbic straight man to the harebrained (but lovable) Gracie, who "skewered common sense and . . . chatted about her bizarre relations."

Always fresh, always funny, always charmingly daffy, Burns and Allen were a unique American phenomenon, filled with innocent good humor and outrageous nonsequiturs.

bush league   Originally applied to small-town or minor league sports teams, the term bears the stigma of the small-time, inferior, second-rate.

See MAKE THE BIG LEAGUE.

Buster Brown   A comic strip character, Buster Brown appeared on May 4, 1902, and was instantly and enormously popular. Buster Brown was the well-dressed, 10-year-old heir to a fortune with an almost insatiable appetite for tricking and annoying his family and friends with explosives, paint, wrecked boats. Buster's constant companion was a "toothily grinning" dog called Tige.

Buster Brown is the archetypal mischief maker, juvenile outrageousness incarnate. He gave his name to a style of haircut.

Butch Cassidy and the Sundance Kid   U.S. western (1969) with Paul Newman and Robert Redford (playing outlaws pursued by a relentless posse); directed by George Roy Hill. In the film the two characters must jump off a cliff into a river to escape a posse. Sundance says he can't swim. Butch answers, "You crazy fool, the fall will probably kill you." The film is a spoof on desperadoes of the Wild West.

See also CASSIDY, BUTCH.

"But I have promises to keep / And miles to go before I sleep"
Penultimate lines of Robert Frost's poem "Stopping by Woods on a Snowy Evening." In the poem, a man on his way home from a New England village stops his horse and buggy on a road bordered by woods on one side and a lake on the other. He watches the snow falling. It is so quiet and so beautiful that he is tempted to stop there forever. His horse, however, gives the harness bells a shake. The sound wakes the man to his duty. He has promises to keep and miles to go before he can "sleep." Frost says that sometimes we long for the peace and stillness of death, but life's responsibilities and opportunities call to us.

Butler, Rhett   Hero of *Gone With the Wind* (1936), novel by Margaret Mitchell. (See also GABLE, CLARK; O'HARA, SCARLETT.)

Byronic   An allusion to the literary style or the life of George Gordon, Lord Byron (1788–1824), one of England's most popular poets at home and abroad. Enormously attractive to women, despite a slight limp, dashing, adventurous, surrounded by glamorous friends, rebelling against conventional morality in his poetry and in his life, Byron was the quintessential romantic. Caught up in liberal, nationalistic causes in Italy and Greece, he died of malarial fever at the age of 36 at Missolonghi.

Much of Byron's tempestuous life and loves finds expression in the archetypical Byronic hero of such poems as *Childe Harold's Pilgrimage* and *Don Juan*. To Thomas Babington Macaulay (1800–59), the Byronic hero appears as "proud, moody, cynical, defiance on his brow and misery in his heart, a scorner of his kind, implacable in revenge, yet capable of deep and strong affection."

The great Russian poet Alexander Pushkin (1799–1837) has been called the "Russian Byron."

Byzantine   Besides having the characteristics of the art, architecture and music of the Byzantine Empire (the Eastern Roman Empire; see BYZANTIUM), "Byzantine" has taken on several meanings having to do with political intrigue.

According to the *Columbia Encyclopedia,* "Byzantine court history is a story of absolute despotism and barbarous cruelty not exceeded at any Asiatic court. . . . Rulers acceded to the throne by blinding or murdering their predecessors, often their closest blood relatives. Treason, intrigue and violence were normal political instruments . . . vice, corruption, and perversion had lost the power to shock."

Today Byzantine, when not associated with art, tends to refer to devious, complicated, exotic machinations.

Byzantium   Originally a Greek city on the Bosporus Strait, it became the capital city of the Byzantine Empire, also known as the Eastern Roman Empire. With the vicissitudes of its political and military fortunes, the name was changed to Constantinople in 330 and again to Istanbul in 1930. Byzantium, however, remains associated with art in the form of highly decorative mosaics and gold icons, pictures of saints shown full face, two-dimensionally flat, as far removed from the reality of organic flesh as possible.

In William Butler Yeats's great poem "Sailing to Byzantium" (1927), in which Byzantium is the central organizing symbol, Yeats writes that "once out of nature" he wishes to be reincarnated as a golden bird. He utters a passionate cry to be gathered "into the artifice of eternity." He wishes, in other words, to remain a poet, but an immortal one, not subject to the ravages of time and the flesh.

Byzantium stands for artful artifice, which is unchanging and immortal, as opposed to nature, which is organic and, therefore, subject to decay and transience.

C

cabal   Although this word derives ultimately from the Hebrew word *cabala,* it received a special political significance during the reign of Charles II in England. The word became an acronym for the names of five of his advisers on foreign affairs: Clifford, Ashley, Buckingham, Arlington and Lauderdale. These five secretly signed the Treaty of Alliance with France in 1672 without the consent of Parliament, a move that plunged England into war with Holland. "Cabal" has ever since meant "a group of conspirators."

Cabala   Although the dominant mode of thought in Hebrew interpretation and exegesis, as in the TALMUD, is rationalism, the Cabala illustrates the deep current of mysticism that runs through alternative modes of interpreting and understanding the Scriptures. The Cabala is a collection of writings that seek to unfold the "hidden wisdom," the secret meanings of Torah. The substance of this mystical revelation was handed down from ancient times by oral tradition to highly select members of the rabbinate, but during the Middle Ages it was codified and set down in writing. The most influential of these writings are the *Sefer Yetzirah* (Book of Creation), the *Bahir* (Brilliance) and the *Zohar* (Splendor).

The methodology by which these Hebrew mystics sought clues to the divine essence within the appearance of things is beyond rational comprehension. It involved the use of the 22 sacred letters of the Hebrew alphabet and a system of numbers attached to them. The mystics sought to discover especially the secret, ineffable names of God, the use of which would enable them to perform miracles like hastening the coming of the Messiah.

"Cabala" is a term that may be applied in modern usage to the esoteric interpretation of any material.

Cadillac   Luxury car produced by General Motors and named for the city in Michigan where it is made. By extension, a Cadillac is something tops in its class.

Use: "Congress is grabbing for a Cadillac salary, but it already has a Rolls-Royce pension." (*Palm Beach Post,* February 4, 1989)

Cagney, James (Jimmy) (1900–1986) American actor James Cagney, born in New York City. This tough, cocky *Yankee Doodle Dandy* film star could act, sing and dance. He started in gangster roles in *Penny Arcade* (1930) and later appeared in *The Roaring Twenties* (1939) with HUMPHREY BOGART. He was known for his quick, jerky, chip-on-the-shoulder body movements and speech.

Calamity Jane Nickname of Martha Jane Cannary Burk(e) (1853–1903). Considerably ahead of her time, she dressed, shot, and cursed like a man. She claimed to have been a scout for General Custer and a Pony Express rider.

By 1867, she was spending time in the mining districts allegedly "drinking and cussing" with the miners and other less respectable characters. She was a companion of Wild Bill Hickock, though probably not married to him. From 1876 till her death, she became a fixture of life in Deadwood, South Dakota. Her last years there were spent in poverty.

There is no definitive account of how or why Martha Cannary came to be called Calamity Jane. The accepted characterization of Calamity Jane stands, however, as "any vociferous female prophet of doom" (*I Hear America Talking* by Stuart Berg Flexner, p. 71).

Calder, Alexander (1898–1976) American artist famous for his mobiles, which are constructions of metal wire and painted aluminum so delicately balanced as to move with the slightest current of air. These mobiles are abstractions of organic forms like flowers, fish, animals, which fascinate by their constantly changing aspect in space.

Caliban In Shakespeare's play *The Tempest,* Caliban is born of the witch Sycorax and a devil. He is deformed and brutish. He hates Prospero who, with his magic powers, has not only robbed him of his rightful claim to the island but also has enslaved him to do all the dirty work.

Once upon a time, Prospero tried to teach Caliban language and other civilizing arts, but Caliban tried to rape the innocent Miranda, Prospero's daughter, and for this he has been punished. Caliban's surly response is: "You taught me language; and my profit on't/Is, I know how to curse."

In spite of his bestial nature, Caliban evokes sympathy. Only half-human, he nevertheless has mortal longings. "I'll be wise hereafter, / And seek for grace," he promises Prospero at the end.

Louis Untermeyer's poem "Caliban in the Coal Mines" deals subjectively and sympathetically with modern-day Calibans who work underground in the cold and the dark. "God . . . fling us a handful of stars!" they plead.

Calvinist   An adherent of the theological tenets of John Calvin (1509–64), the French Protestant reformer; also, anything pertaining to these tenets. In 1533 Calvin experienced a personal conversion. He turned away from Catholicism to the concepts of the Reformation. In 1536 he codified his own special Protestant views in his "Institutes of the Christian Religion."

Like Protestants everywhere, Calvin rejected papal authority and looked to the Bible as the only source of God's law. His theological concepts of immutable original sin and predestination, however, imposed harsh, inflexible restrictions on every aspect of a person's conduct. One was born into and destined to die in a state of sin. No amount of good works could offer any hope of redemption. Only a select few, the elect, were born into a state of grace. Yet Calvin encouraged the doomed mass of mankind to such worthy traits as "thrift, industry, sobriety and responsibility."

In the reformist mood of the 16th century, Calvinism spread throughout Europe through the influence of John Knox in Scotland, the Puritan Revolution in England, and the Huguenots in France.

The term "Calvinist" in modern usage implies joyless, punitive, strict attitudes with respect to life's possibilities.

Camelot   The legendary palace of shining spires and turrets where King ARTHUR and the Knights of the Round Table held court in the Age of Chivalry. Here the idealistic king built what he thought would be an ideal society founded on principles of truth, loyalty, justice, reverence and compassion.

The tragedy of Camelot was that it held within itself the seeds of its own destruction. The adulterous love of Queen Guinevere and Lancelot made a mockery of Arthur's ideals and eventually brought about the downfall of Camelot and the death of Arthur at the hands of the treacherous Modred.

The story of Camelot has been told and retold throughout the ages, from Sir Thomas Malory's *Le Morte Darthur* (1485) through Alfred Lord Tennyson's *Idylls of the King* (begun in 1842) to T. H. White's *The Once and Future King* (1958). In 1960, Alan Jay Lerner and Frederick Loewe wrote the musical play *Camelot*.

"Camelot" suggests a vision of the ideal city, which, through human frailty and corruption, is destined to disintegrate. John F. Kennedy's term of office in the White House (1961–63) has often been referred to as "Camelot" because of the president's youthful vigor, charismatic appeal and bright vision.

Camille   The lady of the camellias, by whatever name, has moved the hearts of multitudes. In the novel by Alexandre Dumas *fils* (1824–95), *la Dame aux camélias* (1848), and in his play of the same name (1852), she is Marguerite Gauthier. In Giuseppe Verdi's opera *La Traviata* (1853), she is Violetta. In the American movies with Norma Talmadge (1927) and Greta Garbo (1936), she is Camille. By any name, she is a beautiful, vivacious Parisian courtesan who, for her station in life, commits the error of falling in love.

She abandons her wealthy nobleman, Count de Varville, and her dissolute life in Paris to live quietly on a country estate with Armand Duval (Alfredo Germont in *Traviata*). For the first time in her life she is blissfully happy. But Duval's father asks her to give up his son for the good of his family. Camille returns to Paris, leaving Armand bitter and shattered, as she has kept his father's visit a secret from him. Although she is dying of tuberculosis, Camille resumes her desperately gay life. When Armand learns the truth of Camille's sacrifice and the two lovers are reconciled in a bittersweet scene, Camille dies.

Camille is the prostitute with the heart of gold, one who is capable of true love and self-sacrifice.

Candid Camera   A very popular, long-running (1948–67) TV program conducted by Allen Funt (1914–99) and his crew of resourceful assistants. *Candid Camera* caught "unsuspecting folks in the act of being themselves" by trapping them in innocent-looking but contrived settings. The results were by turns hilarious and embarrassing, but both audiences and victims hugely enjoyed themselves.

Candide   The hero of *Candide* (1759), a satiric picaresque tale by VOLTAIRE, the French philosopher, historian, dramatist and poet.

Candide starts out as an amiable, naive young man who accepts unquestioningly the philosophy of his tutor, PANGLOSS, that all is for the best in this best of all possible worlds. In the course of this episodic novel, Candide is forced to test the validity of this optimistic view based on the ideas of the German philosopher and mathematician Gottfried Wilhelm Leibnitz (1646–1716). In a series of misadventures all over the world, each more disastrous than the previous one, Candide learns from personal experience that this may be the *worst* of all possible worlds. He observes and feels the ravages of war and of natural disasters (e.g., the earthquake in Lisbon that killed 35,000 people). He and his companions, his beloved Cunegonde and Pangloss, become victims of the savage religious fanaticism of the INQUISITION. He comes to know the lash of political tyranny, the chicanery of the nobility, the fickleness of women and the lechery of men, the prevalence of greed, theft, rape and murder in the affairs of mankind. He finally settles down on a small farm with Cunegonde, now his wife but old and ugly, "to cultivate our garden," for in the end he realizes that only through work and minding one's own business can one avoid the idleness, vice and folly to which mankind is heir.

In all his travels, Candide finds only one ideal society: the mythical realm of Eldorado. There, all people are rich, wise and virtuous, and therefore they have no need of lawyers or priests. Obviously, this is Voltaire's concept of Utopia, against whose standards are to be measured the ugly realities of Candide's experience.

A Candide, then, is the wide-eyed person who learns what is what in the real world.

Canossa, go to   For three days in January 1077, Holy Roman Emperor Henry IV dressed like a penitent and stood barefoot in the snow before the Canossa residence of Pope Gregory VII (Hildebrand). The pope had earlier excommunicated Henry for contesting his right to invest abbots and bishops with ring and staff, symbols of their position in the Catholic Church. Henry was pleading (successfully) to be taken back into the church.

To go to Canossa is to humble oneself, to ask for forgiveness.

Canterbury   Site of the famous cathedral in England that has become a shrine for pilgrims. *Canterbury* is more broadly used to mean any place of pilgrimage. See THOMAS Á BECKET and CHAUCERIAN.

Capone, Alphonse (1899–1947)   Also known as "Scarface," Al Capone was the most powerful and ruthless crime figure of his time.

Early in his educational experience, Capone beat up one of his teachers and was expelled from school. He was clearly cut out for a violent, non-academic career. Raised in New York's notorious Five Points neighborhood, Capone quickly rose in the rapidly burgeoning racketeering hierarchy of the Prohibition era.

In 1925, Capone moved his ruthless expertise to Chicago. By 1930, with an army of 1,000 gunmen and gangsters, he controlled all 10,000 speakeasies in Chicago—and ruled the entire bootlegging business from Canada to Florida.

At his peak, Capone boasted "I own the police" and "I own Chicago." Indeed, he could not have functioned as he did without some official connivance.

On February 14, 1929, St. Valentine's Day, Capone made his great and final mistake. He ordered what became known as the St. Valentine's Day Massacre. A group of his killers, some dressed in police uniforms, surprised seven members of a rival gang, lined them up against a wall and machine-gunned them to death.

Everyone knew that this atrocity could not have been perpetrated without Capone's direct or indirect intervention. The FBI was especially infuriated. For years, it had been trying in vain to get Capone for the murders it "knew" he was responsible for. But the FBI couldn't prove it. The St. Valentine's Day Massacre changed FBI tactics. Shortly thereafter Capone was convicted on a long list of income tax evasions. Result: 11 years in the federal penitentiary at Atlanta. In 1934, Capone was transferred to ALCATRAZ, the toughest prison in the United States. His health rapidly deteriorated and he was released in 1939, suffering from terminal syphilis.

In common parlance, Capone is almost universally regarded as the quintessential crime boss, synonymous with the worst in organized crime.

Use: "The Al Capone of pigeon poaching came home to roost yesterday and the Eliot Ness of the Parks Department got him. Domiano Parasimo, 73, of Brooklyn is suspected of trapping thousands of pigeons and selling them to poultry markets." (*New York Daily News,* June 23, 1988)

Captain Bligh   One of the main characters in *Mutiny on the Bounty* (1932), one of a trilogy of novels by James N. Hall and Charles B. Nordhoff that were made into a successful movie in 1935. Captain William Bligh is the tyrannical commander of a British vessel sailing to the South Sea islands in 1787. On the way home, his crew mutinies and sets him and 17 others adrift in an open boat on the high seas. An excellent mariner, he makes it to England in the sequel, *Men Against the Sea* (1934). When some of the mutineers return to England, Captain Bligh brings charges against them. They are tried, convicted and hanged.

Based on a historical character, Captain Bligh has become a prototype of the rigidly authoritarian and eccentric sea captain for whom discipline represents the highest good.

Captain Kangaroo   Popular children's television show (1955–75) starring Bob Keeshan. For a time, it was the only daily show that treated the very young with kindness and concern. Captain Kangaroo, with his distinctive cap and uniform and heavy gray moustache, was a sweet, kindly, somewhat avuncular presence. He was a departure from the usual loud, silly animated cartoons served up to the impressionable young.

Captain Marvel   In the 1940 comic book of the same name, Captain Marvel is the alter ego of Billy Batson, an orphan without a home, who sells papers and lives in subway stations.

One day, a stranger leads Billy through an underground passage to meet the old Egyptian wizard, Shazam. The wizard, about to retire, passes on his secrets and powers to Billy. When Billy utters the magic word—"Shazam"—he becomes Captain Marvel, wearing a colorful gold and orange hero suit. When, as Captain Marvel, Billy wishes to return to his other self, he again utters "Shazam"—and, presto, he is back in the subways selling papers. The magic word "Shazam" makes Billy into the world's "mightiest mortal"; he can leap great distances, repel bullets and fly at supersonic speeds. The word "Shazam" gives Billy:

Solomon's Wisdom
Hercules' Strength
Achilles' Courage
Zeus's Powers

Atlas's Stamina
Mercury's Speed

Every month, one million readers the world over followed Captain Marvel's breathtaking exploits. "Shazam" and Captain Marvel became part of the English language.

Capulets and Montagues   The two feuding families in Shakespeare's tragedy *Romeo and Juliet* (c. 1596). Juliet, the daughter of the Capulets, and Romeo, the son of the Montagues, fall hopelessly in love. The absolute disapproval of both families, the headstrong nature of the two young lovers and numerous unintentional errors and misunderstandings lead inexorably to the tragic death of the star-crossed pair.

The Capulets and the Montagues are a more romantic as well as a fictional version of other infamous feuding families such as the Guelphs and the Ghibellines or the HATFIELDS AND THE MCCOYS.

Carmen   Tempestuous gypsy heroine of George Bizet's opera *Carmen* (1875), based on Prosper Mérimée's 1846 novel of the same name.

Alternately passionate and calculating, Carmen has her way with men. She seduces the officer Don José, separating him from Micaela, the girl who truly loves him, only to throw him over ruthlessly for a new conquest, the more dashing bullfighter Escamillo. The rivalry between the two men ends in tragedy as Don José stabs Carmen and is led away by officers of the law.

A Carmen is a recklessly flirtatious girl, a femme fatale.

Carnegie, Andrew (1835–1919)   Born in Dunfermline, Scotland, Andrew Carnegie grew up in poverty with little more than an elementary school education. When his parents brought him to America, they settled in Pittsburgh. Beginning with a series of low-level jobs, Carnegie devoted his enormous energy and intelligence to advancing himself, and to the burgeoning steel business, rising to become "rich beyond the dreams of avarice." In 1901, he sold his vastly successful business enterprises to J. P. Morgan's U.S. Steel for $250 million. Thenceforth, he devoted his money and energy to philanthropy and world peace. He built and supported hundreds of public libraries, and was the first philanthropist to make libraries one of his major concerns. He endowed the still functioning Carnegie Institute of Technology (now Carnegie Mellon University), the Carnegie Institute for Teaching and the Carnegie Institute for International Peace. Ultimately, Carnegie put over $350 million into his various charitable endeavors.

In the fullness of his philanthropic career, Carnegie once said "The man who dies rich dies disgraced."

To be called a Carnegie is to be placed high among mankind's enlightened givers, the philanthropist par excellence.

Carnegie, Dale (1888–1955) Teacher, lecturer, author. His book *How to Win Friends and Influence People* (1936) sold almost five million copies up to his death, becoming one of the best-selling nonfiction books of all time.

Encouraged by the phenomenal sales of his book, Carnegie and his associates founded the Carnegie Institute for Effective Speaking and Human Relations. By 1955, the self-improvement courses created and administered by the institute had been taken by more than 450,000 people in 750 U.S. cities and 15 foreign countries.

Today's highly successful Dale Carnegie courses and seminars continue to speak to basic human needs and desires. The book is still selling briskly, a title that has long since passed into the language as a statement of fundamental longings and aspirations.

Carnegie Hall An elegant concert hall built in New York City in 1892 by the philanthropist ANDREW CARNEGIE and faithfully restored in the 1980s. To have given a concert in Carnegie Hall is to have "arrived" and, indeed, the greatest musicians in the world have performed there. An anecdote often repeated goes as follows:

Visitor to New York City: "How do I get to Carnegie Hall?"

Cab driver: "Practice! Practice! Practice!"

Carnegie Hall stands as a MECCA for aspiring musicians and as a temple for concertgoers. It is to instrumentalists what La Scala is to opera singers. The *Smithsonian* has referred to Carnegie Hall as the "Mt. Olympus of musical performance" and "the jewel in every performing artist's crown."

carpetbagger During the 19th century, luggage made out of carpeting was widely used. Bank robbers caught stashing stolen loot in such receptacles were called carpetbaggers.

During Reconstruction after the Civil War, the term "carpetbagger" was applied to the poor Yankee who packed all his worldly belongings into a carpet bag and went South. These unscrupulous adventurers, together with their Southern counterparts, the Scalawags, manipulated the newly enfranchised blacks to gain control of the Republican state governments. Their record of greed and political corruption remains unique in American history.

The American novelist William Faulkner drew a devastating portrait of such Northern scavengers, the Snopes clan, in his novel *The Hamlet.*

A carpetbagger is an opprobrious term for an exploitative, unprincipled, greedy interloper.

carry coals to Newcastle   Newcastle upon Tyne is a port city in the northeast of England, a region formerly known for its coal-mining industry. For centuries, Newcastle shipped coal to other parts of England and to the rest of the world. If there is one thing that Newcastle had a superfluity of, it was coal. To carry coals to Newcastle, therefore, would have been silly, as silly as to send bags of sand to the Sahara. To "carry coals to Newcastle" refers to a redundant act.

Carson, Christopher (Kit) (1809–1868)   American guide and frontiersman. In 1826, he found his way to Taos, New Mexico, which became his headquarters. There he made his living as cook, hunter, and guide for early exploring parties. In the 1840s he joined the American explorer John Charles Frémont's three Western expeditions as guide. Frémont's reports about Carson's role in the expeditions made Carson famous.

In 1858, Carson was appointed agent of Indian affairs, headquartered at Taos. At the outbreak of the Civil War, Carson organized and commanded the first New Mexican Volunteers, who fought the Apache, Navajo and Comanche Indians. In 1864, Carson's forces fought their final battle against the Indians. The 400 poorly armed white men were overwhelmed by 5,000 Indians, but Carson survived.

After the Civil War, in 1866, Carson was made a brigadier general for volunteers.

Carson is the epitome of the American frontiersman.

Carson, Johnny (1925–   )   Nebraska-born former magician, he dominated "late-show" television programming for 30 years (1962–92). With a gifted crew of assistants, Carson created an easy, casual atmosphere within which to express his special brand of wit, slick vulgarity, ridicule of prominent politicos and commentary on current trends in America.

Carson commanded an enormous salary. Tens of millions watched his *Tonight Show* every night from 11:30 to 12:30 and later from 11:30 to 1:00. The style and the content of Carson's show exerted a far-reaching effect on television's other one-man late shows. He also launched the careers of many television entertainers.

Cartesian   Related to the ideas and the methodology of the French philosopher and mathematician René Descartes (1596–1650). Referred to as the founder of analytical geometry, Descartes tried to apply mathematical method to all other fields of knowledge. He began his philosophical inquiries with universal doubt, acknowledging only the existence of doubt itself. From there he went on to establish the existence of God and the existence of the material world as two separate entities. He was a rationalist, tutored in scholasticism, who pioneered in scientific method. He is responsible for the famous phrase *Cogito, ergo sum* (I think, therefore I am).

Carton, Sydney A brilliant but dissolute young lawyer who has wasted his talents, Carton is one of the protagonists in Charles Dickens's *A Tale of Two Cities* (1859). He falls in love with Lucie Manette, but Lucie eventually marries Charles Darnay, a French aristocrat condemned by the Revolutionary Tribunal in Paris. Twice Carton saves the life of Darnay, to whom he bears an uncanny physical resemblance: once, when Darnay is on trial for spying against England; and once again at the end of the book when Carton manages to substitute himself for Darnay at the guillotine. Carton sacrifices his life for Lucie's sake.

In the last moments before Carton is beheaded, he murmurs, "It is a far, far better thing that I do, than I have ever done. It is a far, far better rest that I go to, than I have ever known."

A Sydney Carton is one who achieves nobility through self-sacrifice.

Casanova, Don Giovanni (Chevalier de Seingalt) (1728–1798) Italian adventurer and charlatan, one of the great philanderers of history, an insatiable libertine. His *Mémoires* (12 volumes, 1826–38) contain vivid accounts of his many amorous adventures. The authenticity of some of these writings has been questioned.

Casanova spent a good part of his life wandering in and out of European aristocracy, leading a colorful and dissolute existence, posing as a preacher, alchemist and gambler. In his more respectable years, he was employed as director of the state lottery in Paris, and as librarian to Count Waldstein in Bohemia.

A Casanova is a quintessential, glamorous, irresistible lover, one who boasts of his many sexual conquests.

Casey at the Bat See THERE IS NO JOY IN MUDVILLE.

Caspar Milquetoast This inspired creation of H. T. Webster first appeared as a comic strip character, *The Timid Soul,* in May 1924. He looked and thought and acted the role Webster created for him. Pince-nez perched above droopy white moustache, shoulders stooped, gait shambling, looking lean and tired, he quietly accepted "the slings and arrows of outrageous fortune." Life seemed too much of a burden for him—filled with frightful people and frightening decisions. He was a beleaguered soul in a world he never made and could not control.

Caspar's many faithful readers recognized something of themselves in his self-inflicted dilemmas, in his doubts, his compromises, his self-abasement. He provided an object they could feel sorry for and superior to.

The quintessential Caspar is shown waiting in a pouring rain on a busy downtown street corner, his hat collapsed damply about his face, water puddling around his shoes. The caption reads: "Well, I'll wait one more hour for him, and if he doesn't come then, he can go and borrow that $100 from someone else."

Cassatt, Mary (1845–1926)   American-born painter who lived in Paris most of her life. Cassatt was a student and companion of Edgar Degas and exhibited with the Impressionists. Her paintings often had a mother and her children as their subjects.

Cassidy, Butch (1866–1937?)   American gangster, born Robert Leroy Parker and raised on a ranch in Utah by his Mormon father. While still an adolescent, Cassidy fell in with bad company, engaged in cattle rustling, small bank robberies and other crimes. Released from prison in 1890, he adopted the alias Butch Cassidy and formed the famous Wild Bunch—a gang of ruthless desperadoes devoting their energies to such pastimes as train and bank robberies, stock thefts and murder. To a man, they were fiercely loyal to Butch.

Cassidy was the "brains" of the Wild Bunch, planning and executing their major depredations with exquisite skill and care. He boasted that he had never killed anyone. His associates could not make this claim. They felt quite at ease with the murders they had committed.

The widespread criminal activities of Cassidy and the Wild Bunch put the famous Pinkerton and railroad detectives on their trail. In the hot pursuit and the confrontations that followed, several gang members were killed or arrested. Realizing that he, too, would be caught, Cassidy and his friend the Sundance Kid took off for South America. From this point on, accounts vary as to where the duo settled, what they did and when and where they died.

The prototypical free-lancing criminal, Butch Cassidy is widely regarded as one of the outlaw West's most romantic characters. See also BUTCH CASSIDY AND THE SUNDANCE KID.

Castle, Vernon and Irene (1887–1918 and 1893–1969)   Elegant pair who around the time of World War I developed and demonstrated a new style of ballroom dancing in which couples held each other in embrace. Their most famous dances were the Maxixe, the Castle Walk, the Castle Polka, the Tango and the Hesitation Waltz. Idolized for their stylishness in exhibition dancing, the Castles helped popularize social dancing.

A movie about the couple, *The Story of Vernon and Irene Castle* starring Fred Astaire and Ginger Rogers, was released in 1939 by RKO Radio Pictures.

Catch-22 (1961)   Wildly satirical novel by the American writer Joseph Heller (1923–1999). The protagonist, Yossarian, is a bombardier in an American squadron stationed on a Mediterranean island during World War II. His commander is a fanatic bent on sacrificing his men to his own ambitions. In desperate efforts to survive, Yossarian feigns madness. But, argues the military bureaucracy, referring to regulation 22, how can one be mad if one is trying to get out of the war? There's the catch—catch-22!

"Catch-22" is widely used to mean a paradoxical bind out of which one cannot work one's way, an absurd dilemma.

cat's paw   A cat and a monkey, walking in the woods one day, came upon some chestnuts roasting in a fire. The aroma of the roasting chestnuts was irresistible. How to get them out of the fire? After some discussion, the monkey, traditionally the more clever one, convinced the cat to undertake this delicate, somewhat hazardous job. As the cat proceeded to pull the chestnuts out of the fire, the monkey devoured them as they cooled off. Thus, the clever monkey got the chestnuts. The not-so-clever cat got a pair of sizzled paws. The origin of this old fable is uncertain. See DOG IN THE MANGER.

A cat's paw is a dupe, a tool, someone who is used to do someone else's dirty work to get someone out of a difficult or embarrassing situation.

Caulfield, Holden   Seventeen-year-old hero of J. D. Salinger's novel *The Catcher in the Rye* (1951). In his book-length monologue, Holden reveals his disaffection from almost everybody in the world except his innocent young sister, Phoebe. His classmates and teachers at prep school, his own parents, affected girls, casual acquaintances into whom he runs during his long weekend in New York City, are all phonies, not to be trusted. He has a vision of standing in a field of rye at the bottom of a cliff so that he may catch the little children who fall off. He wants to protect the innocent children from the disillusionment they inevitably face in a world of grown-ups. Holden Caulfield became a cult figure for millions of youths all over the world. Young people dressed like him, with a long scarf trailing around their necks; they used his racy language; and they adopted his attitudes.

caveat emptor   Latin for "let the buyer beware." In other words, if the buyer gets something inferior or defective, he has no one to blame but himself. "Caveat emptor" tells the buyer he should try to be informed and intelligent about what he buys. It does not (as it appears) give the seller a free hand to cheat the buyer.

The complete quotation, however, puts *some* responsibility on the buyer: "*Caveat emptor, quia ignorare non debuit quod ius alienum emit*" (Let a purchaser [buyer] beware, for he ought not to be ignorant of the nature of the property that he is buying for another party).

By a natural extension, the "caveat" applies to a person who "buys" ideas, principles or codes of behavior. He needs to be as careful and as informed as if he were buying goods of any kind.

Cavell, Edith Louisa (1865–1915)   British nurse executed by the Germans on October 13, 1915, on charges of espionage during World War I. She had treated the wounded of both sides, and so her death was viewed on the Allied side as a martyrdom.

"the center cannot hold"   Phrase from "The Second Coming," a poem by William Butler Yeats (1865–1939). He writes:

Things fall apart; the center cannot hold;
Mere anarchy is loosed upon the world . . .

What Yeats means is that Western civilization, as we have known it, is disintegrating. We are no longer bound together by commonly shared values and rituals. We recognize no authority: "The falcon cannot hear the falconer." It's each man for himself. See also SLOUCHING TOWARD BETHLEHEM.

Chagall, Marc (1887–1985)   Born Moyshe Shagal in Russia, he became a world-renowned painter and stained-glass maker who worked variously in St. Petersburg, Paris, Berlin, Jerusalem and New York. Chagall painted dreamlike fantasies out of the nostalgic elements of his boyhood in a Russian shtetl: rural village life, Russian folk tales, Jewish proverbs. Chagall's stained glass windows may be seen in the Hadassah Chapel in Jerusalem, in the cathedral at Rheims, France, and in many other places. Two large Chagall murals can be seen in the Metropolitan Opera House in New York City. A "Chagall" is a bright-colored pictorial folk tale.

chain reaction   This term comes from chemistry and physics. It is what happens, for example, in fission, when a single neutron splits the nucleus of a uranium atom into smaller parts, releasing two or three neutrons, each of which then attacks and splits nearby nuclei. The net result in fission is released energy. It was with this hypothesis that Enrico Fermi first succeeded in producing the chain reaction that made possible the making of the atom bomb.

In everyday use, a chain reaction is any series of happenings linked in such a way that one is the cause of the next, and so on.

Challenger   The explosion of the U.S. space shuttle *Challenger* 74 seconds after launching on the morning of January 28, 1986, at Cape Canaveral, Florida, with all seven astronauts aboard was the worst disaster in the history of space exploration. The tragedy was witnessed on television by millions of stunned viewers. One of the seven who died was Christa McAuliffe, a high school teacher from Concord, New Hampshire, who was supposed to have been the first "ordinary citizen" in space. The others were Francis R. Scobee, commander; Michael J. Smith, pilot; Gregory B. Jarvis; Ronald E. McNair; Ellison S. Onizuka; and Judith A. Resnik.

The cause of the explosion was found by the National Aeronautics and Space Administration (NASA) to be a weakness in the seal of a solid-fuel rocket booster. This terrible accident on the 25th flight of the shuttle brought the American space program to a standstill for about three years.

The *Challenger* has become a grim reminder of the possibility of catastrophe in space.

Use: "When working on the razor's edge of catastrophe, success demands constant training and easy communications from bottom up as well as top down—and that, in turn, demands leaders who are prepared to listen to and learn from their subordinates. . . . These are among the principles that can help us avoid future BHOPALS, Chernobyls, *Challengers*—or mistaken attacks on Iranian aircraft." (John Pfeiffer, *Smithsonian,* July 1989)

Chamberlain, Neville (1869–1940)   British prime minister (1937–1940) whose name has become synonymous with appeasement. In spite of German chancellor Adolf Hitler's broken promises—his rearming of Germany, his reoccupation of the Rhineland, his annexation of Austria—Chamberlain still thought he could do business with Hitler. In Munich on September 29, 1938, at a four-power conference—not including Czechoslovakia—Chamberlain capitulated to Hitler's demand for the German-speaking Sudetenland in return for guaranteeing the rest of Czechoslovakia's independence. Chamberlain acted, he said, "for peace in our time." Six months later, on March 15, 1939, Hitler's troops marched into Prague.

Champs-Élysées   Very wide boulevard of upscale stores and restaurants in Paris, leading from the Place de la Concorde to the Etoile.

Chan, Charlie   Aphorism-spouting Chinese detective character created by the writer Earl Derr Biggers in 1925 and adapted for the screen in a long series of popular B movies from 1926 to 1949. His sayings were repeated by viewers as if they had emanated from Confucius; e.g., "When money talks, few are deaf" and "Man who flirt with dynamite sometimes fly with angels." Unlike hardboiled American private eyes or the menacing Fu Manchu, Chan was courtly and soft-spoken. He was usually accompanied by his klutzy, bungling Number One (or Number Two) son, who supplied the comic relief. Oddly, Chan was never played by a Chinese actor. His two most authentic impersonators were Warner Oland, a Swede, and Sidney Toler, an American.

Chandleresque   Suggestive of the novels and movie scripts of Raymond Chandler (1888–1959), American mystery writer. His books include such novels as *The Big Sleep* (1939), *Farewell, My Lovely* (1940), and *The Long Goodbye* (1954), and *The Simple Art of Murder* (1950), a collection of 12 stories. Chandler depicted racketeers, corrupt policemen, venal politicians and a stoic private detective, Philip Marlowe, against a backdrop of the "mean streets" of southern California.

Chanel, Gabrielle (1886–1971)   Familiarly known as "Coco," Chanel was a French designer of the haute couture whose understated, casual, slim and straight suits with collarless jackets became the standard of ultra-chic women's clothing, just as her Chanel #5 became a perennial favorite among perfumes. A Chanel is said never to go out of style. It is a classic.

Chaney, Lon (1883–1930)   Known as "the man of a thousand faces," Chaney used grotesque masks and horribly contorted physical postures to simulate fiendish characters in the silent movies. His most notable success was in the title role of *The Hunchback of Notre Dame* (1923). Chaney was the undisputed star of horror films. Two actors who succeeded him in this genre were Bela Lugosi (*Dracula*, 1931) and Boris Karloff (*Frankenstein*, 1931).

Chaplinesque   Looking like or having the qualities of "the tramp," a character invented and played by Charles Chaplin (1889–1977), the greatest comic genius of the silent screen. The tramp was a homeless vagabond, a little guy with a derby hat, a cane, baggy pants and a duck-like waddle. He was a slapstick Mack Sennett–type with a soul, wistful and trying to cope in an incomprehensible and intractable world. He first appeared in one-reelers and then in such full-length movies as *City Lights* (1931) and *Modern Times* (1936).

Chappaquiddick   Tiny island in Massachusetts where Senator Ted Kennedy drove off a bridge on the night of July 19, 1969. His 28-year-old companion in the car, Mary Jo Kopechne, was drowned. Kennedy received a two-month suspended sentence and one year's probation for leaving the scene of an accident. Although Kennedy, in a televised speech, said that he tried to save the girl, the unanswered questions of Chappaquiddick have continued to haunt his political career.

Chappaquiddick stands for political nemesis. It is a shady part of one's past that won't go away.

Use: Gary Hart's brief affair with Donna Rice proved to be his Chappaquiddick.

"Charge of the Light Brigade, The"   A poem (1854) by Alfred, Lord Tennyson, that commemorates the heroic but tragic cavalry charge of a British brigade against the overwhelming fire power of the Russians at Balaclava during the Crimean War. Their commander, or "*someone* had blundered." However,

> *Theirs not to make reply,*
> *Theirs not to reason why,*
> *Theirs but to do and die.*
> *Into the valley of Death*
> *Rode the six hundred.*

Out of 637 men, 247 were killed or wounded.

"The charge of the light brigade" is a phrase used to signify a futile, ill-conceived assault against great odds.

Charles, Nick and Nora   Slick couple in the detective novel *The Thin Man* by Dashiell Hammett (1894–1961). As played by William Powell and Myrna Loy in the 1934 film adaptation, the Charleses stand for debonaire sophistication and wit. The name of their little terrier, Asta, often shows up in crossword puzzles.

Chaucerian   In the manner of Geoffrey Chaucer (1343–1400), the greatest English poet of the Middle Ages, as evidenced especially in his most characteristic work, *The Canterbury Tales.*

In this unfinished masterpiece, the author joins a motley company of 29 characters who are setting out on horseback for a pilgrimage to the shrine of THOMAS À BECKET at CANTERBURY cathedral. They stop overnight at the Tabard Inn, where the resourceful host offers to join them. The host also proposes that, to while away the time on the journey, each person should tell two stories on the way there and two stories on the way back. Whoever is judged to have told the best story will win a fine dinner. All accept the challenge. This is the framework of *The Canterbury Tales,* similar to that of BOCCACCIO's *Decameron.* This plan gave Chaucer the opportunity to present every genre of writing current at the time: chivalric romance, fable, bawdy tale, sermon and other forms.

Chaucer starts out by describing in vivid and deliciously tongue-in-cheek detail each one of the pilgrims: appearance, costume, speech, type of occupation, class, idiosyncrasies, foibles and philosophy of life. He paints a panorama of the Middle Ages, representing the middle range of chivalry, the church, the professions and trades, women; he observes them closely and describes them realistically, with all their human blemishes and frailties. He never idealizes, but accepts them as they are. His tone is lightly ironic, tolerant, never rising to shrill condemnation, although he makes his opinions of each character clear. He is not a reformer. He laughs quietly at the obvious ruses and rationalizations with which some of these scoundrels deceive themselves. Chaucer loves the commonplace, even the raw, the rowdy, the vulgar. See *The Miller's Tale* and *The Reeve's Tale*.

Of all the poets in the English language, surely the worldly Chaucer is the most companionable.

Chautauqua   The name of a lake, a town and a county in New York State, it is famous for developing the first and largest venture in adult education in America. It started in 1873 with a proposal to add some secular elements to the religious instruction program at the Methodist Episcopal summer camp. By 1874, the Chautauqua administration developed an eight-week summer program with courses in religion and the arts, humanities and sciences.

Chautauqua lecturers went out to the communities where people lived who wanted to participate but could not attend the meetings. At its peak, the Chautauqua Circuit visited about 10,000 communities.

In the late 1920s, the combined effects of the automobile, the spread of hotels and motels and the growing sophistication of the people led to the decline of the Circuit. The last vestige of the Chautauqua Circuit is now located on Lake Chautauqua, where it offers a wide variety of lectures, concerts and workshops.

William Safire, the *New York Times* columnist, has defined "Chautauqua" as "grass-roots intellectualism."

Checkpoint Charlie   A crossing point through the BERLIN WALL to which was attached this notice: "Attention. You are now leaving the American sector." It was a symbol of the COLD WAR. The hut at the checkpoint was demolished on June 22, 1990. As Robert Frost said, "Something there is that doesn't love a wall." See also IRON CURTAIN.

checks and balances   The fundamental principle embodied in the Constitution of the United States, it is the secret of the flexibility and strength of this great document. The founding fathers, in constructing the Constitution, applied a profound lesson they had learned from their immediate experiences with the king of England, and from the history of past nations and institutions, later given memorable expression by Lord Acton (1834–1902): "All power corrupts. Absolute power corrupts absolutely."

To make sure that no branch of government became too powerful, for virtually every power granted to one branch of government, the creators of the Constitution allocated equal controlling power to the other two branches. Thus, the Congress (the law-making body) could check the powers of the president. The Supreme Court could, by its rulings, "check" the powers of the Congress and/or the president. The president, by his veto, could "check" the powers of Congress. And so, "a careful symmetry and balance" was maintained among the several branches of the government.

A system of checks and balances may be applicable to business as well as academic organizations.

Chekhov, Anton Pavlovich (1860–1904)   Russian short-story writer and dramatist. A practicing doctor, Chekhov had ample opportunity to observe all kinds of people in crisis. The crises he transmuted into literature, however, were not physical but spiritual.

Chekhov is the master of depicting spiritual malaise, the characteristic embodied by the adjective "Chekhovian." Characters hang suspended in time, dreaming of the past, unable to face the future and incapable of decisive action in the present. They are filled with inexpressible, inchoate longings doomed to frustration. For the most part, they belong to the Russian landed aristocracy on the eve of extinction. These are the beautiful, faded people with exquisite feelings who live in the land of nostalgia.

Chekhov presents them sympathetically yet realistically in hundreds of stories, and in four full-length plays: *The See Gull* (1891), *Uncle Vanya* (1897), *The Three Sisters* (1901) and *The Cherry Orchard* (1904).

Chelm   In Jewish folklore and legend, Chelm is a little village in Eastern Europe inhabited by amiable simpletons. It has been told that the angel carrying the bag of the souls of the stupid for world distribution accidentally dropped it. They all spilled out in one place: Chelm.

Chelmniks are the unwitting masters of the nonsequitur. It is not so much that they are irrational or illogical but that they seem to live in a world not governed by logic. Leo Rosten in *The Joys of Yinglish* writes that "Chelm is the equivalent of Holland's 'Kampen,' Italy's 'Cuneo,' and Germany's 'Schildburg'—all famous for boneheads, dunces and nincompoops." Add to that list the village of Gotham in England, where the wise men were all idiots.

The following are Chelmisms, for which we are indebted to Leo Rosten:

1. Sleep faster: we need the pillows.
2. In Chelm, the inhabitants go to a dentist to have wisdom teeth put in.
3. In Chelm, the best cobbler, among all the tailors, is Chaim Yudel, the baker.
4. The council of wise men in Chelm were debating a profound question: Which is more important to mankind: The moon or the sun? After three hours of philosophical wrangling, Rabbi Schmerl had the definitive answer:

The moon! Why? Because the sun shines only in the daytime when we don't need it. But the moon shines at night when we do need it.

SHOLEM ALEICHEM in his tales and Isaac Bashevis Singer in "The Fools of Chelm and Their History" are among the writers in Yiddish who have made good use of the folkloric material of Chelm.

Chelm stands, of course, for a place where fools dwell.

Cherry Orchard, The (1904) A drama, a masterpiece, by the Russian playwright and short story writer Anton Chekhov (1860–1904). (See RANEVSKAYA.)

The cherry orchard is part of an estate forfeited by its aristocratic and impractical owner, Mme. Ranevskaya, who cannot bear to mutilate it in order to hold on to it. The cherry orchard represents her past, the pampered carefree life she led in her youth when feudal forms of loyalty and graciousness and mutual responsibility and love of beauty were the norms of her society. She abhors the new commercialism of changing Russia, but she cannot stem the tide. In the end, the cherry orchard is bought by a former serf who cuts down the trees and breaks up the land into small parcels for the new bourgeois to own and develop.

The Cherry Orchard stands for a way of life to which one is sentimentally attached even though it is no longer viable, such as the antebellum South.

Cheshire Cat In *Alice's Adventures in Wonderland* (1865), by Lewis Carroll, Alice first sees the Cheshire Cat in the Duchess's pepper-filled kitchen. The only two creatures who do not sneeze are the cook and "a large cat, which was lying on the hearth and grinning from ear to ear." Later Alice notices the cat sitting on the bough of a tree, grinning and looking good-natured. A conversation between the two ensues, in the midst of which the cat abruptly vanishes and reappears several times:

". . . I wish you wouldn't keep appearing and vanishing so suddenly; you make me quite giddy!"

"All right," said the Cat; and this time it vanished quite slowly, beginning with the end of the tail, and ending with the grin, which remained some time after the rest of it had gone.

"Well, I've often seen a cat without a grin," thought Alice; "but a grin without a cat! It's the most curious thing I ever saw in all my life!"

To say that a person looks like a Cheshire Cat is to say that he or she is grinning from ear to ear, looking mysterious and feeling quite pleased with himself or herself.

"chicken in every pot, a"   Slogan of the Republican Party in the presidential campaign of 1928; a promise of continued prosperity under a new Republican administration. The entire slogan, the first part of which echoed a quote of King Henry IV of France, read: "A chicken in every pot, a car in every garage."

Connotes general prosperity for the masses. Sometimes used ironically to suggest the opposite.

Chicken Little   The main character in a nursery tale first printed in a collection by J. O. Halliwell in the 19th century. Chicken Little goes for a walk in the woods. An acorn drops on her head. "The sky is falling, the sky is falling," she cries, and runs to warn her friends: Hen-len, Cock-lock, Duck-luck, Drake-lake, Goose-loose, Gander-lander and Turkey-lurkey. They form a procession, with Chicken Little in the lead, to go and warn the king. On the way they meet Foxy-loxy, who offers to take them to the king. Alas, the cunning and skeptical fox lures them to his den, where he and his little ones eat up all the gullible fowl.

A Chicken Little is an alarmist, one who warns of impending doom on the basis of incomplete or faulty evidence.

Chirico, Giorgio De (1888–1978)   Artist born in Greece of Sicilian parents, he studied in Athens, Munich, Italy and Paris. His early paintings, through the juxtaposition of incongruous elements caught in brooding shadows and cold light, suggest sinister events, as of a town just emptied of people. Some of his trademarks are classical buildings with arches and arcades stretching into infinity, a curtain flapping out of an open window in an empty house, a lone figure rolling a hoop down a deserted street. Typical is his painting *Mystery and Melancholy of a Street* (1914). His best paintings are hallucinatory, as in the 1920s series of wild horses galloping along shores strewn with broken Greek columns. His work is metaphysical, eerie, dreamlike and disturbing. It touches the unconscious. In 1938 Chirico wrote: "We who know the signs of the metaphysical alphabet know what joys and sorrows are present in a portico, on a street corner, within the walls of a room or inside a box."

A Chirico is a dreamlike, almost surrealist evocation of scene.

Use: "Ian McEwan's fictional world is a dark and threatening place, combining the bleak, dream-like quality of Chirico's citiscapes with the strange eroticism of canvases by Balthus." (Michiko Kakutani, the *New York Times,* September 26, 1987)

Cinderella (French, *Cendrillon*)   The story of Cinderella, which is founded in oral tradition, first appeared in print in the *Contes du temps passé* (Tales of times past, 1697), a collection of eight fairy tales by the French writer Charles Perrault (1628–1703). On the frontispiece appeared not Perrault's name but, for the first time, the words *Contes de ma mère l'Oye* (Tales of Mother Goose). Perrault's book was translated into English in 1729.

Cinderella is a young girl "of an exceptionally sweet and gentle nature." She is mocked and abused by her stepmother and two stepsisters. She does all the menial tasks uncomplainingly and sits in ragged clothes among the cinders. One day, after her stepsisters have departed for a ball given by the prince, Cinderella sits weeping. Her fairy godmother appears. With her magic wand she turns a pumpkin into a gilded coach; six live mice into horses; a rat into a coachman, and six lizards into liveried footmen. With a touch of her wand, she transforms Cinderella's rags into "garments of gold and silver cloth, bedecked with jewels," and then she gives Cinderella a pair of glass slippers. Cinderella, warned that she must return home by the stroke of midnight, rides off to the ball, dazzles the prince with her beauty and charm, and manages to slip away just before midnight. The next night, at a second ball given by the prince, in her haste to get away by midnight, Cinderella drops one of her glass slippers. The prince orders a search for the unknown princess whose foot will fit into the glass slipper. The stepsisters, try as they may, cannot get their big feet into the slipper. When Cinderella asks to try it, to the stepsisters' amazement and fury it fits. Cinderella then takes the matching slipper out of her pocket. She marries the prince and lives happily ever after.

A Cinderella story is thus the tale of a simple, good-hearted girl whose virtue overcomes meanness and whose fortunes change from rags to riches; any story in which the least becomes the first.

circle the wagons In the days of westward migration in the United States, people and goods moved across the prairies and the Great Plains in covered wagons that could cross the land without benefit of roads. Because of the hazards posed by vast unsettled distances and hostile Indians, wagon trains were developed so that groups could more safely travel together under the guidance and protection of professional wagoners, usually accompanied by a military captain. Contracts were drawn in advance and strict rules enforced. The order of the wagons in the line of march was fixed. At night the wagons were drawn into a circle for defense, and a guard was posted against a surprise attack by Indians.

"Westerns" have presented vivid images to moviegoers of this circling of the wagons, the white emigrant families fighting from within the circle of wagons, the Indians on their horses racing around the circle yelling their war cries and shooting their arrows and throwing torches onto the flammable canvas covering the wagons.

Today the term "circling the wagons" means a concerted defense against a concerted offense.

Circumlocution Office A department of the government, manned by petty, rude, obstructive bureaucrats like the Barnacles in Charles Dickens's novel *Little Dorrit* (1857–58). In his essay "Little Dorrit" (in *The Opposing Self*, p. 55), Lionel

Trilling wrote: "Dickens is far from having lost his sense of the cruelty and stupidity of institutions and functionaries, his sense of the general rightness of the people as a whole and of the general wrongness of those who are put in authority over them. . . . The Circumlocution Office is a constraint upon the life of England which nothing can justify."

Today, a circumlocution office is any government agency whose relations with the public are marked by torpor, red tape and obfuscation.

Citizen Kane   This 1941 film about the life of a controversial publishing tycoon, modeled after William Randolph Hearst, is considered by many critics to be one of the greatest films ever made. It was produced, directed and coauthored (with Herman J. Mankiewicz) by Orson Welles (1916–1985), the onetime "boy wonder," who also played the title role. See also ROSEBUD.

city upon a hill   In a sermon aboard the ship *Arabella* in 1630, John Winthrop (1588–1649), on his journey from England to be the governor of Massachusetts Bay Colony, spoke to his followers:

> For we must consider that we shall be a city upon a hill. The eyes of all people are upon us, so that if we shall deal falsely with our God in this work we have undertaken, and so cause Him to withdraw His present help from us, we shall be made a story and a byword through the world.

Winthrop must have had in mind the passage in Matthew 5.14: "Ye are the light of the world. A city that is set on an hill cannot be hid. . . . Let your light so shine before men, that they may see your good works, and glorify your Father which is in heaven."

The city upon a hill is, therefore, an ideal city, a shining city, a model of virtue for all to see, a righteous community devoted to the good.

Clarissa   The virtuous heroine of *Clarissa: or the History of A Young Lady* (1747–49), an epistolary novel in eight volumes and more than a million words by the English writer Samuel Richardson (1689–1761).

The rather complicated plot can be briefly summarized thus: When Mr. Lovelace, the suitor of Clarissa Harlowe's older sister, transfers his ardor to Clarissa herself, Clarissa's disapproving parents forbid her to see him. They try to force Clarissa to marry the wealthy Mr. Solmes, whom she detests. Rebellious, she is locked in her room. She engages in a secret correspondence with Lovelace, who poses as her sympathetic protector. He convinces her to run away with him. He takes her to a house in London, which she eventually realizes is a high-class brothel. Clarissa resists all of Lovelace's attempts to seduce her. The more she resists, the more he persists. Obsessed with breaking down her virtue, which he mistakenly takes for mere prudery, he finally drugs and rapes her. Clarissa is desolate. Lovelace, conscience-stricken, offers to marry her. Clarissa shuns him and makes her escape. She winds up in a debtor's prison, from which she is rescued by a friend. Inconsolable and alone, Clarissa prepares herself for death. Lovelace is killed in a duel.

If GRISELDA is synonymous with patience, Clarissa is synonymous with chastity.

classic   A thing of such excellence and such elegance, so free of faddism and frou-frou, so well constructed that it stands the test of time, whether it be an epic poem like *The Iliad* or a suit by CHANEL, is a classic.

In ancient Rome, a citizen of the highest class was called a *classicus;* hence, the best authors became known as classical authors and the best books became known as classics. Later, "classics" referred to ancient Greek and Roman works of art and literature and to the rules that governed their creation, as described, for example, in Aristotle's *Poetics.* The dramatic unities of time, place and action were such rules of classic form.

After the exuberance of certain aspects of the late Renaissance, the 18th century saw a return to classical form: neoclassicism, which was, in turn, followed by its opposite, ROMANTICISM. The classical became associated with orderliness, restraint, convention, reason and unity, in contrast with romantic wildness and boldness, freedom, experimentation, imagination, emotion, mysticism. A classical garden is a French garden with its geometrical patterns; a romantic garden is an English garden with abundant natural flowering forms. The 18th-century neoclassicists were concerned with the city, with witty and civilized discourse, with poetic forms like the rhymed couplet. The 19th-century romantics were concerned with country life, with political freedom, with beauty, with stanzaic variety.

Classic has come to have many applications, some of them paradoxical. For example, what is a classic Western? Surely the Western as a genre is romantic in tone, action and character; yet, there seems to be within it certain obligatory elements like the "classic" confrontation scene. So "classic" may mean "true to form" or "serving as a model," as in a "classic" demonstration in science, or as in a "classic" response, a response that conforms to expectations.

Clausewitzean   A reference to the military strategy and theories propounded by Karl von Clausewitz (1780–1831), a Prussian general who fought in the wars against NAPOLEON and participated in the battles at WATERLOO. In 1818 he was appointed director of the German War School.

On War, published posthumously, is considered his masterpiece. In it he develops his concept of total war: namely, an all-out, no-holds-barred attack on the people, land and resources of the enemy.

"clear and present danger, a" See FALSELY SHOUTING FIRE IN A CROWDED THEATER.

Cleopatra The seductive Egyptian queen of whom Shakespeare wrote in *Antony and Cleopatra* (c. 1607):

> *Age cannot wither her, nor custom stale*
> *Her infinite variety; other women cloy*
> *The appetites they feed, but she makes hungry*
> *Where most she satisfies. . . .*

She dazzled great Caesar himself and seduced Mark Antony into giving up an empire for her. When Antony, having finally bestirred himself to return to his duties, was defeated in battle and fell on his sword, Cleopatra committed suicide by holding an asp to her bosom.

Not much more is remembered of the ambitious historical Cleopatra who lived from 69 to 30 B.C.; but who can forget Shakespeare's description of her as she first came into Antony and Enobarbus's sight:

> *The barge she sat in, like a burnished throne,*
> *Burned on the water; the poop was beaten gold,*
> *Purple the sails, and so perfumed, that*
> *The winds were love-sick with them, the oars were silver,*
> *Which to the tune of flutes kept stroke, and made*
> *The water which they beat to follow faster,*
> *As amorous of their strokes. For her own person,*
> *It beggared all description.*

Cleopatra has stood throughout the ages as the most alluring of women—not to mention, the most tragic of heroines. John Dryden saw Cleopatra as a tragic queen in *All for Love* (1678), whereas George Bernard Shaw presented her as a kittenish would-be seductress of the rather amused Julius Caesar in *Caesar and Cleopatra* (1906).

cliffhanger From silent movie serials, where every episode ended with a melodramatic, suspenseful situation designed to make the viewer come back the following week to see the outcome. Literally, the hero might be left at the end of an episode clinging by one hand to the edge of a cliff. How would he escape? Wait till next week.

A "cliffhanger" is any suspenseful situation not immediately resolved.

Clockwork Orange, A   Novel (1962) by English writer Anthony Burgess (1917–93) and film (1971) directed by Stanley Kubrick. The first half of the movie vividly depicts a teenage gang of the future rampaging through streets and homes. These young men are as hard-edged as the decor. Utterly lacking in human compassion or sensibility, they strike terror wherever they attack. They represent Burgess's terrible vision of a society tyrannized by children growing up without restraints of any kind.

Burgess's future seemed to have arrived during the author's lifetime. Under the headline "A Clockwork Orange in Central Park" (*U.S. News & World Report,* May 8, 1989), the copy reads: "The attackers were children wielding rocks and a pipe, and the casual brutality of the crime shattered the springtime countenance of a city long accustomed to a daily drumbeat of murders, muggings and robberies."

clone   Term coined around 1903 from the Greek word *klon,* meaning a slip or a twig. Biologists have discovered that, just as a plant can be reproduced from a small slip, an entire living system can be reproduced from a single cell, since each cell contains the DNA molecules of the whole organism. It is possible, therefore, to make a copy of a complex organic system (theoretically, even a human being) in a science laboratory. In other words, it is possible to produce a clone genetically identical to the ancestral unit from which it was derived.

This theory was proven when the Roslin Institute in Scotland announced that one of its scientists, Dr. Ian Wilmut, had succeeded in cloning the first-ever mammal from an udder cell of a sheep. Thus was Dolly born on July 5, 1996. Since then, Hawaiian mice and Japanese cows have been cloned, and Dr. Wilmut has launched a project for the cloning of human embryos, a source for stem cells that have the capacity to differentiate into any and all cells of the body, in which to grow spare human organs. Research on human cloning has raised controversial ethical questions.

Colloquially, a clone is a copy or a close imitation of someone or something else; e.g., (1) In choosing a vice presidential candidate for the ticket, the presidential candidate was not looking for a clone of himself, or (2) *60 Minutes* has been cloned. We now have *60 Minutes Two,* not to mention a slew of other copycat magazine-type TV shows.

Clouseau, Inspector   Main character played by Peter Sellers in a series of films made during the 1960s and 1970s, including *The Pink Panther, The Return of the Pink*

Panther and *The Revenge of the Pink Panther*. He is an inept, ineffectual, bumbling detective; a farcical parody of the tough private eye.

cockamamie   Probably originally a mispronunciation of "decalcomania," a picture on a small square of paper that children used to transfer to their hands or arms simply by licking it and applying. A childhood fad, it was a quick, easily applied and easily removed substitute for a tattoo; therefore, a fake, of little consequence; easy on, easy off. Today it is used derisively as an adjective almost synonymous with Mickey Mouse, meaning trivial, hare-brained or fake, as in, "What kind of cockamamie excuse is that?"

Cogito, ergo sum   See CARTESIAN.

Cohan, George M. (1878–1942)   Actor, playwright, composer, producer who dominated the Broadway musical theater for two decades. Cohan spent 56 years on the stage. He wrote 40 plays, collaborated on 40 others, produced 150 other plays, wrote over 500 songs and made between 5,000 and 10,000 stage appearances.

Cohan's songs sold millions of copies of sheet music. Among his still popular songs are "Over There," "You're A Grand Old Flag," "Mary," "Give My Regards To Broadway," "I'm a Yankee Doodle Dandy." In 1940, Congress voted Cohan a special Medal of Honor. Cohan is the quintessential "song and dance man."

cold war   All-out hostility, short of a shooting war, between the Western democracies and the Soviet Union following the end of World War II. It denoted ideological, military, economic and political rivalry between these two sides. The expression was coined in 1946 by Herbert Bayard Swope in a speech he wrote for elder statesman Bernard Baruch. Used today to indicate such a feeling between any two parties. The cold war came to an end with the tearing down of the BERLIN WALL in 1989 and the collapse of Soviet communism.

collateral damage   Unintended damage accompanying a hit on a designated target in war. For example, in Yugoslavia in 1999, NATO forces blew up a bridge by firing guided missiles from a plane. The pilot had no way of knowing at that height that a bus full of people was crossing the bridge at that very moment. Thus, the civilian deaths accompanying the strategic military destruction of the bridge were counted as collateral damage.

The application of the term has been extended to nonmilitary events, as, for example, the collateral damage resulting from a bitterly contested divorce.

Collyer brothers Wealthy brothers Homer (1882–1947) and Langley (1886–1947), who lived like poverty-stricken recluses in a Harlem town house. When the police broke in, they found both brothers dead amidst mountainous piles of junk, garbage, old newspapers and magazines.

The Collyer brothers are synonymous with misers and irrational hoarders.

Columbine See LITTLETON.

Columbus, Christopher (c. 1451–1506) Columbus was born in Genoa, Italy, but moved to Portugal in 1477. Like many others in that great era of Portuguese exploration, he dreamed of finding an Atlantic route to Asia. Failing to convince the king of Portugal to sponsor such an expedition, he moved to Spain in 1484. He spent eight years seeking the patronage of Queen Isabella and King Ferdinand before he was finally outfitted with three small ships (the *Santa Maria,* the *Pinta* and the *Nina*) and a crew of 120. They set sail on August 3, 1492. After terrible hardships, despair and even mutiny, they landed in the Bahamas on October 12, 1492, and claimed the land for Spain. Columbus proceeded to explore what is now called the West Indies, and he founded the first Spanish settlement in the New World on Hispaniola (Haiti and the Dominican Republic).

On his return to Spain, Columbus was named "admiral of the ocean sea" as well as viceroy and governor of all the new lands. All in all, Columbus made four voyages of discovery to the New World. Fortune was capricious. Once, he was returned to Spain in chains by Bobadilla, the governor who had been sent to Hispaniola to investigate conditions in the colony. Although Columbus was vindicated and celebrated as a hero, he nevertheless died in poverty and neglect at Valladolid, Spain. In 1542 his remains were unearthed and transferred to Hispaniola.

A Columbus is an intrepid and indefatigable explorer, one who follows a dream, one who discovers a new world, not necessarily geographic.

Comédie humaine (Human Comedy) The title Honoré de Balzac (1799–1850) used for his series of 90 novels about French life—an encompassing, realistic picture of human follies, cruelties and kindnesses. More than 2,000 characters move through this vast pageant of human behavior. In massive, vigorous detail, the *Comédie humaine* touches all classes.

It took Balzac 20 years to complete this "social history of France." His enormous energy and penetrating insights inform this "intensely alive" panorama of the human condition. Today *comédie humaine*—though originally applied to French society—has acquired a universal meaning.

"come up and see me sometime"   See WEST, MAE.

"comin' in on a wing and a prayer"   From a World War II song about a pilot, written by Harold Adamson and Jimmy McHugh (lyrics) in 1943. Quoted now to mean just barely making it.

commedia dell'arte   A genre of improvisational comedy performed by traveling theatrical companies throughout Europe from 1545 to the end of the 18th century. The commedia dell'arte originated in Italy. The actors would receive a bare outline of a plot, from which they had to create extemporaneously a three-act comedy. Each actor specialized in a stock character. Among these standard parts were Pantalone, a greedy and foolish Venetian merchant; Graziano, a pedantic Bolognese lawyer; the "miles gloriosus," a braggart captain; two young lovers, usually called Julia and Octavio; a host of vulgar female servants and male buffoons who tripped over each other like forerunners of the KEYSTONE KOPS; Arlecchino (Harlequin in patched clothes); and Pulcinella, with a large nose and ravenous appetite. The parts were easily identifiable by stock costumes, masks, accents, gestures and props. The end result was uproarious broad comedy.

Commedia dell'arte is today used as a derisive term for predictable stock characters; e.g., the usual bickering personages in government in Washington, D.C.

Como, Perry (1912–   )   In the 1950s, Como was the "epitome of the super star" of television. His relaxed, easy, familiar voice and manner made him one of the most popular performers of his time. His detractors' characterization of his "somnambulant style" had no effect on Como's vast and constant audience.

Comstock, Anthony (1844–1915)   A lifetime crusader against vice, obscenity and pornography. In 1873, Comstock established the New York Society for the Suppression of Vice, and remained as its secretary until he died 42 years later. Under his unrelenting pressure, the United States Congress passed the Comstock Act, which banned "obscene" materials, including prophylactics, from the mails.

The Post Office appointed him as special agent to enforce the law. Comstock pursued his mission as "smut-hunter" with unparalleled zeal. Among his "victories" was getting the Department of the Interior to fire Walt Whitman for his *Leaves of Grass* collection of poetry. At his insistence, New York City banned Margaret Sanger's books on birth control.

But Comstock didn't win all his battles. Sometimes his activities backfired. His attacks on George Bernard Shaw's *Mrs. Warren's Profession* contributed to the play's great success. Similarly, he focused international attention on the innocuous, mildly erotic painting SEPTEMBER MORN.

Eventually, Comstock became part of our language when George Bernard Shaw characterized his activities as "Comstockery," which the *Random House Dictionary* defines as "Overzealous censorship of fine arts and literature often mistaking outspokenly honest works for salacious productions."

Coney Island   Seaside resort bordering the Atlantic Ocean at the southern tip of Brooklyn, New York City. At the turn of the century it was the most famous resort in the world. With its wide sandy beaches, its boathouses and hotels, its boardwalk, its fabled amusement parks and freak shows, it attracted hundreds of thousands of pleasure seekers. On a summer Sunday, the beach would be covered with a million bathers. At night all the electric lights went on, outlining the turrets of its buildings. Then it became the "City of Fire."

Coney Island, though in decline today, remains in the imagination as a symbol of carnival, with all the tawdriness and gaiety and magnificence intrinsic in that word.

Congress of Vienna (September 1814–June 1815)   After the turmoil of the French Revolution and the military, geographic and national upheavals resulting from the Napoleonic Wars, the Congress of Vienna was convened by the victorious allies to accomplish no less than the total restructuring of Europe. Its guiding principles were: 1) legitimacy, or the restoration of territorial and dynastic status that existed before the Revolution; 2) stability, through a balance of power between the Eastern and Western blocs; 3) national self-determination; 4) conservatism and the repression of revolutionary movements.

All the crowned heads of Europe and their chief negotiators met in Vienna. METTERNICH of Austria presided. Castlereagh and the duke of Wellington represented England; Talleyrand, France; Nesselrode, Capo d'Istria and Pozzo di Borgo, Russia; von Hardenberg and von Humboldt, Prussia. The Final Act of Vienna, embodying all the conclusions and compromises and guarantees, was ratified in June 1815, nine days before Napoleon's final defeat at Waterloo.

The Congress of Vienna was one of the most important convocations in the history of Europe.

A "Congress of Vienna" now refers to a convocation of nations or global enterprises with the purpose of reshuffling the balance of power.

Connecticut Yankee in King Arthur's Court, A (1889)   A novel by Mark Twain (1835–1910). One day the superintendent of an arms factory in Hartford, Connecticut, is struck on the head with a crowbar. He loses consciousness and finds himself transported to CAMELOT in King ARTHUR's time. There he meets the famous knights of legend and finds them to be quite bloodthirsty in their chivalry. On the other hand, with his Yankee ingenuity and hindsight, he is quite impressive to the denizens of the court. He can predict an eclipse and manufacture inventions that have not yet been heard of, such as bicycles and gunpowder. The novel is an amusing study of time-warp that smartly derides the illusion of progress on one hand and of chivalric romance on the other.

The plot of casting a character "back to the future" has become popular in modern movies. The possibilities for comedy in such situations are endless.

A Connecticut Yankee is an anachronism, someone out of place and out of time.

Connor, "Bull" (Theophilus Eugene) (1897–1973)   Sheriff in Birmingham, Alabama, notorious for his use of police dogs and fire hoses in trying to prevent black children from entering white schools. A brutish opponent of the civil rights movement in the 1960s.

Use: "The *Wall Street Journal* got its facts wrong when it described James O. Freedman, the liberal president of Dartmouth College, who accused the right wing *Dartmouth Review* of poisoning the intellectual environment of the campus, as the Bull Connor of Academia." (*New York Times,* May 11, 1988)

conquistadores   Spanish adventurers who, in the 16th century, sailed to the New World, subdued the native populations of Central and South America by terror and treachery, and claimed the territories for the Spanish crown. According to the historian L. B. Simpson, "Most conquistadors were ex-soldiers, merchants, craftsmen, ex-convicts—'nobodies who wanted to become somebodies.'" They came supposedly in the service of God and country, but mostly they came to get rich. Their greed for silver and gold knew no bounds.

Among the best known and most infamous conquistadors were Francisco Pizarro (c. 1475–1541) and Hernán Cortés (1485–1547). Pizarro, an illiterate, with only 183 men and guns and horses, conquered Peru. He seized the emperor of the Incas, Atahualpa, and after extracting from his subjects a ransom consisting of a room filled to the ceiling with gold, had Atahualpa executed in 1533. Cortés likewise defeated Montezuma, the emperor of the Aztecs, striking awe into the natives who believed the white men to be gods, and so conquering Mexico.

In modern usage, a conquistador is any ruthless adventurer.

Conrad, Joseph (1857–1924)   British novelist and short story writer of Polish birth whose fiction is often based on his seafaring experiences and adventures. His characters are often caught in strange, almost hallucinatory moral dilemmas, as in *Lord Jim* (1900), *Heart of Darkness* (1902), *Nostromo* (1904) and *The Secret Agent* (1907).

consciousness raising   A deliberate attempt on the part of women in the 1970s to convene in discussion groups for the purpose of making themselves alert to the various forms of their personal oppression. These groups were support groups. The women gained courage to recognize and free themselves of their dependency and feelings of inferiority.

The term (originally used by Mao Tse-tung to raise revolutionary consciousness in China) is now used not only for women's liberation but also for any person or group that makes an effort to become more aware of its identity and integrity.

Cook's tour   An organized but superficial, inadequate, once-over-lightly tour of a country, city, any geographical area. So named after Thomas Cook (1808–92), British travel agent.

Use: As soon as we arrived, Lila gave us a Cook's tour of her apartment.

Cooper, Gary (1901–1961)   Movie star who started his career as an extra in silent Western movies and won an Oscar for his role as the sheriff in the great Western *High Noon* (1952). He is known for his monosyllabic Montana speech, his tall, lean frame, his craggy face, his quiet strength and his ability to ride horses. He won an Oscar for *Sergeant York* in 1941. One of his best-known parts was Frederic Henry in *A Farewell to Arms* (1932).

Use: "Did he have long eyelashes and a boyish grin and gulp a lot, the way honest, upright Gary Cooper gulped in the old movies?" (Russell Baker, satirizing Lt. Col. Oliver North, the "hero" of the Iran-Contra hearings, in his column on the *New York Times* Op-Ed page, August 5, 1987.)

Copernican   See PTOLEMAIC.

Copperhead   During the Civil War in the United States, Northerners who were sympathetic to the Southern cause were called Copperheads, a term coined on July 20, 1861, by a *New York Tribune* editorial writer. Copperheads were mostly anti-Lincoln Democrats who advocated negotiations for peace and the restoration of the Union, even if it meant the continuation of slavery. Under the leadership of Clement L. Vallandigham they created a secret society called the Knights of the Golden Circle.

Originally, of course, the term "copperhead" comes from the poisonous snake that, having no rattles, strikes without warning. A Copperhead during the Civil War, and in modern usage, is a traitor who strikes secretly and silently.

copycat   A juvenile taunt hurled at a child who imitates another child's actions or words, its use has been extended to cover serious crimes committed in imitation of earlier deeds that have been depicted in great detail in the media. For example, news stories of school bombings and shootings, as in LITTLETON, Colorado, are generally followed by a rash of so-called copycat crimes, as in the shooting of six students in a Georgia school by a 15-year-old sophomore. This phenomenon of suggestibility makes newspapers and TV ponder the danger of prolonged and prominent coverage of children's atrocities.

Cortez, Hernando (Cortés, Hernán) (1485–1547) Conqueror of Mexico. See CONQUISTADORES.

Cory, Richard Subject of a short, paradoxical portrait in the poem "Richard Cory" by American poet Edwin Arlington Robinson (1869–1935). Richard Cory is envied by everybody in his town. He seems to have it all: good looks, elegant manners, riches. But "Richard Cory, one summer night, / Went home and put a bullet through his head."

Richard Cory has become a tragic symbol of the despair that may lurk beneath the surface appearance of seemingly fortunate people. His life and death represent a little morality play about envy.

cosa nostra "Our thing," an "alias" for the MAFIA. Allegedly coined by Lucky Luciano and MEYER LANSKY, two of America's most powerful organized crime figures.

Cossacks From the Russian word *Kazaki,* meaning "peasant soldiers." The Cossacks were originally serfs who had fled servitude and settled on the Russian steppes in the 16th and 17th centuries. In return for certain privileges, they joined the cavalry for 20-year stints of military service. They turned reactionary in their political ideas and were used by the czars to suppress revolutionary activity. For their extracurricular pleasure they would raid Jewish villages, sowing fear and hatred with their extreme brutality. To those who suffered their sudden attacks, their daredevil horsemanship was not an object of admiration.

Today a Cossack is any bullying, cruel oppressor tainted with anti-Semitism.

couch potato A slang expression that originated in the late 1980s to describe television addicts; that is, people who spend all their time plopped passively in front of a television screen. The term has come to describe any inert do-nothing.

Use: Lamenting the continuing loss of wilderness in the United States, an op-ed contributor to the *New York Times* wrote of "today's couch-potato culture," which would rather sit than stand, rather ride in an off-road vehicle than walk along forest paths.

Coughlin, Charles Edward (1891–1979) A Great Depression–era radio chaplain who lashed out at the communists and the "money changers" who he believed had brought America to the verge of chaos and hopelessness.

For the 30 to 45 million of his radio listeners, Father Coughlin held out the hope that the nation would survive and "overcome." They wrote over 50,000 letters a week to his Shrine of the Little Flower in Royal Oak, Michigan.

By 1933, Father Coughlin had become a national hero—and a reckless one, as it turned out, hurling bitter invectives at President Franklin D. Roosevelt, whom he called a "scab president" and "a great betrayer and liar."

Because Father Coughlin's weekly broadcasts were becoming increasingly inflammatory, CBS insisted that he submit his speeches in advance. He refused, so CBS did not renew his contract. Undaunted, and emboldened by a sense that he was destined to save America, Father Coughlin returned to the air, his air time paid for by his faithful listeners.

In 1934, Father Coughlin founded the National Union for Social Justice. His rhetoric turned more raucous, his charges wild and outrageous, and his association with anti-Semites and pro-fascists ugly and threatening.

Appalled by his menacing excesses, the Catholic laity and clergy turned against him. In 1942, his church silenced him. His hectic career had come to an end. Deserted by his former admirers and adherents, he vanished from the national scene.

Use: "America has had its peddlers of political hate, its Father Coughlin and its Joe McCarthy." (*New York Times,* June 8, 1989)

Count of Monte Cristo, The (1844) A novel by the prolific French writer, Alexandre Dumas père (1802–1870). Working with his "factory" of collaborators, Dumas produced about 300 volumes of historical romances and tales of high adventure. For *The Count of Monte Cristo,* Dumas had two collaborators, August Maquet and A. P. Fiorentino.

Edmond Dantès, a young seaman, is about to experience the double pleasure of becoming a sea captain and marrying the lovely Mercédès. But Edmond's rivals for the captaincy and for the hand of Mercédès frame him on charges that he is a sinister Bonapartist.

Edmond is sentenced to life imprisonment. After nearly 20 years in the dungeon of the forbidding Chateau d'If, Edmond makes a dramatic escape. He finally reaches the island of Monte Cristo, where he finds the fabulous fortune about which a fellow prisoner had told him.

Several years later, Edmond returns to his native Marseilles—rich, handsome, powerful, mysterious—to seek revenge. No one recognizes him. One by one he picks off each of his old enemies.

One hundred and forty-eight years after its publication, *The Count of Monte Cristo* still has an enormous hold on its readers. Edmond Dantès embodies every man's desire to avenge the wrongs done to him and others, to cleanse the world of evildoers and to establish a reign of goodness.

countdown Literally, counting backward from ten to one in the ultimate moments before a space launch or before a detonation. First used in the dramatic seconds before the atom bomb was tested. Now used to denote the seconds or minutes or hours or days before an important event or, jocularly, a not-so-important event.

counted out In boxing, the referee gives the fallen boxer 10 seconds, counted out loud, to get up unassisted. If he cannot, he is considered "knocked out." The bout is over and he has lost.

In general use, to be counted out is to be beaten, finished, etc.

Use: There's plenty of fight in Allenby, so don't count him out.

Coxey's Army A group of unemployed men who marched on Washington, D.C., following the disastrous Panic of 1893, to petition Congress for help. They were organized and led by Jacob Sechler Coxey (1854–1951), an American engineer and social reformer. He was passionately interested in the plight of the unemployed. He wrote books on monetary problems, held various public offices and served a term as mayor of Massillon, Ohio.

With 100 unemployed men, Coxey left Massillon for Washington on March 25, 1894. By the time he reached Washington, his "army" had grown to 500. But instead of the demonstration he had hoped to conduct to dramatize the plight of the unemployed, Coxey and other leaders were arrested for walking on the Capitol lawn.

"Coxey's Army" has become a synonym for the futile gesture of a ragged, ineffectual, pathetic group.

Crawford, Joan (1904–1977) American film actress. Born Lucille LeSueur in Texas, she starred in more than 80 films and is remembered mainly for sob sister, self-sacrificing roles like that of *Mildred Pierce*—and for her unflattering portrait in Christina Crawford's memoir *Mommie Dearest* (1978).

Crazy Horse (c. 1842–1877) The Indian leader of mythical proportions in the Great Plains Indian Wars.

A master of guerrilla warfare, Crazy Horse managed to elude the United States's drive to keep Indians on their reservations. On December 21, 1866, using decoy warriors, he ambushed and massacred a small force of 80 U.S. soldiers led by Lt. Col. William Fetterman. Later, he joined SITTING BULL to wipe out Custer's cavalry at the battle of Little Big Horn. (See CUSTER'S LAST STAND.) Military forces hunted Crazy Horse relentlessly until he surrendered on May 6, 1877. He was placed on a reservation. On September 5, 1877, he was again arrested on rumors that he was planning to escape. At first, he offered no resistance. But when he saw that he was going to be locked up in a guard house, he struggled with his captors and was stabbed to death.

Crazy Horse, despite his savage attacks on the white man, stands as a symbol of resistance against overwhelming odds, a fighter for independence and freedom.

Crédit Mobilier of America   Following the American Civil War, plans to link the east and west coasts of the United States by railroad opened up vistas of unlimited wealth. They also provided opportunities to cheat the United States Treasury. One of the most corrupt and most lucrative of these scams was the Crédit Mobilier of America.

One of the guiding spirits of this evil enterprise was Oakes Ames, a congressman from Massachusetts. He sat on the board of directors of the Union Pacific Railroad, the company that was building the railroad from Nebraska westward. With the eager assistance of the Union Pacific, Ames created a dummy company called Crédit Mobilier of America. Along the way, general assistance was provided by, among others, Schuyler Colfax and Henry Wilson, vice presidents in Ulysses S. Grant's first and second administrations, respectively. Not surprisingly, Crédit Mobilier got all or most of the government construction contracts. For their role in this corrupt endeavor, the participants received generous helpings of Crédit Mobilier shares. Even James Garfield, later to become president, was implicated in the scandal, though he denied the charges. According to historian Kenneth Davis, Colfax and Wilson gave "the vice in their titles a whole new dimension."

Crédit Mobilier has become a symbol for large-scale greed and corruption.

Crockett, Davy (1786–1836)   Born in Greenville, Tennessee, Davy Crockett grew up on the American frontier without much formal education and became a hunter and scout for Andrew Jackson in the Creek Wars (1813–14). In 1821 he was elected a state legislator. In 1827 he was sent to the U.S. House of Representatives. He died in the battle at the ALAMO.

Although Davy Crockett was a successful politician, his fame rests on his tall tales and frontier lingo as expressed in his fictionalized autobiography of 1834, and in subsequent books that portrayed him as a "frontier superman" caught up in fantastic exploits, able to "whip his weight in wildcats."

Despite his occasional cruelty and bigotry, Davy Crockett has become an ineradicable part of American folklore, the epitome of the rough, unwashed, dangerous West.

Cro-Magnon man   Four skeletons of prehistoric men found in a cave near Les Eyzies, southern France (1868). Approximately 1 to 2 million years old, they have been held to be the prototypes of modern man, *Homo sapiens.* Reconstruction from the skeletal remains indicate that Cro-Magnon man had a long head, broad face, sunken eyes and was about 5 feet 9 inches tall.

"Cro-Magnon" is applied to men whose behavior or speech is primitive, crude, raw or vulgar. See NEANDERTHAL MAN.

Crosby, Harry Lillis "Bing" (1903–1977)   American popular singer. The career of "old groaner," as he was affectionately called, encompassed network radio, television, 50 movies, over 300 million records. In its uniquely unpretentious way, his quiet, intimate baritone made it all look so easy, so relaxed, so natural. Actually, his elegant phrasing, his faultless sense of rhythm, his fastidious diction and his special way with a song were anything but accidental. Crosby's art was the art that concealed art.

Bing Crosby was a legend in his time, a middle-American in taste, dress and inclination. He was the crooner par excellence, associated with the song "White Christmas."

Crown Heights   A neighborhood in Brooklyn, New York, where on August 22, 1991, anti-Semitic rioting by blacks broke out when a Hasidic Jew killed one black child and injured another in a car accident. In the midst of the looting and rioting, which lasted for three days, a gang of blacks attacked and killed a Jewish student from Australia. Several police officers were injured in the mêlée. Mayor David Dinkins was severely criticized for his failure to deal forcibly with this outbreak of ethnic violence—and probably lost his bid for reelection to the mayoralty as a result.

Crown Heights stands as a symbol of Jewish-black tensions in the inner cities of the United States.

Crusoe, Robinson   The hero of the novel *The Life and Strange Adventures of Robinson Crusoe* (1719), by Daniel Defoe (1660–1731).

Robinson Crusoe runs off to sea and is shipwrecked on a desert island, where he lives for 24 years. Here he encounters and solves the problems of the solitary, primitive life. He finds spiritual solace in reading the Bible.

After some years, Crusoe comes upon a young savage, whom he saves from a tribe of cannibals. He calls him MAN FRIDAY because he found him on Friday. Friday becomes Crusoe's faithful, versatile servant and companion, accompanying him on a series of breathtaking island adventures.

Defoe's novel is based on the true adventures of Alexander Selkirk (1676–1721), a Scottish sailing master who spent four years on a desolate South American island (1704–09), was rescued and returned to England, where he became a celebrity.

A Robinson Crusoe is someone who, by choice or necessity, leads a self-sufficient life for long periods of time.

cry wolf   Based on an Aesop's fable, DOG IN THE MANGER.

Once upon a time there was a young shepherd who found tending his sheep boring. To inject a little excitement into his daily regimen, he shouted "Wolf! Wolf!" so loudly that he could be heard in the village. The villagers came running with pitchforks and stones. They returned home irritated with the shepherd's trickery. Delighted with the village's dramatic turnout, a few weeks later the shepherd cried "Wolf! Wolf!" again. Again, the same villagers came to his aid—much to the shepherd's amusement and their chagrin. Some time later, the shepherd sighted a large wolf lurking in the woods. Terrified, he cried for help: "Wolf! Wolf!" This time no one came. The villagers had had their fill of false alarms. The wolf, of course, made off with one of the lambs.

To cry wolf is to sound a false alarm, with predictably tragic results.

"cultivate one's own garden"   See CANDIDE.

Curie, Marie (1867–1934)   Polish-born French chemist and physicist who, together with her husband Pierre Curie, studied radioactivity. She discovered the element radium and received a Nobel Prize for her find in 1911. She remains the prototype for women in science.

Currier and Ives   Famous American printers and lithographers.

Nathaniel Currier (1813–88) began his career as an apprentice to John Pendleton, pioneer lithographer. In 1833, he set up his own shop and started a series of lithographs that would continue for 70 years.

James Merritt Ives (1824–95) joined Ives as a bookkeeper. In 1857, he became a full partner in the firm of Currier and Ives.

From the beginning, the enterprise flourished. Priced from 15 cents to three dollars, these lithographs were popular throughout the United States and Europe. Many were hand-colored by a staff of women working on a production line.

Between 1840 and 1890, Currier and Ives produced over 7,000 individual prints. Their lithographs constituted an unparalleled record of the contemporary life and institutions of America, what its people looked like, what they wore, how and where they worked and played; how, in short, they went about the making of America.

Collectors continue to prize original Currier and Ives prints. The term "Currier and Ives," however, is practically synonymous with unsophisticated Americana.

Custer's last stand   Educated at West Point, George Armstrong Custer (1839–76) fought on the Union side during the Civil War and emerged as the youngest general in the Union Army. Daring, flamboyant, reckless, Custer was frequently in trouble with his superiors.

In 1874, prospectors and trespassers found gold on the Indian Reservation in the Black Hills of South Dakota. In the summer of 1876, Custer was sent to order the Indians off their reservation. The Sioux and Cheyenne, concentrated in the Bighorn River area in southwestern Montana, decided instead to go on the warpath.

On June 25–26, 1876, Custer (acting against specific orders not to attack) led his 250 men against a force of between 2,000 and 4,000 Indians. The Indians, led by chiefs CRAZY HORSE and SITTING BULL, destroyed Custer's entire force.

Custer's last stand has come to mean a valiant (even if misguided) last-ditch fight against overwhelming odds in the face of certain defeat.

Cyrano   Central character of Edmond Rostand's verse play *Cyrano de Bergerac* (1897), based on a 17th-century figure of the same name.

A dazzling swordsman, brilliant wit and inspired poet, a man of quintessential panache, Cyrano is yet afraid to face his true love, the beautiful and spirited Roxanne. How can he woo her, ugly as he is, with his grotesquely enormous nose? No, it would be quite ridiculous, quite incongruous. And what if she laughed at him? How many duels had he fought with fools who had had the temerity to refer even obliquely or quite inadvertently to that appendage, the nose?

Cyrano finds the answer in Christian, a handsome but inarticulate recruit. When Cyrano discovers that Roxanne and Christian are attracted to each other, Cyrano offers to supply the impassioned rhetoric of which Christian is incapable and which Roxanne demands. Cyrano writes the poems, the letters, even the speeches that Roxanne believes emanate from Christian. Not until many years later, after Christian has died in battle and Cyrano, mortally wounded, is visiting

Roxanne in her convent retreat, does Roxanne surmise the truth. She realizes that it is really Cyrano, with his eloquent outpourings of his own love, with his nobility of spirit, with his self-sacrifice, whom she has loved all along.

A Cyrano is a tragicomic figure, a PAGLIACCIO who hides his pain beneath flamboyant flourishes of words and deeds.

Dachau The first of the Nazi concentration camps, erected in Bavaria under the direction of Heinrich Himmler in March 1933, and manned by the SS. Dachau was the model for many other concentration camps. Over the camp gates was the motto ARBEIT MACHT FREI. Those who could work were spared for forced labor; those who were judged incapable of work (women, children, the old, the handicapped) were killed. See also AUSCHWITZ.

Dagwood An unusually thick sandwich stuffed with a variety of meats, cheeses, dressings, vegetables, spices and condiments. This sandwich gets its name from the popular comic strip, BLONDIE, in which Dagwood Bumstead makes these belly-busters for himself.

Dali, Salvador (1904–1989) Surrealist Spanish painter who went to great lengths to publicize his flamboyant persona as well as to promote his strange and disturbing art. His waxed mustache, turned upward like the horns of a bull, made him a caricature in the flesh; his surrealist images of melted watches—*The Persistence of Memory* (1931)—made an indelible impression on the public psyche.

Use: In the 115-degree Las Vegas heat, the ballpoint pen on the dashboard of the car had melted overnight like a Dali watch.

Dallas One of the most popular television shows of the 1980s. It had all the elements of the successful soap opera: larger than life characters; riveting conflicts about money and power; and lots of sex and intrigue.

The episode revealing which of *Dallas*'s 15 characters had shot J. R. (all of them had good reasons) was seen by more people than any other program in the history of television up to that time.

The centerpiece of *Dallas* was Larry Hagman as J. R. Ewing Jr., described by *Time* as "that human oil slick." He was the quintessential villain: power-hungry, cruel, vain, a ruthless womanizer, master of the shady deal. Through J. R.'s dealings and encounters, *Dallas* illuminated the false values and the ruthless pursuit of money and power he represented.

Damien, Father (1840–1889)

Joseph Damien de Veuster, a Belgian Catholic missionary who worked among the natives in Hawaii, was ordained in 1864 in Honolulu. In 1873 he asked to be sent to the leper colony on Molokai Island. There he contracted leprosy and died.

As Susan Sontag has argued in her book *Illness as Metaphor,* certain diseases carry symbolic baggage. Tuberculosis, for example, has been perceived as romantic; cancer, as expressionistic horror. Since antiquity, leprosy has been viewed as a disgusting, unclean scourge. Lepers, whose extremities often rotted away and whose flesh stank, were loathed and shunned. They were segregated in leprosariums as early as the seventh century. In the 13th century, leprosy reached epidemic proportions; it did not subside appreciably until the end of the 16th century.

Father Damien's request, therefore, to live and work among the lepers was an act of rare courage and charity. In our time MOTHER TERESA was another such symbol of selflessness and saintliness.

danse macabre (dance of death)

A ghoulish motif in the art of the late Middle Ages depicting Death as a kind of skeletal PIED PIPER leading a twisting, writhing line of mortals, from peasants to kings, to the inevitable grave and the dissolution of the flesh.

Christianity in the Middle Ages fostered a morbid preoccupation with death, verging on the hysterical. Life on this earth was riddled with temptation, sin and error ending in damnation for eternity. The BLACK DEATH, which carried off almost half the population of Europe, acquainted the people with the reality of death like nothing else.

The dance-of-death theme first appeared on church murals circa 1400 in Paris and somewhat later in England, Switzerland and Germany (*Totentanz*). In one representation there are two panels, the first showing three kings in their fine robes, crowns and scepters, and the second showing them decaying into skeletons. The caption under pictures of such skeletons often read "As I am, so shalt thou be." In 1538 Hans Holbein the Younger created a series of 50 woodcuts on this theme.

The modern artist whose work is imbued with the spirit and motifs of the danse macabre is undoubtedly the Norwegian painter Edvard Munch (1863–1944). In 1874 Charles Camille Saint-Saëns (1835–1921) composed a symphonic poem called *Danse Macabre.*

In modern usage the danse macabre is pictured as a whirling, wild, uncontrollable urge to destruction, as in the nuclear arms race of the 20th century.

Dantesque   In the manner of Dante Alighieri (1265–1321), the Italian poet, especially as revealed in his great Christian epic poem *The Divine Comedy* (1302–21).

> In the middle of the journey of our life I came to myself within a dark
> wood where the straight way was lost.
>
> (Translation by John D. Sinclair, published by
> Oxford University Press, 1939)

These moving opening lines set the tone of confession for an intense spiritual autobiography that reverberates with allegorical overtones. At the age of 35 (in 1300) Dante, exiled from Florence and in a state of turmoil, sets out to rid himself of the temptation to sin. He seeks the way to purify his soul and attain redemption. He will have two guides on this journey: Virgil, the author of the *Aeneid* and the master of classical learning, will lead him through the Inferno (hell) and the Purgatorio (purgatory); BEATRICE, Dante's ideal love and the symbol of divine revelation, will lead him through the Paradiso (heaven).

Along the way Dante meets and converses with many historical personages who have been consigned, according to the gravity of their sins, to the appropriate circle in the nine circles of Hell. Their punishments fit their transgressions. *The Divine Comedy* thus becomes not only a passionate quest for the individual soul's salvation, but also a compendium of Catholic doctrine, philosophy and learning in Dante's time.

This poem is an architectural masterpiece. Besides the one introductory canto, each of its three divisions (Inferno, Purgatorio, Paradiso) has 33 cantos, making 100 in all. The rhyme scheme is the interlocking *terza rima: aba, bcb, cdc* and so on. Dante has designed a system of poetics consistent with his system of Catholic theology. Both are complete and self-enclosed.

However, what makes *The Divine Comedy* the supreme expression of medieval literature is not only its intellectual brilliance, its spiritual intensity and vision, but also its soaring, memorable language, its poetry.

"Dantesque" has come to mean a passage through hell, whatever the nature of that hell may be.

Dark Ages   A misnomer for the Middle Ages. Historians have long rejected the notion that after the fall of Rome in 476 the light of culture was extinguished and the entire Western world experienced a blackout of civilization.

Although classical culture was in decline and the "barbarians" preferred the life of action to that of intellect, this was nevertheless the time when Christianity took root and gradually came to dominate Europe. Monks in their cloistered communities preserved libraries, copied books and eventually produced magnificent illuminated manuscripts. Monasteries conducted schools and were oases of learning and disputation. Great Romanesque cathedrals were succeeded in the High Middle Ages by the far lighter, soaring Gothic cathedrals with magnificent stained glass windows and sculpture.

Crafts flourished, and towns and cities multiplied when improved techniques of agriculture released surplus peasants to find new work in urban centers. Society was organized into well-defined classes, each with its duties and responsibilities. Chivalry provided a code of ethical behavior. If, from a contemporary point of view, the medieval preoccupation with death seems grim, the consolations and even ecstasies of faith were at least as important.

Misnomer or not, "the dark ages" in modern terminology suggests a time of ignorance, superstition, barbarism.

Dark Lady   The mysterious and faithless brunette who, in Shakespeare's sonnet sequence (1590s), seduces the earl of Southampton away from Shakespeare, so that he is bereft of both.

> *Two loves I have of comfort and despair,*
> *Which like two spirits do suggest me still;*
> *The better angel is a man right fair,*
> *The worser spirit a woman colour'd ill.*
> *To win me soon to hell, my female evil*
> *Tempteth my better angel from my side,*
> *And would corrupt my saint to be a devil,*
> *Wooing his purity with her fowl pride.*

(Sonnet 144)

Of Shakespeare's 154 sonnets, numbers 127 through 152 are addressed to the Dark Lady.

The Dark Lady is one who betrays her lover by being unfaithful to him with his friend.

Darkness at Noon (1941)   An influential novel by the Hungarian-born writer Arthur Koestler (1905–83). The hero of the novel, Rubashov, a brilliant intellectual and polemicist, is a top-level Bolshevik who has hewn to party discipline even at the expense of betraying personal friendships. He himself is finally arrested and accused of plotting against the life of Stalin and of having become ambivalent about the regime. During his successive interrogations in a prison cell, he gradually allows himself to be brainwashed. He succumbs to the rationalization that by confessing to false charges and accepting execution he will be performing a last act of selflessness for the revolutionary cause.

Rubashov stands for those who betray their own humanity in the false belief that the end justifies the means. Rubashov was modeled on certain founders of Bolshevism—among them Kamenev, Zinoviev and Bukharin—who were liquidated by Stalin in the infamous political purges of the 1930s in the Soviet Union.

The expression "darkness at noon" represents the extinction of the light of revolutionary ideals in the reality of the Soviet Union. See *THE GOD THAT FAILED*.

Darrow, Clarence S. (1857–1938)   In his day, Darrow was widely regarded as one of America's most brilliant lawyers. He first gained prominence as a "political" lawyer for his successful defense of Big Bill Heywood, a radical leader charged with murder.

Later, Darrow achieved international fame defending Nathan Leopold and Richard Loeb, the "thrill killers" of little Bobby Franks. His plea, that both were "mentally and morally sick," saved them from the electric chair. They were sentenced to life imprisonment.

In his next sensational case, the so-called Monkey Trial, Darrow defended Thomas Scopes, a schoolteacher charged with teaching the theory of evolution. The famous William Jennings Bryan was the attorney for the prosecution. Scopes was convicted and fined $100. In the court of world opinion, however, Darrow won the case.

To be called a Clarence Darrow is to take one's place in the pantheon of great lawyers who represent the underdog and the apparently sure loser. See also LEOPOLD AND LOEB.

Darth Vader   Villain of the epic space movie *Star Wars* (1977) and its sequels, *The Empire Strikes Back* (1980) and *The Return of the Jedi* (1983); all were produced and the first written and directed by George Lucas. As imperial master of the Death Star, Vader pursues the good guys (the rebels)—Princess Leia, Luke Skywalker, Han Solo, Obi-Wan Kenobi, the mystical Yoda, the robots R2D2 and C-3PO and a host of others. He represents the dark side of the Force. Luke learns to master the good side of the Force. The Force "is an energy field. It is all around us . . . It gives us power. You can learn to make it work for you."

Darwinian   Pertaining to the theory of evolution through natural selection formulated by the English naturalist Charles Robert Darwin (1809–82) in *On the Origin of Species* (1859). Darwin's ideas have been reduced in the popular vocabulary to almost a single poorly understood phrase: the survival of the fittest. Interestingly, that phrase was popularized not by Darwin, but by his contemporary, the English philosopher Herbert Spencer (1820–1903). Furthermore, the expression has been distorted to rationalize and justify the so-called law of the jungle: the natural right of the strong to oppress the weak.

The Darwinian theory of evolution is based upon meticulous observation and classification of thousands of species of life during his five-year voyage (1831–36) as official naturalist aboard HMS *Beagle*. The journey of exploration took him to South America, the Galápagos Islands, Tahiti, New Zealand and Australia. Darwin became convinced that the various species of life on earth "had not been created complete and unchanging, but that heredity and environment had produced new forms along ancestral lines. . . . As many more individuals of each species are born than can possibly survive, and as consequently there is a frequently recurring struggle for existence, it follows that any being, if it vary however slightly in any matter profitable to itself . . . will have a better chance of surviving, and thus be naturally selected." (Alan Moorehead, *Darwin and the Beagle*, [New York: Harper & Row, 1969], pp. 258–59).

Darwin's conclusions, especially as extended in his *Descent of Man* (1871), amounted to heresy. According to Genesis, had not God created the world and all its creatures in six days, and had He not created Man in His own image? Although science now generally accepts Darwin's theory, religionists (or Creationists) still do battle against it. The latter scornfully reject any notion that man is descended from the apes. The conflict between the two sides reached a half-mythical, half-ludicrous climax in the "Monkey Trial," the Scopes trial in Tennessee (1925) in which two giants of rhetoric, Clarence Darrow and William Jennings Bryan, contended over the right of John T. Scopes, a biology teacher, to teach evolution in the public schools. Scopes and his defender, Darrow, lost. In 1955, Jerome Lawrence and Robert E. Lee wrote *Inherit the Wind,* a drama based on the trial.

Use: ". . . rock music has yet to win the respect it deserves as the authentic voice of our time. . . . Rock music should not be left to the Darwinian laws of the marketplace. This natively American art form deserves national support." (Camille Paglia, *New York Times,* April 16, 1992)

"date which will live in infamy, a" Words spoken by President Franklin Delano Roosevelt on December 8, 1941, after the previous day's attack by Japanese war planes on the American military bases at Pearl Harbor, Hawaii. The surprise strike had come in the midst of ongoing negotiations between the United States and Japan. Caught off guard, the Americans lost five battleships, 14 smaller ships, 200 aircraft as well as thousands of seamen, soldiers and civilians killed or wounded. The United States immediately declared war on Japan, and on December 11 the United States declared war on the other Axis powers, Italy and Germany.

The components of a day of infamy would seem to be outrageous activity, betrayal and shamefulness.

Daumier, Honoré (1808–1879) French painter, caricaturist and lithographer who in the course of his life produced more than 4,000 cartoons satirizing the bourgeoisie and its professions, such as the law, education and medicine. These were published first in *Caricature* and then in the Paris daily *Le Charivari.*

Although one is tempted to associate Daumier with HOGARTH, that would be a mistake. Like Hogarth, Daumier could be a merciless satirist, but he was a 19th-century romantic who dealt sensitively with realistic subjects. Daumier's sympathy for the poor, the lowly, the oppressed is especially evidenced in his paintings, as in the well-known *The Third-Class Carriage* (1862) and in his studies of Parisian laundresses. His paintings are done in bold brush strokes, which give them an unfinished but powerful force. They were not appreciated in his lifetime.

A Daumier can be a blistering satirist or alternatively a defender of the downtrodden. Often the term "a Daumier" is applied to the product (that is, the cartoon) rather than to the cartoonist.

Davis, Bette (1908–1989) American screen star with huge, expressive eyes, distinctive movements and speech—easy to caricature. Associated with bitchy parts: the destructive waitress Mildred in *Of Human Bondage* (1934); Leslie Crosbie, the murderess in *The Letter* (1940); the title character in *Jezebel* (1938); the jealous aging actress in *All About Eve* (1950). Bette Davis generated nervous intensity, a fierceness and independence bordering on intransigence.

D-day June 6, 1944, the day of the Allied invasion of Europe on the Normandy beaches. It was the opening of the long-awaited Second Front in World War II, under the command of General Dwight D. Eisenhower. "D-day" is generally used to mean the long-awaited day of launching a new enterprise.

Dean, James See REBEL WITHOUT A CAUSE.

Dear Abby Syndicated newspaper column (started in 1956) by Abigail van Buren, answering requests from readers for advice on handling personal moral dilemmas. Used mockingly in general parlance whenever advice in personal matters is sought, and where there are no easy, cliché answers.

Dear John letter A letter to a soldier during World War II, from his girlfriend or his wife, to announce the breakup of their relationship. The salutation "Dear John" and the cruel content of the letter became a bitter paradox.

A Dear John letter is still a letter of rejection, concealing a wallop behind the loving salutation.

Death in Venice (1913)   A novella by Thomas Mann (1875–1955). The hero, Gustav von Aschenbach, an austere classicist and writer in his fifties, is vacationing in Venice. There is a kind of decadence in the air, which exerts a strange fascination over him. He falls in love with Tadzio, a 14-year-old Polish boy of ideal beauty and grace. To overcome his infatuation he knows he must leave Venice, but he stays on. His unexpressed feelings become a passionate obsession. Venice is in the first stages of a cholera epidemic; Aschenbach becomes feverish and dies on the day Tadzio leaves.

The expression Death in Venice has come to stand for the inner plague of self-indulgence and decadence. It exemplifies what may happen when Dionysian passion and license win out over Apollonian reason and restraint.

Decameron   See BOCCACCIO.

Decline of the West, The   Book written by the German philosopher and historian Oswald Spengler (1880–1936) and published in 1918. Its main thesis is that every culture passes through an organic life cycle similar to the human cycle. It predicts the decline of Western civilization and the growing ascendancy of Eastern cultures.

The great problems of Western democracies (crime, materialism, decadence, drugs, possibility of nuclear war) are taken to be proof of the decline of the West.

Deep Throat   Code name (derived from a pornographic movie of the same title) for the person who supplied information about the Watergate conspiracy and cover-up to Carl Bernstein and Bob Woodward, reporters for the *Washington Post,* who received the Pulitzer Prize for their investigative journalism on May 7, 1973. The identity of Deep Throat has so far not been disclosed.

"Deep Throat" is now used to refer to any secret source of information.

Defarge, Madame   A vindictive woman, a revolutionary fanatic who embodies the remorseless spirit of the Reign of Terror in Charles Dickens's novel *A Tale of Two Cities* (1859). Mme. Defarge's hatred of aristocrats has been fueled by a personal vendetta against the Marquis de St. Evrémonde, who years ago violated her sister. She is determined to take vengeance on every member of that detested family. It does not matter to her that Charles Darnay, the hero of the novel and an Evrémonde, has renounced his family and has turned over his inheritance to the peasants.

Mme. Defarge is forever knitting a long, long scarf. Into the scarf she knits the names of those who must be guillotined. She attends every execution, gloating over the last moments of the enemies who have been brought to "justice."

In modern usage, a Mme. Defarge is often simply a woman who is endlessly knitting, but more commonly is an implacable, vengeful fanatic.

Degas, Edgar (1834–1917)   French painter whose name has become synonymous with the world of the ballet. He did pastel studies of ballet dancers, presenting them in all their unselfconscious positions backstage, as well as in their showy attitudes onstage in the glare of the spotlights. Although Degas was a master of portraiture (as in his drawing of the painter Edouard Manet, c. 1865) and a revealing artist of the life of the poor (as in his famous painting of the brooding couple in *The Glass of Absinthe,* c. 1876), it is as a painter and sculptor of ballet scenes that he is fixed in the popular imagination. A Degas is a ballerina in frothy tutu and satin laced-up ballet slippers.

Delmonico's   One of several famous restaurants run by the Delmonico family of New York City in the late 1860s, named after the Swiss founder, Lorenzo Delmonico (1813–81).

The name "Delmonico's" is synonymous with elegant, expensive dining. Something of the special nature of Delmonico's is evident in the fact that George Pullman named the first dining railway car he built the *Delmonico.*

de Mille, Agnes (1909–1993)   American dancer and choreographer whose *Rodeo* ballet (1942) captured the exuberant spirit of the American West and influenced the choreography of many Broadway musicals, including *Oklahoma* (1943) and *Carousel* (1945). Her ballets are not merely decorative; they move the plot forward, as in "Laurie Makes Up Her Mind" in *Oklahoma,* in which Laurie must decide between her rival suitors.

DeMille, Cecil B. (1881–1959)   Pioneer director of epic films, including *The Ten Commandments* (1923) and *The Greatest Show on Earth* (1952). DeMille's name is synonymous with colossal extravaganzas, lavish spectacles.

Dempsey, William Harrison (Jack) (1895–1983)   Boxer who held the world heavyweight title from 1919 to 1925. Born in Manassa, Colorado, mining country, Dempsey started life as a miner, found the work not to his liking, drifted into the tough, grimy existence of a boxer. A small man, Dempsey defeated many bigger men in the ring. Sportswriters called him "Jack, the Giant Killer" and "The Manassa Mauler."

Dempsey has become a symbol of guts and fury in, at best, a not too gentle craft.

Dennis the Menace   First appearing on March 12, 1951, this comic strip achieved vast popularity. In fact, *Dennis the Menace* has become a household word. Dennis, according to Maurice Horn, author of *The World Encyclopedia of Cartoons,* is a ". . . tousle-haired, enterprising tot whose counterfeit innocence, unflattering candor, and joyous vandalism are in delightful contrast to the docile conformity of the adult world. . . ."

Dennis is the unpredictable, unstoppable disrupter of neighborhood and family peace. His helpless parents are often the target of his shenanigans. He is the contemporary counterpart of an earlier terror, PECK'S BAD BOY.

A *U.S. News and World Report* article (March 27, 1989) refers to Representative Newt Gingrich as an "exasperating Dennis The Menace."

devil's advocate   Originally a spokesman appointed by the Roman Catholic Church to challenge the claims of a candidate for sainthood before a papal court. As Advocatus Diaboli (Advocate of the Devil), it was his function to present every possible argument against the proposed canonization. The strongest possible case for the beatification was made by the Advocatus Dei (Advocate of God).

Today, a devil's advocate is someone who takes an unpopular, wrong or losing side of an argument, sometimes to be contrary, mischievous, spiteful, sometimes to maintain a balanced point of view.

Diaghilev, Serge Pavlovich (1872–1929)   Russian-born impresario, famous mostly as the director of the Ballets Russes in Paris with NIJINSKY as its star. Although he himself never choreographed a ballet, he exerted tremendous influence on the development of the ballet in the 20th century by gathering around him luminaries of dance, music and design who created the new ballet (and whom he helped to make into stars). Among these were the dancers Nijinsky, Karsavina, Danilova; the choreographers Fokine, Massine, BALANCHINE; the composers Stravinsky, Prokofiev, Ravel, Debussy; and the artists and designers Benois, Bakst, PICASSO, MATISSE, BRAQUE, Derain, Laurencin, CHIRICO. By force of personality, artistic integrity and brilliance, Diaghilev stamped his name on the world of art in the 20th century.

Diamond, Jack "Legs" (1896–1931)   One of Prohibition's most feared, most hated racketeers. Many unsuccessful attempts were made on Diamond's life. For a time, he was thought to be "unkillable" and "unconvictable": "The bullet hasn't been made that can kill Legs Diamond."

Finally, his luck ran out. He was asleep in an Albany, New York, hotel room when two hired killers entered his room. One held him by the ears and the other shot him three times in the head.

Diaspora The global dispersion of the Jews since 586 B.C.E., when Nebuchadnezzar destroyed Solomon's temple in Jerusalem and led the captive Jews with halters around their necks into Babylonia. The sorrows as well as the longings of the captives are poignantly expressed in Psalm 137:

> By the rivers of Babylon, there we sat down,
>   Yea, we wept, when we remembered Zion.
> We hanged our harps upon the willows
>   in the midst thereof.
> For there they that carried us away captive
>   required of us a song; and they that wasted us
>   required of us mirth, saying,
>   Sing us one of the songs of Zion.
> How shall we sing the Lord's song in a strange land?
> If I forget thee, O Jerusalem, let my right
>   hand forget her cunning.
> If I do not remember thee, let my tongue cleave to the
>   roof of my mouth; if I prefer not Jerusalem
>   above my chief joy

Some historians claim that the dispersion of the Jews started even earlier, in 721 B.C.E., when the Assyrians captured Samaria and deported tens of thousands of Jews to colonize their far-flung empire. It was during the Roman governance of Judea, however, that the greatest dispersion took place. Large colonies of Jews were settled throughout the reaches of the Roman Empire.

It is said that the in-gathering of the exiles, the return to Jerusalem, will take place when the true messiah appears. Meanwhile, there is a concentration of Jews now in the state of Israel and pockets of Jews scattered throughout the world in the Diaspora, a Diaspora decimated by the Nazi murder of six million Jews in Europe in the early 1940s.

Although the term "Diaspora" usually refers to the specific dispersion of the Jews, the word is sometimes used (with a lowercase d) for the scattering of other refugee peoples, such as African Americans, gypsies or modern-day Yugoslavs.

Dickensian In the manner of Charles Dickens (1812–70), arguably England's greatest novelist and certainly the most popular. Dickens's novels appeared in monthly installments in the periodicals of his day before they were published as books. His readers awaited the next episode with the same avid anticipation that TV viewers today await the next day's developments in a soap opera. The question "Is Little Nell going to die?" aroused in followers of *The Old Curiosity Shop* (1840) the same agitation as "Who shot J. R.?" stimulated in addicts of *Dallas* in the 1980s. When Dickens, an enthusiastic and talented thespian, began in 1858 to give public readings from his novels, he filled the theaters to capacity, both enriching and exhausting himself.

Dickens was not only a superb storyteller and entertainer but also an influential social critic. Daniel Webster said that Dickens had "done more to ameliorate the condition of the English poor than all the statesmen Great Britain had sent into Parliament" (quoted in the *New York Times,* September 1, 1991). Much of Dickens's preoccupation with poverty and with cruelty to children arose out of a searing experience in his own childhood. When Dickens was 12 years old, his improvident father was thrown into debtors prison. Young Charles was packed off to London to work in Warren's blacking warehouse in the Strand. The humiliation and despair he experienced during his months there, the sense that he had been abandoned by his own father, that he would never receive the education he longed for, were so traumatic that they colored his imagination for ever after. Dickens kept this shameful childhood experience an absolute secret, even from his wife and children, but at the center of many of his books is a neglected or abused child.

The term "Dickensian" has, in modern usage, become attached to:

1. satiric humor (as in *The Pickwick Papers,* 1837);
2. sentimentality (as in the fortunes of Dora, Little Nell, Tiny Tim, Lucie Manette);
3. eccentricities of character (as in Micawber, Uriah Heep, Bumble, Josiah Bounderby as well as a host of others whose names have become household words and allusions in their own right: Pickwick, Sam Weller, Fagin, Sikes, Sary Gamp, Scrooge, Gradgrind, Miss Havisham and others);
4. indignation, couched in irony, against social injustice: the degrading living conditions of the poor in hovels, in slums, in workhouses and debtors' prisons; the inequities and delays of the law, notably in *Bleak House* (1853); the blighting effects of industrialization and the philosophy of utilitarianism in general, as in *Hard Times* (1854); and most especially the neglect, the abuse and the exploitation of children as in *David Copperfield* (1850), *Oliver Twist* (1839), *Little Dorrit* (1855–57);
5. an expressionist atmosphere, not unlike that in Dostoevsky, in which one gets a sense of teeming crowds of ragged people (*A Tale of Two Cities,* 1859), tiers of grotesque faces (Fagin's trail and Sikes's pursuit in *Oliver Twist;* crooked alleys and precipitous flights of stairs and cramped attics and cellars; shadows and fog (*Bleak House,* 1853) and dust (*Our Mutual Friend,* 1864) in which terror is lurking around the corner.

Dick Tracy   Hero of a comic strip of the same name that first appeared in 1931. Early on, Tracy watches, powerless, as his sweetheart Tess Trueheart is kidnapped and her father murdered. Tracy joins the police force to track down the criminals who are responsible for these two acts. In time, he becomes the symbol of avenging justice, relentlessly pursuing all evildoers at great peril to himself. He embodies retribution in the endless struggle between good and evil.

Dick Tracy was the first "realistic" comic strip. He is "eagle-nosed," "square chinned"; his violent, brutal encounters exerted a great influence, not only on "the cops and robbers" strips but also on all action comics. Warren Beatty starred in the 1990 feature film, *Dick Tracy.*

Didi   See VLADIMIR.

didn't lay a glove on him   In boxing, this describes a boxer who can't hit his opponent, or can't hit him hard or often enough to hurt or harm him. He is, in short, the inferior fighter, outmaneuvered by a more skillful opponent and, hence, likely to lose the match.

"Can't or didn't lay a glove on," in current use, means one is unable to do anything to injure a person's reputation, diminish his public standing, or tarnish his image. The expression is often used in a political context.

Dien Bien Phu   The Vietnamese village where, in May 1954, the French military forces lost a decisive battle against the communist Viet Minh. In July 1954 the French signed an armistice at Geneva. They agreed to pull their troops out of Vietnam and they agreed to the division of Vietnam along the 17th parallel into two parts, North and South, to be reunited in the future by open elections.

The French had staked their national honor at Dien Bien Phu and lost, as the Americans were to lose their war in Vietna, withdrawing in 1973.

Dietrich, Marlene (1901–1992)   Born Magdalena von Losch in Germany, this blonde, wickedly sexy, sophisticated goddess of the screen was a femme fatale with perfect legs and a German-accented, husky singing voice. Her great role was Lola in *The Blue Angel* (1930), directed by Joseph von Sternberg, in which she dressed in a man's tuxedo and sang sexy songs in a cabaret.

different drummer, a   In "Where I Lived and What I Lived For," the American essayist Henry David Thoreau (1817–62) wrote: "If a man does not keep pace with his companions, perhaps it is because he hears a different drummer. Let him step to the music which he hears, however measured or far away."

Thoreau, himself a nonconformist, lived alone for two years (1845–47) in a cabin at Walden Pond in Concord, Massachusetts. He wanted to find out whether he could be self-sufficient and free from slavish attachment to material things. He urged others to be true to their own inner voices, to listen to their own individual drummers.

Use: "Yugoslavia showed that Europe is still a collection of states that have separate political needs and fears and will not march politically to the same drummer for decades—probably never." (A. M. Rosenthal, *New York Times,* May 22, 1992)

Dillinger, John (1903–1934)   The first American criminal to be named Public Enemy Number 1 (1925) by U.S. attorney general Homer Cummings. Until he reached the age of 22, Dillinger led a fairly prosaic existence. The last nine years of his life he devoted to an almost unparalleled succession of robberies, murders and prison escapes. His name spread terror throughout the Midwest. Released from prison in 1933, he shot 17 people, killing 10. His end came on July 22, 1934. Betrayed by female companion Anna Sage, known as "the woman in red," Dillinger was shot and killed by FBI men as he was leaving the Biograph Theater in Chicago.

Dillinger's name has become a metaphor for a brutal, merciless, senseless killer.

Dilsey   Black servant in *The Sound and the Fury* (1929), a novel by William Faulkner (1897–1962). She holds the Compson family together and cares especially for Benjy, the idiot son. She is compassionate and dependable. Sustained by her religious faith, she endures.

Dilsey is the black woman who has often compensated for the inadequacies of the southern white mother. She is a symbol of stability in the family.

DiMaggio, Joe (1914–1999)   New York Yankee centerfielder from 1936 to 1951, known as the Yankee Clipper not only for his outstanding batting achievements (his 56-game hitting streak in 1941 has never been equaled) but also for his physical grace in commanding the playing field. He never played to the stands, but comported himself with great dignity and elegance on and off the field. The son of a poor Italian fisherman in San Francisco, he grew up to become not only an icon in the world of sports—"the greatest team player of all time," according to Connie Mack—but also an authentic American hero. A Hemingway character refers to him as "the great DiMaggio," and indeed DiMaggio almost consciously conformed to the HEMINGWAY CODE of honor, reticence, grace under pressure. When DiMaggio married the world-famous film goddess Marilyn Monroe, "a mismatch made in heaven" according to Bob Herbert of the *New York Times,* his image as an American hero seemed complete, even though the marriage ended in divorce nine months later. DiMaggio mourned Monroe's death by suicide deeply but silently, never commercializing his relationship with her. A mysterious aura clung to him: he was tall, dark, handsome, remote, silent, dignified, elegant—his own man.

At his death, the world recalled Paul Simon's lyrics: "Where have you gone, Joe DiMaggio? / A nation turns its lonely eyes to you."

dime novel   Lurid, exciting, highly colored, cheaply printed novels that first appeared in the United States in 1858. Originally written by Erastus F. Beadle (1821–94), they dealt with episodes in early American history, such as pioneer life, fights with Indians and the Revolutionary War. They were fantastically successful, satisfying the public hunger for adventure and romance. By the mid-1860s, over four million copies had been sold.

The early dime novels were originals. Later, in the absence of effective copyright laws, publishers issued cheap reprints of British publications.

The term "dime novel," like its British counterpart, the PENNY DREADFUL, carries a heavy judgmental freight of literary trash.

Dimmesdale, Arthur   See PRYNNE, HESTER.

dinosaur   An extinct reptile of the Mesozoic era, the dinosaur ranged in size from $2\frac{1}{2}$ feet to 90 feet. Some, like Tyrannosaurus, were carnivorous bipeds; others, like Brontosaurus, were herbivorous quadrupeds. Their fossil remains reveal very small brain cavities for such large creatures, and therefore they must have had low intelligence.

To call someone "a dinosaur" today is to suggest that he or she is an old fossil and that his or her attitudes are so retrograde as to deserve to be extinct.

Disney, Walt (1901–1966)   Hollywood producer of cartoons and animated feature films combining cartoon and live characters. Creator of Disneyland. See also MICKEY MOUSE, SEVEN DWARFS, DISNEYLAND.

Disneyland   Famed amusement park covering 160 acres in Anaheim, California; completed in 1955 by WALT DISNEY. Here a child of any age can see Disney's cartoon characters come to life; he can enter a world of fantasy or history, explore a medieval castle, ride on a stagecoach or a Mississippi steamboat. Disneyland is synonymous with wonderland or fantasyland.

Disraeli, Benjamin (1804–1881)   A rare combination of statesman, novelist and brilliant personality, Disraeli served three times as chancellor of the exchequer and twice as prime minister (1867–68, 1874–80) under Queen Victoria. In 1876 he was made first earl of Beaconsfield.

As a leader of the Tory Party, Disraeli pursued an aggressive imperial foreign policy and yet he extended democracy at home with the enfranchisement of about two million men, mostly workers, through the Reform Bill of 1867.

Most of Disraeli's novels were political, especially the trilogy consisting of *Coningsby* (1844), *Sybil* (1845) and *Tancred* (1847). Many of the characters were obviously based on contemporary figures.

Disraeli was colorful enough to be the hero of a film, *Disraeli* (1929). He was complex: brilliant, witty, cunning; a dandy, a politician, an empire builder, an adoring husband; inherently aristocratic yet democratic in his political programs; born of a Jewish father who converted to Christianity and had the child baptized, yet always drawn to the spiritual essence of Judaism, as is evident in *Tancred.* Such a person is a living embodiment of some fictional character.

A "Disraeli" is the embodiment of the philosopher-statesman.

Dr. Kildare   The hero of a popular American television series (1961–66). Played by Richard Chamberlain, he was an archetypal, dedicated young physician, personable and appealing. Hence, any doctor embodying these characteristics.

"Dr. Livingstone, I presume?"   On November 10, 1871, in the remote village of Ujiji on the shore of Lake Tanganyika, H. M. Stanley found the man he'd been sent to search for "in darkest Africa." "Dr. Livingstone, I presume?" he said. The sheer British understatement of the greeting captured the world's admiration.

Henry Morton Stanley (1841–1904) was a British journalist sent by the *New York Herald* to find David Livingstone (1813–73), who originally went to Africa as a medical missionary for the London Missionary Society. During these years (1841–52) Livingstone was an intrepid explorer, discovering, among other natural sites, Victoria Falls and the Zambezi River. After a two-year interlude in England (1864–66) he returned to Africa to find the sources of the Nile. On this expedition he became ill and returned to Ujiji, where Stanley found him.

Their meeting resulted in a shared exploration of the north shore of Lake Tanganyika. After Livingstone's death in 1873, Stanley continued to explore Africa and to write accounts of his findings. Some of his books include *How I Found Livingstone* (1872), *Through the Dark Continent* (1878) and *In Darkest Africa* (1890).

The phrase "Dr. Livingstone, I presume?" is often used in a jesting way as a greeting between people who are meeting for the first time, or whose meeting has been arranged.

Dr. Strangelove (1964)   British film directed by Stanley Kubrick and based on *Red Alert,* a novel by Peter George. In the movie, Peter Sellers plays three roles: the president of the United States; an RAF captain; and Dr. Strangelove, a mad German-American scientist. When a fanatical USAF general (George C. Scott) mistakenly launches an A-bomb attack on the Soviet Union, and fail-safe attempts do not work and Soviet retaliation seems certain, the movie becomes a suspenseful black comedy about man's propensity for self-destruction in the atomic age. The full title of the film is *Dr. Strangelove: Or, How I Learned to Stop Worrying and Love the Bomb*.

A Dr. Strangelove is a mad eccentric so in love with what he has created that he cannot think of the consequences of his deadly inventions.

Dodsworth, Samuel   The main character in *Dodsworth* (1929), a novel by Sinclair Lewis. He is a retired manufacturer who longs to break through the limitations of small-town life by traveling abroad and being exposed to the culture of the Old World. In Europe, his wife has a series of disappointing love affairs. After many lonely months, Dodsworth himself falls in love with a cultivated American widow, Edith Cartright. At the end he plans to leave his rather immature wife and return to Edith who teaches him much about the possibilities of life even in his home town, Zenith.

Dodsworth is representative of the suppressed bourgeois who under the right circumstances learns to appreciate a more open way of life.

dog in the manger, a   A fable attributed to Aesop (620–560 B.C.), thought to have been a Greek slave or an Ethiopian. He was clearly not the author of all the "Aesop's fables" that have come down to us. Some of these fables have been discovered on Egyptian papyri dating from 1000–800 B.C.

Typically, a fable is a simple story with a moral. The characters are generally one-dimensional animals who think, talk and act like people. In "A *Dog in the Manger*" an ugly, bad-tempered dog is sitting on top of a large stack of hay, snapping and snarling at the hungry cows who want to eat the hay. One cow speaks up, "Look at this selfish animal. He can't eat the hay himself—yet he won't let those who can eat it have any."

Thus, a dog in the manger keeps others from enjoying what he himself cannot enjoy.

Dolce Vita   See *LA DOLCE VITA*.

Doll's House, A   See NORA.

domino effect   Term derived from the game of dominoes. When dominoes are aligned and stood on end, pressure on one will be transmitted to the next and so on, until the entire series topples over one by one. Politically, the domino theory holds that the fall of one nation to communism inevitably leads to the fall of its neighbor and so on until the whole region is communist. The theory was applied in the 1960s to Asia and in the 1970s to Central America.

The cumulative, serial effect created by a single act or cause; e.g., convince the top man and all the rest of the organization will fall like dominoes.

Don Juan   A legendary Spanish nobleman and libertine devoted to womanizing. In psychiatry, Don Juanism is "excessive preoccupation with sexual satisfaction and conquest." Don Juan is the central character in Mozart's opera *Don Giovanni.*

In common parlance, a Don Juan is an indefatigable, irresistible skirt-chaser, perennially involved in numerous amours; the "Great lover," much like a CASANOVA or a LOTHARIO.

Donner Pass   In 1846, a wagon train of westward-moving families from Illinois and Iowa started out for California. Among the families, the most prominent were the Donners and the Reeds. A late start and unforeseen delays caused anxiety that they might not reach their destination before the snows fell. Nonetheless, some of the party opted to proceed along the prescribed route. The others chose to take a shortcut through an untried pass in the Sierra Nevada. The second group was trapped in the pass by an unusually early blizzard. They ran out of food and eventually resorted to cannibalism. A rescue expedition from the Sacramento Valley reached the survivors, but only half of the original migrants reached California.

The Donner Pass has become a symbol of the human tragedies endured in the course of settling the American West. The Donner party's resorting to cannibalism reminds us of the abominations to which even civilized people can be driven in extreme circumstances.

Donnybrook   An annual Irish fair, first licensed in 1204, that usually lasted about two weeks. It was marked by much drinking and disorder. Thoroughly fed up with the drunken antics of many of the fair's guests, the local citizenry finally abolished the fair in 1855. (Donnybrook is now a peaceful suburb about $1\frac{1}{2}$ miles from Dublin.)

A Donnybrook has become a metaphor for any disorderly gathering or meeting. Athletic contests frequently end in a Donnybrook, as opposing teams or spectators assault one another.

Don Quixote   The main character of the satirical novel *Don Quixote de La Mancha* (Part I, 1605; Part II, 1615) by Miguel de Cervantes Saavedra (1547–1616). Don Quixote is a gaunt country gentleman whose brain has been somewhat addled by overexposure to chivalric romances, the popular literary genre of his time. He sees it as his mission to fare forth as a knight on horseback to redress the injustices of the world. His "charger" is an emaciated nag called Rosinante. His "squire," who accompanies him astride a donkey, is a squat, uneducated, but practical peasant called Sancho Panza. His "lady" is a country girl whom he names Dulcinea del Toroso.

Don Quixote, the idealistic romantic, and Sancho Panza, the pragmatic realist, become involved in a series of hapless adventures that eventually send Don Quixote reeling home buffeted and wiser. He has, after all, all along been "tilting at windmills."

Don Quixote has become a prototype of the misguided, well-intentioned idealist. He is a forerunner of CANDIDE in his idealism, a forerunner of Emma Bovary in his addiction to romantic reading, and a forerunner of Charlie Chaplin's tramp in his winsome ineffectuality. He is one of the great tragicomic inventions of all literature, the subject of a series of drawings by Picasso and of a popular musical comedy, written by Dale Wasserman with music by Mitch Leigh and lyrics by Joe Darion, *The Man of La Mancha,* with its theme song "The Impossible Dream."

From Don Quixote comes the word "quixotic," meaning extravagantly chivalrous or romantic, visionary to the point of being impractical or unpredictable.

"Don't fire until you see the whites of their eyes" On June 17, 1775, 1,500 raw recruits of Colonel William Prescott (1726–95) faced a superior force of 3,000 British soldiers. Realizing that every shot would have to find its mark, Prescott ordered his men: "Don't fire until you see the whites of their eyes."

The first British assault on the American position was repulsed with enormous casualties for the British. The second assault was met with the same deadly fire and huge losses. Despite what they faced, the British moved on the Americans for a third time. The Americans, having run out of ammunition, retreated across Charlestown Neck.

Today, Prescott's command means simply: launch your plan under the best possible circumstances, with the best possible chance that it will succeed.

"Don't give up the ship" On June 1, 1813, Commander James Lawrence (1781–1813) lay dying in his frigate, the *Chesapeake.* Cruising well out to sea, the *Chesapeake* locked horns with the British vessel H.M.S. *Shannon* in what turned out to be the bloodiest battle of the War of 1812.

Mortally wounded in the encounter, Lawrence was carried below. As he lay dying, he heard the British boarding party on the deck above. He gave his final orders to his men: "Don't give up the ship! Sink her! Blow her up!" Before the Americans could take any action, however, the British overpowered them and took the ship.

Lawrence's last words to his men have come to stand as symbols of indomitable courage, determination to keep up the fight. Often used in a more casual context, these words may simply mean "hang in there."

Dooley, Mr. One of the great characters of American literature. The creation of Finley Peter Dunne (1867–1936), he first appeared in the *Chicago Post* in 1893 behind the bar of a small saloon in the center of Chicago's Irish immigrant district.

Couched in a salty, irreverent brogue, Mr. Dooley's sharply humorous thrusts at corruption and hypocrisy at all levels won him an enormous audience. By 1899, the country had gone "Dooley-mad." Mr. Dooley's astringent, witty observations on the frauds and follies of his day made him the subject of more than 700 essays and songs.

In 1896, Mr. Dunne introduced Mr. Dooley's inseparable companion, Hennessy, "the great listener." It was to Hennessy that Mr. Dooley addressed some of his most pungent observations:

> "Thrust ivrybody, but cut the cards."
> "Children shouldn't be sent to school to larn, but to larn how to larn. I don't care what you larn thim so long as 'tis onpleasant to thim."

Mr. Dooley, describing himself variously as traveler, archaeologist, social observer, economist, philosopher follows in the tradition of American humor set by Mark Twain, Artemus Ward, Will Rogers and Art Buchwald.

A Mr. Dooley is a sardonic commentator on the foibles of his time.

Dostoevskian Pertaining to the Russian novelist Feodor Mikhailovich Dostoevsky (1821–81), known especially for *Crime and Punishment* (1866), *The Idiot* (1869), *The Possessed* (1872) and *The Brothers Karamazov* (1878).

Dostoevsky lived in a time of social unrest when Western liberal ideas were infiltrating Russian orthodoxy. In 1849 he was arrested for seditious conspiracy and sentenced to death before a firing squad, but at the last moment he was reprieved and his sentence was commuted to eight years of hard labor in Siberia. There he underwent a religious conversion. He accepted his suffering as expiation for his sins. His sympathy for the poor and the wretched, always strong, was reinforced. He exalted the meek and the simple to sainthood.

In Dostoevsky's novels the dualism between free thought and humble acceptance, between intellect (bad) and feeling (good), is a major theme. Raskolnikov in *Crime and Punishment* falls victim to his theory that everything is permissible to certain extraordinary men. He stifles his naturally generous and compassionate nature and commits a murder to test this idea. Sonia, a girl of pure feeling, is the instrument of his redemption.

Dostoevsky's characters are either saints or sinners, and often the saint and the sinner are at war within the same individual. In *The Brothers Karamazov* Alyosha is guileless and pure of heart; Ivan, the cold skeptic; Dmitry, the passionate man at war with himself; and Smerdyakov, the illegitimate half-brother, the evil one. Dmitry is condemned for a crime he did not commit. Nevertheless, he rejects his brothers' plan to help him escape exile in Siberia because he feels that he must expiate his many sins through suffering.

Dostoevsky's books teem with passionate, tormented, often poverty-stricken minor characters who inhabit the slums of St. Petersburg. The Marmeladovs of *Crime and Punishment* are prime examples. A montage of images depicting their life would superimpose pictures of littered courtyards, crowded tenements, low-ceilinged smoky rooms, ragged finery, consumptive coughing, constant quarreling, prostitution, drunken scenes of masochistic self-abasement, all adding up to an expressionistic atmosphere of febrile excitement, delirium and nightmare.

Dostoevsky has given the world what it has come to recognize as the "Russian soul." "Dostoyevskian" refers to the duality of human nature, the good at war with the dark impulses of evil.

doubleheader   Two consecutive baseball games played on the same day. A ticket for this day admits the holder to both games.

Use: We had a busy day. First, Jill's graduation, then a special luncheon at the Baldwin Hotel—a real doubleheader.

double play   See TINKER TO EVERS TO CHANCE.

doublethink   In George Orwell's novel *1984* (1949), doublethink is the hypo-critical and grotesquely flexible mode of thought imposed on society to reconcile its people to tyranny; e.g., in the slogans "War Is Peace"; "Freedom Is Slavery"; "Ignorance Is Strength". "Doublethink," sometimes written as "doublespeak," refers to turning truth upside down to serve one's own interests.

doves and hawks   Two terms representing people with opposite points of view, they first came into use in modern times during the Cuban Missile Crisis of 1962. Doves advocated a conciliatory attitude toward the U.S.S.R.; hawks advocated a tough policy, a showdown. The same terms were then used during the Vietnam War in the 1960s, doves urging a negotiated peace and quick withdrawal, hawks urging a continuation of the war until the communists were thrown out of Southeast Asia.

In general, a dove is a peacenik; a hawk is an advocate of aggressive policy, not only in international relations but, for example, in business as well.

downer   First a slang term for depressant drugs like VALIUM or barbiturates, it has come to mean any depressing experience or situation.

down for the count   In boxing, when the boxer is knocked down and cannot rise before the count of 10, he is said to be "down for the count" (knocked out).

Informally, "down for the count" has a variety of meanings: beaten, defeated, done for, "dead."

Use: The competition was too much for Bullfinch. After a tough fight, having spent a fortune, he went down for the count.

Dracula   Motion picture adapted in 1931 from the 1897 novel by Bram Stoker and the 1920s play by Hamilton Deane and John Balderston. Together with *Frankenstein* it launched the vogue for horror films. Its main character, brilliantly played by Bela Lugosi, became a figure in popular mythology as a human vampire.

Count Dracula is a cultivated Rumanian nobleman, impeccably dressed in white tie, tails and a black cape. His hair is black, his skin alabaster. He welcomes his intended victims to his castle in Transylvania, where he feasts upon their blood.

Dragnet   An allegedly "real life" cops and robbers television drama (1952–59, revived 1967–70). Each episode began with the following introduction: "The story you are about to see is true. The names have been changed to protect the innocent." On this documentary note, *Dragnet* made its television debut. Its tightly written script, skillfully created suspense, and understated acting held its large television audience glued to the screen for 18 years.

Jack Webb, the creator and producer of *Dragnet*, was also its main character, Detective Joe Friday. Joe Friday is the archetypal "honest cop," the implacable foe of evil—tenacious, resourceful, unromantic. His clipped, monosyllabic speech ("Just the facts, ma'am") conceals his true compassion for his troubled and frightened clientele.

Dresden   City in Germany bombed into the ground by Allied air strikes, February 3, 1945. More than 130,000 civilians were killed and cathedrals and museums destroyed by bombs and intense fire storms. Symbol of total devastation of war.

Dreyfus Affair, the   Alfred Dreyfus (1859–1935) was a captain in the French Army when he was accused of passing French military secrets to Germany (1894). He was tried, convicted, stripped of his rank in public and condemned to life imprisonment in solitary confinement at the infamous French penal colony on Devil's Island, off the coast of French Guyana.

In the furor that followed Dreyfus's conviction, it became clear that Dreyfus's only offense was that he was Jewish in an army and a society deeply steeped in anti-Semitism. Indignation ran high in France, and throughout the rest of the world. Among those who fought hardest for Dreyfus was Emile Zola (1840–1902), whose fiery letter "J'ACCUSE," published in *L'Aurore* (Jan. 13, 1898), exposed the sinister part played by the government and other groups in sending the innocent Dreyfus to Devil's Island.

The worldwide outcry finally led to the exoneration and reinstatement of Dreyfus, after 12 years of suffering and humiliation.

The Dreyfus affair has become a symbol of gross injustice and cruelty driven by the basest of passions, and of a cause célèbre shot through with dark deeds and evil intentions.

droit du seigneur, le   Literally, "the lord's right." In the Middle Ages, the lord of the manor claimed as his "right" ("le droit du seigneur") the deflowering of the bride of any of his vassals on their wedding night. While theoretically possible, this "right" was rarely invoked.

In today's parlance, the "droit du seigneur" describes a grandiose, overbearing, arbitrary assertion of authority.

drop one's guard   In boxing, to lower the hand that protects one's chin. Hence, to leave oneself unprotected.

In general use, to relax one's defenses.

Use: Before they went into the courtroom, the defense attorney cautioned his client not to drop his guard under the merciless cross-examination the prosecuting attorney was sure to subject him to.

DuBarry, Comtesse (Marie-Jeanne Béau) (1743–1793)   As mistress of Louis XV from 1768 to his death in 1774, she had enormous influence at court, which she often used to benefit artists and men of letters. She was guillotined in 1793 during the French Revolution.

A DuBarry is a patroness of the arts.

Du Bois, Blanche   Heroine of Tennessee Williams's play *A Streetcar Named Desire* (1947). A faded Southern belle, she comes to live with her sister Stella and Stella's Polish working-class husband, Stanley Kowalski. She is repelled by Kowalski's vulgarity but attracted to his animal physicality. After Kowalski relentlessly exposes her shady past, brutally ridicules her airs and pretenses, spoils her last chance for a stable marriage, and rapes her while Stella is in the hospital giving birth to his child, she suffers a nervous breakdown. At the end of the play, she is taken away to a mental institution. The male guard, understanding her nature, offers his arm. She takes it and goes quietly, uttering the famous words: "I have always depended on the kindness of strangers."

The name describes a sensitive woman unable to cope with the brutalities of life.

Dubuque   City in Iowa, associated with the hinterland, far from cosmopolitan interests or activities—similar to Peoria, Illinois ("Will it play in Peoria?").

Use: Harold Ross, founder of *The New Yorker,* announced that the new magazine was going to be "for caviar sophisticates, not for the old lady from Dubuque."

Duesenberg   The fast, expensive, classic car of the Jazz Age. The Duesenberg vanished from the market after the stock market crash of 1929.

Dumb Dora   A popular comic strip (1925–30) about Dora Bell, a college-age brunette, her boy-girl dating and other related college activities. For obvious reasons, she was soon rechristened Dumb Dora. She had many dumb boyfriends whom she baffled, subdued and, in then-current fashion, "enslaved." Actually, of course, Dora wasn't as dumb as the strip's caption would seem to indicate. The pay-off line, "She ain't so dumb," was closer to Dora's real intelligence. While many girls are, in a sexist society, automatically labeled "dumb," Dora gave the lie to this stereotype.

Duncan, Isadora (1878–1927)   American dancer. Born in San Francisco, she became a legendary figure on two continents, not only because of her revolutionary dance style but also because of her much publicized free lifestyle. She was a precursor of modern dance. She rejected the precise discipline of ballet movement and the traditional costumes of the ballerina. She wanted to be free of restraints. Dressed in Greek tunics, she danced barefoot, responding expressively and emotionally to symphonic music. She won wildly appreciative audiences all through Europe. In 1921, at the invitation of the Soviet Union, she set up a school in Moscow. It lasted until 1928. She became notorious for her many turbulent love affairs (Gordon Craig, the theater set designer; Sergei Ysenin, the Russian poet; Paris Singer, heir to the sewing machine fortune). Her life was triumphant and tragic. She lost her two small children, one by Craig and one by Singer, in a car accident. She herself died when a scarf wound around her neck caught in the rear wheel of an open car on the Côte d'Azur and strangled her. In 1927 her autobiography, *My Life,* was published. In 1969, Vanessa Redgrave starred in the film *Isadora.*

She continues to fascinate people by her legendary beauty, daring, passion and originality.

Dunkirk   Seaport in northern France from which allied troops and a British expeditionary force of about 340,000 men in danger of annihilation were evacuated under German fire from May 29 to June 4, 1940. The channel crossing, although a great military achievement, still claimed the lives of about 30,000 Allied troops.

After the Dunkirk rescue, Churchill declared: "We shall fight on the seas and oceans; we shall fight . . . in the air . . . we shall fight on the beaches, we shall fight on the landing grounds, we shall fight in the fields and in the streets, we shall fight in the hills; we shall never surrender."

A Dunkirk is a successful retreat by heroic means from seemingly sure defeat.

Durante, James (Jimmy, "Schnozzola") (1893–1980) American entertainer. A veteran of vaudeville, movies and the night club circuit, Durante found a new and colorful career in television. The audiences loved his old songs, his comic mugging, his deliberately concocted malapropisms, his unabashed hamming—and last but not least, the endless puns and fun provoked by his sizable nose. No one really knows who first nicknamed him "Schnozzola"; but it stuck—and he played his CYRANO-esque role lovingly.

Each show closed with Durante, caught in a spotlight, reverently removing his crushed hat and taking a melancholy walk away from the camera, paying a ritual farewell: "Good-night, Mrs. Calabash, wherever you are."

Dynasty Inspired by the television prime time soap opera *Dallas, Dynasty* was its main competitor from 1981 to 1987. The plot was a heady mixture of murder, intrigue, the endless struggle for money and power, frustration, finagling and infidelity. Joan Collins as Alexis Carrington Colby, a sort of female J. R. Ewing, was the major source of the venom that permeated all of *Dynasty.* Lacking *Dallas*'s depth of characterization, it compensated for this deficiency by providing a liberal application of "style and glamour."

Though it enjoyed considerable popularity, *Dynasty* never quite achieved the dramatic impact of *Dallas.*

--- 𝓮 ---

East Lynne (1861)   An immensely popular novel by Mrs. Henry Wood, later turned into an equally popular play.

Critics are agreed that *East Lynne* was an unabashedly simple tearjerker, a "four hankie" work, an example of bad taste and sentimentality with little if any literary merit. Yet it achieved immediate popularity on two continents. The announcement on a theater marquee, Next Week: *East Lynne,* assured audiences that they were in for a good cry.

The name *East Lynne* is synonymous with sentimentality in trashy novels, soap operas or real life; a tearjerker.

Eastwood, Clint (1930–   )   Hollywood movie actor. Plays a macho American male, a loner, a tough guy, fast with the fists and the gun, willing to bypass the law and the bureaucracy in dishing out retributive justice on his own. Fulfills the fantasy of being a vigilante who can go out and clean up a mess by himself. He became a superstar with *Dirty Harry* (1971), in which he plays a cop hampered by red tape who relentlessly pursues a sadistic murderer. See also "MAKE MY DAY."

Edison, Thomas Alva (1847–1931)   The greatest inventor of them all. No one has ever equaled him in the number and nature of his epoch-making inventions: the electric light, the phonograph, the telephone transmitter, et al. When Edison died, more than 1,000 patents bore his name.

Edison's life is the archetypal American "HORATIO ALGER" story. He was born in the small town of Milan, Ohio, into a family of straitened and declining fortunes. In his early boyhood, he lost much of his hearing. His schooling was fragmentary at best.

In 1868, having overcome most of his early handicaps, Edison moved to Boston, a center of American science and technology. Here, in the shop of Charles Williams, surrounded by the facilities and skilled workmen to put his ideas into practice Edison's inventive powers flowered.

In 1869, Edison set up his own "invention factory" in Menlo Park, New Jersey, a unique self-sustaining research and development center.

An "Edison" is, naturally, another inventor of extraordinary talents and accomplishments. The term, however, is sometimes used sarcastically to deride a person for a feeble experiment, as in "Look, a veritable Edison!"—just as one might say of a slow-witted person, an "EINSTEIN."

Edsel   Car named after Edsel Ford (1893–1943), son of Henry Ford. Launched with a media blitz in 1957, it became the biggest flop in automobile history.

The Edsel stands for a dud, a flop, an anticlimax to a big build-up.

Edwardian   Pertaining to life, manners, dress and culture during the reign (1901–10) of King Edward VII (1841–1910) of England. The Edwardian period ushered in a change from the stodgy morality and dowdy dress and demeanor of Queen Victoria's court to opulence and elegance. It was a time when a sense of liberation and confidence prevailed until the outbreak of World War I.

Eichmann, Adolf (1906–1962)   Head of the SS Jewish section, Eichmann was responsible for the deaths of millions of Jews in Nazi concentration camps. Kidnapped in Argentina in 1960 by Israeli security agents and tried for crimes against the Jewish people before an Israeli court of law, he claimed as his defense the fact that he was merely obeying the orders of his superiors. Eichmann was hanged in 1962. He inspired the phrase "the banality of evil," coined by Hannah Arendt (1906–75) in her book on his trial, *Eichmann in Jerusalem* (1963).

Einstein, Albert (1879–1955)   German-born physicist who found refuge in the United States from Nazi anti-Jewish persecution. He was perceived as the preeminent brain of the 20th century—so much so that he was asked to donate his brain for posthumous scientific study. He developed the theory of relativity, transforming our understanding of the relationship between space and time. His famous equation for energy, $E = MC^2$, was the theoretical basis upon which the atom bomb was built.

Use: ". . . of me, my mother would say, with characteristic restraint, 'this bandit. He doesn't even have to open a book—"A" in everything. Albert Einstein the Second.'" (Portnoy, in Philip Roth's *Portnoy's Complaint*)

Often used sarcastically, as in: An Einstein he's not.

Elba   A small island off the coast of Tuscany, Italy (in the Tyrrhenian Sea), to which NAPOLEON was exiled in 1814 after his abdication as emperor of the French. After 10 months he escaped and rallied his forces for a final showdown with allied forces. Napoleon's Hundred Days after Elba ended with his defeat at Waterloo, a second abdication on June 22, 1815, and his final exile to St. Helena.

Elba has since stood for a place of exile, or for temporary exile, in a metaphorical sense. One's Elba can be a banishment, a deprivation of status or power for a time.

Eldorado   An imaginary kingdom, presumably somewhere in or near Peru, named after its king—Eldorado, "the gilded one." Legend had it that, on certain festivals, the king was covered with oil and then powdered with gold dust, all of which he later washed off in a nearby lake.

Manoa, the major city, was supposed to be resplendent in gold buildings and decorations, its streets abounding in gold nuggets available to anyone who wanted them. The natives used gold only to beautify their lives.

Driven by an insatiable hunger for gold, explorers set out on a futile search for Eldorado.

In common parlance, an Eldorado is any place that holds out the promise of big, quick, easy money.

El Greco (The Greek)   Nickname of Domenikos Theotokopoulos (1541–1614), the last of the great Renaissance mannerist painters. Born in Crete and probably trained in youth in the Byzantine tradition, he moved to Venice, where he worked in the 1560s with Titian and other Italian masters. In 1577 he moved to Toledo, Spain, where he lived for the rest of his life.

El Greco is famous for his ecstatic religious paintings (see especially *The Burial of Count Orgaz,* 1586) and for his psychologically penetrating portraits of Spanish grandees. (See especially his portrait of Fray Felix Hortensio Paravicino [1609], a scholar and poet who was his friend.) In the mannerist tradition, El Greco's faces and figures are elongated and ascetic. The faces burn with intense spirituality. In the Byzantine tradition, he moved away from the naturalist, three-dimensional space of the high Renaissance painters for a flatter surface. For all these reasons his reputation among the moderns has grown steadily for the last century and a half.

Occasionally, in current usage, we come upon an arresting face that we recognize as an El Greco. It is generally male, elongated, bearded, ascetic, pale, intense, with eyes of burning coal.

Ellington, Edward Kennedy "Duke" (1899–1974)   Black composer and band leader known as "Duke" from childhood. A largely self-taught pianist with little formal training in composition, Ellington nonetheless became a major spokesman for jazz music. In his compositions, he used daring devices, blending, in his own words, "lush melodies with unorthodox, dissonant harmonies . . ."

Ellington composed music for theater, movies, radio, the concert stage. In 1969 he received the Presidential Medal of Freedom, and in 1971 he was inducted into the Songwriters Hall of Fame. Ellington's famous songs include "Sophisticated Lady," "In My Solitude," "Don't Get Around Much Anymore."

Ellis Island   Entry port in New York Harbor for some 17 million immigrants to the United States who were processed there from 1892 to 1954. Most of these were the poorest of the poor, who had traveled in steerage to America to escape the famines, wars and pogroms of the Old World. Ellis Island is located next to the Statue of Liberty, with its engraved lines of poetry by Emma Lazarus:

> *Give me your tired, your poor,*
> *Your huddled masses yearning to breathe free,*
> *The wretched refuse of your teeming shore,*
> *Send these, the homeless, tempest-tossed to me:*
> *I lift my lamp beside the golden door.*

Ellis Island stands for the gateway to freedom and opportunity in the New World.

El Niño   A weather phenomenon set off by warm ocean currents near the Pacific coast of Peru, it results in abnormal storms, torrential rains, tornadoes and mud slides on the one hand, and draught on the other. The term El Niño has come to be synonymous with unpredictable and tempestuous behavior, much like that on a smaller scale of a temperamental prima donna.

eminence grise   French for "gray cardinal," the term has come to mean "the power behind the throne," the shadowy figure who manipulates, advises and influences the actions or policies of government officials.

Cardinal Richelieu (1585–1642), prime minister of France under Louis XIII, played a decisive role in determining and controlling France's domestic and foreign policies. Richelieu's private secretary and confessor was Père Joseph de Trembley, who exerted a decisive, albeit shadowy influence over Richelieu. Because he wore a gray habit, Père de Trembley was called *Eminence Grise,* the "Gray Cardinal."

Louis McHenry Howe (1871–1936), President Franklin Delano Roosevelt's personal secretary and confidant, was often referred to as eminence grise. He played a key, behind-the-scenes role in fashioning and promoting Roosevelt's gubernatorial and presidential campaigns.

emperor's new clothes, the (1836)   This term derives from a fairy tale by the Danish writer Hans Christian Andersen in which an emperor who is excessively fond of finery orders a suit of clothes from two con men. These false "weavers," without any thread in their loom, proceed to weave the finest fabric in the world. The fabric has magic properties: whoever claims not to see the fabric is unfit for his office. In time, the emperor struts about in his new "suit." Nobody dares say anything—except for one little child who blurts out, "He isn't wearing anything!"

The phrase "the emperor's new clothes" applies to people's being hoodwinked by so-called experts or by their own powers of rationalization into rejecting the evidence of their own senses. Many lay people contend that a great deal of what passes for modern art, modern music and modern poetry may simply be a case of the emperor's new clothes.

end run   In football, a play in which the ball carrier outflanks the opposing team by running around one end of the defensive line.

In general use, an attempt to solve a problem without confronting it head on, a diversionary tactic designed to achieve an illegitimate or illegal result.

Enemy of the People, An (1882)   A bitterly ironic polemical play by the Norwegian playwright Henrik Ibsen (1828–1906).

Dr. Stockmann discovers pollution in the municipal baths that have brought tourists and prosperity to his little town. At first hailed as a hero, he becomes an outcast when the townspeople realize that economic disaster could result from shutting down the baths for extensive and expensive repairs. When Stockmann rejects all bribes and resists all threats to change his findings, he is branded "an enemy of the people" by the entire community of vested interests: business, the press, the clergy, the town council. He assails the "compact majority," which, he declares, is always wrong. He vows to hold out against them if he must stand and fight absolutely alone.

An "enemy of the people" is an ironic epithet for reformers whose reforms require sacrifice and are therefore rejected by the unthinking majority. He or she is a whistle blower, in today's parlance, and is treated as an enemy to be fired from a job or even murdered by the vested interests.

enforcer   See MURDER, INC.

Enoch Arden   Main character in *Enoch Arden* (1864), a long narrative poem by England's Victorian poet laureate, Alfred, Lord Tennyson (1809–92). Enoch Arden, a seaman who has been shipwrecked and stranded upon a desert island, returns home after many years to find that his wife has remarried. He resolves not to destroy her newfound happiness, and so he leaves again without disclosing that he is still alive.

Enoch Arden laws have been passed by the United States to protect women whose husbands have deserted them or whose husbands have been soldiers listed as missing in action. After a certain number of years, the missing men are pronounced legally dead and their wives may inherit their estates and remarry.

Enola Gay   The American B-29 bomber from which Col. Paul W. Tibbets, Jr., dropped the first atomic bomb on Hiroshima, a military-industrial city in Japan, on August 6, 1945.

Entebbe   International airport in Uganda, where on July 4, 1976, Israeli commandos staged a spectacularly daring and successful raid to free 105 mostly Jewish hostages held by pro-Palestinian hijackers of an Air France jet. In a dramatic shoot-out, the commandos killed the terrorists, who were being supported by President Idi Amin and his troops. They then hustled the hostages onto three waiting transport planes and flew them 2,000 miles to Israel.

Entebbe stands for epic heroism, exultant victory against international terrorism, and triumph against overwhelming odds.

Erté (1892–1990)   Born Romain de Tirtoff in St. Petersburg, Russia, Erté (the name is derived from the French pronunciation of his initials) moved to Paris, worked for the then reigning French fashion designer Paul Poiret and himself became a great costume designer and illustrator. Like Poiret, his designs are exotic, imaginative, sophisticated and avant-garde. His illustrations are works of art.

An Erté is an exquisite fashion plate.

Estragon (Gogo)   One of the two tattered tramps in Samuel Beckett's tragicomic masterpiece *Waiting for Godot*. See also VLADIMIR and GODOT.

ethnic cleansing   The deliberate policy of removing from their homes and from their native land, by means of harassment, confiscation of property, forced exile and even massacre, a local population for no other reason than their common ethnicity—that is, their religion, language, culture—in order "to create an ethnically unified zone."

The HOLOCAUST is the extreme example of ethnic cleansing, unique in its scope, its brutality, its fanaticism, its dedication to the total annihilation of the Jews on the continent of Europe; ethnic cleansing as a "Final Solution." After their victory over Nazi Germany at the end of World War II in 1945, the Allies echoed the cry taken up by surviving Jews: "Never again!" Never again did they expect to see in Europe the wholesale elimination of an entire population for ethnic cleansing.

Yet, 50 years later, in the Balkans, in the name of Serbian nationalism, Serbian troops and paramilitary bands were ousting from their homes Muslims in Bosnia-Herzegovina and, a couple of years later, Albanians from Kosovo. Their tactics were brutal: surround a village; separate the young men from the others and march them off to be massacred; rape the women; torch the houses; remove identity papers; force the victims into exile.

In the case of Bosnia, the U.N. imposed the Dayton peace accord to be administered by U.N. forces. In the case of Kosovo, after Slobodan Milosevic refused to acquiesce in a diplomatic solution, NATO forces started bombing Serbia on March 24, 1999, to stop the ethnic cleansing. More than a million Albanian Kosovars were driven from Kosovo into Albania, Macedonia and Montenegro. In June 1999, Milosevic finally acceded to NATO terms and of the refugees started the long trek back to their ruined homes in Kosovo. However, the ancient tensions remained, and it was by no means clear that ethnic cleansing had been put to an end once and for all.

"Et tu, Brute?" ("You too, Brutus?")   The words Julius Caesar was supposed to have said to Brutus when he saw his great friend among the conspirators who were about to assassinate him on the Ides of March (March 15), 44 B.C. Suetonius wrote that Caesar was speaking in Greek; it is from Shakespeare's tragedy *Julius Caesar* that we have the phrase in Latin.

Caesar had counted Brutus a friend and supporter. Brutus's collusion with Cassius and the rest of the conspirators was an act of gross professional and personal disloyalty and betrayal. "Et tu, Brute?" in modern usage is an expression of surprise at betrayal, usually in much more trivial circumstances than the original context. The tone today is often joshing.

Eustacia Vye   A character in Thomas Hardy's novel *The Return of the Native* (1878). A proud, passionate beauty, she will do anything to get away from the uncongenial environment of Egdon Heath, a wild, dour place peopled for the most part with provincial, uneducated sheep farmers.

When Clym Yeobright, a successful diamond merchant in Paris, returns to his mother's home on the heath, ostensibly for a visit, Eustacia sees in him her great chance to escape. She dazzles him with her beauty, intelligence and waywardness. They marry against Clym's mother's will. Alas, Clym has returned to the heath to stay. He hates the vain life in Paris and intends to teach and elevate the humble natives of the heath. Thus, the ambitions of the two protagonists are at cross purposes. Clym becomes blind, leaves teaching and turns to furze-cutting (that is, the menial job of cutting heather for fuel) as his occupation. Eustacia's love turns to disgust when she observes Clym's placid acceptance of his humble station.

Eustacia makes one more desperate attempt to escape the heath: elopement with her former lover, Damon Wildeve, now married to Clym's cousin Thomasin. Wildeve has unexpectedly inherited some money and has the means to go to Paris. At the last moment, Eustacia is too proud to submit to Wildeve. She commits suicide by throwing herself into a weir and Wildeve drowns trying to rescue her.

Eustacia Vye represents a tragic figure caught in a web of coincidents, misunderstandings, stubborn wills and impulses of headstrong self-destruction. She is an example of those who, try as they will, cannot escape a hostile environment.

Everyman   The term refers to the subject of a morality play (c. 1500) with a subtitle that sets down the "theme" with chilling succinctness: "A Treatise How The hye Fader of Heaven Sendeth Death to Somon every creature to come and give a counte of theyr lives in this world."

As the play opens, Everyman has been summoned by Death for the final, dread accounting. Fearful of going it alone, Everyman calls upon his friends: Fellowship, Worldly Goods, Kindred, Beauty and other allegorical figures to accompany him on his final journey to his grave. They all desert him. Only Good Deeds, whom he has neglected, remains faithful to him. Knowledge, too, provides support for Everyman in these memorable words:

> Everyman, I will go with Thee and be Thy guide
> In Thy most need to go by Thy side.

Everyman is each one of us.

"every man a king"   Phrase used by Huey Long (1893–1935), governor of Louisiana and later senator from that state, in appealing to the less affluent segments of the nation. Often labeled a demagogue, Long promised these people, in the depths of the Great Depression, a guaranteed annual income of $5,000 per family, thus making "every man a king."

evil empire   An empire in space held in a grip of terror by DARTH VADER, the villain of *Star Wars,* a 1977 film written and directed by George Lucas. In the 1980s President Ronald Reagan referred to the Soviet Union as an evil empire.

Excalibur   In Arthurian legend, KING ARTHUR's magic sword was given to him by the Lady of the Lake, according to Thomas Malory's *Le Morte Darthur* (1469). After his battle with Modred, Arthur, mortally wounded, has Bedivére throw the sword into the lake. An arm reaches up out of the water to take it. In another version of the legend, Arthur proves himself to be the rightful king of England when he alone of all the knights is able to draw the sword from the stone in which it is fixed. With Excalibur, Arthur wins great battles and unifies England.

Excalibur stands for magic or a powerful personal weapon. For example, President Lyndon B. Johnson used the telephone to such powerful effect that it was called his excalibur. See also MERLIN; AVALON.

expressionist   Belonging to a 20th-century movement in art that conceives the true purpose of art to be not the representation of nature but, instead, the expression of fundamental emotions like love, hate, fear, anxiety. Van Gogh, an early expressionist, wrote in one of his letters that he exaggerated the forms and rhythms of nature in order "to express . . . man's terrible passions." Expressionists reject Greek and Renaissance conceptions of beauty and use distortion to convey the force of an emotion. Although expressionism started in France with Van Gogh, Gauguin, and Rouault, it spread throughout Europe: in Norway, Edvard Munch; in Belgium, James Ensor; in Germany, Ernst Kirchner and Emil Nolde; in Austria, Oskar Kokoschka.

"Expressionist" is associated with dark emotions, heavy outlines and mask-like grotesques. It is the opposite of "impressionist," which sees reality in terms of light and joy.

Exxon Valdez   Oil tanker that in 1989 ran aground in Prince William Sound, Alaska, spilling 11 million gallons of crude oil over 500 square miles of water and hundreds of miles of coastline. Bird, fish and plant life were poisoned and destroyed. Although the ship's owner, Exxon, sued by the State of Alaska for billions of dollars for its negligence, tried to clean up the spill and restore the failing fishing industry, it was a case of too little too late. The *Exxon Valdez* became a symbol of environmental disaster.

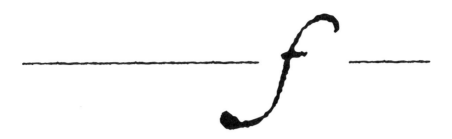

Fagin   The villain in Charles Dickens's novel *Oliver Twist* (1839), he is a loathsome old Jew, master of a den of young thieves whom he instructs in the art of stealing. He kidnaps the innocent Oliver, a boy recently escaped from a poorhouse, and tries, like the devil in an old morality play, to corrupt him and win his soul. With the collusion of Monks, Oliver's evil half brother, Fagin is determined to keep Oliver from discovering his true identity and from coming into his inheritance. In the end, Fagin is foiled. Implicated in Sikes's murder of Nancy, he is tried, convicted and executed.

A Fagin is an evil man, a slimy corruptor of the young.

fail-safe   A signal created by the U.S. Air Force to prevent completion of a retaliatory response to an enemy's preemptive atom bomb strike, in the case of a false alarm. A double-check point at which bombers already on their way to enemy territory can be recalled, a fail-safe is insurance against atomic war by mistake.

Now, any scheme that is foolproof, even in so trivial a matter as a recipe for a souffle.

Fairbanks, Douglas (1883–1939)   Hollywood star associated with swashbuckling roles in derring-do films of historical adventure like *The Mark of Zorro* (1920), *The Black Pirate* (1926), *The Iron Mask* (1929) and *The Thief of Bagdad* (1924). He married Mary Pickford in 1920.

Fair Deal   Term used by President Harry S. Truman in his State of the Union message to Congress in January 1949 to characterize his proposals for the nation. He called for an increase in the minimum wage, more low-income housing, adherence to civil rights laws, and greater social security coverage—a program intended to benefit the aged and the disadvantaged.

fallout   Radiation released into the air from nuclear testing of H-bombs or atom bombs. Radioactive particles fall to earth or into water, contaminating the environment. A disaster in a nuclear power plant, as in CHERNOBYL, also results in a widespread fallout. In general use, fallout is the lingering aftereffect of any unfortunate event in any milieu.

falsely shouting fire in a crowded theater   Phrase taken from the U.S. Supreme Court's decision in *Schenck v. U.S.* (1919), setting limits on the freedom of speech guaranteed by the first amendment to the Constitution. Justice Oliver Wendell Holmes, Jr., wrote: "The most stringent protection of free speech would not protect a man falsely shouting fire in a theater and causing a panic." The test for abridgement of free speech would be "whether the words are used in such circumstances and are of such a nature as to create a clear and present danger." For example, certain words that would be protected by the First Amendment in peacetime would not be tolerated in wartime. Thus, John Schenck's petition to have his arrest for distributing anti-draft pamphlets voided was rejected by the Court.

The phrase is often quoted when someone claims license to say whatever outrageous thing he thinks of, even in family squabbles. "Isn't there free speech in this country?" might be answered with, "But you can't shout fire in a crowded theater."

Falstaff   Probably the greatest comic character ever created, Falstaff appears in Shakespeare's *Henry IV* (Parts I and II) and *The Merry Wives of Windsor*. Fat, unkempt, lazy, drunk, licentious and a blustering braggart, he is the unlikely companion of Prince Hal in the latter's salad days. Falstaff is a foil to Hotspur, who is impetuous, headstrong, patriotic, self-destructive. Falstaff values life too much to be a hero, and rationalizes his cowardice.

When Hal is crowned Henry V, he brutally and summarily rejects Falstaff. The pathos of Falstaff's recognition of his image through the king's eyes is deeply affecting. Shakespeare mixes comic and tragic elements in the same character, violating the precepts of dramatic unity in his time.

In modern film, the outrageousness of W. C. Fields on one hand and the pathos of Charlie Chaplin on the other remind us of the two sides of Falstaff.

A Falstaff is a pathetic, tragicomic fat braggart and blusterer.

Falwell, Jerry (1933–   )   "Born again" Christian evangelist on the nationwide TV program *Old-Time Gospel Hour,* he founded the Moral Majority, Inc., in 1979 to become a formidable political activist, endorsing and supporting conservative political candidates with views similar to his own. He is against abortion, the Equal Rights Amendment and homosexual rights, and for, he says, traditional moral values.

Farewell to Arms, A (1929)   Ernest Hemingway's novel about love against a background of war. Frederic Henry, an American lieutenant in the Italian

Ambulance Corps during World War I, falls in love with Catherine Barkley, an English nurse. When he is wounded, she comes to nurse him. They spend a few idyllic months together while he recuperates. He returns to the front and participates in the disastrous retreat from Caporetto. Disillusioned with the war, he makes his separate peace and deserts. He finds Catherine, who is pregnant, and they flee to Switzerland. There she dies in childbirth and the baby with her. Henry is left desolate. The rain, which has been a melancholy symbol of death throughout the book, falls steadily.

A farewell to arms is generally used to describe a personal truce, a private retreat from any kind of hostility.

far from the madding crowd   A phrase taken from "Elegy Written in a Country Churchyard," a poem by Thomas Gray (1716–71) published in 1751, used by Thomas Hardy (1840–1928) as the title for a novel (1874). Gray's poem is a meditation on "the short and simple annals of the poor" who live in a pastoral setting far from the temptations and possibilities of power and glory.

"fasten your seatbelts"   Refers originally to the command given to airplane passengers on take-off and landing and during turbulent air conditions. The term has come into general use to indicate anticipation of danger or any rough going. For example, toward the end of the movie *All About Eve,* Bette Davis, having just discovered that Anne Baxter, the ingenue she has befriended, has secretly been maneuvering to replace her in a starring role, turns to a roomful of people and says, "Fasten your seat belts. It's going to be a bumpy ride." In other words, "Gird yourselves, the war is on. Watch out for the flak."

fast lane   Usually the left lane of a highway or expressway for speedy driving or for passing slower cars, the term also refers either to a fast track to success or celebrity in a highly competitive environment, or to a glamorous lifestyle ("life in the fast lane").

Fatal Attraction   A 1987 movie thriller directed by Adrian Lyne and starring Glenn Close as a sexy, obsessive "other woman" relentlessly pursuing an unwilling married man (Michael Douglas) after an unfortunate one-night stand. She subjects him, his wife and child to a reign of terror that ends only with her death.

The term "fatal attraction" has since been widely used for any obsessive and damaging relationship, as in this *Newsweek* headline: Teacher, Lover, Schemer, Killer? The "Fatal Attraction" Murder Trial.

Fata Morgana   Translation into Italian of the name Morgan le Fay, the sorceress who played an ambivalent role in the Arthurian legends. KING ARTHUR's half sister by his mother Igerne, she often plotted against Arthur, at one time stealing his sword, EXCALIBUR. Nevertheless, it was she who conducted the mortally wounded Arthur to AVALON to heal him for a second coming.

Morgana was a mysterious figure, said to have lived at the bottom of a lake, where she hoarded her treasures. She appears as the Lady of the Lake in *Orlando Furioso* (1516), a romantic epic by Ariosto.

Today "Fata Morgana" refers, in a meteorological sense, to mirages resembling magical castles reflected in the sea or in the air above the sea in the region of the Strait of Messina on the Calabrian coast. In general, a Fata Morgana is an illusion, a mirage.

fatwa   An edict issued by a Muslim cleric in defense of Islam. The word achieved widespread recognition in the West when Ayatollah Ruhollah Khomeini, the fundamentalist spiritual leader of Iran, on February 24, 1989, issued a *fatwa* against the writer Salman Rushdie, whose novel *The Satanic Verses* he declared to be blasphemous. Declaring Rushdie the enemy of all Islam, Khomeini sentenced him to death and placed a million-dollar bounty on his head. He called for the suppression of the book worldwide and an extension of the *fatwa* to any booksellers who defied the ban. Rushdie went into hiding for years, riots broke out in Pakistan and India, and protests against this violation of free speech were mounted by writers' organizations throughout the Western world.

In 1994, a *fatwa* calling for the arrest and death of another author, young Tashima Nasrin, born and raised a Muslim in Bangladesh, was issued because she had criticized Islamic society for its treatment of women.

Thus, *fatwa* stands for any relentless, arbitrary condemnation of a person for supposed heresy.

Faubourg St-Honoré   District of fashionable shops and of the haute couture in Paris. Synonymous with elegant fashion.

Faulknerian   Having to do with the world, the style, the characters, the setting and themes in the work of William Faulkner (1897–1962), Nobel Prize–winning American novelist and short story writer. Faulkner lived most of his life in Oxford, Mississippi. Using the people and the history of the place he knew best, he became the greatest of the "Southern" writers. He created mythical Yoknapatawpha County with its county seat in Jefferson, Mississippi, and peopled it with declining aristocratic families of the Old South (the Sartorises and the Compsons) soon to be replaced by the rapacious poor white trash of the New South (the Snopes clan). The values of honor, courage, noblesse oblige, patriotism of a stable society are replaced by the cynicism and greed of a people without a past.

Faulknerian themes are many: the meaning of the past and its continued hold on the people of the South; the curse of slavery and its baleful effect upon race relations; the violence attached to Southern religiosity, class differences and sexual puritanism.

The Faulknerian style is often baroque, rhapsodic, using long sentences that seem to come out of the subjective dreams and subconscious of the characters. It is full of large symbols and allegorical overtones, as in *Light in August* (1932). Often Faulkner presents the same story from several points of view, as in *The Sound and the Fury* (1929), where the first version is told from the consciousness of an idiot Benjy, and then by each of his brothers, Quentin and Jason. He uses the same technique in *As I Lay Dying* (1930), the harrowing story of a family's pilgrimage to bury their mother in the town where she was born. Faulknerian humor is large and wild, as in the chapter of the horses rampaging through a house in *The Hamlet* (1940), the first of a trilogy about the Snopes saga. The Faulknerian world is strange, dreamlike, hallucinatory, full of violence and despair, often hilarious, peopled by "crazies," having the tone of remembered events recapitulated with conjecture, speculation and new interpretations. And yet it all hangs together because it bears the stamp of Faulkner as surely as the paintings in the Sistine Chapel bear the stamp of Michelangelo.

Faust   The tragic hero of one of the most powerful and persistent myths about human nature—namely, man's unappeasable drive to learn more than it is, perhaps, wise for him to know and probably more than he can handle.

The two best known treatments of this myth are *The Tragical History of Doctor Faustus* (c. 1593–94) by the British playwright Christopher Marlowe (1564–93) and *Faust,* a much more densely complex and profound drama in two volumes (1808 and 1832) by the German poet Johannes Wolfgang von Goethe (1749–1832).

Johannes Faustus was a brilliant scholar and necromancer of the early 16th century who, in frustration at his failure to plumb the secrets of nature, entered into a pact with the devil. It was upon this legend that Marlowe and later Goethe based their dramas. For 24 years of induction into the secrets of the universe, Faust is willing to sell his eternal soul to Mephistopheles. Faust knows, of course, that with knowledge comes power.

In Marlowe's version, Faustus uses his power in mostly silly and clownish pranks. Near the end of his term, he recants in terror as he faces eternity in hell's flames. Marlowe has created a hero caught between medieval and Renaissance views of man.

Goethe's Faust grows out of the conflict between Enlightenment and Romantic views. By the end of Book One, appalled and contrite over his seduction and destruction of Gretchen, Faust understands the error of his past. In Book Two,

Faust is redeemed by using his knowledge and power to improve the lot of mankind. Compassion and the human spirit have triumphed over sheer intellect.

In modern times, when physicists were delving into the nature of the atom to unleash nuclear power capable of destroying all life on this planet, they also unleashed a debate as to whether they were not making a Faustian pact with the devil. Many people, including many scientists, thought that physicists should desist from seeking knowledge too dangerous to control. Others, however, saw mankind's drive to know as an inevitable concomitant of his nature. Perhaps the idea of a Faustian bargain started in an earlier great myth, that of the Garden of Eden, when Eve and then Adam were tempted to eat of the fruit of the tree of knowledge.

Fauves   A French word for "wild beasts," the term was applied by an art critic to the painters whose work went on exhibit in October 1905 at a Paris salon. So brilliant and violent were the colors of their paintings that this critic felt that he had been thrust into a cage of wild animals. The Fauves wore their epithet proudly. It gave them a sense of liberation to experiment not only with color but also with distortion of form. Most prominent of the Fauves was Henri Matisse (1869–1954). The Fauves liberated all the world from a conventional use of color combinations.

"Fauve" or "Fauvist" is used to describe the riotous use of color, not only in painting, but also in dress and home decoration.

Fawkes, Guy   On November 5, 1605, a group of British Roman Catholics plotted to destroy King James I and his government by the simple device of setting off barrels of gunpowder under the House of Lords on the day that Parliament officially opened. The ensuing conflagration and mayhem was to be the signal for a general Catholic uprising. To Guy Fawkes, one of the plotters, fell the task of setting off the explosion that would bring down the king and the reigning aristocracy. But the plot was foiled and Guy Fawkes was seized before he could set off the explosion. Fawkes was subsequently executed before a large crowd in front of the House of Lords.

November 5 is now officially Guy Fawkes Day in Great Britain, and begins with a ceremonial searching of the vaults in Parliament prior to its annual opening. To complete the memorial ceremony, Guy Fawkes is burned in effigy to the accompaniment of bonfires and fireworks, thus celebrating the thwarting of the gunpowder plot.

A Guy Fawkes is an English analogy to John Brown of Harper's Ferry fame: a hero to one side but a traitor to the other; one who aims to right a grievous wrong through violent means.

federal case   A case that comes within the jurisdiction of a federal court is generally held to be more serious than a case in the local courts. To make a federal case out of something is, with reverse logic, to exaggerate the significance, the weight-iness, of a trivial fault, lapse or misdemeanor. A boy might say to his mother, "O.K. I forgot to take the garbage out. Let's not make a federal case out of it."

Fellini, Federico (1920–1993)   Italian film director who succeeded in mythol-ogizing the materials of his own life by projecting unforgettable images of it upon the screen. For example, in *8$^1/_2$* (1963) he surrealistically shows a human child climbing up the walls and across the ceiling in an attempt to get away from an adult with a whip. In *Amarcord* (1974) the heavy metal shutters of a shop clank down. Caught within is a little boy who is promptly smothered in the enormous breasts of the shopkeeper. See also "LA DOLCE VITA."

Feminine Mystique, The (1963)   Title of a seminal book by Betty Friedan that launched the modern women's liberation movement. Friedan defines the fem-inine mystique as a lie that for generations kept women from realizing themselves as full persons with interests and longings beyond the bedroom, the kitchen and the nursery. Women themselves had been brainwashed into believing that work and interests outside the home were unfeminine. Friedan exploded the myth that the "little woman" was ecstatic in her domesticity. Her book changed the lives of mil-lions of women—and men—worldwide.

Fibber McGee and Molly   Characters in the hilarious radio and TV comedy of the same name who lived at 79 Wistful Vista from 1925 to 1960. What remains in popular memory of this long-running show are: Fibber's tendency to exaggerate (some charitably called it "fibbing"); Fibber's constant trouble with his friends—saved from disaster by Molly's good, old-fashioned common sense; and Fibber's famous overcrowded hall closet, which would unleash its contents when opened. In time, the closet disgorging its motley contents became a symbol of Fibber, his crotchetiness, his helplessness, his all-too-human frailties.

Fields, W. C. (1879–1946)   Screen name of William Claude Dukenfield, come-dian of the silent movies and then the talkies. Paunchy, bulbous-nosed, bibulous, raspy-voiced, caustic, hating children and courting unlovely women, he played in *My Little Chickadee* (1940), *The Bank Dick* (1940), *Never Give a Sucker an Even Break* (1941) and many others.

Fields is remembered for outrageous lines like "Anybody who hates children can't be all bad." He never touched water, he said, because "fish copulate in it."

Fifth Avenue   Street of fashionable shops and department stores (Cartier, Tiffany, Gucci, Bergdorf Goodman, Saks Fifth Avenue, Lord and Taylor, and many others) from 34th Street to 59th Street in Manhattan. It is the route of the Easter parade in which people show off their new spring outfits, as in the popular 1933 song by Irving Berlin. From 59th Street north, it borders on Central Park and becomes a street of fine residences and museums. Fifth Avenue is a symbol of elegance and affluence.

fifth column   Phrase coined during the Spanish Civil War by fascist supporter Lt. General Queipo De Llano, to the effect that Franco had four columns of insurgents marching against Madrid and a fifth column within the city ready to betray it. Generally, the term refers to subversives in sympathy with the enemy of their country and ready to commit sabotage in support of that enemy.

Final Solution   It was Nazi Germany under HITLER that added the word and the concept of "final" to the various "solutions" to the so-called Jewish problem. The problem had been seen by the emerging nation-states of Europe as the tendency of the Jews in the diaspora to remain a separate entity within the state, with their own religion, customs, language. Pre-Nazi "solutions" to this problem had been forced conversion, expulsion, exclusion from certain rights, including the right to engage in trades and professions. The Nazis' "solution" was truly final: genocide, extermination of a whole people.

The term is sometimes trivialized and used colloquially and even mockingly to mean the end, the ultimate solution to any problem.

fin de siècle   French for "end of the century," particularly the last 10 years of the 19th century. This period was characterized in part by an attack on established ideas and conventions; experimentation with new objectives and techniques in literature and music; decadent behavior and extremism in dress and ideas personified in England by Oscar Wilde (1854–1900) and Aubrey Beardsley (1812–98) and in France by J. K. Huysmans (1848–1907), Arthur Rimbaud (1854–91), Stéphane Mallarmé (1842–98) and Paul Verlaine (1844–96).

Although marked by a general sense of "emergent emancipation" (the new woman, political suffrage, and other movements or ideas), the term *fin de siècle* is now narrowly applied to its decadent excesses.

Finnegans Wake (1939)   A novel by James Joyce so dense in word-making, so original and complex in design and content, it almost needs to be translated as from another language. The entire book represents an unconscious dream in which elements of history, mythology, philosophy and art coalesce in individual words and events. Based on Vico's cyclical philosophy of history, it begins with the second half of a sentence, the first half of which is to be found on the last page. Here is a sample:

"Whatif she be in flags or flitters, reekie rags or sundye chosies, with a mint of mines or beggar a pinnyweight. Arrah, sure, we all love little Anny Ruiny, or we mean to say, lovelittle Anna Rayiny, when unda her brela, mid piddle med puddle, she ninny goes nanny goes nancing by."

One might say of a given work that it is so incomprehensible that it might just as well be *Finnegans Wake*.

"Fire and Ice"   Often quoted literally to refer to death of the planet Earth by atomic warfare or a new ice age, the term refers to a short poem by Robert Frost (1875–1963), which begins:

Some say the world will end in fire,
Some say in ice.

fireside chats   Informal radio talks to the nation begun by President Franklin Delano Roosevelt on March 12, 1933. He invariably began "My friends . . ." and spoke in simple language as if to "a mason at work on a new building, a girl behind a counter, and a farmer in his field." He explained to the people his proposals to fight the Great Depression and appealed directly to them for their support. The term has been used by succeeding presidents as well.

first string   In sports, the players who regularly start in games as against those who are held in reserve or are substitutes.

In general use, the best members of a staff, business or professional organization.

Use: "Send only your first string people to the next conference. They'll meet stiff competition."

Fitzgerald, F. Scott (1896–1940)   American novelist and short story writer, a member of the Lost Generation, associated most with the Jazz Age, a term he coined. He described his age as "a new generation grown up to find all Gods dead, all wars fought, all faiths in man shaken." He depicted the aimlessness and cynicism of the post–World War I expatriates in *Tender Is the Night* (1934) and the corruption of the American Dream in *The Great Gatsby* (1925). He and his beautiful wife, Zelda, became legendary figures, so wild, reckless and glamorous that they seemed to have stepped out of the pages of his novels. Both ended tragically, Zelda in an institution for the mentally ill and Scott Fitzgerald drunk, sick, depleted in Hollywood.

five-foot shelf of books   Charles William Eliot was the president of Harvard University from 1869 to 1909. In 1910, the joint efforts of Dr. Eliot and the enterprising publisher P.F. Collier launched *Dr. Eliot's Famous Five-Foot Shelf of Books*.

151

According to a contemporary ad, written by the gifted Bruce Barton,
One hundred thousand businessmen are using the helpful reading courses which Dr. Eliot has laid out.
They are reading the great histories, seeing the great plays, hearing the great orations, meeting the great men of history with Dr. Eliot . . . In all the world, there are only a few books . . . that have really made history. To read these few great works systematically and intelligently is to be well read.
What are these great works? . . . Dr. Eliot has picked the few really worthwhile books out of the thousands of useless ones . . . and he has arranged them as the *Famous Five-Foot Shelf of Books.*

To which Dr. Eliot adds: "I believe the faithful and considerate reading of these books will give any man the essentials of a liberal education, even if he devotes to them only fifteen minutes a day."
At the time and over the years, the *Five Foot-Book Shelf* (as it came to be known) received its share of spoofing. Nonetheless, it has remained a metaphor for the well-read man.

Flaherty, Robert (1884–1951)   Father of the documentary film, although the term documentary was itself coined by a Scottish educator, John Grierson. Flaherty's first film, *Nanook of the North* (1922), which he made while living among the Eskimos in Hudson Bay country for 12 years, followed the daily patterns of existence in the life of one Eskimo and his family. *Moana* (1926) did the same for the people of Samoa. These were followed by *Man of Aran,* commissioned by Grierson; *Elephant Boy;* and *Louisiana Story.* Flaherty's ambition was to film the life of the peoples of Earth.
He stamped his poetic sensibility, his powers of observation, his genius with the camera, on the documentary genre.

flak   Originally a German acronym for anti-aircraft fire in World War II, the term later was used for a barrage of words or complaints. Now used to denote criticism in response to a controversial idea; for example, a book contending that there is no discrimination against women in science, no matter how cogently argued and statistically proved, is sure to get plenty of flak from the feminists.

Flanders fields   Cemetery in Belgium where white crosses mark the graves of Allied soldiers fallen in World War I. The place has been immortalized in a poem written by the Canadian poet John McCrae (1872–1918). The poem begins:

In Flanders fields the poppies blow
Between the crosses, row on row,
That mark our place.

floor   In boxing, to knock down an opponent. The floored fighter is given 10 seconds—counted out loud by the referee—to get up unassisted to continue the fight.
If he cannot, then he is "down for the count," "knocked out," "K.O'd," "Kayoed."

In general, to "floor" means to defeat, overwhelm, surprise, confound, puzzle.

flower children   Young hippies of the 1960s counterculture who would offer a
flower to policemen or military personnel as a symbol of their nonviolent, pacifist
beliefs. Their slogan was "make love, not war." The term often is used to describe
people with naively idealistic views or a style of dress reminiscent of the 1960s.

Flynn, Errol (1909–1959)   Born in Tasmania, this actor experienced real-life
adventures in the South Seas equal to his swashbuckling roles in such movies as
Captain Blood (1935) and *The Sea Hawk* (1940). He is also thought of as a debonair,
charming seducer of women.

Force, the   See DARTH VADER.

Forest of Arden   A woodland refuge to which all the characters eventually
escape from the cares and intrigues of the court in Shakespeare's romantic comedy,
As You Like It (c. 1600). In this natural setting, all classes mingle, from the banished
Duke Senior and his retainers to the lowly shepherds, shepherdesses and country
wenches. The forest is an equalizer and all engage in the pursuit of happiness, each
in his or her own way: the lords to hunt and sing; the lovers to tease, to pursue, and
to be caught; JACQUES to philosophize in melancholy vein. Even Duke Frederick,
the usurper, makes his way to the healing forest and undergoes a change of heart.
In the end, those who were banished return to the court and their responsibilities
in the real world. The forest can be but a temporary escape.

The Forest of Arden stands for an idyll in which nature exerts a beneficent
influence on character.

"form follows function"   See BAUHAUS.

Forrest Gump   The eponymous "hero" of a 1994 movie starring Tom Hanks in
the title role, Sally Field as his mother, Robin Wright Penn as his sympathetic girlfriend, and Gary Sinise as a handicapped Vietnam veteran. The director was Robert
Zemeckis and the story was based on a novel by Winston Groom. The film won six
Academy Awards in 1995.

Forrest Gump is a 20th-century version of the holy fool, exemplified in "GIMPEL THE FOOL" by I. B. Singer, and Alyosha and PRINCE MISHKIN created by Feodor Dostoevsky. He is simpleminded and innocent but well-intentioned and life affirming, transforming, like PIPPA in "Pippa Passes" by Robert Browning, the lives of those he encounters. By means of cinematic special effects, he is shown to be involved in historic events over four decades. His take on these events is idealistic and eye-opening. One of the movie's most famous lines is "Life is like a box of chocolates—you never know what you're going to get."

Forsyte, Soames   "The man of property" in John Galsworthy's novel of the same name, the first volume (1906) of *The Forsyte Saga,* a series eventually comprising three trilogies, which follows the fortunes and changing mores of several generations of an upper-middle-class British family. The BBC adapted the first six novels in a popular TV series in the 1970s.

Soames Forsyte is a hidebound solicitor who manages the family's business interests. He is stable and honest but unimaginative. He has "bought" his beautiful wife Irene as he has bought the paintings in his collection. They are all assets. She leaves him when she falls in love with Philip Bosinney, an architect whom Soames has hired to build a magnificent house for Irene. When Soames learns about his wife's affair, he asserts his property rights and forces himself upon her. The novel ends tragically with the suicide of Bosinney.

A Soames Forsyte is a man of wealth who looks upon the world as a column of assets and liabilities. He cannot create beauty, but he can buy it.

Fort Knox   Since 1936, U.S. depository of gold bullion, located in Kentucky.

Fort Knox has come to stand as a symbol for any treasure house.

Fort Sumter   The Civil War "officially" began at this federal garrison in the harbor of Charleston, South Carolina, on April 12, 1861, when Confederate forces under General Pierre G. T. Beauregard (1818–93) attacked the fort. Short of supplies and ammunition, the Union commander of the fort eventually surrendered to the Confederates. On April 15, 1861, President Lincoln declared that a state of "insurrection" existed, and called for 74,000 Union volunteers. The bloodiest war in American history had begun.

"Fort Sumter" refers to the opening shot in a rebellion.

Fountain of Youth   A legendary, much sought-after fountain said to be located, among other places, in Bimini, in the Bahamas. The fountain, it was widely believed, had the power to bestow eternal youth on those who bathed in its magical waters.

Juan Ponce de León (c. 1460–1521), a Spanish explorer, set sail in 1512 in search of the fountain. He never found it.

Four Hundred, the   During and following the Civil War, great fortunes were made in America. It was the era of the ROBBER BARONS. Not wholly content with the power and prominence that came with their enormous and often ill-gotten wealth, the newly rich yearned to set themselves apart as a social elite. At the time, no established mechanism existed for constituting or perpetuating such an elite. Into this vacuum stepped the social arbiter, sometimes self-appointed, sometimes chosen by the group.

Among the earliest and most influential of these social arbiters was Ward McAllister (1827–95), a leader of Southern society. He early decided to devote himself, full-time, to "society." He went to Europe to see, firsthand, how the European elect managed their social affairs. On his return, McAllister settled in Newport, Rhode Island, where he devoted himself to making Newport the social capital of America. He gave elaborate dinners and arranged balls. Soon he was the acknowledged leader of Newport society. He then moved to New York where, by 1870, with the help of an inner circle, he became the adviser to the city's "smart set."

McAllister is widely credited with creating the notion of the Four Hundred: In his words, they were the persons "whose opinion could be said to count. If you go outside that number (400) you strike people who are either not at ease in a ball room or else make other people not at ease" (1888).

Another origin of "the Four Hundred" has it that Mrs. William B. Astor gave a ball. When she discovered that her ballroom could not accommodate more than 400, she appealed to McAllister for assistance. Applying his own formula, McAllister came up with the "correct 400."

No matter how "the Four Hundred" originated, it still means an inner circle, a social or intellectual elite, a coterie of socially acceptable Americans. To be one of the Four Hundred still carries with it the stamp of exclusivity.

foxhole   A hole dug into the ground in which a soldier can take cover against enemy fire; a defensive position in warfare. Foxhole mentality has come to refer to defensive strategy in nonmilitary situations, as in politics. During the congressional debate on gun control following the LITTLETON / COLUMBINE massacre in 1999, Republican congressmen, who had at first opposed the mandating of safety locks on guns, adopted a fall-back foxhole position to fend off outraged public opinion and passed the very same bill a couple of days later.

Foxy Grandpa   This comic strip appeared in January 1900, when the comic strips were devoting themselves exclusively to the *Katzenjammer Kids* theme. The full-time preoccupation of the Kids was making the lives of their parents, their teachers and other authority figures miserable with their annoying, sadistic pranks.

Foxy Grandpa changed all that. He gave the Kids a taste of their own medicine, turning the tables on them with ingenious tricks of his own. The public relished seeing the Kids finally get their comeuppance. But the strip enjoyed a relatively brief popularity. By the end of the decade, interest in Foxy Grandpa's shenanigans evaporated. Nonetheless, Foxy Grandpa played his part in altering the stereotype of older folks as hapless victims.

Francis of Assisi, St.   See ST. FRANCIS OF ASSISI.

Frank, Anne (1929–1945)   Writer of *The Diary of Anne Frank,* a journal kept while she and her family were hiding out in an attic in Amsterdam during the Nazi occupation of Holland. The diary expresses with keen observation and honesty all of the feelings, the fears, the hopes, the frustrations, the budding sexual awareness of a young girl in such a fearful situation. The family's hiding place was discovered by the Nazis. All were sent to concentration camps and Anne Frank herself died at Bergen-Belsen at the age of 14. Anne Frank has become a symbol of hope in the midst of horror and despair.

Frankenstein or, The Modern Prometheus (1818)   A GOTHIC novel by Mary Wollstonecraft Shelley. In a series of letters written to his sister in England, Robert Walton, on a voyage to the North Pole, tells of a stranger rescued from the sea. His name is Frankenstein. He comes from Geneva. He is being pursued by a fiend.

As a student in the natural sciences and in the occult, Frankenstein conducted laboratory experiments to create by mechanical means a being that he hopes to imbue with the spark of life, with Promethean fire. But the being he succeeds in creating turns out to be a hideous monster. When Frankenstein refuses to create a mate for the lonely monster, the latter turns upon his creator and embarks upon a vicious vendetta. He destroys Frankenstein's brother, best friend and wife, and pursues Frankenstein himself over land and sea with implacable purpose. Frankenstein, worn out and despairing, dies aboard ship as the ghoulish monster hovers over him. The monster then plunges overboard and disappears into the Arctic mists.

By a strange reversal, the name "Frankenstein" is often mistakenly applied not to the scientist, but to the monster itself; people will say of an experiment gone awry, "You have created a Frankenstein that will come back to haunt you." Some people fear that genetic experimentation with DNA, for example, may create uncontrollable Frankensteins.

"Frankly, my dear, I don't give a damn"   Rhett Butler's final words of rejection to Scarlett O'Hara's pleas of helplessness in Margaret Mitchell's best-selling novel of the Civil War, *Gone With the Wind* (1936). The two were played by Clark Gable and Vivien Leigh in a 1939 movie.

"free at last" See "I HAVE A DREAM."

Freudian Pertaining to the psychoanalytic theories, practices and terminology formulated by the Viennese neuropathologist Sigmund Freud (1856–1939). Freud added a new dimension to man's understanding of himself; namely, the subconscious, to which are relegated repressions of instinctual sexual desires. These repressed desires emerge in garbled form in dreams and in free association. Freud postulated within each person the ID (primitive instinct), the ego (the developing self) and the superego (demands of culture), with the ego trying to accommodate the pull of the other two. Central to Freud's theories was the Oedipus complex (the child's natural sexual desire for the parent of the opposite sex). The child's eventual sublimation of this desire was necessary for his healthy development. Neurosis was caused by fixation on an infantile oral or anal phase of sexual development or by unresolved repressions. The psychoanalyst guided the patient, lying on a couch and freely associating, to relive his early experiences and through transference to work out the blocks to his normal development.

Freudian terms have become part of the vernacular but with little understanding of their meaning. Mostly, "Freudian" conjures up sexual obsessions and perversities. Everybody bandies about phrases like "castration complex," "death wish," "Oedipus complex," "Freudian slip," "fixation," "the id."

Use: Hemingway's second novel, *The Torrents of Spring,* was a savage parody of Sherwood Anderson, a writer who had been his mentor and who had befriended him in many ways. Dwight Macdonald theorized that Hemingway "had to kill the Freudian father in order to make his own place in the world of letters." (George Plimpton, *New York Times* Book Review, April 16, 1989)

Friar Tuck Jolly, fat friar in the company of ROBIN HOOD's merry men, a band of outlaws living in Sherwood Forest.

"Friar Tuck" is often used as an allusion to a physical type: fat, short and jolly, as well as a humorous, practical, unceremonious antihero.

Friday, Joe See *DRAGNET.*

Friday, Man/Gal See CRUSOE, ROBINSON.

Friedan, Betty See *FEMININE MYSTIQUE.*

friendly fire Paradoxical term for casualties inflicted not by the enemy but by your own side in combat, your so-called friends. In the Gulf War, more than 20

American servicemen were killed and about 472 were wounded by their own forces in strikes that mistook them for the enemy.

The term, which emerged in the Vietnam War, has come to be applied to damage caused unwittingly by friends and relations on the domestic front.

Führer   This German word for "leader" is now associated with a dictator of a particularly heinous virulence.

full-court press   A term taken from the game of basketball to describe a defensive strategy in which all five members of one team make a concerted effort to prevent the player holding the ball on the opposing team from passing it on to his teammates for the purpose of scoring a basket.

The term has been extended to the fields of business, politics, war and even personal relations to indicate an all-out effort to beat an opponent or to obtain a desired goal.

Use: "The West should apply a full-court press to stop terrorism throughout the world."

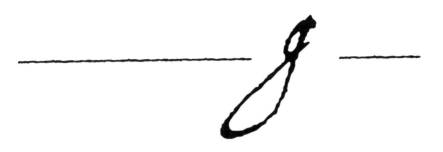

Gable, Clark (1900–1960)   Perhaps the most glamorous male sex symbol and leading man of his time, he became synonymous with Rhett Butler, a role he played in the movie version of *Gone with the Wind* (1939). Butler, handsome, dashing, devil-may-care, dared to stand up to and eventually abandon the tempestuous Southern belle Scarlett O'Hara (Vivien Leigh). Gable starred in many other films, including *It Happened One Night* (1934), *Mutiny on the Bounty* (1935) and *The Misfits* (1961), but he remains, in the popular imagination, the embodiment of Rhett Butler.

Galahad, Sir   In Sir Thomas Malory's *Le Morte Darthur* (c. 1469), he is the illegitimate son of Lancelot and the princess Elaine, who was descended from Joseph of Arimathea. Galahad proved to be the purest of the Knights of the Round Table. He alone could sit in the Siege Perilous reserved for that knight who would succeed in the Quest for the Holy GRAIL, the cup that held a drop of Christ's blood. Many had tried, but all except Galahad had failed in achieving that epiphany.

Galileo (Galileo Galilei) (1564–1642)   Italian philosopher, physicist, mathematician, astronomer, he attracted students from all over the world. In 1632 he published his *Dialogue on Great World Systems,* which defended the theory of the Polish astronomer Nikolaus Copernicus (1473–1543) that the earth and related planets revolved around the sun. Earlier, the Catholic Church had declared that the sun and planets revolved around the earth, and that the Copernican theory was a heresy. In 1633, the church summoned Galileo before the Inquisition. Fearing excommunication and the loss of all opportunities to work and study, Galileo recanted, admitting that he had erred in supporting Copernicus's theory. Legend has it that as he rose from his knees, he stamped his foot and muttered under his breath: *"Eppur si muove"* (and still it [the earth] moves [around the sun]). For the rest of his life, Galileo remained under virtual house arrest.

Galileo remains a symbol of quiet defiance of despotic authority.

game plan   In sports, a team's meticulously planned strategy for winning a game.

In general use, any well-conceived, carefully worked-out plan or course of action designed to achieve a specific goal, as in business, government, one's personal affairs.

Use: "If you expect to succeed in today's risky market, you've got to have a well worked-out game plan."

Gandhi, Mohandas Karamchand (1869–1948)   Also known as Mahatma (great-souled) Gandhi, he was the political and spiritual leader of India in its struggle for independence from British rule. Although he had been born into a rich Indian family and had practiced law in England, India and South Africa, Gandhi ultimately broke with his upper-class traditions and lived the life of an ascetic, taking vows of poverty and celibacy. He inspired and led a mass movement for Indian independence through nonviolent means, civil disobedience, passive resistance, noncooperation, protest marches, boycotts and strikes. He was arrested and imprisoned by the British many times. Periodically, he undertook fasts, "fasts unto death," to achieve his goals. He favored a return to simple village life and promoted, even by personal example, participation in cottage industries. In 1947, having finally persuaded Britain that its position as colonial ruler of India was no longer tenable, he helped negotiate Indian independence. In 1948, at the age of 78, he was assassinated by a Hindu fanatic.

Lean, emaciated, wearing only a loin cloth, Gandhi struck an odd figure in modern times, but he was universally recognized as a symbol of selfless, nonviolent struggle for freedom and justice.

gangbusters   *Gang Busters* was a very popular radio program in the 1930s. It usually featured violent stories of "crime and punishment," opening with sirens, shots, screeching of brakes. The police officers specialized in breaking up organized crime by sensational, forceful, aggressive means.

Over the years, the word "gangbusters" has taken on other meanings: having an unusual impact, done with great speed, force, success, strikingly effective.

Use: The new chancellor of the school came on like gangbusters with his reform program.

Gang That Couldn't Shoot Straight, The   A best-selling book by Jimmy Breslin about a gang of clumsy, inept New York City crooks. In 1971 it was adapted as a comic film directed by James Goldstone with Robert De Niro, Jerry Orbach and Lionel Stander. The term is now applied to any bungling faction, whether in business, sports or politics. For example, the political commentator Kevin Philips referred to the Republicans in Congress as "the gang that couldn't shoot straight," citing several recent political fiascoes, among them shutting down the government just before the presidential election of 1996 and the partisan handling of President

Clinton's impeachment proceedings in 1998–99. National Public Radio commentator Daniel Schorr, referring to NATO's inadvertent 1999 bombing of the Chinese embassy in Belgrade, lambasted the CIA as "the gang that couldn't read its maps straight."

Gant, Eugene   Hero of *Look Homeward, Angel* (1929), an autobiographical novel by Thomas Wolfe (1900–38). One of a large, rambunctious family living in North Carolina, he is a youth eager to break away and get to the "big city," where art lives. He has the ineffable yearnings, large ambitions and poetic sensibilities of certain very bright adolescents convinced of their own specialness and even genius. He is a modern example of "the young man from the provinces" like the hero of Flaubert's *Sentimental Education.*

Gantry, Elmer   Main character in the satirical novel of the same name written in 1927 by Sinclair Lewis and adapted for the movies in 1960. He is a charlatan and hypocrite who becomes a successful evangelist.

Garbo, Greta (1905–1990)   Born Greta Gustafsson in Sweden, hers was perhaps the most beautiful face in the history of cinema. Reserved, mysterious, aloof, private; summed up in her famous but spurious line, "I vant to be alone." Her low, husky, accented voice thrilled moviegoers from the time of her first talkie, *Anna Christie* (1930), advertised simply: "Garbo Talks." She starred in *Flesh and the Devil,* a 1927 silent movie with John Gilbert, and in *Anna Karenina* (1935), *Ninotchka* (1939) and many others. Her retirement in 1941, at the height of her career, only added to her allure.

Garbo stands for feminine mystery combined with exquisite beauty.

Garden of Earthly Delights   See BOSCH, HIERONYMUS.

Gargantuan   Outsized, like Gargantua in *Gargantua and Pantagruel,* a 16th-century satire on French institutions, customs and attitudes, by Francois Rabelais (c. 1494–1553).

Gargantua was the son of Grandgousier and Gargamelle. He was born in the eleventh month out of his mother's left ear, shouting, "Drink, drink, drink!" Whether this injunction referred to spirits or to knowledge, nobody knows—he had a great thirst for both. At any rate, like the hero in medieval folklore upon whom his character is based, he was born a giant, with a giant's appetite. In infancy he daily required the milk of 17,913 cows. Soon wine replaced milk in his diet. When he was two, his blue and white costume was made from 1,350 yards of linen for the shirt, 1,219 yards of white satin for the doublet, 1,657 yards of light wool for the hose, $24\frac{1}{4}$ yards for his capacious codpiece, and 2,400 yards of blue velvet for his cape.

"Gargantuan" has become a common word in the English language and always means huge or tremendous. See RABELAISIAN.

Gaslight (1944)   Movie thriller, directed by George Cukor and starring Ingrid Bergman and Charles Boyer, about a sophisticated man who subtly and insinuatingly tries to make his wife question her own sanity.

–gate   A suffix that alludes to the WATERGATE scandal of the Nixon presidency, and has come to indicate political corruption and scandal in high places. During the Reagan presidency in the 1980s, the term "IRANGATE" was coined, and during the Clinton presidency in the 1990s the term "Travelgate," "Filegate" and "Monicagate" entered the vocabulary.

The suffix has been appended to foreign scandals as well. For example, "Baligate" refers to a bank scandal in Indonesia in which $70 million paid to a finance company was thought to have been diverted into the election campaign of President B. J. Habibie. "Camillagate" refers to the scandal in England when it became widely known that the Prince of Wales, married to Princess Diana, was having an adulterous affair with Mrs. Camilla Parker Bowles.

Even the unsubstantiated rumor of scandal now has "–gate" affixed to it, as in "snortgate," referring to George W. Bush's possible youthful experimentation with cocaine.

Gates, Bill (1955–   )   The richest man in the world, according to the June 1999 issue of *Forbes* magazine, worth about 90 billion dollars.

A brilliant "nerd" who dropped out of Harvard University, he and his friend Paul Allen founded the software company Microsoft in 1975. After Allen left Microsoft, Gates took over the company. In 1980 he got his big break by making a deal with IBM to supply all its computers with the Microsoft disc operating system (MS-DOS), for which Gates received royalties of $200 million a year. Gates proved to be a brilliant businessman. In April 2000 Microsoft was found guilty of monopolistic practices in an antitrust case brought by the U.S. government.

A Bill Gates is a phenomenally successful technological business genius, as in a reference to "Stanley Shih, the Bill Gates of Taiwan."

Gather ye rosebuds   First three words of "To the Virgins, to Make Much of Time," a poem by the English Cavalier poet Robert Herrick (1591–1674). The first stanza advises:

Gather ye rosebuds while ye may,
Old Time is still a-flying;
And this same flower that smiles today
Tomorrow will be dying.

Although Herrick addresses his poem to young girls and warns them to marry before their beauty fades, the phrase "gather ye rosebuds," like Horace's "carpe diem," means, Enjoy the pleasures of life while you can, make the most of every opportunity, and not just for love, because Time is the great destroyer.

Gatling gun   The first practical machine gun, built in 1862 by the American inventor Richard Jordan Gatling (1818–1903). It fired 350 rounds per minute. In 1866, an improved model was approved by the War Department. In 1870, Gatling moved to Hartford, Connecticut, to supervise the manufacture of the Gatling Gun by the Colt Patent Fire Arms Manufacturing Company. Here, Gatling's improvements in the gun's mechanism enabled it to fire 1,200 rounds per minute.

"Gatling gun" now refers to anything with a metaphorical rapid-fire mechanism.

Use: "[Pat] Buchanan is a Gatling Gun firing military metaphors." (George Will, *Newsweek,* March 23, 1992)

Gatsby, Jay   Central character in *The Great Gatsby* (1925), a novel by F. SCOTT FITZGERALD. In Gatsby we see the corruption and vanity of that part of the AMERICAN DREAM that exalts great wealth as the means to happiness and success. Gatsby was a midwestern boy who fell in love with the beautiful Daisy, several notches above him in wealth and social class. To get her, he amassed a fortune from bootlegging and gangsterism. He bought a mansion on Long Island and gave big parties where he felt like a stranger, an outsider. But Daisy had married the enormously rich and brutal Tom Buchanan. Gatsby's life was empty except for his continuing devotion to the dream of Daisy. In the end, his illusions as to the true nature of the very rich betrayed him. Fitzgerald deals sympathetically with this falsely romantic and, some say, tragic character.

Gaudí, Antonio (1852–1926)   Spanish architect who worked mostly in Barcelona. His buildings are like pastry pastiches, as if stone had been made as malleable as clay or wax and shaped into extraordinarily decorative and decorated organic shapes encrusted with glass, ceramics, etc. Some of his best known structures are the Casa Mila (1905–10); the Church of the Sagrada Familia, of cathedral proportions; and the Colonia Guell Church and Park (1914).

Genovese, Kitty   At 3 A.M., the morning of March 13, 1964, Kitty Genovese (1935–64) was murdered on her way home to her Queens, New York, apartment. Her killer, Winston Moseley, attacked her three times. First, he stabbed her on Austin Street in Kew Gardens. As Kitty staggered to her home, Moseley returned and stabbed her for the second time. He drove off. Then he returned again to find Kitty in the hallway of her apartment. There, he stabbed her for the third time— and left her dying. Moseley was later apprehended, tried and sentenced to life imprisonment.

Police investigation revealed that at least 37 people witnessed the murder of Kitty Genovese. Not one called the police.

Some of the people who saw and heard what was happening said:

"I didn't want to get involved."

"Frankly, we were afraid."

"I was tired. I went back to bed."

"I don't know."

The behavior of the onlookers and witnesses has been labeled the Kitty Genovese syndrome, a dramatic illustration of the extent to which fear of crime has saturated our society and created a frightening, deliberate noninvolvement in the lives of our neighbors.

gentleman caller   From *The Glass Menagerie* (1944), a play by Tennessee Williams. Amanda Wingfield, the mother of Tom, the narrator, lives in a largely imaginary past when as a Southern belle she entertained many gentlemen callers. Abandoned by her husband, living in genteel poverty in St. Louis, she urges Tom to bring home a gentleman caller for his very shy, crippled sister Laura. Tom brings home Jim, a kind young coworker in the warehouse. Accidentally, Jim breaks off the horn of the unicorn, Laura's favorite animal in her glass animal collection. Nevertheless, Laura and Jim hit it off. She comes out of her shyness for once, but in a tender moment Jim confesses that he is engaged to another girl. Laura withdraws again into the world of her glass menagerie. The gentleman caller scheme has backfired, with the fragile Laura broken as surely as the unicorn.

A gentleman caller is one who calls on a girl and instantly becomes a prospective suitor.

Genghis Khan (1162–1227)   A Mongol emperor who conquered vast areas of Asia and Eastern Europe and laid the foundations for the Ottoman Empire. True to his name, which means "perfect warrior," Genghis Khan is known as one of the greatest, if most savage generals in history. His grandson, Kublai Khan, cultivated the arts as emperor of China after 1259, and his lavish court inspired the tales of

MARCO POLO as well as the poem "Kubla Khan" by Samuel Taylor Coleridge. Genghis Khan's great-great-grandson, Tamerlane (1336–1405), reverted, however, to Genghis's pattern of conquest and cruelty.

Geritol   A trade name (probably derived from the same root as "geriatrics," the study of diseases of old age) for an elixir to energize mostly tired old people. The word is often used derisively, as in "the Geritol crowd."

Use: "Here in Los Angeles, investigators speak of the Mickey Mouse Mafia and say the mob is so enfeebled that illegal bookmakers refuse to pay it for the right to operate. . . . And in New Jersey . . . the State Police Superintendent calls the Bruno-Scarfo group the 'Geritol gang,' so aged and ineffective does he find its leaders." (*New York Times,* October 22, 1990)

Geronimo (1829–1909)   The last American Indian chief to surrender to the United States Army. After Mexico ceded vast lands in the Southwest to the United States in 1848, the American authorities set limits on where the Apaches could live. The Apaches, understandably, objected to such confinement. Geronimo and his followers periodically broke out of their reservation, and the U.S. Army's attempts to capture them were not conspicuously successful. The Apaches knew the terrain well—much better than their pursuers. In a series of what the authorities called "cunning, brutal raids," Geronimo and his followers terrorized the white settlers in the Southwest.

Finally Geronimo and his men surrendered to General Nelson Miles of the U.S. Army in Skeleton Canyon, Arizona, on September 4, 1886.

Legend has it that once Geronimo, pursued by a U.S. cavalry unit, made a daring leap on horseback from Medicine Bluffs, Oklahoma, into the river below, defiantly crying out "Geronimo!" Although this incident does not appear in Geronimo's autobiography (1909), it has become an ineradicable part of the Geronimo mystique. World War II U.S. paratroopers in the North African invasion (1942) shouted "Geronimo!"—an exclamation of daring and defiance—as they parachuted behind Nazi lines.

gestalt   From the German word meaning "form" or "pattern," gestalt psychology suggests that people respond not to individual elements within a scene or situation but rather to the pattern that they discern these elements to make. The whole is different from the sum of its parts. Different people may see different configurations emerging from the same collection of elements.

Use: Perestroika and glasnost are but two elements in a whole gestalt of revolutionary change introduced by Gorbachev in the Soviet Union.

Gestapo   Abbreviation of *Geheime Staatspolizei,* the German secret state police organized in 1933 by Hermann Göring as a Nazi instrument of terror, for the suppression of all opposition to Hitler. Gradually it became absorbed into the SS (Schutzstaffel) under Heinrich Himmler, and merged with the SS's Sicherheitsdienst (SD), under Reinhard Heydrich.

The term "Gestapo tactics" refers to heavy-handed actions, an arbitrary use of power intended to coerce or intimidate.

get to first base   In baseball, to get to the first of the four bases, in counterclockwise order as seen from home plate.

In general, to succeed in the first phase of an undertaking, to begin well, take a successful first step. In a romantic relationship, getting to first base is commonly understood to be the first step or steps leading to greater intimacy, attaining a status short of actual intercourse.

See also SCORE.

Gettysburg Address, the   On July 1, 1863, General Robert E. Lee invaded Pennsylvania with 70,000 Confederate men. He faced General George Meade's Army of the Potomac at Gettysburg, Pennsylvania. The three-day battle, climaxed by Pickett's disastrous "Napoleonic charge," left 6,000 dead and 40,000 wounded on the battlefield.

It was here at Cemetery Ridge, on November 19, 1863, that President Abraham Lincoln delivered his famous Gettysburg Address dedicating Gettysburg as a national cemetery. The main speaker at the ceremony was Edward Everett, a famous orator of the day. He spoke for two hours. Lincoln's address lasted a few minutes.

Contrary to popular legend, Lincoln did not write his speech on the back of a piece of brown paper or an envelope en route to the dedication ceremonies. Actually, it was a carefully crafted address. At least five versions of the address exist.

Lincoln's prediction about the fate of the address has proved wrong: "The world will little note nor long remember what we say here—but can never forget what they did here." William McFeely, reviewing Garry Will's *Lincoln at Gettysburg* (*New York Times Book Review,* June 7, 1992), calls the Gettysburg Address "our nation's greatest garnering of words—an authoritative expression of the American spirit, perhaps even more influential since it determines how we read the Declaration—the greatest of all political speeches."

ghetto   The origin of this word is in dispute, but sources agree that it is from the Italian, either from *getto* (meaning "cannon factory" and, by association, the Jewish quarter in Venice adjacent to the factory there) or from Il Geto, an island in Venice to which Jews were consigned.

In the early Middle Ages, Jews tended to congregate in certain enclaves around a synagogue, because of common interests, customs, language and religious observances. By the end of the 14th century, Jews in Spain and Portugal were *forced* to live in ghettos, areas enclosed by walls with gates. These gates were locked at night. A Jew who had to work outside the ghetto during the day was required to wear either a yellow badge or a yellow hat so he could be easily spotted. In 1555, Pope Paul IV issued a papal bull requiring all Jews within Vatican controlled territories to be confined in ghettos. In 1870, with the end of papal authority in Italy, the last compulsory ghetto in Italy was abolished.

The Nazis reinstituted walled ghettos in the early 1940s with the most brutal and repressive measures. The most infamous of these was the Warsaw Ghetto, which at one time contained 500,000 Jews who were eventually transported to the death camps at Auschwitz and other locations. The Warsaw Ghetto uprising (1943) of a handful of Jews against the German military machine was an act of valor and glory, even if doomed to failure.

Today the word "ghetto" covers not just neighborhoods where Jews are concentrated, but also neighborhoods where, because of economic necessity, ethnic groups and minorities tend to congregate; such as Harlem in New York City and Watts in Los Angeles. The term "middle-class ghetto" has also come into use for provincial neighborhoods lacking cultural aspirations and opportunities.

GI   A regularly enlisted soldier in the U.S. Armed Forces. Originally an abbreviation from the "galvanized iron" trash cans used in the army; then from all "government issue" items, like GI uniforms, GI blankets, GI mess pans and even GI haircuts; then applied to the soldier himself. GI used as an adjective means regimented, standardized.

Giacometti, Alberto (1901–1966)   Swiss sculptor whose thin, elongated, emaciated, skeletal, open-cage figures suggest the pain and isolation of modern man.

Gibraltar   A fortress and seaport, a British Crown colony since 1704, Gibraltar is located on Spain's southern coast. Only $2.^3/_4$ miles long, $^3/_4$ miles wide, and rising to a height of 1,398 feet, it occupies a virtually impregnable position athwart the entrance to the Mediterranean Sea. Its name derives from an Arab leader, Tarik, who conquered it. The present name "Gibraltar" is a corruption of the Arabic *Jebal-el-Tarik,* Tarik's Mountain.

Gibraltar (widely known as the Rock) has become a symbol of great strength, solidity and endurance. The Prudential Insurance Company, one of America's largest, has used a sketch of Gibraltar on its official stationery and in its advertising, with the slogan "Get a piece of the Rock."

Gibson girl   An image of ideal American femininity created by the New York artist and illustrator Charles Dana Gibson (1867–1944). In pen and ink Gibson drew a wholesome, full-bosomed, small-waisted girl with long hair piled like a halo around her head. She wore a high-necked blouse with puff sleeves and a long skirt slightly flared at the ankles. She engaged in athletic as well as social and romantic activities. Although her time was the turn of the century, the Gibson girl remains a vision of clean, wholesome, lovely womanhood.

Gideon Bible   A cheaply printed Bible found in virtually every hotel room in America. It is provided for the comfort and solace of travelers by an international Christian society established in 1898 by a few traveling salesmen who found themselves alone in a small hotel without Christian services or facilities. They called themselves the Gideons after a judge in ancient Israel who freed the Israelites from their oppressors, the Midianites.

The Gideon Bible has come to be a symbol of ubiquity. You can't leave home without coming upon it.

G.I. Joe   Comic strip created during World War II (June 17, 1942) by David Breger (1908–70) for *Yank,* the United States Army's enlisted man's magazine. The American troops, here and overseas, and the American public embraced *G.I. Joe* with universal affection. Based on Breger's experiences as a rookie, it quickly entered the language as both the military and civilian name for the American foot soldier.

Gilbert and Sullivan   Before William Schwenk Gilbert (1836–1911) and Sir Arthur Seymour Sullivan (1842–1900) teamed up to become the longest running and most successful partnership in musico-dramatic history, each was fairly undistinguished in his own field: Gilbert as a playwright and author of light verse, Sullivan as a composer. Together, they worked magic, creating such immensely popular and seemingly immortal operettas as *Trial by Jury* (1875), *H.M.S. Pinafore* (1878), *The Pirates of Penzance* (1879), *Patience* (1881), *Iolanthe* (1882) and *The Mikado* (1885).

These operettas lightly and charmingly satirize in song and story a variety of Victorian pieties: the law, the navy, the House of Lords, the education of women, aesthetes. Gilbert's witty verse is tempered by Sullivan's good-natured, memorable melodies. In 1999, Gilbert and Sullivan's creation of "The Mikado" was dramatized brilliantly in the film *Topsy-Turvy.*

The name Gilbert and Sullivan, taken together, has become a trademark as inseparable as ham and eggs or fish and chips. It stands for rollicking, irreverent, satirical musical drama. See POOH BAH Bunthorne.

Gilded Age, the   The title of an 1873 novel by Mark Twain and Charles Dudley Warner that came to represent the period of post–Civil War financial speculation, greed, vulgarity and extravagance in America. "Gilded" suggests the period's bogus, superficial quality, its "appearance" of the genuine gold; the moral shoddiness of the characters and their enterprises is the book's central theme. All the characters are modeled after real people. William Weed and his political gang, for example, are none other than Boss Tweed and his unsavory cronies.

"Gilded" applied to any period is a pejorative commentary on its essential hollowness, immorality and cynicism, but "Gilded Age" often loses its negative associations in contemporary use, as in columnist Anna Quindlen's reference to "that gilded age called youth."

"give 'em hell, Harry"   In his 1948 campaign for the presidency, Harry Truman told his running mate, Alben Barkley, "I'm going to fight hard. I'm going to give them hell." "Them" were the "vested interests" and the "do-nothing Congress." At every whistle stop during the campaign, the crowds would shout, "Give 'em hell, Harry!" Against the odds and the polls, Truman defeated Thomas E. Dewey.

To "give 'em hell" is to charge fearlessly at one's opponents by speaking the truth.

"Give me liberty or give me death"   Patrick Henry (1736–99), a fiery orator and a leader of the southern forces of revolt against the king of England, uttered these ringing words on March 23, 1775, before the Virginia convention held in St. John's Episcopal Church, Richmond, Virginia:

> Is life so dear, or peace so sweet, as to be purchased at the price of chains and slavery? Forbid it, Almighty God! I know not what course others may take—but as for me, give me liberty or give me death.

glasnost   The Russian term for speaking out. Initiated by the charismatic leader of the U.S.S.R., Mikhail Gorbachev, glasnost is a relaxation of censorship, a thaw in repression, a new sense of liberation from restraint. Socialism with a human face.

Use: "The best you can say about the Arab world today is that it is finally entering its Gorbachev phase: it is trying glasnost without perestroika." (Thomas Friedman, *New York Times,* February 12, 1999)

glass ceiling   A term originally used by feminists to suggest an invisible and unacknowledged barrier above which women may not be promoted to top positions in business or other professions, this expression also is applied to the seeming inability of minorities to climb to top positions in management, even in professional sports in which they excel as players.

Godard, Jean-Luc (1930–) French film director who made his reputation with *Breathless* (1959), a tradition-shattering movie with Jean-Paul Belmondo as a small-time Parisian punk and Jean Seberg as his American girl. Belmondo, who has stolen a car and killed a cop, is being chased by the police. He has grown up in a movie era and associates himself with the gangster heroes of American movies. Godard is associated with the *Nouvelle Vague* (new wave) films from young French and Italian filmmakers, beginning in the late 1950s, which broke with traditional concepts.

godfather Originally, one who sponsors a child at baptism, the older and still most common use. More recently, however, "godfather" has acquired another meaning: a powerful leader of a criminal enterprise, especially of the MAFIA. In 1972, Mario Puzo's best-selling novel *The Godfather* (1969) was turned into the Academy Award–winning film of the same name, directed by Francis Ford Coppola and starring Marlon Brando.

go the distance In boxing, being able to last the scheduled number of rounds without being knocked out or judged a technical knockout.

In general use, to go all the way to one's goal or destination.

Use: Jack surprised us all when he graduated from college. We never thought he'd go the distance.

Godiva, Lady See PEEPING TOM.

Godot The mysterious character who never shows up in *Waiting for Godot,* a 1952 tragicomedy by Samuel Beckett (1906–89), an Irish playwright who wrote in French. Two tramps, Estragon and Vladimir, wait for Godot, but they are not sure where and when he is supposed to arrive. Two other characters come along: Pozzo, the master, driving the exploited Lucky at the end of a rope. What these characters represent has been a subject of intense speculation. Nobody really knows.

"Waiting for Godot" has entered the language to mean waiting endlessly and helplessly for somebody or something that never materializes.

Use: Waiting for cable TV in the Bronx was like waiting for Godot.

God That Failed, The Title of a book of autobiographical essays by six disillusioned writers who came to realize that their faith in the Russian Revolution, in communism as practiced in the Soviet Union under Stalin, was a misplaced faith. Communism was a false god, the god that failed, and they rejected it. The writers were Arthur Koestler, Ignazio Silone, Richard Wright, André Gide, Louis Fischer and Stephen Spender. The book was edited by Richard Crossman and published in 1949.

Goetz, Bernhard   New York City subway rider who in December 1984 shot and wounded four black youths who tried to mug him. The case aroused passionate controversy because of general revulsion against widespread violence in the cities and the perception that police agencies were unable to protect the public. Indicted originally on four counts of attempted murder, Goetz eventually was found guilty only of carrying an illegal weapon.

Goetz's name has become synonymous, for some, with vigilantism, for others, with self-defense in the absence of police protection.

Gogh, Vincent van   See VAN GOGH, VINCENT.

Gogo   See ESTRAGON and GODOT.

Goldberg, Rube (1883–1970)   Comic strip artist Reuben (Rube) Goldberg drew imaginative drawings of odd, daffy, highly complex machinery or gimmicks designed to achieve the simplest of ends.

Use: "It took parliamentary contortions worthy of Rube Goldberg—but Texas legislators last week finally adopted a spending and revenue blueprint that staved off financial chaos." (*New York Times,* July 26, 1987)

Golden Pond   A serene little lake in the country in the play *On Golden Pond* (1979) by Ernest Thompson. To their cottage on this lake an aged couple have retired to spend their last years in peace and loving tranquility. The couple originally were played by Hume Cronyn and Jessica Tandy on stage and by Henry Fonda and Katharine Hepburn in the screen version (1981).

"Golden Pond" has become synonymous with an unspoiled, idyllic retreat.

Goldilocks   In the nursery tale "Goldilocks and the Three Bears," this little girl wanders into the bears' house. Nobody is home. She tastes their porridge. She sits in their chairs. She goes upstairs and tries out their beds: Baby Bear's is just right.

When the Three Bears return from their walk in the woods, they find Goldilocks asleep in Baby Bear's bed. "Somebody's been eating my porridge!" "Somebody's been sitting in my chair!" "Somebody's been sleeping in my bed!" says each of them in turn. Goldilocks awakens and runs out of the house, never to return. Her name is used to describe a blonde child.

The Three Bears have become just as much an allusion as Goldilocks. They usually stand for differences in size affecting differences in quality, as in references to "Papa, Mama and Baby Bear" computers to suit different customers.

Goldwynism   Any unwitting humorous twist or idiom attributed originally, perhaps apocryphally, to Sam Goldwyn (1883–1974), pioneer film producer. It is a modern version of a MALAPROPISM. Some examples are: "Include me out." "Anyone who goes to a psychiatrist ought to have his head examined." "I'll say it in two words: im-possible." "We have all passed a lot of water since then." See BERRAISM.

"Good fences make good neighbors"   From the poem "Mending Wall" (1914) by Robert Frost (1875–1963). The line is ironic, since Frost questions the need for fences between his apple orchard and his neighbor's pines. Neither has cows that might trespass. Frost writes:

> *Something there is that doesn't love a wall . . .*
> *Before I built a wall I'd ask to know*
> *What I was walling in or walling out*

But his neighbor, "like an old-stone savage armed" who "moves in darkness . . . not of woods only," doggedly clings to the old saw: "Good fences make good neighbors."

The phrase is often quoted to show the futility of outworn barriers between classes or nations—and sometimes *mis*quoted to insist that barriers are necessary to maintain peaceful relations.

Good Housekeeping Seal of Approval   In 1910, *Good Housekeeping* magazine set up its own laboratories to test the products and claims of its advertisers. It accepted advertisements only for those products that passed its own tests for reliability, safety and other standards. It also checked the claims its advertisers made for their products. Originally, the products that passed its battery of tests received the Good Housekeeping Seal of Approval—a much prized award. It was widely accepted as a sign that a product measured up to Good Housekeeping's high standards. The expression "Good Housekeeping Seal of Approval" has now been extended to mean any significant stamp of approval.

Goodman, Benjamin David (Benny) (1909–1986)   Musician, bandleader. After playing with various jazz bands, Benny Goodman put his own band together in 1934. With the help of the gifted arranger Fletcher Henderson, Benny developed his own "big band" style: tightly woven, driving ensemble work overlaid with the improvisations of fine soloists. In short, Benny ushered in a new kind of jazz called swing, and quite naturally was crowned "The King of Swing"—a title he wore with dignity and aplomb.

Goody Two-Shoes   In a story published by John Newberry in 1765 and rumored to have been written by Oliver Goldsmith, the main characters, Margery and her brother Tommy, are orphaned and separated in childhood. Tommy eventually becomes a sailor. Margery, neglected and ragged, goes about with only one shoe. When a benefactor gives her a pair of shoes, she is utterly delighted. Thereafter she is called Little Goody Two-Shoes. She learns to read and becomes a tutor to the children of the neighboring villages. She marries a wealthy man and devotes herself to a program of good works. At her death the poor weep for her.

In modern usage, Goody Two-Shoes is a disparaging term for a too-good-to-be-true, butter-wouldn't-melt-in-her-mouth person.

Gotham   A town in Nottinghamshire, England, one of the several towns all over the world whose inhabitants are in legend supposed to have been simpletons (see CHELM). In the case of Gotham, its people may have been smarter than they let on. They may only have pretended to be silly so that King John would give up his idea of establishing a dwelling there or of building a highway through the town. At any rate, one may read all about the Gothamites in a 16th-century collection of tales called *Merie Tales of the Mad Men of Gotham, gathered together by A.B. of Phisike, Doctour.*

"Gotham" is also a satiric appellation given to New York City by Washington Irving (1783–1859) in his *Salmagundi Papers.* This was a nice way of calling the city a madhouse.

Gothic   An adjective derived from the Goths, the barbarians who sacked Rome in 410. How "Gothic" came to be applied to the architecture of the 12th through 16th centuries in Europe is conjectural. The Goths were a cruel, primitive people; the Gothic cathedrals are among the noblest works of man. Perhaps a new style always seems barbaric to defenders of tradition.

The Gothic style in architecture was introduced at St-Denis, just outside of Paris, by Abbot Suger in the years 1137 to 1144. He transformed the original Romanesque abbey by tearing down the massive stone walls, opening up the interior space and enveloping it in a skin of luminescent stained glass windows, and using pointed arches and ribbed vaults. As cathedrals in France soared ever higher and higher, flying buttresses of stone, invisible from the airy interior, supported these grand edifices on the exterior. Examples of great Gothic cathedrals are Chartres, Notre-Dame de Paris, Amiens and Bourges.

Another leap of conjecture is necessary to understand the "Gothic" in literature. The Gothic romance is usually set in a gloomy castle or mansion haunted by ghosts or demented outcasts. An innocent young person comes to live in such a setting and does not discover the full horror of the place until the end of the book. The Gothic novel flourished in England from the late 18th century (e.g., *The Castle of Otranto,* 1764, by Horace Walpole) to the early 19th century (e.g., *Frankenstein,* 1818, by Mary Shelley). In the novels of the Brontë sisters, Gothic elements were transformed into great literature: *Jane Eyre* (1847) by Charlotte Brontë (1816–55) and *Wuthering Heights* (1847) by Emily Brontë (1818–48).

In *Jane Eyre,* for example, Jane, an orphan, takes a job as governess at isolated Thornfield Hall. Her charge is the illegitimate daughter of the saturnine master of the house, Mr. Rochester. From the attic come the piercing screams and occasional appearances of a disheveled, crazy woman. Rochester falls in love with Jane and asks her to marry him. When Jane discovers that the woman in the attic is really Rochester's mad Creole wife, she flees. Mrs. Rochester sets fire to the house and dies in it, while Rochester is blinded while trying to rescue her. Jane returns to care for Rochester. The famous final sentence of the book is, "Reader, I married him."

"Gothic" in modern use refers to tales, situations, places characterized by intrigue, moody persons, violent passions and supernatural elements.

Götterdämmerung   In Norse mythology, *Götterdämmerung* (German for "twilight of the gods") stands for the end of the world, preceded by a titanic battle between the good and the evil gods. Out of the ashes of this gigantic conflict, a new world will arise.

Richard Wagner (1813–83), German composer and author, drew upon these titanic encounters for his great opera cycle, *Der Ring des Nibelungen* (*The Ring of the Nibelungs*). The last of the four operas in the cycle is *Götterdämmerung* (1876), in which Wagner depicts the destruction of the world of the gods.

In general use, the word *"Götterdämmerung"* describes a cataclysmic struggle resulting in or foreshadowing universal disaster.

"Go west, young man"   This oft-repeated piece of advice originated as the title of an editorial in the *Terre Haute* (Indiana) *Express* in 1851. The editor, John B. L. Soule, urged young people to go out West where challenge and adventure beckoned.

When New York journalist Horace Greeley (1811–72) came across Soule's editorial, he reprinted it in his paper, *The Tribune,* expanding the original title to *Go West, Young Man and Grow Up with the Country.*

The editorial caught and heightened the national mood. Greeley's prominence gave impetus and prestige to its message and also caused the editorial to be widely and wrongly attributed to Greeley.

Today, the essential message of "Go west, young man" is, Seek your fortune wherever you may find it.

Goya, Francisco (1746–1828)   Every history of art introduces Francisco José de Goya y Lucientes as "the great Spanish painter." One goes so far as to call him "the greatest painter of his century, the worthiest successor of the masters of the baroque." He was influenced especially by Tiepolo, Velásquez, Rembrandt.

As a young man in Madrid, Goya painted charming scenes of popular life in the late ROCOCO style: couples on swings; couples courting and similar scenes, which visitors to the Prado can see framed in archways set within the walls.

This is not the work for which Goya is remembered, however. Goya is associated with the following:

1. Realistic, almost cruelly revealing psychological portraits of the Spanish royal families through several régimes—for example, *The Family of Charles IV* (1800) at the Prado.
2. Harrowing images of war. Although Goya had been sympathetic to the aims of the French Revolution and the young French Republic, the savagery of Napoleon's troops incited equally savage resistance. Goya's dramatic painting *The Third of May 1808* depicts the execution of a group of Madrid citizens by a phalanx of faceless, monstrous executioners with drawn bayonets and rifles. We see the victims as martyrs and the killers as hired tyrants.
3. Grotesque, nightmarish, fantastic visions in a series of etchings called *Los Proverbios*. One haunting example is *The Giant,* c. 1820, in which a huge, bare figure sits on the edge of the world, colossal, dwarfing the tiny habitations beneath him.

At the age of 70, Goya retired to his villa where he painted on its walls such macabre subjects as *Saturn Devouring His Children,Witches' Sabbath* and *The Three Fates.*

Goya's prevalent mood was a dark one during most of his life. His work is an indictment of man's vanity, stupidity, brutality and corruption, a nightmarish vision unequaled in terror until the 20th century.

Gradgrind,Thomas   The central character in Charles Dickens's novel *Hard Times* (1845). A retired hardware merchant, Gradgrind has founded a school run strictly on utilitarian principles, and he has raised his own children Tom and Louisa to live by facts alone. He has stifled their every impulse, every sign of affection, every fancy, every play of imagination. He discovers too late that he has crippled his children emotionally and morally.

Gradgrind is a tragic figure who comes to recognize that the values exemplified by Sissy Jupe, the little circus girl who has proved immune to his teachings, are the life-affirming values of kindness, generosity, trust, devotion and love.

A Gradgrind is one who subscribes to the false ideas that practicality alone must be the basis of action and that only facts will nourish a human soul.

Graham, Billy (1918–   )   Born in North Carolina to Protestant fundamentalist parents, he was ordained as a Southern Baptist minister and became a preacher for American Youth for Christ in 1944. Graham launched blockbuster evangelical campaigns that lasted for months. These he called crusades. He packed huge meeting places like Yankee Stadium and Madison Square Garden with 75,000 to 100,000 listeners. The object was to get as many as possible to "decide for Christ." He carried his crusades into England, Hungary, Korea and even the Soviet Union (1984), and served as an informal spiritual adviser to a number of U.S. presidents.

Billy Graham is the model for clean-cut, middle-class, optimistic Christianity.

Graham, Martha (1894–1991)   American dancer, teacher and choreographer who created and codified a new dance vocabulary that was to become the foundation of modern dance in America. Her dance technique was based on contraction and release of the muscles of the diaphragm, back and pelvis. She danced barefoot but with voluminous draperies to mask or reveal emotion. Her dance subjects were often literary in origin and Freudian in their psychological probing. Some of her most acclaimed works are: *Primitive Mysteries* (1931); *Letters to the World,* about Emily Dickinson (1940); *Appalachian Spring* (1944); *Cave of the Heart,* about Medea, (1946); *Night Journey,* about Jocasta (1947); and *Clytemnestra* (1958). All in all she choreographed more than 150 dances using members of her own company.

Grand Central Station   Located in New York City, this station is one of the busiest, most crowded railroad terminals in the world. The name describes any place that is very busy.

Use: At noon, his office is Grand Central Station.

Grand Guignol   A type of drama characterized by macabre and gruesome plots. It originated in 18th-century French puppet shows. The main character was called Guignol. Later, the Grand Guignol, a legitimate theater in Paris, specialized in plays with violent, blood-curdling action.

Grandma Moses (1860–1961)   Born Anna Mary Robertson, this self-taught modern primitive painter had her first one-woman show at the age of 80. In bright, clear colors she painted the rustic scenes and activities of her childhood in upstate New York. Many of her works have been reproduced on Christmas cards. A Grandma Moses has the quality of an old-fashioned sampler or a rural Currier and Ives.

grandstand play   In baseball, an ostentatious play explicitly designed to win the spectators' applause—especially those seated in the grandstands. Hence, a grandstand play—or "grandstanding"—is any action designed to elicit applause or make an impression. It raises questions about the individual's sincerity and intent.

Grant, Cary (1906–1986)   American movie actor. Born Archibald Leach in Bristol, England, in Hollywood he became a star famed for his tall, suave good looks and charm. Grant had a flair for light comedy, appearing in *She Done Him Wrong* (1933), *Bringing Up Baby* (1938), *Topper* (1937) and *To Catch a Thief* (1954), among other films, and playing opposite most of the leading ladies of his day.

Great Wall of China   Now one of the great tourist attractions in China, the wall was originally built in ancient times during the Ch'in dynasty. It was rebuilt in its present form during the Middle Ages by the Ming dynasty (1368–1644). Made of earth, stone and brick, it is about 25 feet high, between 15 and 30 feet wide and about 1,500 miles long, with watchtowers at regular intervals. The wall meanders across northern China. It was built to keep out barbarians from the north, but successive invasions proved the wall to be of little practical use. It is sometimes seen as an expression of Chinese xenophobia.

Any protective barrier, not just against a physical enemy but also against foreign ideas, is referred to symbolically as a Great Wall.

Great White Father   A nickname for a United States president, it appeared in popular Western novels about 1916. Now used to describe any important, influential, beneficent figure in industry, government and other fields.

Great White Hope   The term originated in the early 1900s when Jack Johnson, the first black heavyweight champion of the world, held that title for seven years (1908–15). His unsavory life outside the ring, his falling afoul of the law and his arrogance fed the desire of a considerable body of boxing fans to see the almost invincible Johnson beaten by a white boxer. On April 15, 1915, their wishes were fulfilled. In Havana, Cuba, Jess Willard, the then-current Great White Hope, and now a member of the boxing hall of fame, knocked Johnson out in the 26th round of a fight for the world's heavyweight championship.

"Great White Hope" is now applied generally to anyone who is expected to accomplish much in a specific field. It no longer bears any of its early racist overtones.

Green Hornet, The   Program that ran first on radio and then on television, between 1936 and 1967. A special arrangement of Rimsky-Korsakov's "Flight of the Bumble-Bee" signaled the beginning of another episode of *The Green Hornet*—determined, unvanquishable fighter against crime. Britt Reid, the crusading editor and publisher of the *Daily Herald,* is, of course, none other than the Green Hornet, crime fighter extraordinaire, in disguise. Only Kato, his faithful servant, knows that Britt is the Green Hornet's alter ego.

In his unrelenting battle against the forces of evil, the Green Hornet has a souped-up car with a built-in TV camera that "sees" four miles ahead; exhaust apparatus to spread ice on the road to foil his pursuers; a special nonlethal gun that immobilizes "elements"; and a sting gun that goes through steel.

The Green Hornet is another of television's dramatizations of the "good guys" vs. "the bad guys."

Greenwich Village   A section of lower Manhattan in New York City, which in the early years of the 20th century became the hub of a circle of artists, writers, theater people, radicals and bohemians experimenting with new art forms and unconventional lifestyles. Among them were Eugene O'Neill and the Provincetown Players, Edna St. Vincent Millay, Edmund Wilson, e.e. cummings, Maxwell Bodenheim, John Sloan, Edward Hopper and many more.

Still a neighborhood of town houses, tree-lined streets, antique shops, boutiques, galleries, book shops, restaurants and little theaters, it continues to attract the young and the young at heart.

Grendel   Underwater monster in *Beowulf* (c. 700), the oldest English epic, written in Anglo-Saxon alliterative verse by an unknown poet and newly translated into English in 1999 by Seamus Heaney.

Grendel, a descendant of Cain, lives with his mother in the depths of a murky pond. For 12 years he has emerged periodically to prey upon Danish warriors as they are sleeping in Heorot, the great mead hall built by their king, Hrothgar. Now, after so many raids and so many murders, the hall lies abandoned.

Beowulf, hero of the Geats, a neighboring people, comes to do battle with the monster. Eventually he liberates the Danes and, laden with gifts, returns to his homeland.

Grendel, in modern usage, still stands for a fierce, savage monster.

Gresham's Law   The author of this "law" was Sir Thomas Gresham (1519?–79), English merchant, financier, founder of the Royal Exchange. Simply stated, Gresham's Law holds that bad money drives out good money. Technically, "when cheaper metals are used for currency, the more valuable coins and metals disappear from circulation because they are being hoarded."

The original sense of Gresham's Law does not apply to current local, national or international finance, but as a metaphor and allusion it is widely applicable. Bad art tends to drive out good art. In political contests, bad campaigning and bad politics tend to imperil the survival of good campaigning and good politics.

Gretchen (sometimes "Marguerite" or "Margarita")   The innocent 14-year-old girl in Goethe's *Faust* (Part One, 1808). Faust, rejuvenated by a magic potion, falls in love with Gretchen. With the help of Mephistopheles he succeeds in seducing her. When he abandons her, she goes mad and in despair kills her newborn child. When Faust learns of her arrest and imminent execution, he rushes to save her. She refuses to escape, since she must pay for her sins. In prayer she achieves redemption.

Gretchen is the prototype of the pure young girl who is destroyed by a worldly lover.

Grimm's Fairy Tales   A collection of more than 200 folk stories assembled and edited by the Brothers Grimm. Jacob Grimm (1785–1863) and Wilhelm Grimm (1786–1859) were eminent German philologists. In tune with the Romantic movement's interest in the common man and his folklore, the brothers began to record tales told by peasants in neighboring villages. One source, Katharina Viehmann, a tailor's wife, told them 20 stories that were new to them.

The Grimms published these tales in *Kinder- und Hausmärchen* (Nursery and Household Tales) in 1812 and 1814. The first English translation appeared in 1823, with illustrations by George Cruikshank. Included were such well-known stories as "Rumpelstiltskin," "Snow White and Rose Red," "Hansel and Gretel" and "Rapunzel."

In modern times, Grimm's Fairy Tales—or, for that matter, any fairy tales— have stirred up controversy about their suitability for children. Psychologists disagree about the effect upon children of stories about cruel stepmothers, witches, giants and ogres, magic transformations and elements of the macabre. Nonetheless, these stories have been translated into 70 languages and remain a staple of children's literature.

Griselda   The model of patience, Griselda is the heroine of the last (the 100th) tale in *The Decameron* (1351–53) by Giovanni BOCCACCIO and of "The Clerk's Tale" in *The Canterbury Tales* (1387–1400) by Geoffrey Chaucer.

Griselda, a very poor but beautiful and virtuous peasant girl, marries the Marquis of Saluzzo. She promises to obey him in all things. But the Marquis is not content. He must test her fidelity by subjecting her to a series of trials. He pretends that he has killed their two children. He divorces her and sends her home. He recalls her to prepare his palace for a new wife. Throughout, Griselda remains uncomplaining and true to her vow. Finally, her husband reveals that he has only been testing her and she is restored to his favor and to her children.

Griselda and patience are synonymous.

Grosz, George (1893–1959)
German painter and caricaturist who immigrated to New York in 1932 and taught at the Art Students League. Grosz is identified with a series of savagely satirical studies of beefy German bourgeois types, hypocritical and complacent, which show his disillusionment with militarism, capitalism and conformism in Germany at the end of World War I. For example, in *Germany, a Winter's Tale* we see as if in a collage the pernicious influence of a clergyman, a general and a schoolmaster on an average smug German, against a tangled background of buildings that look like a huge jail.

ground rules
In baseball, special procedures or regulations applying to a specific ballpark or playing field.

In general usage, agreed-upon rules or procedures are often called "ground rules."

Use: Before the conference starts we'll have to draw up some ground rules regarding the length of each presentation, time for discussion and other procedural matters.

Grover's Corners
The setting of *Our Town* (1938), a play by Thornton Wilder about the everyday lives of people in a typical American town, this one being in New Hampshire. A "Stage Manager" narrator introduces the townspeople: the newsboy, the milkman, the druggist, the gossip, the artist, the undertaker. The central characters will be the families of Editor Webb and Dr. Gibb. Young Emily Webb marries George Gibb. She dies in childbirth. She returns after death to observe the people she has been so familiar with and realizes the eternal verities in their simple, everyday actions, duties and relationships.

Grub Street
Defined by Samuel Johnson (1709–84) in his *Dictionary of the English Language* (1747–55) as "the name of a street in Moorsfield, London, much inhabited by writers of small histories and temporary poems, whence any mean production was called Grub Street." Grub Street no longer exists as a street, but the term still refers to something written by literary hacks; hence shoddy, of poor quality. It is also the place where such hacks produce inferior work.

George Gissing (1807–1903), English novelist and critic, wrote with much compassion and insight of his bitter life as a writer in *The New Grub Street* (1891).

Grundy, Mrs.   Unseen, offstage character in the comedy *Speed the Plough* (1800) by British playwright Thomas Morton. One of the main characters, Dame Ashfield, constantly asks, "What will Mrs. Grundy say?" for Mrs. Grundy, her neighbor, is exceedingly proper. "What will Mrs. Grundy say?" has come to stand for "What will the neighbors say?" Mrs. Grundy herself has become a symbol of prudery and conventionality.

As Frederick Locker-Lampson wrote in 1857:

> They eat, and drink, and scheme and plod,
> And go to sleep on Sunday—
> And many are afraid of God—
> And more of Mrs. Grundy.

Guernica   The bombing of the Basque capital of Guernica by German warplanes on April 27, 1937, during the Spanish Civil War, was memorialized by PABLO PICASSO in his masterpiece *Guernica*. The painting depicts the horrors of war in terrifying images of dismemberment, chaos and suffering.

guerrilla warfare   Term that describes an array of unconventional military tactics whereby bands of armed men (and, sometimes, women and even children) recruited from the civilian population are able to outwit, ambush and harry the regular military forces of the enemy. Guerrilla fighters often are lightly armed and operate in small units, but they may have the advantage of familiarity with the rough terrain of their native land. When these guerrillas are motivated by a national liberation movement, they can absorb almost any punishment and can inflict unexpected damage on the enemy, as they did in Vietnam, Cuba and Afghanistan.

Guerrilla in Spanish means "little war," and indeed the term was coined during the Peninsular War (1808–14) in opposition to Napoleon.

Guerrilla attacks prove useful not only in military conflicts but also metaphorically in domestic quarrels and business raids when direct confrontation is best avoided.

guillotine   A device for beheading a person with a heavy blade that is dropped between two guides. It was named after Joseph Ignace Guillotin (1735–1814), a French physician who favored the guillotine as a quick and relatively painless form of execution. The inventor of the guillotine was Anton Louise (1723–92), a French surgeon. The guillotine was widely used during the French Revolution (see REIGN OF TERROR).

The guillotine was not a uniquely French invention. Similar instruments had been used in some countries from the 13th century on. The French simply employed it more dramatically and on a larger scale.

"Guillotine" has come to stand for metaphorical execution.

gulag   Russian acronym for Main Directorate of Corrective Labor Camps, a chain of forced-labor camps in the Soviet Union. The Russian Nobel Prize–winner in literature, Aleksandr I. Solzhenitsyn, drew upon his own experiences as a prisoner to reveal the horrors of the camps in such books as *One Day in the Life of Ivan Denisovich*, *The Cancer Ward*, *The First Circle* and *The Gulag Archipelago*.

Now the word describes any prison or detention camp, especially for political prisoners.

Gulf of Tonkin   Waters off the coast of North Vietnam where communist patrol boats made "unprovoked" attacks against the U.S. destroyer *Maddox*. In August 1964 Congress passed a resolution granting President Lyndon B. Johnson support for whatever action he deemed necessary to defend U.S. forces in Southeast Asia. The Tonkin Resolution was later thought to have been engineered by Johnson and the military, and was held responsible for the expansion of U.S. involvement in the Vietnam War.

Mentioning the Gulf of Tonkin Resolution is generally held to be a cautionary reference to a too-easy yielding to presidential demands for waging undeclared wars.

Gulliver   The main character in *Gulliver's Travels* (1726), Jonathan Swift's savage satire on the nature of man and his institutions.

After Lemuel Gulliver, a doctor on an English merchant vessel, is shipwrecked, he experiences a series of fantastic adventures in four different lands: Lilliput, where the inhabitants are only six inches tall; Brobdingnag, where the inhabitants are 60 feet tall; Laputa, a floating island of absent-minded theoretic scientists; and the country of the Houyhnhnms, horses who rule over humans called YAHOOS. Gulliver has insatiable curiosity about all these creatures. He observes their customs closely and recounts his observations in such exact detail that the reader accepts the veracity of his story.

Gulliver starts out as an average 18th-century Englishman who accepts all the conventional ideas of his time. As he compares the societies he observes in his travels with the one he has known in England, his eyes are opened to man's follies, vices, corruption, even bestiality. He takes the reader along on this more profound voyage of discovery.

A Gulliver, then, is a voyager to strange lands who returns home with a changed insight into his own country and people. His observations have made him a pessimist and a misanthrope.

See LILLIPUTIAN; BROBDINGNAGIAN.

Gumps, The   Sidney Smith, who in 1917 created *The Gumps*, the most widely read comic strip through the 1930s, was fascinated by money and riches. A great storyteller and lover of soap opera melodrama, he made Andy Gump and his dedicated wife, Min (Minerva), the central characters of *The Gumps*, exemplars of the lower-middle-class, materialistic values he admired. Together with his wife and his billionaire uncle Bim, Andy embodied the aspirations of millions of readers.

Gunga Din   The title character in one of Rudyard Kipling's *Barrack-Room Ballads* (1892), Gunga Din is a native water carrier for a British regiment stationed in India. The narrator, who ordinarily would display the mental trappings of colonialism, shouldering what Kipling called "the white man's burden," surprisingly is moved to admit:

> *Though I've belted you an' flayed you,*
> *By the livin' Gawd that made you,*
> *You're a better man than I am, Gunga Din!*

It is the last line that has come into modern usage.

gung-ho   From the Chinese, meaning "work together," this term was adopted by Lieutenant Colonel Evans F. Carlson as the slogan for his marine battalion. Known as Carlson's Raiders, they won a stunning victory over the Japanese in a surprise attack against Makin Island during World War II. This assault became the subject of the 1944 movie *Gung-Ho!* Generally used now to mean enthusiastic, eager, all-out.

Use: After the coach's pep talk, the players were all gung-ho for the game against their arch-rivals.

guns before butter   Slogan coined in 1936 by Nazi political and military leader, Hermann Goering: "Guns will make us powerful; butter will only make us fat." He was urging Germans to sacrifice domestic comforts to an all-out preparation for war.

The phrase is now used to mean the sacrifice of amenities to hard realities.

guru   A wise man, a spiritual guide and teacher with a devoted following. Originally used for leaders in the Hindu religion, but now applied to elder statesmen, industrial geniuses, anyone with disciples.

Gypsy Rose Lee (1914–1970)   Born Rose Louise Hovick, her generation hailed her as the "Queen of Burlesque," America's most famous striptease artist. For perfecting her art "beyond that practiced by all contemporary practitioners," H. L. Mencken invented a word for Gypsy Rose Lee—"ecdysiast."

In the 1920s, Gypsy Rose Lee was taking striptease lessons from the knowledgeable Tessie, the Tassel Twirler. By 1931, she had honed her considerable skills in

Minsky's and other burlesque palaces. In her many subsequent appearances, she succeeded in raising the lowly, somewhat disreputable striptease to a graceful, stylish art.

Beautiful and intelligent, Gypsy Rose Lee became the darling of the New York intellectual set, to whom she was introduced by the famous sportswriter, Damon Runyon. While on tour, she wrote her first, best-selling novel, *The G-String Murders* (actually ghost-written by popular mystery writer Craig Rice). She appeared in the movies, on the Broadway stage and on TV.

Haight-Ashbury   District in San Francisco associated in the 1960s with hippies and other segments of the counterculture.

HAL (HAL 9000)   The talkative supercomputer that controls the spaceship *Discovery* in the film *2001:A Space Odyssey* (1968), directed by STANLEY KUBRICK from a screenplay by Arthur C. Clarke. The *Discovery,* manned by two highly skilled astronauts, attempts to track down a strong radio signal emanating from a 3 million-year-old monolith on the moon, aimed at Saturn (Jupiter in the film). On the way to Jupiter and perhaps the remains of an ancient civilization, a deadly feud breaks out between the astronauts and the psychotic homicidal computer for control of the spacecraft. Who will prevail?

HAL represents a science fiction scenario of man vs. machine. The struggle symbolizes innate human fears engendered by FRANKENSTEIN monsters when we experiment with artificial intelligence.

Hale, Nathan   See I ONLY REGRET THAT I HAVE BUT ONE LIFE TO LOSE FOR MY COUNTRY.

Halley's comet   Comet named after English astronomer Edmund Halley (1656–1742), who concluded that the comets sighted in 1531, 1607 and 1682 all followed the same orbit around the sun and were indeed one and the same comet. He predicted that the comet would reappear in 1758, and was proven correct. The comet takes about 76 years to complete its run. Its most recent appearances have been in 1910 and 1986.

Halley's comet has come to stand for a highly dramatic appearance.

Use: Pausing for a moment in the wings, Callas streaked across the stage with the predictable éclat of Halley's comet.

Hamlet   The tragic hero of Shakespeare's play of the same name (first performed c. 1601). Hamlet, prince of Denmark, is recalled from the University of

Wittenberg to attend his father's funeral at Elsinore, the royal palace in Denmark. Within a month his mother, Gertrude, marries his father's brother, Claudius. Hamlet learns from his father's ghost that Claudius has murdered his father, and Hamlet is sworn to avenge his father's death.

Why Hamlet hesitates so long in taking revenge and whether or not he truly goes mad or feigns madness after his encounter with the ghost are questions that have occupied critics for almost 400 years.

In the popular imagination, Hamlet is the "melancholy Dane" given to philosophical brooding over "To be or not to be." He is a man of too much thought and too little action to take control of events. This, some say, is his tragic flaw.

Use: Mario Cuomo, former governor of New York, was called "Hamlet on the Hudson" and "the Hamlet of Albany" by the media because he could not make up his mind about whether to run for president of the United States in 1992.

Hammer, Mike   Fictional private detective created by Mickey Spillane (1918–). Tough, ruthless, violent in speech and action, he pursues the bad guy with no holds barred, bypassing legalities when he deems necessary. He feels no sentimental remorse when he visits retribution upon a killer. He is in his own way incorruptible and he will risk his life for what he feels is right. He has a voluptuous assistant secretary named Velda. Some of the novels he appears in are *I, The Jury* (1947), *Vengeance Is Mine* (1950), *My Gun Is Quick* (1950), *Kiss Me Deadly* (1952).

Hancock, John (1736–1793)   In his time, he was one of the richest men in New England. During the Revolutionary War, he played an important part in financing the American cause. When the war ended, he served as president of the Continental Congress. He was elected governor of Massachusetts in 1780 and served until his death.

John Hancock was one of the signers of the Declaration of Independence. His is the most noticeable, most distinctive handwriting.

A "John Hancock" has become a synonym for a signature.

hang up the gloves   In boxing, to retire, to withdraw from active participation. In general use, this expression has a similar meaning.

Use: After 10 years as head of the company, Bill Morris decided to hang up his gloves.

Hansel and Gretel   Brother and sister in one of GRIMM's fairy tales who are abandoned in the woods by parents who are too poor to feed them. Hansel leaves a trail by which he and his sister find their way home. Their parents abandon them a second time. Now they are truly lost in the forest. They come upon a house made of sweets, bread and cakes. When they start nibbling upon it, a witch disguised as an old woman comes out and invites them in. She imprisons Hansel in a cage and proceeds to fatten him up to roast him in the oven, while she puts Gretel to work for her. Gretel pushes the witch into the oven, releases Hansel, and together they find their way home, this time laden with the witch's treasure.

The tale was turned into an opera by the German composer Engelbert Humperdinck in 1893.

Use: "[T]he closet's dull odor, the floor's wooden crack, the smug smell of a cleanser around the sink. Every house has a Hansel and Gretel trail of these sensory bread crumbs that lead from the front door to the attic." ("Remembered Roads," *New York Times Magazine,* June 7, 1992)

"Happy families are all alike"   The oft quoted opening sentence of Leo Tolstoy's novel *Anna Karenina,* which continues, "Every unhappy family is unhappy in its own way." In this case, Tolstoy refers to the unhappy family of Anna's brother, Prince Oblonsky, a genial philanderer whose wife Dolly is threatening to divorce him over his latest infidelity. Anna comes to the rescue. With her tact, warmth and understanding she effects a reconciliation of the warring couple.

The famous sentence often is used to make the point that unhappy families or people are inherently more interesting than happy ones.

Happy Hooligan   Fred Opper's great contribution to the pantheon of comic strip characters, *Happy Hooligan* occupied the avid attention of millions of readers from 1900 to 1932.

In a sense, *Happy Hooligan* is an American Candide. The classic Irish tramp with a red nose and a tin can for a hat, he is "a simple innocent whose impulsive undertakings nearly always land him in the hands of the law . . ."

Despite the bad luck that dogs his efforts at making the world a better, sunnier place for himself and for everyone else, Happy remains the unconquerable optimist, always smiling and hopeful. His brother, Gloomy Gus, is as long-faced as Happy is cheerful.

happy warrior   Originally, a reference to William Wordsworth's "Character of the Happy Warrior" (1807), which begins:

Who is the happy Warrior? Who is he
That every man in arms would wish to be?

The expression was used politically when Franklin Delano Roosevelt applied it to Governor Alfred E. Smith of New York in a nominating speech in 1924 and then again in 1928, when Smith became the Democratic candidate for president. A liberal and a Catholic, Smith lost the election to Herbert Hoover.

Later the same nickname was given to Senator Hubert Humphrey, who, though he tried valiantly and with much optimism, never made it to the presidency.

In general use, the term describes one who joyously fights the good fight.

hara-kiri   In centuries past, a member of the Japanese warrior class who was found guilty of a disloyal or dishonorable act was obligated to commit hara-kiri, ceremonial Japanese suicide. The term is considered vulgar in Japan, the more polite *sepuku* being used instead to describe ritual suicide. The disgraced noble would receive from the emperor a jeweled dagger with which he was expected to rip open his own belly.

Obligatory hara-kiri was discontinued in 1868, but to this day prominent Japanese figures will sometimes commit hara-kiri as a form of protest against national policy or as an act of self-inflicted penance for some intolerable personal disgrace. Yukio Mishima (1925–70), the famous Japanese novelist and playwright, committed hara-kiri because of an insult.

Today the term is used in a figurative sense to mean a self-destructive act. For example, any candidate who runs on a platform of raising taxes for the purpose of solving the nation's problems is thought to be committing political hara-kiri.

hard hat   The steel or plastic helmet worn by various workers, especially construction workers.

In general use, a "hard hat" has come to mean a conservative, a reactionary, a "right-winger."

Hardy, Andy   Teenage protagonist played by Mickey Rooney in a series of 15 enormously popular films made by MGM between 1937 and 1947. These movies purportedly portrayed the everyday growing pains of a good, clean-living boy in a typical American family in a small midwestern town. Andy would get into trivial scrapes and his father, a judge played by Lewis Stone, would have man-to-man talks with him. The series was given a special Academy Award in 1942 for "furthering the American way of life."

Use: "I realized how much of themselves these men [the early pioneering movie moguls] invested in the movies. They really believed in that Andy Hardy world. For Goldwyn, America provided a place where everything could be clean" (A. Scott Berg, quoted in a review of his biography *Goldwyn*).

Harlem   Black district in Manhattan with its main artery along 125th Street, site of the Apollo Theater. It is associated not only with the problems of a black urban population—poverty, overcrowding, poor housing—but also with black creativity in jazz, dance and theater. In the 1920s, white patrons flocked to the reviews at the Cotton Club and Connie's Inn, while blacks themselves danced at the Savoy.

Harlow, Jean (1911–1937)   American actress, born Harlean Carpenter in Kansas City, Missouri, she became the "Platinum Blonde" sex goddess of the 1930s. Brassy and often comic, she appeared with CLARK GABLE in *Red Dust* (1932) and *Hold Your Man* (1933).

Hatfields and the McCoys, the   The Hatfields, a violent clan prone to crime, lived in West Virginia. The McCoys, a similarly inclined clan, lived in Kentucky. When the Civil War (1861–65) broke out, the two families found themselves on opposite sides of the conflict: the Hatfields with the South, the McCoys with the North. Over the years following the war, sporadic violence and bloodshed marked the relationship between the clans.

In 1888, the Hatfields decided to "eliminate" the McCoys. They first surrounded Randolph McCoy's house. He was not at home. Undeterred, the Hatfield gang, wearing masks, set fire to the house. When Randolf's daughter ran out of the burning house, the Hatfields shot her to death. His son Calvin met a similar fate. Mrs. McCoy, trying to save her daughter, was clubbed by the Hatfields and left for dead.

Kentucky law officers conducted raids into West Virginia looking for Hatfield men. They seized eleven: two were killed, nine others captured. Of the nine, two were executed, the rest were sent to state prison. In 1890, the Hatfields at last declared an end to the feud.

Any adversarial group relationship characterized as "the Hatfields and the McCoys" varies from incessant wrangling and petty jealousies to physical violence often ending in death.

Haussmannize   To remodel a city, to effect urban renewal in the way that Baron Georges Eugène Haussmann (1809–91) transformed Paris under the direction of Emperor Louis Napoleon during the years 1853 to 1870. Haussmann was a bureaucrat recalled from the provinces to become the prefect of the Seine and to formulate a grand plan for securing Paris against future uprisings by the populace of the inner city.

Haussmann demolished much of the medieval city, including its narrow, winding streets that so easily could be barricaded. He overhauled the Île de la Cité, pushing the people out toward the periphery, opening up vast "places" with splendid buildings and monuments that could be seen at the end of long vistas, building wide boulevards radiating from fixed centers like the Étoile, the Place de l'Opéra, the Place de la République, the Place de la Concorde, and gentrifying residences so that only the rich could afford them. He created and renewed a series of parks—the Bois de Boulogne, the Parc Monceau and others. He built new bridges across the Seine, set grand railroad stations around the limits of the city and, most important, he instituted a freshwater supply system after replacing the horrible medieval sewers.

It cost a fortune, mostly financed by realtors who could gain from the upscaling of the city, since Louis Napoleon was adamant about not raising taxes. Haussmann met with much grumbling. Eventually he had to be retired. He died a forgotten, sour old man with the reward of the Boulevard Haussmann named after him.

Many think that Haussmann made Paris what it is today, a grand city of spacious boulevards amenable to the lifestyle of boulevardiers, the most classically beautiful city in the world. Others regret the passing of the quaint old city, referring to the "vandalism of Haussmann."

Have Gun, Will Travel   The most adult of the 1950s television westerns. The "hero" Paladin, a surly "hired gun," dressed in black and played with subdued conviction by Richard Boone, offered his services to the helpless and oppressed. Despite each episode's expected ending (virtue triumphant over evil), the tight writing and the convincing, understated acting of Boone attracted and held a wide spectrum of viewers.

Originally, Paladin was one of the legendary knights pledged to defend noble causes and protect the weak in the name of King Charlemagne. The modern Paladin's business card expressed this ancient code in a universally understood, contemporary idiom: "Have Gun. Will Travel. Wire Paladin. San Francisco."

Havisham, Miss   In Charles Dickens's novel *Great Expectations* (1860), Miss Havisham is an eccentric old woman who, many years earlier, was jilted at the altar. Since that traumatic day she has been a recluse in her own house. Brooding on the treachery of men, she sits in the room where the wedding feast is still laid out on the tables covered with years of dust.

Her revenge is to turn her beautiful young ward Estella against men, to condition her to break the hearts of men as one of them broke Miss Havisham's. To this end she summons young Pip, the hero of the novel, to her household to play with Estella. Pip satisfies Miss Havisham's hopes by becoming obsessed with the haughty girl who torments him.

In the end, Miss Havisham and her house go up in flames. Pip tears the smoldering draperies down and lets in the light.

A Miss Havisham is an eccentric who nurses an old injury for the rest of her life.

Hawkshaw, the Detective   A very popular comic strip character introduced by its creator, Gus Mager, February 23, 1913. In its time, it became an American version of Sir Arthur Conan Doyle's immortal Sherlock Holmes. Actually, an earlier version of Hawkshaw was called Sherlocko. When it became obvious that Conan Doyle's representatives were about to launch a lawsuit contending that "Sherlocko" was a flagrant plagiarism, the publishers dropped Sherlocko and put Hawkshaw in his place.

Though Sherlock Holmes has displaced Hawkshaw in the minds and hearts of detective story aficionados, Hawkshaw is not entirely forgotten.

Use: ". . . The Times Bureau decided it was a job for Jeff Gerth, a reportorial Hawkshaw." (William Safire, *New York Times*)

haymaker   In boxing, a crushing, devastating punch, which usually results in a "knockout" or "knockdown."

In general use, it carries the same sense of overwhelming force.

Hayworth, Rita (1918–1987)   Born Margarita Cansino, a red-headed, glamorous, voluptuous Amerian movie star and pinup girl. Hayworth was married twice, first to Orson Welles and then to Aly Khan. She is remembered as a Hollywood love goddess.

Heart of Darkness (1902)   Short novel by JOSEPH CONRAD about a journey through the jungles of the Congo to rescue a legendary ivory trader by the name of Mr. Kurtz, who is said to be very ill. It is an allegorical journey of the soul at the end of which the narrator, Marlow, finds that Kurtz has traveled backward into savagery, where he stares into the heart of darkness, the abyss of death and of evil in men's souls.

Use: "Some people were drawn to the story not because of a Conradian 'fascination of the abomination' but out of an obligation to try to make sense of this modern-day heart of darkness." (Edwin Diamond, "Anatomy of a Horror," in *New York Magazine,* May 15, 1989.) See also THE HORROR, THE HORROR.

"Hearts and Flowers"   An immensely popular, sentimental song of the early 1900s. Its melancholy tune tears at the heart strings.

Any maudlin, tearjerking appeal is often labeled a "hearts and flowers" presentation.

Heathcliff   The hero of Emily Brontë's *Wuthering Heights* (1847), a romantic novel with GOTHIC elements of passion and revenge.

Heathcliff is a wild-spirited, gypsy orphan whom the kindly Mr. Earnshaw finds on a street in Liverpool and brings to Wuthering Heights, his home on the Yorkshire moors. Mr. Earnshaw's daughter Cathy falls in love with Heathcliff, but her brother Hindley hates and abuses him. Heathcliff morosely endures Hindley's abuse, vowing ultimate vengeance. When Heathcliff overhears Cathy haughtily saying that she will never marry a person so degraded in social status as he is, he runs away. Three years later, Heathcliff returns to Wuthering Heights a rich and polished man, determined to have Cathy and to ruin Hindley.

A Heathcliff is a dark-natured, brooding, tempestuous person obsessed and possessed by a single-minded love, a romantic hero. Today such a character's intensity lends itself to mockery by those who find such passions embarrassing.

heavy hitter   In baseball, a player whose batting average is high, who can be counted on to get considerably more than the average number of hits per game or per season.

In general, a heavy hitter is an important, influential person.

Hedda Gabler   The neurotic central character of Henrik Ibsen's play of the same name (1890). Faced at the end with being blackmailed into adultery, she kills herself "beautifully" with a pistol-shot to the head. The famous last line of the play is Judge Brack's muttering, "My God, people don't do such things."

The daughter of a general, Hedda is physically courageous. She can ride and shoot and she is often reckless. She feels vastly superior to all the "provincials" around her. She is meant, she thinks, for glory. But she has no constructive talents of her own. She will have to find glory through her association with a man.

She proves, however, to lack moral courage. She has shied away from commitment to Lövberg, the brilliant young Dionysian who has loved her, and she has made a safe marriage with a pedant she despises. When Lövberg, under the rehabilitating influence of Thea Elvsted, publishes a remarkable book and is about to publish an even greater one, thus becoming eligible for the same professorship as Hedda's husband, Hedda embarks upon a jealous frenzy of destruction. She taunts Lövberg into resuming his dissolute life, burns the manuscript of his new book and gives him a pistol to shoot himself with, which he does "unbeautifully" in a brothel brawl.

Hedda thinks of herself as unconventional, yet it is the "ordinary" Thea Elvsted who has left her husband and children in order to advance the work of a genius, Lövberg. Thea, not Hedda, is the heir to NORA in Ibsen's *A Doll's House.* Hedda is discontented, cynical, cruel, bored, restless and unfulfilled. She is a rootless woman without a purpose and without a future, sterile except for her husband's child within her, a pregnancy that disgusts her. At least she has the courage to die.

Hefner, Hugh (1926–   )   Publisher of *Playboy* magazine, which he founded in 1953. From the beginning, *Playboy* appealed to the young, affluent, urban male. It advocated a lifestyle marked by sexual permissiveness and conspicuous consumption. The magazine stimulated these impulses with nude photos of attractive young women surrounded by high-pressure advertising.

Hefner organized and ran a string of private Playboy clubs staffed by girls dressed like "bunnies": an exercise in extravagant hedonism. Hefner himself, through his publications and other enterprises, pursued the kind of lifestyle extolled in the pages of *Playboy*.

Hegelian   In accordance with the theory of dialectical evolution as developed by the German philosopher and historian Georg Wilhelm Friedrich Hegel (1770–1831). Hegel believed that the world is a process of becoming. Every thesis implies an antithesis. The conflict between these two must result in a synthesis. This synthesis in turn produces its own antithesis. Again the conflict is resolved in a synthesis.

To Hegel, a philosophical idealist, reality is mind and spirit. The world-soul develops by a dialectical process, and history is the unfolding of that mind and spirit. History proceeds out of the clash and synthesis of conflicting human interests, all the while progressing toward the "self-realization of human reason and freedom."

Hegel's dialectic had a profound influence upon Marx and Engels, who accepted the process but applied it to their materialist view of the world; dialectical materialism is at the heart of communist theories of class conflict.

Hegel's philosophy is developed in his books *Phenomenology of Mind* (1807), *Science of Logic* (1812–16), *Encyclopedia of the Philosophical Sciences* and *Philosophy of Right* (1821).

One unfortunate byproduct of Hegel's philosophy is the belief in the rightful ascendancy of the state over the individual. Carried to extremes, this notion gives rise to fascism and communism. Indeed, Hegel used his theories to support the repressions of the Prussian state.

Hegira   In the year 622 Muhammad fled from Mecca, his birthplace, to Medina to escape persecution. This date marks the beginning of Islam, the religion of Muslims. Nevertheless, it is Mecca that remains the holiest city for Muslims. Muslims are expected to make a pilgrimage to that city at least once. When Muslims pray, it is in the direction of Mecca that they turn.

Today a hegira represents any flight from one place to another to escape religious or political or economic oppression.

Held, John, Jr.   (1889–1958)   American illustrator and cartoonist. After working, unsatisfied, for several magazines, Held found his style and voice in the pages of *The New Yorker.* Here, he began to capture the mood, feel and look of his skinny, flat-chested flappers of the 1920s.

Hemingway, Ernest (1899–1961)   American novelist, short-story writer and journalist.

In his own life, Hemingway stands for machismo, for pursuit of the manly sports such as big game hunting (*Green Hills of Africa,* 1935; "The Short Happy Life of Francis Macomber" and "The Snows of Kilimanjaro," 1938), deep-sea fishing (*The Old Man and the Sea,* 1952), boxing and bullfighting (*Death in the Afternoon,* 1932; *The Sun Also Rises,* 1926). He became an ambulance driver on the Italian front in World War I (*A Farewell to Arms,* 1929), covered the Spanish Civil War as a war correspondent (*For Whom the Bell Tolls,* 1940) and fought in World War II. His personal stance was pugnacious and challenging. When he could no longer pursue his macho activities because of illness, he committed suicide at the age of 61.

Hemingway has become synonymous with the Lost Generation, a group of American expatriates living in Paris after World War I (*A Moveable Feast,* published posthumously in 1964). See also HEMINGWAY STYLE, HEMINGWAY CODE.

Hemingway code   A standard of behavior stated and exemplified by certain characters in ERNEST HEMINGWAY's novels and short stories. It is the ideal toward which the Hemingway hero strives: knowing how to lose well, courage in crisis, "grace under pressure," stoicism, loyalty to comrades, reticence, skill in manly endeavors. Santiago, the old man of *The Old Man and the Sea,* is an excellent example of the code, one who initiates the boy Manolin into what it takes to become a man. Wilson, the hunting guide in "The Short Happy Life of Francis Macomber," is another exemplar of the code.

Hemingway style   A taut style of writing first forged by ERNEST HEMINGWAY in the interludes and short stories of *In Our Time* (1925). Characterized by monosyllabic vocabulary, short sentences, stark dialogue, understated emotion and dependence upon verbs and nouns rather than adjectives and adverbs, the Hemingway style exerted a strong influence on 20th-century fiction. See also HEMINGWAY CODE.

Henry VIII   King of England from 1509 to 1547, he is remembered for two reasons: 1) he defied the Pope on the matter of being granted permission to marry Anne Boleyn and was subsequently excommunicated, whereupon he established the Church of England with himself as its head; 2) he had six wives: Catherine of Aragon (annulled), Anne Boleyn (beheaded), Jane Seymour (died in childbirth), Anne of Cleves (divorced), Catherine Howard (beheaded) and Catherine Parr.

In modern usage Henry VIII, aside from having fathered Elizabeth I, is generally thought of as a real-life BLUEBEARD.

Hepburn, Katharine (1909–) U.S. film actress who represents high-spirited, independent, outspoken, classy career women. Often teamed with SPENCER TRACY in movies that involve the battle of the sexes, such as *Woman of the Year* (1941) and *Adam's Rib* (1949), she initiated this image as the young Jo in *Little Women* (1933). Her film career spanned more than half a century.

Hessians German mercenaries from the principality of Hesse-Cassel. Their princes "rented" 30,000 of them to the British during the Revolutionary War. Of these, 12,000 reached America and fought unwillingly against the Americans. A few actually deserted to the colonists' side.

"Hessian" has become a synonym for a hired soldier.

Heston, Charlton (1923–) American stage and film star associated with epic roles: Moses in *The Ten Commandments* (1956), the heroes of *Ben Hur* (1955) and of *El Cid* (1961). His sonorous voice and heroic stature are often parodied. He is also known as a political arch-conservative, espousing the views of the National Rifle Association.

High Noon (1951) Directed by Fred Zinnemann, this adult western tells the story of a sheriff (GARY COOPER) who must stand up alone against four desperadoes who will return at high noon on a certain day to kill him and to retake the town they terrorized for years. The townspeople, out of abject fear, have deserted him. His new, young wife (Grace Kelly) is a Quaker who disavows violence, even in self-defense. Caught in a moral dilemma and a situation of great personal danger, the sheriff decides to face the outlaws alone. Eventually he faces the leader of the outlaws in a classic confrontation scene on the town square.

"High noon" has become a parable of citizen responsibility against lawlessness, as well as a metaphor for decisive, often fatal confrontation.

hired gun Originally, a person hired to kill someone; now applied to anyone hired to do a particularly difficult job.

Hiroshima Japanese city destroyed by the first atomic bomb ever dropped upon a civilian population, on August 6, 1945. Four days later a second atomic bomb was dropped on Nagasaki with equally devastating effect. Japan surrendered to the United States, thus ending World War II in the Pacific. The bomb was delivered by the ENOLA GAY, piloted by Col. Paul W. Tibbets, Jr. Hiroshima is a symbol of the destructive power of atomic warfare.

his master's voice   One of the most famous ads ever created shows a fox terrier with his ear cocked to the large horn of an early record player. The ad for *Victor Records* carried the legend: His Master's Voice. In time, the attentive canine became known as "the dog everybody knows."

The English painter Francis Barrand was inspired to paint this picture when he saw his dog Nipper listening intently to the voices and music coming from the horn. The American rights to the painting were acquired in 1901. The expression "his master's voice" is used ironically to indicate taking instruction rather than speaking for oneself.

Hiss, Alger (1904–1996)   Highly respected State Department official sentenced on January 25, 1950, to five years in prison for perjury in denying that in the 1930s he had given secret documents to Whittaker Chambers, an agent for a Soviet spy ring. The evidence hinged on a borrowed typewriter and papers hidden in a pumpkin.

Referred to originally as a victim of Red-scare hysteria, although revisionist theory now holds him to have been guilty of spying.

Hitchcock, Alfred (1899–1980)   British film director famous as the "master of suspense." Almost every one of his many thrillers achieved the status of an instant classic. He made *The 39 Steps, The Lady Vanishes* and *Sabotage* in England. After 1939 he made his pictures for Hollywood: *Rebecca* (1940), *Foreign Correspondent* (1940), *Suspicion* (1941), *Spellbound* (1945), *Dial M for Murder* (1954), *Rear Window* (1954), *Vertigo* (1958), *North by Northwest* (1959), *Psycho* (1960) and *The Birds* (1963).

Once asked whether he ever considered making any other kind of picture, such as a comedy or a musical, he replied: "I'm a typed director. If I made *Cinderella,* the audience would immediately be looking for a body in the coach."

His signature in his films was his appearance in some capacity as a walk-on. But his face became familiar to millions of fans through his commentaries on the TV series *Alfred Hitchcock Presents,* beginning in 1955. He was short, pudgy, double-chinned, bald-pated and had a jutting lower lip from which emanated wry humor delivered with poker-faced imperturbability.

Hitler, Adolf (1889–1945)   Fanatical leader of the National Socialist Party (Nazi) of Germany. Hitler, born in Austria, was appointed chancellor of Germany on January 30, 1933, and became Nazi dictator. Hitler, also known as the FÜHRER, was responsible for German expansionism, World War II and the Holocaust. He was author of *Mein Kampf,* a book setting forth his ideas of a pure Aryan race and society. Not taken seriously at first, he made the world pay heavily for not taking heed. Physically, Hitler was a figure of derision, with a slicked-down lick of hair across his forehead, a short bushy mustache, ramrod spine, arm raised stiffly in the Nazi salute, knickerbocker-uniformed and booted. But he was a mesmerizing orator and a master of propaganda. Hitler committed suicide on April 30, 1945, rather than surrender to the victorious Allies.

To be called a Hitler is to be called evil incarnate; a monster, beyond the limits of the human; a brutal and deranged dictator. A Hitler is also a derisive term for an apoplectic caricature with a short moustache.

hit list   Originally, in Mafia circles, an alleged or actual list of individuals targeted for murder. In non-criminal circles, a hit list contains the names of individuals to be punished, demoted, removed from office or dunned for money.

Use: Nobody had seen it—but everyone knew that the president of the company kept a hit list of employees who were making trouble among their coworkers.

hitting below the belt   In boxing, the belt is an imaginary line above the hips, where a man's belt usually rests. A boxer who punches his opponent below this line ("below the belt") is said to have delivered a "foul blow"—and is penalized a number of points. If he continues to hit his opponent below the belt, he may be disqualified and forfeit the match.

In general use, "hitting below the belt" refers to an indecent, illegal, unsportsmanlike act or remark.

Hobbesian   Related to the ideas of the English political philosopher Thomas Hobbes (1588–1679). Contrary to the tenets of JEAN-JACQUES ROUSSEAU, Hobbes believed that men in a state of nature are selfish, nasty, brutish and bellicose. To curb these destructive tendencies, they enter into a contract with each other to create a state that will be responsible for keeping the peace. They submit to a sovereign who in turn must guarantee them protection. The power of the sovereign derives from the people, who may rebel against him (or a parliament) should he fail to maintain his duties under the compact. These ideas are developed in Hobbes's most famous book, *Leviathan* (1651). "Hobbesian" suggests aggression as the natural state of men.

Use: "The Thai highway, far from being a Hobbesian battleground, is a network of communication . . . as in blinking one's lights to make sure that the other fellow knows you will collide presently unless he gets back in his lane." (Charles Murray, *National Review,* March 30, 1992)

Hobson's choice   Thomas Hobson (1544–1630) was the Cambridge University mail carrier. He also rented horses to university students and others. The October

14, 1712, issue of the *Spectator* (quoted in *A Dictionary of Word Makers* by Cecil Hunt) noted that "Mr. Hobson kept a stable of forty good cattle, always ready and fit for traveling; but when a man came for a horse, he was led into the stable where there was a great choice, but he obliged him to take the horse which stood next to the stable door; so that every customer was alike well served according to his chance, and every horse ridden with the same justice. . . ."

So when you rented a horse from Hobson, you got the most rested horse no matter which one you wanted. Hence a Hobson's Choice is no choice at all.

Use: "If it is reorganization, a new deal and a change you are seeking, it is Hobson's choice. I am sorry for you, but it is really vote for me or not at all." (Woodrow Wilson in a 1910 campaign address, cited in *Political Dictionary* by William Safire)

Hogarthian   In the satirical mode of the English painter and engraver William Hogarth (1697–1764). The 18th century in England is generally referred to as the Age of Satire. In the graphic arts, Hogarth is preeminent.

Hogarth painted and engraved for popular sale three well-known series of pictures: *The Harlot's Progress* (1732), *The Rake's Progress* (1735) and *Marriage à la Mode* (1745). Hogarth, himself, described his pictures as "modern moral subjects . . . similar to representations on the stage." And indeed they have many elements of the drama: one or two characters whom we follow in consecutive action from picture to picture; narrative energy; closely observed and detailed settings; satirical and often didactic themes on the profligacies, inanities and boorishness of society. His scenes are often coarse, raw and brutal as he depicts rowdy men and women in stages of undress and dishevelment in bedrooms, taverns, brothels.

Hogarthian, then, refers to satirical social criticism of what is loutish and cruel in manners.

Hokinson Girls   Inhabitants of cartoons created by Helen Hokinson (1893–1949). They were a good-natured spoof of well-fed, middle-aged, deadly serious clubwomen on the lookout for culture. They are shown at book discussion clubs, at flower shows, in department store mélées, in traffic jams of their own creation, at home wheedling maids. In all these situations, culture is the loser. Hokinson's partner, James Reid Parker, wrote the humorous captions for her drawings. Her *New Yorker* cartoons were collected and published in several books during her lifetime and posthumously, e.g., *The Ladies, God Bless 'Em* (1950), *There Are Ladies Present* (1952) and *The Hokinson Feature* (1956).

"The Hollow Men" (1925)   Poem by T. S. Eliot about modern man's lack of faith or conviction. He inhabits "death's dream kingdom," that is to say, death-in-life, without hope of redemption. Eliot writes:

We are the hollow men
We are the stuffed men
Leaning together
Headpiece filled with straw. Alas!

Today the phrase is usually used to denote people who are shallow, lacking in idealism, or stupid. See also "NOT WITH A BANG BUT A WHIMPER."

Hollywood   Fabled movie capital of the world, located in Los Angeles, California, where the weather is mild and dependable, it has been the home of the big-time film studios from the pioneering days of the industry until today. Here William and Cecil B. DeMille, Sam Goldwyn, Louis B. Mayer, William Fox and the Warner Brothers built their empires. Here, movie stars and goddesses lived and worked amid glamor and glitter. Like the American Dream, it had its shabby side, too. Its power to corrupt has been vividly related in novels like *The Deer Park* (1955) by Norman Mailer and *The Day of the Locust* (1939) by Nathanael West. But in setting and disseminating in vivid screen images the patterns and values of American life, Hollywood has had immeasurable influence on the popular culture of the entire world. Hollywood, in the popular imagination, remains a place of stardust and dreams.

Hollywood Ten   HOLLYWOOD writers and one director who in 1947 were blacklisted by the motion picture industry itself, after they were held in contempt of Congress for refusing to testify before the House Un-American Activities Committee (HUAC) hearings. They are generally considered victims of anticommunist hysteria and witch-hunting.

The 10 are Alvah Bessie, Herbert Biberman, Lester Cole, Edward Dmytryk, Ring Lardner, Jr., John Howard Lawson, Albert Maltz, Sam Ornitz, Robert Adrian Scott and Dalton Trumbo.

Holmes, Sherlock   Master detective created by Sir Arthur Conan Doyle (1859–1930) in *A Study in Scarlet* (1887). He solved a variety of strange, exotic crimes through uncanny observation, intuition, and ratiocination. He shared rooms in Baker Street, London, with his constant companion, DR. WATSON. The phrase "Elementary, my dear Watson," spoken by Holmes to his friend, has become part of the English language.

Holocaust   Nazi Germany's deliberate annihilation of six million European Jews during World War II, Hitler's "FINAL SOLUTION" to the "Jewish problem." The systematic and technical proficiency of the mass murders in the gas chambers of concentration camps irrevocably altered our consciousness of the potential for human brutality and depravity. Although the Nazis also destroyed members of other groups (gypsies, Slavs, homosexuals, political opponents), "the Holocaust" refers specifically to the destruction of the Jews and their culture.

Now used to indicate mass murder of any people.

Holy Grail   See GALAHAD.

Hooverville   A shantytown put together out of crates and cardboard by the poor and dispossessed during the Great Depression in the United States, when Herbert Hoover was president (1929–1933).

The term has come to stand for any haphazard, temporary shelters.

Hopalong Cassidy   One of television's early "heroes" (1949–51), "Hoppy," as he was affectionately called, was the nemesis of the villains of the Old West. Astride his faithful horse Topper, the silver-haired movie star William Boyd (1895–1972), dressed in black, played Hoppy to the delight of old and young and to the consternation of evildoers.

The predictable but nonetheless enjoyable plots of the television series were drawn from Clarence E. Mulford's novels and from earlier low-budget movies.

Hopper, Edward (1882–1967)   American painter whose canvases suggest with compassion and even poetry the loneliness and alienation of ordinary people in ordinary American settings: a woman sitting alone at a window in an all-night cafeteria, or on a bench outside a railroad station, or standing in the lobby of a movie theater. Even his houses and trees and gasoline stations are imbued through the play of light and shadow with a brooding, introspective loneliness. His subjects seem frozen in time. Although often labeled a realist, Hopper is subjective in emotional tone.

"The horror! The horror!"   The last words of the dying Mr. Kurtz, an ivory trader in the heart of the Congo, in HEART OF DARKNESS (1902), a short novel by JOSEPH CONRAD (1857–1924). The words represent the ultimate, despairing vision of a man who went into the jungle not only to find and export ivory but also to bring civilization to barbaric natives. Instead, he found himself using brutal means, including human sacrifice, to subjugate the natives for his own purposes. What he discovered, and what the narrator, Marlow, discovers too, is that beneath the facade of civilized behavior shown by any one of us lies a substratum of savagery waiting to erupt. The jungle is within all of us.

The words "The horror! The horror!" are quoted seriously and sometimes mockingly to connote evil, the dark evil of death and savagery and sin.

Horton, Willie   Willie Horton was a convicted murderer in Massachusetts who had been allowed to leave prison on weekend furloughs. On the last of these releases from prison he killed again. During the presidential campaign of 1988, supporters of the Republican Party candidate George Bush blitzed the TV air waves with commercials showing Horton going through a revolving door and implying that Michael Dukakis, then governor of Massachusetts as well as the Democratic Party's candidate for president, was soft on crime. Although some labeled the commercial racist, many accepted the message. Bush's victory was to a large extent the result of fears aroused by the Willie Horton commercial. It was, of course, a spurious issue: the Massachusetts furlough policy had been adopted before Dukakis became governor.

A Willie Horton issue now means a spurious or invented issue to discredit an opponent.

hot line   Originally referring to a direct telephone link between the heads of state in Moscow and Washington for the purpose of averting a terrible mistake in a presumed nuclear first strike, the term now refers to immediate telephone communication in any crisis. TV stations, for example, cite hot lines for getting help in domestic crises, for child abuse, for suicide threats.

Hotspur   A character in Shakespeare's history play *Henry IV,* Part One. Hotspur is the well-deserved nickname of Sir Henry Percy, son of the earl of Northumberland. In this play about honor, Shakespeare portrays Hotspur as excessively impetuous and fiery in the defense of his honor. On the other end of the spectrum, FALSTAFF is a cowardly braggart who would not dream of risking his life for honor. In the center is Prince Hal, who seems lax about his honor as a king's son when he cavorts with Falstaff, but who rises to the occasion when necessary. It is Prince Hal, representative of the golden mean, who kills the rebellious Hotspur in battle at Shrewsbury.

A Hotspur is a hotheaded, reckless person too quick to take offense and too quick to avenge it.

Hottentot   Originally, the term described a native of West Cape Province, South Africa. The Hottentots, whose appearance and language are similar to those of the Bushmen, were the first tribe to greet the Dutch settlers in the 17th century. A pastoral people, they were pushed back into uncongenial areas of the interior by the Dutch. Their numbers have dwindled.

In today's usage a Hottentot is a wild man, an ignorant savage.

Use: "A dunderhead gets himself in a long-tailed coat, rises behind the sacred desk, and emits such bilge as would gag a Hottentot. Is it to pass unchallenged?" (H. L. Mencken)

Houdini, Harry (1874–1926) Born Eric Weiss, a world-famous American magician renowned for his baffling escapes from straitjacket, chains, handcuffs, locked containers. Houdini's stage performances also included the disappearance and reappearance of men, women, animals. He never revealed the secrets of his extraordinary exploits.

In popular parlance, anyone who escapes from an apparently escape-proof setting is called a "real Houdini." One who causes people to disappear is also referred to as a "real Houdini."

House Un-American Activities Committee (HUAC) See MCCARTHYISM.

Howard, Leslie (1893–1943) Born Leslie Stainer, a British actor who played sensitive, soft-spoken, gentle roles, including Ashley Wilkes in *Gone With the Wind* (1939). See O'HARA, SCARLET.

Howard Beach Blue-collar neighborhood in the Borough of Queens, New York, where in 1986 a gang of white youths attacked four blacks and chased one of them, Michael Griffith, onto a parkway where he was struck and killed by a car. The whites were tried by a special prosecutor and found guilty of manslaughter. The incident raised racial tension in the city, but many blacks felt that justice had been meted out to the white racists.

Howard Beach has become a symbol of racial confrontation as well as a test of racial justice.

Howdy Doody Puppet on the television show of the same name. From 1947 to 1960, this four-foot puppet with 72 freckles (by an official count) provided lively, nonsensical, highly appealing entertainment for children—ably assisted by Clarabell, a clown with "the voice of an autohorn."

The host and creator of the *Howdy-Doody* show was Buffalo Bob Smith (1917–98), a gifted ventriloquist with a true affection for children and an intuitive understanding of what made them tick.

The audience demand for tickets to the show was overwhelming; the waiting list was so long that—the show's managers reported—expectant mothers requested tickets for their unborn children!

How to Win Friends and Influence People See CARNEGIE, DALE.

Huck Finn Thirteen-year-old narrator and main character of *The Adventures of Huckleberry Finn* (1885), a seminal American novel by Mark Twain (Samuel Langhorne Clemens, 1835–1910). Huck also plays a pivotal part in *The Adventures of Tom Sawyer* (1876).

Huck is a homeless, rough-hewn boy in St. Petersburg, Missouri, who resists all attempts to "civilize" him. He runs away from the schooling, pieties and manners to which Miss Watson and the widow Douglas subject him. He also runs away from his brutal, drunken father who beats him and locks him up. By staging his own "murder," Huck successfully prevents any search for the runaway boy.

Huck escapes by canoe to Jackson's Island near Hannibal. There he finds Jim, a black slave who has run away from his mistress, Miss Watson, because she was about to sell him down the river. Huck and Jim embark on an odyssey upon the broad Mississippi River, advancing by night and hiding in coves by day. They have many adventures, experiencing the foolishness, depravity and chicanery of the human species encountered along the river.

The central problem for Huck is his moral dilemma: Should he turn in Jim to the authorities, as the law demands? Ironically, his conscience tells him that he must. After all, he is a boy of the South. But he has come to recognize and appreciate Jim as a loyal, brave, good-hearted, dignified friend, even if his skin is black. After a great inner struggle, Huck decides to reject the dictates of the law and to follow the promptings of his heart. He will help Jim escape from slavery. He will do right by doing wrong. His decision makes him feel good and "all washed clean of sin."

Huck Finn is the prototypical American struggling with the overriding problem of racism in our country. Pure of heart, he is imprisoned for a while in the accepted moral code of his time and place. Lionel Trilling said of Twain's novel, *Huckleberry Finn,* that "it is one of the world's great books and one of the central documents of American culture."

Use: "It is a peculiarity of the American historical imagination to believe that we, as a people—Huck Finns, all—have always just awakened, the day before yesterday from an age of innocence" (*New York Times,* August 23, 1992).

Hughes, Howard (1905–1976)   A billionaire inventor, movie maker, eccentric and recluse, Howard Hughes was born in Texas to a wealthy family. In the late 1920s he became a movie producer with *Hell's Angels* and many other hits to his credit. He studied aeronautics, designed planes and became an aviator who made and broke speed records. In July 1938 he and his crew flew around the world in three days, 19 hours, and 17 minutes, cutting in half the previous world record set by Wiley Post in 1933. He invested in Las Vegas casinos and associated with strange people who made unsubstantiated claims upon his fortune. Eventually he disappeared from public view, becoming a mysterious legend in his own lifetime and after his death. His last years were so mysterious that he became the subject of one of the most infamous publishing frauds of modern times. A writer by the name of Clifford Irving wrote the *Autobiography of Howard Hughes,* based, he claimed, on taped interviews with Hughes. McGraw-Hill and Time, Inc., bought it for $750,000 and spent over a million dollars in publicizing it. The whole publishing world was agog, because nobody knew whether Hughes was dead or alive or mentally fit. A telephone call from Hughes, himself, to the publisher to the effect that he didn't know Irving from Adam exposed the fraud. Irving was sentenced to two and a half years in prison.

Humpty-Dumpty   A nursery rhyme riddle that first appeared in print in the early 19th century:

> *Humpty-Dumpty sat on a wall*
> *Humpty-Dumpty had a great fall*
> *All the king's horses and all the king's men*
> *Cannot put Humpty-Dumpty together again.*

Humpty-Dumpty is, of course, an egg, which, once broken, cannot be made whole again; thus, a Humpty-Dumpty describes anything that has been split irreparably apart.

Use: "My gut feeling about Yugoslavia is that Humpty-Dumpty has fallen off the wall and can't be put together again." (Thomas Friedman on *Washington Week in Review,* 1991)

Hun   See ATTILA.

hundred days, the   Originally, this expression referred to the period of time (March 20 to June 28, 1815) between Napoleon's escape from Elba and his defeat at Waterloo. In our time, "the hundred days" refers to the first hundred days of Franklin Delano Roosevelt's presidency in 1933. Under his dynamic leadership, Congress passed far-reaching, revolutionary legislation to deal with the problems of the Great Depression. Since then the first hundred days of a president's incumbency have become a measure of the direction and style of his administration. See also NEW DEAL.

Huntley-Brinkley Report   Broadcast nightly from 1956 to 1980, this news report was named for the superstars of TV reporting: Chet Huntley (1911–74), conservative, straightforward, somewhat on the serious side; and David Brinkley (1920–   ), liberal, glib, inclined to the sardonic. Both handled the news superbly—with style and distinction. TV has not found their equal. At its peak, the *Huntley-Brinkley Report* reached an audience of over 17,000,000.

The program was famous for its coverage of the news, and for its closing signature:

"Good-night, David."
"Good-night, Chet."

Hurstwood, George   Tragic character in Theodore Dreiser's novel SISTER CARRIE (1900). Infatuated with Carrie, he abandons his wife and his two selfish children, steals $10,000 from the safe of the fashionable bar in Chicago of which he has been the manager, and tricks Carrie into going with him to New York. There the police catch up with him, recover the money, and Hurstwood, accepting more and more meaningless jobs, finally is reduced to a Bowery bum. When he comes unwillingly to depend upon Carrie's rising earning power on the stage, he commits suicide.

Hurstwood is a weak man who is destroyed by his passion for another woman and by hostile forces that undermine his will.

***"Hypocrite lecteur, mon semblable, mon frere"* (Hypocrite reader, my double, my brother)**   Last line of the preface to *Les Fleurs du Mal* (1857), a book of poems by the French Symbolist poet Charles Baudelaire (1821–67). The book achieved instant notoriety when both author and publisher were prosecuted for "offending against public morals."

Baudelaire liked to strike attitudes as a dandy, a profligate Parisian boulevardier, an opium smoker, a decadent who pushed the frontiers of the forbidden. The well-known phrase *"épater les bourgeois"* has been attributed to him. He was addicted to the BYRONIC and the GOTHIC, the dark turbulent sides of romanticism; and he was enormously influenced by the stories and poems of Edgar Allan Poe, which he came upon in 1846 and translated into French between 1856 and 1865. Poe reinforced Baudelaire's tastes for the macabre, the morbid, the perverse, in all of which Baudelaire claimed to find not only beauty but also good. He rejected the conventional distinctions between good and evil.

What Baudelaire is saying to his readers in "Hypocrite lecteur . . ." is that in the profoundest layers of our being we are all attracted to evil as well as to good.

Iacocca, Lee A. (1924–   )   The son of Italian immigrants, Iacocca became a marketing genius and the president of Ford Motor Company. In 1978, forced out of Ford, he took over the failing Chrysler Motor Corporation, and through astute management and an unprecedented $1.2 billion loan guarantee from Congress he turned the company around to make a $2.4 billion profit in 1984. His autobiography *Iacocca* (1984), written with William Novak, sold 2.5 million hardcover copies by 1986.

An "Iacocca" is a business genius, especially at reviving failing companies.

Iago   The archvillain of Shakespeare's tragedy *Othello* (1604). It is impossible to find an adequate motive for Iago's calculated and deliberate destruction of Othello, the Moor of Venice. Iago claims to feel indignant at Othello's passing him over for promotion and favoring the younger and less experienced Cassio, but that motive is too trivial for the magnitude of the crime. The truth is that Iago is a cunning sadist. He takes infinite pleasure in manipulating people out of sheer malevolence, and especially in playing upon the passions of the black Othello. He provokes and prods Othello into a paroxysm of jealous rage. Not until Othello has smothered his innocent wife Desdemona and committed suicide is Iago's lust for evil temporarily slaked.

Iago is a name synonymous with evil for evil's sake.

"I cannot tell a lie"   A phrase attributed to the young George Washington in a story first published by M. L. Weems in his *Life of Washington* (1800). The fictional story of how George Washington cut down a cherry tree when he was a young boy and then confessed his misdeed to his father became the most popular legend about any American president until the proliferation of "Honest Abe" anecdotes in Lincoln biographies.

The tale is used to this day to instruct the young in truth-telling. Of course, just as often, it is said tongue-in-cheek.

Ichabod Crane   A gangly, scarecrowish itinerant schoolmaster in "The Legend of Sleepy Hollow," a story in *The Sketch Book* (1820) by Washington Irving. Ichabod is courting Katrina Van Tassel, a farmer's daughter in a Hudson Valley village. His rival for Katrina, Brom Bones, fills Ichabod's head with scary tales of a headless horseman who haunts the countryside. One night, as Ichabod is riding home from Katrina's, the headless horseman appears in the mist and gallops at top speed after him. Ichabod is so terrified that he rides right out of Katrina and Brom Bones's life.

An Ichabod Crane is a person whose appearance elicits laughter or ridicule: someone timid, gawky, skinny, wearing ill-fitting clothes with pants and sleeves much too short.

"I coulda been a contender"   A rueful remark made by Marlon Brando to his brother (Rod Steiger) in the taxi scene of *On the Waterfront,* a 1954 movie about union corruption on the Hoboken, New Jersey, docks. The phrase, today used ironically, suggests wasted potential, lost opportunities.

I Cover the Waterfront (1932)   Best-selling novel by journalist Max Miller, exposing crime and corruption on the waterfront.

Now expanded to mean a complete account of anything, "the whole story."

Use: The catholicity of what we publish is apparent. We really do cover the waterfront.

id   FREUDIAN term for the primitive side of the psyche, the subconscious, associated with repressed sexual and aggressive instincts. The ego and the superego attempt to keep the id in check, but every once in a while the id blows its top and runs amok, in civilizations as in individuals.

Use: "Père Ubu is a giant id let loose, without any reins on his appetite or his ambitions." (*Columbia Spectator,* July 12, 1989)

"I do not choose to run"   Calvin Coolidge (1872–1933), the 30th president of the United States and a man of few words, announced in his usual laconic manner, on August 2, 1927: "I do not choose to run for president in 1928." That was that.

The phrase has since been used flippantly by anybody who turns down an offer to run for any office, no matter how humble or trivial. It is a way of saying "Thank you, but no thank you."

"I do not like thee, Dr. Fell"   The opening line of a verse written by Thomas Brown, a 17th-century English clergyman, while he was a student at Christ Church, Oxford:

I do not like thee, Dr. Fell
The reason why I cannot tell
  But this alone I know full well
I do not like thee, Dr. Fell.

Though Dr. Fell was highly regarded as a man of courage and high principles, a wholly admirable man, his contemporaries could not, for some inexplicable reasons, "warm up" to him. Thus, a Dr. Fell arouses respect and admiration along with simultaneous distaste or emotional rejection.

"If Winter comes, can Spring be far behind?"   The final line of "Ode to the West Wind" by the English romantic poet Percy Bysshe Shelley (1792–1822).

In this poem, Shelley prays to the powerful west wind, which can drive all before it—leaves, seeds, clouds, waves:

Drive my dead thoughts over the universe
Like withered leaves to quicken a new birth!
And, by the incantation of this verse,

Scatter, as from an unextinguished hearth
Ashes and sparks, my words among mankind!
Be through my lips to unawakened earth

The trumpet of a prophecy! O Wind,
If Winter comes, can Spring be far behind?

Shelley, always a nonconformist, a rebel and a free spirit, became a crusader against all forms of what he considered bondage: religion, marriage, political domination. He was a revolutionary poet and activist. His ideas were obviously not well received by the establishment. Often discouraged but never defeated, except by an untimely death, he wrote in the same poem:

A heavy weight of hours has chained and bowed
One too like thee: tameless, and swift, and proud.

He hoped always that his ideas would prevail. After all, were not poets the "unacknowledged legislators of mankind"?

Thus the line "If Winter comes . . ." is always used to express hope in a better future, hope for renewal, for rebirth after a time of deadness and aridity.

"I have a dream"   Inspirational words, intoned with biblical refrain and cadence, in a speech by Rev. Dr. Martin Luther King, Jr., on August 28, 1963. To a crowd of 200,000 mostly black, peaceful demonstrators gathered at the

Washington Mall to demand passage of a civil rights bill, he said: "I have a dream that one day this nation will rise up and live out the true meaning of its creed: 'We hold these truths to be self-evident, that all men are created equal.'" He ended his stirring speech with the dream that his people would be "free at last."

A person need but say, "I have a dream," no matter how trivial or jocular or profound the dream, to call up overtones of the passionate eloquence of Dr. King's dream.

I Love Lucy   When Lucille Ball (1911–89) died, episodes of *I Love Lucy,* the longest-running show in prime time and syndicated television history (original run: 1951–57), were lighting up TV screens in 80 countries. Conceived by Lucy and her husband, Desi Arnaz, a Cuban band leader, *I Love Lucy* became the most familiar, the most loved, the most rerun of all SITCOMS. Though Desi played his part as straight man well, Lucy was obviously the central character. A flawless comedienne, she acted the part of the wacky but lovable housewife, Lucy Ricardo.

"I'm from Missouri"   Phrase used by Willard D. Vandiner, representative to Congress from Columbia, Missouri, from 1897 to 1905. In 1902, at a dinner given for members of a House Naval Committee inspecting the Navy Yard in Philadelphia, Vandiner expressed skepticism about a statement made by a previous speaker. Jocularly he said, "I'm from Missouri, you've got to show me."

Used (and not only by Missourians) to express doubt, as in "doubting Thomas," to challenge statements, and to demand proof in the form of direct evidence.

"I'm in charge"   Premature statement by General Alexander Haig, the secretary of state, shortly after the assassination attempt on President Ronald Reagan on March 30, 1981.

Generally used satirically for a pushy, rather arrogant assumption of authority.

impressionist   The most important element of an impressionist painting is natural light, or rather the effect of natural light, sunlight, upon a subject. Claude Monet (1840–1926), for instance, painted whole series of canvases on the same subject in different light: Rouen Cathedral, haystacks, poplars and especially the water lilies in his pond at Giverny. His paintings became more and more incorporeal, verging in his last years on the abstract. The word "impressionism" was coined in 1874 by an unfriendly critic looking at a picture by Monet entitled *Impression: Sunrise.* The dazzling patches of flickering color, which at first blinded the conservative critics, have become an accepted way of looking at nature.

The impressionists went outdoors for their subjects, not only in the country but in the city as well. They painted the boulevards of Paris, with their throngs of strollers and people watchers on the terraces of cafés, as well as picnics and fairs and lanes in the country. Camille Pissarro (1830–1903) painted exquisite canvases of both city and country life. The impressionists convey an enthusiasm for life, for gaiety, for leisure. They are the absolute opposites of the expressionists.

in the ball park   Falling within the area where the game of baseball is played. It has come to mean acceptable, within reasonable limits.

Use: Markson offered $28 a share for Bartel Company stock. The company officers considered it well within the ball park.

I Never Promised You a Rose Garden (1964)   Novel by the American writer Joanne Greenberg (Hannah Green) about a 16-year-old girl's psychotic retreat into an imaginary world and her sympathetic psychiatrist's successful efforts to bring her back to the real world, however flawed it may be.

"I never promised you a rose garden" is an admission that whatever has been proffered is not perfect, but perhaps acceptable.

"I Never Saw a Butterfly"   Title of a poem, written by a child in a Nazi concentration camp, and then of a book containing the discovered writings and art work of the children exterminated in the camps. A sad, rueful, touching sentiment, the phrase is a metaphor for all the missed life, the missed experience of beauty, of the one million slaughtered Jewish children. There were no butterflies, no tender frail beauties behind barbed wire and concrete.

Information, Please   A radio show that opened, "Wake up, America. Time to stump the experts." It was the most literate, most urbane, most witty quiz show on radio from the late 1930s to the early 1940s. Every week the listening audience submitted questions about art, music, literature, nature, sports and other topics to a panel of "experts," including Oscar Levant, a concert pianist; John Kieran, a sports writer for the *New York Times,* a nature-lover and classical scholar; Clifton Fadiman, a critic, teacher and editor; and F.P.A. (Franklin Pierce Adams), a newspaper columnist for the *World* and the *New York Post,* whose *Conning Tower* and *Our Own Samuel Pepys Diary* were a rare literary delight.

Innisfree   An idyllic island in Lough Gill, County Sligo, Ireland, to which William Butler Yeats, in his poem "The Lake Isle of Innisfree," dreams of retiring from the "pavements grey" of London.

Inquisition, the   The Catholic Church's method for rooting out heresy and punishing heretics. Beginning c. 1233, Pope Gregory IX designated Franciscan and Dominican monks to investigate religious practices among the Albigenses in southern France. By papal decree, the visiting inquisitors superseded the local bishops, who apparently had not been sufficiently zealous in dealing with heresy. The itinerant inquisitors, holding court in the local monastery, gave everyone a month of grace to come forward "to abjure heresy." Having done this, the individuals were then given a month of penance. Those who did not come forward were tried before a tribunal of laymen and representatives of the bishop. The procedures were secret. Authorized by Pope Innocent IV in 1252, the inquisitors subjected their victims to cruel and relentless questioning and torture. Stubborn heretics were handed over for punishment to the local civil officers, not the church. Burning at the stake was a frequent punishment. Lesser punishments consisted of imprisonment and confiscation of property.

The medieval Inquisition was mainly employed in southern France, northern Italy, Germany and the Papal States. It was abolished in the 19th century.

Any investigation, especially of a religious or political nature, characterized by reckless charges, harsh questioning, cruel punishment, prejudice of the examiners, is often described as "an inquisition" or "inquisitorial." Thus, the U.S. Senate hearings conducted by Senator Joseph McCarthy (1907–57) from 1950 to 1954 on communist infiltration of governmental agencies, were compared to the Inquisition, subverting individual liberties and depriving individuals of their constitutional rights.

invisible hand   In his influential book, *Wealth of Nations* (1776), the Scottish philosopher and economist Adam Smith (1723–90) set forth the doctrine of laissez-faire. In essence, it held that individual self-interest, untrammeled by government regulation or interference, would lead to flourishing economic conditions for all. According to Adam Smith, "Individuals—seeking to further their self-interest will be led—as if guided by an invisible hand. . . ."

Use: "Howe and Longman are correct in arguing that the welfare state can't keep expanding at its present rate; the political market, unlike the economic one, has no self-correcting mechanism, no Invisible Hand to restore equilibrium between supply and demand." (*National Review,* April 27, 1992)

Invisible Man (1952)   Novel by Ralph Ellison (1914–94). The unnamed hero is a talented, idealistic black boy who grows up to be totally disillusioned with society, black and white. "I am an invisible man," he says in the opening sentence of the prologue. He is hiding in the basement of an abandoned New York City apartment house, which he has illuminated with a thousand electric bulbs to make himself visible. He has literally—and figuratively—gone underground to find his identity.

"Invisible man" is a term applied not only to blacks but also to other segments of society whose needs nobody seems to notice or care about.

"I only regret that I have but one life to give for my country" These are the last words reputed to have been uttered by Nathan Hale (1755–76), a captain in the American militia during the Revolutionary War, just before he was hanged as a spy by the British.

Hale volunteered for a hazardous mission behind the British lines to secure badly needed information about the size of British forces on Long Island. Disguised as a Dutch schoolmaster, Hale penetrated the British lines and obtained the information he sought. While attempting to return to the American lines, he was captured by the British. The British commander, General Sir William Howe, condemned him to die on the gallows the next day.

Hale has remained a martyr to the cause of American independence and a model for patriotic Americans in and outside of the military.

This originally fervent expression has come to be used ironically as an apology for lesser offenses, a kind of "so kill me."

iron curtain Phrase coined by Winston Churchill in a speech at Fulton, Missouri, in 1946, shortly after the end of World War II, to describe the absolute division between the Western democracies and the communist bloc of Eastern European nations dominated by the U.S.S.R.: "From Stettin in the Baltic to Trieste in the Adriatic, an iron curtain has descended across the continent." Soviet policies of secrecy and censorship had created an impenetrable barrier to communication and understanding between these two great ideological adversaries.

The term is now used seriously and sometimes ironically to denote a solid wall of secrecy separating two stubborn individuals, groups or nations.

Use: The advertising and editorial departments of the newspaper were separated by an iron curtain.

It Can't Happen Here (1935) A novel by Sinclair Lewis (1885–1951) warning Americans that indeed "it" can happen "here," "it" meaning a fascist dictatorship and "here" being the United States. The action of the novel takes place in 1936, one year after its publication, when fascism in Italy was already established and Nazism was on the rise in Germany. In the book, the newly elected president of the Untied States, Buzz Windrup, takes control of the Congress and the Supreme Court, suppresses labor unions and minorities and uses storm troopers, the Minute Men, to crush all opposition. The hero, Doremus Jessup, is the editor of a small, liberal newspaper in Vermont. In the course of his fight against the dictatorship, he comes to realize that liberalism will not work and he joins the revolutionary forces of the New Underground.

The phrase "it can't happen here" is always used ironically to mean it *can* happen here—whatever "it" is.

"It" Girl   Clara Bow (1905–65) became known as the "It" Girl after starring in the movie *It* (1927), based on Elinor Glyn's titillating, mildly daring novel of the same name. More than any other movie actress of her time, Clara Bow personified the flapper of the 1920s. She was vital, fun-loving, vivacious and very sexy. Her Hollywood producer, B. F. Schulberg, cast her in pictures precisely tailored for her special persona: *Rough House Rosie, Dancing Mothers, Red Hair, The Wild Party.* Although they promised sex and sin, they were, by today's standards, quite innocent, invariably ending with Clara's marrying the "nice guy."

Today, an It Girl is any vivacious, provocative young woman whom men find interesting and irresistible.

I and Thou   Philosophical book (1923; English translation, 1937) by Martin Buber (1878–1965), Austrian-born Israeli theologian. The book postulates two ways of relating to people: (1) the I-It relationship, which "focuses on a functional and manipulative treatment of other persons and things"; and (2) the I-Thou relationship, which "provides for greater interpersonal knowledge and responsibility." The I-It way looks at people as objects; the I-Thou way sees people as subjects, and is, therefore, a more profound and sympathetic way. *I and Thou* had an important influence on psychology, education, ethics and theology.

It is a far, far better thing that I do . . .   See CARTON, SYDNEY.

***It's a Wonderful Life* (1946)**   Movie directed by Frank Capra and starring James Stewart. Partly a fantasy, it tells the story of a sincere, hard-working but depressed young man. When he is about to commit suicide, his guardian angel comes along, shows him the terrible consequences of his act should he go through with it and convinces him that life can be beautiful after all. The young man returns to his family and they spend a happy Christmas together.

The phrase and the movie are optimistic, if sentimental, summations of everyday family life. Like Dickens's *A Christmas Carol, It's a Wonderful Life* has become a Christmas tradition.

"It was the best of times, it was the worst of times"   Opening words of *A Tale of Two Cities* (1859), a novel about the French Revolution by Charles Dickens.

The novel is set in 1775; the two cities are Paris and London; and the fates of Sydney Carton, Charles Darnay, Lucy Manette and Dr. Manette unravel to the sound of the guillotine presided over by Madame DEFARGE and her revolutionary compatriots.

Use: For some families, Christmas can be the best of times and the worst of times.

Iwo Jima   On February 23, 1945, men of the 28th Regiment of the Fifth Division of U.S. Marines scaled heavily fortified Mount Suribachi on the island of Iwo Jima (750 miles south of Tokyo) and planted the American flag on its summit. The scene has been immortalized in a famous photograph, which is now a symbol of the "can-do" attitude of the marines.

"Jabberwocky"   A poem in *Through the Looking Glass* (1871) by Lewis Carroll. Alice must hold it up to a mirror to read it, but even then "she couldn't make it out at all." Most of the words are invented.

Actually, the poem is a spoof. A young man goes out into the world to make a name for himself. His mother tells him to beware the jabberwock, "the jaws that bite, the claws that catch." He slays the dragon with his "vorpal sword" and with its head the "beamish boy" comes galumphing back to his mother. The last stanza repeats the first, which sets the scene:

> 'Twas brillig, and the slithy toves
> Did gyre and gimble in the wabe;
> All mimsy were the borogoves,
> And the mome raths outgrabe.

Jabberwocky is playful gibberish.

"J'accuse" (1893)   On the morning of January 13, 1898, the readers of the French newspaper, *L'Aurore,* were electrified by a fiery letter, "J'accuse," written by Emile Zola (1840–1902) and addressed to President Faure of France. In passionate, irrefutable detail, France's great naturalist novelist proved that the government had railroaded French army captain Alfred Dreyfus into a lifetime prison sentence in solitary confinement on Devil's Island—an appalling sentence in an appalling prison. (See DREYFUS AFFAIR.)

Zola's charges aroused France and the world. Subsequently prosecuted and vilified, Zola was forced to flee to England. One year later, he returned to France a hero. He had played a crucial role in reversing the verdict against Dreyfus and winning him his eventual freedom.

Today, *"J'accuse"* applies to anyone who publicly exposes individuals guilty of corrupt, illegal, criminal acts or practices.

Jack Armstrong, the All-American Boy   Radio show of the 1930s that met all of the demands of the network's code for children's programs.

The code excluded "torture, horror, use of the supernatural or superstition likely to arouse fear." It banned vulgarity (in speech or action), kidnapping and "cliff hanging."

Jack Armstrong proved that the themes of law and order, clean living, good sportsmanship and decent behavior could attract and hold large, young audiences.

Jack and the Beanstalk   A folktale first published in *Tabard's Popular Stories* (1804) by Benjamin Tabard of London, it tells the story of a poor, feckless boy named Jack who sells his mother's cow for a handful of beans. Exasperated, the mother throws the beans into the garden. Overnight they take root and grow entwined into a sturdy beanstalk reaching into the sky. Jack climbs up the beanstalk into a country terrorized by a giant. Jack steals the giant's goose, the goose that lays the golden eggs, and returns to earth. He makes several more trips. Eventually, the giant pursues Jack, but Jack cuts the beanstalk down and the giant falls to his death.

Jack's beanstalk has come to mean anything that grows or expands so rapidly as to get out of hand.

Use: During the political scandal, rumors grew like Jacks's beanstalk.

Jack the Ripper   In 1888–89, in Whitechapel, in the East End of London, a number of prostitutes were killed and mutilated. The murderer, never caught, was called Jack the Ripper.

Today, a serial killer is often called a Jack the Ripper, especially if he remains at large and if the victims are mutilated. The name also is used to describe any particularly evil villain. The expression sometimes is used sarcastically, as when someone, hearing the doorbell, asks "Who's there?" The mocking answer: "Jack the Ripper."

Jacobin   At the time of the French Revolution, some Breton deputies to the States General of 1789 met at a monastery of the Jacobins, also known as the Dominicans. These deputies, who came to be known as the Jacobins, grew into a political party that turned more and more to extremist views. They derived their support eventually from the Paris commune and the working class. Danton and Robespierre headed the party. After Danton was guillotined, Robespierre ruled as a virtual dictator during the REIGN OF TERROR.

A Jacobin is a radical political extremist.

Jacques   In Shakespeare's play *As You Like It* (c. 1600), Jacques accompanies the banished duke to the Forest of Arden. In that pastoral setting, he sounds the only sour note. He is a poseur who is in love with his own role—that of the melancholy philosopher, the world-weary traveler. His musings confer upon him, he believes, distinction and superiority. Among all the couples playing out their games of love, he alone remains aloof and uncommitted. To him,

All the world's a stage,
And all the men and women merely players.

A Jacques, in modern usage, is melancholy, cynical and hollow, someone who is in love with the sound of his own voice.

James, Jesse (Woodson) (1847–1882)   Born in Clayton, Missouri, Jesse James at age 15 joined Quantrill's Raiders, then one of the most vicious guerrilla bands in Civil War America. With this early start, he soon became the legendary "badman" of the "Wild West."

With his brother Frank and other associates, he took part in spectacular criminal exploits, supposedly becoming a kind of Robin Hood. Actually, the James boys returned none of their booty to the admiring public. Jesse changed his name to Thomas Howard and hid out in St. Joseph, Missouri, where in 1882 two gang members surprised him and shot him in the head for the $10,000 reward that had been offered for his capture.

Jesse James has become the symbol of the daring, ruthless criminal.

Jamesian   Suggesting the subtle psychological nuances of the thought processes and moral dilemmas in characters created by Henry James (1843–1916), the American novelist and short story writer. These niceties and ambivalences of thought are reflected in the Jamesian style, with its long, complex sentences full of modifying clauses and phrases and balanced elements. James can spend 20 pages having his heroine consider whether or not to accept a dinner invitation.

James concerns himself with the upper classes, their refinements of taste, etiquette and morality. He writes especially of the interaction of two cultures: the American seeming more honest, more robust, more unpolished; the European seeming more devious, more aesthetic, more compromised.

The following novels best embody these Jamesian characteristics of substance and style:

The Portrait of A Lady (1881). Isabel Archer, a young, free-spirited American girl who inherits a fortune, turns down her sturdy American suitor, Caspar Goodwood, as well as a British aristocrat, Lord Warburton, only to be manipulated by the devious Mme. Merle into marrying a cultivated bounder, Gilbert Osmond, whose illegitimate child Mme. Merle has secretly borne.

The Ambassadors (1903). The upright American hero, Lambert Strether, is sent to France to bring home a young American friend who has fallen for the charms of Mme. de Vionnet. Strether himself comes to appreciate the pull of the sensual and the aesthetic in European culture. He concludes: "Live all you can; it's a mistake not to."

The Golden Bowl (1904). Maggie Verver, an American heiress, marries an Italian prince. She does not know that her best friend, the beautiful and brilliant Charlotte Stant, has had an affair with the prince. Maggie's devoted father falls in love with and marries Charlotte. These four characters then try to work out a palatable modus vivendi. Eventually, the solution is that the father and Charlotte return to live in America.

Jane Eyre   See GOTHIC.

Javert   A character in *Les Miserables* (1862), by Victor Hugo (1802–85).

A Javert is a totally humorless, totally legalistic, totally implacable police inspector.

Kenneth Starr, the independent counsel appointed to investigate the Whitewater land deal in Arkansas, has been referred to as a Javert in his relentless pursuit of President Clinton.

See VALJEAN, JEAN.

Jazz Age   The period of the 1920s in the United States. The Jazz Age took its name from the new syncopated black music, which was in great part improvisational and seemingly abandoned. F. Scott Fitzgerald labeled his time the Jazz Age. In his books this signified unconventionality, a get-rich-quick mentality, defiance of Prohibition in speakeasies, wild partying.

At the end of *The Great Gatsby* (1925) the narrator says of Tom and Daisy Buchanan, Jazz-Age types, "They were careless people, Tom and Daisy—they smashed up things and creatures and then retreated back into their money or their vast carelessness, or whatever it was that kept them together, and let other people clean up the mess they had made . . ." See also JAY GATSBY.

Jeeves   The impeccable, omniscient and ever resourceful valet to Bertie Wooster in the comic stories of P. G. Wodehouse (1881–1975), collected in *My Man Jeeves* (1919), *The Inimitable Jeeves* (1923), *Carry On, Jeeves* (1925) and other volumes.

A Jeeves is an imperturbable servant with more savvy and elegance than his master.

Jeffersonian   In the manner or style of, expressing the point of view of, embodying the principles of Thomas Jefferson (1743–1826), the principal author of the Declaration of Independence and third president of the United States.

The French historian Alexis de Tocqueville (1805–59) referred to Jefferson as "the greatest democrat whom the democracy of America has produced." Statesman, diplomat, lawyer, scientist, architect, writer, among American presidents Jefferson comes closest to being America's RENAISSANCE MAN. Clearly, Jefferson was "the most versatile intellectual" to occupy the White House.

The principles that guided Jefferson find expression in his first Inaugural Address (1801):

- belief in the "natural rights of man" as embodied in the Declaration of Independence
- faith in people and their ability to govern themselves
- faith in the power of reason to regulate human affairs
- "absolute acquiescence in the decision of the majority"—but "the minority must possess their equal rights which equal laws must protect—and to violate would be oppression"
- "equal and exact justice to all men of whatever state or persuasion, religious or political"
- "supremacy of civil over military authority"
- zealous protection of all minority rights and civil liberties
- simple and compassionate government
- limited central governmental authority

Jekyll and Hyde   The prototype of the split personality, Dr. Jekyll is a respectable London physician by day who, at night, by means of an experimental drug, turns himself into the repulsive Mr. Hyde, a criminal scouring the sleazy slums of London, in Robert Louis Stevenson's novel *The Strange Case of Dr. Jekyll and Mr. Hyde* (1886). Gradually the evil self gains ascendancy. Hyde commits a murder, and Jekyll, no longer able to control the changeover, commits suicide.

Use: Police described the murder suspect as a Jekyll-Hyde figure who seemed to lead a normal life but was driven by violent urges.

Jesuitical   In the manner of the Jesuits, or the Society of Jesus, a Roman Catholic order founded by St. Ignatius of Loyola in the 16th century. The Jesuits have had the reputation of being the most scholarly and the most rigorously trained intellectuals in the church. They have also had a reputation for deviousness, because they have in the past engaged in political intrigue and have always been effective in debate.

To be accused of being Jesuitical is to be accused of using ingenious or crafty reasoning, of practicing casuistry or equivocation.

Jewish mother   Proverbial over-solicitous Jewish mother who suffocates her children, especially her sons, with too much tender loving care, too much chicken soup, too many sexual and moral restrictions, too many admonitions. Satirized in innumerable skits, plays, novels and movies, including Philip Roth's PORTNOY'S COMPLAINT (1969) and WOODY ALLEN's *New York Stories* (1989). The term has been extended to include any all-embracing, hovering, over-feeding, over-worrying mother of any ethnic background.

jihad   A holy war waged by Muslims against infidels, as when Arabs incite a jihad to drive the Israelis into the sea. By extension, a jihad is any crusade for a deeply felt cause.

Jim Crow   In 1829, Thomas D. Rice, a popular white entertainer made up in blackface, introduced the following old song into a Louisville minstrel show:

Wheel about and turn about
And do jis so.
Every time I wheel about
I jump Jim Crow.

By 1838, observes the historian Jerome Bennett, Jr., the expression *Jim Crow* "was wedged into the language as a synonym for Negro," and a highly unflattering one at that.

Following Reconstruction a series of widely discriminatory regulations called Jim Crow laws were keeping black people from associating with and enjoying the same rights as white people.

In 1890, Homer Plessy, a black American, was arrested when he tried to take a seat in a section of a railroad car reserved for whites only. The cars reserved for blacks were called Jim Crow cars. The same kind of segregation had taken place in other public places such as schools, hospitals, restaurants, waiting rooms, washrooms and factory entrances.

Plessy appealed his case to the U.S. Supreme Court. In its 1896 ruling on *Plessy v. Ferguson,* the Supreme Court established a new judicial concept—"separate but equal"—which held that states could legally segregate the races in public places so long as the facilities or services were equal.

It would be 60 years before another Supreme Court decision, *Brown v. Board of Education* (1954), would overturn the *Plessy v. Ferguson* "separate but equal" doctrine, beginning with the order that all schools be desegregated "with all deliberate speed."

Jiminy Cricket   See PINOCCHIO.

Joads   The "Okie" (Oklahoma) family of sharecroppers in John Steinbeck's epic novel *The Grapes of Wrath* (1939). Driven from their home in the "dust bowl" by bank takeovers and absentee landlords, by poverty and drought, the Joads (all 12 of them plus Jim Casy, an itinerant preacher) pile into a dilapidated truck with their meager possessions and head for California, the land of milk and honey, where jobs supposedly await them. The journey turns into a desperate odyssey with Ma Joad bent on keeping the family together at all costs. In California, the conditions of migrant workers turn out to be a nightmare of cheap labor and brutal deputies. Tom Joad, the central character and Ma's son, becomes a man with a mission. He joins Jim Casy in organizing the workers for better wages, working conditions and liberties.

The Joads are the oppressed and the poor among farm workers in America. They struggle. They endure.

Joan of Arc   In February 1429, an illiterate 17-year-old farm girl, dressed in men's clothing—Jeanne d'Arc, from the French village of Domrémy—was presented to the rather foolish and ineffectual dauphin at Chinon. He was so taken with her that he gave her a suit of armor and a white horse to start her on her avowed mission, which was nothing less than to save France from the occupying English and to have the dauphin crowned at Rheims. Her "voices," to which she had been listening from the age of thirteen, had commanded her to do so.

Joan's army swept across France, recapturing town after town from the stunned English. On July 17, 1429, at Rheims, the dauphin, with Joan at his side, was anointed as the legitimate king of France, Charles VII.

A year later Joan was captured by the Burgundians, sold to the English and tried for witchcraft by the venal bishop Cauchon. After months of inquisitorial questioning, during which she was threatened with torture, Joan signed a paper of abjuration. When she realized that she would be imprisoned for life anyway, she recanted. She was pronounced a heretic, and Cauchon handed her over to the English army. On May 30, 1431, in Rouen, Joan of Arc was burned at the stake.

In 1456 Joan of Arc was rehabilitated and cleared of all charges against her. In 1920 she was canonized and became Saint Joan. In literature, Joan fared badly in Shakespeare's historical play *Henry VI* (c. 1590). The patriotic English bard vilified her as a French slut. She was more than redeemed, however, in George Bernard Shaw's play, *Saint Joan* (1923).

A "Joan of Arc" is a woman who, through faith, is capable of extraordinary heroism.

Joe Palooka   This comic strip champion boxer appeared in 1928 when boxing was in especially bad odor. Joe Palooka's simple, corny charm immediately caught on with the public. Joe is a lovable character—not too bright, but not corrupt or vicious. His somewhat gauche, not quite literate, commonplace utterances on home, motherhood and fair play did not sit too well with sophisticated readers. But the vast "general public" found Joe irresistible.

In his speech and behavior, Joe Palooka embodied the great simplicities—still immensely attractive to most Americans.

Joe six-pack   The ordinary blue-collar American male, given to consuming six-can or six-bottle cartons of beer.

John Bircher   Member of rightist, quasi-secret political organization founded in 1958 by Robert Welch, a Massachusetts businessman. The John Birch Society was named after a United States intelligence officer killed in 1945 by Chinese communists.

The term describes anybody with extremist, reactionary, rabid anticommunist views.

Johnsonian   In the manner of Samuel Johnson (1709–84), also known simply as Dr. Johnson, the English dramatist, critic, essayist, poet, lexicographer, pundit, wit and legendary conversationalist; the quintessential 18th-century man of letters. He was also the subject of the greatest biography, BOSWELL's *Life of Samuel Johnson.*

Although Johnson was poverty-stricken and seriously depressed throughout most of his life and had to resort to hackwork until his prodigious *Dictionary of the English Language* appeared, he was fiercely independent. The story is told of how Johnson in 1747 addressed the Plan of his dictionary to Lord Chesterfield, with the hope that Chesterfield would support it. But Chesterfield seems to have neglected Johnson until the Dictionary was actually published, after which he wrote two papers in praise of it. Johnson's reply to Chesterfield has become a famous rebuff to privilege:

> Is not a patron, my lord, one who looks with unconcern on a man struggling for life in the water, and when he has reached ground encumbers him with help? The notice which you have been pleased to take of my labors, had it been early, had been kind; but it has been delayed till I am indifferent, and cannot enjoy it; till I am solitary, and cannot impart it; till I am known, and do not want it."

(February 7, 1754)

Johnson loved to consort with brilliant people. In 1764 he founded the Literary Club, where he conversed with such eminent contemporaries as Sir Joshua Reynolds, David Garrick, Oliver Goldsmith, Edward Gibbon, Edmund Burke, Adam Smith and, of course, James Boswell, who sedulously recorded the words of the great man.

Johnson is noted for his balanced, witty aphorisms, including:

Patriotism is the last refuge of scoundrels.

A second marriage is the triumph of hope over experience.

A woman preaching is like a dog's walking on his hind legs. It is not
    done well, but you are surprised to find it done at all.

Sir, you have but two topics, yourself and me. I am sick of both.

Depend upon it, sir, when a man knows he is to be hanged in a
    fortnight, it concentrates his mind wonderfully.

To be Johnsonian is to be erudite yet witty, to be measured and balanced in the classic 18th-century mode.

Johnstown flood   In the 1880s such prominent families as the Fricks, the Carnegies and the Mellons summered at the exclusive South Fork Fishing and Hunting Club located on a human-made mountain lake 14 miles above Johnstown, Pennsylvania. On the shores of the lake these tycoons had built their 14- or 16-room "cottages" and their spacious clubhouse. There they picnicked, rowed, cruised on their battery-powered catamaran, held musicales, romanced and gossiped in their moneyed, carefree ways.

On May 31, 1889, the dam holding the lake burst. Four and a half billion gallons of water roared down the narrow Conemaugh Valley, inundating Johnstown, a city of immigrant steelworkers. More than 2,200 men, women and children drowned or were buried in the mud. The city was in ruins. Houses, bridges, machinery were all destroyed.

In the litigation that followed the flood, the denizens of the South Fork Fishing and Hunting Club refused to take responsibility for the tragedy, even though they owned and were supposed to maintain the dam. The dam had failed once before and was generally considered unsafe. The prominent families fought to evade liability. The court ruled that the Johnstown flood was an act of God.

To invoke the memory of the Johnstown flood is to allude to an overwhelming calamity. Nevertheless, the popular imagination is always ready to protect itself against disaster by means of deflation or derision. At the turn of the century, signs posted in saloons read "Don't Spit on the Floor: Remember the Johnstown Flood."

Jolson, Al (1886–1950)   The life of this American singer and actor was the great American rags-to-riches story. Born Asa Yoelson in Srednicke, Russia,

223

the son of a rabbi, he was brought to America as a child. At the age of eight, he was singing in the streets of Washington, D.C., where his father had settled. Extraordinarily talented and irresistibly drawn to the world of entertainment, Jolson by turns was boy soprano, whistler, singer in bars, burlesque, minstrel shows, vaudeville, appeared on Broadway and, finally, in the movies with the stellar role in the first talkie, *The Jazz Singer* (1927).

Appearing in blackface in vaudeville and musical comedy, kneeling on one knee, his arms extended, Jolson made entertainment history with his singing of such hits as "Rock-A-Bye My Baby With a Dixie Melody," "Swanee," "Mammy," "Sonny Boy," "April Showers," "You Made Me Love You."

Jonestown   Town in Guyana set up by the Rev. Jim Jones, leader of a cult called the Peoples Temple. There, in the jungle of South America, in November 1978, more than 900 American men, women and children were persuaded by their fanatical leader to take part in a mass suicide by drinking a potion of Kool-Aid and cyanide. This gruesome ending was triggered by an impending congressional investigation of the cult's totalitarian slant and bizarre sexual practices. Jones had just murdered several people, including California congressman Leo Ryan, who had come to investigate the goings-on in Jonestown.

Jonestown has become a symbol of the brainwashing practiced by perniciously fanatical religious cults.

Joycean   Linguistically adventurous and exuberant, life-affirming, as in the works of James Joyce (1882–1941), Irish novelist, short-story writer and poet. Some of Joyce's identifying techniques were the stream of consciousness and the interior monologue (see MOLLY BLOOM), diversity of architectural form in the novel, especially in *Ulysses* (1922), and experimentation with language bordering on the incommunicable, as in FINNEGANS WAKE (1939). In substance Joyce was anticlerical, robust in his appreciation of the sensual and whatever else was life-enhancing. As Joyce wrote at the end of *A Portrait of the Artist as a Young Man* (1914): "Welcome, O life! I go to encounter for the millionth time the reality of experience and to forge in the smithy of my soul the uncreated conscience of my race."

joy ride   Originally referred to the sense of freedom conferred by the mobility of automobiles. Now, "joy ride" may refer to any irresponsible fling, to an action that is fast and reckless without regard to consequences.

Jude the Obscure (1896)   A tragic novel by Thomas Hardy (1840–1928) in which the main character, Jude Fawley, is thwarted in his every endeavor to acquire an education and "the finer things of life."

Poverty, class distinctions, the snobbery of the academic community, Victorian prudery, and intolerance all combine to place insurmountable barriers in Jude's way. Add mistakes of judgment, misunderstandings and accidents, misplaced passions, malevolent fate or chance, and you have all the ingredients for the darkest, most pessimistic of Hardy's novels. In fact, *Jude the Obscure* was received with such critical and popular hostility that Hardy never wrote another novel, instead devoting the last three decades of his life to poetry.

Jude is the ultimate victim, truly a man of sorrows.

Jug of Wine, a Loaf of Bread, and Thou, A

A Book of Verses underneath the Bough,
A Jug of Wine, a Loaf of Bread—and Thou
Beside me singing in the wilderness—
Oh, Wilderness were Paradise enow!

These lines appeared in London in 1859 in an anonymous translation of *The Rubáiyát of Omar Kháyyám,* written by a 12th-century Persian poet and astronomer.

From the first, the translation was hailed by Danté Gabriel Rossetti (1828–82) and others of the Pre-Raphaelite Brotherhood as an authentic masterpiece. But it was not until the early 1870s that the name of the translator was revealed: Edward Fitzgerald (1809–83). His translation of the *Rubáiyát* helped establish the mood of fin-de-siècle poetry in England.

The leitmotif of the *Rubáiyát* was simple and deeply felt: We know nothing about life in the hereafter, so let us make the most of the here-and-now. In Fitzgerald's graceful translations, a mood of sweet, resigned melancholy suffuses the poems.

Jukes   In *A Study In Crime, Pauperism, Disease, and Heredity,* Richard L. Dugdale advanced the thesis that criminal tendencies are inherited. He traced the criminal careers of 540 blood relations to bolster his theory.

The best known of Dugdale's "cases" were the Jukes, dubbed "the most depraved family in America," a group of rapists, thieves, prostitutes, murderers. To be labeled a "Jukes" still carries the original stigma.

Jungian   Pertaining to the theories of Carl Gustav Jung (1875–1961), a Swiss psychiatrist who broke with Freud in 1913. Jung exalted the power and importance of the unconscious over reason. A life based on reason alone was an impoverished life, he thought. He predicated, moreover, a collective unconscious of the race made up of archetypal patterns recurring throughout the history of man. These took the form of powerful myths common to all cultures.

Jung believed that personal psychic health could be achieved only by bringing the conscious and the unconscious selves into harmony. He divided personalities into two types: introvert (in touch with the inner self) and extrovert (diverted by the outside world at the expense of the inner self).

The term "Jungian" is usually applied to large, overriding, mythic symbols, as in William Butler Yeats's poem "Leda and the Swan," or to the mystical sense of déjà vu in large, recurrent historical patterns.

Jurassic Second period of the Mesozoic Age, about 150 to 200 million years ago, when huge dinosaurs roamed the Earth and small flying reptiles evolved. The term Jurassic became popular when the film *Jurassic Park* (1993), directed by Stephen Spielberg and based on the 1990 novel of the same name by Michael Crichton, stirred moviegoers' imaginations and fears with its vividly realized special effects of cloned dinosaurs out of control and on the rampage. A sequel, *The Lost World: Jurassic Park* (1997), also a film directed by Spielberg, reenforced people's recognition of the term as well as their fear of these appallingly huge creatures.

"Jurassic" is used to describe anything huge and menacing, such as a Jurassic national deficit.

Kafkaesque   Having the nightmarish atmosphere of a short story or novel by Franz Kafka (1883–1924), a Jewish writer born in Prague who wrote in German. Kafka's works, all published posthumously by his friend Max Brod, express the anxiety, the alienation, the terror, the irrationality inherent in major events of the 20th century. They may be seen as parables and allegories open to various interpretations: political, psychological and theological.

On the most obvious level, Kafka attacks the unwieldy bureaucracy of Eastern European countries. On the psychological level, Kafka works out his subconscious struggle against an overpowering father figure. On the theological level, Kafka questions the morality of the invisible God and His Law, and he is tortured by man's inability to achieve salvation.

The Trial (1925), surely one of the seminal novels of the 20th century, tells the story of Joseph K, an ordinary, sober, rational bank manager who awakes one morning to be told by two strangers at his door that he is arrested. They cannot tell him his crime, nor do they haul him away to court or prison. Ostensibly, he can continue as usual with his normal routines. But he becomes obsessed with his "case" and he seeks help in identifying his crime and clearing himself of it. He finds himself in airless, crowded, dreamlike chambers suffused with an erotic atmosphere. At the end of a year, to the day, still ignorant of his crime and unsuccessful in finding his judges, he is taken out of his flat by two executioners who slash his throat and leave him to die in the street "like a dog."

Kafka's material seems related to that of the German expressionist painters; his settings evoke the atmosphere of Raskolnikov's guilt-haunted attics; yet his prose is simple, direct and completely accessible. It is his meaning that eludes us. As Churchill once said of Russia, Kafka is "a riddle wrapped in a mystery inside an enigma."

Anyone who has ever fallen victim to some computer error on the part of a department store clerk or a traffic violations bureau clerk and has tried in vain to disentangle himself from it will have found himself, on a very minor scale, in a Kafkaesque situation.

Victims in the Nazi death camps, cramped together in tiers of bunks, awaiting certain extermination yet not knowing exactly when they would be called, nor what their crime was, outside of being born Jewish, found themselves in a Kafkaesque nightmare from which they would never awake.

kamikaze   Literally, "Divine Wind": Japanese pilots who performed the suicide mission of crashing their planes loaded with explosives into enemy (American) warships during World War II. A kamikaze is one who performs a reckless, seemingly suicidal act.

Kangaroo court   Any connection between the Australian marsupial and a kangaroo court, an ersatz court so constituted as to make a fair trial impossible, seems entirely conjectural. The Oxford English Dictionary has the expression originating in the American West around 1850–55. That places it in the midst of the Gold Rush, when indeed Australian '49ers were among those panning for gold. Could the phrase have been used in the arbitrary settling of conflicting claims under frontier conditions?

At any rate, a kangaroo court is a hastily convened tribunal that metes out arbitrary and summary justice, or rather injustice.

karate   A Japanese method of self-defense without the use of weapons. The practice of karate involves striking the body's sensitive areas with hands, elbows, knees and feet. These strikes are called "karate chops." Administered by someone trained in karate, they can have a devastating effect on the attacked.

In general use, a "karate chop" can mean any well-aimed blow to an individual, an institution, or a plan.

Kate   The shrewish wife tamed by Petruchio in Shakespeare's comedy *The Taming of the Shrew* (c. 1594). Critic Richard Hosley notes that Kate is variously described within the play as "shrewd, rough, sullen, headstrong, intolerable curst, stark mad or wonderful forward, impatient, angry, envious, revengeful, proud-minded, bent on pleasing herself, a wildcat, a chider, a railer, an irksome brawling scold, a devil, the devil's dam, a fiend of hell, and a hilding of a devilish spirit. In short, she is a shrew. . . ."

Petruchio undertakes to marry and tame this harridan, not by brutality but by psychological strategy. In this war between the sexes, Petruchio fights Kate with her own weapons, pretending to be as much of a bully as she is and yet leading her inexorably, with alternating carrot and stick, to her transformation into a gentle, obedient wife who recognizes her husband's authority.

Kaye, Danny (1913–1987)   An actor, born David Daniel Kaminsky in Brooklyn, New York, who starred in 17 movies, including *The Secret Life of Walter Mitty* (1947), *Hans Christian Andersen* (1952) and *White Christmas* (1954). He was known for his lightning-speed rhyming patter songs, written by his wife Sylvia Fine, and for his good-natured, zany clowning.

Keaton, Buster (1896–1966)   Slapstick comedian known for his stony-faced stoicism. He appeared in *Day Dreams* (1922), a kind of early version of Walter Mitty; *The Three Ages* (1923), in which he played a Christian martyr thrown to the lions; *The Navigator* (1924); and *The General* (1927).

Kent State   Kent State University, Kent, Ohio. On May 4, 1970, National Guardsmen opened fire on Kent State students peacefully demonstrating against the U.S. invasion of Cambodia during the Vietnam War. Four students were killed and nine injured. The nation was shocked and outraged. Kent State has become a symbol of the excessive use of force against peaceful demonstrations guaranteed by the U.S. Bill of Rights.

Kevorkian, Dr. Jack   Known as "the death doctor," Kevorkian took part in the assisted suicide of about 130 terminally ill people in the 1990s. On November 22, 1998, more than 16 million viewers witnessed Dr. Kevorkian on the TV program *60 Minutes* administer an intravenous injection of potassium chloride to Thomas Youk, who was terminally ill from Lou Gehrig's disease. Millions of viewers were outraged by this blatant display of so-called mercy killing. Dr. Kevorkian is the spokesman for the right-to-die movement, the campaign to legalize euthanasia and assisted suicide. He is actively engaged in a political rather than a medical campaign, and has openly solicited volunteers for assisted suicide. After standing trial five times in 1999, he was convicted of second-degree murder in the death of Thomas Youk and sentenced to a term of imprisonment of 25 years to life.

Dr. Kevorkian's name has become a household word, so that in moments of distress, no matter how trivial, a person with tongue in cheek can be heard calling, "Get Dr. Kevorkian."

Keynesian   In accord with the theories of John Maynard Keynes (1883–1946), one of the most influential economists of the 20th century. Born in England and educated at Cambridge University, Keynes foresaw the terrible economic consequences facing all of Europe and stemming from the harsh treatment of Germany under the Versailles Treaty. He set forth his reasoning in *Economic Consequences of the Peace* (1919).

229

In 1929, at the start of the worldwide Great Depression, Keynes abandoned his classical concept of a free economy to endorse Lloyd George's campaign promise to generate employment through a program of public works. This became a major tenet of Keynesian economics: government must step in with plans for large-scale spending to stimulate a faltering economy. Keynes developed these ideas in his major work, *The General Theory of Employment, Interest, and Money* (1936). Clearly, Franklin Delano Roosevelt resorted to Keynesian means to pull the United States out of the Depression.

At the end of World War II, as consultant to the chancellor of the exchequer and as a director of the Bank of England, Keynes urged the establishment of a world bank to promote the development of third-world economies.

Keystone Kops   Characters in Mack Sennett's short movie comedies. They are a crew of inept, idiotic policemen engaged in slapstick antics in silent films like *In the Clutch of a Gang.*

Generally, the term refers to ineffectual and bumbling figures of authority.

KGB   Komitet Gosudárstvennoi Bezopásnosti (Committee for State Security). Intelligence agency of the former Soviet Union organized in 1954, responsible for internal security and for clandestine operations abroad. Associated with secrecy, brutality and terror, it was the fist of BIG BROTHER.

KGB is sometimes applied to any official using high-handed methods of investigation; an agent of oppression.

kill the goose that lays the golden egg, to   Once upon a time there was a poor woman who came into possession of a goose that laid one golden egg a day. She tried to get the goose to lay all its golden eggs at once so that she would be truly rich. When the goose refused to cooperate, she went into such a rage that she killed the goose who laid the golden egg.

In modern usage, the meaning of the phrase is similar to "cutting off one's nose to spite one's face." Of course, this is a little morality tale: Don't be so impatient or irritable that you cut off the source of your wealth, power or status.

Killing Fields, The (1984)   American film based on the Pulitzer prize-winning articles by *New York Times* journalist Sidney Schanberg. The film depicts the experiences of Schanberg and Dith Pran, his native aide, in the shifting fortunes and horrors of Pol Pot's reign of terror in Cambodia. The term now applies to similar horrors in other wars, such as "the killing fields of Mozambique."

"Kilroy was here"   Ubiquitous inscription left by victorious American troops on walls and other surfaces all over the world during World War II. The mysterious and fictitious Kilroy has been adopted as a sign of one's passing through.

kindness of strangers   "I have always depended on the kindness of strangers," says BLANCHE DU BOIS at the end of Tennessee Williams's play *A Streetcar Named Desire* (1947), as she takes the arm of a gentlemanly guard on her way to a mental institution. She is referring to the many men who gave her solace—sexual and financial—in the years before she arrived at her sister Stella's flat in New Orleans.

The expression often is used for the most casual favors by strangers, such as the changing of a dollar bill for four quarters at a parking meter.

King, Martin Luther, Jr. (1929–1968)   Foremost leader of the Civil Rights movement in the United States. Espousing the nonviolent means successfully employed in India by Mahatma GANDHI, King organized mass demonstrations, marches and boycotts to protest racial discrimination, to implement equal rights legislation and to foster harmony between blacks and whites. In 1963, he led a march on Washington, D.C., where he thrilled 250,000 demonstrators with his now-famous "I HAVE A DREAM" speech. In 1964 he was awarded the Nobel peace prize.

Often misunderstood and vilified, beaten and jailed, King was assassinated by James Earl Ray in Memphis, Tennessee. In 1983, Congress declared January 15 a national holiday to commemorate his life and achievements. His name is synonymous with America's moral conscience in seeking to attain racial harmony and justice. See also MONTGOMERY, ALABAMA; PARKS, ROSA.

King Kong   RKO movie (1933) about a monster, conceived by Merian C. Cooper, with special effects by Willis O'Brien. The plot: A movie producer, Carl Denham, and his crew arrive on Skull Island in the Indian Ocean to film a legendary creature, a huge, monstrous ape. The natives seize the heroine, played by Fay Wray, and are about to sacrifice her to King Kong, when the ape himself appears, snatches the girl and flees with her. A thrilling chase follows in which Kong kills prehistoric animals. Denham finally subdues the giant ape with sleeping gas. He brings him back to New York to exhibit him. Enraged by flashbulbs, Kong breaks his chains and runs amok in the city, causing general panic. Fay Wray is "safe" in a hotel room when Kong smashes through a window, seizes the screaming actress and carries her to the top of the Empire State Building. The military is called out. Fighter planes pump bullets into his body. Kong sets Fay Wray down gently on a ledge and falls to his death.

Kinsey Report   Formally titled *Sexual Behavior in the Human Male* (1948), this was a groundbreaking scientific study based on 12,000 personal interviews and questionnaires, conducted by Dr. Alfred Kinsey (1894–1956), a professor of zoology at the University of Indiana. Kinsey switched from observing the birds and the bees to studying the sexual habits of homo sapiens. He presented statistically sound evidence on the frequency in white males of masturbation, orgasm, oral sex, marital and extramarital intercourse. The Kinsey Report shocked and titillated the nation, but it also exploded many false preconceptions about sexual activity in the human male and probably served unwittingly to spread sexual freedom or, as some contend, license. In 1953, *Sexual Behavior in the Human Female* was published with similar effect.

Kiplingesque   Displaying the imperialistic attitudes contained in the phrase "the white man's burden," coined by Rudyard Kipling (1865–1936), British author born in India, the locale of most of his tales and poems.

Kirche, Küche, Kinder   German for church, kitchen and children. The Nazi slogan for the proper sphere of women, a sexist concept of women's interests, the phrase now describes a stereotype of woman's place in the world.

kitchen cabinet   A group of influential advisers to a president. Though they are not elected to serve as advisers, they often exert more influence on the president than does his "official" staff.

Andrew Jackson (1767–1845) was the first president to set up a kitchen cabinet after he suspended formal cabinet meetings. Jackson's inner circle consisted of two newspaper editors and three minor Treasury Department officials. Other presidents before Jackson had depended heavily on a coterie of close, trusted advisers. Jackson's, however, was the first such group to be designated a "kitchen cabinet."

William Safire, in his *Political Dictionary,* speculates that Jackson and his informal advisers were called a kitchen cabinet "presumably because of his and their reputation for unpolished manners."

Klee, Paul (1879–1940)   Swiss painter influenced by cubism, primitive African art and children's drawings, Klee developed a pictorial language uniquely his own. In his later years he studied ideographs of all kinds; indeed, some of his works seem to have incorporated ancient hieroglyphics as well as cabalistic signs. His paintings are playful, inventive, witty, imaginative and musical.

Klondike, the   On August 17, 1896, George Cormack and his Indian wife and relatives discovered large quantities of gold in the gravel of a creek three miles from

Dawson, northwest Canada. They fittingly called the creek Bonanza—a tributary that fed into the Klondike River in Canada's Yukon Territory.

The outside world got news of the find in June 1897. It started the famous gold rush, which attracted gold prospectors from all over. Many of them died of cold, starvation and disease. More than 10,000 made it to the boom town of Dawson, now teeming with successful prospectors and strange, failed characters, some of whom come alive in the masculine, romantic verse of the Canadian poet Robert W. Service (1875–1958). Probably the most famous tales of the gold rush are *The Call of the Wild* (1903) and *White Fang* (1906), by Jack London (1876–1916).

Gold production in the Klondike peaked at $22 million in 1900 alone. A zealous, skillful prospector could make as much as $1,500 per day panning for gold.

The Klondike and the gold rush have come to stand for man's unslakable thirst for profit, for the fast buck. Many an entrepreneur keeps searching for "the last Klondike," for a killing.

K Mart   Chain of department stores carrying inexpensive items at cut-rate prices. Its name is a symbol of bargain-basement products.

knockout (also kayo, K.O.)   To win a boxing match by literally knocking an opponent unconscious or rendering him unable to get up unassisted after the referee has counted 10 seconds over him.

In general use, an overpoweringly attractive woman, or a highly successful action.

Use: Tarleton's sales campaign was a knockout. It put sales for the latest model ahead of all the competition.

Know-Nothings   An American nativist movement, formalized in the 1850s, opposed to the increase of immigrants and "outsiders" in general. Its major thrust, however, was anti-Catholic. It published anti-Catholic books, magazines and newspapers, stoned Catholic buildings and was said to be involved in the burning of the Ursuline Convent School in Charlestown, Massachusetts (1834).

To the Know-Nothings, the spectacular growth of the immigrant population posed the palpable threat of "cultural dilution," "economic competition" and "growth of immigrant power."

The early Know-Nothings formed a secret society called the Order of the Star Spangled Banner. Members were sworn to secrecy about the society's program and membership. When queried about their activities, they all professed to "know nothing."

Today, "Know-Nothing" is applied broadly to groups and individuals displaying bigotry, gross ignorance, appeal to base emotions or reactionary politics.

Kojak   In this long-running 1970s television drama of crime, pursuit and punishment in New York City, Telly Savalas was Kojak, a tough, crafty, unglamorous detective lieutenant with a curious appetite for lollipops. Kojak's low-key manner concealed his fierce hatred for the criminals who constituted his daily fare. Stocky and bald, Kojak was not the typical nemesis of wrongdoers. Underneath his rough exterior was a reservoir of great tenderness and concern for the injured and the oppressed. Despite his unorthodox manner and appearance, Kojak is recognized and cherished all over the world as the embodiment of the "good cop."

Kowalski, Stanley   Character in *A Streetcar Named Desire* (1947), a play by Tennessee Williams (1914–83). Uncouth, animalistic, macho, beer-guzzling and poker-playing, he is a blue-collar worker of Polish immigrant stock. He is married to Stella, who comes of finer Southern sensibilities. In the course of the play he ruins Stella's visiting sister BLANCHE DU BOIS, whose pretensions to culture and refinement are as a red flag to a raging bull. He destroys Blanche's last chance for marriage, and when he sneeringly rapes her, he destroys her sanity. There is little doubt that the playwright meant Kowalski to be the villain, and yet it is Kowalski who fathers a child with Stella, a child who will probably turn out to be more robust than the faded southern gentility represented by Blanche. The role of Stanley was brilliantly played on stage and screen by Marlon Brando.

See also BRANDO, MARLON.

K.P.   Originally, an abbreviation for the enlisted men who were the U.S. Army's "kitchen police"; later applied to the kitchen chores themselves.

Krantz, Judith (1928–)   American writer of blockbuster novels with mass appeal, she writes modern fairy tales about heroines who fight their way from impoverished, if aristocratic, beginnings to great wealth and power in the glamorous worlds of fashion and advertising. Along the way, Krantz indulges her sexual fantasies. Her novels include *Scruples* (1978), which was adapted for a TV miniseries; *Princess Daisy* (1980), which reportedly netted Krantz over $5 million in prepublication sales; and *Mistral's Daughter* (1980), about a French painter and the three women in his life, also adapted for TV.

A Judith Krantz novel is an easy read about women on the make in a glamorous world. See also JACQUELINE SUSANN.

K-ration   Named for Ancel Keys, an American physiologist who devised a small packet of food containing all necessary nutrients for a soldier's emergency ration out in the field. K-ration now stands for minimalism in the taste or aesthetics of food preparation or service.

Kristallnacht   Literally, crystal night, the term for the night of November 9, 1938, when booted Nazis in civilian clothes under orders from Josef Goebbels rampaged through Berlin, smashing thousands of store windows of Jewish merchants. The streets were littered with glass. They set fire to synagogues, beat people with truncheons and killed at least 90 Jews.

The ostensible justification for this outrage was the assassination of Ernst von Rath, the third secretary of the German Embassy in Paris, by a young Polish Jew, Herschel Grynspan.

Kristallnacht is a term for the urban pogrom, sometimes used to describe mob violence—destruction of property, looting, personal assaults—especially when aimed at a particular segment of the population.

Use: The streets were littered with broken glass. It was *Kristallnacht* in Watts.

Kubrick, Stanley **(1928–1999)**   American movie director who put his personal stamp on such seminal films as *Dr. Strangelove* (1964), *2001: A Space Odyssey* (1968) and *A Clockwork Orange* (1971). With SWIFTIAN savagery and wit, he expressed his misanthropic view of human nature and its institutions: the hypocrisy and ineptitude of the military, the violence of our youth culture, the flirtation with Armageddon via the atom bomb. In *2001,* based on a novel by Arthur C. Clarke, Kubrick created a space epic of spectacular grandeur and eerie suggestiveness that pioneered such film adventures as the *Star Wars* trilogy by George Lucas. Technically he was a perfectionist, taking as many as 100 shots of a single scene, and sometimes taking years to complete a movie. He assumed control of every aspect of his filmmaking.

Ku Klux Klan   A group of white Confederate men met secretly on Christmas Eve, 1865, in Pulaski, Tennessee, to form a social club designed to regain "white supremacy" in the defeated South. By 1867, the basic thrust of the Pulaski organization had spread to other parts of the South. What eventually became widely known and feared as the Ku Klux Klan started in Nashville, Tennessee. By 1872, its members adopted elaborate white robes for its officers and sheets for the rank and file. Essentially vigilantes and terrorists, they were largely rural and local and southern. They rode forth at night, claiming to be the ghosts of Confederate dead. They "intimidated, lynched, murdered, and burned blacks—and sometimes whites and CARPETBAGGERS who were active in liberty and union leagues or otherwise seeking full civil and human rights." So grave a threat had the KKK become that the federal government stepped in (1871–72) to destroy the organization through military arrests, trials in federal courts, and federal legislation. However, the Klan has been reborn several times during the 20th century. The group is synonymous with racist bigotry.

"La Belle Dame sans Merci" (1819) A ballad by the English poet John Keats (1795–1821) in which a knight "alone and palely loitering," haggard and woebegone, tells how he was bewitched by a beautiful lady, a fairy's child. With false shows of love, she led him to her elfin grotto and there she lulled him to sleep.

La Belle Dame sans Merci is a seductress without pity for the victims she ensnares and abandons. In modern usage, La Belle Dame may stand for Lady Luck or the lure of money or fame. These may promise gleaming rewards but end with ruthless betrayal.

La Belle Époque French for "the beautiful era," it extends from 1871, the end of the Franco-Prussian War, to the beginning of World War I (1914). *La Belle Époque* was marked by great elegance, security, social stability, high confidence, and a kind of innocence. It is typically associated with an extraordinary flourishing of the arts (Manet, Degas, Monet, Toulouse-Lautrec) and great discoveries in science (Madame Curie, Louis Pasteur).

But, as the historian Barbara Tuchman points out, these golden times were only for the privileged few. Underneath, "doubt, fear, ferment, protest, violence" assailed the people at large.

La Belle Époque refers to a veneer of glamor at the top echelons of society.

La Dolce Vita (1961) Italian movie directed by FEDERICO FELLINI. Marcello Mastroianni stars as a gossip columnist disenchanted with the trivial, cynical, shallow lives of Rome society. He senses that he is no better than the paparazzi (photographers) who swarm around these social butterflies, but he is too spoiled, too indolent, too corrupted by "the sweet life" to change his ways, even after he glimpses a vision of innocence and purity in the form of a young girl. Literally, *"la dolce vita"* means "the sweet life," the life of pleasure, idleness and self-gratification.

Use: "His looks, his town houses and chateaux and yachts, would have qualified him for a role in *La Dolce Vita*." (Saul Bellow, *A Theft*)

Lady Bountiful   Mother of Dorinda and Sullen in *The Beaux' Stratagem* (1707), a comedy by George Farquhar (1678–1707). A rich woman, she devotes herself to tending the sick. She is "the wisest and kindest" nurse in Litchfield and has "cured more people—although by strange methods—in ten years than the doctors have killed in twenty."

A Lady Bountiful is true to her name, generous, caring, charitable.

Lady Chatterley   Heroine of *Lady Chatterley's Lover,* a novel by D. H. Lawrence (1885–1930), privately printed in Florence in 1928 and finally published in an unexpurgated edition in Britain and the United States in 1960. The wife of a wealthy but crippled land owner, Lady Constance Chatterley is sexually awakened and fulfilled by the gamekeeper on the estate, Oliver Mellors, the son of a miner. In committing adultery with a man of lower social class, she has doubly transgressed. She bears Mellors's child and asks for a divorce. D. H. Lawrence describes her sexual encounters with Mellors with such explicit detail and language that his publishers were prosecuted for, but eventually acquitted of, obscenity.

A Lady Chatterley is a woman awakened to ecstatic sexual passion.

laissez-faire   Originally the motto of 18th-century French physiocrats, who deplored the imposition of customs duties by the government, the phrase meant "let things alone," "don't interfere," "hands off."

The doctrine of laissez-faire was taken up and popularized by the Scottish economist Adam Smith in *The Wealth of Nations* (1776), in which he espoused free trade, a hands-off policy by government. A nation's health was supposedly best served by the natural laws of supply and demand, self-interest and competition, and needed no artificial stimulus or regulation. This basic individualistic principle was extended to political affairs, and during the Industrial Revolution the British Parliament was forced to repeal the corn laws, which sought to regulate the price of food for poor workers. Laissez-faire policies have always been touted by conservatives, whereas liberals have always been for government intervention to create some equality between the rich and the poor.

Today, "laissez-faire" may describe an individual or agency's handling of behavior problems, such as a laissez-faire approach to rearing children.

lame duck   The term for a duck whose wings have been clipped, it refers to an elected official—most notably, the president of the United States who is known to be serving his last weeks or months in office—because he was either defeated for reelection or, in the case of the president, he has served the allowed two terms. Lame duck incumbents have lost their power; they have had their wings clipped.

The 20th Amendment to the Constitution (the "Lame Duck" amendment, 1933) shortened the time between the November election day and the March inauguration day (now January 3 for Congress and January 20 for the president), thus curtailing the period of ineffectiveness.

A lame duck is any person in an important position who has no clout because he is on his way out.

Lancelot and Guinevere   See ARTHUR, KING.

Lansky, Meyer (1902–1983)   One of the founders of the national crime syndicate, he was widely regarded as "the most shadowy of the organized crime leaders." He was said to be the brains of the combination, respected, feared and frequently consulted by all the Mafiosi. He handled their money and deposited their millions in secret Swiss bank accounts. Lansky's personal wealth was somewhere between $300 million and $400 million.

Laputa   The floating island in Book Three of *Gulliver's Travels* (1726) by Jonathan Swift. There, theoreticians who scorn practical knowledge and experience have led the country to ruin: clothes are absurdly ill-fitting; houses are crooked; agriculture is a shambles; poverty and famine are universal. Absentminded scientists try to extract sunbeams from cucumbers and silk from cobwebs. Physicists and mathematicians have so terrified the population with prophecies of imminent disaster, like the sun's burning out or a comet's striking, that they cannot enjoy everyday pleasures.

Laputa is a satire on any congregation of impractical intellectuals.

Lardner, Ring (1885–1933)   Sports writer, newspaper columnist, humorist, sardonic pessimist and short-story writer who had a keen ear for the nuances of the vulgar American speech used by lowlife, uneducated, quirky characters in the world of sports and entertainment. He wrote *You Know Me, Al* (1916), a collection of stories devoted to baseball's more moronic practitioners.

Last Hurrah, The (1956)   A novel by Edwin O'Connor, in which a consummate politician of Irish extraction, Frank Skeffington, at the age of 73, announces his candidacy for reelection as mayor: "Much as he loved to win, he loved the fight to win even more, and in his appraisal of his own strengths he put in first place that of the born campaigner." Skeffington is based on the career of Boston mayor James Curley. A last hurrah is a final farewell.

Last of the Mohicans (1826)   One of a series of novels called collectively *The Leatherstocking Tales* (1823–41) by James Fenimore Cooper (1789–1851). The central character in the series is Natty Bumppo, the uncorrupted natural man. Although he is white, he dislikes the white man's values, especially his ruthless exploitation of nature. He prefers the moral code of the Indians. Loyal, courageous, an expert hunter, he is at home in the wild and follows the wilderness trail westward.

Natty Bumppo's companion and mentor is Chingachgook, the archetypal Indian chief, the quintessential NOBLE SAVAGE: strong, brave, silent, wise; a fierce enemy, devoted friend, the soul of honor and master of woodlore.

Both Chingachgook and Natty Bumppo stand in sharp contrast to their cruel, exploitive contemporaries. They are, in a sense, the shining knights of their respective societies. They exemplify what is noble in their people and their time.

The essential struggle between the "good guys" and the "bad guys" is sharply drawn in *The Last of the Mohicans*. In this book, Uncas, the son of Chingachgook, is the last of the Mohicans, the last in the line of a noble breed. With his death, a certain nobility passes from the scene.

In current use, the expression "the last of the Mohicans" has lost much of its original purity. It has come to refer to the last holdouts in defending or practicing a vanishing way of life, even so reprehensible a way of life as that of a Mafia mobster. Sometimes it is applied simply to the last stragglers—in a marathon, for example.

Las Vegas   City of gambling casinos and night clubs in Nevada, a Mecca of tinsel and gaming.

Laurel and Hardy   Stan Laurel (1891–1965) and Oliver Hardy (1892–1957), a slapstick comedy team who made their best silent movies from 1927 to 1929: *You're Darn Tootin, Battle of the Century, Big Business, Two Tars*. Some of their best-known talkies are *The Music Box* (1931), *Fra Diavolo* (1933), *Sons of the Desert* (1934), and *Way Out West* (1937). Laurel played the role of the trusting innocent; Hardy, the more worldly type whose pompous airs and inflated ego were constantly punctured. Together, they managed to create chaos with the response of "Who? Me?" Their violence might start with pushing and pie-throwing and end with a crescendo of destruction all around them. They stand for escalating mayhem in an absurd and petty vein.

law of the jungle   See DARWINIAN.

lead with one's chin   In boxing, to leave one's weakest point unprotected, to expose one's most serious weakness, to invite a knockout.

In general use, to leave oneself vulnerable to attack or serious trouble.

Lear, King   Tragic hero of Shakespeare's play of the same name (1604–05). Lear is an old man who misjudges the character of his three daughters. Foolishly, he divides his kingdom between Regan and Goneril, who falsely profess unlimited love for him, and he disinherits Cordelia, his youngest daughter, who disdains to follow their example. Soon enough he realizes "How sharper than a serpent's tooth it is / To have a thankless child" when he finds himself dependent upon the mercies of Regan and Goneril. Ousted in turn from each of their castles, he wanders alone, except for his mordant fool, upon a barren heath in a howling storm. There, for the first time, he understands what it is to be "unaccommodated man . . . a poor bare forked animal. . . ."

Compassionately, he murmurs:

Poor naked wretches, wheresoe'er you are,
That bide the pelting of this pitiless storm,
How shall your houseless and unfed sides,
Your looped and windowed raggedness, defend you from seasons such as these?

This is the beginning of Lear's redemption. He is no longer the fatuous king who bases a momentous decision upon mere flattery. He is to suffer and atone even more in the great reconciliation scene with Cordelia. Joyful at first to find her again, he tells her tenderly:

Come, let's away to prison;
We two alone will sing like birds i' the cage;
When thou dost ask me blessing, I'll kneel down,
And ask of thee forgiveness. . . .

But when she lies lifeless in his arms, he cries out against the pitiless heavens: "Howl, howl, howl, howl!" He dies with full recognition of what he has done.

Lear stands as a warning against divesting oneself of all money and power before death, and against trusting in the kindness of your children after you have given up such independence.

Use: "If caring parents help us learn to care for ourselves, the first step in learning to care for others, we break the cycle of anger that can oppress us into a Lear-like dotage." (*Columbia,* Fall 1991)

Lebanon   Small Middle Eastern country on the shores of the Mediterranean, once a prosperous and civilized paradise, but virtually destroyed by contending religious factions. It was reduced to rubble and anarchy after 14 years of civil war in the 1970s and 1980s.

The name, along with the name of its capital, Beirut, has become a symbol of the disintegration of a political or national entity.

Lebensraum   The German word for "living space," it became HITLER's justification for his expansionist policies in Europe.

Now, it means the need for more space. For example: In violating the zoning law, the developer claimed he needed *Lebensraum* to remain profitable.

Lecter, Hannibal   Sinister central character played by Anthony Hopkins in the movie *The Silence of the Lambs* (1991), based on the novel of the same name by Thomas Harris. A former psychiatrist turned cannibalistic serial killer, Lecter is imprisoned in an FBI cage under strict restraints and surveillance. A young and inexperienced female FBI agent, Clarice Starling, played by Jodie Foster, receives permission to try to enlist his psychological insights for the purpose of tracking down another serial killer on the loose. A dangerous cat-and-mouse game subtly infused with sexual attraction and repulsion ensues between the two in this great psychological thriller, which won four Academy Awards. In 1999 Harris published *Hannibal,* a sequel to *The Silence of the Lambs.*
   Hannibal Lecter has come to embody brilliant but unspeakable criminality.

Lee, Lorelei   The predatory, blond flapper heroine of *Gentlemen Prefer Blondes* (1925), an immensely popular novel by Anita Loos (1893–1981). It was adapted for Broadway in 1926, made into a movie in 1928 and staged as a musical comedy with Carol Channing in 1949. Another film adaptation was released in 1953, starring Marilyn Monroe. The hit song of the musical, "Diamonds Are a Girl's Best Friend," sums up the philosophy of the Lorelei Lees of this world.

Léger, Fernand (1881–1955)   French painter enraptured by and fixated on the machine age, so that even his human figures seem made up of tubular, mechanized parts and geometric shapes. He paints bicyclists, acrobats, workers, all happy in a machinelike utopia.

Legree, Simon   Brutal overseer who beats the slave Uncle Tom to death in *Uncle Tom's Cabin* (1852), a novel by Harriet Beecher Stowe. The author's vivid depiction of slavery on a Southern plantation had a profound influence on readers just before the Civil War.
   A Simon Legree is an unspeakably cruel, unjust supervisor.
   See also UNCLE TOM'S CABIN.

Lennie   Character in John Steinbeck's popular novel *Of Mice and Men* (1937), which was made into a play (1937) and a film (1939). Lennie Small and George Milton are a pair of itinerant farm workers in Salinas Valley, California, who dream of some day owning their own place. Lennie is strong but retarded. George is small-boned but cunning. George protects Lennie. Lennie "loves" soft furry things and has been known to hug animals to death. When Lennie accidentally kills the promiscuous wife of the boss's son Curly, George protects him from an angry mob by first calming him with stories of their dream-place and then shooting him in the head.

A Lennie is a brawny but dimwitted person who can unwittingly destroy fragile things because he doesn't know his own strength.

Leonardo da Vinci (1452–1519) In the entire history of mankind, it would be hard to find a handful of people to equal the many-sided genius of Leonardo. He was the quintessential RENAISSANCE MAN: painter, illustrator, architect, sculptor, musician, inventor, engineer, naturalist, city planner, scientist. His curiosity was all-encompassing, as evidenced in the 3,500 pages of his notebooks filled with minute observations in words and meticulously drawn sketches.

The illegitimate son of a notary and a poor peasant woman, he was born in the little Tuscan town of Vinci. When he was 14, he moved to Florence and was apprenticed to Verrocchio. He began to paint his remarkable canvases stamped by his special use of sfumato, a subtle shading of contour and color that makes the figures emerge three-dimensionally from a kind of hazy mist and lends mystery to his subjects.

Leonardo said that the highest aim of painting is to depict the intention of the soul. This is apparent in all of his paintings, but especially in the two most famous: the *Mona Lisa* and *The Last Supper.* The ambiguity, the mystery of the Mona Lisa smile has intrigued viewers through the centuries. The expressions on the faces of the disciples in the *The Last Supper* register each one's deep psychological response to Christ's announcement: "One of you shall betray me."

From 1482 to 1499, Leonardo worked for Lodovico Sforza, the duke of Milan, designing military weapons, organizing elaborate festivals and executing commissions for paintings, sculpture and architecture. After Milan capitulated to the French army, Leonardo returned to Florence to work for Cesare Borgia as a military engineer. In 1515, at the invitation of King Francis I of France, Leonardo settled at the castle of Cloux, near Amboise, to pursue his own studies until he died.

Use: In *A Child's Christmas in Wales,* Dylan Thomas lists the presents he used to receive at Christmas. Among the "Useless Presents": "Bags of moist and many-colored jelly babies . . . And Easy Hobbi-Games for Little Engineers, complete with instructions. Oh, easy for Leonardo."

Leopold and Loeb In 1924, when Nathan Leopold was 19 and his friend Richard Loeb was 18, they murdered their 14-year-old friend, Bobby Franks, son of a Chicago millionaire—just for the intellectual challenge of committing the perfect crime. Both Leopold and Loeb were brilliant, gifted college students, sons of prominent, wealthy Chicago families.

The parents of the two murderers hired Clarence Darrow, the famous criminal lawyer, to defend their sons. In his brilliant defense, Darrow depicted Leopold as a paranoiac and Loeb as a dangerous schizophrenic, arguing eloquently against putting them to death. The jury returned a verdict of guilty by reason of insanity and sentenced them to life imprisonment for murder, plus 99 years for kidnapping.

A Leopold-Loeb crime is marked by calculated, cold-blooded sadism carried out for "kicks," for thrills.

"less is more"   Dictum coined by Ludwig Mies van der Rohe (1886–1969) of the Bauhaus School, which also gave birth to another slogan: "Form follows function." "Less is more" encapsulated the aim of clean, unadorned, economical forms in architecture, crafts and industrial design.

Use: This summer less is more. Shorts are shorter. Swimsuits are skimpier.

L'État c'est moi **("I am the state")**   This bit of royal arrogance has been ascribed to King Louis XIV (1638–1715), the most powerful of France's absolute monarchs. When the president of the parliament objected to Louis's exorbitant demands for money because they were against the interests of the state, he replied *"L'État c'est moi."*

Louis XIV remains the archetype of the regal absolutism that the French Revolution finally uprooted and destroyed.

"let them eat cake"   This heartless and cynical expression is usually—and mistakenly—attributed to MARIE ANTOINETTE when she was told that the starving masses had no bread. Actually, it was Jean-Jacques Rousseau in his *Confessions* (1767) who wrote about "a great princess, who, on being informed that the country people had no bread, replied, 'Let them eat cake.'" The saying illustrates the total ignorance of the rich with respect to the conditions of the poor.

Levittown   Housing development consisting of practically identical one-family houses mass-produced by the builder, William Levitt, on Long Island, New York, and throughout the post–World War II United States. Actually these were attractive and moderately priced and have become a standard for low- to middle-income housing, in spite of their uniformity, which some critics saw as emblematic of the conformist 1950s.

Lidice   Village in Czechoslovakia demolished by the Nazis in retaliation for the murder of a top-ranking German official, Reinhard Heydrich, the "Hangman of Europe." The Germans executed 1,300 of its civilian inhabitants.

Commemorated by Edna St. Vincent Millay in her verse play *Lidice,* the name is a reference to brutal and ruthless destruction for the sake of revenge.

life of Riley   A luxurious lifestyle, living "in clover," free from care of any kind. Perhaps based on early 1900s songs about one "Reilly," especially "The Best of the House Is None Too Good For Reilly."

Use: If you win the lottery, you can lead the life of Riley for the rest of your days.

lightweight   A professional boxer weighing between 126 and 135 pounds. Officially, he boxes in the lightweight division against men of comparable weight.

In general use, "lightweight" has derogatory overtones: inconsequential, unimportant, small-time.

Use: Pay no attention to Raymond's opinions about current trends in international trade. He's an intellectual lightweight.

light year   A term taken from astronomy, it is the distance traveled by light in a single year. The speed of light multiplied by the number of seconds in a year equals 5.88 trillion miles. The distance between stars is so great that it is measured in light years. For example, the distance from our sun to the nearest star is more than four light years.

Used colloquially for a great distance, as to express progress, or for a long time, e.g., man's full understanding of the interaction between body and mind is still "light years" away.

Li'l Abner   Al Capp's enduring contribution to the mythology of the comic strip. Since he appeared in 1934, Li'l Abner has remained one of the most popular comic strip characters. Actually, the 19-year-old Li'l Abner is six-foot-three. Throughout the strip's long life, he has played the endearing role of "NOBLE SAVAGE"—a figure American readers have been especially fond of since the days of James Fenimore Cooper's Chingachgook in *The Last of the Mohicans*.

The strip's skillful mixture of surprise, suspense and humor proved irresistible. The comings and goings of such characters as Sir Cecil Cesspool and Lady Cesspool, the appearance of the Schmoo, the potent Kickapoo Joy Juice, and other inhabitants of Dogpatch provided a delicious, bizarre brew for its readers all over America.

Lilliputian   In Book One of *Gulliver's Travels* (1726), a satire by Jonathan Swift (1667–1745), the narrator, Lemuel Gulliver, a surgeon on a British merchant vessel, is shipwrecked on the island of Lilliput. There he discovers that all the inhabitants are only six inches tall and everything else is in proportion to their diminutive size. He soon observes that the Lilliputians' frenetic parliamentary and religious squabbles, their wars over silly differences—as, for example, whether an egg should be broken at the little end or big end—as well as their sense of self-importance, are all ridiculous in light of their puny size. By analogy, so do our own institutions, attitudes and wars seem absurd.

Thus, "Lilliputian" refers to any small, insignificant, preposterously posturing person or endeavor.

Lincoln, Abraham (1809–1865)   The 16th president of the United States and, by almost universal agreement, the greatest. His life, which began in a Kentucky log cabin and took him to the White House, epitomizes the American experience.

Lincoln presided over the most turbulent period in American history—the Civil War. The very existence of the United States was at stake. The South was girding itself to preserve slavery and secede from the Union. Lincoln was determined that the Union remain indivisible. He guided the country through what proved to be one of the most bitter and most costly wars in America's history. When the guns fell silent, more than 620,000 men had been killed—more than in all of America's other wars *combined.*

The South lay in ruins. One-quarter of the Confederacy's white men of military age were dead, two-fifths of its livestock destroyed, one-half its farm machinery, factories, railroads gone.

Throughout these terrible years, Lincoln adhered to the course he thought morally and militarily right, even though it brought him a kind of vilification unique for American presidents.

Something of the toll these years took of Lincoln is visible in the deep anguish in Mathew Brady's eloquent Lincoln photographs of the war years. Yet there was no bitterness in Lincoln's heart as he called for mercy and healing in his second inaugural address (1865):

> With malice toward none, with charity for all, with firmness in the right
> as God gives us to see the right, let us finish the work we are in, to bind
> up the nation's wounds, to care for him who shall have borne the battle,
> and for his widow and orphans, to do all which may achieve and cherish
> a just and lasting peace among ourselves and with all nations.

A few months into his second presidential term, on the evening of April 14, 1865, Lincoln was watching a performance of *Our American Cousin* at Ford's Theater when he was shot and killed by a deranged actor, John Wilkes Booth (1838–65).

Abe Lincoln stands for nobility of spirit, for steadfastness in conflict, for dignity in suffering and for honesty ("Honest Abe").

lineup   A list of players taking part in a game, as in baseball, football.

By extension, "lineup" has come to mean a list of participants in any activity or event.

Use: The lineup for the Constitution Forum contains some well-known speakers and scholars.

litmus test   A chemical test in which a piece of litmus paper is moistened with a solution. If the paper turns red, the solution is acid; if the paper turns blue, the solution is alkaline. The term is used figuratively today to mean a test of attitude in which there is only one decisive factor, e.g., the litmus test for any candidate sponsored by the Christian right is his or her stand on abortion.

Little Lord Fauntleroy (1886)   A children's novel by Frances Hodgson Burnett (1849–1924), the author of *The Secret Garden*. Cedric Errol, a seven-year-old American boy whose mother has him wear long golden curls and a black velvet suit with a lace collar, discovers that he is the grandson of an English earl. Summoned to England, the good-natured boy, now Lord Fauntleroy, exerts a beneficent influence upon his bad-tempered old grandfather. The latter begins to make long overdue improvements in the living conditions of his poor tenants. In the course of the book, a false claimant to the title is exposed as a fraud and all ends happily.

Little Lord Fauntleroy has become a term of derision based on the golden curls and the velvet suit. In effect, it became an epithet meaning "sissy."

Little Nell   Nell Trent is the good little orphan girl who is the heroine of *The Old Curiosity Shop* (1840), a novel by Charles Dickens. She lives with and cares for her aged grandfather, the proprietor of the old curiosity shop. To provide for the child's future, the old man borrows money in the hope that he will be able to increase his store through gambling, but he loses everything. He and Little Nell are evicted from the shop, and are reduced to homeless wandering and begging. After a while they are given safe haven in a little cottage by a kind schoolmaster, Mr. Marton. But it is too late. Worn out, yet uncomplaining to the end, Little Nell dies. Her heartbroken grandfather dies soon after.

When Dickens was writing his installments of *The Old Curiosity Shop* for one of the periodicals of the time, crowds of his readers would stand outside his house weeping and waiting to hear whether Dickens was going to allow Little Nell to die. Little Nell has become an emblem of Dickens's penchant for excessive pathos and sentimentality.

Little Orphan Annie   This comic strip, which made its debut in 1925, consisted essentially of a series of morality plays. The heroine, Little Orphan Annie, with her only friends, her dog Sandy and her doll Emily Marie, stands alone against the world. Daddy Warbucks, originally a munitions manufacturer, acquires extraordinary powers that enable him to mete out justice "arbitrarily, ruthlessly, and quietly."

The strip embodied its creator Harold Gray's conservative political and social views, and made it to the movies, to radio, to the phenomenally popular Broadway play *Annie,* and into the world of popular song with Annie's rendition of "Tomorrow, Tomorrow."

Little Rock   City in Arkansas where a major struggle for school integration took place throughout September 1957. Not until after President Dwight Eisenhower sent in federal troops, in a showdown with Governor Orval Faubus and a mob of white segregationists, were nine black children permitted to enter Central High School.

Little Rock has become a landmark in the continuing expansion of civil rights for blacks. It represents a hard-won triumph over school segregation.

Littleton   A middle-class suburban town in Colorado, where on April 20, 1999, two students, Eric Harris and Dylan Klebold, armed with a variety of guns and homemade bombs, gunned down 12 of their classmates and one teacher at Columbine High School and then turned the guns on themselves. With 15 dead and many wounded, the episode was the worst school massacre in American history.

What followed after the mourning was a national orgy of questioning the usual suspects: the National Rifle Association; the juvenile justice system; violence in the movies, TV, rap music and video games; the Internet; the breakdown of family values; and, of course, the widening generational gap between parents and children. Blame was scattered in all directions, but in truth nobody could adequately explain what had caused this ultimate rampage of youth violence. Nor, in spite of a flurry of legislation to "do something," did anybody know exactly what to do. Perhaps, it was thought, one would have to fall back on the notion of the BAD SEED, innate evil.

Rumors of planned copycat shootings followed almost immediately throughout the nation, closing down schools with bomb threats and shooting scares.

Littleton and Columbine have already entered the language as a metaphor for school violence. One pundit referred to Littleton as the CHERNOBYL of guns in popular culture.

Lloyd, Harold (1893–1971)   Silent film comedian. Lloyd, with his horn-rimmed glasses, played hayseed characters who earnestly set out to make good in the big city. Along the way he had to take some pratfalls, but eventually his eternally optimistic Horatio Alger–type character succeeded. Slapstick stunt episodes involving chases and dangling from tenement roofs were both chilling and hilarious. His films include *Never Weaken* (1921), *Safety Last* (1923), *Girl Shy* (1924), *The Freshman* (1925).

Lochinvar   The young Highlander hero of Sir Walter Scott's (1771–1832) romantic poem *Marmion* (1808):

> *Oh, young Lochinvar is come out of the West*
> *Through all the wide world his steed is the best.*
> *So faithful in love, and so dauntless in war*
> *There never was Knight like Young Lochinvar.*

His lady love, Ellen, against her will, has been betrothed to another: ". . . a laggard in love, and a dastard in war."

Lochinvar appears at the wedding and asks for the last dance with the bride. He dances her out the door and takes her away on his waiting steed.

A Lochinvar is a brave, bold, handsome, romantic, dashing hero lover. The term often is used satirically.

Lolita   A nymphet in Vladimir Nabokov's satirical novel *Lolita* (1958). The sexually precocious Lolita inflames a college professor. Together they run away, from motel to motel, in a series of comic adventures across the breadth of the United States, with every scene offering readers a devastating picture of American manners, mores, morals and glitz.

Loman, Willy   Main character in *Death of a Salesman* (1949), a play by Arthur Miller (1915–   ). Willy Loman is a pathetic (some say tragic), confused, traveling salesman who is a failure at everything. Unable to make a living as he grows older, he daydreams about past glories (mostly imagined) and about missed opportunities as an entrepreneur. Having foisted his shoddy values about success onto his two sons, he cannot understand why success eludes them. At the age of 60 he feels discarded. Only his wife understands his perplexity at the disparity between his dreams and his reality. At the end, he commits suicide so that his son Biff may make a new start with the insurance money.

A Willy Loman is a person who thinks he can make it on a smile and a slap on the back. He is discarded when he can no longer bring in profits for his boss.

Lonely Crowd, The (1950)   Scholarly work in sociology that became a best seller in spite of its subtitle: "A Study of the Changing American Character." Written by David Riesman, it showed the relationship between socioeconomic development and national character. Reisman coined the now popular terms "inner-directed" and "other-directed." His phrase "the lonely crowd" has become a catchword for alienated residents of cities.

Lone Ranger, The   One of the most popular Western series programs, first on radio (1933) and then on television (1949–61). The opening of each episode captured the essence of the Lone Ranger's character and mission:

"A fiery horse with the speed of light . . . a cloud of dust and a hearty Hi-Yo Silver, the Lone Ranger. With his faithful Indian companion Tonto, the daring and resourceful masked rider of the plains led the fight for law and order in the early West. Return with us now to the thrilling days of yesteryear . . . The Lone Ranger rides again. Hi-Yo Silver and a-w-a-y"—to the accompaniment of pounding hoofs and Rossini's pulsating *William Tell* Overture.

So popular had the Lone Ranger and his horse Silver become, that the "Hi-Yo Silver" call was, according to historian Irving Settel, actually used as a password by American troops entering Algiers during World War II.

The Lone Ranger is the sturdy archetype of the one good man against the evils of the world.

Use: The vice president was as self-effacing as Tonto to the president's Lone Ranger.

Lonigan, Studs   Main character in James T. Farrell's trilogy: *Young Lonigan: A Boyhood in Chicago Streets* (1932), *The Young Manhood of Studs Lonigan* (1934) and *Judgment Day* (1935). Studs travels a path of moral and spiritual degradation as he changes from an outwardly tough but inwardly sensitive 15-year-old growing up in the squalor of Chicago's South Side to an out-and-out hoodlum who dies of alcohol and venereal disease at the age of 29. He is seen as a victim of our time, a boy who receives no meaningful direction from church, family, school or community. Farrell paints his character's world with an immense accumulation of naturalistic detail, including crude language, lewd attitudes toward sex, brutality against minorities.

loose cannon   Military term applied in 1986–87 to Marine Lt. Col. Oliver North, aide to National Security Advisor Admiral John Poindexter. From his office in the White House, North managed the various deals in what came to be known as the Iran-Contra affair: selling arms to Iran for the release of American hostages in Lebanon and diverting the profits to the Contras in Nicaragua. When these secret deals, made outside legitimate government channels, came to light, North shredded incriminating documents. He was dismissed from his job. North took the Fifth (see TAKE THE FIFTH) until he was granted limited immunity in testifying before the Senate panel hearings on Iran-Contra. Although he testified that he had acted on orders from Poindexter, he seemed generally to have had a free hand in far-reaching military and political transactions—for somebody who had the rank of lieutenant colonel.

A loose cannon is an unpredictable person (so called because a loose cannon might shoot in any direction without warning or control), since he seems not to be responsible in a chain of command.

Lord Jim   Tragic hero of the novel *Lord Jim* (1900) by JOSEPH CONRAD. Guilty of a youthful, cowardly act in a moment of great confusion and indecision when, together with the rest of a ship's crew, he abandons ship before its passengers can be rescued, he spends the rest of his life trying to redeem his honor by some noble deed. In the end, his death is his salvation.

A Lord Jim is a romantic who cannot come to grips with his own human frailty.

Lorelei   A siren in "Die Lorelei" (1827), a ballad by the German-Jewish poet Heinrich Heine (1797–1856). The ballad tells the story of a beautiful young woman who sits upon a rock cliff jutting into the Rhine. As she combs her long golden hair with a golden comb, she sings a song with a *"wundersame, gewaltige melodei."* The glinting gold, the haunting melody, and the maiden lure unwary sailors to their death upon the rocks.

A Lorelei is a seductress, a siren.

Use: "The Lorelei of youth and social status who accompanied the '80s epicurean revival continues to purr . . . 'Indulge yourself.'" (*New York Times,* February 26, 1992)

Lost Generation   A term coined by GERTRUDE STEIN. "You are all a lost generation," she said to ERNEST HEMINGWAY. She was referring to him and his co-expatriate writers and artists who remained in Paris after World War I, without roots, without commitment, without illusions. See *The Lost Generation* by Malcolm Cowley and *A Moveable Feast,* a posthumous autobiography by Hemingway.

Lothario   A character in Nicholas Rowe's *The Fair Penitent* (1703), he is a ruthless, compulsive libertine.

A Lothario has come to mean a womanizer, a seducer of women. Over the centuries, it has lost some of its earlier, crueler overtones.

Louis, Joe (Joseph Louis Barrow) (1914–1981)   Boxer whose long string of ring victories, mostly by knockout, earned him the sobriquet the Brown Bomber, and the world's heavyweight championship. He retired undefeated, having defended his title 25 times (but he later returned and lost two fights).

Joe Louis was universally regarded as "one of the most beloved sportsmanly figures in boxing." In 1954, he was inducted into the Boxing Hall of Fame.

"love that dare not speak its name, I am the"   This is a line from "The Two Loves" (c. 1892), a poem by Lord Alfred Douglas, lover of Oscar Wilde (1854–1900). Douglas was referring to homosexual love, a punishable crime in Victorian England. Wilde came to grief when, after he was publicly insulted, he unwisely sued Douglas's irate father, the marquess of Queensberry, for libel. Wilde lost his case and was sentenced to prison with hard labor at Reading Gaol from 1895 to 1897.

Variations on this phrase all suggest a disgraceful thing about which we do not speak.

In the following citation, Anna Quindlen says:

"This is about race, the thing today that dare not speak its name." (*New York Times,* June 28, 1992)

low blow   A boxer who hits his opponent below the belt is said to have delivered a low blow. For this infraction of the rules, the boxer may lose points, or lose the round, or, in some instances, be disqualified and lose the match.

In general use: an unfair, unsportsmanlike, cowardly attack.

Use: During the presidential campaign the candidates traded low blows in their TV ads. See also HITTING BELOW THE BELT.

Lower East Side   Immigrant ghetto, principally Jewish, of New York City in the early decades of the 20th century. Within this overcrowded, squalid area, in tiny railroad flats in dingy tenements on filthy streets were housed about a million Jewish emigrants from Eastern Europe (especially Russia and Poland), who had sailed in steerage across the Atlantic to seek freedom from persecution as well as economic opportunity in the Golden Land. With them they brought the Yiddish language and the ghetto culture of the shtetl. However, they were ambitious to enter the mainstream of America through education and hard work. Upward mobility sent these immigrants "uptown" and into the outer boroughs of New York.

The Lower East Side is a nostalgic symbol of poverty-stricken immigrants of all nationalities who eventually made it as full-fledged Americans and in the process contributed significantly to the economic, educational and artistic growth of the United States. The term evokes the smells, the foods, the pushcarts, the Sabbath preparations, the Yiddish-English argot, the sweatshops, the noisy vendors, the crowds of a bygone era.

Lucy Stoner   Follower of Lucy Stone (1818–93), American suffragist who insisted on the right to keep her maiden name after marriage. Although her father had opposed her feminist efforts, her husband Henry Brown Blackwell took an active part in furthering her cause. In 1869 Lucy Stone organized the American Woman Suffrage Association.

A Lucy Stoner is a woman who retains her own name after marriage.

Luddite   In the early 19th century, the process of industrialization in England caused large-scale layoffs in textile factories. Enraged workers, first in Nottingham and then in many other industrial towns, broke into factories at night and demolished machinery. These rioters came to be known as Luddites, a name taken from one Ned Ludd who was supposed to have destroyed stocking frames in a Leicestershire factory 30 years earlier.

Today, a Luddite is any person who opposes automation as well as the depersonalization of the workplace.

lunatic fringe   Phrase used by Theodore Roosevelt at the end of his public career to describe men of excessive zeal within reform movements: "The foolish fanatics always to be found in such a movement and always discrediting it—the men who form the lunatic fringe in all reform movements."

Now the term is used mostly to describe violent advocates of fundamentalist doctrines.

Lunt and Fontanne   Alfred Lunt (1892–1977) and Lynn Fontanne (1887–1983). Although each was a Broadway star before they were married, they became, after their marriage in 1922, the most glamorous couple in the history of American legitimate theater. They appeared together in 27 plays, most of them sophisticated comedies like *The Guardsman* (1924), *Design for Living* (1932) and *Idiot's Delight* (1936). However, they were capable of brilliant ensemble acting in such serious dramas as Friedrich Dürrenmatt's *The Visit* (1960). They were stylish and urbane.

Lunt and Fontanne are as inseparable in theater history as caviar and champagne.

Lusitania   British-owned luxury liner sunk by a German submarine off the coast of Ireland on May 7, 1915. Among the 1,198 passengers who drowned, 128 were Americans. This was one of the events that eventually propelled the United States into World War I. The sinking of the *Lusitania* was condemned by Theodore Roosevelt as "an act of piracy."

Luther, Martin (1483–1546)   A German Augustinian monk who "split the Christian world in two," Luther was outraged by contemporary immoralities in the Roman Catholic Church at home and in the Holy City, Rome.

Luther was not alone in his outrage. Widespread revolt was spreading in Germany and elsewhere in Europe. Only a spark was needed to start the conflagration. Luther provided that spark. In 1517, he nailed to the Wittenberg Church door his 95 Theses.

Luther's 95 Theses are the original document of what became the Reformation. Luther's action marks the beginning of the movement that changed Christianity forever.

The church, once it saw the implications of Luther's attack on what it considered to be fundamental, unchallengeable doctrine, charged him with heresy and summoned him to Rome. Luther refused to accept the invitation and refused to recant. Instead, he attacked the primacy of the papacy itself. The pope excommunicated him. In further defiance, Luther burned the papal bull of excommunication. In 1520, the pope ordered Luther's books burned. Again Luther defied the pope. The church summoned Luther to the Diet of Worms and banned him from the Holy Roman Empire.

By this time, support for Luther's defiance of the church had spread through all of Germany and other European states. Supporters of Luther called themselves Protestants—and received the emperor's guarantee of "freedom from molestation." The church would strive to bring the Protestants to heel until the Augsburg Confession (1530), which legalized Protestantism for one half of the German people.

In 1525, in a final act of defiance, Luther married a former Catholic nun, Katherine von Bora.

Luther's actions are the heady spectacle of one man against the formidable power of the Catholic Church. His successful conversion of one-half of the Christian world as well as his zeal, passion and tenacity place him among the true heroes of Christianity.

m

Macavity   The mystery cat in T. S. Eliot's book of poems *Old Possum's Book of Practical Cats* (1939), which became the basis for *Cats,* the longest running musical on Broadway. He is humorously described as "a fiend in feline shape," "the Napoleon of crime" and the elusive "bafflement of Scotland Yard," for

> *He always has an alibi, and one or two to spare:*
> *And whatever time the deed took place—*
> *MACAVITY WASN'T THERE!*

Macavity is a lightly ironic allusion to the sort of "criminal" who would steal a cookie out of the cookie jar.

Macbeth   Protagonist of Shakespeare's play *Macbeth* (c. 1606). Of all Shakespeare's tragic heroes, Macbeth least fits the Aristotelian definition of an otherwise noble person defeated by a single flaw in his character.

Tricked by the Weird Sisters (three witches) and tempted by his own ambition, Macbeth allows his wife, LADY MACBETH, to override his scruples. Against his better judgment and contrary to his moral nature, he kills King Duncan. Macbeth becomes king of Scotland, and to protect his ill-gotten throne, he becomes a confirmed murderer, picking off all who seem to stand in his way. When he cannot get at Macduff, he has Macduff's wife and all their children murdered. He has become a butcher, "in blood / Stepped in so far, that, should I wade no more, / Returning were as tedious as go o'er."

What redeems Macbeth is his recognition of his moral collapse and his bitter understanding of the emptiness of life in the absence of moral imperatives.

> *I have lived long enough: my way of life*
> *Is fall'n into the sere, the yellow leaf,*
> *And that which should accompany old age,*
> *As honor, love, obedience, troops of friends,*
> *I must not look to have; but, in their stead,*

Curses, not loud but deep, mouth honor, breath,
Which the poor beast would fain deny, and dare not.

An allusion to Macbeth is an allusion to the ravages of unbridled ambition.

Macbeth, Lady   Wife of MACBETH in Shakespeare's play. Lady Macbeth stiffens her husband's faltering will to achieve his ambition and to realize his fate as prophesied by the witches. It is she who spurs him on to kill Duncan. She plans all the details of the murder and has the presence of mind (when he does not) to cover for him and to implicate the guards in the crime.

She has no foreboding, however, that one killing will necessitate "another and another and another" until their lives are steeped in blood. In her famous sleep-walking scene the iron Lady Macbeth reveals the psychological toll on her of her husband's total moral breakdown. Whereas initially she had said to Macbeth, "A little water clears us of the deed," now she moans, "Out, out damned spot" as she vainly struggles to rub the blood off her hands and off her conscience.

A Lady Macbeth is generally thought of as a cruel, ruthless, iron-willed woman who will stop at nothing to further her husband's ambitions.

McCarthyism   A political movement named for Joseph R. McCarthy (1907–57), Republican senator from Wisconsin. As chairman of the Senate Committee on Government Operations, he first achieved notoriety by charging that communists and communist sympathizers had infiltrated the State Department. From 1950 to 1954 his witch-hunt for communists in every agency of government and the media paralyzed dissent and threatened to subvert constitutional liberties. He wrecked the careers and even the lives of many innocent people by unsubstantiated accusations, innuendo and bullying.

Today "McCarthyism" generally refers to the impugnment, by unfair and even malicious investigations, of a person's political loyalty, integrity or general character in order to squelch dissent.

McGuffey, William Holmes (1800–1873)   Educator and author of America's most famous textbooks, *The Eclectic Readers,* affectionately known as *McGuffey's Readers.* The *Eclectic Reader* was published in 1836, the sixth and last in 1845. In all, more than 122 million copies of the *Readers* were sold from 1836 to 1920. The *Readers* were the first books many American children encountered, and the first to use illustrations. Of McGuffey, it has been rightly said that "he taught America to read." He helped form the tastes of generations of Americans.

The McGuffey graded readers consisted of extracts from literature that reflected the cultural and religious beliefs and values of McGuffey's society, with heavy stress on Calvinist values of salvation, piety and righteousness. Later editions tended to move somewhat away from exclusive emphasis on these values.

"A McGuffey" has become a nostalgic term for reading primers.

Machiavellian   A term referring to the ideas espoused by Niccolo Machiavelli (1469–1527), a statesman of the Florentine Republic, in his book *The Prince*. Machiavelli analyzed what an aspirant to political power must—and must not—do in order to achieve and retain that power. At the time of the Renaissance, Italy was segmented into numerous little city-states constantly at war with each other. *The Prince,* intended as an objective analysis, turned out to be a handbook for cunning and unscrupulous rulers.

Although Machiavelli himself was an advocate of republicanism and Italian unity, his name has become synonymous with ruthless, cynical, shrewd manipulation. To be Machiavellian is to be, above all, pragmatic, cunning and duplicitous.

Use: Circumstantial evidence suggests that Ronald Reagan's campaign managers may have used Machiavellian means to delay the release of the American hostages in Iran in order to thwart the reelection of President Jimmy Carter.

McPherson, Aimee Semple (1890–1944)   Also known as Sister Aimee, this Canadian-born American evangelist and faith healer founded the Four-Square Gospel movement in 1918, which grew to encompass 400 branch churches in the United States and Britain. "Are you four-square?" is the greeting used by her followers. In 1923, she opened the lavish, 5,000-seat, permanent home of the movement, the Angelus Temple in Los Angeles, California. A consummate showwoman, she used all kinds of theatrical effects (music, lighting, costumes, tableaux) to attract followers. She made a fortune. In 1926 she and her mother (her manager) were indicted for fraud, but the charges were dropped. With her various love affairs, escapades, even a false claim to having been kidnapped, she made sensational headlines. She died of an overdose of sleeping pills in 1944.

She was a prototype of all those "healers" who make money out of religion and sensation.

M.A.D.   Acronym for Mutually Assured Destruction, a term coined in 1955 by Lester Pearson, then prime minister of Canada. During the cold war, it was thought that a balance of terror (that is, an equal capability to launch weapons of mass destruction against each other) between the United States and the Soviet Union would serve as a deterrent to atomic war. The principle still prevails: For example, when India and then Pakistan first tested their newly developed atom bombs in the 1990s, joining the small circle of nations that already possessed such weapons, some experts tried to assuage fears by referring to M.A.D. as the greatest deterrent.

This cautionary acronym has come to be used for lesser causes, such as in corporate takeovers, bitterly fought political contests or acrimonious divorce proceedings.

madeleine   An oval-shaped French cookie that plays a key part in stimulating the train of reminiscences within Marcel, the narrator of *À La Recherche du Temps Perdu (Remembrance of Things Past)* (1913–27) by Marcel Proust (1871–1922). One day, Marcel's mother serves him some madeleines. He dips one into his tea to soften it, and suddenly his entire childhood at Combray comes flooding back to him. Thus begins *Swann's Way,* the first novel of the series.

A madeleine suggests any object or gesture, anything that opens the floodgates of memory.

Mad Hatter, the   A character in *Alice's Adventures in Wonderland* (1865) by Lewis Carroll. Alice meets the Hatter, the March Hare and the Dormouse at a tea party at a table under a tree. Uninvited, she joins them and becomes embroiled in a truly mad conversation full of puns, nonsequiturs, hair-splitting distinctions and altogether delicious nonsense with more than a soupçon of meaning. "It's the stupidest tea-party I ever was at in all my life!" concludes the befuddled Alice. Nevertheless, a mad hatter is logically not mad at all.

Madison Avenue   Street in Manhattan now lined with elegant international boutiques but usually associated with the world of high-powered, slick advertising.

Use: The selling of the Republican presidential candidate in the '88 election campaign had all the earmarks of a Madison Avenue media blitz.

Madonna (1958–   )   Born Louise Veronica Ciccone to an Italian-American father and a French-Canadian mother, she became an American pop icon emblematic of female sexual emancipation.

Always a free spirit, she dropped out of the University of Michigan after two years to seek her fortune in New York City, first as a dancer and then as a rock-and-roll singer. After a brief spell in Paris as a backup singer, she returned to New York, began to write her own songs and started to perform them in 1982. After trying other names, she became known as Madonna. Her first two albums were not very successful, but her brash, sexy music videos began to attract attention.

In 1985 she began her acting career as a kooky, liberated character in the film *Desperately Seeking Susan.* She went on to act in other films, including *Dick Tracy* (1989) and *Truth or Dare* (1990), and played the title role in *Evita* (1996), based on the life of Eva Peron. She also appeared in David Mamet's Broadway play *Speed the Plow* (1987).

In 1992 she published the highly successful book *Sex,* containing erotic photographs and titillating copy. She has boasted of innumerable lovers, but finally she decided to have a child. Since then she has somewhat changed her image, but she remains in the public imagination a daring, unconventional sex symbol.

Mafia   A secret organization engaged in such criminal activities as loan-sharking, gambling, drug smuggling, prostitution, racketeering, infiltrating legitimate businesses, controlling unions.

The exact origin of the Mafia is not entirely clear, but on this much there is some agreement: It was founded in Italy in the 1300s to fight French oppressors. By the 1880s, it had established itself in America. From then on, it has devoted its energies to exclusively criminal activities.

In its present form, the Mafia was organized by Lucky Luciano and Meyer Lansky in the 1930s. The Mafia structure is usually built around crime families (about 24) located in major American cities. Each family is headed by a boss. Serving as his "assistants" are under-bosses (consigliere), lieutenants (capos) and soldiers (rank and file).

When Mafia families are not feuding or killing each other, they work together under a network of agreements, which, under the leadership of master criminals Luciano and Lansky, unified gangs into a national criminal syndicate with a board of directors, assigned territories and areas of influence, plus an enforcement arm— MURDER, INCORPORATED (defunct since 1940s).

"Mafia" is often applied to a small, powerful, highly organized clique or a group of "insiders" within a larger organization.

Use: In President John F. Kennedy's time, some of his confidants and assistants were referred to as the "Irish Mafia."

Mafia kiss (kiss of death)   In Mafia circles, a kiss on the lips, when administered by a fellow Mafioso, is a warning of impending danger or death. It is said that Vito Genovese, a Mafia boss, gave Joe Valachi, an associate, such a kiss "for old times' sake." Fearing that his days were numbered, Valachi turned informer and provided the government with some of the most sensational revelations in underworld history.

magic bullet   Popular name for salvarsan, a chemical compound for the treatment of syphilis. Syphilis had been a deadly scourge for centuries until Paul Ehrlich, a German physician and bacteriologist (1834–1915), discovered a substance effective against it. It is also known as "606" because it was the 606th substance that Ehrlich was experimenting with. In 1908 Ehrlich shared the Nobel Prize in medicine with Elie Metchnikoff for their work in immunology. Ehrlich named his dis-

covery Salvarsan, meaning "salvation," but "magic bullet" has taken over in the popular imagination. Today, by extension, a magic bullet may be the longed-for cure for
any deadly disease, whether medical or economic or social—in other words, a
panacea.

Magic Mountain, The (1924)   In German, *Der Zauberberg,* one of the great
novels of the 20th century, by the German writer Thomas Mann (1875–1955). It
is a study of disease—specifically, the tuberculosis that brings the characters, as
patients or visitors, to the Berghof Sanatorium in Davos, Switzerland, but symbolically, the malaise that infects all of Europe before the outbreak of World War I.

Hans Castorp, the main character, a German engineer of no special talent or
virtue, comes to visit his sick cousin Joachim. He falls under the spell of the mountain, develops a touch of tuberculosis himself and stays for seven hermetic years.
He falls in love with a languorous Russian woman, Claudia Chauchat, "the Asiatic
principle," who carelessly lets doors slam behind her. He also becomes the intellectual bone of contention between Settembrini, an Italian liberal humanist, and
Naphta, a rigid absolutist and neofascist. The atmosphere on the mountain is
febrile, erotic, contentious and self-absorbed.

The Magic Mountain is a place where one can let go. It is a place where one
needn't bother with the duties or the constraints of the real world. It is a place to
which people have withdrawn to concentrate on their own disease, their own psyche, a place where time is of no importance, where endless talk substitutes for
action, where X rays are exchanged instead of snapshots, where shadows replace
reality, where vague romantic and mystical notions replace the pragmatism of the
bourgeois way of life in the flatland below.

Maginot Line   Named after André Maginot, French minister of defense from
1929 to 1932, this supposedly impregnable 200-mile-long system of fortifications
was built by France along the Franco-German border. Unfortunately, the guns were
fixed to face east. In 1940, early in World War II, the invading German armies simply outflanked the line by advancing through Belgium, thus rendering it useless. The
term is a symbol of a fixed, inflexible system of defense that can be outmaneuvered.

Magna Carta   At Runnymede on the Thames River in 1215, after two years of
negotiations with his barons, the despotic and irresponsible King John of England
was forced to sign the Magna Carta, a royal charter "freely granted by the king."
This written document for the first time severely limited a monarch's absolute and
arbitrary power.

Although it was, indeed, only a feudal pact reaffirming the rights of the barons,
it represented a giant step forward in asserting the rights of the individual and in

establishing the ascendancy of the rule of law. The Magna Carta is a written declaration of such basic rights as trial by jury, habeas corpus, no taxation without representation. It is the precursor of such protections as are guaranteed by the American Constitution and the Bill of Rights.

It has become emblematic of all such charters.

Magritte, René (1898–1967)   Belgian surrealist painter who used incongruous juxtaposition of ordinary objects (a man's hat, a cane, an apple) for haunting effect. His planes of color were clear, flat and precise. His canvases make the viewer do a double take: Can he have seen what he thought he saw?

Use: Mark Lamas, an innovative director of Shakespeare's plays, proposes that *Pericles* be produced "as a Magritte landscape with a rocking chair floating in the sky."

Maigret, Inspector Jules   A detective in the novels of prolific Belgian writer Georges Simenon (1903–89), Maigret is of bourgeois origin. He is married and has a shabby little apartment on the Boulevard Richard-Lenoir. His chief recreation is going for walks with his wife and going to the movies. He smokes pipes, wears an overcoat and a bowler hat, and is clean-shaven. He is an intuitive detective who gets the feel of a crime by acclimatizing himself to the environment in which it was committed. Unlike Sherlock Holmes, he does not use the process of ratiocination in solving his cases. Maigret's patience and compassion often get the criminal to confess.

Main Street (1920)   Novel by Sinclair Lewis (1885–1951) in which the Main Street of Gopher Prairie, Minnesota, comes to stand for the provincialism of the majority of small towns in the United States. The heroine, Carol Milford, who is married to the kindly but rather ordinary town doctor, Will Kennicott, struggles in vain to rouse its inhabitants from their apathy and to introduce them to culture.

major league   See MAKE THE BIG LEAGUE.

make the big league (or major leagues)   In baseball, to be chosen to play in either of the two major professional leagues: the National or the American.

"Big league" or "major league" means to attain the highest professional recognition, the best, the highest, the most important, most respected.

Use: When Carlton was invited to join the front office staff, he knew he had at last made the major leagues.

"make my day"   Provocative words spoken by CLINT EASTWOOD in the movie *Dirty Harry* (1971) as he aimed his gun at a thug. The words are associated with vigilantes fighting crime on their own, without benefit of police. They may also be spoken as a challenge, sometimes jocular, in a variety of contexts.

"Make my day" laws in several states legitimize the killing of intruders who use force after breaking into one's home.

malapropism   An unwitting and often amusing substitution of one word for another that sounds similar, a practice immortalized by Mrs. Malaprop, a character in Richard Brinsley Sheridan's play *The Rivals* (1775). For example, she describes one of the characters "as headstrong as an allegory [alligator] on the banks of the Nile" and another "the very pineapple [pinnacle] of politeness."

Malcolm X (1925–1965)   Born Malcolm Little, a powerful, charismatic black American activist. In the political ferment of the 1960s, Malcolm X split from the movement led by Elijah Muhammad (The Nation of Islam) and formed his own group, The Organization of Afro-American Unity. The growing hostility and bitterness that had grown up between these groups reached its peak with the assassination of Malcolm X in a Harlem mosque on February 21, 1965.

Malcolm X has become a symbol of radical, militant black activism and separatism. In his time, he was a rallying point for the energies and aspirations of militant, revolutionary American blacks.

Maltese Falcon, The (1941)   Film classic directed by John Huston, based on a detective novel of the same title by Dashiell Hammett. HUMPHREY BOGART plays Sam Spade, a private eye hired by Mary Astor to retrieve a valuable piece of sculpture, the Maltese Falcon, from various sinister characters (Peter Lorre, Sydney Greenstreet), all of whom are plotting against each other. In an antiromantic reversal, Bogart at the end of the film turns Astor in to the police for murder.

Use: "Stevie Smith is a rare bird, a Maltese Falcon." (Clive James)

Malthusian   In accordance with the "laws" of British economist Thomas Robert Malthus (1766–1834). In *An Essay on the Principle of Population* (1798), anonymously published, Malthus argued that since population increases geometrically while the food supply increases arithmetically, poverty will forever plague the human species. He accepted war, famine and disease as natural ways of checking the growth of population. He was, therefore, opposed to social programs to help the poor. He did urge "moral restraint"—that is, birth control.

Malvolio   Olivia's self-important, arrogant steward who becomes the butt of a cruel practical joke within the subplot of Shakespeare's comedy *Twelfth Night* (c. 1600). Because he constantly upbraids the backstairs characters in Olivia's household for their riotous behavior, he rouses their resentment and ultimately their lust for revenge.

"Dost thou think, because thou art virtuous, there shall be no more cakes and ale?" challenges Sir Toby Belch. Olivia's maid Maria, with the connivance of Sir Toby Belch, the servant Fabian and the foolish Sir Andrew Aguecheek, hatches a scheme whereby Malvolio will come upon a love letter, ostensibly written to him by his mistress Olivia but really forged by Maria. Since Malvolio is "sick of self-love," they are sure that he will snatch at the bait, hook, line and sinker.

Of course, he does, and makes an ass of himself in confronting the bewildered Olivia. The plotters, declaring him mad, incarcerate him in a dungeon-dark room. Eventually the plot is revealed to Olivia, who releases the victim and commiserates with him. But to Malvolio it has been no joke. He retires from the stage at the end of the play, screaming, "I'll be revenged on the whole pack of you." This is a sour note, indeed, and an unresolved denouement in a comedy that ends by pairing all the lovers in conjugal bliss.

Malvolio is a prototype of the puritanical, disapproving, sour-grapes egoist who can't bear to see others enjoying themselves. He invites retaliation and often gets his comeuppance.

Mandela, Nelson Rolihlahla (1918–)

Associated with the dissolution of APARTHEID in South Africa, Nelson Mandela has become one of the most highly respected and beloved political leaders of the 20th century, a popular icon for grace under pressure and for reconciliation with one's former enemies. He was imprisoned from 1964 to 1990 for his leadership role in the African National Congress. In 1991 he was elected president of the ANC and on May 10, 1994, he was elected the first black president of South Africa. At his inauguration he declared: "Let there be justice for all. Let there be peace for all. Let there be work, bread and salt for all. The time for the healing of the wounds has come." It was in this spirit that he led the peaceful transition from apartheid to majority rule in South Africa, and it was in this spirit that he called for an end to factional violence among the blacks themselves. In 1999, Mandela retired and witnessed a peaceful succession to his presidency through a democratic election.

Mandrake the Magician

Comic strip character who first appeared in the strip bearing his name on June 11, 1934. Mandrake was the music-hall magician par excellence—complete with slicked, parted hairdo, waxed moustache and magic wand. Originally, Mandrake possessed supernatural powers. Later in the script, he assumed a more credible persona, relying only on his mastery of hypnotism and illusion, his extraordinary intelligence, ingenuity and courage to subdue his formidable enemies.

Man Friday   A man Friday is a trusted companion, often indispensable helper or assistant. By extension, a GAL FRIDAY functions somewhat similarly in a professional or business establishment accountable generally to one highly-placed executive.

See CRUSOE, ROBINSON.

Manhattan Project   Code name given to the massive, all-out, secret American effort to develop the atomic bomb before Germany could produce one during World War II. A group of internationally eminent physicists (Enrico Fermi, Nils Bohr, Harold Urey, Ernest O. Lawrence, Robert Oppenheimer) were brought together at various locations in the United States (Los Alamos, New Mexico; Oak Ridge, Tennessee) to harness atomic fission. On July 16, 1945, they exploded the first atomic bomb at Alamogordo, New Mexico. See also ATOM BOMB.

Manifest Destiny   On October 20, 1803, the United States bought all the land between the Mississippi River and the Rocky Mountains from France for $15 million. Known as the Louisiana Purchase, this transaction added 828,000 square miles to the country's domain, practically doubling its size. By the mid-1800s, the territorial thrust of the United States into the southwest and to the Pacific Ocean was regarded as inevitable.

The first statement of this developing policy, appeared in the July-August 1845 issue of *U. S. Magazine and Democratic Review,* in an essay by John L. O'Sullivan (1813–95): "It is our manifest destiny to overspread and to possess the whole of the Continent which Providence has given us for the development of the great experiment of liberty and federated self-government entrusted to us."

Twenty years later the full-blown thrust of this policy of expansionism found its expression in a *New York Herald* editorial by James Gordon Bennett (April 3, 1865): "It is our manifest destiny to lead and to rule all nations."

Over time, manifest destiny has taken on the hues of rationalization of and justification for national ambitions (not always legitimate) involving acquisition of territory or domination of a people.

Man in the Gray Flannel Suit, The (1955)   A novel (filmed in 1956) by the American writer Sloan Wilson. A Madison Avenue–type executive of the 1950s who commutes daily from his suburban home to the big city.

man in the street   This term, describing the average person of ordinary intelligence, was used by Ralph Waldo Emerson in his *Essay on Self Reliance* (1841): "A Greenwich nautical almanac he has, and so being sure of the information when he wants it, the man in the street does not know a star in the sky."

Emerson obviously had little respect for the man in the street's intelligence. Today's prevailing opinion of the man or woman in the street seems not to have moved much beyond his appraisal.

man of the people   Usually a man of humble origins, a common man, identified with the larger concerns of his fellow men; often applied to politicians. Andrew Jackson (1767–1845) was such a man.

In modern times, to be a man of the people one need not necessarily come from humble origins. Franklin Delano Roosevelt (1882–1945), for example, was wealthy, yet he identified closely with the needs and aspirations of the common man.

man on horseback   This expression was introduced into American politics in 1860 by General Caleb Cushing. He viewed with alarm what he saw as the impending Civil War over slavery, the Union and secession. The war could lead to a danger to democracy, ". . . a man on horseback with a drawn sword in his hand, some Atlantic Caesar or Cromwell or Napoleon."

A man on horseback who emerges to restore order in a time of social and political unrest and confusion may be welcomed by some because he seems to represent hope, but feared by others because he represents a threat to democracy.

Manson, Charles (1934–)   Cult leader of a "family" of drifters and hippies. They lived, totally dominated by Manson, in a commune outside Los Angeles where they practiced free love, experimented with drugs and held pseudoreligious rites with Manson as the central, Christ-like figure.

On the night of August 9, 1969, Manson and three of his female followers, Patricia Krenwinkel, Susan Atkins and Leslie Van Houten, entered the Beverly Hills home of Roman Polanski and murdered his pregnant wife, Sharon Tate, and four others—all shot, stabbed, clubbed to death. They used the victims' blood to scrawl messages—such as "Pig," "War"—on the walls.

Two nights later, the murderers committed similar atrocities at the home of Leo and Rosemary La Bianca.

All the killers were captured, tried and sentenced to death. But a Supreme Court ruling outlawed the death penalty and gave them life sentences instead.

Manson and his bizarre crew are typical of the "crazies" of the time—essentially deranged, living in a world of their own, totally surrendering their will to their "leader," guided by homegrown, off-the-wall, exotic principles and practices.

See JONESTOWN.

Man Who Came to Dinner, The (1939)   Play by Moss Hart and George S. Kaufman about a character based on Alexander Woollcott, a drama critic and original member of the Algonquin Round Table, infamous for his vicious wit. In the play,

Sheridan Whiteside, a dinner guest in the home of a midwestern family, breaks his leg. He remains for several weeks, virtually a dictator, commandeering the entire household and hurling gratuitous insults at everybody. When in the last scene he is finally getting ready to depart, to the infinite relief of his enslaved hosts, he breaks his leg again.

"The man who came to dinner" is a guest who has overstayed his welcome.

Man With the Golden Arm, The (1949)   Naturalistic novel by American writer Nelson Algren (1909–81), and a film (1955) based on it. The main character, Frankie Machine, is a Chicago gambling house dealer whose addiction to heroin ruins him and drives him to suicide on Skid Row.

The term now generally refers to heroin users.

March Hare   See MAD HATTER.

March of Time, The   A phenomenally popular radio news broadcast (1931–45), it presented highly colorful dramatizations of important news events (also a movie theater newsreel, begun in 1935 by Time Inc.). Each program ended in a riveting, crescendo "TIME . . . marches O-N-N-N." For years, the identity of the announcer was kept secret. Probably the most distinctive voice of its time, it was eventually revealed as that of Westbrook Van Voorhis.

Marie Antoinette (1755–1793)   The queen of France as wife of Louis XVI, she seems to have been a frivolous woman. Unhappy in her marriage, she took up with a circle of dissolute characters at court. She lived for pleasure, borrowed constantly from her ministers, spent money extravagantly and became involved in many scandals. Legend has it that when she was told that the people were starving, that there was no bread to be had in Paris, she replied, "LET THEM EAT CAKE."

The people hated her. She remained forever a foreigner, *l'Autrich ìenne,* in their eyes. They suspected her of spying. Accused of treason, she was tried before the Revolutionary Tribunal and found guilty. On October 16, 1793, she was guillotined. For all her silliness, she is said to have died with dignity.

Marie Antoinette stands for frivolous and unfeeling behavior in high places.

Use: "Even her staunchest defenders concede that Nancy Reagan is more Marie Antoinette than Mother Teresa." (*Newsweek,* April 22, 1991)

Mariel   A port on the northwest coast of Cuba from which refugees sailed in open boats to the coast of Florida in 1980. Mariel has come to be associated with mass migration from Central America.

Use: "Some 300 Nicaraguans arrive in Miami each week. We have a Mariel in slow motion." (*Newsweek,* November 14, 1988)

Marlboro Man   The central, commanding figure in the ads for Marlboro cigarettes since the late 1950s. Dressed in a shearling jacket, cowboy hat and boots, a faint smile playing over his deeply tanned features, he gazes, supremely confident, over the vast terrain, the archetypal "strong, silent man." He is master of all he surveys: the cattle, all the known and unknown rigors and perils around him. He radiates a quiet fearlessness. He is the quintessential embodiment of the virile American male. As a result of litigation against the tobacco companies in the 1990s, many of the cigarette ads appealing to children were withdrawn from use.

Use: The police thought of themselves as Marlboro Men on motorcycles.

Marlowe, Philip   A fictional detective created by Raymond Chandler (1888–1959), he is the chief character in *The Big Sleep* (1939), *Farewell, My Lovely* (1940), *The Lady in the Lake* (1943), *The Long Goodbye* (1953). He epitomizes the private eye. Trouble is his business. He operates from a one-man agency in Los Angeles and is only marginally financially successful. He is honest and loyal, witty, more educated than most private eyes and is able to quote Browning and Eliot, play chess for relaxation and enjoy classical music and art. He has been portrayed on screen by a number of actors (Alan Ladd, Dick Powell, Robert Mitchum and, most notably, HUMPHREY BOGART).

Marple, Miss   An amateur detective in the rather amusing, contrary-to-usual form of an elderly, gossipy spinster, created by Agatha Christie, British mystery writer (1890–1976). Miss Jane Marple assumes disguises in order to get information about a crime. She may pose as a maid, as a member of a repertory group or riding lodge. A shrewd judge of human nature, she invariably solves her case. Miss Marple first appeared in *Murder at the Vicarage* (1930). Other Miss Marple stories include *The Body in the Library, 4:50 from Paddington, What Miss McGillicuddy Saw, After the Funeral* and *Mrs. McGinty's Dead.*

Miss Marple was played by Margaret Rutherford in a series of four British films: *Murder, She Said* (1961), *Murder at the Gallop* (1963), *Murder Ahoy* (1964) and *Murder Most Foul* (1964). Joan Hickson portrayed her in a series of adaptations for British television (1984–92).

Marranos   During the late Middle Ages, Spanish Jews who under duress converted to Christianity were suspected of secretly continuing to observe the rituals of Judaism. These converts were called Marranos, an opprobrious Spanish term meaning swine. The Spanish Inquisition could then treat the Marranos as heretics, subject to humiliation, torture and death.

The Marranos were damned if they did and damned if they didn't confess. Confession to being a secret Jew would guarantee you a more merciful death: strangling before burning at the stake. Failure to confess meant being consigned to a public auto-da-fé. Of course the Inquisitors were impelled by the best of motives: saving the eternal souls of those they tortured and murdered. Many Marranos escaped to Holland. Those who remained alive in Spain and Portugal eventually assimilated into the rest of society.

A Marrano in modern parlance is someone who professes one faith or political affiliation but secretly believes in another.

Marshall Plan   Successful plan proposed by United States secretary of state George C. Marshall on June 5, 1947, for the economic recovery of Europe after World War II.

Use: "We need a Marshall Plan, a Berlin airlift for the cities." (Stella Schindler)

Marx, Groucho (1895–1977)   Comedian, one of the zany Marx Brothers, prominent on stage, television and in film. The team consisted of Harpo, a mute kleptomaniac, master harpist and pantomimist; Chico, a pianist, philosopher, confidence man, master of broken English; Zeppo, fairly normal in speech and behavior, who left the group in 1933; and Groucho, the madcap ringleader.

Groucho wore a long frock coat, sported an oversize cigar and a large, painted-on moustache. The mere appearance of an attractive woman activated his lascivious leer as he coyly wagged his eyebrows at his "prey." Bent over, lurching (not walking), Groucho seemed propelled by some interior mechanism. A "crack-shot wit," quick on the repartee, a lover of atrocious puns and insults, he "made mince-meat of logic and personalities."

Groucho wrote many of his own lines. Others were turned out by such gifted writers as S. J. Perelman, George S. Kaufman, Ben Hecht. Typical of Groucho's style and substance are these lines from one of his films: "I could dance with you 'til the cows come home. On second thought, I'd rather dance with the cows 'til you come home."

Marx Brothers   See MARX, GROUCHO.

Marxist   In accordance with the economic, political and social theories of Karl Marx (1818–83), German author of *Das Kapital* (1867) and coauthor with Friedrich Engels (1820–95) of *The Communist Manifesto* (1848). Marx's revolutionary ideas were to exert a profound influence on the history of the 20th century.

Some of the tenets of *The Communist Manifesto* sound almost utopian (e.g., "from each according to his ability; to each according to his needs"). According to Marx, all history is the history of economic class struggle, the struggle of the exploited against their exploiters. In this struggle the state is identified with the oppressors. In the final revolution that Marx envisioned as the inevitable outcome of the process of dialectical determinism (see HEGELIAN), the workers would rise up against their enslavers, the capitalists, and produce a classless society and the gradual withering away of the state. The rousing song of "The Internationale" is a clarion call:

> *Arise ye prisoners of starvation*
> *Arise ye wretched of the earth*
> *For justice thunders condemnation*
> *A better world's in birth.*

Marx expected that the revolution of the workers, the proletariat, would first break out in a highly industrialized society like Germany. There the disparities between workers and bosses would be most acute. In Marx's view, value comes from labor, the time, the effort and the skill that workers put into the manufacture of a product. But workers never get their fair share of the profits from their labor. The surplus value the workers produce, the profits, go to the capitalists. The rich get richer and the poor get poorer. Inevitably the workers will rebel and seize the means of production from the capitalists and create a dictatorship of the proletariat.

Marx's prediction proved wrong. The proletarian revolution broke out not in Germany but in Russia, an agrarian society for the most part, when Russian losses at the front in 1917 during World War I, combined with starvation at large, provided the spark for what would lead to the Bolshevik Revolution. Marx did not live to see this. It was left to Lenin to establish a communist state in Russia along Marxist lines, and to Stalin to brutalize it into one of the most oppressive governments in history.

Along with economic and political change, Marx foresaw a social revolution. Religion, for example, "the opiate of the people," would be outlawed. Atheism would be taught. Through education a new kind of human being would evolve, one interested not in competition and self-aggrandizement but in cooperation and the collective good.

Today, Marxist is still equated with communist, with revolutionary left-wing ideology, although some say that Marxist communism has never actually been tried, that Stalin's iron rule represented a perversion of Marx's ideas.

M*A*S*H Popular film (1970) and television series (1972–83) based on a fictional medical unit operating close to the front during the Korean War. *MASH* is an acronym for "mobile army surgical hospital." In the show, dedicated doctors and nurses cope with bloody war casualties by adopting a veneer of cynicism akin to black comedy. The last episode, in December 1983, was seen by 12.5 million viewers in the United States.

The term has become synonymous with the kind of mordant wit that permits people in the midst of mayhem to distance themselves from their natural responses and feelings.

Use: "Hospital emergency rooms are the M*A*S*H units of the drug wars, places where rhetoric is irrelevant and 'cool' turns deadly." (*U.S. News & World Report,* March 21, 1988)

Mastroianni, Marcello (1924–1996)   Italian film star idolized by women for his romantic good looks and his world-weary persona. Achieved international fame as the rueful, yet wistful journalist enmeshed in the decadent society of modern Rome in Fellini's LA DOLCE VITA (1960).

Mata Hari (1876–1917)   Margaretha Geertruida Zelle, a Dutch femme fatale, spied for the German secret service. She betrayed military secrets confided to her by Allied officers and was executed by the French on October 15, 1917, at the age of 41. A Mata Hari is a female spy who seduces men to obtain secrets.

Matisse, Henri (1869–1954)   French painter and sculptor who was the leading figure among the fauvists. As such, he liberated the world's conventional conception of color and color combinations. His canvases were vibrant with flat planes of brilliant color used to delineate not only his women and the decorative textiles of their dress but their backgrounds as well. Walls, carpeting, table cloths, household objects dazzled with an almost Moorish lavishness of color. Even late in life, when Matisse turned to découpés, his paper cutouts were riotous with unorthodox juxtapositions of color, except for his Blue Nudes, which were simply blue on white. The stained glass windows that he designed for the Dominican Chapel of the Rosary in Vence, France, glowed with color.

Matisse's aim, philosophy and practice in painting can be summed up in one word: joy. He wanted to give the viewer the pleasure he experienced in the art of painting. And he painted what was joyful. His *Joy of Life* (1905) is a pagan bacchanal. *The Dance* is a huge painting of a circle of figures holding hands and stomping with Dionysian ecstasy. His odalisques are women luxuriating in sensuous repose.

Mau-Mau   Anti-white terrorist society in Kenya, an East African British colony formed in 1925. Consisting mostly of Kikuyu tribe members under the leadership of Chief Jomo "Burning Spear" Kenyatta, the Mau-Mau murdered and pillaged all through the 1950s in an attempt to drive the white settlers from the fertile highlands. Kenyatta was sentenced to seven years of hard labor, but eventually became the first president of Kenya. Today, the term "Mau-Mau" is associated with brutal revolutionary tactics and is applied to extremists, especially among black militants.

Mayflower   The ship that in 1620, after a two-month voyage from Plymouth, England, landed with 102 Pilgrims at Plymouth harbor, Massachusetts. Before disembarking, the Pilgrims agreed that they would set up a temporary government in which the will of the majority would prevail. Thus, the Mayflower Compact became a model for constitutional democracy in North America.

Ironically, the only true self-styled "aristocrats" in the United States are those who can prove that they are descended from the original voyagers on the *Mayflower*. In 1894 the Society of Mayflower Descendants was founded in New York, and in 1897 the National Society of *Mayflower* Descendants was organized.

America has little patience with or tolerance for aristocracy, and so the "descendants of the *Mayflower*" are frequently lampooned, as are their spiritual next of kin, the Daughters of the American Revolution (D.A.R.).

Mecca   The birthplace of Muhammad and therefore the holiest city of Islam. It is situated in what is today Saudi Arabia. Every religious Muslim tries to make a pilgrimage to Mecca at least once in his lifetime. By extension, Mecca has come to mean the goal of any pilgrimage.

Medici   An Italian Renaissance dynasty that produced four popes (Leo X, Clement VII, Pius IV and Leo XI), two queens of France (Catherine dè Medici, who married Henry II, and Marie dè Medici, who married Henry IV) and a long line of rich, powerful bankers who virtually ruled the city-state of Florence.

Outstanding among the latter were Cosimo dè Medici (1389–1464), who established the family's political power, and his grandson Lorenzo dè Medici (1449–92), who came to be known as Lorenzo the Magnificent. Lorenzo was a RENAISSANCE MAN: a statesman who through diplomacy promoted the unity of Italy; a poet, dramatist and literary critic; a banker with business interests throughout Europe. Furthermore, he was a dedicated patron of the arts, subsidizing geniuses like the philosopher Pico della Mirandola, and the painters Verrocchio, Della Robbia, BOTTICELLI, LEONARDO DA VINCI and the young MICHELANGELO.

If the BORGIAS are remembered for their evil, the Medicis are remembered for their cultivation of the arts. They were Renaissance princes in the grand style.

Use: "The new industrialists were America's Medicis, and they dictated American policies as surely as those Italian bankers had owned Popes and principalities . . ." (Kenneth C. Davis, *Don't Know Much About History*)

medieval   Historically, the word "medieval" describes anything having to do with the Middle Ages, from the 6th through the 12th centuries: the organization of society, art and architecture, events and people of that period. In modern, informal usage, however, "medieval" strikes a pejorative note when applied to certain attitudes. To call a person's point of view medieval is as disparaging as to call it CRO-MAGNON; that is, benighted, unenlightened, outdated, belonging to the DARK AGES.

"medium is the message, the"   A phrase formulated by the Canadian social scientist Marshall McLuhan (1911–80). Just as the means influence the end (the other side of the notion that the end justifies the means), McLuhan perceived that the medium of communication in an electronic age would have more potential influence than the message it carried. In fact, the medium *is* the message. He recognized that radio, TV, films, computers would radically alter the ways in which we experience the world, since these mass electronic media would make a global village of the world. He saw that these new forms of communication would have far-reaching sociological, aesthetic and philosophical consequences.

The phrase is a catchword for powerful methods of presentation, as in violent video where the meaning is not clear but the brutality imprints itself.

Meet the Press   Since 1947, a weekly TV press conference with newsmakers from around the world. Originally conducted by the knowledgeable, skillful newspaperman Lawrence Spivak, at the turn of the 21st century this influential Sunday morning program on NBC was hosted by Tim Russert, whose incisive interviews with movers and shakers of the political world gave *Meet the Press* a new vitality.

Me Generation   The generation after the activist, revolutionary, anti–Vietnam War, anti-nuclear, pro–civil rights generation of the 1960s seemed to observers to be "complacent and self-serving" and came to be labeled the "Me Generation." They seemed to lack altruism and commitment to any ideal. They sought college degrees to get rich quick. They became the YUPPIES instead of the hippies of the previous generation.

The term "Me Generation" is applied to any individual or group that seems to act from selfish, self-aggrandizing motives.

meltdown   An ultimate nuclear reactor accident in which the core of radioactive material gets very hot and melts down into the earth. In 1979 the Three Mile Island reactor suffered a partial meltdown with little external radiation. In 1986 the Chernobyl reactor in Russia suffered a complete meltdown, with radiation spreading from the site to many parts of the world.

The concept of meltdown was quickly adapted to fit many disparate and often desperate situations, as in meltdown in the U.S. steel business caused by dumping of steel at low prices by Russia, Brazil and other countries in the 1990s. "Meltdown" also is used to describe a tantrum or emotional crisis.

melting pot, the   The notion that the vast majority of American immigrants have been or will be blended into a simple entity—Americans. A memorable statement of this concept is expressed in Israel Zangwill's *The Melting Pot* (1908).

Use: A melting pot is boiling over with the neighborhood's resentment toward the newest arrivals.

Member of the Wedding, The (1946)   Novel by Carson McCullers about Frankie Adams, a 12-year-old motherless girl whose only companions are her six-year-old cousin John Henry and the black cook Berenice. When her brother is about to be married and asks her to be a member of the wedding, she mistakenly thinks that she is going to make a threesome with him and his bride. She suffers terrible anguish when she realizes her error. Frankie has a lot of growing up to do within the year of the novel.

To be a member of the wedding is to "belong" to a group, whether a family or a club; to be an insider.

Mengele, Dr. Josef (1911–1979)   Infamous doctor guilty of horrendous "medical" experiments, especially on Jewish children, at the Auschwitz death camp. Known as the "Angel of Death," he aided in the torture of four million helpless victims of the Nazis, became a fugitive from justice, and probably died in South America in 1979. His name is synonymous with one who commits inhuman atrocities in the name of science—a 20th-century monster.

Mephistopheles   The devil has many shapes and goes by many names, among them Satan, Lucifer, Beelzebub and Mephistopheles. But whereas the Devil in medieval morality plays was an ugly creature with horns and a tail, half terrifying, half comical, Mephistopheles in Renaissance and modern literature is usually portrayed as an urbane, sophisticated, cunning villain.

He initiates the scholar FAUST into worldly and satanic pleasures in such works as Christopher Marlowe's *The Tragical History of Doctor Faustus* (1593), Goethe's *Faust* (Part One, 1808; Part Two, 1832), Gounod's opera *Faust* (1859), Boito's opera *Mefistofele* (1868) and Thomas Mann's novel *Doctor Faustus* (1947). The function of Mephistopheles in all of these works is to capture the eternal soul of Faust by luring him away from God's ways to the ways of damnation in both intellectual and sensual experience.

A Mephistopheles, in modern usage, is a cynical, diabolical tempter and manipulator.

Use: "[Wilkie] Collins . . . seems to have acted as Mephistopheles to Dickens's Faust, organizing sybaritic nights out and accompanying him on trips to Paris for a taste of its sophisticated diableries." (Claire Tomalin, *The Invisible Woman*)

Mercedes-Benz   High-priced, excellently tooled, German-made luxury car. Like a CADILLAC, it is tops in its class.

merchants of death   From the title of a book by H. C. Engelbrecht and F. C. Hanighan, who in the 1920s sought to prove that nations go to war to advance or protect financial interests. Originally the merchants of death were munitions makers who stood to profit from war. Now the term is applied to the manufacturers and sellers of any product that is potentially lethal; e.g., drugs, tobacco, guns.

Use: *Merchants of Death: The American Tobacco Industry* is a book written by Larry C. White.

Mercutio   Mercurial friend of Romeo in Shakespeare's *Romeo and Juliet* (c. 1595) who is killed in a street brawl by Tybalt, a cousin of Juliet. Romeo in turn kills Tybalt and is banished from Verona. This engenders the chain of events leading to the death of the two lovers.

Some critics have argued that Shakespeare had to get rid of Mercutio as early as act 4, scene 1, because he was threatening to steal the show. Mercutio's role is a coveted one in an actor's repertory. He is quick-witted and sardonic, ribald and fanciful. It is he who, when dying, repeats three times the oft-quoted phrase: "A plague á [on] both your houses!"

Merlin   A magician and seer who sets in motion many of the events in the Arthurian legends: the very birth of Arthur through the union of Igrain and Uther Pendragon; the upbringing of Arthur away from the court; the contest in which Arthur alone is able to draw the sword from the stone, proving him to be the "Rightful King of All Britain"; the gift of the sword EXCALIBUR from the Lady of the Lake to Arthur; the building of the Round Table; the creation of the myth that some day KING ARTHUR, though mortally wounded, will return from Avalon to save his people.

Merlin is the prototype of the sage with magic powers.

Use: The scientists demonstrated how their "Merlin Project," a computer, could forecast world events.

Merriwell, Frank   The hero of one of America's most popular boys' book series. From 1896 through the 1920s the Merriwell books sold over 125 million copies. Unabashedly espousing honesty, courage, hard work, devotion to duty however difficult, fair play in sports and in life, the books were an inspiration to two generations of young Americans.

To be a Frank Merriwell means simply to live the clean, wholesome, exciting life—to exemplify the virtues embodied in the life and work of Frank Merriwell— or to be a "GOODY-TWO-SHOES," even though Frank Merriwell was not, by any means, a "sissy."

Mersault   Central character and narrator of *The Stranger* (1942), an existential novel by the French-Algerian writer Albert Camus (1913–60).

Mersault is a young Algerian who is a totally uncommitted man. He is bound to no person, although he has a mother living in a nursing home and a mistress whom he sees on weekends. When his mother dies, he attends the funeral but feels no grief. As a result of a series of incidents in which he has played only a passive or acquiescent role, he comes to shoot an Arab who had pulled a knife on him. Mersault is tried, convicted of murder, and at the end of the book awaits execution. He has refused apathetically to defend himself, for what difference does it make? We are all condemned to die sooner or later. He has refused the consolation of God or a chaplain. He believes God is dead. Life is absurd and meaningless. There is no causality. We live only in the moment. That's all there is—the moment.

Mersault is modern man who must learn to live in an absurd universe without the constraints or consolations of God or religion.

"Message to Garcia, A"   Title of an essay by Elbert Hubbard (1899) describing the hazardous mission of Lt. Andrew Summers Rowan of the U.S. Bureau of Naval Intelligence. During the Spanish-American War, Rowan was sent by the U.S. chief of staff to deliver a message to General Calixto Garcia, leader of the Cuban insurgents. No one knew where the general and his forces were hiding. It was Rowan's job to find him. Taking off in a small boat, Rowan managed to slip through the Spanish blockade. On April 24, 1898, he landed at Torquino Peak. There the local patriots led him to Garcia. Shortly thereafter, undaunted by the perils he had faced, Rowan was back in the United States with the information he had been sent to find out: the number of followers Garcia had under his command.

Hubbard's essay, read by millions, made a hero of Rowan and added a new expression to the language. To "carry a message to Garcia" means to accept responsibility, face difficulties, persevere against all hazards and obstacles until the job is done.

method acting   A naturalistic style of acting developed by Konstantin Stanislavski (1863–1938), the great Russian theater director, actor, producer and teacher who founded the Moscow Art Theater. The "method" calls upon the actor to remember and use experiences and emotions in his own life, which will help him to identify with his role. The actor's performance thus depends upon psychological truth rather than on tricks and mannerisms. The method was adapted by the Actors Studio in New York, which has trained such exemplars of method acting as MARLON BRANDO and Paul Newman.

The "method" has become associated with such realistic and almost inarticulate roles as that of STANLEY KOWALSKI, played by Brando in Tennessee Williams's *A Streetcar Named Desire*.

Metternich, Fürst von (1773–1859)   So pervasive was his influence throughout Europe after the Napoleonic Wars that the period came to be known as "the Age of Metternich." It was a time in which, as a brilliant Austrian diplomat and as the guiding spirit of the CONGRESS OF VIENNA, he stamped his conservative views on the entire continent from 1815 to 1848.

As a student at Strasbourg he had witnessed revolutionary excesses. He was determined to impose order even if he had to resort to espionage and brutal censorship to suppress nationalist movements. He was despised by liberals, and when the Revolution of 1848 broke out, he had to seek refuge in England for three years.

Metternich sought to maintain the balance of power in Europe through a system of opposing alliances, strengthening the position of Austria and pursuing a middle course between France and Russia.

A Metternich in today's parlance is a skillful, conservative negotiator on an international scale. In the 20th century, Henry Kissinger was sometimes called a modern Metternich.

Micawber, Wilkins   Impecunious but incurable optimist who tries to keep his wife and four children solvent but inevitably lands in debtors prison in Dickens's autobiographical novel *David Copperfield* (1850). Micawber is a well-meaning, happy-go-lucky fraud who hides his shabbiness of character behind well-brushed threadbare clothes, artificially inflated speech and a glad-hand manner.

It is at Mr. Micawber's home that David boards when he is pasting labels on bottles in a rat-infested warehouse in London. And it is Mr. Micawber who helps to expose URIAH HEEP. At the end of the novel, Micawber immigrates to Australia, where he is sure that something good is bound to turn up.

The character of the drunken, improvident Micawber was realized to perfection by W. C. Fields in George Cukor's film version (1935).

Michelangelo (1475–1564)   His full name was Michelangelo Buonarroti. An Italian High Renaissance genius of monumental power in sculpture, painting, architecture—and a good poet, to boot. A cult figure in his own day, he somehow seems modern in the way he wrestled with his personal demons. Subject to violent changes of mood, torn between the Greek ideal of physical beauty and the spiritual appeal of a SAVONAROLA, conscious above all of the truth of his divine inspiration and yet plagued by the shifting demands of his worldly patrons, he infused his creations with psychic energy and tension.

Perhaps Michelangelo's most famous statue is the larger-than-life *David,* commissioned when he was only 26 years old. The supremely beautifully modeled figure is imbued with pent-up energy, and the marble is polished to flesh. Even more suggestive of power is *Moses* (1513–15), a seated figure of a patriarch almost eight feet tall, endowed with *terribilitá*—awesome force—and potential wrath. *The Rebellious Slave* and *The Dying Slave,* each more than seven feet tall and sculpted from 1513 to 1516, exhibit that expressiveness of the psyche for which Michelangelo is famous. For his own tomb he sculpted the *Pietà Rondanini* (c. 1555–64), so devoid of Greek physicality, so spiritualized in bareness of form that it could be a medieval piece of sculpture attached to the cathedral at Chartres.

As a painter, Michelangelo's supreme masterpiece was the painting of the Sistine Chapel ceiling in Rome (1508–12). His theme was no less than the Creation, the Fall of Man, and man's ultimate reconciliation with God. His technique is sculptural in the monumental contouring of the figures, and architectural in the overall framework of the design. The profundity of its theme and the sublimity of its execution make the Sistine Chapel ceiling one of the most awe-inspiring works of man.

How then has "Michelangelo" or "Michelangelesque" become a word in our language? What a freight for a single word to bear! Let us say it stands for largeness of spirit incarnated in transcendent works of art.

Mickey Finn   A potent, doctored drink named after a Chicago bartender who operated in Chicago's notorious Whiskey Row. Finn's "ingredients," secretly added to whiskey or water, caused the victim to fall into a deep sleep from which he could not be aroused until the effects of the drink wore off. Finn's employees slipped this potion to lone customers. When they lost consciousness, they were robbed of everything they owned, including their clothes. They were dressed in old rags and dumped in a strange, distant place. Finn is alleged to have sold his recipe to other criminally-inclined saloon keepers.

A "Mickey Finn" now refers to any drink or act deliberately intended to "knock out," or immobilize, the victim—sometimes in fun or as a practical joke; at other times, with sinister, criminal intent.

Use: "Top Court Slips Unions a Mickey—Dealing a stinging blow to organized labor, the U.S. Supreme Court yesterday said airlines and railroads do not have to guarantee jobs for some workers who go on strike." (*New York Daily News,* March 1, 1989)

Mickey Mouse   Engaging animated cartoon character conceived by WALT DISNEY (1901–66), named by Mrs. Disney and drawn by Disney's associate Ub ("Ubbe") Iwerks in 1928. Mickey was soon joined by his female counterpart, Minnie Mouse. Mickey Mouse has come to mean somebody or something silly or inconsequential.

Mildred   Mildred Rogers, the vulgar little Cockney waitress with whom Philip Carey becomes slavishly infatuated in the novel *Of Human Bondage* (1915) by the British author W. Somerset Maugham (1874–1965). Mildred is common, selfish, restless, petty and vindictive. She feels superior to the sensitive Philip because he has a club foot, but she uses him and very nearly succeeds in wrecking his life, as she wrecks his apartment one day in a fit of rage.

Mildred's image has been stamped upon the consciousness of every moviegoer who has seen Bette Davis in the movie adaptation of the book.

Miller, Henry (1891–1980)   Prolific American writer whose explicit, lusty and often hilarious treatment of sex shocked the censors into banning his books in the United States. Miller spent nine years as an expatriate in Paris. His novels *Tropic of Cancer* (1934) and *Tropic of Capricorn* (1938), when purchased in Paris, had to be sneaked into the United States by intrepid travelers. Miller had much to do with loosening the puritanical sexual and social mores of his native land. In spite of his public image as practically a pornographer, he remained as in his boyhood an innocent, if exuberant, New York City street kid who had seen it all, the degradation as well as the glory. Miller's essays on literary censorship, "Obscenity in Literature" and "Obscenity and the Law of Reflection," reveal his attitudes on freedom of expression.

Miller, Joe (Joseph or Josias) (1684–1738)   A popular English comic actor who performed at the Drury Lane Theater. Offstage, however, Joe Miller was of "grave, taciturn" demeanor, not an outgoing teller of tales, ribald or otherwise.

The story goes that, at some point, Miller's stage friends began ascribing to him jokes that they had heard or had told. It was something of a joke itself to credit a joke to the rather humorless Miller. After Miller's death, his playwright friend, John Mottley, published a compilation of jokes he erroneously attributed to Joe Miller: *Joe Miller's Jests; or, the Wits' Vade Mecum* (1739). It was full of outrageous puns, corny wisecracks and "chestnuts" of various kinds.

The "Miller" jokes were repeated so often that an inevitable dullness settled over these too-oft-told tales.

A "Joe Miller" is any stale oldie of a joke that provokes an "I've-heard-this-before" sigh of boredom.

Miltonic   In the lofty, high-minded and sonorous manner of the great English poet and pamphleteer John Milton (1608–74). This manner is evident in the famous opening lines of *Paradise Lost* (1667), an epic poem in 12 books about Satan's rebellion against God and Adam and Eve's expulsion from the Garden of Eden.

> *Of Man's first disobedience, and the fruit*
> *Of that forbidden tree whose mortal taste*
> *Brought death into the world, and all our woe,*
> *With loss of Eden.*

The Miltonic manner is evident in Milton's description of Satan's ejection from Heaven:

> *Him the Almighty Power*
> *Hurled headlong flaming from the eternal sky*
> *With hideous ruin and combustion down*
> *To bottomless perdition, there to dwell*
> *In adamantine chains and penal fire,*
> *Who durst defy th' Omnipotent to arms.*

It is also evident in Milton's sonnets, such as these lines from "On The Late Massacre in Piedmont" (1655):

> *Avenge, O Lord, Thy slaughtered saints, whose bones*
> *Lie scattered on the Alpine mountains cold*

Milton was a man of enormous erudition. He was as fluent in Greek, Latin and Hebrew as he was with Italian and other modern languages. He had an encyclopedic knowledge of history, mythology, poetry, rhetoric, theology and science. Some critics believe that his learning got in the way of his poetry, making it heavy with classical allusions and proper names that hardly anybody recognizes any more. And yet he could write simply with telling emotional effect, as in the last lines of *Paradise Lost*:

> *Some natural tears they dropped, but wiped them soon;*
> *The World was all before them, where to choose*
> *Their place of rest, and Providence their guide:*
> *They hand in hand with wandering steps and slow,*
> *Through Eden took their solitary way.*

Among Milton's greatest poetic works are "L'Allegro" and "Il Penseroso," "Lycidas" (1637), *Paradise Lost, Paradise Regained* (1671), "Samson Agonistes" (1671) and some 19 sonnets.

As a prose writer, Milton was a powerful polemicist, inveighing against the perceived abuses of the Church of England, espousing the legitimacy of divorce for reasons of incompatibility, defending freedom of the press (see AREOPAGITICA) and arguing the right of a people to rid itself of a bad king.

When Charles II ascended the throne of England in 1660, after the fall of the Commonwealth, Milton was arrested and imprisoned. He had been Latin Secretary to Oliver Cromwell. He was released, however, shortly thereafter through the intervention of the poet Andrew Marvell. By that time, Milton was totally blind, having "lost his sight as he supposed in defence of England's liberties." But like other blind seers (Homer and Tiresias), he was already embarked on writing his masterpiece. That work was *Paradise Lost,* in which he sought nothing less than "to justify the ways of God to men."

Minute Men   Originally a special military force organized by the Continental Congress, ready to fight the British forces "at a minute's notice." Joined by local volunteers, they were "the embattled farmers" who faced the British at Concord and Lexington, and "fired the shot heard 'round the world."

"Minute Man" has come to mean any individual or group of individuals trained to respond immediately to threats to their individual or communal concerns.

Miranda Decision   A landmark Supreme Court decision (*Miranda v. Arizona,* 1966) requiring law enforcement officials to tell anyone taken into custody that:
1. He has the right to remain silent.
2. Anything he says can be used against him.
3. He has the right to have his lawyer present while being questioned.
4. If he cannot afford a lawyer, the Court will appoint one to represent him.
   Miranda stands as a symbol of continuing concern for the rights of the accused.

Miro, Joan (1893–1983)   Spanish surrealist painter known for his brightly colored, amoeba-like forms floating in rhythmic fantasy.

Miss Lonelyhearts (1933)   A short novel by Nathanael West (1903–40), about a man who writes a column of advice to the lovelorn in a New York newspaper. His correspondents address their problems to "Miss Lonelyhearts." He agonizes over their sufferings. He becomes unwittingly entangled in the sordid life of one of these women, Mrs. Doyle. The result is that this Christ-like figure, who has taken upon himself the woes of the world, is murdered by her crazed husband.

Miss Lonelyhearts has become a generic term for practitioners of advice to the lovelorn.

Mr. Chips Main character in *Goodbye, Mr. Chips* (1935), a novel by James Hilton, made into a movie starring Robert Donat in 1939. Mr. Chipping starts out as a young, inexperienced Latin teacher in Brookfield, a boys' prep school in England. Shy, aloof, somewhat rigid in his adherence to rules, he is both feared and ridiculed by his students. Marriage to a warm and understanding girl changes him. After the death of his wife, Katherine, during childbirth, he devotes himself entirely to the school. Even after retirement, he remains on the campus, a living legend. In his 80s, on his deathbed, he overhears one of the masters saying to the doctor, "Poor old chap. Must have had a lonely life. Pity he had no children." "You're wrong," Chips says, "I had thousands of them, thousands of them—and all boys."

Mr. Chips is the prototype of the idiosyncratic but totally dedicated schoolmaster.

Mr. Clean The trademark of a popular liquid household cleaner, the name frequently is applied to an individual of a perfect, unblemished character, scrupulously observant of all his duties, untouched by scandal or corruption.

Mr. Rogers' Neighborhood Public television's low-key children's show. From a set designed to look like his own home, Mr. Rogers, a Presbyterian minister, examines with kids the values, feelings and fears that are the staples of their lives.

In a slow, easy, gentle manner, he deals with matters that concern kids: nightfall, rejection, disappointment, going to the dentist, and so on.

Mr. Rogers' neighborhood is a nice place to be—and a nice place to grow up in. However, Mr. Rogers also can be an object of ridicule because he is so slow of speech as to appear dull-witted.

Mr. Smith Goes to Washington (1939) Movie produced and directed by Frank Capra and starring Jimmy Stewart. Mr. Jefferson Smith, a simple, honest man, head of the Boy Rangers, is tapped by the political machine of a western state to fill an unexpired term in the Senate. The party bosses think they can manipulate him for their own greedy ends. But, of course, they are mistaken. Mr. Smith is educated quickly and outwits and outfights the bad guys.

Mitty, Walter The henpecked, ineffectual husband in "The Secret Life of Walter Mitty," a 1939 short story by JAMES THURBER (1894–1961). Mitty escapes the indignities of a humdrum life in daydreams of glamorous adventures in which he plays the hero—as an intrepid commander-pilot; as a famous surgeon; as a tough gunman on the witness stand.

A Walter Mitty is an inconsequential person who compensates for the pettiness of daily life in self-dramatizing daydreams.

Mix, Tom   Popular cowboy star in the silent movies of the 1920s who rode a black horse named Tony. He exemplified all the virtues and none of the vices of the typical cowboy. Although he eschewed violence, his pictures were full of action and daredevil stunts. His films included the Zane Grey westerns *The Lone Star Ranger* and *The Rainbow Trail*.

Moby Dick   The great white sperm whale of legendary depredation who made off with AHAB's leg and who was pursued with monomaniacal obsession by the avenging Ahab in Herman Melville's novel *Moby Dick* (1851).

Ahab's titanic struggle with the white whale has elicited innumerable interpretations from literary critics: some simple, some fanciful, some profoundly allegorical. Is Ahab motivated merely by intense personal feelings of revenge or is he locked into a cosmic struggle between good and evil? If the latter, who represents evil: Moby Dick or Ahab? According to the critic Richard Chase, the white whale is not truly allegorical: "It is part of Captain Ahab's madness that he understands the white whale allegorically, thinking of it (and thus thinking of nature itself) as representing Evil. In Ahab we see a man alienated from mankind by a fanatical will and intellect which have distorted all the genial emotions into a vindictive hatred of life itself."

The object of a relentless pursuit, a Moby Dick is a formidable combatant.

Model T   Car introduced by Henry Ford in 1909. It originally sold for $850 "in any color you choose, as long as it's black," but by 1926, Ford's mass production assembly line had reduced the price to $350. Over 15 million cars had been sold by 1927.

The Model T now refers to anything sturdy, strictly utilitarian, basic, with no frills added.

"Modest Proposal, A" (1729)   A political pamphlet by the Dublin-born satirist Jonathan Swift (1667–1745). The full title reads: "A Modest Proposal for preventing the Children of poor People in Ireland, from being a Burden to their Parents or Country; and for making them beneficial to the Publick." Swift argues that the children of the poor should be fattened up to feed to the rich, thus eliminating poverty and famine from Ireland. The argument is made with deadpan seriousness and irrefutable logic, with the savage irony that is Swift's hallmark.

A "modest proposal" today is any outrageously ironic prescription for a seemingly intractable problem.

Modigliani, Amedeo (1884–1920) Sculptor and painter who was born in Livorno and moved to Paris in 1906, where he lived in extreme poverty and died of tuberculosis. Influenced by Brancusi and African carvings, he developed his own individual style in the mannerist tradition. A Modigliani woman is instantly recognized by the elegant elongation of the head, the neck, the body and the hands.

Molly Maguires, the In 1843, a group of Irish men formed a secret society called the Molly Maguires, disguising themselves as women to avoid and surprise zealous rent collectors. The rent collectors collected more than they had come for—ruthless beatings, ducking in bog holes and other punishments. In the United States from 1865 to 1875, Irish mine workers, most of whom were members of an Irish-American secret society, organized to resist the exploiting mine owners, remedy their hazardous working conditions and to fight against denial of normal methods of alleviating grievances, the prohibition of unions, collusion between police and mine owners. The society called itself the Molly Maguires after its Irish counterpart.

Despite their laudable motives, the Molly Maguires were soon intimidating their fellow workers, resorting to murder and arson. Finally, in 1875, the miners formed a union and promptly called a strike. The mine owners called in the Pinkerton Agency to help put down the strike. One of the Pinkerton men, James McParlan, infiltrated the union. The testimony of McParlan and other witnesses at a public hearing destroyed the union. Twenty union members were hanged in 1877.

Today, the Molly Maguires are ambivalently remembered for their acts of brutality and violence or their heroic sacrifices for the American labor movement.

Molotov cocktail Simple grenade that can be made by amateurs. It consists of a bottle filled with flammable liquid, like gasoline, and a wick that is ignited just before throwing. It was first used against tanks during the Spanish Civil War. Named after Vyacheslav Molotov (1890–1986), minister of foreign affairs for the U.S.S.R. from 1939 to 1945.

Mona Lisa One of the most famous paintings in the world, it hangs in the Louvre in Paris. It was painted c. 1503–05 by LEONARDO DA VINCI. Its subject is purportedly the wife of Francesco del Giocondo, and, indeed, the painting itself is often called "La Gioconda." It shows the upper half of a seated, full-bosomed, dark-haired woman with her hands folded, her left arm resting on the arm of a chair, her right hand resting on the left wrist. Her gaze is serene, composed, and yet an enigmatic smile hovers over her lips. Behind her is a complicated landscape of rocks and water. The whole is suffused by the air of mystery that Leonardo so often achieved through his famed use of sfumato (creating an illusion of mist by blurring the outline between one area of color and another).

In modern usage, a Mona Lisa smile connotes psychological ambiguity, mystery, teasing.

Monday morning quarterback   Anyone who criticizes the individual football players or the football team after the game or the play has been completed. Monday morning quarterbacking requires no experience or expertise, just a smattering of gall and ignorance—chutzpah.

Now the term is applied to anyone who second-guesses any individual or group for the outcome of a game or performance, anyone with 20/20 hindsight.

Mondrian, Piet (1872–1944)   Dutch painter who lived in Paris, London and New York City. A Mondrian is a geometric composition of intersecting horizontal and vertical lines forming rectangles of various sizes, painted in primary colors plus black and white. Typical examples are *Composition in Red, Blue, and Yellow* and *Broadway Boogie-Woogie.* One sees Mondrians in all kinds of commercial designs.

Use: From the air, the town, with its precisely laid out streets and patches of color, looked like a Mondrian.

Monet, Claude (1840–1926)   Preeminent and prolific French IMPRESSIONIST famous for his studies of light and color, as in his series on Rouen cathedral seen at various times of the day under different conditions of light. Influenced by Turner's canvases, Monet began to paint the water lilies in his pond at Giverny until he seems to have become obsessed with them. He created a series of huge murals, his Nympheas paintings, for the Musee de l'Orangerie in Paris.

Monroe, Marilyn (1925–1962)   Film actress who became a cult figure, not just as a sex symbol but also as a fascinating study in contradictions for many intellectuals who continue to produce books about her. Born Norma Jean Martenson in 1925, she committed suicide in 1962. The ultimate pinup girl, she was sultry, exquisitely proportioned, played dumb blonde roles, but in real life read Dostoevsky and studied with Lee Strasberg. She was both brazen and vulnerable. Her second husband was JOE DIMAGGIO, the baseball hero; her third husband was Arthur Miller, the playwright. Into adult life she brought her childhood traumas from foster homes and orphanages. Her talent was for light comedy in such films as *The Seven Year Itch* (1954), *Bus Stop* (1956) and especially *Some Like It Hot* (1959).

Montaigne, Michel de (1533–1592)   French writer, creator of the personal essay as a literary genre. After the age of 38, Montaigne retired to his manor house in the Dordogne, there to live in seclusion and to set down his civilized, temperate reflections on how best to know oneself and how best to live one's life. These thoughts were published in his *Essais* (Essays), beginning in 1580.

Among Montaigne's best known essays are the stoical "To Study Philosophy Is to Learn to Die"; "Apology for Raimond Sebond," which attacks dogmatism in religion and philosophy and yet questions the power of reason to know all things; and "Of the Education of Children," which suggests that in order to get children to love the good, one must make the most of their appetites and affections, for "the most manifest sign of wisdom is a continued cheerfulness."

These are rather long essays that trace Montaigne's intellectual evolution from stoical humanism through skepticism to the man of good will. But he also wrote about all the basic experiences and emotions: fear, pain, death, friendship, constancy, loss, solitude, love, books, faith, self-knowledge. In examining himself he examined all mankind.

Montgomery, Alabama   Scene of organized boycott of buses, a movement led by Dr. Martin Luther King, Jr., to force, through the technique of passive resistance, an end to segregation of whites and blacks on city buses. Since Alabama law prohibited organized boycotting, thousands of blacks were arrested and jailed. But on April 23, 1956, the Supreme Court of the United States ruled that segregation in public transportation is unconstitutional.

Montgomery has become a symbol of the struggle for civil rights and of the successful use of civil disobedience in removing unjust laws.

Moore, Henry (1898–1986)   An English sculptor, Moore rejected classical Greek and Renaisssance ideals of beauty. A work must have, he said, "a pent-up energy, an intense life of its own, independent of the object it may represent. When a work has this powerful vitality, we do not connect the word Beauty with it." His figures look like primeval boulders that time and weather have eroded into almost human shapes. Moore's massive sculptures, carved out of stone, are noted for their spaces or holes within the framework of the statue. It is these empty spaces that are his signature.

Mother Teresa (1910–1997)   Nobel Peace Prize winner (1979) for her work with the poor. Born Agnes Gonxha Bojaxhiu in Skopje (now in Yugoslavia), of Albanian parents, she took her first vows as a nun in 1928 after training with the Sisters of Loretto, a community of Irish nuns with a mission in Calcutta. She took her final vows in 1937. In 1950 she founded the Missionaries of Charity, a Catholic religious order dedicated to "whole-hearted free service to the poorest of the poor." Mother Teresa said, "To be able to love the poor and know the poor we must be poor ourselves."The vow of poverty is exceptionally strict among the Missionaries of Charity. They care for and live among orphaned and abandoned children, sick and dying poor adults, lepers, battered and raped women.

Mother Teresa remains the symbol of saintliness for the active life of service she led among the very poor and desolate.

Mt. Everest   Situated in the Himalayas, it is the highest mountain peak in the world (29,028 feet) and, therefore, a supreme challenge to climbers and, metaphorically, to anyone struggling to reach a summit.

Mouse That Roared, The (1959)   British film satire with Peter Sellers, based on Leonard Wibberley's 1955 novel. The tiny, bankrupt duchy of Grand Fenwick declares war on the United States in order to be defeated (naturally) and so be eligible to receive MARSHALL PLAN aid. Ah, but suppose the penny-sized duchy were in danger of winning the war? Therein lies the comedy and the topical fun.

moxie   Once the name of a popular American soft drink (also called "tonic," or "pop" in the New England area), "moxie" has acquired a variety of related meanings: dash, vigor, verve, strength, aggressiveness, heartiness, pep, courage, skill.

Use: "If we are going to succeed, we need a sales staff with more moxie."

The movie is a parable of how an everyday citizen, an everyman, can fight corruption in high places and win.

muckraker   When President Theodore Roosevelt first popularized the expression muckraker as an opprobrious term for overly zealous reformers, he was alluding to the man with the Muck Rake in John Bunyan's *Pilgrim's Progress* (1678). This allegorical character was so busy mucking about with the filth on the ground that he could not gaze up to the celestial crown being offered him.

In the first decade of the 20th century, journals such as *McClure's, Collier's,* the *Independent* and *Cosmopolitan* featured articles exposing corruption in government and industry by such writers as Lincoln Steffens, Ida Tarbell and Ray Stannard Baker. They took on Standard Oil, the railroad barons, corruption in the cities and more. Novelists, too, turned to exposés; e.g., Upton Sinclair in *The Jungle* so vividly described the horrors of the Chicago stockyards that Congress passed the Pure Food and Drug Act that very year. "Muckraker" lost its disparaging connotation and became a badge of honor.

Today, as William Safire suggests, muckrakers are known as investigative reporters who work not only for newspapers and magazines but for television as well.

Mudville   See THERE IS NO JOY IN MUDVILLE.

mugwump   From "mugquomp," a word meaning "big chief" in the language of the Algonquin Indians, the term was used sarcastically at first to designate a "big shot." In 1884 it assumed another connotation when regular Republicans leveled it at renegade Republicans who refused to endorse the corrupt James G. Blaine as their presidential candidate and instead supported the Democratic candidate, Grover Cleveland. Now "mugwump" is generally used in that sense: one who breaks with his political party.

One must not omit the immortal 1930s definition of a mugwump by Ben Travato in *The Blue Earth Post*. A mugwump, he wrote, is "a bird that sits on a fence with his mug on one side and his wump on the other."

The term is edged with contempt.

Munch, Edvard (1863–1944)   Norwegian painter and graphic artist whose morbid view of life has touched the nerve of our century. He sees and depicts the skeleton beneath the living flesh and makes us aware, as did the medieval preachers, that death and corruption are the inevitable end of every joy in life. Munch's painting *The Scream* has particularly epitomized the anguish, frustration and desperation of the time, and might today be called the primal scream that psychiatrists advise us to express.

A Munch is always a reminder of death.

Münchhausen, Baron Karl von (1720–1797)   Drawing on his alleged service in the Russian cavalry in the Russo-Turkish war, Münchhausen put together a collection of incredible tales with himself as the central, heroic figure. With the help of a friend, Erich Raspé, these fantastic yarns were published in England (1875) as *Baron Munchausen's Narrative of His Marvellous Travels and Campaign in Russia*. Though many of the adventures were highly derivative, the book met with immediate success—perhaps because the baron's picaresque tales reached new heights of preposterous mendacity. The so-called marvelous travels were obviously a tissue of prodigious lies. They nonetheless seemed to have a charm of their own.

So, a Munchausen is an outrageous, inventive liar.

Munchkins   The little, elfin-like people in the land of Oz from THE WIZARD OF OZ (1900) by L. Frank Baum. Now, any person of dwarfish appearance or low-level stature, or simply a child.

Munich   Four-power conference in Munich, Germany, on September 29, 1938, to decide the future of Czechoslovakia. The participants were Prime Minister

NEVILLE CHAMBERLAIN of England, French premier Edward Daladier, Generalissimo Benito Mussolini of Italy and Chancellor ADOLF HITLER of Germany. No representative from Czechoslovakia was present. England and France consented to Germany's annexation of the Czech Sudetenland for the promise of no further aggression against Czechoslovakia and for the hope of "peace in our time." Hitler invaded and conquered the rest of Czechoslovakia on March 15, 1939.

Munich stands for appeasement.

Muppets, The   According to reliable industry estimates, in the 1970s, *The Muppets*—an American TV program produced in England—was seen in 100 countries by over 235 million people, certainly the most widely viewed program in the world.

The presiding genius of this whimsical mix of muppets and people was Jim Henson (1936–90), a fantastic puppeteer, comedian, character actor, writer, master of many voices. Ably assisted by a group of versatile, ingenious puppeteers, Henson created an American mythology equal, in some measure, to the magical kingdom of Disneyland.

Among the lovable, endearing, unforgettable muppets (a combination of marionettes and puppets) were:

The host of the show, Kermit the Frog, the vaguely genial and bewildered master of ceremonies, trying to contain and direct the motley cast of monsters, animals, guest stars. With the very best of intentions, it all ends up in shambles.

Miss Piggy, a coyly corpulent "actress" determined to become the star of the show, in vain.

Rowlf, the shaggy dog, playing the piano with a demoniacal passion.

Fozzy Bear, he of the peaked head and tiny hat.

Statler and Waldorf, two aging, tart-tongued friends observing the madness on stage, demolishing each segment with what can at best be called "awful jokes."

More than 400 characters, with their corny gags and odd skills, gave *The Muppets* universal appeal. Their wit, warmth, vulnerability, their desperately futile and hilarious attempts to make some sense and order out of a world they never made and could not control gave them an almost human dimension.

Murder, Inc.   The enforcement arm of the national crime syndicate. Organized in the 1930s, it consisted of a group of professional killers available only for the business of organized crime in America. With the concurrence of its top leadership—MEYER LANSKY, Lucky Luciano, Frank Costello, et al.— Murder, Inc., is alleged to have committed between 400 and 500 murders— most unsolved.

Murder, Inc. (so called by the media) never acted against political figures, prosecutors, reporters. In the words of Bugsy Siegel, a high official in organized crime's hierarchy, "We only kill each other."

In the 1940s, Murder, Inc., began to fall apart, its disintegration hastened by the trial and conviction of a number of central crime figures.

Murder, Inc., enriched our language with such terms as "hit," "contract," "rubout." See MAFIA.

Murdstone, Mr. Edward David's cruel, tyrannical stepfather in Charles Dickens's autobiographical novel *David Copperfield* (1850). Murdstone imposes an austere, repressive, life-denying regime upon David's heretofore happy childhood with his mother Clara and his jolly nurse Peggotty. When David rebels against his bullying, Murdstone banishes him to the school run by the sadistic Mr. Creakle. And after David's mother dies, Murdstone sends the 10-year-old David to work at pasting labels on bottles in a London warehouse.

A Mr. Murdstone is one who lives up to his name: hard as stone and cruel as murder.

Murrow, Edward Roscoe (1908–1965) American broadcast journalist. Murrow's *See It Now*—a sophisticated television news presentation produced by Fred Friendly—set new standards for American reporters and commentators and became a "document of its times." To the practitioners of the new "advocacy journalism," Murrow was a saint. Essentially, the program was the world as seen by Murrow—a very personal, passionate view. Before his television career, Murrow had made memorable radio broadcasts covering World War II from London.

In 1954, Murrow broadcast a brilliant exposé of the tactics of Senator Joseph R. McCarthy (see MCCARTHYISM). Murrow's broadcast contributed significantly to alerting his listeners to the dangers Senator McCarthy posed to democracy.

Murrow was one of the most influential radio and TV commentators of his time.

mushroom cloud White radioactive smoke rising in the shape of a mushroom to about 20,000 feet above the earth—when a nuclear bomb is exploded.

Mutt and Jeff Two famous characters in a comic strip of the same name, they are remembered mostly for their physical disparities. Mutt is the tall one, with an unruly, scraggly moustache; an insatiable bettor on the horses, perennially hopeful that the horse he bets on will hit the jackpot. Jeff is Mutt's pint-sized partner who imagines himself to be James Jeffries, the famous prizefighter.

Very little of Mutt and Jeff's character, adventures and misadventures are remembered today. What remains in our collective memory is the disparity in their height. When we encounter two individuals of markedly different heights, our almost automatic comment is likely to be, "There they go—Mutt and Jeff."

My Lai   Hamlet in South Vietnam where 22 old men, women and children were massacred by an American detail under Lt. William Calley, Jr., on March 16, 1968. Calley was court-martialed and convicted in March 1971, but his conviction was later overturned by a federal court. My Lai has become symbolic of the savagery that generally ordinary men can be guilty of under the stress of hatred and suspicion in wartime.

Myshkin, Prince   Protagonist of *The Idiot* (1869), a novel by the Russian writer Feodor Dostoevsky (1821–81). In a letter to his niece, Dostoevsky wrote: "The chief idea of the novel is to portray the positively good man." Prince Myshkin is the embodiment of that idea. He is a Christlike figure, pure, innocent, not good by virtue of good deeds but by virtue of his simple, spiritual nature. He cannot lie or deceive even when it would be better perhaps for others if he did. He is the inspired idiot of folklore, somewhat like Isaac Bashevis Singer's Gimpel the fool.

Whereas other characters of this kind are comic (Don Quixote, Pickwick), Myshkin is tragic. He is subject to epileptic fits, at the onset of which he experiences a moment of mystical ecstasy. It is a divine affliction. When Myshkin interacts with people who are worldly and driven by greed or passion, he attracts them by his radiant goodness, but he has no lasting beneficent effect on them. In fact, he seems to make matters worse. His compassion is confused with love in the case of the two women who love him, Natasha and Aglaia. He is devoid of sensuality and cannot marry either of them. The end result is that Ragozhin, who is passionately in love with Natasha, becomes insanely jealous and murders her. Prince Myshkin, appalled, sinks into idiocy.

A Prince Myshkin is an absolutely good, incorruptible man with childlike simplicity, a holy fool.

nabob   From *nawab,* a Hindi word meaning viceroy or deputy governor under the Mogul Empire in 16th-century India, it became an honorary title for eminent Muslims in India or Pakistan. Accepted into English, a nabob is any wealthy, influential or powerful person. Former vice president Spiro Agnew once called Democrats "nattering nabobs of negativism."

Nader, Ralph (1934–   )   Consumer ombudsman and muckraker whose book *Unsafe at Any Speed* (1965) was an exposé of the automobile industry that led to the passage of the National Traffic and Motor Vehicle Safety Act (1966). He set up consumer advocacy groups like the Public Interest Research Group. With dedicated volunteers called Nader's Raiders, he investigated coal mine hazards, radiation dangers, insecticide use, slaughterhouse conditions and many other abuses. In the year 2000 he was the Green Party's nominee for president.

Ralph Nader's name is synonymous with consumer advocacy.

Nagasaki   City in Japan destroyed on August 9, 1945, by the second, and last, atom bomb used by the United States to end World War II. Japan surrendered five days later. Thirty-six-thousand people were killed by the one bomb, dropped by the B-29 Superfortress *Great Artiste.* See HIROSHIMA.

Naphta   See *MAGIC MOUNTAIN, THE.*

Napoleon (1769–1821)   A commoner born in Corsica and educated in French military schools, Napoleon Bonaparte became a military legend and eventually emperor of the French.

His victorious armies swept across Europe but could not succeed in the frozen terrain of Russia, where the Napoleonic Corps, in retreat, lost two-thirds of its men. Nor could Napoleon prevail in naval battles against England, the French fleet having been crushed by Britain's naval hero, Admiral Nelson, at Trafalgar in 1805. Napoleon was decisively defeated by the allied forces of Europe under the command of the Duke of Wellington at the battle of WATERLOO on June 13, 1815. He was exiled to the island of St. Helena for the rest of his life.

Napoleon was extremely popular with his troops, who in the early years of his career called him "the Little Corporal." As he steadily realized his dreams of conquest, glory and political power, he became the "Man of Destiny." The incongruity of his physical attributes (he was very short and stocky) with his grandiose ambitions made him an easy butt of caricatures. The Napoleonic stance was born: With left arm bent at the elbow and left hand against his chest inside his jacket, the squat little man in the huge tricornered hat was shown standing astride the world like a ridiculous colossus.

In modern parlance, the epithet "Napoleon" is pejorative, meaning someone who compensates for the insufficiency of his stature by being overbearing, grandiose, dictatorial. A Napoleonic complex refers to overweening, unrealistic ambition and pride.

Nash, Ogden (1902–1971)   American writer of light verse marked by outrageous rhymes and lines of comically uneven length.

For example, "Introspective Reflection":

I would live all my life in nonchalance and insouciance
Were it not for making a living, which is rather a nouciance.

or

Candy is dandy
But liquor is quicker.

Ogden Nash stands for wit in versification.

Nation, Carry (Amelia Moore) (1846–1911)   An early, fanatical leader of the Women's Christian Temperance Union. Her passionate hatred of "drink" grew out of her ruined first marriage to Dr. Charles Gloyd, a confirmed alcoholic. Her second marriage to David Nation, a minister and lawyer, ended in divorce on the grounds of desertion: She was spending too much time away from home fighting alcoholism.

Carry Nation was by no means alone in her desire to rid her time of the evils of alcoholism. Her sisters in this battle contented themselves with using the conventional legal means for keeping their states free of saloons and alcoholics. But because saloons were illegal in Kansas, Carry Nation reasoned they were outside the protection of the law, so she embarked on a crusade for their systematic destruction. Her unorthodox technique consisted of using a hatchet to smash saloon furniture, fixtures and mirrors. The saloons she called "joints"; their habitués, "rummies"; and her method of closing the saloons, "hatchetation."

Carry Nation was arrested and jailed for destruction of property. Although she was fined and even shot at by saloon keepers, nothing seemed to dim her ardor for reform.

Carry Nation stands as a symbol of the possessed activist and crusader, especially in temperance movements.

Neanderthal man   In 1856, some scientists digging in the Neander Valley Düsseldorf, Germany, came upon the skeletal remains of a primitive man who roamed the Earth from around 100,000 to 50,000 years ago. They named him Neanderthal man for the place where they had found him, the Neander Valley (itself named after Joachim Neander [1650–80], a poet and writer of hymns).

Usage has grafted several meanings onto the original primitivism of Neanderthal man. Thus, any person or institution exhibiting crude, oppressive, brutish, arrogant, grossly ignorant attitudes or behavior is often pejoratively labeled "Neanderthal."

Nero (A.D. **37–68**)   Emperor of Rome (A.D. 54–68). Born Lucius Domitius Ahenobarbus and adopted by Emperor Claudius, he took the name of Caius Claudius Nero.

Nero's name has become a synonym for depravity, mad cruelty and irrational bloody-mindedness. He had his wife Octavia murdered to please his mistress, Poppaea. When Poppaea, his second wife, was pregnant, he kicked her to death. He poisoned his rival Brittanicus, and ordered the philosopher Seneca and the poet Lucan to commit suicide for conspiring against him.

It is pure legend that Nero "fiddled" while Rome burned (A.D. 64). Still, the legend persists. Now Nero's name is applied to anyone who seems to neglect his or her duties while a regime, business or other enterprise is crumbling.

Ness, Eliot   See UNTOUCHABLES.

"Never in the field of human conflict was so much owed by so many to so few"   Winston Churchill's tribute in August 1940 to the Royal Air Force for its defense of Britain against the German aerial blitz during World War II.

The phrase has come to be used in other contexts, as when one attributes the gains in civil rights for black Americans in the 1960s to such outstanding heroes and martyrs as Dr. Martin Luther King, Jr., Rosa Parks, James Meredith, Medgar Evers, James Chaney, Michael Schwerner and Andrew Goodman.

Never-Never Land   The imaginary land of the Lost Boys in the play PETER PAN by James M. Barrie.

"Never underestimate the power of a woman"   Originally, this simple, powerful statement appeared as part of an advertisement for *Ladies' Home Journal* in the early 1940s—just at the dawn of the modern feminist movement in America.

New Deal   Program of reforms promised by Franklin Delano Roosevelt in accepting the Democratic nomination for president in 1932. In his first 100 days in office he proposed and Congress approved many bills to ease the effects of the Depression and ensure economic stability in the future. From 1933 to 1938 he established so-called alphabet agencies to carry out his reforms: WPA (Works Progress Administration); SSA (Social Security Administration); FDIC (Federal Deposit Insurance Corporation); NLRB (National Labor Relations Board); FHA (Federal Housing Administration); TVA (Tennessee Valley Authority); SEC (Securities and Exchange Commission) and many more. A wave of optimism swept through the country; a capable leader was at the helm.

"New Deal" now is used not only in its original context, but also for any sweeping new program or agenda for reform, whether on a domestic level or a political level. In Britain, Prime Minister Tony Blair called one of his main reform programs the New Deal.

New Jerusalem   See CITY UPON A HILL.

Newport   Seaside town in Rhode Island known for its great mansions, "cottages" to the super-rich.

newspeak   In George Orwell's novel *1984* (1949), newspeak is the reduced and simplified language designed to impoverish thought and ultimately to cripple the mind so that the people can accept totalitarian rule. "Newspeak" has come to mean any kind of doubletalk.

Newtonian   Related to the theories, hypotheses and discoveries of the great 17th-century English physicist Sir Isaac Newton (1642–1727). His formulation of the laws of motion and the principle of gravity sufficed as an explanation of the entire physical universe until the beginning of the 20th century and the advent of Albert Einstein. The world according to Newton came to be seen as a clockwork universe; that is, the universe worked like a clock that God had wound up and left running according to His unchanging laws. It was a rational, harmonious system created by a benevolent deity.

For all his great contributions to the understanding of the physical universe, Newton was extremely modest: "I do not know what I may appear to the world; but to myself I seem to have been only like a boy playing on the seashore, and diverting myself in now and then finding a smoother pebble or a prettier shell than ordinary, whilst the great ocean of truth lay all undiscovered before me."

Nietzschean   Pertaining to the German philosopher and poet Friedrich Wilhelm Nietzsche (1844–1900), who exerted a profound and disturbing influence on 20th-century morals.

The concept of the Superman (*Übermensch*) is central to Nietzsche's philosophy: Man, through the exercise of his will, his most important asset, can free himself of the slave mentality imposed by Christian ethic and rise "beyond good and evil" to extraordinary greatness. This advance is not possible for all. Most people will remain slaves, conditioned by an effeminate Christianity to be fearful and obedient, to learn how to die but not how to live. The Superman in his pride creates his own law, his own values: "He sees through the pretenses of philosophers and moralists; he laughs and creates a new world."

The potentially devastating effect of such a challenge was not lost upon the Russian novelist Feodor Dostoevsky (1821–81), whose work anticipates and refutes the Nietzschean outlook. In *Crime and Punishment* (1866) RASKOLNIKOV discovers, after rationalizing the murder of the pawnbroker, that he is not, after all, a Napoleon, a Superman. He suffers when he transgresses against his innate sympathies. On the other hand, Adolf Hitler had no such scruples. He was bound to create a nation of Aryan supermen and superwomen, pagan, free of the constraints of Christian values, free to torture and kill for their own cause, free to be masters over the rest of the world, free to scorn the decadence of democracy. Although Nietzschean ideas are often equated with Nazism, Nietzsche abhorred the power of the state, and Nazism represents an evil perversion of his tenets. This is not to say, however, that Nietzschean philosophy is not dangerous and not easily misunderstood.

Nietzsche throughout his life suffered bad health and nervous disturbances. He was always an intense and passionate man given to intemperateness and missionary zeal. He could not keep friends. In 1889 he became hopelessly insane, probably from a syphilitic infection. He spent the last 10 years of his life in a mental hospital in Basel. Among his best books are *The Birth of Tragedy* (1872), *Thus Spake Zarathustra* (1883), *Beyond Good and Evil* (1886) and *The Genealogy of Morals* (1887).

The present-day popular cartoon character of comic books and animated film, Superman, who can fly and leap over tall buildings, who rights wrongs as he judges right and wrong, is, of course, a gross vulgarization of Nietzsche's *Übermensch*.

Nietzschean is almost synonymous with the exuberantly amoral, and with setting the individual will against societal restraints.

Nightingale, Florence (1820–1910)   Born into a wealthy British family in Florence, Italy, Florence Nightingale trained to be a nurse. Deeply moved by stories of the wounded soldiers in the Crimean War, she recruited 38 nurses to go with her to take care of the sick and injured on the Crimean battlefields. Appalled at the medical care the soldiers were receiving, she organized a hospital at Scutari in 1854 after the bloody battle of Balaklava. Here she introduced sanitary nursing procedures, which decreased the incidence of typhus, cholera and dysentery from 50 percent to 2 percent. Very much the "hands-on" administrator, Florence Nightingale worked tirelessly day and night making rounds, lamp in hand, tending to the sick and wounded, seeing to it that the hospital was run as she and her staff wanted it run. Quite naturally, she soon became known as the Lady of the Lamp.

When she returned to England, Nightingale set up a nursing institute at St. Thomas's Hospital in London. Her advice on nursing and hospital care was widely sought. In 1907, she became the first woman to receive Great Britain's Order of Merit. Original, dedicated, strong-minded, she is regarded as the founder of modern nursing.

To be called a Florence Nightingale is one of the highest tributes one can pay a caring, supportive, courageous woman.

Nighttown　In *Ulysses* (1922), the novel by James Joyce, Nighttown is a section of Dublin in which Leopold Bloom, the protagonist, visits brothels in the course of his wanderings on June 16, 1904.

Use: "Following the reception, [Oscar] Wilde was taken to a club. There some of the young men are supposed to have importuned him to sample earthly examples of that beauty which he had been diffusing on a more ethereal level. Wilde seems to have gone along to nighttown, and perhaps did what they proposed." (Richard Ellmann, *Oscar Wilde*)

See also BLOOMSDAY; JOYCEAN.

Nijinsky, Vaslav (1889–1950)　Russian ballet dancer. Nijinsky dazzled audiences with his technical virtuosity and exotic sensuality. He had sensational elevation. Leaping into the wings offstage, he seemed to be soaring in flight. As a youth, he studied at the Imperial Ballet School in St. Petersburg and then joined the Maryinsky Theatre, where he soon became a star. His chief association, however, was with the DIAGHILEV Ballet in Paris. There in 1912 he created the erotic role of the fawn in *L'Après midi d' un faune* to the music of Claude Debussy. He pioneered modern ballet with his innovative choreography in *Jeux* (1913), and in *Le Sacre du Printemps* (1913), to music by Igor Stravinsky. The latter caused a riot on opening night. When Nijinsky married a Hungarian dancer, his outraged lover, Diaghilev, threw him out of the company. Nijinsky declined from that time on and eventually showed signs of dementia praecox. He spent his last years in mental hospitals.

911   This telephone number for emergencies, to summon police, firefighters, ambulance or rescue squad, has become a symbol for distress, much as SOS on the high seas. Sometimes, in everyday banter, it may be invoked mockingly for some trivial perceived distress: Call 911!

1984   A novel by George Orwell published in 1949, *1984* depicts a utopia in reverse: a totalitarian society of the future in which every aspect of life is debased, mechanized and regimented. Winston Smith, the hero, wages a brief but hopeless struggle for independent thought and personal love. Arrested, tortured and brainwashed by the Thought Police, he ends by submitting to the overwhelming power of the police state.

The year 1984 has come and gone, but *1984* still stands as a warning against totalitarian repression. The novel has added many phrases to the language: 1984, BIG BROTHER, NEWSPEAK, DOUBLETHINK, as well as such topsy-turvy slogans as "War is Peace," "Freedom is Slavery," "Ignorance is Strength."

ninety-day wonder   In World War II, a disparaging, scornful description of an enlisted man who is commissioned as an army officer after a 90-day course in officer candidate school. The term describes someone obviously callow and inexperienced—and arrogant, too.

Use: The department is falling apart. So whom do they send to keep it from collapsing? This ninety-day wonder.

99 44/100% pure   From the first line of the first ad for Ivory Soap: "The 'ivory' is a laundry soap with all the fine qualities of a choice toilet soap, and is 99 44/100% pure."

This slogan, part of Ivory Soap advertisements for more than 100 years, is universally recognized as one of the most effective in the history of advertising: simple, direct, unforgettable.

The expression *99 44/100%* has slipped into the language and become synonymous with absolute, 100% purity.

nirvana   In the Buddhist and Hindu religions, nirvana is the attainment of a calm, sinless state of mind achieved by the extinction of passion, freedom from pain and worry; an ideal state characterized by the perfect balance of rest, harmony, stability, joy, a consummation achieved in the afterlife.

In today's parlance, nirvana is a state of euphoria, often induced by drugs.

Nisei   A Japanese word for Americans of Japanese descent. During World War II, Nisei were forcibly evacuated from Oregon, Washington and California and relocated in guarded internment camps. Although they were American citizens, their rights were violated in the anti-Japanese hysteria after Pearl Harbor. Their property was confiscated. This action became a source of national guilt and disgrace. In September 1987 the U.S. House of Representatives made reparations to each of the 66,000 survivors with an apology and a payment of $20,000.

The Nisei are a reminder that citizens of the United States were punished without due process of law for suspicion of disloyalty simply because they belonged to a certain ethnic group.

Nixon vs. Kennedy debate   For the first time in American political history (1960), two candidates for the presidency, Republican Richard Milhous Nixon (1913–94) and Democrat John Fitzgerald Kennedy (1917–63), faced each other in a televised debate. Nixon looked tired, ragged, ill-at-ease. His jowly five o'clock shadow made him appear somewhat ominous. Kennedy looked young, handsome, vigorous, bright, eager and confident.

Nixon lost the election. Commentators and voters alike agreed that, in some measure, the merciless TV camera had contributed to his defeat; many who listened on radio thought Nixon the stronger debater.

Nobel Prize   Prize presented annually since 1901 in accordance with the will of Alfred Nobel, Swedish inventor of dynamite and other explosives, to "those who during the preceding year, shall have conferred the greatest benefit on mankind" in the fields of medicine, physics, chemistry, literature and peace. These categories have been expanded to include economics and physiology. The prize money comes from a fund administered by the Nobel Foundation, but the Nobel laureates are chosen by an independent committee. The Nobel Prize is widely regarded as the most prestigious prize in the world.

noble savage   The ROMANTIC notion that man in a state of nature is morally superior to so-called civilized man. JEAN JACQUES ROUSSEAU promoted this unsubstantiated picture of primitive man free from the inhibiting emotional and political constraints of a corrupting society.

The noble savage became a literary archetype, especially in the characterization of American Indians, as in James Fenimore Cooper's *Leatherstocking Tales* (1823–41), in which the wilderness exerts a noble influence not only on the Indian Chingachgook but also on the woodsman Natty Bumppo.

"No man is an island"   Phrase from one of the devotions of John Donne (c. 1572–1631), English metaphysical poet and theologian. The best-known section reads:

No man is an island, entire of itself; every man is a piece of the continent, a part of the main; if a clod be washed away by the sea, Europe is the less, as well as if a promontory were, as well as if a manor of thy friends or of thine own were; any man's death diminishes me, because I am involved in mankind; and therefore never send to know for whom the bell tolls; it tolls for thee.

The phrase "no man is an island" is often quoted to express our interrelatedness and our responsibility for each other. It shows the fallacy in isolationism, in separatism. It is a moral imperative for concern for our fellow men, whether in the matter of poverty or crime or political oppression or AIDS.

no-man's-land   The disputed land between the opposing lines of deeply dug trenches on the western front in World War I. Allied and German forces faced each other and fired at each other and tried to overrun each other across this hellish space of land mines, barbed wire, dead bodies and torn-up earth. The term refers to a space, in any conflict, to which neither side has a right.

Use: "Unless covert actions can be carried on covertly, the United States will have one arm tied behind its back in a deadly serious struggle in that no-man's-land between peace and war." (Raymond Price, *New York Times,* July 12, 1987)

Nora   When Nora Helmer, the protagonist of *A Doll's House* (1879) by Henrik Ibsen (1828–1906), slammed the door at the end of the play and walked away from her husband and her assigned role as a silly, petted, docile, irresponsible "little wife," her act became a symbolic gesture in the launching of the women's liberation movement. She was asserting her divine right to live as a complete human being, with all the privileges and responsibilities of that condition.

Nostradamus (1503–1566)   Born Michel de Nostredame, he was a French astrologer and physician whose book of rhymed prophecies, *Centuries* (1555), drawn from medieval prophetic literature, gained him a reputation as a seer. Some of his predictions came true, and therefore his book has been used throughout the centuries to forecast events even though it was condemned by a papal court in 1781. Nostradamus, who is said to have effected some marvelous cures during the plagues in southern France, was appointed personal physician to Charles IX.

Today, "Nostradamus" carries the pejorative connotation of a fake prophet.

Use: "Although Tennyson did not assume the prophetic mantle of a Nostradamus, some of his poems embody prophecies much less veiled than the cryptic French astrologer's" (Louis Untermeyer, *Great Poems*).

"Not Waving but Drowning"   Title poem (1957) of a book of verse by the English poet Stevie Smith (1902–71), about whose life with her aunt the movie *Stevie* was made. It is an ironic poem, with a tinge of black humor, about a man who is drowning and calling for help, but passersby on the shore think he is just waving high spiritedly.

The phrase "not waving but drowning," with which the poem ends, is used as a cri de coeur for help when one is floundering.

"not with a bang but a whimper"   The final line of T. S. Eliot's poem "The Hollow Men" (1925), in which the poet laments the spiritual stagnation, the emptiness, and the paralysis of will of modern man, including himself. He concludes that his world will end without any kind of affirmation, "not with a bang but a whimper."

The phrase often is quoted to express anticlimax, a kind of petering out of big beginnings or big expectations. Sometimes the line is reversed to read "The world will end not with a whimper but a bang," especially in connection with the threat of the end of the world in an atomic war.

not worth a continental   Worthless, like the paper money (the continental) issued by the American Continental Congress (1774–81) during the American Revolution.

Nude Descending a Staircase   Cubist painting by French artist Marcel Duchamp (1887–1968), which caused a scandal at the 1913 Armory Show in New York City. It shows successive superimposed images of a fragmented and mechanized figure moving down a staircase. Although it represented a revolutionary departure for art in its time, it was greeted with derision and disbelief by laymen.

nuke   Short for nuclear bomb. Used as a verb, to "nuke" an enemy is to atomize him, to hit him with ultimate power.

Nuremberg Laws   Laws enacted in September 1935 by the Nazi regime in Germany; they deprived German Jews of their citizenship and forbade intermarriage or sexual relations between Jews and Germans. These laws were called "The Law Respecting Reich Citizenship" and "The Law for the Protection of German Blood and German Honor." Together with 13 supplementary decrees, they outlined the course of Hitler's war against the Jews. The Jews became pariahs with no civil, political or economic rights.

The Nuremberg Laws are often referred to in connection with the definition of a Jew.

Nuremberg Trials (1945–46)   Post–World War II Allied trials of top Nazis accused of war crimes. The international tribunal in Nuremberg, Germany, sentenced Nazi war criminals to death by hanging and established the principle of personal responsibility for crimes against humanity. Although the accused claimed (falsely) that they were following orders and thus were powerless to stop the crimes, the verdicts made clear that even following orders from an upper command could no longer be used as an excuse for such offenses.

Nureyev, Rudolf Hamitovich (1938–1993)   Soviet-born and trained ballet dancer, he asked for political asylum while on a tour with the Kirov Ballet in Paris in 1961. He achieved sensational success in many companies in the Western world. One of the greatest male dancers of the century, he was a natural heir in expressiveness and virtuosity to NIJINSKY. He was Margot Fonteyn's principal partner for many years at the Royal Academy of Dance in London. He appeared in the 1972 film *I Am a Dancer* as well as in many filmed versions of his ballet performances.

Nurse Ratched   The antagonist in *One Flew Over the Cuckoo's Nest,* a novel (1962) by Ken Kesey and later a movie (1975) directed by Milos Forman. Randall Patrick McMurphy (played by Jack Nicholson), to avoid a prison sentence with hard labor, feigns insanity in order to be consigned to a mental hospital as the lesser of two evils. His ruse backfires: the hospital is run by the absolutely rigid disciplinarian Nurse Ratched, played by Louise Fletcher. A battle of wits and personalities ensues between the hedonistic, rebellious McMurphy and the strictly-by-the-rules Nurse Ratched.

Use: "After President McMurphy, we will want Nurse Ratched. And now she wants us. We have been without adult supervision for too long. Elizabeth Dole is turning in her crisp Red Cross uniform to give us our meds." (Maureen Dowd, *New York Times,* January 6, 1999)

O

Oblomov   The main character in *Oblomov* (1859), a realistic Russian novel by Ivan Goncharov (1812–91). Oblomov is a gentle, good-natured, rather naive 30-year-old bachelor who does absolutely nothing. He lies in bed most of the day, lounges in a dressing gown and slippers when he does get up, daydreams a little about his childhood and occasionally receives visitors who try unsuccessfully to rouse him from his vegetative life. He lives in an apartment in St. Petersburg on an income from his modest estate of about 300 serfs in the country. He is waited on by a lazy, dirty, quarrelsome but devoted servant, Zahar.

The foil to Oblomov is his best friend Andrey Stolz, half-German, an engineer and entrepreneur, a can-do efficiency expert. Stolz introduces Oblomov to the young, animated and intelligent Olga Ilyinsky. Wonder of wonders, they fall in love and become engaged. Olga has plans to change Oblomov into a more Stolz-like person. Oblomov instinctively knows this. He procrastinates and procrastinates on marriage. He doesn't want to change his lethargic way of life. Finally Olga breaks their engagement and marries Stolz.

Oblomov eventually marries his landlady, the widow Agafya Pshenitzyn, who smothers him with motherly attention and indulges him in his indolence. Oblomov's estate, unsupervised except by corrupt, thieving managers, declines into bankruptcy. Oblomov, himself, drifts peacefully with the years into death.

Oblomov is almost pathologically passive, lazy, overcome by physical and mental torpor. We do not admire him, and yet we like him; in fact, we prefer him to Stolz much as we prefer, in Chekhov's *The Cherry Orchard,* Mme. Ranevsky, the charming, generous, impractical aristocrat of the old order to Lopakhin, that practical bourgeois of the new order who buys the orchard and builds mass-produced houses on the land.

Oblomov has given us the word "Oblomovism," that psychological tendency, present to some degree in all of us, of wishing to return to the dark, warm, parasitical life within the womb. An "Oblomov" is inertia personified.

Ockham's (or Occam's) razor   The principle of parsimony first stated and championed by the Franciscan English theologian and scholastic philosopher

William of Ockham (Occam) (1280?–1349?). The principle holds that the simplest explanation for a phenomenon is probably the correct one. The word "razor" in the phrase may refer to a shaving away of unnecessary detail.

Odd Couple, The (1965)   Broadway play by Neil Simon, made into a film in 1968 and later into a TV situation comedy, about two ill-assorted men—fastidiously tidy Felix and slovenly Oscar—who share an apartment with hilarious results. Now, the term describes any ill-matched pair.

Odessa steps   Unforgettable scene in *Potemkin,* a 1925 film masterpiece by the Russian director Sergei Eisenstein. The movie depicts the suppression by czarist troops of an insurrection aboard the Russian warship *Potemkin* in 1905. The memorable scene is a montage of boots and fixed bayonets inexorably advancing down the steps, red flag waving over the ship in the harbor and a baby carriage, with a baby in it, bouncing out of control down the long flight of steps leading to the harbor.

The scene produces a horrifying but symbolic effect by the juxtaposition of images of brute force with images of utter defenselessness.

off base   In baseball, this means not touching one of the four bases. The player whose hit or whose teammate's hit has put him on first, second or third base must remain on or near that base while the ball is in play. If he is caught not touching the base by the defensive team and is tagged with the ball, he is "off base," out, and leaves the field.

In general use, "off base" means wrong, in error, badly mistaken.

Off with her head! Off with his head!   See QUEEN OF HEARTS.

"often a bridesmaid but never a bride"   One of the most potent slogans of the 1920s, this advertisement for Listerine mouthwash started out like this:

> Edna's case was really a pathetic one. Like every woman, her primary ambition was to marry. Most of the girls of her set were married—or about to be. Yet not one possessed more grace or charm or loveliness than she.
>
> And as her birthdays crept gradually toward that tragic thirty mark, marriage seemed further from her life than ever.
>
> She was often a bridesmaid; but never a bride.
>
> That's the insidious thing about halitosis (unpleasant breath). You yourself rarely know when you have it. And even your closest friends won't tell you.

Prominently centered over this doleful copy is the picture of the deeply distressed girl—the unknowing carrier of halitosis.

This ad sold millions of bottles of Listerine mouthwash—and added to our language "always a bridesmaid," a metaphor for any kind of frustration and disappointment.

O'Hara, Scarlett   Flirtatious, fiery, indomitable heroine of *Gone with the Wind* (1936), a novel about the Civil War by Margaret Mitchell. A Georgia belle, rejected by her true love Ashley Wilkes, she spitefully or opportunistically is twice married and twice widowed. She then marries the dashing Rhett Butler, who is more than a match for her. After their child is killed in a horseback riding accident, Rhett Butler realizes that Scarlett's heart has always yearned for Ashley. Disgusted, he abandons her. The novel ends with the suggestion that Scarlett will endure and will somehow reconstruct her ruined but beloved antebellum Southern mansion, Tara.

Scarlett O'Hara has become a legendary figure who stands for a fiery-spirited, enduring woman.

O. Henry   Pseudonym of William Sydney Porter (1862–1910), a prolific American writer of humorous, ironic and poignant short stories known for their surprise endings and their observation of everyday New York types. One of his best known stories is "The Gift of the Magi," in which at Christmas a husband sells his only valuable possession, a gold watch, to buy his wife combs for her magnificent long hair, only to discover that she has cut her hair and sold it in order to buy her husband a fob for his watch.

An O. Henry situation is one marked by coincidence, ironic twists and surprise.

O'Keeffe, Georgia (1887–1986)   American painter whose style is so uniquely her own that she never had to sign her canvases. She is known for her sensual treatment of flowers. The viewer is drawn into the secret downy heart of a single flower, which is magnified to occupy a large canvas. After she moved from New York City to New Mexico, she painted desert landscapes with animal skeletons, Southwestern architecture and Indian artifacts. Her forms are always organic and monumental.

Okie   Derisive epithet for any impoverished farmworker from Oklahoma who in the 1930s tried to escape the dust storms of the ravaged land by moving to greener territories. In John Steinbeck's *The Grapes of Wrath* (1939), Okie "means you're scum." See JOADS, THE.

Old Guard   Originally, "Old Guard" was applied to NAPOLEON's most loyal troops: an honorable, influential group of men.

However, as early as 1844, "the Old Guard" became identified with the conservative, hidebound, reactionary wing of the Republican Party of the United States. Today, members of "the old guard" of any party or group are deeply, immovably conservative. For the opposite of the Old Guard, see YOUNG TURK.

on the ball   In baseball, to be on the ball is to be alert, effective, extremely able, smart, knowledgeable at whatever position a player is playing.

In informal use, being on, or having something on, the ball indicates exceptional intelligence or ability.

Use: Seth is always on the ball. He knows which way the market will go.

on the button   In boxing, the button is the point of the chin, considered to be a boxer's most vulnerable spot. A well-directed blow here is often enough to knock out the boxer.

In general use, "on the button" means in the precise spot or at the precise moment.

Use: He showed up for the appointment at 7 o'clock on the button.

"One-Hoss Shay, The Wonderful"   Or, "The Deacon's Masterpiece." A satirical poem by Oliver Wendell Holmes, Sr. (1809–94), New England doctor, professor, poet and essayist. The poem begins:

Have you heard of the wonderful one-hoss shay,
That was built in such a logical way
It ran a hundred years to a day,
And then, of a sudden, it—ah, but stay,
I'll tell you what happened without delay . . .

The deacon was determined to build a chaise (or shay) to last. Since most things break down at a weak spot, the Deacon saw to it that every single part and joint of his shay was equally strong and durable. And indeed it worked without need of repair for a hundred years. And then one day "it went to pieces all at once."

Holmes intended the poem to be a satire on Calvinist dogma and syllogistic logic. The one-hoss shay, though, is a metaphor for anything that seems to be indestructible and then collapses all at once.

Use: If Soviet Communism could collapse in an afternoon like the one-hoss shay, might American politics also slough off the old usual ways? (Russell Baker, *New York Times,* March 14, 1992)

Oneida Community   A group of utopian socialists calling themselves the Society of Perfectionists founded the Oneida Community and settled in New York State in

1847. The original leader of the community, John Humphrey Noyes (1811–66), shared with his followers the belief that the Second Coming of Christ had taken place, and now they were all living in a state of "sinlessness."

Among the beliefs and practices that held the group members together were the following:

- Monogamous marriages were not appropriate. A new kind of "complex marriage" encouraged sexual freedom and romantic friendships.
- Childbearing was regulated by a group of elders. Women had babies when and with whom they wanted.
- Babies, after they were weaned, were communally cared for.
- Wives were held in common. (This practice was abolished in 1879.)
- The community was held to be one family.
- Mutual criticism and vigorous expressions of opinion took the place of formal government.
- Property was communally held.
- Manual labor was encouraged. Community enterprises centered around the manufacturing of bags, traps and other practical items.
- Business enterprises were run by department heads. Men and women held equal rank.
- Talented men were sent to the universities. Young people of both sexes went to the factories to learn manufacturing techniques.

By 1870, a new generation, not moved by the theories and practices of the founding perfectionists, strained the solidarity of the movement. In 1881, the community collapsed, torn by disaffections and disagreements.

An Oneida community is any idealistic, unorthodox community held together by benign sounding but generally unworkable rules and assumptions.

one man, one vote   In *Baker v. Carr* (1962), the United States Supreme Court ruled that unequal election districts violated the Fourteenth Amendment to the Constitution. The Court mandated fair reapportionment according to the democratic principle of one man, one vote. The effect was to shift power from the sparsely populated rural areas to the densely populated cities.

"One man, one vote" has become a catchword in any kind of decisionmaking, whether on the political level or on the domestic level.

one on one   In sports, "one-on-one" refers to a single player facing or covered by one member of the opposing team.

In general, the term applies to any circumstance in which an individual reacts face to face with another individual.

Use: They are going to have to resolve their differences in a one-on-one meeting.

"one-third of a nation" "I see one-third of a nation ill-housed, ill-clad, ill-nourished." These words were spoken by Franklin Delano Roosevelt at his second inaugural on January 20, 1937. He said he spoke not out of despair but out of hope. He promised to go forward with New Deal reforms to alleviate the plight of the poor. The term refers to the poor and the disadvantaged.

one-two In boxing, "one-two" is a two-punch combination, usually a short left jab then a hard right to the jaw of the opponent.

In general use, the term refers to a two-part action or program.

Use: Fairlee beat the competition with a one-two program of brilliant advertising and low prices.

on the ropes Description of a boxer who has been battered into virtual helplessness, leaning against or holding on to the ropes around the ring. He is clearly at the mercy of his opponent and just seconds away from defeat.

In general use, on the ropes means on the verge of defeat, ruin, failure.

Use: Neglect and bad judgment had landed the once prosperous Harlan Fiske on the ropes.

"on the shoulders of giants" The earliest use of this intriguing phrase occurs in the work of Lucan (A.D. 39 to A.D. 65), a Latin poet who lived in Nero's time. He wrote in *Pharsalia,* an epic on the war between Caesar and Pompey, "Pygmies placed on the shoulders of giants see more than the giants themselves." Sir Isaac NEWTON (1642–1727), the great English mathematician and physicist who discovered and formulated the laws of universal gravitation and the laws of motion, modestly repeated Lucan's phrase: "If I have seen further [than you and Descartes] it is by standing upon the shoulders of Giants." Robert K. Merton, the eminent American sociologist, traced the origins and uses of this phrase in his book *On the Shoulders of Giants: A Shandian Postscript* (1965), a satirical spoof on scholarship.

"On the shoulders of giants" is an apt and vivid image to convey the idea that knowledge is cumulative. It rejects the notion that progress is the work of isolated geniuses. It suggests that knowledge proceeds not only on tradition, on building little by little upon the work of others who have preceded, but also on a contemporary community of scholars.

oomph girl In the 1930s and 1940s, this was the term for a girl generously endowed with a constellation of "virtues," such as sexual attractiveness or "compelling carnality." Frequently referred to as a sex goddess or sex queen.

In 1939, some press agents bestowed the accolade of "oomph girl" on the movie actress Ann Sheridan.

open city   An undefended city. During World War II, Rome and Paris became open cities when their defenders chose to abandon them rather than risk destruction of their art and architectural treasures.

open sesame   Magic words that must be spoken to open the door of a cave in "Ali Baba and the Forty Thieves," a tale from the *Arabian Nights.*

Hidden among the leaves high up in a tree, Ali Baba, a poor woodcutter, observes a band of 40 thieves entering and leaving a secret cave full of treasure. Using their magic code—"open sesame"—he enters the cave, steals some of the treasure and becomes a rich man. His envious rich brother, Cassim, decides to enrich himself still further by also robbing the cave. However, once in the cave, he forgets the magic words. He remains locked inside, and the thieves murder him. The thieves try to catch Ali Baba, too, but they are outwitted again and again by his slave girl, Morgiana, who in the end pours hot oil into the huge jars in which they are hiding, thus killing them all. As a reward, she wins her freedom.

"Open sesame" in modern usage is still a phrase that means opening doors, the doors more often being figurative than literal.

Use: A degree from the elite Harvard Business School is an open sesame to employment in a prestigious Wall Street firm.

opiate of the people, the   This phrase first appears in Karl Marx's *Critique of the Hegelian Philosophy of Right* (1884): "Religion is the sigh of suppressed creatures, the feeling of the heartless world, just as it is the spirit of unspiritual conditions. It is *the opium of the people.*"

Today, "*opiate* of the people" is more commonly used. See MARXIST.

Orchard Street   Narrow, crowded street of pushcart vendors selling every conceivable ware at bargain prices to inhabitants of New York's LOWER EAST SIDE. A vestige of Yiddish immigrant life in the first part of the 20th century, Orchard Street is a symbol of cheap goods and animated bargaining.

Oreo   The name of a cookie in which a white cream filling is sandwiched between two chocolate wafers, "Oreo" has become a slang epithet for an UNCLE TOM.

Use: "Some of the posters announcing his address were defaced with the epithets 'Oreo' and 'Uncle Tom'—evidently referring to his rather mainstream political stance in opposition to racial preference." (Stephen L. Carter, *Reflections of an Affirmative Action Baby*)

Orwellian   Pertaining to the subject matter and style of the British writer George Orwell, the pen name of Eric Arthur Blair (1903–50), especially in those works that are satires on totalitarianism: *Animal Farm* (1945) and *1984* (1949). Orwellian acts or situations refer to the suppression of liberty or the distortion of truth. See also BIG BROTHER; DOUBLETHINK; *1984*; NEWSPEAK.

Othello   The tragic hero of Shakespeare's *Othello* (1604). A Moor, a great victorious general in the service of Venice, an imposing man, he has married Desdemona, the daughter of a Venetian senator. The play reveals how the devilish machinations of his ensign IAGO rouse Othello to such a pitch of jealous rage that this honorable and loving man kills his innocent wife and then, in remorse, kills himself.

Othello has become a symbol of the terrible power of uncontrolled, passionate jealousy.

Our Gang   Variegated group of children whose antics in silent films of the 1920s entertained the children of the world. Original members of the "gang" were Mary Kornman, Mickey Daniels, Joe Cobb, Farina (Allen Hoskins) and Jackie Condon.

The term now is applied to any cute cluster of kids or zany adults, for that matter, who are acting up.

Use: In a *New York Times* book review of a biography of Andy Warhol, the critic cites the strong aberrant behavior of Warhol's associates, and concludes: "And so it goes, this perverse 'Our Gang' comedy, with Warhol as charismatic—though always detached—ringleader."

Our Town   See GROVER'S CORNERS.

out of the closet   Phrase originally used by homosexuals for abandoning secrecy and openly declaring their sexual orientation. This was a tenet of the Gay Liberation Movement. By extension, the phrase means to come out into the open with any hitherto concealed or camouflaged difference, whether personal or political.

out of left field   In baseball, left field, seen from home plate, is the left side of the outfield past third base. Because of the vastness of the outfield and its distance from home plate, "to come out of left field" is a metaphor for something remote, unexpected or slightly looney.

Use: Miller's odd comments on the way the company was being run seemed to come out of left field. They took everyone by surprise.

overkill   Expression coined between 1945 and 1950 for the enormous capacity of a nation (at that time, only the United States) to destroy an enemy many times over with a plethora of nuclear bombs. The arms race between the United States and the Soviet Union, especially in strategic nuclear weapons, was denounced by pacifists as a foolish buildup for overkill.

In general parlance, overkill may refer to any over-zealous sales pitch, market saturation or propaganda campaign.

over the top   From World War I trench warfare, when the troops charged out of the trenches by literally scrambling over the top. The British expression was "to jump off." To go over the top now means the launching and conclusion of a successful advertising or sales campaign. It also can mean a no-holds-barred effort that strikes observers as inappropriately extreme.

Oz   See *WIZARD OF OZ;* YELLOW BRICK ROAD.

"Ozymandias" (1818)   Poem by Percy Bysshe Shelley (1792–1822) about an ancient king who in his pride of power had a monument built in his likeness. On its pedestal he had stonecutters inscribe: "My name is Ozymandias, king of kings: / Look on my works, ye mighty, and despair!"

The poem begins innocently enough and builds to its mordantly ironic conclusion: "Nothing beside remains. Round the decay / Of that colossal wreck, boundless and bare / The lone and level sands stretch far away."

Ozymandias is a symbol of what the preacher in Ecclesiastes said: "Vanity, vanity, all is vanity."

Ozzie and Harriet   One of television's longest running family comedies (1952–66)—a story of the day-to-day life of a decent, loving and lovable American middle-class family. What made this show unique was that Ozzie and Harriet were played by the real Ozzie and Harriet Nelson. David and Ricky, their two growing sons, played themselves, too.

Ozzie and Harriet was a "real" show about real people playing themselves in an especially sweet, comfortable, believable America.

In 1998, the film *Pleasantville* raised profound questions about the family values of Ozzie and Harriet and of the '50s in general. A teenage brother and sister step through the TV screen into a world resembling *Ozzie and Harriet* and find a false Eden, a world in which every single thrown basketball sinks into the basket and every bowling ball makes a strike; in which, every morning, Mother, in a neat apron, has a perfect stack of pancakes ready for her two neatly dressed children (a boy and a girl, of course) and her cute bow-tied hubby all seated at the breakfast table in an immaculate kitchen just before they all go happily off to school or work at the office; in which sex does not exist, not even as a word, but racism permeates society. The world of Ozzie and Harriet, so touted as ideal by social conservatives, is shown to be shallow, hypocritical and unrealistic.

pabulum   Originally food for nourishment (as in pap, food pre-chewed by mothers for their infants or softened in milk or water for invalids), Pabulum became a trade name for bland cereal to be mixed with milk for infant feeding. The significance of the word "pabulum" was transferred from the feeding of the body to the feeding of the mind: soft, bland, inane drivel.

Use: "If people in this country weren't fed all that pabulum [on television], they could figure out what their real interests are." (Eva Hoffman, *Lost in Translation*)

pack the court   In February 1937, shortly after his election to a second term, President Franklin Delano Roosevelt proposed to add as many as six justices to the Supreme Court. These new justices would support his New Deal legislation. The "nine old men" on the court, some of whom were over 70 but still disinclined to retire, had struck down as unconstitutional the National Recovery Act (NRA) and the Agricultural Adjustment Act (AAA). A furor arose over this blatant attempt to pack the court and Roosevelt had to back down.

To pack the court is to influence a vote or an action by padding membership in a committee or club or political organization with people of the desired views.

Pagliaccio   A character within a play performed by a troupe of actors in the one-act opera *I Pagliacci* (1892) by the Italian composer Ruggiero Leoncavallo (1857–1919). The actors' unhappy real-life situation parallels the action of the play they are performing.

Nedda, the wife of Canio (the chief actor), plans to run away with her lover Silvio. Tonio, the clown, overhears them and warns Canio. Silvio runs away before Canio can ascertain his identity. That night, in the middle of these actors' play about Columbine, her cuckolded husband Pagliaccio and her lover Harlequin, Canio steps out of character and demands to know the name of Nedda's lover. She refuses to tell her distraught husband. Canio stabs Nedda and then stabs Silvio, who has returned to help her. As the curtain slowly comes down, Canio sobbing says *"La commedia e finita."* The comedy is over.

A Pagliaccio is one who laughs and plays his part even though his heart may be breaking over a personal tragedy. Like an actor, he covers up his true emotions, either to please the crowd or to be true to his art. The play must go on.

Paine, Thomas   See "THESE ARE THE TIMES THAT TRY MEN'S SOULS."

palace guard   The probable origin of the term "palace guard" is the Praetorian Guard, established in 27 B.C. by the Roman emperor Augustus (63 B.C. to A.D. 14). The Praetorian Guard guarded the emperors and their families at home and abroad until the reign of Constantine (306–337). During this period, the guard acquired considerable powers of its own.

Today's palace guard is a powerful, unofficial inner circle, a tight coterie designated to "protect" the president from powerbrokers, influence peddlers and so on. The term also is applied to the inner circle around any powerful head of a corporation or political party, or even a sports team. See KITCHEN CABINET.

paladin   Any one of 12 legendary peers who served under Charlemagne (742–814), ruler of the Franks and the Romans. Each paladin pledged himself to serve the king, to defend noble causes, fight evil, right wrongs and protect the weak.

In 1957, the enormously popular TV series *Have Gun Will Travel* made its debut. The central character, played with understated éclat by Richard Boone, made himself available to righteous causes or to victims of evildoers. Boone clearly embodied the virtues of his ancient models.

In any general context, a paladin is a defender and champion of a cause.

Pal Joey   Main character, a "heel," in a series of 12 stories originally published in *The New Yorker* and gathered in *Pal Joey* (1940) by John O'Hara, the American short story writer and novelist. The book was made into a successful musical in 1940 by Richard Rodgers and Lorenz Hart.

Pal Joey is the epitome of opportunistic, cynical Broadway types.

Palmer Raids   The post–World War I period in the United States ushered in a series of strikes. At its height, many citizens, thought to be anti-labor, received bombs in their mail. One of these bombs, mailed to A. Mitchell Palmer, U.S. attorney general, exploded on his stoop. Palmer, something of a fanatic, vowed to stamp out the "Bolshevik Revolution," which he held responsible for the current unrest.

On January 1, 1920, using the wartime Sedition Act, he authorized hundreds of his agents to invade homes in 33 cities: More than 4,000 American citizens and aliens were swept up in these raids. Many were held for a week without being charged. Friends and relatives who came to visit were themselves arrested on the grounds that they were likely to be revolutionaries or "Bolshies."

The Palmer Raids, as they came to be known, enjoyed brief public support. But challenges from the legal profession and the Wilson administration soon led to the release of almost all the victims for lack of evidence. The raids yielded no signs that individuals or organizations were giving aid to America's enemies. Not a single spy was discovered. Nonetheless, Palmer succeeded in deporting some 600 aliens and two "anarchists": Emma Goldman and Alexander Berkman.

The Palmer Raids have come to stand for governmental persecution of unpopular groups and individuals, the filing of baseless charges and the violation of civil rights. In a sense, they foreshadowed the hysteria of the McCarthy era. See MCCARTHYISM.

palooka   An athlete, especially a boxer, unskilled, incompetent or having lost much of his ability. Usually, the term describes an older boxer who has seen his best days in the ring, his senses and reflexes now dulled and erratic. By extension, to be given a one-way ticket to Palookaville is to be washed-up and forgotten.

In general use, a palooka is a crude, stupid, physically unattractive person inclined to senseless violence, easily led.

Pangloss   The incurable optimist whose Leibnitzian philosophy is tested and found wanting in Voltaire's satire CANDIDE. Although Candide himself eventually rejects Pangloss's point of view, Pangloss holds to the faith in spite of all evidence. After every calamitous episode Pangloss nevertheless insists that this is the best of all possible worlds.

Panzer   Referring to German armored divisions, especially tank units, used in World War II for lightning assaults. Swift, effective and brutal, as in a phalanx attack for a specific goal. See BLITZKRIEG.

paper chase   From the English game of hare and hounds, in which the hares drop pieces of paper as they run toward a fixed destination. The hounds try to follow the paper trail and catch up with the hares before they reach the designated spot. In 1973 the movie *The Paper Chase,* adapted from John Jay Osborne, Jr.'s, novel, popularized the term, as did the long-running TV series that followed. The movie dramatized the scholastic pressures upon a group of students in their first year at Harvard Law School, especially in a class intellectually tyrannized by a professor of law played by John Houseman.

"Paper chase" has come to mean running after a diploma or degree, especially in law school. It implies also the writing of many papers in pursuit of such a degree. Later the term included the paperwork in applying for financial aid.

Use: "Loss of predictable Federal operating support condemns major institutions like the library to an endless paper chase for public and private funds. A thousand forms must be filled out to win grants . . ." (*New York Times* editorial)

paper tiger   An expression of contempt first used by Chinese leader Mao Tse-tung (Zedong) in 1946 ("All reactionaries are paper tigers. In appearance, the reactionaries are terrifying, but in reality they are not so powerful") and later by other communist nations to characterize the ineffectiveness of United States intervention. In 1965, however, Raul Castro, armed forces minister of Cuba, warned: "United States imperialism is no paper tiger."

Now, a paper tiger is any person or thing that appears strong and powerful but is actually weak or ineffectual.

Use: Is NATO through divisiveness becoming a paper tiger?

Paradise Lost (1667)   An epic poem by John Milton (1608–74). In 12 books of sonorous, majestic blank verse, Milton recapitulates the story in Genesis of the temptation, the fall and the expulsion of Adam and Eve from the Garden of Eden. Milton's stated purpose is "to justify the ways of God to man." However, as in many a morality tale, the villain, Satan, is not only the most vividly but also the most sympathetically drawn character.

In modern usage the phrase "paradise lost" is often trivialized, as in a vacation over and done with. But it is also used to refer to loss of innocence, as in growing out of childhood.

Park Avenue   Wide center-islanded street in Manhattan with elegant residential apartment buildings for the rich.

Use: Her upward mobility was marked by a mink coat, a Cadillac and a Park Avenue address.

Parker, Dorothy (1893–1967)   Witty, sardonic American writer of poetry, short stories and criticism. She wrote drama reviews for *Vanity Fair* and later *The New Yorker*. She was a member of the Algonquin Round Table together with such other luminaries as F.P.A. (Franklin P. Adams). She is known for her "Parkerisms":

Men seldom make passes
At girls who wear glasses.

You can lead a horse to water
But you can't make him drink;

You can lead a horticulture
But you can't make her think.

She ran the whole gamut of emotions from A to B.

Parks, Rosa   First black person to defy the Alabama law that relegated black passengers to the back of the bus. For refusing to budge from the whites-only section in January 1956, she was arrested and fined. When she refused to pay the fine and threatened to appeal the decision to a higher court, she was jailed. Her case sparked the widespread boycott of buses in MONTGOMERY, ALABAMA.

Patton, General George S. (1885–1945)   Nicknamed "Old Blood and Guts," Patton achieved major victories with his tank units in World War II. A war hero, he was twice reprimanded, once for slapping a common soldier suffering from mental fatigue. His arrogance, outspokenness and eccentricities were immortalized in a brilliant portrait of him by George C. Scott in the film *Patton* (1969).

Use: "Let me confess right off that I was an early Lee Iacocca fan. I cheered when the Patton in pinstripes stormed Capitol Hill and won a reprieve for his troops." (*New York Times* Book Review, July 17, 1988)

Pavlova, Anna (1881–1931)   Ballerina born in St. Petersburg, Russia, Pavlova became the greatest dancer of her age, famous especially for her solo "The Dying Swan," created for her by Mikhail Fokine. She studied at the Imperial Ballet School, made her debut at the Maryinsky Theater and became a prima ballerina there in 1906. She toured Europe, danced with DIAGHILEV's Ballets Russes in Paris and London and performed at the Metropolitan Opera in New York City in 1910. She excelled in such classics as *Giselle, Swan Lake* and *Les Sylphides.* In 1913, she resigned from the Imperial Ballet, moved to London and opened her own school of mostly English dancers. She and her company toured all over the world, even in South America and Australia.

Pavlova's name became a household word in her time, a word synonymous with airy lightness and grace of movement suggesting poetic spirituality.

Pavlovian   Pertaining to the experiments and theories of the Russian physiologist, Ivan Petrovich Pavlov (1849–1936), who won a Nobel Prize in 1904 for his work on digestive glands. In his experiments with salivating dogs he coined the term "conditioned reflex" and then showed how the behavior of human beings could also be modified by conditioning. His theories became the basis of a school of psychology, behaviorism.

Pax Americana   The theory that the United States, the only country in the world in 1945 to possess the atom bomb, could impose world peace on its own terms. Reminiscent of the "Pax Romana" at the height of the Roman Empire.

Now, an imposed peace by one who assumes the frustrating role of policeman.

Peaceable Kingdom, The   The title of each of a number of paintings by the self-taught American Quaker and primitive painter, Edward Hicks (1780–1849). The theme of the peaceable kingdom, a moral allegory, is based on a biblical passage from *Isaiah* (11:6–9):

6. The wolf shall also dwell with the lamb, and the leopard shall lie down with the kid; and the calf and the lion and the fatling together; and a little child shall lead them.

7. And the cow and the bear shall feed; their young ones shall lie down together, and the lion shall eat straw like the ox.

8. And the suckling child shall play on the hole of the asp, and the weaned child shall put his hand on the cockatrice' den.

9. They shall not hurt nor destroy in all my holy mountain; for the earth shall be full of the Knowledge of the Lord as the waters cover the sea.

So great was Hicks's fascination with this scene that between 1830 and 1840 he painted more than 100 versions of it.

Use: Despite the fanfare after his election, the new mayor had not turned the city into a peaceable kingdom.

Peace Corps   Organization of volunteers established by President Kennedy in 1961 for the purpose of training American men and women for peacetime service in mostly third-world or developing countries. Volunteers work in such areas as agriculture, education, health or child care.

Use: Allan Bloom, in *The Closing of the American Mind,* writes of college students' attitudes: "It is the Peace Corps mentality, which is not a spur to learning but to a secularized version of doing good works."

Peanuts   See BROWN, CHARLIE.

Pearl Harbor   See DATE WHICH WILL LIVE IN INFAMY.

Peck's Bad Boy   A little hellion who devotes most of his waking moments to wreaking havoc and dismay upon his parents and the adult world in general. He does not spare his peers—but they get what mischief and malice he has leftover. Peck's Bad Boy is the creation of the humorist George Wilbur Peck (1840–1916).

Now the term is applied to anyone—child or adult—who is mischievous, troublesome, breaks the accepted rules, makes a "pest of himself," creates trouble, whose behavior embarrasses his friends or colleagues.

Pecksniff Like URIAH HEEP in *David Copperfield,* Pekcsniff is an unctuous hyp-ocrite in Charles Dickens's *Martin Chuzzlewit* (1843). His name has become syn-onymous with hypocrisy.

"peel me a grape, Beulah" Famous line spoken by the well-padded, indolent movie star Mae WEST in one of her films. It represents the essence of laziness and false refinement.

Peeping Tom In 1040, so the story goes, Leofric, lord of Coventry, levied cer-tain onerous taxes on his tenants. His wife, Lady Godiva, pleaded with him to remove these taxes. Leofric agreed to do so—if Lady Godiva would ride naked through the town. She did, covered only by her flowing tresses.

This legend was amplified during the reign of Charles II. In the expanded ver-sion, everyone in Coventry was ordered to stay indoors and keep all windows shut-tered while Lady Godiva rode through the town. The whole town obeyed the royal order—except for a certain tailor named Tom. Unable to contain his curiosity, he peeped through the shutters of his window at the passing Lady Godiva and instantly was struck blind.

Today a Peeping Tom is a man who secretly looks through windows to see women undress. A Peeping Tom is a voyeur.

Peer Gynt Hero of the 1867 epic verse drama of the same name by the Norwegian playwright Henrik Ibsen (1828–1906).

Peer Gynt is the essence of self-absorption and egotism. He believes that he was born to achieve greatness in some special destiny. Yet he comes to realize, after many fantastical adventures that constitute a quest for true identity, that he is a nobody, empty and hollow. He is like the onion that, as an old man, he peels layer after layer only to find that there is no center.

Peer has been selfish, irresponsible and opportunistic. He has cared for nobody but himself. In fact, he has consorted with the evil trolls and their Mountain King, whose motto is "Troll, to thy self be—enough!" He has rejected the true love of Solveig, who waits for him; he has abducted and seduced all kinds of women; he has stolen and killed to become rich. When the button-molder (Death) comes to melt him down with the common mass of humanity, Peer is appalled. He is, after all, no more special than anybody else. He begs for, and is granted, another chance. Peer Gynt hears Solveig's song coming from a hut in the forest. He realizes that she offers him salvation "in my faith, in my hope and in my love."

A Peer Gynt is a person given to fantasies, especially of his own specialness and greatness.

Penrod   Twelve-year-old boy in Booth Tarkington's novel *Penrod* (1914) who lives in a small midwestern city and has the typical, amusing adventures of a growing boy in a middle-class family of that time; e.g., he blackmails his older sister's suitor into giving him a dollar, with which he buys enough sweets to make him violently sick.

Penrod is a genre youngster in the tradition of PECK'S BAD BOY, TOM SAWYER and HUCK FINN.

Pentagon Papers   On June 13, 1971, the *New York Times* caused a sensation by publishing a summary of the findings of a top-secret inquiry (commissioned by Secretary of Defense Robert McNamara) into the origins and history of the United States involvement in Vietnam. These findings became known as the Pentagon Papers. They were leaked to the *Times* by Daniel Ellsberg, former deputy secretary of defense, who had come to assess the Vietnam War as immoral and the administration's presentation of it to the American people as dishonest. The publication of the secret Pentagon Papers became a cause célèbre. Ellsberg was tried and acquitted.

The Pentagon Papers have become a symbol of whistle-blowing in the highest levels of government and a reminder of the people's right to know just what their government is doing.

Peoria   Peoria is a small town in Illinois supposedly typical of average America. The ultimate test of commercial success is, Will it play in Peoria?

Pepys, Samuel (1633–1703)   Famous English diarist. Pepys's *Diary* opens on January 1, 1660, and closes on May 31, 1669. It was written in a kind of short-hand and was not decoded until 1825, when it was discovered at Magdalene College, Cambridge, where Pepys had received his university education. The *Diary* was published in ever larger editions in 1825, 1875 and 1893. Finally it made up 11 volumes, transcribed in an unbowdlerized edition from 1970 to 1983 by R. Latham and W. Matthews.

Because Pepys never intended his diary for the public eye, he wrote a completely spontaneous and honest account of the events and personages of that time. He wrote of the plague, the London fire, the Dutch war. He tells us what plays, operas and other cultural events he attended and the cost of admission to each. He tells of events and intrigues at court, and of his flirtations and affairs; in a word, all the minutiae of public and private life.

Pepys frequently ended his daily entries with the closing "And so to bed." In our own time, Franklin P. Adams (F.P.A.) adopted this ending for his Saturday columns, modeled on Pepys. These F.P.A. columns from "The Conning Tower" were gathered into the two-volume *Diary of Our Own Samuel Pepys* in 1935.

Père Goriot   Main character of *Père Goriot* (1835), one of the novels in the series *La* COMÉDIE HUMAINE by the prolific French writer Honoré de Balzac (1799–1850). Père Goriot has a single consuming passion: devotion to his two vain and selfish daughters. Although Anastasie and Delphine are both married to wealthy men of the aristocracy, they never have enough money to satisfy their taste for luxury, gambling and lovers. They milk their doting father of his last sou and repay him with scorn and shame for his bourgeois manners. Père Goriot is reduced to penury, to a dingy room in a shabby boardinghouse, without even his annuity to live on. When he dies, his daughters send their empty carriages to the funeral, paid for by two kind medical students.

Père Goriot represents a foolish sacrifice of a parent's life for ungrateful children.

perestroika   A Russian term for the restructuring of the Soviet economy; title of a book by Mikhail Gorbachev, secretary general of the Communist Party of the U.S.S.R. Popularized during Gorbachev's visit to the United States for a summit meeting with President Ronald Reagan in 1987. Gorbachev favored a mixed-market economy rather than rigid Stalinist collectivization.

The word was adapted quickly from Russian into the English vocabulary to mean an overhauling of unsatisfactory conditions.

Use: The city council has called for "perestroika in the public schools."

Perils of Pauline, The (1914)   Silent movie serial with Pearl White as its star. Stock ingredients were a scheming villain, a trusting girl and a hero who rescues her. Every episode was hair-raising, and the "perils" went on from week to week in seemingly never-ending succession.

Perry Mason   An hour-long television show based on Erle Stanley Gardner's phenomenally popular detective novels. Perry Mason, the "hero," is a successful lawyer-detective—played by Raymond Burr. Mason has never lost a case. He usually discovers the real thief, killer or embezzler in the last minutes of the drama, thus clearing his own innocent client.

Perry Mason embodies the virtues of his profession: tenacity, resourcefulness, intelligence. His quick insights and finely honed logic invariably lead him to the guilty ones. Essentially, Perry Mason is a protagonist in that oldest of struggles—the battle between good and evil.

Peter Pan   The boy who wouldn't grow up, in James M. Barrie's 1904 play, *Peter Pan*. One night he flies in through the open nursery window and teaches the Darling children—Wendy, John and Michael—to fly. He takes them to NEVER-NEVER LAND, a country inhabited by all the wonderful characters of children's tales: Indians, mermaids and villainous pirates, the latter led by Capt. Hook. After the one-armed Hook is killed, the children return home to their distraught parents and their St. Bernard dog Nana. But Peter chooses to live with the rest of the Lost Boys in Never-Never Land.

A Peter Pan is an adult who remains locked into childhood, who refuses to relinquish the ways and attitudes of a child; in fact, he crows over his youthfulness and arrested development.

Use: "He's the hit-and-run lover. This darling, involved, sensitive man of your dreams turns out to be not your future husband, but rather your garden-variety Peter Pan, cringing at the thought of real love." (Dalma Heyn in *Mademoiselle,* March 1989)

Peter Principle   One of several mythical "laws" concerning how individuals advance in business, the civil service, not-for-profit organizations or other hierarchical organizations. As set forth by Laurence J. Peter, author of the book *The Peter Principle,* "People tend to be promoted up to the level of their incompetence."

Use: Carton's dismal performance in his new job is just an illustration of the Peter Principle at work.

Petrovich, Porfiry   The police investigator responsible for solving the murder of the old pawnbroker and her sister Lizaveta in Dostoevsky's novel *Crime and Punishment.* Porfiry is convinced that RASKOLNIKOV has committed the crime—not because he has any hard evidence, but because he has a psychological grasp of Raskolnikov's odd behavior. Even after the painter Nikolai makes a "confession," Porfiry is ever more certain of Raskolnikov's guilt. He plays cat and mouse with his suspect, driving him to a frenzy. He is genuinely interested in Raskolnikov and his theories of the superman, and, as a matter of fact, he even feels affection for his tormented quarry. Porfiry urges him to confess his crime, take his punishment (Porfiry will mitigate the sentence) and still the turbulence in his guilt-ridden soul. Eventually, of course, with Sonia's help, Raskolnikov does just that.

Porfiry is the prototype of the enlightened criminal investigator who takes his time and uses psychological means to nail his suspect. Just as *Crime and Punishment* can be thought of as a detective story raised to the highest degree, so can Porfiry be regarded as the detective character transmuted into high art.

Peyton Place   A television program (1964–69) based on Grace Metalious's best-selling novel of the same title, it was the first soap opera to become a major hit on prime time.

The show was set in the small New England town of Peyton Place where, according to popular stereotypes, all is sweet, good, kind and simple. The Peyton Place of the novel, film and of television turns out, instead, to be "something with extra-marital affairs, dark secrets, assorted skull-duggery . . ." Events run the gamut from infidelity to murder.

Peyton Place is a synonym for dark deeds in dark places. Underneath its soap opera-ish plot and characterization, it is an unlovely portrait of human meanness, cruelty and ruthlessness. It was something of a "first" for television to strike so unsparingly at America's fond illusions about small-town life and people.

philosopher's stone   The "stone" or substance obsessively sought by medieval alchemists for the purpose of converting base metals into gold. They never found the philosopher's stone, but in their quest they did lay the foundations of the science of chemistry.

Metaphorically, the philosopher's stone has become the secret answer to the quest for happiness, the cure for spiritual malaise. In one of Jakob Wassermann's novels, the hero discovers the philosopher's stone to be work, work, work to exhaustion and sleep; and then the same tomorrow and tomorrow and tomorrow. In Hans Christian Andersen's story "The Philosopher's Stone," the secret turns out to be faith, and it is discovered by a blind girl.

Picasso, Pablo (1881–1974)   Spanish-born painter, sculptor and ceramist who worked in Paris from 1900. The most protean artist of the 20th century, he went from the poetic pathos of his Blue Period (e.g., *The Old Guitarist,* 1903) to the cerebral abstraction of cubism and collage cubism (e.g., *Les Demoiselles d'Avignon,* 1907, and *Ambroise Vollard,* 1910), to his Classic or Rose Period of monumental figures tenderly modeled (e.g., *Mother and Child,* 1922), to the "cut-paper style" of *Three Musicians* (1921) and *Three Dancers* (1925). Picasso was quicksilver, constantly experimenting. His name in the popular mind, however, stands for a kind of perverse distortion of the figure and for fragmentation, as in his powerful GUERNICA. A Picasso seems deliberately misshapen and angular.

Pickett's charge   One of the most celebrated battles of the American Civil War was fought at Gettysburg on July 3, 1863. Here, the Confederate major general George Edward Pickett (1825–75) launched what was to be the last desperate attack on the entrenched Union forces facing him on Cemetery Ridge.

Across a half-mile of open ground, Pickett marched his 15,000 troops, in parade formation, into the Union's withering artillery fire. Pickett's men fell by the thousands. When General Robert E. Lee ordered Pickett's soldiers to withdraw, fewer than one-quarter of the pitiful remnants found their way back to the

Confederate lines. It was one of the most disastrous retreats of the Civil War. General Lee was never again able to inflict a decisive blow on the Union Army. Three days after the battle, Pickett wrote a friend that "The Cause" was "lost."

Pickett's charge has come to mean a misconceived, unrealistic, yet gallant action doomed from the start.

Pickwick   The genial, unsophisticated founder and chairman of the Pickwick Club in Charles Dickens's picaresque novel *The Pickwick Papers* (1837). The members of the club, cronies of Mr. Pickwick, set out to explore the remote byways of the countryside. They have all sorts of amusing adventures that give the reader an insight into the customs of 19th-century England.

In the course of the novel, the innocent Mr. Pickwick is convicted in a breach of promise suit initiated by his landlady, Mrs. Bardell, a widow who imagines Pickwick is in love with her. Outraged at this miscarriage of justice, Pickwick refuses to pay the fine and spends the next three months in the Fleet Street debtors prison, accompanied, however, by his ever resourceful servant, SAM WELLER. When Mrs. Bardell herself is thrown into the prison for failure to pay her attorneys, Pickwick, always benevolent, pays her the fine and all ends happily.

"The immortal Pickwick," as Dickens describes him in the first sentence of the book, is the essence of cheerful benevolence. He radiates good will. He is the positively good man à la Dickens.

Pickwickian sense, in a   This phrase refers to the use of words in a way different from the way in which they are commonly understood. It originates in Charles Dickens's *The Pickwick Papers*. In chapter one, for example, Mr. PICKWICK accuses Mr. Bottom of acting in "a vile and calumnious manner." Mr. Bottom, in turn, calls Mr. Pickwick "a humbug." This verbal exchange is prevented from escalating when it is pointed out that these seeming slurs were used in a Pickwickian sense; that is, that far from reviling each other, Mr. Pickwick and Mr. Bottom have the highest regard for each other.

Picture of Dorian Gray, The (1891)   A novel by Oscar Wilde (1854–1900), Irish-born English playwright, poet, wit extraordinaire.

Dorian Gray, an extraordinarily beautiful, untouched youth, has had his portrait painted by Basil Hallward, a skilled artist, who considers it his masterpiece. Dorian ruefully observes that the portrait will remain forever young and fresh, even as he in real life grows old and ugly. He says that he would give his soul if the reverse were true; that is, if he himself were to remain forever young and handsome and the picture were to age and grow ugly. By some miracle, the FAUSTIAN bargain is struck.

Hallward reluctantly introduces Dorian to Lord Henry Wotton, who has fallen in love with the haunting portrait. Wotton, a sensualist and a cynic, initiates the young man into a life of vice. As Dorian sinks deeper and deeper into debauchery, the portrait keeps changing, reflecting his growing coarseness and cruelty, while he himself seems unaffected by his own depravity. The portrait, not his face or body, has become the mirror of his corrupted soul.

Dorian hides the portrait from everyone, keeping it in a locked room, but he is drawn to it every day to watch in horror its deterioration. One night, after having committed unspeakable atrocities, including the murder and dismemberment of Hallward, he lunges at the picture with a knife. Household servants, hearing a terrible shriek, break down a door and discover the body of an unrecognizable, withered, ugly old man stabbed through the heart. On the wall above him hangs the picture of the radiant youth, Dorian Gray.

The Picture of Dorian Gray is, astonishingly for Oscar Wilde, a moral tale: The sins of the flesh inevitably corrode the soul.

pied piper   In the year 1284 a pestilence caused by rats broke out in the German town of Hamelin. One day, legend has it, a handsome, mysterious young stranger carrying a silvery pipe entered the town. He offered to rid the town of its rats for a certain sum of money. The town agreed. The stranger began to play his pipe. All the rats came out of their holes and followed him to the river, where they drowned. But the townspeople reneged on their contract, and the stranger exacted a terrible revenge. He played his pipe once more, this time leading all of the children out of the town to a door in the side of a hill, through which they disappeared, never to be seen again.

This folk legend first appeared in written form around 1450. Most people know it, however, from Robert Browning's poem "The Pied Piper of Hamelin" (1842).

A pied piper in modern usage is anyone who attracts gullible followers, especially with false and seductive promises.

Use: "[Allen Ginsberg] transformed himself into a Pied Piper of radical youth." (*New York* magazine, February 15, 1999)

Pilgrim's Progress, The (part one, 1678; part two, 1684)   An allegory by John Bunyan (1628–88), a British writer and a lay preacher in the Baptist Church. His impassioned sermons were banned by royal edict. Nonetheless, Bunyan continued to preach. For his defiance, he was twice imprisoned. During these incarcerations, he wrote *Pilgrim's Progress.*

Pilgrim's Progress opens in the form of the author's dream in which he sees Christian, the central character, a burden on his back, reading a book predicting that the city where he and his family live will be destroyed. He is fleeing the city. On his pilgrimage to his final destination, the Celestial City, Christian is confronted by a series of trials, temptations and hazards. He meets many allegorical characters such as Faithful, Hopeful and Despair. He passes through the Slough of Despond, the Valley of the Shadow of Death, Vanity Fair and other places. He overcomes them all and eventually enters the Celestial City.

Pilgrim's Progress has become the universal symbol for *Everyman's* troubled journey through life to his ultimate salvation.

Piltdown Man   Fossil remains of early man, found in Sussex, England, in 1908; proved to be a hoax. They had been put together from a human skull and the jaw of an ape. Synonymous with scientific fraud.

pinch hit   In baseball, this involves sending in a player to take another player's turn at bat—to pinch-hit for him. The pinch hitter is used in various situations, including: (1) to bat for a poor hitter at a critical point in a game; or (2) to face a particular pitcher from whom he may get a hit.

The term "pinch hitter" was coined by sportswriter Charlie Dryden in 1892, to indicate that the player sent into the game was expected to get his team out of a "pinch" or difficult or tight spot. Now used in any similar situation.

Use: Bernard was asked to pinch hit in the boys' wear department until a new manager was hired.

pinch hitter   See PINCH HIT.

Pinkerton, Allan (1819–1884)   The founder of the famous detective agency that bears his name. Born in Scotland, Pinkerton came to America in 1850. An ardent abolitionist, he worked in the Underground Railroad smuggling runaway slaves into Canada.

He joined the Chicago Police Department and became its first detective. In 1852, he opened his own detective agency. He gained prominence for his role in the sensational capture of the thieves who had stolen more than $700,000 from the American Express Company. In 1861, Pinkerton uncovered a plot to assassinate President Lincoln. During the Civil War, he organized the Secret Service of the North, which did important espionage and counterespionage for the Union.

After the Civil War, Pinkerton became an unsavory ally and tool of the big business interests of the North, and Pinkerton guards played a ruthless part against the workers in the Homestead Strike of 1892.

In common parlance, a "Pinkerton" has come to stand for the private detective or "private eye."

Pinocchio   The main character in a children's book titled *Le Avventure di Pinocchio: Storia di un burattino* (1883) by Carlo Collodi, a pseudonym for Carlo Lorenzini (1826–90). Translated from Italian into English in 1892, the book became an international best-seller. In 1940 the Walt Disney Studios turned it into an immensely successful full-length animated cartoon.

Pinocchio is a boy puppet carved out of wood by an old man named Gepetto. The puppet can walk and talk and seems almost human. His distinguishing physical feature is a large nose that grows longer and longer every time he tells a lie. And Pinocchio lies very often, for he is no better than he should be. He is mischievous and sassy. He plays hooky from school, keeps bad company, gets himself into a hundred scrapes, runs away from home and is kidnapped, and generally ignores the good advice and warnings not only of his "father" Gepetto, but also of his conscience Cricket and his fairy godmother. After some hair-raising, fantastic escapades, Pinocchio finally learns his lesson. Like the Prodigal Son, he returns home to care for his father. As a reward, he becomes a real boy.

What remains in modern usage of Pinocchio is his propensity for lying and the ever-growing nose that gives him away. A Pinocchio, therefore, is one who is caught lying outrageously.

Pinteresque   Like the style and subject matter of the British playwright Harold Pinter (1930–   ) in such provocative and difficult plays as *The Caretaker* (1960), *The Homecoming* (1965) and *Betrayal* (1978). Elements of his style include seemingly ordinary colloquial speech with hidden or ambivalent meaning, long pauses and silences almost musical in effect, an atmosphere of menace or eroticism or derangement. The totality of effect is unsettling, almost surreal.

pinup girl   Popular term for free publicity pictures of movie actresses distributed to men in the U.S. armed forces during World War II. The girls in these pictures were all provocatively clad and immensely appealing. Their pictures were pasted, glued and pinned in barracks, crew's quarters, airplane cockpits, footlockers and bars all over the world. Wherever soldiers, sailors, pilots or Marines were stationed, the pictures followed them.

The most popular pinup girl was Betty Grable.

"Pinup girl" is now used for any sexually attractive girl.

Pippa   In "Pippa Passes" (1841), a short verse drama by the English poet Robert Browning (1812–89), Pippa is a ragged little girl who winds silk in the mills of Asolo in Italy. She works all day long, every day of the year except New Year's Day. The drama begins with her waking at dawn on her one day at leisure. She is full of eagerness to enjoy her day. As she walks through the streets of the town, she sings:

The year's at the spring,
And day's at the morn;
Morning's at seven;
The hill-side's dew-pearled;
The lark's on the wing;
The snail's on the thorn:
God's in His heaven—
All's right with the world!

With her song of the world's perfection, with her cheerful, innocent, untouched demeanor, she unconsciously affects the fate of several people at a critical moment in their lives. She has unwittingly been a force for good.

Pitcher, Molly (1754–1832)   American Revolutionary War heroine. Her real name was Mary Ludwig Hayes.

At the battle of Monmouth (1778), she carried water in a pitcher for her husband and other American soldiers; hence her epithet, Molly Pitcher. Legend has it that after her husband collapsed in battle, she took his place at his gun for the rest of the battle.

Molly Pitcher is the prototype of the heroic woman.

"plague on both your houses, a"   In Shakespeare's ROMEO AND JULIET, a tale of star-crossed lovers from two feuding families, MERCUTIO defends his friend Romeo, a Montague, from an attack by Tybalt, a Capulet. In the brawl that ensues, Tybalt kills Mercutio and is himself killed, in revenge, by Romeo. As Mercutio lies dying, he jests about his wound's being "not so deep as a well, nor so wide as a church door; but 'tis enough, 'twill serve." Despairingly he cries: "A plague à both your houses!" The feud has resulted in many skirmishes and deaths and will engender many more before the play is over.

In modern usage, "A plague on both your houses" expresses disgust with, and a washing of one's hands of, a seemingly endless conflict. The conflict may be trivial domestic bickering or world-shaking tension, as between the Israelis and the Palestinians.

plastic   A synthetic polymer made from long chains of molecules strung together in chemistry laboratories, plastic was a truly original invention since it was not made out of any raw materials in nature. The miracle plastics have been cellophane (1912), acetate (1927), vinyl (1928), plexiglass (1930), acrylics (1936), melmac (1937), styrene (1938), formica (1938), polyester (1940), nylon (1940), polyethylene (1942) and others. Plastic has revolutionized everyday, useful objects, and decorative ones as well. It can be used as a coating for the preservation of paper, as in plastic credit cards. In fact, credit cards are often referred to as plastic money. The whole concept of plastic is one of ersatz materials, and by extension one hears of plastic emotions, plastic tears, plastic smiles.

play hardball   Literally, to play baseball, because the ball used in baseball is smaller and harder than the ball used in the game of softball. The smaller, "hard" ball is more difficult to hit and field than the larger and softer "soft" ball. Hence, baseball is considered the more difficult and more dangerous game.

In general use, the person who is said to play hardball "means business." He is not concerned about the niceties or the amenities or even the rules—if he can bend or disregard them. He is determined to win at all costs.

plumbers   From a sign tacked up by Nixon aides on the door of Room 16 in the old Executive Office Building across the street from the White House. One of the aides' assignments was to investigate and plug up leaks of information to the press, such as the leak to the *New York Times* of the PENTAGON PAPERS, on the Vietnam War, by Daniel Ellsberg. Their obsessive hunt led to the hiring of ex-CIA men for illegal break-ins (as into the office of Ellsberg's psychiatrist and into the headquarters of the Democratic National Committee in the Watergate complex). G. Gordon Liddy and E. Howard Hunt were eventually convicted of conspiracy to break in, together with many others involved in what has come to be known as the WATERGATE scandal.

A plumber is one who tries to stop leaks of information.

Podunk   The mythical small town, with all that it implies in limited access to cultural activities, narrow points of view, constricted aspirations and experiences.

Pogo   Comic strip created in 1948 by Walt Kelly, a "graduate" of the Walt Disney Studios.

All the inhabitants of *Pogo* live in the great swamp of Okefenokee. They represent various "herbivores" and "carnivores," a fascinating melange of social types and classes. Dominating this teeming scene are Pogo, an opossum, wise, warmhearted, kind, outgoing and self-effacing; and Albert the Alligator, Pogo's friend, a self-centered anarchist.

One of the memorable *Pogo* lines has found a secure place in our language: "We have met the enemy, and they are us."

pogrom   From the Russian word for devastation, pogroms were deliberate attacks by Coassacks on Jewish villages.

After the assassination of Czar Alexander II in 1881, and again after the 1905 Russian Revolution, the czar's secret police whipped up hatred against the Jews, using them as scapegoats. Pogroms increased in number and violence, setting off a mass immigration of Russian Jews to the United States and to Palestine.

In modern usage, a pogrom is any violent attack, usually anti-Semitic, against a defenseless community.

Pollock, Jackson (1912–1956)   An abstract expressionist American painter who conceived the unique method of laying huge canvases flat on the ground and dribbling paint all over them. Although he started with color, by 1951 he was using only black and white. The philistine public at first hooted at his marbleized effects, but gradually he was perceived, at least by the critics, on his own terms: an innovator to whom the act of painting was more important than the painting itself. His seemingly formless works were imbued with the rhythms of his own controlled frenzy. His works include *One* (1950), *White Light* (1954) and *Blue Poles* (1953).

Pollyanna   Title character in a 1913 novel by Eleanor H. Porter. An 11-year-old girl who comes to live with a rather dour maiden aunt in Vermont after her father dies, she evinces a totally sunny disposition in the face of every negative circumstance. She makes a game, in fact, of finding "something to be glad about." A Pollyanna is generally a derogatory name for one who sees good in everything, who is excessively and saccharinely optimistic. "Don't be such a Pollyanna!" is a put-down for one who constantly looks at the bright side of things.

Polo, Marco (1254–1324)   Venetian merchant, adventurer and storyteller who spent 17 years in China at the court of Kublai Khan.

With his father and uncle, Marco Polo traveled overland by the Great Silk Road. It took him almost four years on foot to reach what is now Beijing and four more years to return to Venice. He became a favorite of Kublai Khan, who used him for many missions. Marco Polo described all the exotic splendors of the court in *The Book of Marco Polo*.

A Marco Polo is the ultimate traveler. He not only ventures forth into strange territory and observes with wonder and appreciation, but he also sets down the record of his experiences for others. We have had several glamorous Marco Polos since the 13th century; for example, T. E. Lawrence in Arabia, Sir Richard Burton in Africa and Richard Byrd and Roald Amundsen in Antarctica.

Polonius   Father of Laertes and Ophelia, and counselor to Claudius in Shakespeare's *Hamlet*. He is full of sententious advice and long-winded admonitions, which his children receive with knowing winks and gentle mockery. He advises Ophelia to reject Hamlet's advances and he then becomes convinced that Hamlet's madness is the direct result of unrequited love. In the course of trying to prove this theory to the guilt-ridden king, he takes to spying on Hamlet. He is hiding behind an arras in Gertrude's room when Hamlet runs his sword through him.

> *Thou wretched, rash, intruding fool, farewell!*
> *I took thee for thy better . . .*
> *Thou findst to be too busy is some danger.*

And indeed, Polonius *has* been a busybody.

A Polonius, then, is a sententious, garrulous, meddlesome old man giving unwanted counsel in windy phrases. He has not learned his own dictum: "Brevity is the soul of wit."

Pompadour, Marquíse de (1721–1764)

Of middle-class origin, Madam Pompadour (née Jeanne Antoinette Poisson) nevertheless became the mistress of Louis XV at Versailles in 1745, and as such attained enormous power. Beautiful, witty, intelligent, extravagant, she maintained her influence over the king in spite of much opposition. She championed writers of the *Encyclopédie*, such as Voltaire, and supported artists who redecorated her residences. In foreign policy she opposed Richelieu and was partly responsible for France's disastrous Seven Years War with Austria.

"Mme. Pompadour" is synonymous with "courtesan." As a child, she was trained for the job by her mother's lover. She came to fill the job extremely well. As a leader of fashion, she gave her name to a hair style.

Ponce de León

See FOUNTAIN OF YOUTH.

Ponzi, Charles (1877–1949)

Ex-dishwasher, ex-forger, ex-smuggler of aliens into America, high-living Charles Ponzi became the arch-swindler of his time. His get-rich-quick scheme promised a gullible public a 50 percent profit on their investment in three months. The money came pouring in.

Ponzi's scam was simplicity itself. As the new money rolled in, he used part of it to pay interest to the investors. Part went to defray the expenses of running the elaborate enterprise. The rest Ponzi squirreled away for himself. Ponzi banked on an endless flow of new money, but that didn't happen. Eventually the money stopped coming. The scheme collapsed. Ponzi went to prison for his elegant swindling.

In the long and colorful history of larceny, "Ponzi scheme" has become a synonym for cheating on a grand scale.

Pooh-Bah Central character in the highly popular W. S. Gilbert (1836–1911) and Sir Arthur Sullivan (1842–1900) operetta *The Mikado* (1885). Pooh-Bah is the bureaucrat par excellence. He holds many offices simultaneously without sensing any conflict of interest. He is highly amenable to bribes of substantial size. He is, at once, Lord Mayor, First Lord of the Treasury, Lord Chief Justice, Lord High Admiral, Master of the Buck Hounds, Groom of the Backstairs, Archbishop of Titipu. When Ko-Ko is nominated as Lord High Executioner, Pooh Bah becomes Lord High Everything Else.

Always used pejoratively, a Pooh-Bah is a pompous, powerful figure holding several (or many) positions of bureaucratic importance.

Use: "One political Pooh Bah . . . actually introduced a bill in the state legislature forbidding the publication of uncomplimentary cartoons." (*American Heritage,* September 9, 1991)

Poor Richard's Almanac This annual publication (1733–87) written by Benjamin Franklin (1706–90) was a vehicle for his commonsense philosophy. Under the assumed name of Poor Richard, Franklin stirred up a rich and inviting brew of maxims and humorous observations on temperance, cleanliness, chastity and other virtues. All of this was meant to lead its many faithful readers to clean, ethical, frugal, sensible living. Peppered with memorable proverbs old and new, it was one of the most popular publications of its day. Even today, its wry humor, unashamed concerns for the goodness and decency of individual and communal conduct strike a responsive chord in the modern reader.

pop art Art that uses the images of popular culture. Examples include the flags of Jasper Johns, the comic strips of Roy Lichtenstein and the Campbell soup cans, Coke bottles and Marilyn Monroes of Andy Warhol. These images, popularized by the mass media, are shown up as the icons of modern American taste and values. Thus American painters and sculptors of the mid-1960s attempted to transmute "camp" into high art.

Popeye Character in the comic strip *Thimble Theater.* The strip first appeared on December 19, 1919, and as a full-color Sunday page, April 18, 1925. Other characters were Olive Oyl; her cantankerous brother, Castor Oyl; and the hero, Ham Gravy.

Popeye, the Sailor Man, appeared in January 1929 and made *Thimble Theater* one of the most successful strips of the 1930s. The readers had never met anyone like Popeye—a tough-talking, wise-guy, all-powerful sailor. The source of Popeye's omnipotence was uniquely, disarmingly simple—a can of spinach he always carried with him. Faced with some seemingly impossible challenge, Popeye would whip out his old reliable can of spinach and slurp down its contents. Thus fortified, he was up to any Herculean task—equal to, if not surpassing, *Superman.*

Popeye appeared in a movie and in movie and TV animated cartoons produced for Paramount Studios by Max Fleischer.

Portia   The clever young heroine who resolves the conflict in Shakespeare's *The Merchant of Venice* when Shylock insists upon the payment due him of a POUND OF FLESH.

Bassanio loves Portia. He needs 3,000 ducats to woo her. His merchant friend Antonio, short of cash for the moment, borrows the money from Shylock to give to Bassanio. Antonio signs a bond to return the money on an appointed day or forfeit a pound of his flesh to Shylock. When Antonio's ships are wrecked, he cannot repay the loan. Shylock insists upon his pound of flesh. Enter Portia, disguised in male attire as a lawyer. When her appeals to mercy fail, Portia insists upon carrying out the very letter of the bond. Shylock can get his pound of flesh, but not one drop of blood as there is nothing about blood in the bond. Portia has succeeded in outwitting Shylock.

A Portia is a high-minded, intelligent woman who can adjudicate conflicts with reason, wit and wisdom.

Portnoy   Alexander Portnoy is the main character in *Portnoy's Complaint* (1969), an exuberant Rabelaisian tale of hilarious woe by American novelist and short story writer Philip Roth. In a book-length monologue addressed to his psychiatrist, Portnoy presents himself as the victim of an over-solicitous JEWISH MOTHER and an ineffectual Jewish father. His mother is an expert in all the tricks of inducing guilt in her rebellious son. Outwardly a good little Jewish boy, secretly Portnoy seeks refuge in masturbation and other sexual perversities that only aggravate his guilt and shame.

Post, Emily (1873–1960)   Author of *Etiquette: The Blue Book of Social Usage* (1922), a book on manners for a democratic, upwardly mobile American population desiring standards for polite behavior. It made the top of the nonfiction bestseller list, and by 1945 had sold 666,000 copies. "What would Emily Post say?" became the criterion for resolving any social dilemma.

postal, to go   To go berserk, to lose control. The term originated in the 1990s with a series of violent random incidents in which post-office workers, seemingly crazed by their boring, repetitive tasks and moved to vent ancient grudges, gunned down their fellow workers. An interesting reverse use of this newly minted term occurred in a recent *New Yorker* headline reading "Jackson Pollock Finally Goes Postal" above an article revealing that the artist, who had long been considered somewhat daffy for his method of dribbling paint on canvas laid out on the floor, was about to be recognized as a great artist of the 20th century by having his portrait on a postage stamp.

Potemkin village   A cardboard facade with nothing behind it, as on certain B-movie sets; a showy exterior to hide real and embarrassingly poor conditions. From Prince Potemkin, a favorite of Catherine II of Russia, for whose visit to the Ukraine in 1787 he had cardboard villages constructed.

Potsdam   In Germany, site of July 1945 conference to iron out the emerging post–World War II disagreements among the victorious Allies vis-à-vis spheres of influence in Europe. Stalin represented the U.S.S.R., President Harry Truman the United States and Clement Attlee, newly elected prime minister, Great Britain.

Often referred to as the place where the freedom of Eastern European countries such as Bulgaria, Rumania and Hungary was sacrificed to communist control by the U.S.S.R.

pound of flesh   In Shakespeare's *The Merchant of Venice* (1596), SHYLOCK drives a hard bargain with Antonio, a merchant. He agrees to lend Antonio a certain sum of money, but should Antonio fail to repay it on time, he will have to forfeit a pound of his flesh to Shylock. The terms seem ludicrous at the time of the signing of the bond; but when Antonio loses his ships and is unable to repay the loan, the terms become sinister. Portia steps in and ingeniously circumvents Shylock's intransigent demands.

To give, or get, a pound of flesh has come to mean conforming to the letter of an agreement, whether in the form of a contract or a promise, whatever grossly excessive return is called for.

preemptive strike   A nuclear attack in anticipation of an imminent nuclear attack by an enemy. First-strike capacity was considered an absolute necessity in the nuclear age since that might be all it would take to destroy an enemy country. The Soviet Union unilaterally abjured first strike. The United States refused to follow suit. A preemptive strike may be launched with conventional weapons, as in 1967, in what was to become known as the Six-Day War, when Israel made a preemptive strike against the Arab armies poised to strike at its borders.

The term "preemptive strike" may be used in any highly competitive field, as in stock takeovers.

Pre-Raphaelite   In 1848, Dante Gabriel Rossetti (1828–1882), together with some other English painters and poets, founded the Pre-Raphaelite Brotherhood in

England. Their object, as expressed in *The Germ,* their own publication, which folded after four issues, was to reject academism as well as the materialism of industrialization. They proposed a return to medieval spirituality and the simplicity of art produced prior to Raphael and the High Renaissance.

The paintings of the Pre-Raphaelites are dreamlike in mood and use religious themes and mystical iconography. They often are inspired by the poetry of Dante, Shakespeare, Keats and Tennyson. Some well-known Pre-Raphaelites, besides Rossetti, were Edward Burne Jones (1833–98), George Frederic Watts (1817–1904) and William Morris (1834–96).

The Pre-Raphaelites engendered fierce debate among artists and critics. They were accused of morbidity, perverted sensuality, and sentimentality, but they were championed by William Morris and Algernon Charles Swinburne (1837–1909). Pre-Raphaelite paintings, especially the portraits of women, have a pervasive soulful beauty, although some contemporary critics find them out of step with the more robust taste of modern times.

Presley, Elvis Aron (1935–1977)   Dubbed the "King of Rock 'n' Roll," Elvis Presley, like all great popular singers, was an original. Of himself he once said, "I don't sound like nobody."

Elvis represented a fusion of various musical currents in America's subcultures: black and white gospel, country and western, rhythm and blues. Within two years of his appearance on the musical scene, he was easily its dominant figure despite the criticisms that were leveled at him for what one reviewer called his "novocaine lips, hormone hair, pale poached face, his guitar a sort of phallic tommy gun . . . he seemed to be sneering with his lips—Elvis, the pelvis, virtuoso of the hootchy-kootchy—his undistinguished whine."

Elvis was a symbol of youth in revolt, providing an opportunity for a restless, irreverent generation to thumb its nose at society. His rendering of songs like "Heartbreak Hotel," "Love Me Tender," "Jail House Rock" and "You Ain't Nothin' But A Hound Dog" left an indelible mark on American popular singing style, sold millions of records—and won him faithful audiences that make their year-round pilgrimages to his home and shrine, Graceland, in Nashville, Tennessee.

priceless ingredient   This term alludes to the famous ad written by Raymond Rubicam for E. R. Squibb and Sons (1921). The essential point of what was to become a permanent part of Squibb advertising is made in the opening parable:

> In the city of Bagdad lived Hakeem, the wise one, and many people went
> to him for counsel, which he gave freely to all, asking nothing in return.
> There came to him a young man, who had spent much but got little, and

said: "Tell me, wise one, what shall I do to receive the most for that which I spend?"

Hakeem answered, "A thing that is bought or sold has no value unless it contains that which cannot be sold. Look for *The Priceless Ingredient.*"

"But, what is this *Priceless Ingredient?*" asked the young man.

Spoke then the wise one, "My son, the *Priceless Ingredient* of every product in the marketplace is the *Honor* and *Integrity* of him who makes it. Consider his name before you buy."

In common discourse, the concept of "The Priceless Ingredient" has been extended into social and professional relationships.

prima donna   The leading female singer in an opera, usually a soprano. Examples of a prima donna are Joan Sutherland as Lucia in Donizetti's *Lucia di Lammermoor,* Leontyne Price in the title role of Verdi's *Aida* and Maria Callas in Puccini's *Tosca.*

Unfortunately, prima donnas have acquired the reputation of being temperamental, demanding and generally difficult. The term "prima donna" has been extended to any self-dramatizing person who puts on airs, demands special attention or throws a tantrum.

Prince Hal   In Shakespeare's *King Henry IV, Parts One* and *Two,* young Prince Hal, heir to the throne of England, sows his wild oats with riffraff like FALSTAFF, Bardolph, Nym and Pistol at the Boar's Head Tavern—lechers, pimps, drunkards, cowards and liars all. His father despairs of him. But when the time is right, Hal sheds his devil-may-care demeanor, repudiates his lowlife companions and assumes his royal responsibilities as Henry V, a man of valor and honor.

Use: Some critics have called John F. Kennedy an American Prince Hal.

Prince and the Pauper, The   (1882)   A novel by Mark Twain in which Prince Edward (the future Edward VI of England) discovers a little pauper boy, Tom Canty, who is his double. The prince and the pauper exchange clothes for a lark. When grownups mistake their identity, the prince is driven out into the streets to live the life of a pauper, and the pauper must pretend to be a prince in the court. Eventually this mistaken identity is rectified, but not until the real prince has learned something of the life of the poor. When he becomes king, he is a more compassionate ruler because of his unusual experience. He makes Tom Canty the king's ward.

The theme of *The Prince and the Pauper* has mythical overtones: What a difference the accident of birth can make!

"Princess and the Pea, The"   In this tale published in 1836 by Hans Christian Andersen, a prince is determined to marry a real princess. He travels far and wide to find one, but every one is flawed. He returns home. One day in the midst of a terrible storm a young woman appears at the city gate. She is soaked through and bedraggled, but she says that she is a real princess. The Queen Mother devises a test: She places a single pea on the girl's bed beneath 20 mattresses and 20 eiderdown quilts. In the morning, the girl complains of not having slept because of a hard lump in the bed. She is black and blue all over, thereby demonstrating that she is a true princess.

An allusion to the princess and the pea generally concerns someone overly sensitive or delicate. It is not complimentary.

Prospero   The main character in Shakespeare's last play, *The Tempest* (1611). Prospero was the duke of Milan, more interested in books, philosophy and magic arts than in affairs of state. Ousted by his brother Antonio and set adrift upon the sea with his infant daughter Miranda, he is washed ashore upon an island inhabited only by spirits. Prospero releases the spirit ARIEL from imprisonment in a tree and enslaves the grotesque and misshapen CALIBAN. These do his bidding.

Twelve years later, Prospero, with his magic powers, engineers a shipwreck upon his island of a party from Milan, including those who were responsible for his dethronement. Now Prospero uses his white magic to effect a transformation for the good. Antonio and his coconspirators, including Alonso, king of Naples, confess their former crimes and have a change of heart. Miranda and Ferdinand, the son of Alonso, fall in love and marry. Ariel and Caliban will remain sole possessor of the island once more. Prospero renounces his magic and returns to his dukedom in the real world.

A Prospero is a magician using his art and imagination benevolently to control nature and influence human nature. By extension, a Prospero is an artist of any kind.

Protocols of Zion   *Protocols of the Wise Men [or Elders] of Zion* is a fake document purporting to reveal a Jewish plot for world domination. It first appeared in Russia in the early part of the 20th century. The idea was revived by Arabs to undermine plans for a Jewish state in Israel.

The term now refers to spurious anti-Semitic documents or hate propaganda.

Proustian   Suggestive of the style and subject matter of Marcel Proust (1871–1922), French novelist who wrote but one novel (in many volumes) throughout his life: *À La Recherche du Temps Perdu (Remembrance of Things Past)*. It has many autobiographical elements.

Proust is known for his exhaustive, almost mesmeric immersion in the past in order to retrieve it whole. His sentences are often a full page long, convoluted, so that no nuance of feeling or observation is lost. The reader is taken by the narrator, Marcel, with the first taste of a MADELEINE dipped into tea, back to Marcel's childhood at his grandparents' house in Combray. He relives the sensitive boy's clinging dependence upon his mother. He meets the personages who are to play important roles in Marcel's memory: Swann and his daughter Gilberte; the lady in pink, Odette, the demi-mondaine whom Swann unhappily marries; the opportunistic Verdurins; the Duchess of Guermantes and her aristocratic circle; the writer Bergotte; the musician Vinteuil; the great painter Elstir; the insidious homosexual Baron de Charlus, and others.

The novel is permeated with the memory of sickly jealousies and heartaches, which are essential to Proustian love. Overwhelmingly, the novel depicts in infinite detail the life of the French bourgeoisie from the second half of the 19th century to the outbreak of World War I. Sadness pervades the book as Marcel notes the changes that Time, the villain, has wrought. He decides to recapture the past, to transmute the suffering into a great work of art.

Use: The remark unleashed a Proustian flood of memories.

Prufrock, J. Alfred   Persona assumed by T. S. Eliot (1888–1965) in his early poem "The Love Song of J. Alfred Prufrock" (1910–11)—that of an aging, inhibited man who daydreams of erotic encounters but is too timid, fastidious and indecisive to bring them to fruition when real opportunities are offered.

Prussian   Formerly, an inhabitant of Prussia, the most militaristic state within Germany. In 1870, Prussia defeated France in the Franco-Prussian War and became the dominant force in a militaristic, newly unified German nation. Following the defeat of Germany by the Allies in World War II, Prussia was abolished as an entity and was divided among West Germany, East Germany, Poland and the Soviet Union.

The epithet "Prussian" evokes the image of a straight-backed, stiff, arrogant German officer-aristocrat. In today's parlance, a Prussian may be simply a martinet: rigid, strict, cruel, domineering, expecting absolute obedience to authority.

Prynne, Hester   The heroine of the novel *The Scarlet Letter* (1850) by Nathaniel Hawthorne (1804–64). In mid-17th-century Puritan Boston, Hester Prynne commits the crime of adultery. She refuses to disclose the identity of the father of her illegitimate child. She is condemned to wear upon her breast the scarlet letter *A,* embroidered by her own hand. Furthermore, she must endure public humiliation by standing in the pillory with her child.

Hester accepts her punishment, even though she does not feel guilty of sin. "What we have done," she says to her lover, "had a consecration of its own." Her lover, the respected minister Arthur Dimmesdale, is haunted by his secret sin, but he does not have the courage to confess it before his congregation. He is hounded by the diabolic Roger Chillingworth, Hester's husband under an assumed name, who has arrived in America two years after he sent Hester ahead. Chillingworth suspects Dimmesdale and seeks revenge.

Not until Hester proposes that she and her lover and their child flee to Europe does Dimmesdale, near death, mount the pillory and publicly confess his sin.

Hester Prynne embodies the romantic notion that individual passion supersedes conventional rules of morality. More simply, she with her letter *A* stands for adultery.

Ptolemaic   Referring to the theories of Claudius Ptolemaeus, second-century Greco-Egyptian astronomer and mathematician of Alexandria. Ptolemy posited an Earth-centered universe in which the Earth stood still while the Sun, the Moon and the stars revolved around it in circular orbits at a uniform rate.

Not until 1530 was this theory challenged. In his treatise *On the Revolutions of Heavenly Bodies,* Nicolaus COPERNICUS (1473–1543), a Polish astronomer, presented the heliocentric theory of the organization of the universe; that is, that Earth turned upon its axis and revolved around the Sun. Copernicus died shortly after the publication of his thesis in 1543; otherwise, he would have borne the brunt of the fierce theological opposition that denounced his theory as heretical. In the Copernican system, man could no longer be seen as the center of the universe, created in the image of God. The very stability of the world seemed to be at stake.

It was GALILEO (1564–1642), the Italian physicist-astronomer, who espoused the theories of Copernicus and amplified them in his *Dialogue on the Great World Systems* (1632), who suffered the full fury of the church. Tried by the INQUISITION, he sensibly recanted when he was threatened with death. Under his breath, he is said to have muttered, *"Eppur si muove!"* (And yet it moves!).

The term "Ptolemaic" is used in modern parlance to describe a discredited system or theory according to which man is the center of the universe.

public enemies   A term applied in the 1930s by J. Edgar Hoover, director of the United States Federal Bureau of Investigation, to a group of professional, career criminals. They were widely sought by local and federal police.

Now, generally used to describe individuals who are a constant threat to the peace, security, stability of a society or a segment of a society.

public enemy number 1   See DILLINGER, JOHN.

Puck   Otherwise known as Robin Goodfellow, he is a mischievous imp who carries out the whims of Oberon, king of the Fairies, in Shakespeare's *A Midsummer*

Night's Dream (c. 1595). He is a fleet messenger, for he can "put a girdle round the earth in forty minutes." However, he causes many of the mixups in the plot by applying magic love juice upon the eyelids of the wrong lovers at the wrong time. Having caused much mischief in this way, he stands aloof and observes, "Lord, what fools these mortals be."

From this character comes the term "puckish" to describe someone impish, mischievous and whimsical.

pull chestnuts out of the fire   See CAT'S PAW.

pull a punch or punches   In boxing, to punch an opponent with less than one's full power, to hold back.

In informal use, to pull one's punches means to moderate one's speech or actions, to act with less force than one is capable of.

pumpkin papers   Microfilmed documents alleged to have been passed by ALGER HISS of the State Department to Whitaker Chambers, a member of a communist cell, and hidden in a hollowed-out pumpkin on Chambers's Pipe Creek Farm. When Chambers renounced his communist past, he implicated Hiss. Hiss pleaded innocence. When Chambers produced the pumpkin and its papers, Hiss was convicted of perjury and imprisoned for 44 months.

The term now refers to hidden and farfetched evidence, evidence produced almost like a rabbit pulled out of a hat.

punch drunk   In boxing, the characteristically slow speech, hand tremors and uncertain movements of a boxer who has been badly and frequently beaten about the head. His speech and gait indicate that he has suffered some brain damage.

By extension, the term describes any dazed, uncertain, unsteady, befuddled speech or behavior.

Puritan; puritanical   In the late 16th and early 17th centuries the Puritans were religious dissenters who wanted to eradicate all remaining traces of Roman Catholicism from the Church of England. They came from the ranks of the middle class, the landed gentry, merchants and tradesmen, and allied themselves with the parliamentarian party to curb the absolute power of the Stuart kings, James I and Charles I.

The continued intransigence of both sides culminated in civil war. In 1645, under the leadership of Oliver Cromwell (1599–1658), the Puritans (now a political and military power) defeated the king's forces and set up a protectorate. In 1649 Charles I was convicted of treason and beheaded. Cromwell, as lord protector, ruled England until his death, when he was succeeded briefly by his eldest son, Richard Cromwell. With the restoration of the Stuarts in 1660, Charles II was crowned, the Cavaliers drove out the Roundheads and the Puritans were once again suppressed. The theaters, which the Puritans had closed in 1642, were reopened and lyric poets once more sang songs of love.

In the early 17th century, many of the Puritans had been driven into exile. These founded the Puritan colonies in New England at Plymouth and at Massachusetts Bay. By 1640, the Puritan Holy Commonwealth comprised about 35 churches. Their religion had turned Calvinist, believing in predestination, some being born among the elect and others among the damned. Their ministers, such as Cotton Mather, delivered fiery sermons about damnation. Until 1692 they were bound by the terrible strictures of a theocracy. Perhaps the most infamous episode in their history was the SALEM WITCH TRIALS (1692).

The Puritans' moral code was rigid and unforgiving (see HESTER PRYNNE). At the same time they were industrious, frugal, stoical, austere. Their attitudes and ethics profoundly infiltrated the fabric of American society until the 20th century.

The terms "puritan" and "puritanical" have become pejorative, standing for narrow-minded rigidity. H. L. Mencken said it well: A Puritan is one who suspects that "somewhere someone is having a good time."

Purple Heart   U.S. medal awarded to a member of the armed forces for wounds inflicted by an enemy. Now used colloquially, as in "You should get the Purple Heart for what you have had to endure from your so-called best friend."

push the envelope   (or, push the edge of the envelope) To extend the limits, to go beyond the perceived limits. The expression began to be used extensively in the late 1940s when test pilots were seeking to break the sound barrier. It was as if they were pushing through a near-solid envelope of air, causing a shock wave against the aircraft. Finally, in 1947, Chuck Yeager broke through the barrier and was the first to fly at supersonic speed.

Today, to push the edge of the envelope may refer not only to physical barriers but to social and moral barriers as well. For example, when media reporters invade the privacy of public figures, they are pushing the envelope against previously accepted journalistic restraints. A movie or work of art may push the envelope for provocative subject matter.

Use: "I suspect there are people who travel to exotic places because they want to push the envelope. . . . Of course . . . when you sign on for a journey to a place without electricity, telephone or running water, you have to accept that the going will be rough. But that doesn't mean you're looking for an encounter with a band of killers wielding machetes." (Lynn Sherr, *New York Times,* March 6, 1999)

pygmy   "Pygmy" (with a capital *P*) refers to a member of various tribes living mostly in Africa but also in Malaysia, the Philippines and Melanesia. They are on average less than five feet tall.

Today "pygmy" means not necessarily small in stature but, instead, small in intellect, accomplishment or values.

Use: "The Likud came to power 15 years ago, under Menachem Begin. But for all his ideological commitment Mr. Begin was a big man, quite unlike his Pygmy successors. He was able to make peace with Anwar Sadat at Camp David." (Anthony Lewis, *New York Times,* June 28, 1992)

quantum leap   Originally from the word "quantum," meaning "amount," and then from the phenomenon in physics where an electron jumps from one orbit in an atom to another.

"Quantum leap" is used in everyday language to mean simply a significant or very great jump from one dimension to another.

Quasimodo   The protagonist in *Notre-Dame de Paris* (1831), a GOTHIC novel by Victor Hugo (1802–85). Left as a foundling on the steps of Notre Dame cathedral, Quasimodo has been raised by the Archdeacon Frollo, to whom alone he clings. Deformed, ugly, repulsive, grown deaf from ringing the huge bells in the tower, savage when ridiculed, Quasimodo is an isolate who haunts the cathedral.

He falls in love with Esmeralda, a beautiful young gypsy girl, when out of compassion she holds a cup of water to his lips as he is being flogged by the authorities for having accosted her. But it is the priest, Frollo, who initiated the attack.

Frollo, sick with repressed passion for Esmeralda and unable to corrupt her, denounces her as a witch. Quasimodo seizes her, carries her to refuge in the tower, and rains down stones and scaffolding upon the mob below. Frollo, however, removes her from the tower and hands her over once more to her executioners. Ultimately Quasimodo, convinced of Frollo's demonic nature, hurls the priest from the tower to his death.

A Quasimodo is a grotesque creature who nevertheless can feel pure love.

Queeg, Captain Philip   Commander of the World War II minesweeper *Caine* in *The Caine Mutiny* (1951), a novel by Herman Wouk (1915–). The novel was later adapted as a play and, notably, as a film (1954), with Captain Queeg brilliantly portrayed by HUMPHREY BOGART. Like his prototype, Captain Bligh in *Mutiny on the Bounty,* Queeg is tyrannical, cowardly and paranoid. He is forcibly relieved of his command. At the court-martial of the mutineers, Queeg is manipulated by a clever lawyer for the defense into exhibiting his extreme psychological instability. A neurotic idiosyncrasy of Queeg was to keep nervously rolling some steel ball-bearings in his fist.

Use: Questioned on the details of his reported investigations of friends and foes, Mr. Perot's laugh seemed a bit too intense, his tone a bit too sarcastic and his dismissals a bit too snappish. At moments, in his television appearances, his mood was more Captain Queeg than Harry Truman.

Queen of Hearts   Character in *Alice's Adventures in Wonderland* (1865) who, when crossed in any way, screams "Off with his head!" or "Off with her head!" Although everybody is condemned, nobody is ever executed. At the end of the trial of the Knave of Hearts who stole the tarts, all the characters turn into a pack of cards, which come fluttering down upon Alice as she wakes from her dream of Wonderland.

"The Queen of Hearts" refers to a somewhat mad, arbitrary ruler or judge. See use in TWEEDLEDUM AND TWEEDLEDEE.

quisling   From Vidkun Quisling, founder of the Fascist National Unity Party of Norway who collaborated with Hitler in the conquest and occupation of Norway. He was found guilty of high treason by a Norwegian court and executed in October 1945 at the end of World War II.

The term "quisling" was coined by Winston Churchill to signify a traitor.

Quiz Kids   This popular radio program of the 1940s was a kind of juvenile *Information, Please* featuring exceptionally bright kids answering questions that stumped adults. Clifton Fadiman was the moderator.

"Quiz kid" has come to mean any unusually bright kid.

rabbi A graduate of a theological seminary, a rabbi is the spiritual and religious leader of a congregation of Jews who meet in a synagogue. Different rabbis stress different functions. Historically, rabbis have been great scholars, interpreters of TORAH and TALMUD, teachers and holy men.

The word "rabbi" comes from the Hebrew "rabh" (master) and "i" (my), thus meaning "my master," a title of great respect in religious terms. In colloquial usage, however, the term "rabbi" may have pejorative connotations. It is sometimes used for anyone who closets himself away from the world in order to pore over abstruse books on esoteric subjects far removed from general interest or utility; e.g., "rarefied rabbis of the universities." In slang, a rabbi is a high-placed patron or sponsor, as in "To get a job in Washington, you gotta have a rabbi."

Rabelaisian In the style of Francois Rabelais (c. 1494–1553), French author of *Gargantua and Pantagruel,* a comic masterpiece.

At the age of about 25, Rabelais joined the order of Franciscan friars. Disenchanted, he subsequently switched to the Benedictine order, but could not tolerate the monastic discipline or hypocrisy. He abandoned the religious life in 1530 and took up the study and practice of medicine. These two different careers had a profound influence on his thought and style. He turned from orthodox religious beliefs to humanism, and in his work he mocked the church and its teachings as well as other institutions of 16th-century France. Thus, he incurred the wrath of both religious and civil authorities.

At the same time, his experience as a doctor cured him of the fastidiousness with which most people until the 20th century wrote about bodily functions. Not until James Joyce's *Ulysses* (1922), Henry Miller's *Tropic of Cancer* (1934) and Philip Roth's *Portnoy's Complaint* (1969) did writers equal the sheer exuberance, zest, earthiness and hilarious extravagance of Rabelais's writing on sex, appetite, elimination and the various other absurdities that flesh is heir to.

"Rabelaisian," then, has become a synonym for ribald, earthy, boisterous, licentious, even gross in the unbounded enjoyment of the pleasures of the flesh. "Drink and feast" and "do as you will" are Rabelaisian mottoes.

radar   Acronym for *ra*dio *d*etection *a*nd *r*anging, a device for ascertaining the position and speed of a moving object (an automobile or a plane, for example) by bouncing a radio wave off it and analyzing the reflected wave. The American Stealth bomber is supposed to be able to fly so low that it escapes radar detection. "Radar" is used for any sensitive ability to detect, as if one had antennae.

radical chic   Phrase coined in 1970 by Tom Wolfe, American journalist and novelist, in an essay of the same name. It referred to a party given for the Black Panthers by Leonard Bernstein, famous American composer and conductor. Then the sponsorship of various radical causes and dinner invitations to members of radical leftist groups became fashionable in some sections of high society; hence, radical chic.

Raft, George (1895–1980)   American movie actor who played with great authenticity the role of menacing gangster, the slicked-back dark-haired variety.

rain check   When a baseball game or other outdoor sports event or concert has been postponed or interrupted by rain or other unforeseen circumstance, the spectators are given a ticket to be used at a future performance. This is called a rain check.

In general use "an invitation or requested postponement of an invitation" until a more convenient time: "Sorry you can't make it this Saturday. We'll give you a rain check."

raising the barn   In the days of the American frontier when westward migrants and settlers had to depend upon one another not only for security but also for labor, raising the barn was an economic necessity for new arrivals. Neighbors from near and far came to lend a hand in laying the foundation, setting up the frame, putting up the walls and the roof. Raising the barn also provided an occasion for a common festival of merrymaking in a land where entertainment was scarce and opportunities for social intercourse even scarcer.

Raising the barn has come to mean a common effort to help one's neighbors. The modern organization Habitat for Humanity, sponsored by former president Jimmy Carter, carries on the frontier tradition of raising the barn, only Habitat raises human dwellings for the needy.

Raisin in the Sun, A (1959)   Play by Lorraine Hansberry (1930–65). The title was taken from a poem, "Harlem," by the American poet Langston Hughes (1902–67), in which he asks:

> *What happens to a dream deferred?*
> *Does it dry up*
> *Like a raisin in the sun?*

A raisin in the sun stands for frustrated hopes and withered ambitions.

rake's progress   See HOGARTHIAN.

Raleigh, Sir Walter (c. 1552–1618)   Raleigh was a soldier, adventurer, mariner, courtier, statesman and poet: a RENAISSANCE MAN. Handsome and charming, he became a favorite of Queen Elizabeth I, who knighted him and provided him with rich estates and high office. But the queen could be whimsical and fortune capricious. When Raleigh had an affair with Elizabeth Throckmorton, one of the queen's maids of honor, the queen imprisoned him in the Tower of London. Later she released him.

Raleigh organized colonizing expeditions to Roanoke Island, Virginia. These ended in mysterious tragedy: The colony simply disappeared, overcome perhaps by adverse conditions, disease or Indian raids. Twice Raleigh sailed up the Orinoco in search of gold in ELDORADO. He engaged in raids against Spanish settlements. Finally, he incurred the wrath both of James I, who had succeeded to the throne after the death of Elizabeth, and of the Spanish ambassador. James had Raleigh imprisoned in the Tower for 12 years. After a short reprieve, he was arrested once more and beheaded.

Legend often enhances the achievements and character of historical personages, but in the case of Sir Walter Raleigh, legend has trivialized him. His life should have inspired highly romantic, derring-do films of the Douglas Fairbanks variety, but instead the average person thinks of Raleigh only as the courtier who spread his cloak over a mud puddle so that Queen Elizabeth would not soil her royal shoes.

A Sir Walter Raleigh, in today's usage, is courtly and gallant, almost exaggeratedly so.

Rambo   Strongman hero of a series of global action films with Sylvester Stallone in the leading role. Rambo, as a mightily muscled lone crusader, takes on the evils of the world—in Southeast Asia, in Afghanistan and who knows where next.

Rand, Ayn (1905–1982)   A Russian-American writer of novels, plays, film scripts, essays and tracts, she became a cult figure, and her best known novel, *The*

Fountainhead (1943), became a cult book that embodied her more or less libertarian ideas.

Born Alice Rosenbaum in St. Petersburg, Russia, she immigrated to the United States in 1926 and became a naturalized American citizen in 1931. Because she had personally experienced the Bolshevik revolution and life in the early years of Soviet rule, she developed a passionate antipathy against totalitarian political systems. She espoused laissez-faire capitalism, on moral grounds, as the system most likely to allow individual liberties to flourish. On a personal level, she championed rugged individualism and the pursuit of rational self-interest: "Greed is good." Her creed can be deduced from the titles of two of her nonfiction works: *The Virtue of Selfishness: A New Concept of Egoism* (1984) and *Capitalism: The Unknown Ideal* (1966).

In *The Fountainhead,* Rand created a memorable protagonist in the person of Howard Roark, supposedly modeled on the architect Frank Lloyd Wright. He is Rand's version of an Übermensch, an egocentric genius who hews to his own ideals against the corrupting influences of the herd. Roark has become the model for the allusion to the Ayn Rand hero.

Rand, Sally (1904–1979)   A dancer and actress. Sally Rand's "act" was the sensation of the Chicago Century of Progress Exposition (1933–34). Her performance in the Streets of Paris concession was said to have made the fair a financial success. It was simplicity itself: Sally did a slow dance with two ostrich plumes to Debussy's *Clair de Lune.* Lit by lavender lights, she slowly rotated the plumes around her nude body—revealing absolutely nothing of what the frenzied audiences thought they would be vouchsafed at least a peek at.

Nudity, Sally maintained, was nothing new. She simply made it financially rewarding through her "sales methods." For 30 highly profitable years, Sally "presented" her act to virtually insatiable audiences.

Sally created a new genre—and helped pave the way for more kinds of "provocative" dancing.

Raphael (1483–1520)   Considered in his own time the equal of Leonardo and Michelangelo, Raphael (Raffaello Sanzio) remains one of the greatest painters of the Italian High Renaissance. He was born in Urbino; his father was a painter, and he himself was apprenticed before age 17 to Perugino. He was a natural. At the age of 21 he moved to Florence, came under the influence of LEONARDO DA VINCI and the next year (1505) painted the *Madonna del Granduca,* a definitive work with Raphael's special signature. His Madonna is full-bodied, self-possessed, serene, meditative, tender—not enigmatic like the *Mona Lisa,* but with the *Mona Lisa*'s composure and ideal beauty. Like Leonardo, Raphael achieves a haziness and softness of contour through the use of sfumato (smokiness).

Critics generally agree that Raphael's masterpiece is *The School of Athens,* one of a series of frescoes he painted on the walls of the Stanza della Signatura, the pope's library in the Vatican Palace in Rome, and which owes much to Michelangelo's influence. Nevertheless, to the layman, Raphael is the painter of lovely, rosy madonnas. "She looks like a Raphael" is high praise indeed of a woman's beauty and serenity.

Rapunzel   The central figure in the fairy tale of the same name, one of more than 200 fairy tales collected and published in 1812–14 by the German folklorists the BROTHERS GRIMM, Jacob and Wilhelm.

Rapunzel, a girl with very long hair, is imprisoned in a high tower by a witch. When the witch wants to ascend to the tower, she calls out: "Rapunzel, Rapunzel, let down your hair." A prince, observing this, calls to Rapunzel. She lets down her hair and draws the prince up. The witch, learning of these goings-on, cuts Rapunzel's hair as the prince is being lifted. He falls and is blinded, but eventually he and Rapunzel are reunited, the prince regains his sight and the two live happily ever after.

In modern use, a Rapunzel is simply a girl or woman with very long hair.

Rashomon (1950)   Japanese film directed by Akira Kurosawa. The central event of the movie, the rape of a young bride and the murder of her noble husband as they are riding through a forest in ninth-century Kyoto, is reenacted four times from four different points of view: those of the bride, her husband, the bandit and a woodcutter who witnessed the crime. The film suggests the unreliability of evidence and poses the question, What is truth?

Thus, Rashomon is an allusion to the flickering nature of truth, and perhaps to our inability ever to know the real truth.

Raskolnikov   The main character in *Crime and Punishment* (1866), a masterpiece by the Russian novelist Feodor Dostoevsky, he embodies the duality of character, the conflict between heart and mind, that is a major motif in Dostoevsky's work.

Rodion Raskolnikov is a brilliant student who has had to drop out of the university in St. Petersburg because of extreme poverty. He conceives the idea of murdering an old, rapacious pawnbroker and using the valuables he steals from her to finance his education. He rationalizes: Of what worth is the life of one despicable old woman compared with the many lives he might save in the future? It seems to him to be "a question of simple arithmetic." Besides, a great man, a superman like Napoleon, for instance, does not allow himself to be hindered by conventional morality. He creates his own law. And so Raskolnikov murders the pawnbroker and also her poor harmless sister who unexpectedly appears on the scene.

But Raskolnikov does not have the nature of a murderer. He is a compassion-ate man in whom generosity of impulse wars with cynicism of intellect. After the murder he becomes ill and delirious. He experiences extreme alienation from every living being.

In the end, he is persuaded by SONIA, a meek, pious girl who has become a prostitute in order to feed her impoverished family, to confess his crime. Sonia fol-lows him to Siberia. Her pity for his suffering and her unquestioning love for him will perhaps be the means of his redemption.

Raskolnikov represents the inevitable suffering of a person who violates his own moral nature. Pride of intellect has led him astray. In Dostoevsky's world, sim-ple goodness of heart and humility are more important than the most brilliant tricks of reason and the self-assertion of the will.

See PETROVICH, PORFIRY.

Rasputin, Grigory Yefimovich (1872–1916)   An illiterate, licentious Russian peasant mystic, Rasputin was introduced into the Russian court in 1908. Here, his reputation as a mystic and a healer brought him to the attention of the czar, who soon became convinced that the destinies of his hemophiliac son, his family and his court were irrevocably linked to Rasputin. This burgeoning influence with the czar was seen as sinister. A small group of conspirators, led by the czar's cousin, decided to get rid of Rasputin. At a special dinner, held in the luxurious palace of Prince Yusupov, they poisoned Rasputin's wine, shot him twice, bound him hand and foot and threw his body into the Neva River.

Rasputin exercised mysterious powers over others—especially women. Esssentially, he was an evil man. Never hesitating to use his powers, Rasputin was always moved by deep, dark impulses.

"read my lips"   A phrase that generally means "mark my words," it now alludes to a gaffe that may have cost President George Bush reelection to the presidency in 1992. His 1988 pledge to the people, in its entirety, stated vehemently: "Read my lips: no new taxes!" Later, with public opinion poll approval ratings at an unprece-dented 90 percent at the triumphant conclusion of the Gulf War, he raised taxes. His popularity plummeted, and he lost the next election to Bill Clinton.

This phrase is used as a cautionary tale: Do not make absolute promises that you may not be able to keep!

Reaganomics   See TRICKLE-DOWN THEORY.

real McCoy   Around 1890, Norman Selby (1873–1940) left his farm in Indiana. A year later he appeared as a boxer under the name of Kid McCoy. He was a phe-nomenal fighter, challenging anyone, anywhere. For years he averaged a fight a month and won most of them by knockouts. Quite naturally, many imitation Kid McCoys began to appear. On March 24, 1899, the Kid settled any possible confusion. In a brutal 20-round match, he knocked out the formidable Joe Choynski. In the words of the *San Francisco Examiner*'s boxing reporter, "Now you've seen The Real McCoy." There are other accounts of how this phrase came into being. Like this one, none of them have been authenticated.

In general use, the real McCoy is what is promised, stated or implied.

Rebel Without A Cause (1955)   Movie starring James Dean (1931–55), a cult hero for disaffected youth. Dean played the part of Jim Stark, a confused, inarticulate teenager searching for the meaning of manhood, feeling betrayed by the hypocrisy and weakness of adults. He had a desperate need for love and understanding. Dean's death in an auto accident at the age of 24 turned him into a tragic symbol. He became, himself, the "rebel without a cause." He starred in only two other films, *East of Eden* and *Giant*.

Récamier, Mme. Juliette (1777–1849)   Born Jeanne Francoise Julie Adelaide Bernard, at age 15 she married a middle-aged Paris banker who afforded her the wherewithal to run a fashionable salon. Her beauty, wealth, wit and charm drew distinguished literary and political figures, including Mme. de Staël, Sainte-Beuve and Chateaubriand, to her soirées. Her famous portrait by David hangs in the Louvre.

Mme. Récamier stands for that elegance and social grace that permitted certain women to wield much influence upon the intellectual life of their time by providing a congenial gathering place for the great.

Use: Many a social hostess in Washington, D.C., sees herself as a Mme. Récamier, bringing together eminent celebrities from government and the media.

red herring   A smoked herring turns red and has a powerful scent. Pursuit dogs used to be trained to follow a trail with a red herring; escaped criminals would use red herrings to cross their own trail and thus divert bloodhounds from their real pursuit.

Now a "red herring" is a diversionary tactic in argument, used to throw one's opponent off the scent of the real issue in the debate and have him bogged down in answering an irrelevant matter. It is also a literary device in mystery and detective fiction, whereby the author plants false clues to divert the reader's attention from the identity of the character who really committed the crime.

redneck   Originally an unlettered farm laborer, especially from the South, it has now taken on a number of related meanings: a person who is bigoted, reactionary, prejudiced, narrow-minded. Frequently used as an intensifier with HARD HAT.

Reign of Terror (1793–1794)   A brief period during the French Revolution (1789–99) when all governmental powers were concentrated in the hands of the Committee of Public Safety. In the newly installed tyranny, headed by the archtyrant Robespierre (1758–94), terror became the instrument of government. Armed with virtually unlimited power, the new regime executed 2,300 people in Paris alone. In a similar manner, in the rest of France, according to the French historian Tainè, more than 17,000 French men and women lost their lives. Robespierre was overthrown and executed July 27, 1794.

A reign of terror is any period of official ruthlessness and oppression.

Rembrandt van Rijn (1606–1669)   One of the greatest painters of all time. He was born in Leyden of affluent parents, studied painting and at the age of 25 moved to Amsterdam. There he married a beautiful, rich girl called Saskia, who modeled for him and bore him four children, only one of whom, Titus, survived. Rembrandt became a successful portrait painter of the Dutch burghers, bought an elegant house and collected fine works of art. Then everything changed. Saskia died, his commissions dwindled, he went into bankruptcy and lost all his possessions, and eventually even his faithful housekeeper-mistress as well as his son died. Rembrandt spent the last years of his life in poverty, loneliness and despair.

Rembrandt's story has been told best in a remarkable series of self-portraits, about 60 in all, each one of which is a chapter in a visual autobiography of overwhelming emotional power. These portraits span an individual life but they illuminate the universal human condition. If, as LEONARDO said, the chief aim of painting is to show "the intention of the soul," then Rembrandt, of all the painters who ever lived, best fulfilled that mission.

Rembrandt left a legacy of about 700 paintings, hundreds of etchings and numerous line drawings. A great many of them were inspired by scenes and characters in the Bible. In all of these, Rembrandt's intuitive grasp of the emotional and dramatic situation is rendered with utmost compassion. Outstanding examples are *The Reconciliation of David and Absalom* (1642), *The Return of the Prodigal Son* (1665), *Jacob Blessing the Sons of Joseph,* and many more.

The associative word for Rembradnt is usually CHIAROSCURO, that blending of light and shade whereby foreground objects and figures seem to melt out of the background with no clear line of demarcation. In a Rembrandt painting, the face emerges as if the flame of spirit were lighting up neutral matter. It is this sense of the deepest understanding of the human soul that emanates from a Rembrandt painting that sets him apart from all other artists.

"Remember the Alamo!"   Texas was originally a part of Mexico. When Mexican president Antonio Santa Anna made public the new Mexican constitution for all

Mexican territories, the Texans voted to secede. On February 23, 1836, Santa Anna, leading a military force of several thousand, moved into Texas to put down what he interpreted as treasonous conduct. The American garrison of 187 men was holed up in a former Franciscan monastery, the Alamo. The battle was long and bloody. The Americans fought valiantly but succumbed to the superior Mexican force on March 16, 1836. All the American defenders were killed. Among the casualties was DAVY CROCKETT (1786–1836), the famous backwoodsman.

Determined to avenge the disaster at the Alamo, the Americans attacked the Mexicans six weeks later (in April 1836) at San Jacinto, where a small American force, rallying to the battle cry "Remember the Alamo!" drove the Mexican army back across the Rio Grande.

"Remember the Alamo!" has become a symbol of extraordinary bravery against great odds, and an inspiration for beleaguered, determined individuals or institutions fighting back against former oppressors.

Renaissance   Literally meaning "rebirth," the Renaissance is that era between the waning of the Middle Ages and the advent of modern times when a rekindled interest in classical learning and an extraordinary flowering of the arts swept across Europe beginning with Italy in the 14th century to England through the 16th century. Humanism began to replace the orthodoxies of the church. The here and now began to be more important than the hereafter. The idealized Greek form of the human body once more appeared in painting and sculpture to replace two-dimensional, ascetic icons. Intrepid explorers expanded man's sense of his physical universe and cartographers changed the maps of the world.

The roster of great names of the Renaissance is endless and dazzling. Leonardo da Vinci, Michelangelo, Botticelli, Giotto, Fra Angelico, Bernini, Verrocchio, Donatello, Palladio, Petrarch, Shakespeare, Marlowe, Rabelais, Columbus, Magellan, Vasco da Gama, the Medici and Elizabeth I are but a few of the superstars.

"Renaissance" still means "rebirth" in modern parlance, whether it be the rebirth of an individual, an idea or a nation.

Renaissance man   When Ophelia says of Hamlet:

O, what a noble mind is here o'erthrown!
The courtier's, soldier's, scholar's, eye, tongue, sword,
The expectancy and rose of the fair state,
The glass of fashion and the mould of form,
The observed of all observers—quite, quite down!

she is describing the fall of a Renaissance man.

At the time of the RENAISSANCE, a man of the aristocracy received an all-around education that prepared him for all aspects of his life. He was trained in the manly arts of fencing, riding, combat; as a courtier, he had to be able to turn out a sonnet or a song, play a musical instrument and be adept in conversation; as a statesman, he had to have a classical education, a proficiency in languages and skill in diplomacy. There was no division at that time between a man of action and a man of learning and the arts. A Renaissance man was expected to be both.

Sir Francis Bacon (1561–1626), a Renaissance man in England, wrote grandly: "I have taken all knowledge to be my province." Perhaps the outstanding example of such a Renaissance man was LEONARDO DA VINCI (1452–1519), one of the greatest artists of all time, who filled his notebooks with minute observations of nature, with schemes for inventions of all kinds of machines from military projectiles to airplanes, with engineering projects for the state, with anatomical studies and sketches. In England, among the courtiers surrounding Queen Elizabeth I, SIR WALTER RALEIGH was a soldier, statesman, explorer and poet.

Today, a Renaissance man (or woman) is more loosely defined as one who is gifted in several different areas. For example, he/she may be a successful executive who can put together a gourmet meal, advise a president of the United States, play the piano and quote Shakespeare.

In the history of the United States, surely the preeminent Renaissance man was Thomas Jefferson (1743–1826), author of the Declaration of Independence, third president of the United States, architect of the University of Virginia and of Monticello, inventor of many ingenious and useful household improvements, guardian of the liberties of the people.

In our time, almost everybody will agree that Winston Churchill (1874–1965), the wartime prime minister of Great Britain, was a Renaissance man: soldier, statesman, scholar, historian, writer, painter, wit, maker of memorable phrases.

It is interesting to note that "Renaissance man" is always a term of admiration, even awe. No villain, no matter how many-sided or famous, has ever been called a Renaissance man.

Renoir, Auguste   See IMPRESSIONIST.

Revere, Paul (1735–1818)   American silversmith and patriot.

Listen, my children, and you shall hear
Of the midnight ride of Paul Revere . . .

At one time, practically every American knew these lines from Henry Wadsworth Longfellow's "Paul Revere's Ride" (1861). They also knew who Paul Revere was and where he was riding that fateful night of April 18, 1775.

Paul Revere was born of French Huguenot parents who came to America to practice their Protestant religion in peace and freedom. Like his father, Paul was a silversmith. He was also a member of Sam Adams's "circle of rebels" and took part in all of the events leading to the Revolutionary War (1775–81). He is most famous, however, for riding from Boston to Lexington, to warn his countrymen of the approaching British troops, as immortalized in Longfellow's poem.

A Paul Revere is a passionate, courageous patriot giving his all for his country in its hour of need.

Right Stuff, The (1979)   Book about the training of the first astronauts, written by Tom Wolfe and adapted for the movies in 1983, with John Glenn played by Ed Harris. Having the right stuff is having what it takes to complete a dangerous mission.

Rip Van Winkle   The main character in a story of the same name (1819) by the American writer Washington Irving (1783–1859).

In the days of colonial America, a lazy, henpecked farmer named Rip Van Winkle one day wanders with his dog into the Catskill Mountains. He meets a dwarfish old man who asks him to carry a keg of gin up the mountain to where his friends are playing ninepins. Rip steals a sip of the gin and falls into a deep sleep.

When he awakens, his dog is gone, his gun is rusted and he himself has grown a long gray beard. Terrified of his wife, Rip descends to the village. Everything has changed: his wife has died; his little daughter has grown up and married; in the local tavern the picture of King George has been replaced by a portrait of George Washington. Rip has been asleep for 20 years. He has slept through the American Revolution and now must adjust to new times.

A Rip Van Winkle is someone who has been absent a long time and returns to an altered world.

"Road Not Taken, The"   A lyric poem by Robert Frost (1875–1963), the last three lines of which are:

> *Two roads diverged in a wood, and I—*
> *I took the one less traveled by,*
> *And that has made all the difference*

These lines refer to the choices we make at every step in our lives and to the consequences of our choices. We cannot help wondering how our lives would have differed had we taken other paths, and especially had we taken the less conventional road.

robber barons Between the end of the Civil War and the early years of the 20th century, America witnessed the greatest concentration of wealth in the hands of a few men. For their greed and rapacity, Matthew Josephson aptly labeled them the robber barons (1934) in his book of the same name. He compared these American financiers and industrialists to the "predatory nobles" of the Middle Ages who exacted tribute from all travelers whose destinations took them past the barons' strategically placed strongholds. The Americans, as Josephson portrayed them, amplified and refined the techniques of their medieval counterparts. Some of the more notorious robber barons included John D. Rockefeller (1839–1939), J. P. Morgan (1837–1913), Cornelius Vanderbilt (1794–1877) and ANDREW CARNEGIE (1835–1919).

The term "robber baron" is applied to individuals who lavishly enrich themselves through extensive, unscrupulous exploitation of public resources.

Robbins, Jerome (1918–1998) New York–born dancer and choreographer who with GEORGE BALANCHINE codirected the New York City Ballet, where he created such ballets as *Dancers at a Gathering* and *The Goldberg Variations,* among many others. He is most widely known, however, for his energetic, freewheeling American-style choreography and direction in such Broadway musicals as *On the Town* (1944) and *West Side Story* (1957), both of which were done to the music of Leonard Bernstein.

Robert I Bruce In 1306, Robert Bruce (also known as Robert the Bruce [1274–1329]), king of Scotland was battling against King Edward I of England for domination over Scotland. Fleeing from Edward, Bruce went into hiding on the island of Rathlin. According to legend, one day, as he lay despondent and exhausted, Bruce noticed a spider trying to spin its web on a beam on the ceiling. Six times the spider tried. Six times the web tore. Undiscouraged, the spider tried for the seventh time and succeeded. Taking his cue from the spider's determination, Bruce, who had failed six times, set out for the seventh time to fight for what he felt was rightly his.

So in 1307, Bruce left the island with 300 men, landed at Carrick, and there surprised and overcame the English garrison. He continued to challenge the English until he routed them at the Battle of Bannockburn.

Bruce and the spider stand as symbols of the ultimate rewards of perseverance.

Robespierre (1758–1794) Born Maximilian Marie Isidore, he was an extremist of the left, a tyrant who during the REIGN OF TERROR of the French Revolution had thousands of "enemies," including his rivals in power, Georges Jacques Danton and Desmoulins, guillotined. Finally, in the reaction against his despotism, Robespierre, together with his followers, was summarily executed on July 28, 1794.

Ironically, Robespierre had trained as a lawyer and turned down a judgeship because he opposed capital punishment. Equally ironic is that under the influence of ROUSSEAU he accepted democracy and deism as his true values, but raised these to the rigidity of dogma. A despot is a despot, whether of the right or the left. See JACOBIN.

Robin Hood   A legendary outlaw who robbed the rich to give to the poor, Robin Hood was the central figure in a cycle of medieval ballads (14th–16th centuries) about the "greenwood." With his band of merry men, Little John and Friar Tuck among them, and with Maid Marian, he hid out in the forests of Nottinghamshire. With wit, sass and derring-do he overcame his enemies, chief among them the sheriff of Nottingham.

There must be something soul satisfying in the Robin Hood formula, for it has continued to inspire storytellers and moviemakers right up to the present day.

A Robin Hood is now thought of as anyone who works to benefit a less privileged group at the expense of a more privileged group.

Robinson, Bill (Bojangles) (1878–1949)   At the peak of his phenomenal dancing career, this American tap dancer was the toast of Broadway night clubs and musical comedy. Bojangles was equally successful in Hollywood where he appeared in 14 films. Among the most memorable were *The Little Colonel* (1935), *The Little Rebel* (1935) and *Rebecca of Sunnybrook Farm* (1938), all with Shirley Temple.

Almost universally known as Bojangles, Robinson continued dancing until his mid-60s. His versatility, endurance and inventiveness won him the title of "satrap of tap." His performances epitomized the spirit of tap dancing. It was said of Bojangles, that "his feet responded directly to the music—his head had nothing to do with it."

Use: "[Sammy] Davis was above all an entertainer. . . . In the moments before a 1987 Vegas show . . . Davis warmed up backstage . . . then the curtain opened and it was . . . Mr. Bojangles." (Arthur Schwartz, *Newsweek,* May 28, 1990)

Robinson, Edward G. (1893–1973)   Actor Robinson was the personification of the gangster in films such as *Little Caesar* (1930) and *Key Largo* (1948).

Robinson, Jack (Jackie) **Roosevelt** (1919–1972)   Black baseball player. While Robinson was playing in the Negro National League, Branch Rickey, president of the National League Brooklyn Dodgers, asked him to join the Dodgers as the first black major league player. Robinson accepted, breaking the color barrier and paving the way for many other black players into the major leagues.

In 1949, Robinson won the Most Valuable Player Award. In 1972, he was the first black man to be inducted into the National Baseball Hall of Fame.

In the long and troubled history of race relations in America, Jackie (as he was affectionately called by millions of fans) was a true pioneer.

Use: "There had not been a Jewish manager in the entire history of Boston and Northeastern [not quite our class, as they used to say on the Mayflower], and my father, with his eighth grade education wasn't exactly suited to be the Jackie Robinson of the insurance business." (Philip Roth, *Portnoy's Complaint*)

Rockefeller   American business and philanthropic dynasty founded by John D. Rockefeller (1839–1937) on the basis of an oil fortune amassed by Standard Oil Company of New Jersey. In 1911 this corporation was ordered dissolved by the U.S. Supreme Court as a result of an antitrust suit. It owned three-fourths of the entire oil business in the United States and was a symbol of the concentration of business power in the hands of a few individuals.

John D. Rockefeller's only son was John D. Rockefeller, Jr. (1874–1960), who devoted himself primarily to philanthropic and civic causes: the restoration of Colonial Williamsburg; development of Rockefeller Center in New York City; the purchase and building of the United Nations permanent headquarters in New York City; the management of the Rockefeller Foundation; and the development of the Rockefeller Institute for Medical Research, set up by his father in 1901 and now known as Rockefeller University. John D. and John D., Jr., are estimated to have given more than $750 million for philanthropic causes.

John D. Jr. and Abby Aldrich had five sons: John D. 3rd (1906–78); Nelson (1908–79); Laurance (1910–   ); Winthrop (1912–73); and David (1915–   ).

The sons devoted themselves not only to business and philanthropy but to politics as well. Winthrop Rockefeller was twice elected Republican governor of Arkansas. Nelson Rockefeller was elected four times as governor of New York and served as vice president of the United States under President Gerald R. Ford. The fourth generation of Rockefellers continues to be active on all fronts.

In the modern world, "rich as Croesus" has been replaced by "rich as Rockefeller."

rocket scientist   Any aeronautics scientist, especially any superstar like Konstantin E. Tsiolkovsky (Russian) or Robert H. Goddard (American, author of *A Method for Reaching Extreme Altitudes*) or Wernher von Braun (German), who played a major part in developing the science of rocketry for the purposes of war or space exploration. Rockets went from early one-stage projectiles to later multistage liquid fuel projectiles such as the Saturn V, which could achieve orbital velocity.

Today, "rocket scientist" is sometimes used sarcastically as a synonym for genius, as in "You don't need to be a rocket scientist or even a pediatrician; mere motherhood teaches you that a child masters a new skill when he or she is developmentally ready. . . . (*New York Times,* January 18, 1999)

Rockettes   A long line of female dancers famous for their precision high-kicking in Radio City Music Hall shows in New York.

Rockwell, Norman (1894–1978)   American illustrator and cartoonist who between 1916 and 1963 painted 317 covers for the popular magazine *The Saturday Evening Post.* Rockwell painted hundreds more for *Boy's Life,* a publication of the Boy Scouts of America. He seems to have captured, with humor and sentiment, the pleasant and homey spirit of American small-town characters and their everyday concerns: visits to the doctor, the dentist, the teacher; eating at luncheonette counters; dunking in the old swimming hole; expressions of puppy love.

A Norman Rockwell is truly as American as apple pie.

Rocky   Main character in the 1976 Academy Award-winning film of the same name. SYLVESTER STALLONE stars as Rocky Balboa, a boxer who wins against formidable odds in a fairy-tale ending. His street-smart cunning combined with true grit and a spaniel-eyed innocence turned him into a new popular hero.

rococo   A lavishly decorative style of architecture and interior design using curvilinear motifs of leaves, shells and other organic forms. It originated in France during the reign of Louis XV (1715–74) and quickly spread throughout Europe, especially in Germany and Austria, where churches, castles, sculpture, furniture and objets d'art took on a superfluity of ornamentation. Stemming from the baroque, rococo exaggerated that ornateness and became pretty or, as some would have it, graceful.

In painting, Jean-Honoré Fragonard (1732–1806) exemplifies the rococo; in music, Francois Couperin (1668–1733) and Georg Philipp Telemann (1681–1767); in architecture, Balthasar Neumann (1687–1753), who designed the Episcopal Palace in Würtzburg, with its Kaisersaal elaborately decorated in gold, white and pastels.

Today, "rococo" refers to any exuberant, flamboyant, overly decorated style.

Rogers, Will (1879–1935)   Actor and humorist Will Rogers's unique act in the *Ziegfeld Follies* (1916–25) consisted of rope-twirling, chewing gum and telling jokes. Underneath his innocent-looking performance, Rogers was an unusually perceptive political commentator. His thrusts at shenanigans in high places, though delivered with a smile and a drawl, unerringly found their mark. He soon became known as America's "cowboy philosopher." In 1922, he wrote a daily syndicated column that was published in the *New York Times* and 350 other newspapers.

Rogers reached a vast (40 million) and hugely appreciative audience. For his good-natured, homely satire, he found himself compared with "Mr. Dooley," Artemus Ward and Mark Twain.

Successful as he was on stage and in the news media, Rogers achieved even greater success in the movies: *The Connecticut Yankee* (1931), *State Fair* (1933), *David Harum* (1934).

On August 15, 1935, Rogers died with his pilot-friend Wiley Post in an airplane crash near Point Barrow, Alaska.

rogue elephant   A vicious elephant that refuses to conform to the ways of the herd and therefore must live apart in exile. The expression came into use around 1855. The term is now applied to someone who takes a stand apart from or in contradiction to the group to which he or she belongs.

Roland and Oliver   Two of the 12 peers in the court of Charlemagne (742–814), king of the Franks, they are the legendary heroes of the 11th-century epic *La Chanson de Roland* (*The Song of Roland*), which tells the story of their betrayal and death at Roncesvalles.

Roland and Oliver were knights so evenly balanced in prowess that they once engaged in single combat for five full days without either one gaining the advantage. They became inseparable friends. Charlemagne sent them with an army into Spain to fight the Saracens. On the march back from Spain through the narrow pass at Roncesvalles in the Pyrenees, they were surprised and outnumbered by the enemy. One of their own peers, Ganelon, had betrayed them. Although Oliver persuaded Roland to blow his ivory horn as a signal for Charlemagne to send reinforcements, help came too late. Roland and Oliver, together with 20,000 of their men, were slain.

Roland and Oliver were bound in friendship and loyalty. Such a relationship, in certain epochs, was more binding than the one between a man and a woman. Like Damon and Pythias or David and Jonathan, Roland and Oliver stand as a prototypical pair of devoted friends.

roller-coaster   A series of open cars connected into a train, which moves along the tracks of a high, sharply winding trestle, gathering momentum on the upward incline and then plunging down the steep-tilted decline to the accompaniment of screams from thrill-seeking passengers in amusement parks.

By extension, a roller-coaster has come to be any sharply swinging up and down movement, so that one may refer to the stock market being on a roller-coaster or a person being on an emotional roller-coaster.

Rolls-Royce   The aristocrat of expensive, hand-tooled cars, made in Great Britain. Originally driven by chauffeurs, for the very rich. Named for its original designer-builders, Charles Stuart Rolls (1877–1910) and Frederick Henry Royce (1863–1933).

By extension, the symbol of the best, the most elegant, the most expensive, the classiest.

Use: "Congress is grabbing for a CADILLAC salary, but it already has a Rolls-Royce pension." (*Palm Beach Post,* February 4, 1989)

roll with a punch   In boxing, to move one's head or body in the same direction as an opponent's punch in order to diminish its effect.

In general use, to deal successfully or vigorously with a downturn in one's fortunes.

Romanesque   Referring to a style of medieval architecture from the ninth to the 12th centuries, especially in the building of cathedrals throughout Europe.

Patterned on ancient Roman edifices, Romanesque cathedrals are built of heavy masonry. They look solid as compared with the later soaring lightness of the GOTHIC cathedrals. The Romanesque is characterized by round arches, vaulted ceilings, an exterior shape in the form of a cross and bold surface ornamentation and sculpture. Unlike the Gothic, with its skin of colored glass, the Romanesque looks like a fortress.

These churches are to be seen all along the route of the pilgrimages to SANTIAGO DE COMPOSTELA in northwestern Spain. Some outstanding examples of Romanesque churches are St-Sernin, Toulouse (c. 1080–1120), Durham Cathedral (1093–1130), the abbey church at Cluny (981), St-Etienne at Caen (1068), the Cathedral of Worms (1110–1200).

Romantic/Romanticism   Near the end of the 18th century, a comprehensive revolt against CLASSICISM began to spread throughout the Western world. The Romantic revolution affected philosophy, literature, art, music, politics, religion and social mores. Conformity to convention was out, experimentation and freedom of expression were in. Reason and judgment gave way to imagination, intuition and emotion as chief sources of inspiration. The era of the common man and of individual rights was about to begin.

Jean-Jacques ROUSSEAU is generally considered to be the father of Romanticism. His ideas about man's goodness in a state of nature (see NOBLE SAVAGE), the beneficent effect of nature itself, the importance of the child and his or her education, the social contract as the basis for government, all profoundly influenced the Romantic revolution.

The movement had German progenitors as well—among them Schiller, Schlegel, Lessing, Goethe—who in turn influenced the English poet and literary critic Samuel Taylor Coleridge. In 1798 Wordsworth and Coleridge, in Wordsworth's preface to *Lyrical Ballads,* sounded a Romantic manifesto for poetry: to make the faraway and long-ago, the strange and the supernatural, seem familiar; and to invest the everyday, the familiar, the simple folk with an air of wonder and mystery. This was to be done in the language of everyday speech. Wordsworth and Coleridge had been preceded in 1765 by Thomas Percy's *Reliques of Ancient English Poetry,* a collection of about 180 old English and Scots ballads that had awakened interest in the past, in the folk and in their simple manner of expression.

The excesses of Romanticism culminated in the BYRONIC HERO, passionate, rebellious, daring, demonic, and in the GOTHIC novel, with its saturnine hero, its violent passions, its supernatural elements and its overheated atmosphere. From these aspects of Romanticism flow its dangers and parodies.

Romeo and Juliet "Star-crossed" young lovers of Verona in Shakespeare's tragedy of the same name (c. 1595) who lose their lives because of the opposition of their feuding families, the Montagues and the Capulets; because of accidental errors and misjudgments; and because of their headstrong, impetuous passion.

Romeo and Juliet have taken their place in the galaxy of legendary tragic lovers including ABELARD AND HÉLOISE, TRISTAN AND ISOLDE, Antony and Cleopatra.

Rommel, Erwin (1891–1944) German general in World War II. Field marshal of the African Theater of War, commander of the Afrika Korps, Rommel was known as the "Desert Fox" for outwitting and outflanking Allied forces in Egypt, Libya and Tunisia. Eventually beaten by Field Marshal Montgomery at El Alamein and sent to the Normandy area, he was suspected of participating in the 1944 assassination attempt on Hitler and forced to commit suicide.

Rorschach test Introduced by Hermann Rorschach, a Swiss psychiatrist, it is a psychological probe for personality traits based on an individual's interpretation of a series of random ink blots. What the subject sees is a configuration not in the inkblots but in his own mind. Many jokes have arisen out of patients' interpretations. Often the jokes are at the expense of the psychiatrist who, in the eyes of his patients, is a dirty man showing dirty pictures.

Use: A person's interpretation of certain modern plays like *Waiting for Godot* is often a Rorschach test of his own obsessions and predilections rather than an understanding of what may have been the intention of the author.

rosebud   Mystery word uttered with his last breath by the dying tycoon in the opening scene of Orson Welles's film CITIZEN KANE. The movie is a search for the real Kane behind the wealth, power, acquisitions, achievements. What makes him tick? "Rosebud" is thought to be the key. Who is Rosebud? In the closing scene, when workmen are throwing into the flames the accumulated junk in Kane's castle, they pick up a sled. On it we see the faded letters "Rosebud." It is the sled Kane played with when he was a poor boy, before he was thrust out of his home by his mother to live with a guardian in the style necessitated by his unexpected inheritance. "Rosebud" is a symbol of the unspoiled happiness of one's youth.

"rose is a rose is a rose, a"   Quotation from the works of GERTRUDE STEIN (1874–1946), American writer who lived in Paris most of her life. The line is from "Sacred Emily" in *Geography and Plays* (1922). It illustrates Stein's theory of naming (the use of nouns) in poetry. She wrote: "You can love a name and if you love a name then saying that name any number of times only makes you love it more," and poetry is "really loving the name of anything." Stylistically, Stein is famous for her experimentation with language and composition. She loved repetition, rhyme, automatic writing coming from the subconscious, and she hated punctuation.

The phrase is always quoted playfully to indicate the inadequancy of description; that is, what more can one say about something, since everything is subsumed in the one word "rose."

Roseland   The brainchild of Louis J. Brecker, Roseland opened in New York City at 51st Street and Broadway on New Year's Eve, 1919. Mounted police had to control the crowds clamoring to get in. On a dais behind a silken rope sat 150 taxi dancers (hostesses) waiting to be summoned by gentlemen with tickets ("ten cents a dance"). It was all very proper, jacket and tie de rigueur, no dating the clients. Nevertheless, there is a record of 550 couples meeting at Roseland and subsequently marrying. Roseland was open seven nights a week, with music by the big bands of Glenn Miller, Benny Goodman, Artie Shaw and other bandleaders.

With the advent of rock 'n' roll, disco dancing replaced traditional social dancing and Roseland went into decline, although it has never closed permanently. In 1956, Roseland moved to 52nd Street between Broadway and 8th Avenue. The taxi dancers had been eliminated. In 1977, Albert Ginsberg bought Roseland and brought back the taxi dancers, who now also included men for female patrons. The price went up to a dollar a dance, open Thursdays only.

Rosetta Stone   During Napoleon's Egyptian military expedition in 1799, one of his soldiers came upon an odd stone in an excavation at Port St. Julien at the mouth of the Nile River near the town of Rosetta. The stone, now appropriately called the Rosetta Stone, was made of basalt and stood three feet, nine inches high and two feet four inches wide. Chiseled into its surface were thousands of characters that no one at the time could understand. Somewhat later, the great French Egyptologist, Jean Francois Champollion (1790–1832), decoded the Rosetta Stone. Here was the dramatic history, religion, custom, language of the ancient Egyptian civilization. Later Egyptologists enlarged Champollion's original discoveries.

In contemporary usage, a Rosetta Stone furnishes clues, crucial bits of knowledge or information that provide answers to hitherto unsolved problems, puzzles or questions.

Rosie the Riveter   Character in popular patriotic song and in a satirical poster by NORMAN ROCKWELL, she symbolized the women who took over men's jobs on the home front, especially in defense plants, during World War II under the government policy of "equal pay for equal work." Women, who no longer had to be traditionally "feminine," have been entering the work force in greater and greater numbers ever since.

Rothko, Mark (1903–1970)   American artist born in Russia; he immigrated to the United States in 1913. An abstract expressionist, he covered huge canvases with horizontal bands of luminous color, suffused in focus and seemingly floating in air.

Rothko said that he was searching for the most simple means to express universal truths. He hoped that the effect of his paintings would be calm and contemplation.

In looking at certain dawns and sunsets one may say, "Look, a Rothko sky!"

Rothschild   A family whose members constituted one of the chief international financial powers in the 19th century. Its influence was reduced after World War II.

The family fortune was founded by Meyer Amschel Rothschild (1743–1812), son of a minor Jewish moneychanger in Frankfurt, Germany. During the Napoleonic wars, Meyer and his five sons consolidated their financial resources and played a key role in financing the war effort. After Napoleon's defeat, Meyer and his sons were made barons by Emperor Francis I of Austria. By this time, the Rothschilds had become one of the most influential international bankers, with branches and contacts in all the major financial centers.

Throughout their financial dominance in the international community, the Rothschilds continued to follow their Jewish religious practices and traditions.

Their lavish philanthropy supported Jewish and non-Jewish causes as well as the arts and sciences.

A "Rothschild" has come to mean a person of enormous wealth and influence.

Rouault, Georges (1871–1958)   French expressionist whose early training in the restoration of medieval stained glass carried over into the black-outlined jewel-like colors of his paintings of judges, clowns, outcasts, prostitutes, saints and kings. He wanted to create "the passion mirrored upon a human face," as in *The Old King.* Of deep religious faith, he was haunted by the image of the suffering Christ, e.g., in *Head of Christ* and in *Christ Mocked by Soldiers.* His slashing brush strokes as well as his mixture of rage and compassion mark him as heir to van Gogh.

round table   A circular table is featured in all the stories about King ARTHUR and his Knights of the Round Table. It is first mentioned in Robert Wace's *Roman de Brut* (1155), then by Layamon (c. 1205) and fully described by Sir Thomas Malory in *Morte d' Arthur* (c. 1469).

The legendary Round Table was made by MERLIN, the magician, for Arthur's father, Uther Pendragon. He passed it on to King Leodegraunce of Camiliard, who in turn gave it to Arthur as a wedding present on his marriage to Guinevere.

The table could seat 150 knights. However, one place was always vacant. That was the Siege (chair) Perilous, which awaited the knight who would attain the Holy Grail. Eventually, he would be GALAHAD, the pure. Around the table were seated such famous knights as Lancelot, Kay, Modred, Belvedere and Gawain.

The round table was a brilliant diplomatic invention. It precluded all quarrels over precedence. All were equal. Today a round table has the same significance. Whether it is used for heads of state or for business executives or for students and faculty, it is meant to avoid distinctions of status.

"Round up the usual suspects"   A line spoken by the police prefect, Captain Louis Renault (Claude Rains), near the end of the movie *Casablanca,* directed by Michael Curtiz in 1942 and starring HUMPHREY BOGART, INGRID BERGMAN and Paul Henreid. Bergman and Henreid (a leader of the underground movement against the Nazis) are racing to board a plane leaving Casablanca. Bogart has engineered their flight to safety. Bogart is holding Rains at gunpoint so that he will not prevent them from boarding the plane. At this moment Major Strasser arrives in hot pursuit. He draws a gun to shoot Henreid, but Bogart shoots the Nazi. Covering up for Bogart, Claude Rains tells his men that Strasser has been shot; after a dramatic pause, he orders them to "round up the usual suspects." For Bogart and Rains, this is the beginning of a "beautiful friendship."

Rousseau, Jean-Jacques (1712–1778)   Although his life fell entirely within the 18th century and therefore properly within the scope of the Enlightenment, with its emphasis on reason, order, stability, decorum, Rousseau was an original thinker, a harbinger of 19th-century romanticism.

He was born in Geneva, Switzerland. His mother died in childbirth and he was raised by an indifferent father and assorted relatives. By the age of 16 he was on his own, drifting from country to country, supporting himself with a variety of secretarial jobs as well as work in musical notation, and acquiring patrons along the way.

In 1749 Rousseau burst upon the intellectual world's horizon by winning first prize for an essay taking the negative point of view on the question, Has the progress of the sciences and arts contributed to the corruption or to the improvement of human conduct? Rousseau argued that man is born good but is corrupted by civilization. This gave rise to the romantic concept of the NOBLE SAVAGE in a state of nature.

Because it was impossible for modern industrial man to return to a state of nature, Rousseau proposed, in his pedagogical novel *Emile* (1762), a system of education to reduce the gap between primitive innocence and corrupt "civilization." A child must be allowed to develop his own natural gifts from within. Learning from books should be secondary to learning from nature. Nature has a beneficent influence on the human soul; therefore, contact with landscape, trees, water and birds should be encouraged. Rousseau advocated breast feeding, fresh air and hygiene, and abandonment of swaddling clothes in the rearing of children. He had a profound influence on progressive educators such as Pestalozzi, Montessori and Piaget.

In the field of political philosophy Rousseau is known for *The Social Contract* (1762), a book-length extension of his argument in an essay on "the origin of inequality among men." He argued that man can attain civil liberty by entering into a social contract with his fellow men. Sovereignty is inherent in society as a whole; it cannot be delegated and must not be abrogated, no matter what the form of government.

Rousseau is perhaps best known for his *Confessions* (1781–88), a posthumous autobiography so self-revelatory, so free of the restraints of prudishness or shame, that it practically opened the way for a new genre of self-expression.

Rousseau has become a symbol for the romantic sensibility, for the freedom of the individual from the contraints of overbearingly oppressive institutions.

Use: "[Tolstoy] started a school for his tenants, organized on the Rousseauan principle that the unsophisticated life of the peasant is morally and intellectually sounder than the artificial standards of civilization." (Brooks Wright, *50 European Novels*)

Rubenesque   In the style of Peter Paul Rubens (1577–1640), Flemish painter of Antwerp who spent eight years studying masterpieces of art in Italy. His name has become associated with such large-scaled, full-bodied, full-bosomed, fleshy, golden-haired women as are to be found in his *Garden of Love* (1632–34) and in his *Allegory on the Blessings of Peace* (1630).

The expression "Rubenesque" is now often applied to a voluptuous woman of generous proportions.

Rubik's Cube   A puzzle invented and patented in 1975 by the Hungarian architect and professor Erno Rubik (1944–   ) for the purpose of teaching his students three-dimensional design. It is a multicolored cube with moveable tile-like squares that can be arranged in only one correct way, but in an almost infinite number of incorrect ways. This daunting challenge became a world-wide craze. By extension, a Rubik's Cube has come to stand for any extremely difficult problem.

Use: "Trying to form a government from such pieces . . . is turning out to be Mr. Barak's Rubik's Cube. Every time he thinks he's got all his squares right, one pops up that doesn't fit." (Thomas Friedman, *New York Times,* June 11, 1999)

Rumpelstiltskin   Character in a GRIMM BROTHERS fairy tale of the same name. Once upon a time a miller boasted that his daughter could spin straw into gold. The king challenged her by locking her into a room full of straw with a spinning wheel. Of course, she could not do it.

A gnome appeared and accomplished the miracle in return for her necklace. The second time he received her ring. The third time he demanded her first-born child. She married the king and bore him a child. The gnome demanded his payment unless within three days she could guess his name. Couriers were sent far and wide, but they were unsuccessful in their efforts to learn his name. On the third day one of them spied a little man dancing up and down in a forest. "Rumpelstiltskin is my name," he chanted. When the queen triumphantly produced his name, Rumpelstiltskin went wild, stamping his feet and running, howling, out of the palace.

Now, to "do a Rumpelstiltskin" is to burst into a temper tantrum when frustrated.

Runnymede   Meadow on the south bank of the Thames near Windsor where, in 1215, King John had to accept from his barons the MAGNA CARTA. The place has become synonymous with the charter itself.

By extension, a "Runnymede" is any birthplace of political emancipation from absolute authority.

Ruritania   A mythical, central European country just a short train-ride from Dresden, it is the locale of Anthony Hope Hawkins's (1863–1933) once-popular novels, *Prisoner of Zenda* (1894) and *Rupert of Hentzau* (1898). Outwardly, Ruritania appears quaint, colorful, romantic, but underneath its charming surface run dark currents of outré and violent court intrigues.

A "Ruritania" may be just a place of glitter and romance—or it may, as in the original, conceal ugly realities beneath its surface charm.

Russian roulette   A dangerous game, often played on a dare, in which losing means instant death. The player holds a pistol to his own temple, a pistol in which only one of six cylinders has been loaded. After spinning the cylinder, he pulls the trigger. He has one out of six chances of blowing his brains out. The game is supposed to have been popular with czarist troops.

Figuratively, to play Russian roulette is to take a great chance entailing grave consequences.

Ruth, George Herman (Babe) (1895–1948)   Starting in baseball as a left-handed pitcher, by 1919 Ruth was the best in the American League. When his Red Sox manager moved him to the outfield that season, Ruth took off like the proverbial rocket, piling up one home run record after another.

Following the White Sox scandal of 1919–20, public interest in baseball fell to its lowest point. Ruth's spectacular playing arrested baseball's precipitous slide. He was widely hailed as the "savior of baseball."

Ruth's performance as a Yankee player was a major factor in attracting vast numbers of fans to the new Yankee Stadium, which some inspired writer called "the House that Ruth built."

In 1936, Ruth was inducted into the Baseball Hall of Fame.

A man of heroic, mythic proportions, he taxed the ingenuity of the writers of his time to capture, in words, his essential qualities. "The Bambino" and the "Sultan of Swat" seem to be the most promising contenders. The most durable—and the simplest—of all is probably "the greatest slugger of them all."

A measure of Ruth's worldwide fame and prestige turned up during World War II when the Japanese hurled at the Americans what they considered the supreme insult, "To Hell with Babe Ruth."

Sacco-Vanzetti   Political anarchists Nicola Sacco, a shoemaker, and Bartolomeo Vanzetti, a fish peddler, became the central figures in an international cause célébre. Italian immigrants to the United States, they were convicted of murdering the paymaster and guard of a shoe factory in South Braintree, Massachusetts, during a payroll holdup in 1920. In spite of worldwide protests and demonstrations, they were finally executed on August 23, 1927. Many people still think of them as victims of a frame-up, punished for their political convictions and labor affiliations. Books continue to be written trying to prove either their guilt or innocence.

sacred cow   In Hindu India, cows may wander through the streets without interference. No one may harm them because they are sacred. They are believed to contain the souls of the dead.

Today a sacred cow is any subject that may not be criticized.

Sade (Donatien-Alphonse-François, Count and Marquis de) (1740–1814) French writer of the pornographic novels *Justine* (1791), *Juliette* (1798) and *The Crimes of Love* (1800), which are filled with characters who derive sexual pleasure from humiliating, dominating or hurting their partners.

In his own life, de Sade experimented with the violent practices of the characters in his novels. His sexual practices and his incessant battles with his enemies kept him in prison for a total of 30 years.

From "de Sade" comes the word "sadism," which technically means sexual pleasure or gratification derived from torturing or inflicting pain but has also come to mean any pleasure (not necessarily sexual) derived from causing pain or suffering to others.

Sad Sack, The   Comic strip created by George Baker, an ex-Disney animator. *The Sad Sack* first appeared in 1942, in *Yank,* the U.S. Army enlisted man's weekly magazine. According to Baker, the Sad Sack was just "an average soldier" reflecting the soldier's way of looking at and responding to the world around him: "resigned, helpless, tired, and beaten."

The world, it seemed, had conspired to deprive the Sad Sack of the simple, expected joys. He never got the girl he wanted. Army regulations seemed especially set up to confuse and frustrate him. His superiors took advantage of him. In Army parlance, he was just "a sad sack of s—t."

The Sad Sack was enormously popular. In a sense, he was, according to Maurice Horn, an authority on comics, the classic comic figure "reflecting the frustrations of the common man but at the same time . . . something for the common man to look down on." Hence a Sad Sack is any ordinary mortal, helpless against the system that seems stacked against him. Also applied to anything lackluster, lacking in vitality or distinction, poor quality, below average.

Sagan, Carl (1934–1996) A professor of astronomy and astrophysics at Cornell University, he popularized his subjects by drawing an audience of about 400 million to his 1980 public television series *Cosmos*. With his contagious enthusiasm, his passionate belief in the existence of life in outer space and his youthful good looks, he mesmerized his viewers and his reference to the "billions and billions" of stars in the universe was parodied by comedians.

Sahara A vast desert in North Africa covering about three million square miles. It has become a generic term for a desert, both in the literal sense of dry sands or in the figurative sense of aridity of spirit or intellect.

St. Francis of Assisi (1182–1226) Born into a wealthy merchant family in the town of Assisi, Giovanni di Bernardone (or Francis, as he was called) experienced a religious conversion at the age of 21. He gladly gave up all his possessions and, clad in rags, became a mendicant friar preaching the gospel and working at menial tasks for his material needs. Soon disciples gathered around him, all dedicated to a life of poverty. They called themselves *Joculatores Dei,* God's Minstrels, for wherever they went they sang joyous songs in God's praise. Francis, himself, wrote such a paean called the "Canticle of the Sun."

He was, in a way, a child of nature. He loved contemplating wild mountain landscapes. He preached, we are told in the *Fioretti di San Francesco,* to the birds and beasts at Alviano. He kissed the hands of lepers. He wanted to live without organization, without rules, although these were imposed upon him by the church, and he became willy-nilly the founder of the Franciscan order.

In 1224 he had a vision of an angel nailed to a cross, and he found upon his own body the stigmata of Christ's wounds. In 1228, two years after his death, he was canonized by Pope Gregory IV and became St. Francis of Assisi.

Of all the saints, surely St. Francis is the most lovable. His simplicity, perhaps naiveté, his compassion for the lowly, his humility, his gentleness, his childlike joyousness, all mark him as the quintessentially good man, a man in harmony with nature, a saint. He is analogous to the genre of the holy fool.

St. George and the dragon   Any number of saints are supposed to have slain dragons, including St. Michael, St. Margaret, St. Sylvester and St. Martha; but St. George, the patron saint of England, is the one most often pictured in combat against the dragon, a symbol of evil. Legend has it that St. George rescued a captive princess from a dragon who had been preying upon her people.

St. George was probably a historical person (not merely an allegorical character), a soldier martyred in the fourth century A.D. for his Christian beliefs. He was buried in Palestine.

St. George has been sighted several times; once, when he came to the rescue of Crusaders at the battle of Antioch in 1089; and again when he was seen by Richard the Lionhearted. He became a favorite saint of English soldiers and was associated with the cult of chivalry. In 1347 he became the patron saint of England.

A St. George is a figurative slayer of dragons.

St. Sebastian   An early Christian martyr who dies for his faith in A.D. 266 at the hands of his fellow Roman army officers. He was pierced by arrows in mock intimation of the death of Christ. St. Sebastian has been the subject of several Renaissance paintings, most famous of which is the one by Andrea Mantegna (c. 1455–60) now hanging in the Kunsthistorisches Museum in Vienna.

St. Sebastian is a symbol of suffering and martyrdom.

Use: "What makes Pat [Buchanan] so sore? He is a soul from the '50s, permanently at war with the '60s, and now reaching for power in the '90s. He likes playing the role of a conservative Saint Sebastian, pierced by arrows from the left for thinking so far right." (*Newsweek,* January 27, 1992)

Salem witch trials   In 1692, two little girls in Salem Village, Massachusetts, acting strangely, were brought to their doctor. After examining them, the doctor pronounced them "bewitched," under the influence of the "Evil Hand." Tituba, a West Indian slave, and two local women were, in due course, accused of practicing witchcraft upon the girls, and were jailed. Their trial loosed a frenzy of witchcraft accusations in the surrounding countryside. Dozens of innocent, frightened people were hauled before the local courts, accused of weird doings, found guilty and punished. Under extraordinary stress, the victims confessed to bizarre behavior, from broomstick riding to having sex with the devil. Refusal to implicate a neighbor drew a death sentence. Eventually, 19 "witches" were hanged. One husband was crushed under a pile of stones because he refused to plead guilty.

The widespread public outcry against the trials brought witchcraft to an end in New England and elsewhere.

Arthur Miller's *The Crucible* (1953), ostensibly dealing with the Salem witch trials, draws a sharp parallel with the destructive congressional hearings on communists conducted by the eventually discredited Senator Joseph McCarthy in the 1950s.

The Salem witch trials have become a symbol for any mass accusations based on hysteria rather than on evidence and reason.

samurai   Warriors attached by feudal bonds to the great landholding barons of medieval Japan. Arrogant, schooled in martial arts, quick to find offense, stoically indifferent to pain or death, they protected the honor of their overlord according to the code of conduct called *bushido*. A samurai was privileged to carry two swords and had the right to strike down any commoner whom he perceived to have insulted him.

In modern parlance, "samurai" is used as an epithet to designate a proud, belligerent man.

Sancho Panza   See DON QUIXOTE.

Sand, George   The pen name of the French writer Amandine-Aurore-Lucile Dupin (1804–76) who became at 18 the baroness Dudevant after her marriage of convenience to a country squire. The pseudonym was taken from one of her lovers, Jules Sandeau, with whom she collaborated on her first two novels, signed "J. Sand." All of her subsequent novels, about 80 in all, were signed George Sand.

Although George Sand was brought up by a severe aristocratic grandmother on the family estate at Nohant and educated in a convent, she was an extremely unconventional woman. She left her husband and with her two children settled in Paris, where she earned her living by writing popular novels. A romantic feminist, she espoused free love and took many lovers, of whom the most famous were the writer Alfred de Musset and the Polish composer Frédéric Chopin, whom she nurtured for nine years until he died of tuberculosis.

George Sand was politically to the left and wrote many novels of social conscience, as well as pastoral novels of the countryside and its simple people. Her best novels are said to be *La mare au diable* (*The Haunted Pool*) (1846) and *les Maîtres sonneurs* (*The Master Bell-Ringers*) (1853).

Perhaps her most fascinating book was her autobiography in several volumes *Histoire de Ma Vie* (*Story of My Life*) (1854–55). George Sand survives as the embodiment of an emancipated yet womanly woman, free yet unselfish, daring yet maternal, aristocratic in upbringing yet democratic by belief and practice.

Santiago de Compostela   One of the most famous shrines in Christendom during the MIDDLE AGES, it was the destination of innumerable devout pilgrimages. For a thousand years, penitents from all over Europe took the route to Compostela in northwest Spain, where the tomb of the apostle St. James, the brother of Christ, had been miraculously discovered. All along the way they stopped at a network of hospices, gathering places where ideas were exchanged that eventually filtered into every part of the continent. Although the original sanctuary was destroyed by the Moors in the 10th century, a ROMANESQUE cathedral was built in its place during the 11th and 12th centuries when Spain was retaken.

To take the route to Compostela is still to go on a pilgrimage of some sort, making stops along the way.

Sarajevo   City in Yugoslavia (then Austrian) where Archduke Francis Ferdinand, heir to the Austrian throne, was assassinated by a Serbian nationalist, Gavrilo Princip, on June 28, 1914. Within days Austria-Hungary declared war on nearby Serbia. Soon all of Europe was involved and World War I began. By the end of the war the number of dead on both sides was nine million; the number of wounded, 20 million. Sarajevo is associated with political assassination and its awesome consequences.

During the war among the ethnic Serbians, Bosnians and Croats in the 1990s, Sarajevo, a predominantly Bosnian city, came under siege by Serbian forces and suffered much damage. Sarajevo was once again a focus of international attention, a symbol of strife in Europe.

Saturday night massacre   President Richard Nixon's abrupt dismissal on Saturday night, October 20, 1973, of Archibald Cox, the special Watergate prosecutor who had insisted that Nixon release the tapes of Oval Office conversations. On the same night, Attorney General Elliot Richardson resigned rather than fire Cox. Then Nixon fired William D. Ruckelshaus, the deputy attorney general, who also had refused to fire Cox. That left Solicitor General Robert H. BORK to do the actual firing of Cox.

The term is now used to connote the threat of arbitrary, wholesale firing.

saved by the bell   When a boxer is knocked down by his opponent in a boxing match, he is allowed 10 referee counts to get on his feet without assistance. If he cannot arise unassisted at the count of 10, the bout is ended and he is declared "out"—the loser. If, however, the gong sounds before the referee has counted 10, the boxer is said to be "saved by the bell."

In general use, being "saved by the bell" means to be rescued just in time from trouble or disaster by some unforeseen, unanticipated, lucky incident or interference.

Savonarola, Girolamo (1452–1498)   An Italian reformist preacher who became the scourge of Florence. Born in Ferrara, he joined the Dominican order and was called to the monastery of San Marco in Florence. He began to preach sermons of such fiery eloquence that he gathered thousands of followers. He exhorted them to rid themselves of "vanities" and he started great bonfires into which they tossed cards, dice, ornate clothing, paintings. With terrifying zeal he unearthed hidden vices and subtle heresies, and he taught people to spy upon and denounce each other.

After the fall of the Medicis, he gained political power. He became the virtual ruler of Florence. When he attacked Pope Alexander VI for "scandalous" practices at the papal court, he incurred that potentate's implacable vengeance. The pope ordered him to stop preaching. When Savonarola refused, the pope excommunicated him for disobedience. Savonarola denounced the pope. The city was torn by warring factions and riots. Eventually Savonarola was arrested, tortured into confessing, convicted of heresy and hanged in a public square.

Although Savonarola appears to us today to have been an evil figure givern to fanaticism, he won many adherents in his own day, among them Botticelli and the young Michelangelo. An interesting portrait of Savonarola as a healing influence was drawn by George Eliot in *Romola* (1863). If he is the more interesting for being controversial, a "Savonarola" in today's usage still is a dangerous zealot.

Sawyer, Tom   The central character of *The Adventures of Tom Sawyer,* a novel by Mark Twain, pen name of Samuel Langhorne Clemens (1835–1910).

The story of Tom Sawyer is Mark Twain's boyhood vividly and lovingly remembered. Actually, Mark Twain once said, he didn't *invent* the story. He *recalled* it.

Tom is a 12-year-old boy endowed with a "wildly romantic imagination and an inordinate love of mischief"—and, not unexpectedly, no tolerance for school and even its most modest demands on his free spirit. So it naturally follows that Tom will play hookey with some regularity and abandon. It follows, too, that when Aunt Polly sentences Tom to whitewash the fence, he will *allow* his young confreres to "help" him for a price. Tom's running away with Huck Finn, his subsequent appearance at his own funeral and finally the enduring and endearing "romance" between Tom and the blonde, blue-eyed Becky Thatcher make *The Adventures of Tom Sawyer* an irresistible story of youth, adventure and puppy love.

"Say it ain't so, Joe"   In the 1919 World Series, the Chicago White Sox were overwhelmingly favored to beat the Cincinnati Redlegs. But it was not to be. Eight Chicago players decided to throw the series by deliberately and uncharacteristically underperforming. The honest bettors lost heavily. The gamblers, who knew about the "fix" in advance, made the proverbial "mint." Most of the corrupt players got about $5,000 apiece.

A year-long investigation revealed who the players were in this sordid, corrupt transaction. The Chicago White Sox emerged with a stigma that remained with them for a long time. They were, unofficially of course, called the Chicago Black Sox.

When the players emerged from the grand jury room, a group of admiring young fans were waiting for them. One tearful small boy approached the Chicago centerfielder, Shoeless Joe Jackson.

"It ain't true, is it, Joe?" the boy asked.

"Yes, boys, I'm afraid it is," Jackson mournfully replied.

Crushed, the small boy plaintively looked up at his fallen idol.

"Say it ain't so, Joe."

Never actually proved or disproved, this touching encounter has become an inseparable part of baseball folklore. It remains a moving account of youthful idealism tarnished or destroyed by its awareness of the harsh realities of the real world.

scarlet letter, the An embroidered scarlet *A* (for adultery), which HESTER PRYNNE, the heroine of Nathaniel Hawthorne's novel *The Scarlet Letter* (1850), is forced to wear as a shameful emblem of her sin. She has refused to divulge the name of her lover, the father of her child, and so, in 17th-century Puritan New England, she stands condemned.

The term "scarlet letter" has come to stand as an emblem of sin for anyone pilloried by the public for moral transgression. In our "free" society the term is often used in a spoofing way.

Use: "Ken Starr, with destructive cheerleading from the Christian right, helped turn Republicans into a party of scolds brandishing scarlet letters." (Maureen Dowd, *New York Times*, February 10, 1999).

Scheherazade The superb storyteller of *The Arabian Nights*. Desperately trying to avoid execution by her husband. Scheherazade hits upon the ingenious scheme of starting a suspenseful story each night, leaving the conclusion for the following evening. The sultan is spellbound by these cliffhangers. By the time a thousand and one nights and stories have gone by, the sultan is ready to spare Scheherazade's life.

The tales told by Scheherazade date from the 14th and 15th centuries, perhaps earlier, and are of Persian, Indian and Arabian ancestry. They were collected and published in France by Antoine Galland under the title *Mille et une Nuits* (The thousand and one nights) and included such well-known stories as "Aladdin and His Wonderful Lamp," "Ali Baba and the Forty Thieves" and "Sinbad the Sailor."

A Scheherazade is a spinner of tales, one who holds people enthralled with stories.

School for Scandal, The (1777)   A comedy of manners by Richard Brinsley Sheridan (1751–1816), Irish-born English dramatist. A group of fashionable friends meet regularly at the home of Lady Sneerwell to exchange malicious gossip. Their names reveal their character: Sir Benjamin Backbite, Crabtree, Mrs. Candour, Lady Teazle and Lady Sneerwell herself. They are said to "strike a character dead at every word." Society of their ilk constitutes the school for scandal.

The play itself, using plenty of farcical elements as well as witty dialogue, has a complicated plot in which two brothers, Charles and Joseph Surface, vie for the same girl, Maria, the ward of Sir Peter Teazle. All ends well when Joseph is exposed as a conniving hypocrite, Charles, somewhat impulsive but good-natured, wins Maria, and Lady Teazle, a young flirt, comes to appreciate her generous old husband.

The expression "school for scandal" generally refers to social slander.

Schweitzer, Albert (1875–1965)   A scientist and exemplary figure whose central precept was "reverence for life," he gave up very successful careers as an organist, a scholar and a theologian (he wrote *The Quest of the Historical Jesus* in 1906 as well as a biography of J. S. Bach in 1905) to study medicine. He had determined that when he reached the age of 30 he would devote the rest of his life to serving mankind. He founded the Schweitzer Hospital in Lambarene, Gabon, Africa, to treat the native population. In matters of healing, he became a benevolent despot. The compound at Lambarene became a mecca for all those inspired by Schweitzer's humanitarianism to follow his example in other parts of the world. In 1952 he was awarded the Nobel Peace Prize. His name has become a spiritual symbol, a symbol of dedication to the poor, the ill.

scorched earth   Military policy of a retreating army, to burn and destroy the land and its contents so that a pursuing enemy can make no use of it. This was a recurrent tactic of the Russian army, as it retreated from Napoleon in the 19th century and from the Nazi German divisions in the 20th century.

The term's use has been extended to difficult domestic battles, as in a particularly hostile divorce. You burn your bridges behind you almost out of spite.

Use: "The practice is 'hardball,' and the practitioners talk of 'scorched earth' or 'taking no prisoners' or 'giving no quarter' in advocating a client's cause: 'When I go into the courtroom, I come in to do battle—I'm not there to do a minuet,' was how the lawyer Gerry Spence explained his philosophy in the American Bar Association Journal." (*New York Times,* August 5, 1988)

score   To accumulate "points" in a game or match. In football, the score is expressed as points for touchdown, field goal etc. In baseball, the score is given in runs.

In general usage, to score means to succeed, to win, to triumph.

Scotland Yard The official name of the London Metropolitan Police. The "force" got its name in the following way: During his reign (959–975), King Edgar of England gave a piece of London real estate to King Kenneth of Scotland. Thereafter, when the Scottish kings made their annual visits to London, they lived in this area, officially recognized as a piece of Scotland.

The first English police force (1829) was housed at 4 Whitehall Place. The entrance was from the yard formerly owned by Scotland. So, the London police force was, from the beginning, called Scotland Yard, its present designation even though it moved to the Embankment in 1890. The current headquarters, called New Scotland Yard, is located on Victoria Street.

"Scotland Yard" has become a generic name for any sizable police force, sometimes ironically or humorously.

Scottsboro Boys One of the greatest civil rights battles of the 1930s centered on nine black youths accused of raping two prostitutes. It all started as a fight on a freight train between white and black men. The blacks won and tossed the whites off the train. The two prostitutes remained on the train.

At Scottsboro, Alabama, the authorities stopped the train and removed the black men and the two prostitutes: Victoria Price, 19, and Ruby Gates, 17. The women accused the men of gang rape.

The trial of the Scottsboro Boys (as they came to be known) was marked by widespread hysteria and threats of lynching. During the trial, the defense introduced evidence that the women showed no physical sign that they had been raped. Nonetheless, the all-white jury found the men guilty. Eight were sentenced to death. The ninth (a 13-year-old) was sentenced to life imprisonment.

The verdict was appealed to the Supreme Court, with Samuel Leibowitz, a brilliant New York City lawyer, heading the defense. The Court threw out the original guilty verdict, holding that the defendants were not allowed adequate counsel. A later ruling held that the exclusion of blacks from the jury was unconstitutional. Under pressure, the state eventually dropped charges against four of the Scottsboro Boys—and later placed the remaining four on probation.

The case of the Scottsboro Boys stands as a complex symbol of justice denied/justice triumphant.

Scrooge, Ebenezer The central character in Charles Dickens's novella *A Christmas Carol* (1843). Scrooge is the quintessential skinflint. One Christmas Eve, in his dismal, old house, Scrooge has a dream in which he is visited by three spirits: the Ghost of Christmas Past, the Ghost of Christmas Present, the Ghost of Christmas Yet to Come. The visions the spirits present to Scrooge touch him deeply. He awakens a new man, a convert to a life of kindness, decency and generosity.

A Scrooge is a man from whose soul all vestiges of humanity have been squeezed. Although Scrooge suffers a change of heart and mind, he is remembered mainly as a repulsive miser.

Scud   A Russian-made surface-to-surface missile, capable of carrying warheads of mass destruction, which came into prominence during the Gulf War of 1991 when Iraq launched them against Saudi Arabia and Israel (a noncombatant). Because they were usually launched from mobile launch pads, their attacks proved difficult to preempt. They were often intercepted in midair by allied Patriot antimissile systems, but falling debris caused severe damage and death, especially in urban areas.

A Scud has come to be associated with a hit or miss sneak attack.

Use: "The Reverend Jesse Jackson maintains that many black officials are receiving 'scud missile attacks on their reputations'." (*New York Times,* March 11, 1991)

SDI   Strategic Defense Initiative, also referred to as Star Wars. A comprehensive laser cover over the United States to knock out any incoming Soviet atomic missiles before they can land. This massive military project was ardently sponsored by President Ronald Reagan. It threatened to upset the existing balance of terror called Mutual Assured Destruction (MAD), which was credited by many as having prevented nuclear war. The Soviet Union understandably balked at this so-called "peace" program and it was eventually dropped. However, in 1999 the program was again proposed by Congress as a defense, not against the defunct Soviet Union but against terrorist, outlaw states and organizations. Actual tests of the new antimissile technology were conducted in 1999 and 2000.

Use: "Now that spring is upon us, every gardener should develop his or her own Strategic Defense Initiative. Here's a list of nonlethal safe guards." (Article on animal destruction of gardens, *Metropolitan Home,* April 1989)

search-and-destroy   This term refers to the mission of U.S. patrol units in the Vietnam War to search for pockets of Viet Cong resistance in the jungle and to wipe them out. Now used for any such mission, as in fighting drugs or, comically, even in fighting cockroaches and other pests.

second front   "Open up that second front" became a rallying cry in 1943–44 during World War II for a propaganda campaign in Great Britain and the United States to take the pressure off the Russian armies on the fiercely contested Eastern front. Finally, on June 6, 1944, the Allies launched an amphibious attack on German-occupied western Europe and established a beachhead in Normandy.

A second front is a strategy for dividing an enemy's resources by attacking on more than one front.

send someone to the showers   In baseball and football, this means to remove a player from the game for poor play or for engaging in illegal plays on the field.

In general use, someone who has been dismissed from his position is said to have been sent to the showers.

send to Coventry   A phrase meaning "to ostracize." Although the origin is uncertain, speculation has it that the great cathedral town of Coventry in England was at one time so antimilitarist that any soldier posted there was shunned and completely cut off from any contact with the townspeople.

Sennett, Mack (1880–1960)   Silent film pioneer in the field of slapstick comedy. Founded the Keystone Company using zany actors recruited from vaudeville and the circus: Slim Summerville, Fatty Arbuckle, Mabel Normand, Ben Turpin, Buster Keaton, Chester Conklin, Louise Fazenda and Charlie Chaplin.

A Mack Sennett comedy situation is any sequence of events that is illogical, irreverent, farcical, extravagantly slapstick. Pratfalls, pie-throwing, grotesque physical types and bathing beauties are some of the ingredients. See also KEYSTONE KOPS.

separate but equal   The notion that no discrimination existed if separate but approximately equal facilities were provided for blacks and whites was enunciated by the Supreme Court of the United States in *Plessy v. Ferguson* (1896). This doctrine in effect condoned segregation in schools, restaurants, theaters and transportation. In 1954, the Court reversed itself and unanimously ruled in *Brown v. Board of Education* of Topeka, Kansas, that the doctrine of separate but equal was discriminatory and damaging to the educational development of black children. It ruled that all children were entitled to the equal protection of the laws guaranteed by the 14th Amendment. Therefore, state laws requiring segregation in public schools were unconstitutional.

September Morn   An early 20th-century painting by Paul Chabas, it is a portrait of a young woman bathing nude in a pond. Not a great work of art, it was made into a lithograph designed for a calendar. It achieved international fame as the most famous "pornographic" painting because it was attacked by ANTHONY COMSTOCK, "The great American Blue Nose" and head of the New York City Society for the Suppression of Vice.

When *September Morn* was brought to his attention, Comstock ordered the dealer to remove the "filthy" picture from his window. The dealer refused.

Comstock brought suit. He lost the case. Ironically, in the years following the trial, over 7,000,000 copies of *September Morn* were sold. It still sells.

Sergeant Bilko   Leading character of a highly popular television SITCOM, played for belly laughs by Phil Silvers (1912–65). TOP BANANA on the burlesque circuit, Silvers brightened television with his high-spirited antics. Working with a superb supporting cast from scripts by the not yet famous Neil Simon, Silvers and his company created one of television's zestier comedy classics.

The action of *You'll Never Get Rich* (later known as *The Phil Silvers Show*) takes place on an army base presumably run by Colonel John Hall, played by Paul Ford, whose looks alone produced wild laughter. Actually, however, the scheming, money-hungry, motor pool sergeant Ernie Bilko (Phil Silvers) runs the base. His mind teems with endless harebrained schemes for bilking everyone he meets.

Bilko is the archetypical con man: fast-talking, endlessly inventive, thoroughly, incurably manipulative.

Sesame Street   This pioneering educational television program for children began in the late 1960s.

Sesame Street makes children aware of letters and numbers by using a variety of dramatic and musical techniques, including animation and an unusual combination of live actors and puppets.

Many of the MUPPETS who appear on *Sesame Street* are cherished by millions of adults and children all over the world: Kermit the Frog, the inseparable companions Bert and Ernie, Oscar the Grouch, the insatiable Cookie Monster and, of course, Big Bird, who towers over the whole cast.

Settembrini   See *MAGIC MOUNTAIN, THE.*

Seven Deadly Sins, the   According to St. Thomas Aquinas (1227–75), the great Roman Catholic theologian, there are seven fundamental vices that lie at the root of all sinful acts. These are Pride, Wrath, Envy, Lust, Gluttony, Avarice and Sloth. Committing any of these sins constitutes "purposeful disobedience to the known will of God." St. Thomas considered pride the worst of them. Man's struggle against and his contamination by these sins is a central concept in the Christian religion. They are authoritatively described in St. Thomas's great work, the *Summa Theologica* (1265–74), a full description of God's omnipresence, man's relation to God and the role of faith and reason in man's ultimate salvation beyond this vale of tears.

Seven Dwarfs   Animated cartoon characters in WALT DISNEY's full-length movie *Snow White and the Seven Dwarfs* (1937). The seven dwarfs were named Happy,

Sneezy, Bashful, Grumpy, Doc, Dopey and Sleepy, an assortment of types, but all friendly. They made famous the songs "Whistle While You Work" and "Heigh Ho, Heigh Ho."

Use: In the 1988 Democratic primaries for president of the United States the original contenders were called "the seven dwarfs." They did not seem to have presidential stature and they seemed to be all alike in their programs.

Shakespearean   Suggestive of the work of William Shakespeare (1564–1616), English dramatist and poet, born and buried in Stratford-upon-Avon.

When George Bernard Shaw stated that he had a better mind than Shakespeare, he may have been right, but Shakespeare stands for more than the intellectual brilliance so dominant in Shaw. Nobody has ever been another Shakespeare. He stands alone, Mt. Everest among foothills. But certain qualities of perception, a certain breadth of understanding, an ability to give life to an enormous variety of human characters, a certain grandeur of poetic expression can be said to be Shakespearean.

Shakespeare wrote 154 sonnets in a rhyme scheme known as Elizabethan or Shakespearean: *abab cdcd efef gg.* They are among the greatest poems in the English language. Time, or rather the ravages of time, is their profoundly moving Shakespearean theme.

Shakespeare wrote 36 plays; these were collected and published only after his death in the First Folio of 1623 and in the Second Folio of 1632. They were immensely popular in his lifetime and made him a fairly rich man, but plays were not considered literature then. Among them are comedies, histories, tragedies, problem plays. He created a wide range of memorable characters—Falstaff, Hotspur, Hamlet, Lear, Iago, Shylock, Portia, Juliet, Lady Macbeth and many others. No other writer has so enriched our experience of human nature.

Nor has any other writer given us so many memorable passages of dramatic poetry, rich in psychological insight, expressive of human emotion, and just plain beautiful.

"Shakespearean" alludes to the deepest thoughts spoken by the widest range of characters in the most eloquent and appropriate language.

Shandian   In the manner of *Tristram Shandy,* an unconventional, whimsical novel (1759–67) by Laurence Sterne (1713–68), who was born in Ireland. The narrative, seemingly plotless but full of amusing characters, proceeds not by chronology of events but by association, or rather dissociation and capriciousness of ideas, characteristic more of 20th-century stream of consciousness than of 18th-century fiction.

Furthermore, as in the fiction of James Joyce and in certain modern poetry (e.e. cummings, for example), the printed pages are full of typographical eccentricities and mannerisms: dots, dashes, asterisks, lack of capital letters, unfinished sentences, blank pages, one-sentence chapters. The term "Shandian" usually means digressive, whimsical, with many asides.

Shanghai   One of the greatest shipping ports in the world, Shanghai, China, was the destination of many a vessel that, from the mid-19th century, filled its required component of sailors by kidnapping hapless young men off the streets and out of the bars of Western cities. Press gangs would get these boys drunk or drugged or beaten and drag them off to a ship in need of a crew. Once aboard, they were prisoners of absolute maritime discipline. This practice used to be called "to ship a man to Shanghai." Then it was shortened simply "to Shanghai."

To "shanghai" now means to impress somebody unwillingly into service or an activity of any kind.

Shangri-La   A fictional lamasery situated on a remote and hidden plateau high up in the mountains of Tibet. This tranquil place, isolated from the tensions of the world below, is the setting for *Lost Horizon* (1933), a novel by the British writer James Hilton (1900–54), which was made into a Hollywood movie starring Ronald Colman. Shangri-La is a utopian refuge where nobody grows old.

Sharpeville   Town in South Africa where on March 21, 1960, police fired submachine guns into a crowd of thousands of black Africans demonstrating against the government requirement that black Africans carry identification passes. In what has become known as the Sharpeville massacre, 56 black Africans were killed and 234 protesters against APARTHEID were arrested. The government declared a state of emergency.

Sharpeville became a symbol of South African oppression of blacks in the years of apartheid.

Shavian   Witty and iconoclastic, in the style of George Bernard Shaw (1856–1950), Irish playwright, novelist, critic, essayist, lecturer, reformer. In literature, an admirer of Ibsen; in politics, a Fabian socialist; in language, a would-be reformer of the English alphabet and spelling, Shaw wrote over 50 plays, in which dramatic tension comes from the brilliant clash of ideas via sparkling dialogue; from paradoxical reversals of conventional opinions rather than from the conflict of passions or wills. Among his best plays are *Man and Superman* (1903); *Major Barbara* (1907); *Pygmalion* (1913), which was adapted for the stage as *My Fair Lady;* and *Saint Joan* (1924). The published plays are valued as much for their pungent introductory essays as for themselves. A vegetarian who never drank alcohol, coffee or tea, Shaw lived to the age of 94, a delightful, acerbic curmudgeon to the end.

Use: He writes with insight, humor and a firm grasp of human and Shavian perversity!

Sheen, Bishop Fulton J. (1895–1979)

An auxiliary Roman Catholic bishop of New York who became a radio and TV personality. He was the first evangelist to preach regularly on a radio program, *The Catholic Hour,* in 1930. In 1951 he started a TV ministry with the show *Life Is Worth Living.* His orotund voice, passionate eloquence and mannered, dramatic gestures attracted an audience of 20 million. His views were anticommunist, antiliberal, anti-Freudian, antimonopolistic. He converted many well-known people to Roman Catholicism, including Clare Boothe Luce, Fritz Kreisler and Henry Ford II. He wrote a regular newspaper column as well as almost 50 books.

He became a target of satire because of his over-dramatic, elocutionary manner.

Shelley, Percy Bysshe (1792–1822)

Most people know this English Romantic poet for his excessively emotional lines such as "I fall upon the thorns of life! I bleed." It is easy to parody such intense and often self-dramatizing short lyrics, but Shelley was a poet of noble thoughts and aspirations. Freedom was all to him: freedom from cant, from convention, from dogma, from oppressive governments. He held a high view of the function of the poet: "Poets are the unacknowledged legislators of the world." And he did try to right wrongs with his poems, pamphleteering and active participation in causes. For all that, Matthew Arnold concluded that Shelley was "a beautiful and ineffectual angel, beating in the void his luminous wings in vain."

The term "Shelleyan" sometimes refers to the poet's own physical beauty, but more often to his romanticism or to his passionate advocacy on individual and political freedom. See "IF WINTER COMES."

"shiver me timbers"

An expletive habitually used by Long John Silver, a one-legged ship's cook who assembles the crew for the *Hispaniola* on its search for buried treasure in the novel *Treasure Island* (1883) by Robert Louis Stevenson (1850–94). The hearty cheeriness of the expression belies the brutality of Silver and his pirate crew (Black Dog, Blind Pew, Billy Bones), each of whom seeks to outsmart the other as well as to rob the good guys, Jim Hawkins and Squire Trelawney.

Use: "Avast ye swabs and shiver me timbers. Or is it timber me shivers?. . . Something about sea talk makes a landlubber feel like—well, like a landlubber—but I can't resist talking it when I fall under the spell of the smell of the ocean brine." (Russell Baker)

"Shocked! Shocked!" A mock expression of horror and surprise uttered by the police prefect in the film *Casablanca* (1942), Captain Louis Renault (Claude Rains), when he is asked self-righteously whether he knows that illegal gambling is going on in the back room of Nick's Café—something, of course, that he has known and condoned and profited from all along. Often used with exaggerated sarcasm when the obvious is "revealed."

Sholem Aleichem (1859–1916) Pen name of the Russian Jewish writer Solomon Rabinovitch. He wrote in Yiddish and was instrumental in forging the spoken idiom of that language into an instrument of modern Yiddish literature. A master of humor, pathos and folk philosophy, he has been called the Jewish Mark Twain. His tales, rooted in the folkways of Eastern Europe, are read aloud wherever Yiddish is understood.

Sholem Aleichem's best-known creation is Tevye the Dairyman, the protagonist in a series of tales (1894–1916) subsequently adapted and translated for the stage and screen under the title *Fiddler on the Roof.* Tevye lives in a shtetl with his wife and seven daughters. His greatest hope is to arrange good marriages for these girls. But his hopes come to naught. The oldest girl falls in love with and marries a poor tailor. The second daughter falls in love with a young Jewish revolutionary and when he is arrested and sentenced, she accompanies him into exile. The third daughter falls in love with a non-Jew, converts to Christianity, and Tevye is forced to disown her. A fourth commits suicide when her love affair is broken up by the boy's wealthy mother. And so it goes for Tevye.

Throughout the course of these adversities, Tevye, confused and perplexed, carries on gentle philosophical monologues with God, questioning His purposes, methods and wisdom. Tevye is a survivor. He may be oppressed by Cossacks, circumstance, poverty, fate, but he survives by laughing at his own misfortunes.

Sholem Aleichem represents the essence of that special ironic Jewish humor in the face of adversity.

shopping mall A commercial center in which a large number of diverse retail stores, restaurants and entertainments is concentrated. Often, these are connected within an enclosed structure with a central promenade. The shopping mall started as a suburban phenomenon that displaced colorful "Main Street" mom-and-pop shops, but it has gradually invaded the cities as well.

Use: *The Shopping-Mall High School*—title of a book that criticizes schools that offer anything the students want in the way of easy courses, as if they could shop around for the least expensive bargain in credits.

shot heard 'round the world, the On the morning of April 19, 1775, 800 British troops faced 200 American farmers and MINUTE MEN across the bridge at

Concord, Massachusetts. Over the years, the colonists had grown angry and restive under the oppressions that England, their mother country, had laid upon them. So far, no actual armed insurrection had taken place. The British were alarmed by signs of a revolt in the making, so they had come to Concord to seize stores of hidden arms.

Ordered to disperse, the farmers stood their ground. Suddenly, a lone, "unordered" shot rang out, beginning the Revolutionary War. In the battle that followed, the British were routed. In their retreat, they lost 300 men.

Sixty-one years later, Ralph Waldo Emerson (1803–82) wrote the stirring "Concord Hymn" (1836), which begins:

> By the rude bridge that arched the flood,
> Their flag to April's breeze unfurled,
> Here once the embattled farmers stood,
> and fired the shot heard 'round the world.

Today, a shot heard round the world is an apparently small action with far-ranging consequences.

Shylock   The villain who demands his pound of flesh in Shakespeare's *The Merchant of Venice*. As a Jew and a usurious moneylender, he is vilified, spat upon and tormented. Small wonder that his suppressed rage turns to revenge.

As a great dramatist, Shakespeare humanizes the villain and allows Shylock to speak for himself:

> I am a Jew. Hath not a Jew eyes? Hath not a Jew hands, organs, dimensions, senses, affections, passions? If you prick us, do we not bleed? If you tickle us, do we not laugh? If you poison us, do we not die? And if you wrong us, shall we not revenge?

When Shylock rejects a merciful solution offered by PORTIA, the full force of the letter of the law is brought to bear upon him. He loses his ducats, his property and his daughter Jessica, who has eloped with a Christian gentleman. Shylock is a pathetic man at the end, once more tricked, ridiculed and abused.

In modern usage a Shylock is not viewed with any SHAKESPEAREAN sympathy. He is a usurer, a person greedy for money, one who drives a hard bargain.

Siamese twins   Born in Bangkok, Thailand, in 1811, Chang and Eng were physically joined together at the chest by a "short, tubular cartilaginous band." When they grew up, they were taken on a worldwide tour by an enterprising Englishman. They amassed a fortune and settled in North Carolina. The twins died almost simultaneously on January 16, 1874—Chang first, Eng three hours later.

Although, medically, Siamese twins are physically conjoined, the term has colloquially come to refer to any two people who think, speak, behave alike.

Siberia   Remote region in the Asiatic portion of Russia with a sparse population spread out over about 5 million square miles. From the 17th century onward, Siberia was used as a vast penal colony—not only for criminals but also for political prisoners, who were forced to labor in the gold mines, the salt mines and on building the Trans-Siberian Railroad. Great Russian writers from Dostoevsky (*The House of the Dead*) to Solzhenitsin (*One Day in the Life of Ivan Denisovich* and *The Gulag Archipelago*) have portrayed, sometimes from personal experience, the inhuman, brutal conditions of the labor camps in Siberia.

To be relegated to Siberia, in modern usage, is to be cast out, to be exiled to some remote, icy place or condition far from civilized life.

Siege Perilous   See ROUND TABLE; GALAHAD.

silent majority   Term applied approvingly—first by Vice President Spiro Agnew and then by President Richard Nixon—to the vast majority of Americans who did not express their opposition to the Vietnam War in mass demonstrations, draft card burning, marches on Washington, D.C., or in other forms of public activism. The question is, What does the silent majority think?

Silicon Valley   The name comes from silicon wafers used in semiconductor devices. Silicon Valley itself is an area in northern California, south of San Francisco, which has become famous for its concentration of high-technology design and manufacturing companies in the semiconductor industry. Here young geniuses almost overnight built great empires and great fortunes.

silk stocking   Originally a term of disparagement applied to the upper classes, now it largely applies to a high income area.

In the 1700s, when men wore knee britches, only the wealthy could afford silk stockings. More recently, silk stocking has taken on connotations of wealth, snobbery, "spoiled people."

A silk-stocking district is today a privileged area.

Silvers, Phil   See SERGEANT BILKO.

Simple   A folk character—a humorous Everyman—who spoke his mind to generations of black readers through Langston Hughes's weekly newspaper column in

The Chicago Defender. These pieces were gathered into a book called *Simple Speaks His Mind* in 1950.

Simple exemplifies a common man speaking in everyday street language the wisdom that comes from fresh perceptions.

Sinatra, Frank (1917–1998)   American popular singer and actor. At the height of his popularity, Sinatra attracted hordes of hysterical, Sinatra-smitten teenagers. The "Sinatrance" that came over the female adolescents in the 1940s at the sound of his warm, tender, vulnerable-sounding voice turned Sinatra into one of the sociological phenomena of the century—much like the BEATLES.

There is a misguided tendency to dismiss Sinatra as just "the Voice" or "the crooner." He was an accomplished jazz singer as well as a movie and television star. In a career that stretched over more than five decades, he established himself as the preeminent interpreter of classic American popular songs.

Sinbad   A Baghdad merchant in "Sinbad the Sailor," one of the tales in the ARABIAN NIGHTS. He goes on seven voyages to strange places where he has adventures and enriches himself in every one of them. See SCHEHEREZADE.

Sister Carrie   In Theodore Dreiser's realistic novel of the same name (1900), an innocent country girl who goes to Chicago to find work but who discovers that it is much more pleasant to be somebody's mistress. After her first affair with Charles Drouet, a traveling salesman, she forms a liaison with George HURSTWOOD, an affluent manager of a fashionable bar and a married man with a family. She is tricked into running away with Hurstwood, who has stolen $10,000 from the bar. In New York, her star rises as she embarks on a stage career, while Hurstwood sinks lower and lower until he becomes a Bowery bum and eventually commits suicide.

Sister Carrie belongs to the genre of novels concerned with "the young man from the provinces," as Lionel Trilling has called them; only this time it is the young girl from the provinces who makes her fortune in the big city. Carrie is a prototype of the shallow, pretty, ultimately unfulfilled young woman caught up in materialistic dreams of success and quite willing to sacrifice virtue to attain it.

sitcom   Short for "situation comedy," the simplistic, fabulously profitable staple of television programming. Each episode puts its characters into a crisis or series of crises, from which they try to extricate themselves in a half-hour, the usual length of a sitcom episode. The actors and actresses play familiar, recognizable stock characters to which TV audiences relate quickly and easily. The humor is usually basic and obvious, crafted to evoke a predictable, satisfying audience response. The serious, tragic scenes are similarly constructed.

Recent sitcoms have involved the characters in more mature, more real-life problems and solutions, with more complications extending over several episodes—this to build and sustain suspense and interest. Real-life situations are often referred to as sitcoms.

Sitting Bull (1834–1890)   A leader of the Sioux Indians in their struggle for the survival of their lands and their way of life, Sitting Bull (Tatanka Yatanka) taught his people to shun the white man's world and never to sign a treaty that would force them to live on a reservation.

He led his people to the "pristine" Powder and Yellowstone Valleys. There, they found peace and plenty of buffalo. The Indians used every part of the buffalo for food, clothing, decoration, tools.

Westward expansion brought Sitting Bull into conflict with white settlers and the buffalo hunters, hired by the railroads, who systematically wiped out the buffalo herds without which the Sioux were "hungry, homeless, and unemployed."

On June 25, 1876, Sitting Bull fought against the U.S. forces at the Battle of Little Big Horn, site of General George Armstrong Custer's last stand. Sitting Bull escaped to Canada. He returned to the United States (1881) on promise of a pardon. For a time, he toured with Buffalo Bill's Wild West Show.

Eventually the U.S. government, fearful of Sitting Bull's influence, sent a military detachment to arrest him. In a melee outside his cabin, he was killed by one of the military police.

The name Sitting Bull is used as a caricature of the stony-faced, tight-lipped, stoic Indian of myth and legend.

Six-Day War (June 5–11, 1967)   In only six days the tiny nation of Israel won a great victory over the massed armies and air forces of Egypt and its Arab allies, Syria and Jordan. Israeli forces under the command of General Moshe Dayan and Chief of Staff Itzhak Rabin took the holy city of Jerusalem, rolled over the Golan Heights on the north, and swept through Gaza and the Sinai Desert all the way to the Suez Canal. The Israelis found themselves occupying territories four times as large as Israel itself.

The Six-Day War has attained mythical status: David once more defeated the giant Goliath in a stunning reversal of expectations.

$64,000 Question, The   The most-watched of the big-money television quiz shows of the 1950s. Each contestant (a self-declared expert) appeared in an "isolation booth" to sweat out the answers to the questions prepared by the Columbia Broadcasting System's staff. The top prize: $64,000. Successful contestants were allowed to compete until they were stumped, thus increasing suspense.

For years, the quiz shows ran very successfully until a Tennessee preacher on *Lotto,* another quiz show, revealed that he had been fed an answer before he appeared on the show. At a congressional investigation that followed, some contestants testified that they had been given answers before they entered the booth and faked their emotions in the booth. Dan Enright, CBS producer of six quiz shows, admitted on the stand that his quiz shows had been rigged and that some of the contestants had been coached.

The players in this sordid drama suffered public and private degradation. Prominent among them was Charles Van Doren, an instructor at Columbia University and son of Mark Van Doren, a member of the Columbia University faculty. For participating in the rigged quiz show *Twenty-One,* Van Doren lost his jobs at Columbia and at the National Broadcasting System. Ironically, the corporate sponsors who polluted the media and perverted the contestants got off scot-free.

The $64,000 question (sometimes shortened to the $64 question) is any fundamental, vital question the answer to which is crucial to the solution of a problem or the successful execution of a project or enterprise.

skid row   From "skid road" or "skidway," a logger's slippery decline for rolling heavy logs. By extension, an area frequented by loggers, and then an area of cheap hotels, flophouses and saloons for those on the skids (those who are down and out): alcoholics, vagrants, derelicts.

skin you love to touch   One of the most famous advertising slogans, it first appeared in the *Ladies' Home Journal* for May 1911, touting the cosmetic and romantic virtues of Woodbury Soap.

Skokie   Suburb of Chicago, Illinois, and the home of hundreds of survivors of the Nazi concentration camps. The Supreme Court ruled on June 12, 1978, that the National Socialist Party of America (American Nazis) had the right to march through the town. At the last moment, the Nazis, defended by the American Civil Liberties Union, called off the parade in Skokie and held a demonstration in Chicago's Marquette Park instead.

Skokie has become a symbol of the stretching of principles by which freedom of assembly and freedom of speech may be protected under the U.S. Constitution. It has become for many the low-water-mark of the ACLU's defense of civil liberties for those who would destroy civil liberties if they ever came to power.

Sleeping Beauty   Originally *La Belle au bois dormant* (1696), a fairy tale by Charles Perrault (1628–1703) in which a disgruntled old fairy lays a curse on a newborn princess: The child will prick her finger with a spindle and die. A friendly fairy attenuates the curse: The princess will not die but she will fall into a deep sleep for a hundred years. A prince will make his way to her through a forest that will have sprung up around her and he will awaken her with a kiss. And in spite of every precaution, so it happens when the blossoming princess pricks her finger at the age of 15.

Sleeping Beauty has been read as an allegory for the sexual awakening of the pubescent girl. But it may represent in modern usage any awakening, a coming into awareness.

slouching toward Bethlehem   Phrase adapted from "The Second Coming," a poem by William Butler Yeats (1865–1939). Yeats believed in the cyclical progression of history. We are approaching the end of Christ's 2,000-year-old ideal of compassion and forgiveness, and Yeats sees in 20th-century events an adumbration of the evil to come. He has a vision of the Second Coming and asks at the end of the poem:

And what rough beast its hour come round at last,
Slouches toward Bethlehem to be born?

Slough of Despond   A foul, treacherous bog in John Bunyan's (1628–88) allegory, the *Pilgrim's Progress* (1678). Here, Christian, the central character, is unhappily mired on his way to his ultimate salvation, Celestial City. His sins, symbolized by the burden on his back, weigh him down as he wallows in the slough. Help, another character, comes upon Christian, shows him the way out of the slough and sets him on his journey.

In current parlance, to be in a slough of despond is to experience intense emotional depression, to be overcome by a sense of hopeless despair.

smoking gun   Indisputable proof of evidence of a crime. In the WATERGATE scandal (1972–74), President Nixon's tapes of Oval Office conversations turned out to be the smoking gun, the absolute evidence that he had been a coconspirator in the Watergate break-in and in the cover-up of the crime. During the Iran-Contra hearings, no "smoking gun" was discovered to implicate President Reagan in the diversion of funds from Iranian arms sales to the Nicaraguan Contras.

Snake-Pit, The (1946)   Novel by Mary Jane Ward about a girl who becomes mentally deranged and is placed in an insane asylum where she experiences horrifying conditions. It was made into a movie in 1948 starring Olivia de Havilland. The book was a muckraking piece and aroused people to seek more sympathetic treatment of the mentally ill.

The term "snake pit" is used to describe a mental institution or any place or situation that is chaotic, unfeeling, squalid, where people are treated with cruelty or indifference.

Snopes   See FAULKNERIAN.

"Snows of Kilimanjaro, The" (1936)   Short story by ERNEST HEMINGWAY about Harry, a writer who has wasted his talent. Together with the woman who has been keeping him, he goes on safari in Africa, hoping to recapture the discipline of his vocation. But he develops gangrene, and in his delirium, he sees on the summit of Kilimanjaro the legendary frozen leopard, a symbol of death.

soap operas   Radio or television serials (also known as soaps) dramatizing the everyday problems of one-dimensional, stock characters. Generally the programs are sentimental and melodramatic. The "soap opera" name for these programs derives from the soap manufacturers who were their original producers and sponsors. In general usage, soap opera is applied to a melodramatic situation.

Use: She lost her job and her husband left her. Her life is a regular soap opera.

soccer moms   Suburban women whose lives are centered on their children's everyday needs and activities: schooling, extracurricular sports (like soccer), hot lunch programs, day care, health coverage. What concerns them are not the big national or international issues, like campaign finance reform or U.S.–China relations, but the local issues like school uniforms or time out for parent-teacher conferences. In the 1996 presidential election, soccer moms were perceived to be a formidable voting bloc. President Clinton, a master at addressing small, domestic concerns, easily won over the soccer moms. In the ubiquitous public opinion polling mania of today a key question is, What do the soccer moms care about?

Sojourner Truth (1792–1883)   Born Isabella Van Wagenen to slave parents owned by a wealthy Dutch family in Ulster County, New York, she had five children by a fellow slave. Three were "sold away."

In 1827, she escaped slavery and lived with a Quaker family in New York State. There she worked as a domestic, gradually becoming involved in moral reform and religious evangelicism.

Six feet tall, possessed of a powerful voice and an aggressive platform manner, she was a riveting presence when she started preaching in 1843, adopting the name of Sojourner Truth. Essentially an "illiterate mystic," she somehow acquired a great knowledge of the Bible. As an itinerant orator, she attracted large audiences with popular songs and stories and her passionate espousal of abolitionist, evangelical, feminist causes. During the Civil War, she was appointed by President Lincoln to help the "freed men" of the capital by collecting food and clothing for the black regiments.

Sojourner Truth is an eloquent, archetypal figure: the woman fighter for freedom.

–something   A suffix originally added to "thirty" in the television series *Thirty-something* (1987) about a group of friends of approximately the same age, from 30 to 39, who supposedly shared common attitudes, problems and lifestyles. Since then, the suffix has been added to "forty," "fifty" and beyond to indicate the common characteristics of each decade of age.

"Something is rotten in the state of Denmark"   Line from Act 1, Scene 4 of SHAKESPEARE'S HAMLET. Hamlet, Horatio and Marcellus are on the platform of the watch at Elsinore Castle. At the stroke of midnight the ghost of Hamlet's father, as expected, appears once again. It beckons Hamlet to a removed spot. Horatio and Marcellus try unsuccessfully to prevent Hamlet from following. "My fate cries out," say Hamlet, running after the ghost. Marcellus concludes that "Something is rotten in the state of Denmark" as he and Horatio prepare to follow Hamlet.

What is rotten, as Hamlet is soon to hear from the ghost, is that Claudius, Hamlet's uncle, has murdered Hamlet's father, married Hamlet's mother, and now rules as king of Denmark.

The quotation is often used in a bemused or joking way to express a conjecture that something, who knows what, is amiss.

Sonia   The cliché of the prostitute with a heart of gold achieves transcendence in the character of Sonia in DOSTOEVSKY's novel *Crime and Punishment* (1866).

Sonia Marmeladov comes from an abjectly poor family living in a curtained off section of a room in a St. Petersburg tenement. To feed her family she turns to prostitution, but remains pure of heart and full of faith and Christian piety.

When RASKOLNIKOV, sensing in Sonia the nonjudgmental, accepting girl she is, confesses to her his murder of the pawnbroker, she is filled with overwhelming pity for him. "How you must be suffering," she cries. She urges him to confess to the authorities and to do penance for his crime: Only thus will he free himself of his soul-sickness. At the end of the novel she accompanies him to Siberia.

Sonia thinks of herself as a sinner, but actually she is a saint, the very soul of selflessness. Like Dante's BEATRICE, she represents "the divine grace that transcends morality."

Son of Sam   From July 1976 to August 1977, David Berkowitz terrorized New York City. Berkowitz, who signed his letters to the newspapers "Son of Sam," shot

13 young women and men—girls alone or couples parked in cars at night. Six died, seven were wounded. On August 10, 1977, 11 days after he killed Stacy Moskowitz and blinded her escort, Robert Violante, Berkowitz was caught.

Sentenced to a long prison term, Berkowitz announced his plans to sell his "memoirs," which he would write while in prison. The New York State Legislature put an end to Berkowitz's plans. It passed a law forbidding convicted killers from capitalizing on their crimes. Subsequently, 42 states passed similar "Son of Sam" laws.

Sophie's Choice (1979)   A novel by the American writer William Styron (1925–) in which a beautiful Polish Catholic woman, Sophie Zawistowska, recalls how she was forced, immediately upon her arrival at the Auschwitz concentration camp, to choose which one of her two young children should be saved and which one should be consigned to the gas chambers. Of course, it was a paralyzing choice that only a sadistic Nazi could have presented. At the last moment, rather than have both children torn from her, she selects one. Her guilt, her sin, has haunted her ever since, even as the reader meets her years after World War II as a survivor living in Brooklyn.

Sophie's Choice was made into an award-winning movie in 1982 directed by Alan J. Pakula and starring Meryl Streep as Sophie.

Today, a Sophie's Choice is an agonizingly impossible choice, a moral dilemma. For example, an anti-abortion pediatrician who had to decide whether human embryos, which were going to be discarded anyway, should be used for stem-cell research, which had great promise for curing fatal diseases, declared that he probably would vote for the use of the embryos but that he was faced with an agonizing Sophie's Choice.

Sorrows of Young Werther, The (1774; 2nd version, 1787)   An epistolary novel by Johann Wolfgang von Goethe (1749–1832) in the style of *Pamela* (1739) and *Clarissa* (1747) by the English novelist Samuel Richardson.

Werther is an impressionable youth of infinite dreams and longings. He falls in love with Lotte, a girl who prefers a man with a steady income to one with artistic sensibilities. Overcome by his unfulfilled and rejected passions, he kills himself. This rather sentimental novel in the STURM UND DRANG manner started an avalanche of suicides in Germany.

South Bronx   Neighborhood in New York City that has become a symbol of urban blight in the form of poverty, abandoned buildings, drugs and crime.

Use: "entropy—things going from a state of relative order to one of disorder—is the upshot of all natural actions . . . It's what happens when you move into a nice neighborhood and within a few years it turns into the South Bronx." (Judy Jones and William Wilson, *An Incomplete Education*)

South Sea Bubble   In 1710, Sir John Blunt, a British lawyer with a flair for the outré, offered to buy up Britain's national debt in exchange for control of trade in the South Seas and South America. Spain refused to surrender any of its trading facilities to Sir John. Not a whit daunted, Sir John and his operatives used the money they had gotten from potential investors to rig the stock market. To begin with, the venture seemed to grow and prosper, at times rivaling in size the Bank of England, founded in 1694. As with so many "best-laid schemes," Sir John's failed. The speculative mania triggered by inflated stocks contributed to England's great crash in 1720. Thousands of investors were ruined in the ensuing débacle. Sir Robert Walpole's last-minute stock plan provided a partial rescue.

A "South Sea Bubble" is any glamorous-sounding, get-rich-quick scheme that bears within itself the seeds of its own destruction.

Spade, Sam   Famous hard-boiled detective who made his first appearance in THE MALTESE FALCON (1930), a novel by Dashiell Hammett (1894–1961). The book was adapted for the movies three times. The third version, with Humphrey Bogart as the private eye, became a film classic. Sam Spade's milieu is the world of cops and hoods in San Francisco, where he wins the admiration of both sides. He is a man who can take care of himself in any situation. He is tough, tight-lipped, seemingly cynical; but, oddly, he does not carry a gun.

Spanish Armada   In May 1588, King Philip II of Spain launched his "Invincible Armada," a fleet of about 130 ships and 30,000 men, upon what would become a fateful mission: nothing less than the invasion of England and the capture of Queen Elizabeth's throne. Three days after its initial engagement with the British fleet in the English Channel, the Spanish Armada, outmaneuvered by English seamanship, outmanned by Dutch reinforcements, buffeted by storms, went reeling back toward Spain. Only half of the fleet reached home.

The defeat of the Spanish Armada represents one of those stunning and decisive events that mark the shift of power on a world scale. It meant the end of Spain as a dominant nation and the ascendancy of England as a world power.

Spanish Inquisition   See INQUISITION.

spark plug   A device for producing the electrical spark in each cylinder, which starts up a gasoline-powered internal combustion engine.

By analogy, a "spark plug" came to be, in the 1930s, an enthusiastic leader who supplies vital energy and inspiration to any undertaking.

spear-carrier   Someone playing an insignificant, nonspeaking part in a play: simply carrying a spear, standing at attention on stage as part of an entourage or an army.

391

Carried from the theater into current idiom, a spear-carrier is a modest, unobtrusive individual faithfully carrying out his insignificant duties "unhonored and unsung." "They also serve who only stand and wait," as Milton might have said of the spear-carrier.

Spenglerian   See *DECLINE OF THE WEST, THE*.

Spielbergian   Having the qualities associated with the films produced, directed or written by Steven Spielberg (1947–   ), the director of such action pictures as *Jaws* (1975) and *Raiders of the Lost Ark* (1981), as well as fantasies like *Close Encounters of the Third Kind* (1977) and *E.T.* (1982), a film about a lovable creature from outer space. With *Schindler's List* (1993), about the HOLOCAUST, and *Saving Private Ryan* (1998), about World War II, he has embarked on epic films of social consciousness. His films have been blockbusters at the box office.

Use: "The high point is Cymbeline with its Spielbergian supernatural touches (ghosts appearing in dreams, Jupiter descending from the heavens) and robust battles." (Wm. A. Henry III, "London's Dry Season," *Time,* July 18, 1988)

Spillane, Mickey (1918–   )   Creator of the fictional private eye MIKE HAMMER. He belongs to the tough, realistic school of detective fiction, using abrasive diction, violent action and steamy sex. His detective often seems brutally sadistic.

Spirit of '76, The   A painting by the American artist Archibald M. Willard (1836–1918), first exhibited at the 1876 Centennial Exposition in Philadelphia. It is one of the best-known works by an American artist. The familiar figures are a bareheaded elderly man with white locks flowing as he bravely beats a drum; a sturdy young soldier blowing a fife; a boy in uniform beating a drum; and, in the background, marching troops carrying an American flag. The painting is a vibrant symbol of the ideals and aspirations that animated the patriots of the American Revolution.

To invoke "the spirit of '76" is to call upon the past for inspiration and for continued devotion to deep-rooted American ideals and passions.

Spock, Benjamin (1903–1998)   American pediatrician. One of the most influential mass market books ever published, Dr. Spock's *Common Sense Book of Baby and Child Care* (1946) has sold over 30 million copies. Spock liberated parents from the rigid childrearing "advice" of the time. He encouraged them to be kinder, more flexible and to rely on their good judgment and common sense.

Many people blamed Spock and his permissive theories of child-training for the rebellious behavior of youth in the 1960s. Despite these criticisms, Spock still remains a standard guide in the field—the mother's bible on bringing up baby.

As a political activist, Spock was involved in opposing America's role in the Vietnam War.

In the mid-1930s, American mothers were "massively" under the influence of the dogmatic teachings of Dr. Luther Emmett Holt, Jr., professor of pediatrics at Columbia University. Dr. Holt was the author of *The Care and Feeding of Children*, then the unchallenged household authority on the subject. The *New York Times* called the book "the Dr. Spock" of its time.

Spoon River A small fictional village modeled on Petersburg, Illinois, and Lewistown, Illinois, in *Spoon River Anthology* (1915) by Edgar Lee Masters (1868–1950). The anthology contains about 250 free-verse poems in the form of epitaphs or, more precisely, monologues, spoken from the grave with the utmost candor. Sometimes they contradict each other as we read of the same series of events from different points of view. All in all, these life summations reveal the "buried" secrets, the hopes, the frustrations, the pettiness and boredom, the crimes, as well as the satisfactions and even epiphanies of the inhabitants of a small midwestern town. See also WINESBURG, OHIO.

SS (Schutzstaffel) A German term meaning protective echelon, it originally consisted of a few dozen fanatical Nazi Party members who acted as black-shirted personal guards to Hitler and other Nazis. By the end of the Third Reich, they numbered five million and, under Heinrich Himmler, controlled every department of government. A law unto themselves, they were brutal and ruthless "storm troopers," an apparatus for terrorizing the population into submission to Hitler. They later manned the concentration camps and the death camps. The name is synonymous with brutal, inhuman oppressors.

Staël, Mme. Germaine de (1766–1817) A formidable intellectual in her own right, Mme. de Staël was the center of a Parisian salon that attracted some of the most brilliant minds in Europe.

Born Anne Louise Germaine Necker in Switzerland, she grew up in a Parisian household frequented by members of her mother's literary and political circle. Her father was the French minister of finance. At 20, she married Baron Staël-Holstein, a Swedish diplomat. She was forced to leave France several times, once during the French Revolution in 1792, and twice again because of her opposition to Napoleon. She became enamored of German romanticism, wrote *De l'Allemagne,* a comparison between French and German culture to the detriment of the former. The entire first edition (1811) was confiscated as "un-French" by Napoleon's police and she fled to Russia and to England. The book, republished in London in 1813, exerted a great influence on European thought. She also wrote feminist novels, literary criticism and political essays.

Mme. de Staël led an unconventional life. She was involved in many love affairs, including her long and tempestuous relationship with Benjamin Constant, a writer and political philosopher. "Love is the whole history of a woman's life," she said, "it is but an episode in a man's."

Mme. de Staël is an exemplar of those brilliant 18th-century women who through their salons were influential in the dissemination of ideas throughout Europe.

Stakhanovite   From Aleksei Grigorevich Stakhanov (1906–77), a Soviet coal miner who became a hero in 1935 because of his prodigious productivity on the job.

A Stakhanovite is any person who regularly exceeds production quotas and is used as an example to be emulated by the rest of the workers.

Stallone, Sylvester (1946–   )   American film actor and producer who created the immensely popular roles of ROCKY (1976), a prize-fighter, and RAMBO (1982), a tough soldier. Stallone's name has become synonymous with the kind of role he plays.

Use: In an article on summer restaurant-discos: "On a drizzly Tuesday evening, we pull up to the unmarked portals and confront the Stallone Twins poised behind a velvet rope. They are unsubtly informing a couple of casually clad beach combers that they have about as much chance of getting inside as piloting the next space shuttle." (*New York Times,* August 12, 1988)

Standish, Miles   See WHY DON'T YOU SPEAK FOR YOURSELF, JOHN?

star chamber   Originally a room in Westminster Palace that took its name from the gilt stars painted on its ceiling, it was the setting for the trial of nobles too powerful to be curbed by the regular courts during the 14th and 15th centuries. The "judges" were the king's own councilors, who were empowered to use torture to obtain confessions. Under the early Stuarts, King James I and King Charles I, star-chamber proceedings became increasingly arbitrary and tyrannical. In 1641 they were abolished by the Long Parliament.

In modern usage, a star chamber is any arbitrary and oppressive tribunal without a jury.

Star Wars (1977)   Epic space movie directed by George Lucas (1944–   ) about the interplanetary struggle of the forces of good against the forces of evil. At the end, the hero, young Luke Skywalker, blows the Death Star space station, commanded by the Grand Moff Tarkin (and DARTH VADER), into smithereens. Lucas produced two sequels to *Star Wars: The Empire Strikes Back* (1980) and *Return of the Jedi* (1983).

Use: When President Ronald Reagan announced his plans for the development of an ambitious Strategic Defense Initiative (SDI), a laser shield to protect the United States against all enemy nuclear missiles, skeptics derisively dubbed the plan "Star Wars."

Steerforth, James   David Copperfield's handsome, romantic schoolboy friend who turns out to be a cad in Charles DICKENS's novel *David Copperfield* (1850). He seduces and abandons Little Emily, who was already engaged to a simple fisherman, Ham Peggotty, at Yarmouth. Poetic justice is satisfied when Steerforth drowns in a storm at sea just off the coast at Yarmouth; but, unfortunately, Ham dies in the attempt to rescue him.

A Steerforth is a kind of Byronic hero gone wrong.

Stein, Gertrude (1874–1946)   American expatriate writer whose salon in the Rue de Fleurus in Paris became a meeting place for many of the young writers and artists of the "LOST GENERATION," a term she coined. She lived with her companion and factotum, whose name she used for her own *Autobiography of Alice B. Toklas* (1933). An eccentric in her own person and in her work, she stamped her name upon the general consciousness, and not only among the literati. Few people have ever read her work, but everybody supposedly knows her cinematic quirks of style. Sherwood Anderson said of her: "She may be, just may be, the greatest word-slinger of our generation." Her portrait by Picasso is known to all. Picasso's retort to Stein, who upon first viewing the painting complained that it didn't look like her, was prophetic. "It will," he said. And it does! She was opinionated, egotistical, thoroughly convinced of her genius.

In common parlance, Gertrude Stein stands for crazy, incomprehensible, repetitious, disconnected use of language, as well as for eccentricity of manners. See also "ROSE IS A ROSE IS A ROSE."

Stonehenge   This awe-inspiring prehistoric megalithic monument on Salisbury Plain in Wiltshire, England, consists of a great circle (97 feet in diameter) of huge upright stones about $13\frac{1}{2}$ feet tall, supporting horizontal slabs or lintels. Within this circle are two concentric circles of smaller stones, and in the center is an altar-like slab of stone 18 by 4 feet. Nobody really knows precisely where these stones came from, how they were transported, who arranged them in their present position or for what purpose. "The entire structure is oriented toward the exact point at which the sun rises on the day of the summer solstice, and therefore it must have served a sun-worshiping ritual." (H. W. Janson: *History of Art*). It is possible that Druids used it as a temple to a sun god. Legend has it that Merlin transplanted the stones from Killarans in Ireland, to which place a race of giants had originally brought them from Africa.

Stonehenge is a place of awesome, brooding mystery, of monumental proportions that dwarf mere human size and destiny.

Use: News reports after the hillside fire described "ruins reminiscent of Stonehenge."

Stonewall   On June 28, 1969, police raided the Stonewall Inn, a gay bar in the Greenwich Village section of New York City. The patrons fought back against police brutality and harassment, and their resistance sparked a riot that spilled into the neighboring streets. "Stonewall" has entered the popular lexicon as the event that ignited the gay and lesbian civil rights movement, or, as Frank Rich of the *New York Times* referred to it, its BUNKER HILL. Thirty years after this defining event, in June 1999, the Stonewall Inn was listed as a landmark on the National Register of Historic Places. Every year in late June a gay and lesbian pride march along Fifth Avenue commemorates the uprising. Similar celebrations take place throughout the United States to demonstrate that homosexuality is no longer "LOVE THAT DARE NOT SPEAK ITS NAME."

stonewall   For his stubborn resistance to the Union Army at the First Battle of Bull Run, Thomas J. Jackson (1824–63), a brilliant military tactician and Confederate general in the American Civil War, earned the nickname "Stonewall." His superior officer, General Robert E. Lee, is said to have characterized Jackson's tenacity thus: "There stands Jackson like a stone wall."

At the Battle of Chancellorsville (May 1863), Jackson was fatally wounded by the fire of his own troops who mistook him and his staff for Union officers. Jackson's dying words still resonate in the national memory: "Let us cross the river and rest in the shade."

Today, "to stonewall" has acquired somewhat pejorative meaning: to stall, to refuse to cooperate. In the Watergate scandal, the conduct of several of the guilty officials was characterized as stonewalling—in effect, obstructing justice.

Stradivarius   A violin, viola or cello made by violin maker Antonius Stradivarius (1644–1737). A pupil of the great Niccolo Amati, he soon surpassed his master. The violins he made, often called Strads, represent violin-making at the peak of perfection. Over the centuries, many gifted violin makers have tried, in vain, to imitate Stradivarius.

Stradivarius's peerless achievements span the period from 1666 to 1737. He made his last violin in 1737, the year of his death. Several hundred of the 1,116 instruments he created still survive, about half of them in the United States. They are still much prized and sought after.

The name Stradivarius has come to mean excellence of the highest order. To say, for example, that the new Rolls-Royce is the Stradivarius of automobiles is to pay it the highest possible tribute.

strategic bombing   Saturation bombing of an enemy target, not only to knock out a military or industrial installation, but also to strike terror into and cause demoralization of the civilian population, as in the bombings of Schweinfurt, Dresden, Rotterdam during World War II. Saturation bombing was used by the U.S. Air Force against North Vietnam, devastating entire areas but without the intended effect of reducing morale.

straw man   Literally, a dummy stuffed with straw and dressed in man's clothing to look like a man, as in a scarecrow set up in a field to frighten the crows away.

Metaphorically, a straw man is an argument attributed to, but not actually held by, one's opponent in debate so as to avoid the real point of contention. A straw man is a clever fallacy in logic and argumentation.

strike out   In baseball, a player strikes out (or is struck out) when he swings at and misses three pitched balls; does not swing at three pitched balls that pass through the "strike zone"; or hits a foul ball for the first and/or second strike and then misses for the second and/or third pitch.

Thus, to strike out means "to fail"—in baseball, and in informal usage, too.

Use: "Were you able to get any concessions from Abernathy?" "Not a thing," replied the negotiator. "Struck out."

Stroheim, Eric Von (1885–1957)   A film actor and director born in Austria, Von Stroheim immigrated to the United States in 1913 and moved to Hollywood, where he became "the man you love to hate" in war films. As an actor he played the stereotypical Prussian general, with a German accent, straight spine, bald head, monocle, high polished boots and clipped, barking speech.

As a director he made films exposing the decadence of the pre–World War I Austro-Hungarian Empire.

Sturges, Preston (1898–1959)   Movie writer-director who revived the slapstick tradition and coupled it with satire. Among his films are *Hail the Conquering Hero* (1944), about a 4F army reject (Eddie Bracken) who is mistaken for a war hero and becomes the object of hero worship in his home town, and *The Great McGinty* (1940), the tale of a crooked politician who meets his Waterloo in the performance of a single honest deed.

Sturm und Drang   German for "storm and stress," this was a late 18th-century German literary movement that took its name from *Die Wirrwarr; oder Sturm und Drang* (1776), a play by F. M. von Klinger. Perhaps the outstanding example of this genre was *The Sorrows of Young Werther,* an influential early novel by Goethe, in which a sensitive, gifted young man, rejected by a girl with bourgeois values, commits suicide.

Sturm und Drang, essentially a revolt against classicism, became part and parcel of the Romantic movement that swept across the entire European continent in the 19th century. With its emphasis on the individual passions, its exaltation of sensibility and intuition above reason, it led inexorably to the phenomenon of the BYRONIC hero.

Sturm und Drang is a phrase often used to describe the stage of adolescence, a period marked by emotional turmoil, rebellion against authority, defiance of conventional modes of thought and behavior, and the absolute conviction of one's own uniqueness. *Sturm und Drang* now refers to any time of turbulence in the life of an individual, such as a mid-life crisis.

Stutz-Bearcat   Named after Harry Clayton Stutz (1876–1930), a U.S. car manufacturer, it was the sports car of the Roaring Twenties, the Jazz Age.

Sullivan, Edward (Ed) **Vincent** (1902–1974)   A sports reporter for the racy, sensation-mongering *New York Graphic* in the 1920s, Sullivan signed on with the *Daily News* (1932) as a Broadway "gossip"—the *News*'s answer to the unique Walter Winchell.

In 1948, Sullivan started a weekly TV show, eventually called *The Ed Sullivan Show.* It ran for 23 years. Rather awkward and nervous in speech and manner, not especially telegenic, full of mannerisms and malapropisms—by all standards *not* a showman—Sullivan managed to produce and to present the most popular variety show on TV. The acts ran the gamut from Shakespeare to the Beatles, from trained dogs and cats and ventriloquists to Elvis Presley and grand opera stars. The *Ed Sullivan Show* launched many a career in show business.

Sunday, Billy (1863–1935)   William Ashley Sunday was an American evangelist born in Iowa who turned the old-time revivalist camp meetings into a three-ring circus with parades, marching bands, large choirs and audience participation. Having sown his wild oats in his youth and having started out as a professional baseball player with the Chicago White Stockings (1883–90) before he got religion, he was able to pepper his fiery sermons with colorful colloquialisms. He inveighed against drinking, gambling, whoring in a "degenerate, God-forsaken gang you call society." His revivals were attended by millions of Americans who enjoyed his ranting and clowning. Naturally, he made a fortune. After 1920 his popularity waned as more sophisticated fundamentalists entered the field.

Superman   *Superman,* "the quintessential comic strip," first appeared in June 1938 as a comic book. Superman is now part of American mythology, embodying three major themes or clichés. First, he is a visitor from another planet, the doomed Krypton. Threatened with death in infancy, he is launched to Earth by his wise and powerful father. Second, he is a superhuman being. He can fly limitless distances. He can leap tall buildings. No bullet can penetrate him. In time, he acquires X-ray vision. Third, he has dual identity. Superman's alter ego is Clark Kent, a humble reporter on the *Daily Planet,* devoting his life to fighting for "truth, justice, and the American way." When evil "rears its ugly head," Clark changes into his Superman costume and sallies forth to subdue or eradicate it. After each such mission, Superman again becomes Clark Kent, "mild-mannered reporter."

Superman is a symbol of extraordinary physical strength and power. He decides what is good and what is evil. He acts on his judgment, recognizing no higher authority. Superman is omnipresent and omnipotent.

The character of Superman has appeared in all the major media: radio, movies, animated cartoons, TV, even a Broadway play.

survival of the fittest   See DARWINIAN.

Susann, Jacqueline (1921–1974)   American author of the best-selling, blockbuster novels *Valley of the Dolls* and *The Love Machine,* each of which sold millions of copies. Susann offered an escape for the average housewife into the glamorous worlds of show business and the media where sex, money and power are the driving forces. These spun-out novels, akin to gossip columns, are easily accessible to the reader because of their easy, fast-paced narrative style and their ample use of dialogue.

A Jacqueline Susann type of novel is essentially a phenomenally successful soap opera between covers.

Svengali   Central character in George du Maurier's novel *Trilby* (1894). Svengali is a dedicated Austrian musician, physically unattractive and with a malicious personality to match. When Trilby O'Ferrall, the heroine of the novel, meets Svengali, she is an artist's model and an indifferent singer. At first repelled by Svengali, whom she regards as a "spidery demon," she soon succumbs to his hypnotic spell. Under his tutelage she becomes a famous singer; but when not under Svengali's influence, she sings wretchedly. When Svengali dies of heart failure, Trilby loses her voice, sickens and dies too.

A person who through sheer force of personality exercises control or influence over others is called "a Svengali."

sweetness and light   Although this phrase first appeared in Jonathan Swift's preface to *The Battle of the Books* (1697), in which he stated that the two noblest things of mankind are sweetness and light, it was the English poet and critic Matthew Arnold (1822–88) who made the phrase a cornerstone of his critical work. In *Culture and Anarchy* (1869), Arnold stated that the two things a culture should strive for are "sweetness" (moral righteousness) and "light" (intellectual truth): "He who works for sweetness and light united, works to make reason and the will of God prevail." He thought that the culture of his time was dominated by "Hebraism" (moral fervor and rigidity) and that it needed to be balanced by a greater element of "Hellenism" (sweet reason and the recognition of things as they are).

Arnold's phrase has become debased in common contemporary usage. It is often used to suggest a saccharine quality and carries a touch of sarcasm.

Swiftian   Resembling the point of view and style of Jonathan Swift (1667–1745), one of the foremost prose satirists in the English language, especially as evidenced in his masterpiece, GULLIVER'S TRAVELS, and in his political pamphlet *A MODEST PROPOSAL.*

Satire may take very mild, good-natured forms, as in the novels of Jane Austen and the witty plays of Oscar Wilde. But in Swift's work, satire turns savage with outrage and misanthropy. Swift directs his withering scorn and disgust against the political and religious institutions of 18th-century England and then against the very nature of man, whom he sees as deformed, brutish, avaricious and depraved YAHOOS. Yet the first two sections of *Gulliver's Travels* ("A Voyage to Lilliput" and "A Voyage to Brobdingnag") have often been published separately as children's books because of their fairy tale–like fantasies and their comic inventiveness. Children do not detect and, of course, could never understand Swift's irony.

In the last years of his life, Swift had to be institutionalized because of madness. He wrote his own epitaph: *Ubi saeva indignato ulterius cor lacerare nequit* ("Where savage indignation can no longer lacerate the heart [. . . Turn aside, traveller, and imitate, if you can, the resolute vindicator of human freedom"]).

tabula rasa   Latin for "blank slate." The English philosopher and political scientist John Locke (1632–1704), the father of British empiricism, declared in his "Essay Concerning Human Understanding" (1690) that the mind of every human being at birth is a tabula rasa, upon which personal experience inscribes itself. Only with this experience, which comes through the senses, can one reason.

Some people's talent for forgetting the unpleasant is so great that they can be said to start each time from a tabula rasa.

Taj Mahal   A mausoleum at Agra, India, built from 1630 to 1648 by the Mogul emperor Shah Jahan to commemorate his love for his wife, Mumtaz Mahal, who died in 1629. An exquisite example of Islamic architecture, the domed, minareted white marble building seems weightless as it seemingly floats and shimmers in the oblong reflecting pool before it. Set within a walled garden with fountains and cypress trees, it invites peaceful contemplation.

The Taj Mahal has become the ultimate example of architectural splendor, elegance and airy beauty, as well as a monument to love.

take the Fifth   To seek the protection of the Fifth Amendment to the Constitution of the United States. (The first 10 amendments collectively are known as the Bill of Rights.) The Fifth Amendment reads in part: No person "shall be compelled in any criminal case to be a witness against himself."

The phrase "to take the Fifth" was often invoked by witnesses called to testify in 1954 before the House Un-American Activities Committee, presided over by Senator Joseph McCarthy. The hearings were held to investigate communist infiltration into government and the media. Witnesses often refused to testify on the grounds that they might be incriminating themselves.

More recently, in 1987, Lt. Col. Oliver North took the Fifth. He refused to testify about his activities as a member of President Reagan's National Security Council until the Senate and House panel on Irangate granted him limited immunity from prosecution.

Although taking the Fifth is a perfectly legal, constitutional right, invoking it suggests, perhaps erroneously, that the witness has something to hide.

In popular or jocular use, it means to refuse to answer a question for fear of self-incrimination or embarrassment.

taken for a ride   This is a criminal underworld euphemism for being murdered, coined in the Chicago bootleg wars of the early 1920s. The victim was usually taken in a car driven by the individual who was charged with "rubbing" him out. The actual murder was committed by the "hit man" or "trigger man" hidden in the back of the car. It was he who shot the victim in the back of the head or neck.

The Chicago gangster Hymie Weiss is alleged to have called this method of disposing of one's enemies a "one-way" ride. Now, when someone is taken for a ride, he is tricked into something, cheated or swindled.

take no prisoners   The exact origin of this phrase is hard to trace. In ancient times, the victors in war held the right of life or death over their captives. It was common practice to take them home as slaves. During the Middle Ages, wealthy prisoners of war were held for ransom. What was done with prisoners of the lower classes was not regulated. In many cases, they were exchanged. In all ages, brutal military commanders on the march have been known to have prisoners killed rather than provide for them. Not until the 1929 Geneva Convention did the international community subscribe to a set of rules governing the treatment of prisoners of war. The International Red Cross, a neutral organization, is empowered to determine whether these rules are being enforced. There have been and still are serious lapses.

"Take no prisoners" means give no quarter, show no mercy, kill everything in sight. The phrase is now applied not only to military tactics but also to ruthless business, legal, and political operations.

Talleyrand (1754–1838)   His full name was Charles-Maurice de Talleyrand Périgord. Although he was born and died in Paris, he lived for a short time in exile in England and the United States. A consummate master of diplomacy, he managed to wield power under a bewildering succession of diverse governments in France: the ANCIEN RÉGIME, the French Revolution, Napoleon, Louis XVIII and the July Revolution. He represented his country at the CONGRESS OF VIENNA (1814–15) so skillfully that one might have thought France to be a victorious power rather than a defeated one. His abiding policy was aimed at the peace and stability of Europe as a whole.

Talleyrand is the prototype of the manipulative, successful diplomat, always a controversial figure: saint or sinner, patriot or traitor, according to one's point of view. Henry Kissinger is a kind of Talleyrand of recent times.

Tallulah   Tallulah Bankhead (1903–68) was a flamboyant American actress famous for her low, husky voice and racy language. A beauty from an aristocratic Alabama family, she starred in many Broadway plays, including *Dark Victory* (1934), *Rain* (1935), *The Little Foxes* (1939) and *The Skin of Our Teeth* (1942). She was one of the wits at the Algonquin Round Table.

When one calls a woman "Tallulah," it is because of the woman's unusually deep voice and her salty stevedore's vocabulary.

Talmudic   Like the Hebrew Talmud; given to intense study, examination and interpretation of any given rule, law or text. The term "talmudic" is sometimes used derisively to mean quibbling, overly legalistic, hair-splitting.

The Talmud, codified in the fourth to sixth centuries, consists of two parts: 1) Mishna, the text of the Oral Law of the Jews, derived mostly from the Pentateuch; and 2) Gemara, the commentary on the Mishna by various scholars, teachers and rabbis. One of the most influential of these commentators was the French-born Rashi (1040–1105), known for the exactness and the clarity of his exegeses.

Tar Baby   A character in a tale from *Uncle Remus: His Songs and Sayings* (1880) by Joel Chandler Harris (1845–1908). The narrator is Uncle Remus, an aging black man full of warm humor, not at all the stereotypical "devoted slave." He is talking to a small white boy in what Harris presents as a transcription of black plantation speech derived from the original African. Actually, both the characters and their speech were largely "invented" by Harris, a humorist, journalist, writer of short stories and novels, one of the prominent representatives of the "local color" school in the 1870s and 1880s.

In "The Wonderful Tar Baby" story, Brer Rabbit, ambling down the road, spots a doll held together with tar. The doll had been skillfully constructed by the prankster Brer Fox, who is not overly fond of Brer Rabbit. Brer Rabbit, in a genial mood, starts a conversation with the Tar Baby. Receiving no response, he tries again and again. Finally, he strikes the Tar Baby, with predictable results: His paw sticks to the Tar Baby. Angered and frustrated, Brer Rabbit begins thrashing around, trying to free himself. The more frenetic his efforts, the more tenaciously the Tar Baby sticks to him—first to one paw, then to the other, and then to both his legs, until Brer Rabbit is immobilized.

To come up against a Tar Baby is to find oneself inextricably involved with an unwanted situation, something one can't get rid of. The more one struggles, the more deeply enmeshed one becomes.

Tartar   Originally, a member of a Mongolian tribe who fought under GENGHIS KHAN when he overran Asia and much of eastern Europe during the Middle Ages.

Tartars achieved the same reputation for savagery as their leader. Today, to be a tar-tar is to be stubborn, ill-tempered, even tyrannical.

Tartuffe The central character in Molière's comedy *Tartuffe* (1664), he is a pious hypocrite whose name has become a symbolic word in the French language. He cons the gullible Orgon into deeding his property to him in advance of his marry-ing Orgon's daughter. When Orgon discovers Tartuffe's lechery, he orders him out of the house. But Tartuffe now owns the house and evicts Orgon and his family. In the end, all is set right as Tartuffe is exposed as an impostor and hauled off to jail.

A Tartuffe is a sanctimonious hypocrite, an impostor, a humbug.

Tarzan The hero of the jungle in a series of stories by Edgar Rice Burroughs (1875–1950). The son of an English noble, he is abandoned in the jungle and reared by apes. He learns the language of the animals, marries an American girl named Jane and has a son. Burroughs's stories were translated into 56 languages, adapted into a comic strip and used in many movies.

"Me Tarzan, You Jane" is a phrase derived from a movie version and is often used to connote inarticulate, primitive reactions.

Teapot Dome Political scandal during President Warren G. Harding's adminis-tration (1921–23), over the leasing of navy oil reserves to private oil companies; it was not exposed until after Harding's sudden death in 1923. One of the reserves was called Teapot Dome, in Wyoming; another, Elk Hills, was in California. Secretary of the Navy Edwin Denby resigned from office. Secretary of the Interior Albert B. Fall was convicted of accepting a bribe of $223,000 and was sentenced to jail for a year. The Supreme Court voided the leases.

Teapot Dome has become synonymous with scandal in high government office, equaled only by Watergate and Iran-Contra.

Teddy Boy Any post–World War II, rebellious British teenager who affected Edwardian costume. By the 1960s the Teddy Boys were in competition for disaf-fectedness with the "Mods," the "Rockers" and the "Punks." Gang fights along the King's Road in London were not uncommon.

Teflon A thin plastic coating of tetrafluoroethylene applied to industrial machine surfaces to reduce stress, it was later applied to cooking utensils to render them non-stick. Called the slipperiest substance on Earth, Teflon was discovered by the DuPont chemist Dr. Roy Plunkett in 1938.

As applied to human beings, teflon has come to mean slippery, immune to blame or responsibility, as in *Teflon president.*

Temple, Shirley (1928–   )   Blonde, curly-haired, appealing little girl who sang and danced her way into the hearts of moviegoers all over the world. She was one of the most popular stars of the 1930s, outranking even GRETA GARBO. *Little Miss Marker* (1934) was one of her best-known films.

Tess of the D'Urbervilles (1891)   The subtitle of this novel by Thomas Hardy (1840–1928) is *A Pure Woman*. Tess Durbeyfield is an innocent girl led by malevolent circumstance to have a child out of wedlock (she was seduced by Alec D'Urberville), to be abandoned by the good but self-righteous man she truly loves and marries (Angel Clare) and to end up being hanged as a murderer (of her persistent tormentor, Alec).

Tess is portrayed as an honest, compassionate, hardworking girl motivated by the desire to help her poverty-stricken family. From Hardy's point of view, Tess is much more sinned against than sinning. She remains pure of heart in spite of the terrible fate that befalls her. Hardy ends his novel thus: "Justice was done, and the President of the Immortals, in Aeschylean phrase, had ended his sport with Tess."

Tess is a portrait of the victimized woman.

Thatcherism   The policies as well as style of governing associated with Margaret Thatcher (born Margaret Hilda Roberts in 1925), Conservative prime minister of Great Britain from 1979 to 1990. She was the first female prime minister in England's history and the only one in 160 years to be elected for an unprecedented third term. During her governance she was considered the most powerful woman in the world.

As head of the Conservative government, she aimed to remove most hallmarks of the welfare state introduced by previous Labour governments: She curbed the power of the trade unions by breaking the miners' strike in 1984. She privatized government control of the gas, electricity, water and telecommunications industries. She sold over a million municipal homes to their tenants. She instituted a poll tax to replace local property taxes, thus breaking the power of the municipal councils. She championed a free-market economy and in foreign policy she steadfastly and vigorously opposed communism.

Her grand and ultimate goal was to restore the former glory of Great Britain among the nations. Her popularity, which during her first term had been waning as a result of her domestic policies, surged when she triumphantly sent an armada to reclaim the Falkland Islands from Argentina in 1982.

Her autocratic intransigence, haughty aloofness, absolute self-confidence and indomitable will earned her the nickname of the "Iron Lady." It was a sign of respect as well as of fear and hatred. On November 22, 1990, she was forced to resign after the defection of three of her cabinet ministers. Two years later she was elevated to the peerage as Baroness Thatcher of Kesteven.

Theater of the Absurd   A revolutionary departure from the well-made play, it seeks by new forms to express the meaninglessness of the human condition. Theater of the Absurd rejects the conventions of traditional drama: plot, resolution of crisis, developing characters, a well-defined theme and rational dialogue. It does not hold the mirror up to nature but creates, instead, the atmosphere that dreams, or rather nightmares, are made of. It is not a self-conscious school of drama with a manifesto or purpose. It happened that at a certain time in 20th-century history individual playwrights began to express their sense of isolation, their sense of loss of all integrating values. They perceived that we are all strangers in a strange land where God is dead and reason is dead. In their anguish they wrote savage, bitter, often mordantly funny plays attacking hypocrisy, conformity and spiritual sterility.

Among the playwrights associated with Theater of the Absurd are Samuel Beckett (Irish), Eugene Ionesco (Romanian), Jean Genet (French), Harold Pinter (English) and Edward Albee (American). They wrote, respectively, *Waiting for Godot* (1952), *Rhinoceros* (1959), *The Balcony* (1956), *The Caretaker* (1960) and *The American Dream* (1961).

Thelma and Louise   A feminist road movie (1991) analogous to the male buddy movie *Butch Cassidy and the Sundance Kid*. Two friends, Thelma (Geena Davis) and Louise (Susan Sarandon), get away for what they plan to be a two-day vacation from their daily routines as a housewife and waitress, respectively. On the way, they come afoul of the law when they decisively get rid of a male sexual predator. A police chase follows. The two women, driven to further crimes in their getaway, begin to feel a heady exhilaration in their newfound freedom as outlaws. At the end, they gun the accelerator of their car over a cliff rather than face a return to everyday life or actual imprisonment. *Thelma and Louise* has become a symbol for getting even with men.

"there is no joy in Mudville"   "There is no joy in Mudville—mighty Casey has struck out" is the wrenching last line of that immortal baseball ballad "Casey at the Bat" (1888) by Ernest L. Thayer.

Here, in brief, is how it happened on that unforgettable day:

> *The outlook wasn't brilliant for*
> *the Mudville nine that day.*
> *The score stood four to two*
> *with but one inning more to play.*
> *So when Cooney died at second*
> *and Burrows did the same,*

A pallor wreathed the features of
The patrons of the game.

With defeat almost a certainty:
Flynn lets drive a single
to the wonderment of all
And Blake the much despis-ed
tore the cover off the ball.
There was Jimmy safe at second
and Flynn a-hugging third.

Radiating confidence, the mighty Casey stepped up to the plate, to the delighted roar of thousands in the stands: Casey would save the day. But the dirge-like mood of the last line tells it all.

Use: The day after the New York Yankees lost the 1963 World Series (October 7, 1963), the *New York Herald-Tribune* carried the following headline: "The Mighty Yankees Have Struck Out."

"These are the times that try men's souls"   In the fall of 1776, General George Washington's tattered, demoralized army was in retreat from the British. Desertions were increasing and lack of confidence in the leaders of the Revolution was everywhere. At this low point, Thomas Paine, a British immigrant and member of Washington's forces, decided to address an appeal to his dispirited fellow soldiers. So, it is said, by the light of a campfire, he wrote "The American Crisis No. 1," which first appeared in the *Pennsylvania Journal* of December 23, 1776.

The ringing opening lines were "These are the times that try men's souls. The summer soldier and the sunshine patriot will, in this crisis, shrink from the services of their country, but he that stands it now, deserves the love and thanks of man and woman."

These stirring words continue to rally beleaguered men in desperate moments.

"They also serve"   The last line of "On His Blindness," a sonnet by the English poet John Milton (1608–74), reads: "They also serve who only stand and wait." Although Oliver Cromwell was the military and political leader of the Puritan revolution, John Milton was its impassioned spokesman. In pamphlet after pamphlet, Milton championed the rights of the common man as opposed to the divine right of kings. He wrote on liberty, on divorce, on freedom of the press. He worked, as he saw it, for a great cause in his function as Latin secretary to the Council of State during the Protectorate.

But he was hindered by poor eyesight. Eventually he became blind and even had to be read to by his rebellious daughters. In the poem, quoted above, he asks, "Doth God exact day-labor, light denied?"

Patience replies,

God doth not need
Either man's work or his own gifts, who best
Bear his mild yoke, they serve him best. His state
Is kingly: Thousands at his bidding speed,
And post o'er land and ocean without rest;
They also serve who only stand and wait.

In modern usage the phrase applies to those who loyally perform their duties, no matter how lowly, with good faith and modest demeanor. See SPEAR-CARRIER.

Thimble Theater   See POPEYE.

third degree   Police use of torture, brute force, psychological manipulation, intense and prolonged questioning, to extract confessions from suspects. Subjected to the "third degree," many suspects confessed to crimes they hadn't committed, or implicated innocent people. The rich and influential were rarely, if ever, subjected to the third degree. That was reserved for the poor, the friendless, the ignorant.

Within recent times, the Supreme Court's MIRANDA DECISION has sharply reduced the use of the third degree.

Now, "third degree" has acquired broad meanings such as: a severe rebuke from one's superiors, a "bawling out" or "chewing out," a searching interview full of sharp, probing questions.

third rail   Besides the two rails along which a train travels, for electric trains there is often a third rail, adjacent and parallel to them, which supplies the electric current to the engine through "contact shoes." Anyone unfortunate enough to come in contact with the third rail, either through accident or a criminal act, would be instantly electrocuted. The third rail is therefore a feared and fatal danger point.

Use: "Social security has been considered the third rail of politics. Touch it and you're dead." (Sam Donaldson, *David Brinkley Show*)

third world   Developing, usually poverty-stricken nations of Africa, Asia and South America. Now often used to describe the poor, the uneducated and the unemployed minorities within a developed society, as in "We have a third world nation inside America, growing radically poorer, more violent and more hopeless as the rest of America gets its BMW's."

Thomas à Becket (1117–1170)   The story of Thomas à Becket's friendship with King Henry II, their subsequent quarrels over the supremacy of church or state, the martyrdom of Becket at the inadvertent instigation of the king, and the king's penance at the cathedral of Canterbury are the stuff of high drama. Indeed, high drama has been fashioned of this material, as in *Murder in the Cathedral* (1935), a verse play by T. S. Eliot.

Henry II appointed Becket royal chancellor in 1155, and in 1162 he appointed the reluctant Becket archbishop of Canterbury. He did not anticipate that Becket would drop his roistering fellowship with him and assume the serious responsibility of his new office; namely, defending the prerogatives and liberties of the church against the encroachments of the Crown. Exasperated by Becket's adamant resistance, Henry is said to have blurted out, "Who will free me of this turbulent priest?" Four of Henry's knights thereupon traveled to Canterbury and murdered Becket inside the cathedral.

In 1173 Thomas à Becket was canonized, and his tomb in Canterbury became a shrine for pilgrimages. It is to Canterbury that CHAUCER's pilgrims wend in *The Canterbury Tales.*

A Thomas à Becket is known as a martyr for his strong and incorruptible beliefs.

Three Mile Island   Nuclear power plant in Middletown, Pennsylvania, where on March 28, 1979, an accident exposed some 36,000 people living within five miles of the plant to a slight increase of radiation (two to eight millirems). The facility, owned by General Public Utilities Corporation, was closed down. Widespread fear led to an investigation of the rules and procedures governing nuclear power plants and of the Nuclear Regulatory Commission in charge of them.

Three Mile Island has become a code name for all those opposed to the construction and operation of nuclear power plants. These people fear a recurrence of accidents and claim that no orderly evacuation of nearby residents is possible. See CHERNOBYL.

Three Musketeers, The   (1844)   A novel by the French writer Alexandre Dumas père (1802–70). Set in 17th-century France, it deals with the exploits of d'Artagnan, a swashbuckling Gascon, and his three comrades in arms: Athos, Porthos and Aramis.

The novel opens with D'Artagnan's arrival in Paris. He is dashing, romantic, an expert duelist with a zest for intrigue and adventure who wants to enter the famous corps of King Louis XIII's musketeers. His first encounter is with Porthos, Athos and Aramis, musketeers in the service of the king. In peace they are his bodyguards. In war, they serve the regular army.

D'Artagnan's brilliance as a duelist wins the admiration of the three. Subsequently, when he becomes one of the musketeers, he utters the now famous declaration: "And now—all for one, one for all. That is our motto, is it not?"

The Three Musketeers has become a symbol of a special kind of friendship grounded in loyalty, affection and common concerns.

three-ring circus   The term originated with the merger of P. T. Barnum's "Greatest Show on Earth" and James Anthony Bailey's Circus. The Barnum and Bailey Circus boasted three rings in which three separate acts appeared simultaneously. Colloquially, a three-ring circus means confusion and noise arising from too many activities going on at the same time, as in a farce.

throw a curveball   In baseball, a pitch thrown in such a way that the ball will spin to the right, the left or downward. The curveball is usually more difficult for the batter to hit than is the straight ball.

In general parlance, being thrown a curveball is being given something difficult to deal with, something unexpected, something embarrassing, being caught off guard.

throw in the towel   In boxing, a boxer's trainer or seconds may concede that he is beaten by throwing a towel into the ring. This is done to keep the badly hurt boxer from suffering further injury. In practice, the referee usually stops the match when he feels that the boxer has been decisively beaten and can no longer safely absorb his opponent's blows. He names the opponent as winner by a technical knockout.

In general usage, to throw in the towel is to admit one is beaten, defeated.

Thurber, James (1894–1961)   American writer and cartoonist who caught the popular imagination with a series of cartoons called "The Battle of the Sexes" for *The New Yorker*. The woman, gigantic, always loomed over her timid, self-effacing husband in a menacing way. Somewhere in the picture was a big dog, also dwarfing the husband. No captions were really necessary.

Use: The bride and groom were the embodiment of a Thurber cartoon: she Amazonian, he shrunken. Only the ubiquitous dog was missing. See also MITTY, WALTER.

Tiananmen Square   Huge plaza in Beijing, China, where, in the early morning hours of June 4, 1989, the 27th People's Army massacred hundreds of unarmed students who had been demonstrating since April 18 for democratic political reforms like freedom of speech and freedom of the press.

The students' marches into the square, their hunger strikes, which evoked sympathy from the workers, their heroism in the face of tanks and troops who at first disobeyed orders to fire at them, brought the country to the brink of civil war. Zhao Ziyang, the Communist Party general secretary who wanted to negotiate with the students, was forced out. Hardliners Li Peng and Deng Xiaoping won out. Martial law was declared on May 20. Army units from the provinces rolled into the capital to clear the square.

After the carnage, student leaders were hunted down, arrested and executed or imprisoned as "counter-revolutionaries." The government propaganda machine tried to mask its brutality, but the BIG LIE did not work, since millions of people all over the world had watched on TV the events in Tiananmen Square.

"Tiananmen Square" has become a term associated with a totalitarian government's savage massacre of unarmed demonstrators for democracy.

Tiffany   Ultra-swank Fifth Avenue store in New York City. Tiffany stands for luxury, the highest quality, the best.

tilting at windmills   Fighting against imaginary foes or injustices. The phrase comes from one of the most absurd episodes in DON QUIXOTE. Under the delusion that 30 or 40 windmills in the distance are giants, Don Quixote, his lance raised, charges against them to "sweep so evil a breed off the face of the earth." His lance gets caught in one of the sails and he and his horse, Rosinante, are lifted up into the air. They crash to earth with nothing for their pains but pain. So much for chivalric adventure!

Timbuktu   Founded in 1087, this city in Mali, the former French Sudan in western Africa, was once a center of Muslim trade and culture, renowned for its gold and slave market. In 1591 it was ransacked by a Moroccan army; thereafter it deteriorated, until it was just a mass of ruins when the French occupied it in 1893.

Today, Timbuktu stands for any remote, strange place.

Times Square   The crossroads of Manhattan at 42nd Street and BROADWAY, the hub of the theater district, site of huge neon advertisements, the square where throngs gather every December 31st to welcome in the New Year. Once a center of prostitution, pornography and crime, Times Square has in recent years undergone a facelift and a cleansing.

Synonymous with the bustle and activity of great crowds.

Tinker to Evers to Chance   In the early 1900s, Joe Tinker, Johnny Evers and Frank Chance were known as the "peerless trio" of the Chicago Cubs baseball team.

They were all superb infielders and great hitters, but they won their place in baseball's Hall of Fame for their legendary ability to execute double plays. The frequent appearance of DP (double play) in the box scores of the day made "Tinker to Evers to Chance" a part of the American language. It has now come to mean any successful maneuver or operation involving the deft, highly coordinated effort of several individuals—that is, excellent teamwork.

Tinkertoy   A child's toy consisting of detachable wooden wheels and spokes that can be easily assembled into various shapes.

It has come to mean something with interchangeable parts that can be readily disassembled and reconstructed.

Use: "Nations are not Tinkertoys to be pulled apart and reassembled casually." (George Will, *Newsweek*)

tin lizzie   Generally, the nickname for a Model T Ford. Now, any broken-down, shabby but still serviceable car.

Tin Man   Character in L. Frank Baum's novel *The Wonderful Wizard of Oz* (1900).

Dorothy discovers the Tin Man as she travels along the YELLOW BRICK ROAD on her way to see the wizard. She persuades him to accompany her. He is stiff and rusted, but some squirts of oil from an oil can enable him to move. He is hollow and has no heart. As played by Jack Haley in the movie, he sings, "I could be human if I only had a heart." At the end he discovers that he does indeed have a heart when he sheds tears because of Dorothy's imminent return to Kansas.

Tobacco Road (1932)   Novel by the American writer Erskine Caldwell, dramatized in 1933 by Jack Kirkland and made into a film in 1941. Jeeter Lester, the main character, and his family are sharecroppers and what used to be called "poor white trash." They live in squalor and degradation on Tobacco Road in Georgia. Their degenerate antics shocked, amused and titillated wide audiences.

Tobacco Road has become synonymous with squalid and morally obnoxious conditions among the rural poor, especially in the South.

"To be or not to be"   That is the question that occupies HAMLET in his soliloquy of act 3, scene 1. In this speech the melancholy Dane ruminates on the existential question of suicide.

What is interesting about the phrase "to be or not to be" is that it is used allusively not so much for substance (that is, the problem of suicide) as for form. The neat, succinct, balanced opposition invites parody. So that we may be reminded of Hamlet's great soliloquy by something as trivial as: to eat or not to eat an ice-cream cone. When Mario Cuomo, former governor of New York, agonized like a "Hamlet on the Hudson" about becoming a candidate for president in 1992, the media paraphrased his indecision as "To run or not to run."

toe-to-toe   In boxing, when the boxers face each other and continue to exchange punches, making no effort to defend themselves. The purpose of this apparently unplanned exchange is to land as many damaging blows as possible on each other.

In general use, hostile, unyielding confrontation or opposition.

Use: The meeting started out peacefully enough, but before long, the participants discarded the rules of civilized discourse and went at each other toe-to-toe.

Tokyo Rose   Alias for Iva Togori, born in Los Angeles, who broadcast daily appeals from a radio station in Tokyo to GIs in the Pacific theater of World War II to desert the armed forces. She was arrested on September 8, 1945, in Yokohama and tried for treason.

The term Tokyo Rose is applied rather sneeringly to subversives because Tokyo Rose was so ineffectual.

Tolstoyan   Relating to the life, ideas and literary works of Count Leo Nikolaevich Tolstoy (1828–1910), considered by many critics to have been the greatest novelist who ever lived. In scope and magnitude of action, in realization of character, in exploration of human emotion and intellect, in unobtrusiveness of style, in great-heartedness of moral attitude, he is a giant. What one ultimately comes away with from reading Tolstoy is the stunning yet sober realization that this is life itself.

His masterpieces include *War and Peace* (1865–69), an epic novel of three families set against the background of the Napoleonic Wars; *Anna Karenina* (1873–77), a novel of the tragic love of Anna and Vronsky set against the normal life of Levin, Tolstoy's protagonist and most autobiographical character; *The Death of Ivan Ilyich* (1884), a novella written with such psychological insight and nuance that seemingly only a man come back from death could have written it.

Tolstoy's life reads like a Tolstoy novel. It parallels the life of Levin in *Anna Karenina*. Levin's experiences in the real world are contrasted with the glamorous, all-else obliterating, self-destructive passion of Anna and Vronsky. The woefully shy, stammering Levin woos and eventually marries Kitty, a pretty girl from a generous, open family. (Kitty has lost Vronsky to the more dazzling Anna.) He retires with her from the corrupt society of the upper classes in Moscow and St. Petersburg to the comparative tranquility of his country estate. Here Levin devotes himself to domestic problems with wife and children, to working on the land with the peasants, to developing theories about social and political reorganization, to figuring out his relationship with God, and the very meaning and purpose of life. Like Tolstoy himself, Levin experiences a spiritual conversion. Like Tolstoy, he wishes to divest himself of all property by dividing it among the peasants. The last sentence of the book reads: "Now my life . . . regardless of anything that may happen to me . . . is not only not purposeless as it used to be, but has the unmistakable purpose of goodness that I have the power to provide to it."

Tolstoy became a cult figure in Russia and, indeed, in the world. As a pacifist, he had a profound influence upon the young Gandhi, who corresponded with him. He ran into fierce opposition only at home, where his wife fought to protect the property rights and royalty rights for their 10 children.

Tombs, the   Built in 1838, this New York City prison has been rocked by scandals from its beginning: mistreatment of prisoners; unsanitary, crowded conditions; inadequate security; escapes. A second Tombs was built in 1905. It shortly acquired the same kind of bad name as the first Tombs.

To compare any prison facility to the Tombs is to place it in the lowest possible category.

"Tomorrow and tomorrow and tomorrow"   The first line of a cry of despair uttered by Macbeth in act 5, scene 5 of Shakespeare's tragedy.

Macbeth's world has crumbled: "I am in blood / stepped in so far, that, should I wade no more, / Returning were as tedious as go o'er." He has murdered again and again to cover up his original murder of King Duncan and to protect his ill-gotten crown. He has come to realize the ambiguity of the witches' prophecies, which have given him a false sense of invulnerability, and he has just received word that his wife, Lady Macbeth, who had been the spur to his ambition, has committed suicide. With extreme bitterness he projects his disgust with his own deterioration onto the very condition of man:

> *Tomorrow and tomorrow and tomorrow,*
> *Creeps in this petty pace from day to day,*
> *To the last syllable of recorded time;*
> *And all our yesterdays have lighted fools*
> *The way to dusty death. Out, out, brief candle!*
> *Life's but a walking shadow, a poor player,*
> *That struts and frets his hour upon the stage*
> *And then is heard no more; it is a tale*
> *Told by an idiot, full of sound and fury,*
> *Signifying nothing.*

"Tomorrow and tomorrow and tomorrow" is used to express the ennui, futility and meaninglessness of life.

Tonio Kröger   Main character in *Tonio Kröger* (1903), a novella by the German writer Thomas Mann. Within him we find personified a recurrent theme in Mann's works and in his personal life: the conflicting claims of his artistic and bourgeois heritage. The sensitive Tonio Kröger, a writer who has always felt isolated and set apart, longs for the vitality, the animal spirits, the everyday commonplaceness and the comradeship enjoyed by the burger types around him. Kröger realizes that *they* are the true inspiration for his writing.

Toonerville Trolley   The most famous "character" in Fontaine Fox's comic strip, *Toonerville Folks* (1915). The Toonerville Trolley was unforgettable: tall, angular, equipped with an interior stove and a smokestack and a twisted antenna, traversing miles and miles of twisted country track.

The colorful, irascible skipper—with cap, spectacles and beard as unruly as his temper—is the "living adjunct" of the Toonerville Trolley.

Until fairly recently, Americans relied heavily on the trolley for surface transportation within cities and towns. When a trolley or trolley line went to its final rest, the residents frequently mourned its demise as "the passing of our Toonerville Trolley."

In the 1950s, Fox folded the real Toonerville Trolley with all its colorful passengers and villagers.

Fox's Toonerville Trolley has entered our language as any aging, aged, broken-down, erratic, uncomfortable, yet fondly regarded public transportation.

tooth fairy   A fib told to nursery age children who are persuaded that the tooth fairy will exchange a tooth left under the pillow for a coin. This is a compensatory tale for all the gaps little children must suffer as their baby teeth fall out.

The expression "the tooth fairy" is commonly used today in referring to childish nonsense.

top banana   The leading comedian in musical comedy, vaudeville, burlesque. By extension, the chief executive officer, the most important individual in a group, a business or any undertaking.

Use: It didn't take Farrell too long to become top banana in the newly-organized steel company.

Topsy   Mischievous little black sprite in Harriet Beecher Stowe's novel *Uncle Tom's Cabin* (1851). Topsy's upbringing as a slave child has made lying and stealing her normal behavior pattern. She remembers nothing of her family or origins. "I s'pect I growed," she says. "Don't think nobody ever made me."

Thus, a "Topsy" grows, matures, flourishes, without any apparent care or attention.

Torquemada, Tomás de (1420–1498)   A Dominican monk, he was appointed an inquisitor in 1482 by Pope Sixtus IV. By 1483, he had become grand inquisitor, charged with centralizing the activities of the INQUISITION. With merciless zeal, he hunted down those he hated and distrusted the most: the Maranos (Jewish converts to Catholicism) and the Mariscos (Moorish converts to Catholicism).

In a period noted for its fanatical pursuit of "heretics" and other nonconformists, Torquemada stands out as one of the most ruthless prosecutors and torturers. Under his malevolent administrations, about 2,000 innocent souls were executed.

Torquemada also played a key role in the expulsion of 200,000 Jews from Spain in 1492.

Torquemada has become a symbol for cruelty incarnate: a man, driven by almost maniacal determination to rid his religion and his society of what he sees as threats to purity and stability.

touch base   In baseball, the player who has hit the ball must touch each base in sequence: 1st, 2nd, 3rd, home plate. If he touches each base and home with one hit, he has hit a home run. If he doesn't hit a home run, he must either physically touch the base his hit has taken him to or in a position to touch base when he is approached by a member of the opposing team. If he is tagged by an opposing player while he is not touching the base, he is "off base" and hence "out"—and must leave the field.

In general use, to touch base means to make contact with or keep in touch with, confer with.

Use: During the campaign, Matlock touched base with every voter group in town.

town and gown   Two groups of inhabitants of a college or university town, the "town" representing those not connected with the university and "gown" representing those who are. Traditionally this mix has given rise to resentment and friction. The town residents are supposed to be less intellectual, less educated, less sophisticated. They consequently are hostile and resentful, finding the university group snobbish, aloof and generally richer, too. The juxtaposition can lead to confrontations.

In recent times, however, the town and gown people have learned to live peaceably together—at least superficially. "Town and gown" is a symbol for the resentment and clash between the intellectual haves and have-nots.

Tracy, Spencer (1900–1967)   U.S. movie actor who projected a craggy, strong, upright, self-sufficient image with natural good humor, as in *Captains*

Courageous (1937), *Boys' Town* (1938), *Bad Day at Black Rock* (1954) and *The Old Man and the Sea* (1958). Tracy made memorable film comedies with KATHARINE HEPBURN.

trench warfare   From 1915 on, both Allied and opposing German forces dug in on the Western Front. World War I was in many ways a war of attrition with both sides fighting bloody battles for patches of land, advancing and retreating to their trench positions. Between the opposing lines of trenches was a NO-MAN'S LAND, the land of crossfire.

trial balloon   Originally a helium- or hydrogen-filled balloon launched to test weather conditions in the atmosphere. In modern usage, a trial balloon refers to the tentative launching of an idea or project in the media to test public reaction or opinion. For example, when Daniel Patrick Moynihan of New York announced his intended retirement from the Senate, a trial balloon was launched by Democrats suggesting that Hillary Rodham Clinton might be a possible successor.

Triangle Fire   On Saturday, March 25, 1911, fire raged through the top three floors of a 10-story factory building at the corner of Washington Place and Greene Street in New York City. Within half an hour, 146 workers of the Triangle Shirtwaist Company (mostly young Jewish and Italian immigrant girls) died in the flames or died leaping from windows, their clothes and hair ablaze. Charred bodies littered the pavement below.

This traumatic disaster galvanized the movement for reform of sweatshop conditions in the garment industry. The Triangle Fire remains a symbolic warning against indifference to sweatshop violations that threaten the lives of exploited workers.

trickle-down theory   President Ronald Reagan's economic policy in the 1980s of encouraging production by cutting taxes was referred to as the trickle-down theory. Supposedly the flood of advantages to the rich would trickle down to the poor in the form of more jobs and more income. But Reagan balanced decreased revenues from the rich with decreased social expenditures on housing, hospitals and education for the poor. Thus, the expression often is used ironically to describe a system in which the rich become richer and the poor become poorer.

triple threat   In sports, a player who is efficient or outstanding in three skills as, for example, a football player who can run, kick and pass—or, in baseball, a pitcher who can pitch, hit and steal bases.

In general, a triple-threat person is master of three disciplines in the same or separate fields.

Tristan and Isolde   Two doomed lovers in a Celtic romance of 1185 that has continued to inspire poets and composers to the present day.

Tristan (sometimes spelled Tristram) is sent to Ireland to bring back Isolde (sometimes spelled Iseult) as a bride for his uncle, King Mark of Cornwall. On the return voyage, Tristan and Isolde unwittingly drink a magic love potion and fall helplessly in love. When Mark discovers their liaison, Tristan flees to Brittany. There, in a vain attempt to escape his inescapable passion, Tristan marries another Isolde, Isolde of the White Hands. When Tristan is dying of a poisoned wound, he sends to Cornwall for Isolde, who he knows has healing powers. A white sail is to be the signal of her approach. Tristan's wife, jealous, reports untruthfully that a black sail has been hoisted. Without hope now, Tristan dies, and Isolde, arriving too late, commits suicide.

Richard Wagner composed soaring music for his opera *Tristan and Isolde* (1865), based on the German version of the tale (1210) by Gottfried von Strassburg.

Tristan and Isolde are prototypes of tragically enmeshed lovers, whose passion can be appeased only by death.

troglodyte   A prehistoric man who lived in caves. The earliest mention of the troglodytes occurs in the work of Pliny (A.D. 23–79), a Roman historian and naturalist.

Today, "troglodyte" is applied to individuals who act or think in a coarse or primitive manner; degraded, brutal. See CRO-MAGNON MAN; NEANDERTHAL MAN.

trump card   In card games such as bridge, whist, pinochle, a trump card—that is, a card within the suit that won the bid—will prevail over all other cards. For example, a low trump card like a two will win over even the highest card, like an ace, in any other suit. Sometimes a trump card is produced unexpectedly and triumphantly to take a set.

In areas outside card games, playing a trump card is often a surprise move with decisive consequences: "The defense won its case by playing its trump card at the last moment: a surprise witness who confessed to having committed the crime himself."

In *Crime and Punishment* by Dostoevsky, the detective Porfiry is interrogating the suspect Raskolnikov. He urges Raskolniknov to confess to the murder of the old pawnbroker and her sister. Should his efforts at persuasion fail, Porfiry plans to produce his trump card, sequestered in an adjoining room: a house painter who actually saw Raskolnikov at the scene of the crime.

Turner, Nat (1800–1831)   A slave leader who saw himself "divinely appointed" to free his fellow slaves, he led a revolt of about 60 slaves in 1831. Before the insurrection was put down, 55 whites had been killed. Sixteen slaves were caught and hanged; Turner escaped, but six months later, he, too, was caught and hanged. The aborted insurrection led to more tyrannical slave laws.

Turner, despite his abortive efforts, remains a symbol of liberation.

William Styron's *Confessions of Nat Turner* (1967) is an eloquent portrayal of Nat Turner.

Tweed, ("Boss") William Marcy (1823–1878)   Starting as a mechanic in the New York City municipal work force, William Marcy Tweed became the unchallenged "boss" of the Democratic Party's powerful political machine at Tammany Hall. As such, he exerted wide control over contracts, patronage, appointments and the choice of candidates for political office. Tweed was the master of all the known tools of curruption: kickbacks, faked invoices, padded bills, bribery of officials. It is estimated that Tweed and his "associates" bilked the city treasury of between $50 million and $300 million.

For a time, Tweed seemed untouchable. But finally, a combination of Samuel Tilden, a future governor, the *New York Times* and Thomas Nast's *Harper's Weekly* political cartoons of Tweed and his fellow predators, rallied law enforcement officials and succeeded in jailing Tweed for larceny and forgery. He escaped jail and fled to Spain; was caught and returned to New York City where he died, unmourned, in the Ludlow Street Jail in 1878.

For massive greed and corruption, Tweed and Tammany Hall have few equals in American history. They have come to stand for unbridled corruption.

Tweedledum and Tweedledee   Characters in *Through the Looking Glass* (1865) by Lewis Carroll, they are two fat little men, identical in appearance, who live in the same house and echo each other's pronouncements. The expression, however, seems to be of earlier coinage. It was first used about 1715 to mock Giovanni Bonancini and George Frederic Handel, two rival composers (the verb "tweedle" meaning to make a shrill, high-pitched sound).

Tweedledum and Tweedledee are two identical persons or repetitive ideas. They evoke a response of boredom, since there's nothing to distinguish between them. In Friedrich Duerrenmatt's sinister play *The Visit* (1956) Claire Zachanassian, out of revenge for their having borne false witness against her, has two men blinded and reduced to an impotent pair, a Tweedledum and a Tweedledee who echo each other's words.

Typhoid Mary   Mary Mallon (1870–1938), an Irish-born cook employed in a home in Oyster Bay, Long Island, New York, was suspected of being a typhoid carrier as early as 1904. She ran away from the authorities and was not captured until 1907. She spent almost all of the rest of her life confined in Riverside Hospital on

North Brother Island, New York City. She herself was immune to typhoid but she transmitted the disease (through her handling of food) to at least 50 people.

Today, a "Typhoid Mary" is anyone who is suspected of being a carrier of anything unpleasant, harmful or even disastrous; therefore, someone who is to be shunned. Most often the term is used jocularly, as when one pretends to shrink from a person who may have been employed by two companies that went bankrupt.

$$\mathcal{U}$$

"Ugly Duckling, The"   A story by the Danish writer Hans Christian Andersen (1805–75) about a duckling who stands out from the rest of a duck's brood because he is ugly. All the ducks attack him. He runs away and one day finds himself among three swans who accept him as one of their own. He discovers that he is a swan, a beautiful swan, not a duck.

An ugly duckling is a misfit who grows up to be perfectly acceptable.

Uncle Tom   The central character in Harriet Beecher Stowe's novel UNCLE TOM'S CABIN (1851). He is the "noble slave," sold to a series of slaveowners and beaten by his master, Simon Legree. Through all his sufferings and degradations, he maintains an almost Christlike demeanor.

The expression "Uncle Tom" has come to suggest a black lackey willing to bear any kind or amount of humiliation to remain in the good graces of whites.

Uncle Tom's Cabin (1851)   When President Lincoln met Harriet Beecher Stowe (1811–96), the author of *Uncle Tom's Cabin,* he said, tongue in cheek, of course, "So you're the little lady who wrote the book that caused the great war."

Actually, Mrs. Stowe had not intended to beat the drums for the Civil War. The Civil War would have come anyway. She wrote *Uncle Tom's Cabin* to reveal the horrors and cruelties of slavery, as seen through the suffering of slaves and especially a saintly old slave, Uncle Tom, who dies at the hands of Simon Legree, his sadistic overseer.

Uncle Tom's Cabin made a profound difference in the way people all over the world thought and felt about slavery.

United Nations   An international peacekeeping organization founded after World War II, with headquarters now in New York City. Its charter was drafted at Dumbarton Oaks in 1944 and ratified on October 24, 1945. By 1998 the number of member countries was 185.

In colloquial use, the United Nations connotes variety and heterogeneity, more in its composition than in its peacekeeping function. Looking at a schoolroom containing black, white, Asian and Hispanic children, one might say, "Why, it's a regular United Nations."

Untouchables   Nine incorruptible, unbribable agents assembled by Eliot Ness (1903–57), head of a special Prohibition unit, to fight the Al Capone gang of bootleggers in Chicago in the 1920s. Dubbed "The Untouchables" by the underworld itself, their adventures formed the basis of a TV series and then of a 1987 movie, *The Untouchables,* with Kevin Costner as Eliot Ness.

Up the Down Staircase   On November 11, 1962, the *Saturday Review of Literature* published a modest little story, "Up the Down Staircase." The author, Bel Kaufman, granddaughter of SHOLEM ALEICHEM, after some difficulties had finally landed a job as teacher of English in a New York City high school.

The story was composed of scraps of paper found in a teacher's wastebasket. Ironically, those papers told a story of "chaos, confusion, cries for help, bureaucratic gobbledygook, and one teacher's attempt to make a difference in one child's life."

In 1963, Prentice Hall published an expanded version of the story as a novel under the same title. An instant, international success, it brought fame and fortune to its author. It was translated into many languages.

The "Up" and "Down" in the title refer to stairwell signs designed to facilitate the orderly movement of students throughout the school day. The title, now a part of the language, has become a metaphor for going against traffic or bucking the system.

upper   A drug (e.g., amphetamines) that stimulates and provides a temporary feeling of exhilaration or elation.

By extension, "upper" has come to mean a pleasant, stimulating experience, condition or set of circumstances or events.

Upstairs, Downstairs   Enormously popular British TV series that traced the fortunes of an upper-class family and their servants through the first few decades of the 20th century. Lord and Lady Bellamy and their son and daughter represent the upstairs contingent; the butler, the cook, assorted maids, chauffeurs and governesses represent the downstairs contingent. All inhabit the same town house on Eaton Place in London. Both groups are bound by the respective privileges, duties, responsibilities, manners and even linguistic differences of the British class system. Both groups are affected not only by domestic affairs but also by such public events as the sinking of the *Titanic,* the suffragette movement and World War I. The entire series is marked by consummate acting, riveting plot development and absolutely authentic settings.

Weekly episodes ran for four years on Masterpiece Theatre (Public Broadcasting System in the United States). Eventually the series was seen by about one billion people in 50 countries.

"Upstairs, Downstairs" has come to be shorthand for class differences.

Uriah Heep   An unctuous, hypocritical clerk in Charles DICKENS's novel *David Copperfield* (1850). Professing himself to be "an 'umble servant" as he subserviently bows his head and wrings his hands, Uriah Heep is secretly embezzling funds from his employer, the solicitor Mr. Wickfield. He has brought Mr. Wickfield almost to the point of bankruptcy and tries to blackmail Wickfield into allowing him to marry Wickfield's beautiful daughter Agnes. With the help of Mr. MICAWBER, Uriah Heep is eventually exposed.

Utopia   Greek for "no place" and the title of a book (1516) by Sir Thomas More (1478–1535), chancellor to Henry VIII, in which Utopia is an island paradise where people and institutions are governed by reason. It is a society without crime, poverty or injustice—free of the social, moral, physical evils of the England of More's time.

Other utopias that have not achieved quite the fame or durability of More's:

Samuel Butler, *Erewhon* (1872)
Edward Bellamy, *Looking Backward—2000–1887* (1888)
H.G. Wells, *Modern Utopia* (1905)

"A utopia" has come to mean any ideal, perfect society. George Orwell's *1984* (1949) and Aldous Huxley's *Brave New World* (1932) deal with purely imaginary but hardly perfect worlds. Bitter, sardonic, frightening by turns, they qualify as dystopias, "utopias in reverse."

$\mathcal{V}$

Valentino, Rudolph (1895–1926) Sinuous, dark and sleek silent screen star, the heart-throb of millions of women, Valentino played the lover in exotic movies like *The Sheik, Blood and Sand, The Young Rajah, Cobra* and *The Son of the Sheik*. Valentino became a cult figure for whom women swooned. He died at the age of 31.

A "Valentino" is a parody of the romantic, exotic, passionate lover, one who exhibits these qualities in excess, an "image of smoldering male sexuality."

Valhalla In Norse mythology, Valhalla is the banquet hall to which the souls of heroes slain in battle were immediately conducted. They were scooped up in the very heat of combat by the VALKYRIES, the beautiful blonde handmaidens of Odin, god of war, wisdom and poetry, and brought to the paradise where they would enjoy eternal feasting, drinking and games of war. The walls of Valhalla were made of gold; and the roof, of warriors' shields. Everlasting life in Valhalla was the inducement, the promise and reward for fearless conduct in battle.

By extension, in modern usage, a Valhalla has become a place set aside for people worthy of special honors, a heaven of sorts.

Valium Trademark for *diazepam,* one of the most widely prescribed medications for stress and anxiety. Now past its 30th anniversary, it has become part of our culture—a sort of metaphor of our high-strung, agitated, hard-driving age. Thus, mellow, popular music has been described as "audio-valium," and columnist John Leonard has referred to the women of New York City's East Side as "the Valium Girls."

Valjean, Jean When the reader first meets Jean Valjean, the hero of Victor Hugo's epic novel *Les Miserables* (1862), he is a bitter and surly ex-convict. He has just spent 19 years as a galley slave for the crime of stealing a loaf of bread to feed his starving family.

Upon his release, Valjean is shunned by everybody except the saintly Bishop Myriel, who gives him shelter in his own home. Valjean repays the bishop's trust by absconding with the silver. When the police catch him with the stolen goods, the bishop insists that the silver was a gift to Valjean. The bishop's act of compassion exerts a profound influence on Valjean. Thereafter, under an assumed name in another town, he leads an exemplary life. But his travails are not over. A fanatical police inspector by the name of JAVERT suspects Valjean's true identity. Many of the complicated events that follow revolve around Javert's unremittingly maniacal pursuit of his quarry.

During a socialist uprising in 1832, Valjean comes face to face with his implacable enemy. Valjean can kill him and be rid of him forever, but he spares his life. This act of mercy affects Javert as deeply as the bishop's act of mercy had affected Valjean. Javert, realizing that his whole life had been based on false premises about "criminals," commits suicide.

A Jean Valjean is a victim of a cruel, impersonal criminal justice system that operates on the principles of punishment and revenge, not of rehabilitation.

Valkyries   In Norse mythology, "choosers of the slain." Brandishing drawn swords and sitting astride swift-flying horses, these handmaidens of Odin swoop down upon battlefields to select the worthiest warriors in order to conduct their souls to VALHALLA.

In Richard Wagner's opera cycle *The Ring of the Nibelungs* the chief of the Valkyries is BRUNHILD, who rebels against Wotan (Odin) and eventually brings about the destruction of Valhalla with her own immolation.

See GÖTTERDÄMMERUNG.

Vance, Philo   Aristocratic young amateur detective created by S. S. Van Dine (1888–1939), a pseudonym for Willard Huntington Wright. A graduate of Harvard and several European universities, Philo Vance has knowledge of all kinds of esoteric subjects, which helps him in his criminal investigations. He is not above lecturing on these subjects in a rather pedantic way. He is an intellectual detective, a sophisticated poseur with a British accent. There are 12 Philo Vance cases, among them *The Benson Murder Case* (1926), *The Canary Murder Case* (1927) and *The Bishop Murder Case* (1929).

Vandals   A Teutonic people from central Europe who began a massive migration southward during the fifth century. These barbarian tribes invaded first Gaul, then Spain, North Africa and Italy, sacking towns and villages, pillaging and looting, preying on ships in the Mediterranean, plundering the shores of Sicily and southern Italy. In 455 they attacked Rome, where they wantonly destroyed irreplaceable works of art and great buildings.

Vandals are barbarians in a modern sense, too. They are guilty of vandalism, destroying or defacing what others have created.

van Gogh, Vincent (1853–1890)   A Dutch painter, he is sometimes called a postimpressionist, like Cezanne and Gauguin, and sometimes a forerunner of the EXPRESSIONISTS. Van Gogh wrote that he exaggerated the forms and rhythms of nature in order "to express . . . man's terrible passions." Many viewers have seen in the thickly applied paint, the bold swirling brush strokes, the frenzied torturous rhythms and the blazing colors of van Gogh's landscapes and self-portraits evidence of the madness that would confine him to an institution and eventually lead him to suicide at the age of 37. His final paintings (*Cornfield with Black Crows, Starry Night, Cypress Road, Wheatfield and Cypress Trees*) vibrate with a force that seems to animate all of nature.

Van Gogh is the archetype of the tortured artist striving to break through mere material paint and canvas into a vision of spiritual faith and meaning.

Vanity Fair   In *PILGRIM'S PROGRESS* (1678) by John Bunyan (1662–88), a year-round fair held in the town of Vanity. The populace is preoccupied with the buying and selling of honors, titles, kingdoms, with a variety of follies, frivolities, lusts and pleasures. Quite appropriately this bazaar of vices, corruptions, sins and temptations is set up by Beelzebub and his assistants.

Any city, country, locality dominated by these motives and emotions rightly earns for itself the appellation of Vanity Fair.

When he wrote his novel *Vanity Fair* (1848), William Makepeace Thackeray (1811–63) obviously had *Pilgrim's Progress* in mind: "What I want to make is a set of people living without god in the world . . . greedy, pompous men, perfectly self-satisfied for the most part, and at ease about their superior virtues."

V-E Day   Victory in Europe, May 8, 1945.

The allies accepted the unconditional surrender of Germany, signed in Rheims and in Berlin. World War II was over in Europe, but not yet in Japan.

velvet divorce   The severance of a marriage or intimate relationship without the usual acrimony and court battle over the division of assets and custody of the children. On January 1, 1993, Czechoslovakia, only 74 years after its birth as a nation, split without any bloodshed into two separate countries—the Czech Republic and Slovakia—a velvet divorce.

Venice   An Italian city built on 118 islets dotting a lagoon in the Gulf of Venice at the northern end of the Adriatic Sea. Its main arteries are not streets but 160 canals crossed by countless bridges, and the main means of conveyance are gondolas, water taxis and *vaporetti* (water buses). It is a unique city, yet other cities have described themselves in tourist brochures as Venices; e.g., St. Petersburg, Russia, is called the Venice of the North, since it, too, has many canals; Bruges is the Venice of Belgium; and Amsterdam can certainly lay claim to being another Venice because of its ubiquitous canals.

Although Venice is a city with an illustrious history, magnificent Renaissance buildings and works of art, it is known chiefly for its physical, geographical features.

Verdun   City in France where the longest single battle in history was fought in 1916 during World War I. In the 10 months the battle lasted, the front line moved less than four miles. Almost a million men were killed, wounded and shell-shocked. Verdun symbolizes the horror and brutality of war.

Vermeer, Jan (1632–1675)   Dutch genre painter whose canvases usually depict a solitary woman sitting in the light filtering in from above through a single window. She is writing or receiving a letter, pouring water from a pitcher, holding a stringed instrument or performing some simple household task. She is rapt in a serene moment. While the interior is boldly broken into geometrical patterns on tiled floors, picture-hung walls, doorways, the figure itself sits realistically rounded and solid.

Verne, Jules (1828–1905)   A popular French pioneer in the genre of science fiction, he wrote tales of adventure that incorporated, for his time, astoundingly prophetic technological inventions. His works include *Five Weeks in a Balloon* (1863); *A Voyage to the Center of the Earth* (1864); *A Trip to the Moon* (1865); *Twenty Thousand Leagues under the Sea* (1870); *Around the World in Eighty Days* (1872). His imagination anticipated the submarine, the landing on the moon and air travel, as well as the exploration of space.

V for Victory   Hand sign using the index and middle finger to form the letter *V.* It was made popular by Winston Churchill during World War II. Actually, the use of *V* was introduced by a Belgian exile in a radio broadcast from London to his native land in 1941. His *V* stood for "Vrieherd" (freedom), but all the allies adopted the *V* for "victory" over the Nazis. It was ubiquitous all during the war, appearing in posters, slogans, V-mail.

The V for Victory hand sign is still used today to anticipate or to celebrate winning, whether in a football game, a political campaign or a personal triumph over adversity.

Viagra   A drug developed and produced by Pfizer, Inc., to counteract ED, erectile dysfunction, or sexual impotence in men. Sales of the expensive pill, which went on the market in April 1998 shortly after its approval by the Food and Drug

Administration, immediately went through the roof, substantially increasing the value of Pfizer stock.

Viagra became the butt of late-night TV jokes, especially after former senator Bob Dole, the defeated Republican Party candidate for president in 1996, announced that he had begun to use Viagra to good effect. Subsequently, Senator Dole became the spokesman in TV ads for Viagra, asserting that a man could show courage not only on the battlefield (as he obviously had done) but on the home front by admitting and confronting his sexual impotence.

In spite of the gravitas of its spokesman, the mention of Viagra is still pretty much accompanied by a wink or a leer. By extension, "Viagra" stands for a needed boost to one's inadequacy in any macho endeavor.

Vicar of Bray, the   A vicar of the village of Bray (Symon Symonds), a highly "adjustable" man determined to "retain his living" under all the religious changes that took place during the reigns of the English rulers: Henry VIII, Edward VI, Bloody Mary and Elizabeth I. So, in his lifetime the vicar twice embraced the Catholic faith and twice the Protestant.

A popular 18th-century song caught the vicar's unswerving determination:

And this is the law I will maintain
Until my dying day, Sir,
That whatsoever King shall reign
I'll still be the Vicar of Bray, Sir!

In current usage, the Vicar of Bray is someone who changes his or her beliefs or affiliations based on political expediency.

Vichy   Collaborationist, fascist government formed by Marshal Henri Philippe Pétain in that part of France not occupied by German troops after Pétain signed an armistice with Germany on June 22, 1940. Vichy became a puppet government of the Third Reich in the south of France. It rounded up thousands of Jews and German refugees and handed them over to the Nazis for deportation to the concentration camps. Pétain was followed by Pierre Laval, who was executed for treason at the end of World War II.

Vichy has become a symbol of betrayal, of easy surrender to and collaboration with a detested enemy.

Victorian   Characteristic of the time of Victoria's 64-year reign as queen of England from 1837 to 1901 as evidenced in literature, art and architecture, politics, philanthropy, social engineering, industrialization and especially in moral and sexual attitudes.

Victoria's reign was remarkably peaceful, stable and prosperous, symbolized best perhaps by the domestic bliss enjoyed by the queen and her beloved consort, Prince Albert. It was a time of the rising middle class when Englishmen took great pride in the virtues of "industriousness, self-reliance, temperance, piety, charity, and moral earnestness" (*Benet's Reader's Encyclopedia*). But at the same time, people tended to be stodgy, smug and prudish. The subculture, as Steven Marcus has described it in *The Other Victorians,* was another matter.

In modern usage, to have one's behavior or attitude called Victorian is to be accused of being old-fashioned, inhibited and narrow-minded.

Vietnam   Refers to the U.S. involvement in the Vietnam War, an undeclared war to oppose communist expansion in Southeast Asia. It was the most divisive war in modern American history. From 1965 to 1973 more than 55,000 Americans died in the conflict in Vietnam. Although the U.S. Air Force dropped more bombs on North Vietnam than in all of World War II, the United States was unable to achieve a victory. Vietnam has become a symbol of U.S. defeat abroad and of disunity at home. Vietnam taught the United States that it could not win an unpopular war. Many refer to Vietnam as the American agony, which has resulted in the paralysis of the American will in foreign affairs.

The Vietnam War Memorial wall, with the names of all the dead carved into its polished granite surface, attracts more visitors than any other memorial in Washington, D.C.

Vikings   A seafaring Scandinavian people who, for reasons unknown, left their peaceful occupations as farmers, shipbuilders and fishermen to become the most dreaded pirates and marauders of the early Middle Ages. From the eighth to the 10th centuries, these powerful "yellow-bearded" men in vividly painted, square-sailed long ships raided the coasts from Byzantium in the east to Iceland, Greenland and even North America in the west. Their object was plunder: gold, silver, jewels, coins and valuable chalices and reliquaries from monasteries.

They struck such terror in their victims and gained such a reputation for ferociousness that the mere threat of an attack produced the desired result: protection money or ransom. In prayers was regularly added the plea, "From the fury of the Northmen, good Lord deliver us."

It is interesting to note that, today, a Viking, unlike a Hun, is associated not with cruel rapaciousness but with positive qualities: blond Nordic manliness and a thirst for exploration and adventure on the sea.

Vladimir (Didi)   One of the two tattered tramps in Samuel Beckett's *Waiting for Godot* who while away their time in poignant antics as they wait and wait. "At this

429

place, at this moment, all mankind is us, whether we like it or not," says Vladimir. See GODOT.

Volpone   Main character in *Volpone* (1606), a savagely satirical comedy on greed by Ben Jonson (1573–1637), the foremost man of letters in Elizabethan England.

Volpone worships wealth. In the opening lines of the play, he sings a hymn to gold: "Thou art virtue, fame, honor, and all things else. Who can get thee, he shall be noble, valiant, honest, wise." Accumulating more and more treasure is a challenging game for him: "Yet I glory more in the cunning purchase of my wealth, than in the glad possession." He is as cynical as he is avaricious, certain that his cronies are stamped out of the same greedy mold as he is.

With the exuberant connivance of his parasite, Mosca, he concocts a plot to defraud them of their treasure. He pretends to be dying; childless, he lets it be known that he will name as his heir one of his three "friends." Each one tries to outdo the other with extravagant gifts. But Volpone is not satisfied with money alone. What else will each one sacrifice for the promise of a fortune? Voltore (the vulture) prostitutes his profession of law; Corbaccio (the raven) disinherits his own son; and Corvino (the crow) delivers his young wife to Volpone's bed to comfort him in his "dying" moments.

When the agile, quick-witted, pandering Mosca is on the verge of outsmarting Volpone, Volpone exposes the plot to the authorities and all receive their just punishment.

If all of these characters sound like forerunners of our contemporary Wall Street junk-bond manipulators and inside traders, they are. A Volpone is not just a rich Venetian merchant in a play; he is cunning greed incarnate, universal and ubiquitous.

Voltaire   Pen name of François Marie Arouet (1694–1778), born in Paris of bourgeois parents and educated by the best teachers of his day, the JESUITS. He came to hate organized religion and the authoritarian state. He was a skeptic, a rationalist, a towering figure of the 18th-century Enlightenment. Although he was imprisoned for his unorthodox ideas several times and had to flee France, he eventually won the homage of his age. In 1760 he retired to his estate at Ferney on the French-Swiss border, where he received the most distinguished thinkers of Europe.

Voltaire was a philosopher, an historian, novelist, poet and playwright. A friend of the English satirists Jonathan Swift and Alexander Pope and an admirer of the rationalists Isaac Newton and John Locke, Voltaire used his brilliant wit to inveigh against superstition, fanaticism, intolerance and injustice. He paved the way for the French Revolution, although he probably would have been appalled at its excesses.

Strangely enough, Voltaire's most enduring work has turned out to be his rather lighthearted satire on optimism, CANDIDE.

The true cast of his mind may perhaps be ascertained from the following well-known quotations from his work:

> If God did not exist, it would be necessary to invent him.
>
> I disapprove of what you say, but I will defend to the death your right to say it.
>
> In general, the art of government consists in taking as much money as possible from one class of citizens to give to the other.
>
> I have never made but one prayer to God, a very short one: 'O Lord, make my enemies ridiculous." And God granted it.
>
> I am very fond of truth, but not at all of martyrdom.
>
> Men use thought only to justify their wrong doings, and speech only to conceal their thoughts.

In our own time, H. L. Mencken has been called a modern Voltaire.

wag the dog Concept that gave its name to a movie (1997) directed by Barry Levinson from a screenplay by David Mamet and Hilary Henkin, which was based upon the novel *American Hero* by Larry Beinhart.

When a president of the United States is about to be engulfed in a sex scandal, White House officials hire a political manipulator (Robert DeNiro) to divert the public's attention. DeNiro in turn enlists the skills of a brash Hollywood producer (Dustin Hoffman). Using faked photos and "reliable sources," they fabricate a little war against a small, practically unknown country, Albania. Mission accomplished!

This "wag the dog" scenario seemed prescient to opponents of President Clinton when, in 1998 at the height of the Monica Lewinsky scandal, the president ordered the bombing of Iraq because of Iraq's refusal to grant full access to an UNSCOM team of inspectors. Suspicions of a "wag the dog" scenario were again engendered when Clinton subsequently ordered cruise missile attacks against terrorist sites in the Sudan and Afghanistan in retaliation for the terrorist bombings in August 1998 of U.S. embassies in Kenya and Tanzania.

"A wag the dog scenario" refers to a diversionary tactic to change the focus of public outrage.

Wagnerian In the manner of the German composer of operas, Richard Wagner (1813–83). Wagner revolutionized opera, rejecting the Italian and French styles of separating arias and recitatives for a continuously melodic style (*Sprechgesang*). He completely integrated music and drama and made much use of musical leitmotifs to characterize the recurrent appearance of persons, things, situations and emotions.

Everything about Wagner's operas was large; some would say, grandiose. He took his subject matter from Nordic and Teutonic myths and legends that involved titanic struggles among the gods. To treat his material adequately he decided to compose a tetralogy, *Der Ring des Nibelungen* (1876), for the proper presentation of which he had to build a specially designed theater, the Festival Theater (*Festspielhaus*) at Bayreuth in Bavaria. He enlarged the orchestra to express his grand themes of tragic love and redemption with soaring musical power. And his operas are notoriously long.

Among Wagner's masterpieces are *Tristan and Isolde* (1865), *Die Meistersinger von Nürnberg* (1868), the four operas of the *Ring* cycle and *Parsifal* (1882). Some of his other operas are *The Flying Dutchman* (1843), *Tannhaüser* (1845) and *Lohengrin* (1848).

The term "Wagnerian" applies to anything larger-than-life, grandiose, inflated, overblown or melodramatic. Because Wagner's music has unfortunately come to be associated with Germanic nationalism, Teutonic pretensions and even Adolf Hitler, the term is often used in a politically negative context.

Walden (1854)   A book by Henry David Thoreau (1817–62). Subtitled *Life in The Woods,* it is an account of the two years Thoreau spent living alone in a cabin he built in the woods at the edge of Walden Pond in Concord, Massachusetts. He aimed to simplify his life, to arrive at its essential meaning away from the distractions of the town, to be in touch with nature and the passing seasons.

Walden has become a romantic symbol of escape from civilization. It is a term associated with the back-to-nature movement that echoes WORDSWORTH in averring "The world is too much with us."

See DIFFERENT DRUMMER, A.

Wallenberg, Raoul (1912–?)   Swedish attaché in Hungary during World War II. He made it his mission to save as many Hungarian Jews as he could during the Nazi occupation. By giving them Swedish identification papers and hiding them in safe houses flying the Swedish flag, he literally snatched Jews from SS roundups and deportation lines. On January 17, 1945, Wallenberg went to a meeting with Soviet officers, whose troops had entered Budapest just a few days before. He disappeared on that day and has never heard from again. It is known that he was taken prisoner by the Russians and sent to a camp in the GULAG. But why? The Russians say that he has died; other prisoners claim that he still lives on in a prison camp. The mystery has never been solved.

Wallenberg has become a heroic symbol of what a single individual can achieve against evil.

Wall Street   A street in lower Manhattan that has come to be known as the financial center of the world. It is the location of the Stock Exchange. The term is also used as an indicator of economic trends.

Wall Street has become the symbol for mammoth financial dealing, for insider trading, for greed and ruthlessness.

Wandering Jew, the   In medieval legends of the 13th century, the Wandering Jew was a sinister figure doomed to roam over the face of the Earth until the Second Coming of Christ. With his long gray beard, malevolent eyes and crooked figure, he became a bogeyman to frighten unruly children. More alarming, he became an archetype in anti-Semitic mythology, an ever recurrent reminder that the Jews were Christ-killers.

The legend was supposedly based on the account in Matthew of how Jesus, dragging his heavy cross along the Via Dolorosa to Calvary, was mocked, spat upon and stoned by a mob in Jerusalem. In 1228 in *Flores Historiarum,* an English monk by the name of Roger of Wendover embellished the account in the New Testament by introducing a fictional character among the jeering mob, one Joseph Cartaphilus, who would not permit Jesus to rest upon a stone for a few moments, but prodded him on toward his execution. Jesus replied: "I sure will rest, but thou shalt walk / And have no journey stayed." Here was the inception of the myth of the Wandering Jew. Repeated again and again by chroniclers and poets, clergy and theologians, the story took on the aspect of truth and indeed became part of the canon law of the church. The legend justified the "righteous" hatred of the Jews by Christians and the anti-Semitic policies of Christian rulers. Among writers of note who have used the legend of the Wandering Jew are Goethe (1774), Edgar Quinet (1833), Eugene Sue (1845) and Lew Wallace (1893).

In today's usage, the expression "the wandering Jew" has been trivialized to describe any restless person who changes domicile frequently, who cannot seem to find a permanent home.

Warhol, Andy (1930–1987)   Painter associated with POP ART, maker of experimental and outrageous films, man-about-town and member of café society.

Warhol stands for the most avant of the avant-garde.

Warsaw Ghetto   On November 26, 1940, German troops began herding the Jewish population of Warsaw, Poland, into a ghetto enclosed by an eight-foot-high wall. The Jews were systematically forced into labor for the German war machine, starved, beaten and finally decimated by mass deportations to concentration camps. By April 1943 only 60,000 of more than half a million Jews remained. A handful of Jewish resistance fighters made a last-ditch stand against heavily armored SS troops commanded by General Jurgen Stroop. With a meager supply of arms, they fought the Nazi troops from house to house and in the sewers in a desperately heroic but losing battle. By May 16 there were no Jews left. They'd all been killed or had committed suicide. Symbol of Jewish resistance to the Nazis.

By extension, the Warsaw Ghetto is a symbol of heroic resistance.

war to end all wars   The war that came cynically to be called World War I, when it became obvious that the terms of the peace were inevitably leading to a World War II. The "war to end all wars" was a World War I slogan to make the slaughter seem palatable, as were other shibboleths like "making the world safe for democracy."

war to make the world safe for democracy   The purpose of waging World War I, according to President Woodrow Wilson. The phrase has been used cynically in view of the spread of totalitarian governments all over the world during the 20th century, especially in Fascist Italy, Nazi Germany and Communist Russia.

Washington, Booker T. (1856–1915)   Born a slave, Washington educated himself, eventually working his way through school and college. In 1889, he founded Tuskegee Institute, which, at first, prepared blacks for farm, factory and domestic service. Later, as its program and facilities expanded, it educated its students for the trades and professions.

In *Up From Slavery* (1900), his autobiography, Washington looks back at the long, hard road that brought him from a Southern log cabin to the presidency of Tuskegee Institute. Washington stands as a symbol of success won against extraordinary obstacles. In his own time, Washington's life and achievement became a legend for his fellow blacks.

Waste Land, The (1922)   A poem of 434 lines, in five sections, written by T. S. Eliot. By means of symbols and myths, especially that of the impotent Fisher King, it deals with the fragmentation and sterility of modern civilization. It contrasts the splendor and richness of the past with the sordidness and decadence of the present. We live in a spiritual wasteland.

Use: Newton Minow, head of the FCC (Federal Communications Commission), caused a national stir when he declared that American television was a "vast waste land."

Watergate   An apartment-office complex in Washington, D.C., which gave its name to one of the biggest political scandals in American history, a scandal that culminated in the resignation of President Richard M. Nixon on August 8, 1974, two years into his second term.

On June 17, 1972, five men were arrested for breaking into the executive quarters of the Democratic National Committee in Watergate. Through the investigative reporting of two young journalists for the *Washington Post,* Carl Bernstein and Bob Woodward, what appeared at first to be a simple robbery turned out to be a conspiracy involving a Republican Party espionage network with a secret fund at its disposal. Top White House aides (H. R. Haldeman, John D. Ehrlichman, John W. Dean etc.) as well as former attorney general John N. Mitchell were implicated. President Nixon was forced to turn over tapes of conversations in the Oval Office, which proved conclusively his own involvement in the conspiracy and the cover-up. On July 30, 1974, the House Judiciary Committee recommended impeachment proceedings against Nixon for "obstruction of justice, abuse of power, and contempt of Congress." Ten days later Nixon resigned.

Watergate stands for political scandal involving abuse of power, corruption and cover-up on the part of high government officials. See also DEEP THROAT; SATURDAY NIGHT MASSACRE; —GATE.

Waterloo   On June 18, 1815, there took place near the village of Waterloo, about 50 miles south of Brussels, one of the most decisive confrontations in military history. NAPOLEON Bonaparte, risen like the Phoenix out of his defeat and exile on ELBA, had once again taken command of the French forces, had defeated the Prussians under the command of Field Marshal Blücher, and was now marching west to attack the British army under Wellington. It was a classic face-off: the "Iron Duke" against the "Man of Destiny." Napoleon miscalculated. Wellington received reinforcements from the Prussians and routed Napoleon's troops, which suffered 32,000 casualties. Napoleon abdicated on June 22, 1815, and was exiled for good to the island of St. Helena.

The Battle of Waterloo marked the end of the Napoleonic Wars, the end of the career of a military and organizational genius whose armies had marched into Spain and down the boot of Italy and across the rest of the European continent, failing to conquer only Russia and England. Waterloo was the stuff that legends, novels and poems are made of.

Since that time, the word "Waterloo" has become synonymous with downfall, utter defeat.

Watson, Dr.   Constant companion and admiring audience to Sherlock Holmes in the detective stories of Sir Arthur Conan Doyle. Steady, deliberate, loyal, often amazed, he acts as a foil to the nervous and erratic energy of Holmes.

"Elementary, my dear Watson," are the words purportedly used by Sherlock Holmes to the openmouthed Dr. Watson as he launched into an explanation of his solution to a crime.

The phrase has become a popular opening to any explanation.

Watts   Black ghetto in Los Angeles, California, which erupted in rioting, looting and arson in August 1965. The violence raged for five days before 20,000 National Guardsmen, called by Governor Edmund Brown, restored order to the ravaged area. Results: 30 dead; hundreds injured; 22,000 arrested; property worth millions destroyed. Watts established a pattern for riots in other depressed black ghettos, like Newark and Detroit in 1967.

Watts has become synonymous with racial rioting during "the long hot summer," when people tend to gather in the streets and the heat makes tempers flare.

waving the bloody shirt   This phrase has its origins in post–Civil War politics. It was used by Republicans who kept bitterness alive by blaming the Democrats for the war. The bloody shirt was an emblem of the war's casualties. Oliver P. Morton (1823–77), Republican U.S. senator from New York, made waving the bloody shirt popular when he introduced it into his political campaign. The Republicans, he insisted, were loyal to the Union. Their party saved the Union. The Democrats supported secession, the rebels and the war against the Union.

"Waving the bloody shirt" has come to mean rabble-rousing, playing upon deep-seated emotions and prejudices, arousing or intensifying social unrest and instability.

Wayne, John (1907–1979)   Born Marion Morrison, this movie actor was the archetypal western hero: strong, silent, stoic, incorruptible. One of his many starring roles was the hero in *Stagecoach* (1939), directed by John Ford.

Use: "Bush is Jimmy Stewart after Reagan's John Wayne." (*Newsweek,* 1989)

Weems, Parson Mason Locke (1759–1825)   United States clergyman and biographer, known chiefly for *The Life and Memorable Actions of George Washington* (c. 1800) in which first appeared the famous fictional story of Washington and the cherry tree. Parson Weems was not above creating fictional anecdotes in his biographies for the purpose of heightening interest while teaching a moral. A Parson Weems is someone who stretches the truth to make a moral point.

Use: "I've never dealt with an American President whose life owed so little to Parson Weems and so much to Pirandello." (Gore Vidal on Edmund Morris's use of fiction in *Dutch,* a biography of President Ronald Reagan)

"we have met the enemy and they are us"   See *POGO.*

Welk, Lawrence (1903–1992)   The band leader of the *Lawrence Welk Show,* (1955–82) a popular, all-musical TV program appealing to older Americans, sometimes uncharitably referred to as the "geriatric set." For them, Welk and his attractive company provided unabashedly sentimental music—danceable, singable, listenable.

Weller, Sam   The loyal, witty and resourceful cockney manservant of PICKWICK in Charles Dickens's *The Pickwick Papers* (1837). When Pickwick goes to debtors prison, Weller arranges to get himself arrested and packed off to prison, too, so that he can be close to his master and be of service to him. Weller is "street smart" and full of aphorisms, proverbs and paradoxes. In slang terminology, he may be viewed as an ever-present sidekick.

"We Shall Overcome"   Signature song of hope and resolution during the Civil Rights movement, sung at innumerable rallies, demonstrations and marches throughout the United States. It was adapted by Pete Seeger in 1955 from a Baptist hymn. Now the phrase is used to express faith in the ability to overcome any obstacle, not only the obdurate obstacle of bigotry or racism.

West, Mae (1893–1980)   Movie star comedienne whose special variety of femme fatale was that of a bordello madame: openly, brazenly, vulgarly sexual. Her ample hourglass bulk swaddled in sequined silk or satin, swaying her indolent hips and batting her false eyelashes, she could insinuatingly greet a male visitor to her suite with a drawled: "Is that a gun you've got in your pocket, or are you just glad to see me?" Some of her famous lines were "Come up and see me sometime"; "Beulah, peel me a grape"; and the song "I Like a Man Who Takes His Time." She opened in *Night after Night* (1932), then made *She Done Him Wrong* (1933), *Goin' to Town* (1935) and many other films.

A Mae West is (1) a large-bosomed parody of unabashed sexuality; (2) an inflatable life-preserver, suggesting the shape of Mae West.

What Makes Sammy Run? (1941)   Satirical novel by Budd Schulberg about Sammy Glick, a tough young New York City Jew whose ambition and unscrupulous opportunism take him to a position of power in the movie industry. The title refers to the ambitious drives that make people trample each other to get to the top.

What Price Glory?   Title of a 1924 play by Laurence Stallings and Maxwell Anderson about the stupidity and cynicism of war. At the end of the play, when the main characters, weary soldiers, are once more deprived of furlough and ordered to the front, Sergeant Quirt says: "What a lot of God damn fools it takes to make a war!"

The phrase is now generally used ironically to question the sacrifices or compromises one makes for fame or even ephemeral recognition.

"What's It All About, Alfie?"   Song from the 1966 British film *Alfie,* about a philandering cockney playboy (Michael Caine) who can't make up his mind whether his "freedom" is really better than marriage. The phrase is used to express puzzlement about the purpose of life itself.

"When a new planet swims into his ken"   A line from "On First Looking Into Chapman's Homer," a sonnet by the English poet John Keats (1795–1821).

Keats expresses his awe and excitement at discovering the greatness of Homer's epic poems through George Chapman's English translation of the *Iliad* and the *Odyssey*. He compares his feelings with those of an astronomer amazed at seeing through his telescope for the first time a great new heavenly body—a planet, no less—which nobody had suspected was there. It is the same feeling that Balboa must have had when, unsuspectingly, he came upon the Pacific Ocean.

The line, in general use, has come to stand for a sense of tremendous excitement at the discovery of something vast and unknown.

"When you call me that, smile!"   Phrase spoken by the hero of *The Virginian: A Horseman of the Plains* (1902), an early Western by Owen Wister (1860–1938). It is a tale set in Wyoming cattle country and has to do with the hero's adventures among cowpunchers as well as with his courtship of Molly Wood, a schoolteacher from Vermont.

The phrase is now used banteringly to counter any derogatory remark.

"Where are the snows of yesteryear?"   This is the English translation by Dante Gabriel Rossetti (1828–82) in "The Ballad of Dead Ladies" of a line in a poem written by the French poet François Villon (1431–c. 1465): "*Mais où sont les neiges d'antan?*" The sentiment and the image by which it is expressed seem to be universal, for long before Villon, Geoffrey Chaucer (1344–1400) in *Troilus and Criseyde* wrote: "Ye, fare wel al the snow of ferne yere!"

The phrase is a lament for the transitoriness of all things: not just snow, but youth, beauty, love, glory, life itself. Poets start with *ubi sunt* (where are the lost days?), proceed to *lacrimae rerum* (oh, the tears, the sadness of everything) and conclude with a stoical or a hedonistic warning, *carpe diem* (seize the day!).

"Where Have All the Flowers Gone?"   Antiwar song written and popularized by Pete Seeger in 1961. It is an elegiac lament for the young boys gone to war, "gone to graveyards everywhere," and for the women they left behind. It was inspired by a passage from Mikhail Sholokhov's novel *And Quiet Flows the Don* (tr. 1934). It became a hit record done by the Kingston Trio under the Capitol label. The phrase has a dying cadence and is used to bemoan the disappearance of fragile things and people, somewhat akin to the refrain of Villon: "Where are the snows of yesteryear?"

Where the Wild Things Are (1963)   A children's picture book written and illustrated by Maurice Sendak. It tells the story of Max, a little boy who is sent to his room without supper. He imagines himself in the forest where the wild things are. These are frighteningly grotesque creatures with beaks and claws and prominent eyes, but they make him their king and obey him. Nevertheless, Max decides that he wants to be back where he is loved. He goes home to his room, where supper is waiting for him.

The phrase "where the wild things are" has come to represent our subconscious fears and imaginings and our desire to master them.

whistle stop   Any town too small or too insignificant for a regularly scheduled train stop. When a passenger wishes to descend at such a place, the conductor notifies the engineer by pulling the signal cord and the engineer responds with two toots of the whistle. President Harry Truman confounded the prognosticators when he campaigned successfully against Thomas Dewey for the presidency in 1948 by speaking from his train at innumerable whistle stops.

"White Man's Burden, The" (1899)   The title of one of Rudyard Kipling's poems. Addressed to the American people as the United States assumed control of the Philippines at the end of the Spanish-American War, it is a ringing justification for colonization, British- and continental-style, at the end of the 19th and the beginning of the 20th centuries. It declares the whites a superior race whose moral duty it is to uplift the inferior races, provide paternalistic care for "your new-caught, sullen peoples."

This point of view was especially popular during the later years of Queen Victoria's reign when the Sun never set on the British Empire.

Here it is in Kipling's words:

Take up the White Man's burden
Send forth the best you breed.
Go blind your sons to exile
To serve the captives' needs.

Today, imperialism has been discredited and the white man's burden is regarded as outmoded racism and elitism. The phrase is used pejoratively to suggest the presence or persistence of a distasteful, unworkable ideology.

Whitmanesque   Resembling the style, the content or the attitudes of the American tradition-shattering poet, Walt Whitman (1819–92), as evidenced in *Leaves of Grass* (1855).

Although Whitman could use traditional stanzaic patterns creditably (as in "O Captain, My Captain" [1865], on the death of Lincoln), he chose to forge a new style that would be uniquely American. His lines were long and unrhymed, given to cumulative and exhaustive series of phrases and lists, biblical in cadence, rhapsodic in tone. Having eschewed European models, he could defiantly proclaim in "Song of Myself": "I sound my barbaric yawp over the roofs of the world."

In many ways it was indeed a barbaric yawp in its unashamed proclamations and revelations. He sang of himself, he sang the body electric, he sang of the open road. He sang of America, its pioneers, its immigrants, its workers, its soldiers. He was all-embracing in his love and his optimism. He sang paeans to life and to death. He could be brash and yet he could be lyrical and elegiac, as in "Out of the Cradle Endlessly Rocking" and in "When Lilacs Last in the Dooryard Bloomed."

Whitman's poetry was appreciated by Europeans before it was appreciated by Americans. From across the ocean, they recognized it as a new, revolutionary, authentic voice of the New World—unafraid, liberating, democratic, full of promise.

In the 20th century, "Howl," by the BEAT poet Allen Ginsberg (1926–97), best illustrates and continues the Whitmanesque tradition of the long prophetic line and the uninhibited subject matter.

Whitman Sampler   Box of assorted chocolates with the familiar cover designed like a cross-stitched, early American sampler. It has the convenience of easy accessibility since it can be bought in any candy shop, stationer's or drug store.

Use: "I started my lessons at a dance school in an introductory course, the Whitman Sampler approach to ballroom dancing." (Alice J. Kelvin, in *Smithsonian*)

"Why don't you speak for yourself, John?"   In Henry Wadsworth Longfellow's narrative poem "The Courtship of Miles Standish" (1858), Miles Standish, captain of the Plymouth colony, asks his friend, the better-educated John Alden, to woo Priscilla for him. Alden, who is also in love with Priscilla, is torn between love and loyalty to his friend. Loyalty wins out, but he is rendered awkward and stammering as he delivers the message. Priscilla, no fool, thereupon asks coquettishly, "Why don't you speak for yourself, John?"

The question is often used to reject surrogate pleas and arguments, not to mention wooing, and to encourage forthright self-assertion.

Wicked Witch of the West   One of four (two of them good, two of them wicked) witches in the Land of Oz in *The Wonderful Wizard of Oz* by L. Frank Baum. This formidable, evil witch melted away when Dorothy threw a pail of water at her. Her attempts to wrest the magical ruby slippers from Dorothy were thus foiled.

See also OZ; YELLOW BRICK ROAD; WIZARD OF OZ.

Wiesel, Elie (1928–   )   A survivor of the concentration camps at AUSCHWITZ and BUCHENWALD, where his whole family was murdered, Wiesel has dedicated his life to bearing witness to the Nazi atrocities against the Jewish people. To this end, he has written several autobiographical novels that have caught the attention of the world: *Night* (1958), *Dawn* (1960) and *The Gates of the Forest* (1966). He has written many other books about the Jewish experience, both contemporary and historical. He has taught and lectured and insisted upon remembrance. Yet he has inveighed against all attempts to commercialize, vulgarize or sentimentalize the HOLOCAUST.

Wiesel became the conscience of the world when he pleaded eloquently but unavailingly with President Ronald Reagan to cancel a state visit to BITBURG cemetery in Germany, where a group of SS officers were buried beside regular army troops. In 1986 he received the Nobel Peace Prize.

Wiesenthal, Simon (1908–   )   Having lost 89 relatives in the HOLOCAUST and being himself a survivor of Nazi concentration camps, he became the chief hunter of Nazi war criminals in the world. Wiesenthal located over a thousand of them. He stalked Adolf Eichmann, notorious former chief of the Gestapo's anti-Jewish operations, and was instrumental in having Eichmann spirited out of Argentina to be tried, convicted and hanged in Israel. He wrote *I Hunted Eichmann* (1961) and *The Murderers Among Us* (1967).

Wiesenthal is a modern-day nemesis, hunting down and bringing to justice those responsible for the murder of 6 million Jews in the Holocaust.

Wife of Bath   One of the 31 pilgrims in *The Canterbury Tales* (1387–1400) by Geoffrey Chaucer (1343–1400). Vividly delineated, she is a bold, earthy, large-hipped woman who wears scarlet stockings. She has had five husbands, not to mention other lovers, and is well schooled in the arts of love:

Five men in turn had taken her to wife,
Omitting other youthful company—

. . .

All remedies of love she knew by name,
For she had all the tricks of that old game.

Like the devil, she can quote Scripture:

But plainly this I know without a lie,
God told us to increase and multiply.

The Wife of Bath is a prototype of the full-blown, coarse-grained woman who cashes in on her sexuality and revels in her dominance over men.

Wild Bunch, The   A small group of outlaws put together and held together by BUTCH CASSIDY circa 1890. They were absolutely loyal to Cassidy and to each other. By 1902, their bank and train robberies, their assaults on guards and police officers, were over and most of the gang members were dead or imprisoned.

Wimsey, Lord Peter   Aristocratic amateur detective in the novels of Dorothy L. Sayers (1893–1957). Witty, sophisticated, eccentric, epicurean, he has a wide range of interests, such as rare books, history, classical music (he is an accomplished pianist) and criminology. His character was played by the British actor Ian Carmichael in TV versions of *Clouds of Witness, The Unpleasantness at the Bellona Club, The Nine Tailors* and *Murder Must Advertise,* and later by Edward Petherbridge in further adaptations.

Winesburg, Ohio (1919)   Written by Sherwood Anderson (1876–1941), this work contains 23 stories about characters who live in a small midwestern town with limited horizons. Each is seen through the eyes of a young reporter, George Willard. Anderson tears the veil from the idealized, sentimentalized picture of American small-town life and shows the loneliness, cruelty and boredom beneath the calm exterior. Winesburg became the prototype of a whole series of novels (*Main Street* by Sinclair Lewis) and poetry (*Spoon River Anthology* by Edgar Lee Masters) that expose the steamy, inbred, passionate entanglements of a town's inhabitants.

Winnie-the-Pooh   The lovable, ostensibly stupid but strangely wise, honey-eating bear who is the hero of A. A. Milne's Christopher Robin books for children, *Winnie the Pooh* (1926) and *The House at Pooh Corner* (1928).

"Pooh's way is amazingly consistent with the principles of living envisaged long ago by the Chinese founders of Taoism." (Benjamin Hoff, *The Tao of Pooh*)

"winter of our discontent, the"   From the first line of Shakespeare's *Richard III* (c. 1592):

> *Now is the winter of our discontent*
> *Made glorious summer by this sun of York;*
> *And all the clouds that lowered upon our house*
> *In the deep bosom of the ocean buried.*

These lines are spoken in the opening soliloquy by Richard, not yet king but duke of Gloucester, youngest brother of the ailing Edward IV. Richard alludes not only to the historical moment of the play (the triumph in the person of Edward IV of the house of York over the house of Lancaster in the long

Wars of the Roses) but also to his gleeful anticipation of the MACHIAVELLIAN schemes by which he means to rid himself of all the obstacles between himself and the throne of England. He will engineer the imprisonment and execution of his older brother, Clarence; he will make himself protector of the little princes after their father Edward IV dies, and he will send them to the Tower of London there to be murdered; and he will woo and marry the Lady Anne, widow of the son of Henry VI, whom Richard murdered. And all this he will do in spite of or perhaps because of his misshapen, hunchbacked body. In the opening soliloquy Richard notes, "Grim-visaged war hath smoothed his wrinkled front"; however, the Wars of the Roses will not really end until Richard himself is killed at the end of the play in the Battle of Bosworth Field by a Tudor who will be crowned Henry VII.

The "winter of our discontent," which Shakespeare contrasts metaphorically with "this sun (son) of York" is used frequently now simply to refer to hard times, perhaps to be followed by better times.

with all deliberate speed   In 1954 in *Brown v. Board of Education,* the United States Supreme Court struck down the concept of separate but equal and ordered the desegregation of public schools. Many states in the South were loath to comply. In *Brown II* (1955) the Supreme Court ordered recalcitrant school districts to integrate the schools "with all deliberate speed."

without redeeming social value   For years the courts have had to adjudicate cases in which charges of obscenity leveled against printed material have been countered by charges of First Amendment violations of freedom of the press. One of the most famous cases involved the government's attempt to ban James Joyce's *Ulysses.* Judge John M. Woolsey in 1933 concluded: "I am quite aware that owing to some of its scenes, *Ulysses* is a rather strong draught to ask some sensitive, though normal, persons to take. But my considered opinion after long reflection, is that whilst in many places the effect of *Ulysses* on the reader undoubtedly is somewhat emetic, nowhere does it tend to be aphrodisiac. *Ulysses* may, therefore, be admitted to the U.S."

In 1966 the Supreme Court, in a case involving the banning of John Cleland's *Fanny Hill: Memoirs of a Woman of Pleasure* (1748–49) ruled that henceforth the burden of proof of obscenity rested squarely on the censors. They would have to prove that the material (1) appealed to prurient interest, (2) was patently offensive and (3) was utterly without redeeming social value.

Wizard of Oz, The   Film musical (1939) made from the popular children's book of the same name written by L. Frank Baum.

Dorothy (Judy Garland), a young girl, lives with her aunt on a farm in Kansas. During a tornado, Dorothy is hit on the head by flying debris and knocked unconscious. She and her dog Toto are borne away to the Land of Oz, ruled by a wizard known only by his dreaded stentorian voice. Dorothy follows the YELLOW BRICK ROAD to meet the wizard and enlist his help in finding her way home. Along her path she encounters a host of strange characters whose names have become metaphors: the Tin Man, who has no heart (Jack Haley); the Cowardly Lion (Bert Lahr); the Scarecrow, without a brain (Ray Bolger); the wicked Witch of the West; and the diminutive Munchkins.

At the end of the road, Dorothy is brought before the Wizard's hidden presence and tearfully begs him to help her and Toto home. The Wizard's voice is fierce, but Dorothy pulls the curtain aside and unmasks the Wizard as a genial, bumbling fraud. Armed with a pair of ruby slippers and counseled by the Good Witch Glinda, Dorothy has but to will herself home to get her wish. All ends happily in Kansas.

Wolfe, Nero   Fictional detective created by Rex Stout (1886–1975). Wolfe has been called a "corpulent recluse." Weighing "a seventh of a ton," he abhors all unnecessary physical activity and relegates all leg work to his assistant, Archie Goodwin, the narrator. He is a gourmand with a Swiss chef, lives luxuriously in a brownstone on West 35th Street in New York City, grows orchids on his roof, speaks seven languages and has an extraordinary command of English.

"woman I love, the"   Phrase used in his abdication speech of December 11, 1936, by Edward VIII, king of Great Britain, to describe Wallis Warfield Simpson, a divorcee from Baltimore, Maryland, whom he afterward married. The context of the phrase runs: "You must believe me when I tell you that I have found it impossible to carry the heavy burden of responsibility and to discharge my duties as King as I would wish to do without the help and the support of the woman I love." Edward was succeeded by his brother, the duke of York, who became George VI.

Every man feels himself a tragic king of romance when he points to his wife and says, "the woman I love," for whom he is mockingly willing to sacrifice his all.

Wonder Woman   Appearing on the comic book scene in 1942, *Wonder Woman* was later hailed by feminists as an embodiment of some of their tenets. It was sharply condemned by such critics as Dr. Frederic Wertham who, in his *Seduction of the Innocent* (1954), took it to task for being one of the most harmful crime comics.

Originally, Wonder Woman was an Amazon princess who lived on Paradise Island. No men were permitted on the island. Wonder Woman came to America to help win World War II. Clad in a flashy red, white, blue and yellow costume, she performed her fantastic feats. She was virtually all-powerful—unless a man linked together her "bracelets of submission."

Female readers simply identified with Wonder Woman, the superheroine, just as the male readers were drawn to Superman. Psychological experts of all sorts, however, had a field day with *Wonder Woman,* claiming to find in the comic book evidences of lesbianism and sadomasochism.

Woodstock   Town in New York State near the farmland where, in August 1969, thousands of counterculture young people sprawled on a field to listen to rock music or ballads by performers like Joan Baez, Arlo Guthrie, Jimi Hendrix, Richie Havens, the Jefferson Airplane and the Who. Antiestablishment dress and behavior and the longing for peace marked the attitudes of youth in the 1960s at Woodstock. A documentary of the same name about the festival won an Academy Award in 1970.

Wordsworthian   Marked by the worship of nature and by the sympathy with the lives of simple rural folk central to the work of the English ROMANTIC poet William Wordsworth (1770–1850).

Wordsworth's feelings and thoughts about nature find their fullest expression perhaps in "Tintern Abbey," a poem in his first book, *Lyrical Ballads,* published in 1798. In that poem he traces his developing response to nature. When he was a boy, he reacted with sheer animal spirits:

> *I cannot paint*
> *What then I was, the sounding cataract*
> *Haunted me like a passion; the tall rock,*
> *The mountain, and the deep and gloomy wood,*
> *Their colours and their forms were then to me*
> *An appetite; a feeling and a love,*
> *That had no need of a remoter charm,*
> *By thought supplied, nor any interest*
> *Unborrowed from the eye.*

Later he learned

> *To look on nature, not as in the hour*
> *Of thoughtless youth; but hearing oftentimes*
> *The still, sad music of humanity,*
> *Nor harsh nor grating, though of ample power*
> *To chasten and subdue.*

And finally he came to feel the mystical power of nature, the immanence of God in nature:

And I have felt
A presence that disturbs me with the joy
Of elevated thoughts; a sense sublime
Of something far more deeply interfused,
Whose dwelling is the light of setting suns,
And the round ocean, and the living air,
And the blue sky, and in the mind of man;
A motion and a spirit, that impels
All thinking things, all objects of all thought,
And rolls through all things.

In Wordsworth's poems, nature exerts a beneficent influence, whether in remembered images that "flash upon that inward eye / Which is the bliss of solitude" (from "The Daffodils") or in the formation of character of those who live in rural places and follow simple rural pursuits (the Lucy poems, "Michael," "The Leech Gatherer," "The Solitary Reaper"). It follows that Wordsworth cried out against the baleful influence of industrialization, as in the sonnet (1807):

The world is too much with us; late and soon,
Getting and spending, we lay waste our powers;
Little we see in Nature that is ours;
We have given our hearts away, a sordid boon!

See ROMANTICISM; ROUSSEAU.

Wright, Frank Lloyd (1869–1959) Controversial American architect who pleaded for an end to America's "lust for ugliness." Although in his youth he studied with Louis Sullivan, "the father of the skyscraper," Wright came to detest steel and stone cities. He rejected box-like structures, saying "a box is more of a coffin for the human spirit than an inspiration." He promoted organic architecture, that is, architecture that uses poured reinforced concrete, takes its shape from organic forms of nature and looks as if it has "grown" upon its site rather than been imposed upon it. He is famous for his dramatic prairie homes in which interiors merge with the landscape, e.g., the Robie House, with its low, horizontal planes (1908); the Kaufman House, cantilevered over a waterfall (1936); and the various Taliesins (1911, 1914, 1925), which housed his school for architects.

Wyeth, Andrew (1917–) American painter whose canvases depict with photographic realism lonely people against a rural background of wide skies, open fields and poor farmhouses. His painting *Christina's World* (1948), showing an isolated girl half-sprawled upon an upland pasture and looking toward a gaunt farmhouse on the horizon, has become almost a cliché because it is so popular. Wyeth succeeds in evoking the girl's mood: a mixture of desolation and yearning. His Helga paintings, a group of pictures of a neighbor done over a number of years, were first exhibited in 1986. A Wyeth is synonymous with pictorial realism.

$\mathcal{X}$

Xanadu   These are the opening lines of "Kubla Kahn," a poem written in 1798 by Samuel Taylor Coleridge (1772–1834):

> *In Xanadu did Kubla Khan*
> *A stately pleasure dome decree:*
> *Where Alph, the sacred river, ran*
> *Through caverns measureless to man*
> *Down to a sunless sea.*
> *So twice five miles of fertile ground*
> *With walls and towers were girdled round.*

He is describing the exotic and splendid palace of a Mongol emperor of the 13th century KUBLAI KHAN, already vividly described by MARCO POLO.

In 1927, John Livingston Lowes wrote *The Road to Xanadu,* in which he analyzed the probable sources of Coleridge's "dream" poem.

A Xanadu is a place of beauty and splendor, like the TAJ MAHAL.

Use: "The largest private house in the United States, George Vanderbilt's version of Xanadu was designed by Richard Morris Hunt and Frederick Law Olmsted." (*American Heritage,* May–June 1992)

X-rated   For adults only, according to the self-regulatory Code of the Motion Picture Industry. X-rated films carry the warning "This movie contains scenes of explicit sex, not suitable for children's viewing."

The term "X-rated" may be applied to any verbal or graphic material: language, magazines, newspapers, comics, as well as movies and theater.

Actually, films are no longer X-rated. The new Code of the Motion Picture Industry has replaced the X with NC-17: No children under 17 admitted.

𝒴

Yahoo   In Book Four, the final book of *Gulliver's Travels* (1726) by Jonathan Swift, GULLIVER comes to a land where the Houyhnhnms, a breed of noble horses, are the rulers, and the Yahoos, in the shape of men like Gulliver, are their brute servants. The Houyhnhnms are beautiful and graceful; the Yahoos are ugly and vicious. The Houyhnhnms live by reason alone (they are without passion or jealousy or deception) and have created a UTOPIAN society in which friendship and benevolence are the highest virtues.

When Gulliver describes his own land to them, England, a land of Yahoos, the Houyhnhnms conclude that Yahoos have perverted their reasoning power to indulge their natural inclination toward vice, folly and corruption through wars, avarice and political chicanery. When Gulliver realizes that he, himself, belongs to the species of Yahoo, he is filled not only with disgust but also with suicidal despair.

The Yahoo represents the ultimate expression of Swift's misanthropy.

Yalta   Russian seaport on the Black Sea where American president Franklin Delano Roosevelt, British prime minister Winston Churchill and Soviet leader Joseph Stalin met from February 4 to 12, 1945, to carve out their separate spheres of influence following the end of World War II. History has accused Roosevelt of giving the store away to Stalin, with concessions that led to the domination of Poland, Romania, Bulgaria, Hungary, Czechoslovakia and Eastern Germany by the U.S.S.R.

Yalta has come to stand for a betrayal of Western democratic entities to communist domination; a cynical or perhaps pragmatic bargaining away of freedom in a quid pro quo.

Yellow Brick Road   The golden paved road along which Dorothy, Toto, the Tin Man, the Scarecrow and the Cowardly Lion travel in search of the wizard in *The Wonderful Wizard of Oz*. The wizard supposedly has the power to grant each one of them what he or she desires, but he turns out to be a fraud. In the 1939 MGM musical made from L. Frank Baum's 1900 fantasy, the characters sing a happy song, "Follow the Yellow Brick Road."

The Yellow Brick Road suggests a quest, a journey in a fantasy land to find one's heart's desire.

Yes, I can! From the children's picture book *The Little Engine that Could* (1945) by Watty Piper, illustrated by Lois Lenski. It tells the story of a little railway engine that chugs up a steep slope panting all the way, "I think I can—I think I can—I think I can," and concludes, "Yes, I can!"

The phrase has become an optimist's triumphant cry.

Yes, Virginia, there is a Santa Claus From an editorial written by Francis Pharcella Church in the *New York Sun*, September 21, 1897, in reply to an inquiry by a little girl named Virginia O'Hanlon. Virginia wrote that her friends had told her there was no Santa Claus. Church replied in part: "No Santa Claus! Thank God, he lives, and he lives forever. A thousand years from now, Virginia, nay, ten times ten thousand years from now, he will continue to make glad the heart of childhood."

This affirmation has been used not only for the existence of Santa Claus, but also for the "truth" of all those beliefs and myths that have taken hold of our imaginations and have given us joy or solace.

Yippies Self-styled, tongue-in-cheek acronym for Youth International Party; coined by leaders of the student demonstrators against the Vietnam War at the Democratic National Convention in Chicago in August 1968. Riots started by Mayor Daley's police against the demonstrators led to the arrest and trial of the "Chicago Seven," including Abbie Hoffman and Jerry Rubin; all seven were acquitted.

Yoknapatawpha See FAULKNERIAN.

York, Sergeant Alvin C. (1887–1964) Originally a conscientious objector from Tennessee, he became a World War I hero in the U.S. infantry. In the battle of the Argonne on October 8, 1918, he charged a German machine-gun emplacement and captured 90 Germans almost single-handedly, then repeated the exploit, capturing 42 more.

young Turk Expression derives from a reformist Turkish political party, which took control from 1908 to 1918. Now a young Turk is any insurgent, usually of a reformist persuasion, who tries to take control of an organization by political maneuver.

yo-yo A toy introduced in the 1920s to the United States by an American toy manufacturer named Donald Duncan, although similar toys were in use in China as early as 1000 B.C. The toy consists of two wooden disks and a string wound around the connecting dowel. When let out, the yo-yo returns to the hand.

A yo-yo may be a stupid person who can be wound around one's fingers and manipulated up and down. The word also describes something or someone that fluctuates repeatedly, e.g., one's emotions, stock market prices, foreign policy.

yuppie   An acronym for young urban professional, "yuppie" carries a slightly derogatory connotation since it implies an inordinate interest in upward mobility through materialistic goals: money, clothes, fashionable addresses, physical fitness, social climbing.

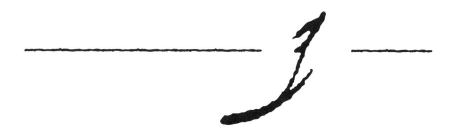

Zelda Zelda Sayre (1899–1948), beautiful, madcap, reckless wife of writer F. SCOTT FITZGERALD, the model for his heroines. A JAZZ AGE flapper, she drank, smoked, danced the days and nights away and eventually died in a hospital for the mentally ill.

Zenger, John Peter (1697–1746) American printer and newspaper publisher, he became a champion of freedom of the press when Lewis Morris, chief justice of the provincial court, asked him to print the *New York Weekly Journal,* started and founded by him and his friends.

In 1733, William Cosby, royal governor of New York, suspended Morris for ruling against him in a salary dispute. Morris and a group of lawyers and merchants banded together to publicize their opposition to Cosby's arbitrary action, but discovered that the only newspaper in town, the *New York Gazette,* would not print anything critical of Cosby's actions or policies. Having no other access to public media, they started a paper of their own, the *Journal,* which quite naturally was sharply critical of Cosby.

In 1734, Cosby had Zenger arrested on charges of "seditious libel." In 1735, however, Zenger was tried and acquitted. He was defended by Andrew Hamilton of Philadelphia, who argued that Zenger had not committed seditious libel because he had printed the truth.

John Peter Zenger's name is invoked as a fighter for freedom of the press.

Ziegfeld, Florenz (1869–1932) American theatrical producer famous for his Ziegfeld Follies (1907–31), "glorifying the American Girl." He chose the music for his productions, approved the lavish costumes and stage effects, directed every scene and musical number. His taste and judgment brought the musical show to heights it had never attained before. Ziegfeld left his mark on the American musical revue.

Among the famous composers who wrote scores for the Follies were Irving Berlin, Rudolf Friml, Victor Herbert, Jerome Kern. Various stars contributed their own material: Eddie Cantor, Fannie Brice, W. C. Fields, Will Rogers, Ann Pennington. Among the enduring songs that were first heard in the Follies: "Shine on, Harvest Moon," sung by Nora Bayes (1908); "A Pretty Girl Is Like a Melody," composed by Irving Berlin and used as a theme song for the Follies; "My Man," sung by Fannie Brice (1921). See also ZIEGFELD GIRLS.

Ziegfeld Girls   They were "the most beautiful girls ever to walk across an American stage," and they were all personally selected by the legendary FLORENZ ZIEGFELD (1869–1932) for his fabulously successful Ziegfeld Follies, which, with only a few interruptions, ran from 1907 to 1931.

Just as Charles Dana Gibson created the GIBSON GIRL, so did Ziegfeld create the Ziegfeld Girl. Tall, slender and elegant, she displaced the more amply endowed female as the "ideal" woman.

From this point on slenderness was in, plumpness out. Any tall, statuesque woman might find herself, not unhappily, labeled a Ziegfeld Girl.

Index

Munchkins 286
Munich 286
Muppets, The 287
Murder, Inc. 287
Murdstone, Mr. Edward
 288
Murrow, Edward R. 288
mushroom cloud 288
Mutt and Jeff 288
Mutually Assured Destruction.
 See M.A.D.
My Lai 289
Myshkin, Prince 289
mysticism. *See* Cabala

N

nabob 290
Nader, Ralph 290
Nagasaki 290
Naphta. *See Magic Mountain,*
 The
Napoleon 290
Nash, Ogden 291
Nation, Carry 291
Neanderthal man 292. *See*
 also Cro-Magnon man
Nell (Little) 246
Nero 292
Ness, Eliot *See* Untouchables
"Never in the field of human
 conflict..." 292
Never-Never Land 292
"Never underestimate the
 power..." 293
New Deal 293
New Jerusalem. *See* city upon
 a hill
Newport 293
newspeak 293
Newtonian 293
Nietzschean 294
Nightingale, Florence 294
Nighttown 295. *See also*
 Bloomsday; Joycean
Nijinsky, Vaslav 295
911 296
1984 296

ninety-day wonder 296
99 44/100% pure 296
nirvana 296
Nisei 296
Nixon *vs.* Kennedy debate
 297
Nobel Prize 297
noble savage 297
"No man is an island" 297
no-man's-land 298
Nora 298
Nostradamus 298
"Not Waving but Drowning"
 299
"not with a bang but a
 whimper" 299. *See also*
 "Hollow Men, The"
not worth a continental 299
"(Now is the) winter of our
 discontent" 443
Nude Descending a Staircase
 299
nuke 299
Nuremberg Laws 299
Nuremberg Trials 300
Nureyev, Rudolf 300
Nurse Ratched 300

O

Oakley, Annie 10
Oblomov 301
Ockham's razor 301
Odd Couple, The 302
Odessa steps 302
off base 302
"Off with her head! Off with
 his head!" *See* Queen of
 Hearts
"often a bridesmaid but never
 a bride" 302
O'Hara, Scarlett 303
O. Henry 302
O'Keefe, Georgia 303
Okie 303
Old Guard 303
"One-Hoss Shay, The
 Wonderful" 304

Oneida Community 304
one man, one vote 305
one on one 305
"one-third of a nation" 306
one-two 306
on the ball 304
on the button 304
on the ropes 306
"on the shoulders of giants"
 306
oomph girl 306
open city 307
open sesame 307
opiate of the people, the 307.
 See also Marxist
Orchard Street 307
Oreo 307
Orwellian 308
Othello 308
Our Gang 308
Our Town. See Grover's Corners
out of the closet 308
out of left field 308
overkill 308
over the top 309
"Ozymandias" 309
Oz. *See Wizard of Oz*
Ozzie and Harriet 309

P

pabulum 310
pack the court 310
Pagliaccio 310. *See also*
 Cyrano
Paine, Thomas. *See* "These are
 the times that try men's
 souls"
palace guard 311. *See also*
 kitchen cabinet
paladin 311
Pal Joey 311
Palmer Raids 311
palooka 312
Pangloss 312
Panzer 312
paper chase 312
paper tiger 313